Figures of Thought
for College Writers

Figures of Thought
for College Writers

Dona J. Hickey

University of Richmond

Mayfield Publishing Company

Mountain View, California

London · Toronto

Library of Congress Cataloging-in-Publication Data

Hickey, Dona J.
    Figures of thought for college writers / Dona J. Hickey.
        p.   cm.
    Includes index.
    ISBN 1-55934-652-3
    1. College readers. 2. English language — Rhetoric — Problems,
exercises, etc. 3. Figures of speech — Problems, exercises, etc.
4. Academic writing — Problems, exercises, etc. I. Title.
PE1417.H48 1999
808′.0427 — dc21
                                98-47191
                                CIP

Manufactured in the United States of America
10 9 8 7 6 5 4 3 2 1

Mayfield Publishing Company
1280 Villa Street
Mountain View, California 94041

Sponsoring editor, Renée Deljon; production editor, Lynn Rabin Bauer; manuscript editor, Margaret Moore; art director, Jeanne Schreiber; design manager, Susan Breitbard; text and cover designer, Joan Greenfield; cover art: bowl of cherries, image copyright © 1997 PhotoDisc, Inc.; hammer and nail, Stockbyte; and surfer, copyright © Greg Huglin/Adventure Photo; art editor, Robin Mouat; manufacturing manager, Randy Hurst. The text was set in 10.5/13 Minion by ColorType and printed on 45# Highland Plus by Malloy Lithographing, Inc.

Acknowledgments and copyrights continue at the back of the book on pages 652–656, which constitute an extension of the copyright page.

 This book is printed on recycled paper.

For Monica and Julie

A Note to Instructors

It's never easy, if ever truly possible, to trace the development of a book. Ideas take many turns, as we all know, even though in the end it may appear as if they marched in a straight line to a clearly visible goal. As the narrator says in L. P. Hartley's *The Go-Between*, "The past is a foreign country; they do things differently there." I can, however, describe generally one line of development. After reading *Metaphors We Live By* (by George Lakoff and Mark Johnson) and *More Than Cool Reason* (by George Lakoff and Mark Turner), I understood more clearly the nature and patterns of conceptual metaphor as well as the interplay between metaphor and culture. That understanding, in turn, influenced my work in writing across the curriculum, sparking and sustaining my interest in metaphor's role as a means of constructing theory in the academy. In addition to consulting with scholars and teachers on my campus and beyond, I read widely, both metaphor theory and introductory textbooks within academic disciplines. In general, I found that students are routinely introduced to metaphorical thinking in their college courses — without necessarily having their attention explicitly drawn to the language use. *Figures of Thought for College Writers* is my response to that realization.

Because metaphor is basic to human cognition, because we act according to the way we perceive and conceive of things, because our cultural values are embedded in metaphor, and because all across the disciplines metaphor figures prominently, conceptual metaphor is a suitable — and promising — focal point for first-year college writers. As an area of academic focus, metaphor lends itself to achieving various goals common to the writing classroom: heightening students' language awareness, improving students' critical thinking abilities, fostering a purposeful study of culture, and introducing students to a wide range of academic disciplines. Students long ago acquired the habit of metaphor (though they may be unaware of it), so the analogical thinking that they are asked to develop in college is not very different from the thinking in which they are daily engaged. Learning that metaphor is not just a matter of words, but also a matter of beliefs and values that affect human behavior, can help student writers and readers recognize the artificial separation made between words and action, and content and style. That recognition, I believe, fosters a finer sense of language use, both others' and one's own.

The goal of this book, then, is ultimately threefold: (1) to encourage greater language awareness; (2) to introduce some of the dominant metaphors of our culture, and, therefore, also those of the academy; and (3) to provide numerous occasions for meaningful writing. *Figures of Thought* takes students on a journey from ordinary language habits to language and thinking skills that college writers are asked to cultivate in their academic studies — the ability, in particular, to see resemblances among ideas and objects in the world. Seeing resemblances is first an act of imagination; pursuing their implications is then an act of critical thinking; and, finally, structuring and expressing those implications in a meaningful way for a specific audience is an act of persuasion.

In my own writing classes that focus on conceptual metaphor, students are quick to become engaged with this material, and they clearly enjoy becoming increasingly conscious of the role metaphor has played, and continues to play, in their own lives and academic learning. They discover how metaphor helps them get hold of an abstract subject; how the same metaphor becomes unsatisfactory as they gain more knowledge of a subject; and, finally, how the original metaphor can rarely be replaced by the literal, but is instead replaced by other, often competing, metaphors. For example, a future communications major studied the names of commercial products, focusing on how names change in response to changes in social and cultural values. Her favorite cereal, "Super Sugar Crisp," is now called "Super Golden Crisp." The company didn't change the product, just the name. The emphasis is now on the golden color instead of the sugar ingredient, thus replacing one value with another of higher cultural currency.

Another student, skeptical about the cultural and social value of cyberspace, studied a variety of metaphors related to computing and discussed their influence on the way she thinks about and engages the World Wide Web. Finally, several international students corresponded with John Lawler, the linguist whose lecture "Metaphors We Compute By" is included in this book. After their e-mail exchange, the students co-authored an essay for their American classmates, arguing that cultural differences between their countries and the United States make some metaphors in Lawler's list less attractive and less meaningful in describing their own computing experience. The importance of these students' questions and observations led Lawler to include their initial correspondence with him on his Web site.

As writers in my classes analyze the use of metaphor in readings, in the writing of their peers, and in their own writing, they also become more critically conscious of the dignity as well as the deception in the names people give things.

That is, names are important; we need to know the names of things and we need to take care in our own acts of naming. Natalie Goldberg, writer and teacher, says, "Give things the dignity of their names." Yet no one name can capture the complexity of a person or thing. Reg Saner, a nature writer and the author of "Naming Nature" (chapter 3), argues, "In answering to the aptest word we can give it, each thing in creation asks to be seen, thus known, even more truly. Just as we do."

My students ultimately pay closer attention to the metaphors they invent as well as those that they borrow or receive from others, and they begin to see one of their roles as creator of the world in which they conduct their lives. Through acts of imagination, we all make meaning and order from the data — visual, aural, and verbal — that pass swiftly through our perceptual fields. We select, we name, we connect, and, through this process, we construct reality not once but over and over in our lives. This book's thematic focus on conceptual metaphor — across domains of knowledge and across a variety of experiences — helps writers examine the cognitive necessity as well as the social, political, and cultural importance of metaphor.

ORGANIZATION AND FEATURES

After an extensive introduction to conceptual metaphor, "What Is a Figure of Thought?" (chapter 1) and a chapter devoted to metaphors for writing, "A Writing Life" (chapter 2), six thematic chapters explore various conceptual metaphors in popular and academic culture: "Naming and Claiming" (chapter 3); "Illness and Health" (chapter 4); "Mind and Body" (chapter 5); "Minds and Machines" (chapter 6); "War and More War" (chapter 7); and "Games and Not Games" (chapter 8). You and your students will no doubt think of other compelling conceptual metaphors that could have served as the focus of an entire chapter.

The book's first three chapters follow what I believe is an especially set, and necessary, sequence. After the first three chapters, other sequences could have worked, but there is a discernible progression, one that begins with perceptions of the self, moves to our relationship to objects in the world, and ends with our social and cultural relationships with others. The general progression from the personal to the public makes the organization flexible so that you may decide on the order that best suits you and your students' interests and needs.

- Chapter 1, "What Is a Figure of Thought?," provides the groundwork of the book. It explores metaphor from its use in everyday language and thought to its use in academic and professional writing. This chapter includes numerous examples and exercises ("Applying the Idea") throughout so that students have opportunities to write in response to their reading. After exploring the use of metaphor across disciplines, students will find a demonstration of reading and responding to metaphors as one way to question a writer's assumptions or the premises on which an argument is based. The chapter ends with a sample essay followed by discussion and writing topics that invite students to apply the principles themselves.

- Chapter 2, "A Writer's Life," is the first thematic chapter. It invites student writers to examine metaphor within the framework of writing itself, thereby offering immediate relevance. Ultimately, the chapter offers useful metaphors that writers can draw on and that will help them see the limitations of any one metaphor for describing the experience of writing.

- Chapter 3, "Naming and Claiming," is at the heart of the book. Metaphor's primary business involves naming, both its power and limits. This chapter explores the importance of names in science and nature, and the importance of our own names to our self-image and to our relations with others.

- Chapter 4, "Illness and Health," moves from physical to mental illness, exploring conceptual metaphors and the personal, social, and cultural responses to health and disease as a consequence of those metaphors.

- Chapter 5, "Mind and Body," begins with metaphors for particular mental activities and then explores the relationship between the mind and images of the body as revealed by popular metaphors in our culture.

- Chapter 6, "Minds and Machines," focuses on our ambivalence toward machines, particularly computer technology. It invites readers and writers to consider a variety of metaphors used to conceptualize technology and the effects of those metaphors on our relationship to it.

- Chapter 7, "War and More War," explores metaphors for describing and defining the experience of war. It begins with World War II, moves to the Vietnam War and the Gulf War, and ends with a cultural study of "war worship."

- Chapter 8, "Games and Not Games," progresses from traditional, culturally sanctioned games to controversial games to those games that people invent for themselves that carry emotional and physical risks.

The Readings

Figures of Thought offers 62 selections by professional writers. Representing various perspectives, and levels of difficulty, the readings in this collection are principally, but not exclusively, nonfiction (including a few selections of creative nonfiction). The readings vary in length and are drawn from popular culture and disciplines across the curriculum. Each of the thematic chapters (chapters 3–8) also includes at least one student essay (there are a total of seven student essays). Student writers represent various cultural backgrounds, ages, and levels of writing experience.

Apparatus

Every chapter includes the following apparatus:

- Chapter introductions include a preview of the readings as well as their sequence, and they pose some of the larger questions that the collected readings suggest.

- Prereading questions serve as discussion or journal-writing prompts ("Starting to Think about It"). These questions help writers see what they already know about the topic, help them examine their assumptions, and can lead to new insights as students engage each other and the selections in the chapter.

- Discussion questions ("Talking about It") follow each reading. These questions encourage readers to explore the rhetorical features of each selection and are divided into three categories: "Seeing Metaphor," "Seeing Composition," and "Seeing Meaning." The questions can also be used as writing prompts.

- Questions to prompt writing ("Writing about It") also follow each reading. These questions invite a variety of essay forms and sometimes include collaborative writing.

- End-of-chapter writing assignments ("Permeable Boundaries") ask students to explore connections between two or more readings. These questions encourage synthesis and critical analysis by moving the "boundaries" of each selection so that writers may discover points of overlap, intersection, and uncrossable distance.

ACKNOWLEDGMENTS

Describing the writing process is, for me, a ceaseless exercise in mixing metaphors: traveling and sewing, dancing and cooking, gardening and flying—all those and more. Writing can be like any one or a combination of such activities, none of which I perform well entirely alone. Thus, I am grateful to many people. Elizabeth Hodges of Virginia Commonwealth University was my traveling companion and sometime guide from starting point to destination. Without her, some roads would have been impassable. Renée Deljon, sponsoring editor, has a designer's eye for pattern; she helped me weave ideas and better envision the texture and color of the whole cloth. Mark Gallaher waltzed in gracefully with creative and pedagogically sound contributions to the discussion questions that follow readings.

Reviewers helped prune the best and weed out the worst. Thanks go to: Wendy Bishop, Florida State University; T. M. Brown, Diablo Valley College; Alice Gillam, University of Wisconsin, Milwaukee; Georgina Hill, Western Michigan University; Victor Luftig, Brandeis University; Jill A. Makagon, Kapi'olani Community College; Mary Paynter, Edgewood College; Jay Prefontaine, Eastern Illinois University; Lawrence C. Roderer, J. Sargeant Reynolds Community College; Hephzibah Roskelly, University of North Carolina, Greensboro; LeAnn Smith, Eastern Illinois University; Elizabeth Sommers, San Francisco State University; Elena Tapia, Eastern Connecticut State University; and Lawrence Tobin, Boston College.

Without Margaret Moore's careful copyediting; without Lynn Rabin Bauer, production editor; and without the collaborative talents and goodwill of the production staff at Mayfield, I'd have never sewn this up. Finally, thanks go to Gordon for studiously ignoring the writing of the manuscript, and to Tony for being a superb paperweight, even on very windy afternoons.

A Note to Students

The greatest thing by far is to be a master of metaphor.
—Aristotle

What do we commit ourselves to when we conceive of time as money, illness as war, or fitness and diet as virtue? These popular conceptions in our culture commit us to personal, social, and political realities that are defined by metaphor. You might be familiar with metaphor as a kind of figurative language, a figure of speech in which one object or idea is used in place of another to express a likeness, for example, "She's *swimming* in money." But contrary to popular belief, metaphor is not just ornamental; it is an ordinary and integral part of thought and language, fundamental to the way we think about and experience our world.

Metaphor may in fact already be most familiar to you when it operates as analogy (a form of direct comparison). "Try to picture it like this," a teacher might say. "The notes in this musical composition are like pearls on a string. Each one is separate, but part of an unbroken chain." Or, "Picture the mind as a computer, an information-processing system." Or, "Neurons are like messengers, carrying information from cell to cell." All of us have learned new or abstract concepts by thinking about them in terms of more familiar, concrete objects. Seeing resemblances through analogy is how we connect new and old information so that we can increase our knowledge and build coherence among our experiences and ideas.

Like analogy, then, metaphor informs our conceptions of ourselves, our relationships, our jobs, time, everything. Metaphor becomes, in this sense, not a figure of speech but a figure of *thought*. For instance, Americans commonly talk about (and therefore think about) time as if it were money, something that can be "saved" or "invested." Similarly, politicians talk about the "war" against AIDS or drugs or poverty, and military leaders "up the ante" or "raise the stakes" on the battlefield. *Figures of Thought for College Writers* provides opportunities for you to examine the implications of these and other of our culture's most familiar conceptual metaphors.

This book also asks questions such as, What is at stake when, even in our most ordinary communication, we are likely to be unaware of metaphor? And it provides an occasion for you to experience what changes when we uncover metaphor's seemingly invisible way of operating—what happens when we pull up and look closely at the roots of our conceptual system. The dominant metaphors in a culture carry social and often political implications that affect people's ideas, judgments, and lives. The readings in chapters 2–8 focus on metaphors that influence us and therefore have far-reaching consequences, such as "The mind is a computer," or abnormal behavior or unwanted conduct is evidence of "illness," as in mental illness. *Figures of Thought* will help you become more aware of how our culture's metaphors affect our ideas and influence our behavior, and that awareness will give you choices; it will enable you to read and write more consciously about the connections among language, thought, and action.

Metaphors are necessary not only to our conceptual structure of everyday experience but also to the structure of theories across academic disciplines. Theorists often begin with analogy, a perceived resemblance between a thing as yet not identified and another known, familiar thing. Researchers then pursue the analogy to see how far the resemblances between two phenomena can be extended. This pursuit is a primary way theories are tested, advanced, or replaced by others. Of the sciences, Kenneth Burke says, "Whole works of scientific research, even entire schools, are hardly more than the patient repetition, in all its ramifications, of a fertile metaphor." Two examples from physics are black holes and chaos, both of which are metaphors that have seized the imagination of theorists in other domains of knowledge, such as business, political science, and literature, and have influenced the direction of study in these secondary fields. The first phrase, black hole, is, in fact, now so popularized that it is even used metaphorically to express fear of our fate and that of the universe, or to explain the sudden and complete disappearance of anything lost—from a dream to a weekend to a book of stamps.

As you write in response to the readings in the following chapters, I hope you will understand more deeply the relationship of metaphorical language to thought and actions, and that such understanding serves you both personally and academically.

Contents

Chapter 4: Illness and Health   201

Chapter 5: Mind and Body   287

Chapter 6: Minds and Machines   363

Chapter 7: War and More War   457

Chapter 8: Games and Not Games   569

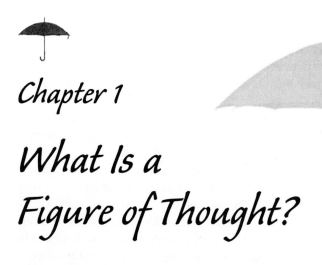

Chapter 1

What Is a Figure of Thought?

The most profound social creativity consists in the invention and imposition of new, radical metaphors.

— R. Kaufmann

INTRODUCTION TO METAPHOR

At one time or another, who hasn't been labeled as "too literal-minded"? In some failed act of communication, we didn't hear the prompt to disregard the literal truth of an utterance and go hunting for implied comparisons. We missed a cue, as if in response to the command "Chill out," we had applied ice to our foreheads instead of just "calming down." That's an extreme example to make a simple point: We've all had the experience, especially with ever-evolving slang expressions, of not understanding that a person was speaking metaphorically, that is, talking about one thing in terms of another. At best, we're confused. At worst, we might act in response to a literal expression and, in the case of "Chill out," reach for the ice. Or maybe we just secretly wish to drop a bag of it on the speaker's head for slighting our mental acuity. And we'd rightly feel offended. No one is unpracticed in the use of metaphor. In fact, everybody is an expert.

What Is Metaphor?

Metaphor, as it is broadly defined, is the act of partially, not totally, structuring one idea in terms of another. We understand, for example, that calming down is not really the same as physically chilling ourselves. Yet there is some physical basis for this metaphor because emotions can cause our blood pressure to rise and our faces to redden. The point is that metaphors reveal some, not all, aspects of an idea, and they necessarily hide others. Additionally, a metaphor can be stretched only so far until the correspondences between two phenomena collapse. If that were not so, one thing would actually be the other. Altering one's body temperature from hot to cold does not necessarily alter one's emotional state. Taking a cold shower, for example, may not put out the fire in your heart. And some anger is not visible as physical heat or charged emotion. People can look and sound calm but be highly annoyed. We say sometimes, "She coldly ordered him from the room," or "His behavior frosts her." Metaphors may sometimes look like equations (to calm down is to cool off), but they offer only some understanding of a concept. Not all properties of one phenomenon can be applied to another.

Let's take a closer look at "Chill out." The phrase more than likely derives from the metaphorical concept—anger is heat. That metaphor structures how we perceive anger, and it is reflected in our everyday language through expressions such as "She blew her top," "He's hot under the collar," "That behavior makes his blood boil," and "She's fired up." Other emotions, too, are described in terms of heat, such as lust—"She's hot for him" or "There are sparks between them." In contrast, we commonly conceptualize reason as "coolness" and "control," thus artificially separating reason from emotion: "Despite conflicting obligations, she made up her mind coolly," "He's cool under pressure." As you can see, these expressions carry value judgments.

Typically in this culture, reason is valued more than emotion. Not all cultures, nor all subcultures—or individuals within them, for that matter—share this belief. For example, in some subcultures and for some individuals, emotion is a greater sign of concern for an idea or another person than reason is: "He must love me; he's jealous of all of my friends," or "She must not care about him; she's unwilling to fight back." Consequently, our personal or social and cultural values are embedded in the everyday metaphors that we use to describe experience. "Chill out" carries a judgment: someone perceives another as "too emotionally charged," as if electrified, or "out of control," as can be the case with fire. "Cool down," "Get a grip," we might say. Other variations spun from "Chill out" are these: "Take a chill," as in a cold shower, perhaps, and "Take a chill pill," such as a tranquilizer.

☙ *Metaphor Awareness Is Language Awareness*

We acquire the metaphor habit early and effortlessly. As children, we develop it as a simple matter of course because we are language-makers as well as language-users. So intrinsic is metaphor to thought and language, we could scarcely get from morning to night without it. Yet because metaphor is such an ordinary part of our experience with language, we're rarely conscious of it. That's just the trouble. People don't often think about how metaphor operates in their understanding of others, themselves, and the world—of how it makes ideas visible, gives form to the unknown, and helps integrate otherwise discrete experiences. Through metaphor we discover meaningful resemblances among things, and, through that process, we connect the abstract to the concrete. It is a primary means of getting hold of the world and, as some would argue further, of creating the world in which we live.

Traditionally, the subject of metaphor tends to come up in literature classes where everyone learns that a metaphor is a *figure of speech*: "No man is an island." It's learned first as an element of style, a way to embellish ideas. Its closest neighbor is the simile: "No man is like an island." Metaphors are first brought to our attention in poems, mostly, but we're taught to recognize them in stories and songs too: "She's got the moon in her eyes." Consequently, many people associate metaphors most readily with the literary arts and understand them as a matter of language—*a figure of speech.* But metaphors are also a tool for discovering and connecting ideas—*a figure of thought.* And it's that role of metaphor that is emphasized in this book.

Just as metaphor is intrinsic to everyday thought and language, it is intrinsic to thought and language within the academy. Metaphor has itself become an object of academic study. Within this study, metaphor is defined broadly as partially understanding and experiencing one thing in terms of another. The critical questions are these: how does metaphor structure concepts? what is its role in theory-making and research? These questions apply to testing grounds as vastly different from each other as astrophysics and Pepsi Cola marketing. Thus, we need to be highly aware of how metaphorical language within and beyond the academy affects our perceptions of reality and our behavior in response to those perceptions.

Whether ornamental or conceptual, metaphors are acts of imagination. To see one thing in terms of another is to think associatively. That is, we set up correspondences between two concepts. This usually involves partially structuring our understanding of an abstract object (love, for example) by seeing it in terms of a concrete object (say, a garden). Thus we can think and talk about "cultivating," "nurturing," and "tending to" our friendships. The process of setting up such correspondences is called "mapping." By mapping gardens onto love, which are otherwise two separate conceptual domains, we invite a comparison and give visible form to an abstract idea. "Gardens" is the source domain from which we draw properties that can be applied to "love," the target domain. Through metaphors, both conventional and unconventional, we build and lay claim to coherence among otherwise discrete phenomena. The habit of metaphorical thinking belongs to everyone—from the child learning to name and organize her experiences to the poet, the physicist, the philosopher, the social scientist, and the mathematician. Metaphor is very much involved in the way they conceptualize, talk about, and, most of all, experience the world.

Metaphor and College Reading and Writing

No one is a blank slate. Everyone arrives at college with experience and practice in language and learning. *Figures of Thought,* therefore, incorporates what you already know through everyday thought and language (though you may be unaware of it) in order to explore a primary means of constructing knowledge within and beyond the academic community. The general goals are

1. to show how the use of language, specifically metaphor, informs particular ways of seeing and writing about the world and ourselves; and

2. to foster an awareness and appreciation of the richness, flexibility, and vitality of language so that you will use it more consciously in reasoning and writing.

More specifically, the goal of this book is to illustrate how metaphorical thinking functions to define our reality and form the basis of our actions. In this approach to reading and writing, you will learn

1. how metaphor leads to general principles of understanding based on seeing one experience in terms of another;

2. how metaphor helps to connect ideas and experiences;

3. how metaphor structures concepts, revealing some features of a phenomenon, but concealing others, and thus how it can both broaden and limit understanding;

4. how we need many metaphors for an experience so that our understanding is not limited by one direction of vision, thereby cutting off alternative ways of conceptualizing experience;

5. how people in power — lawyers and judges, the media, politicians, doctors, scientists, for example — get to impose their metaphors; and

6. how cultural constructions of knowledge are connected to the construction of knowledge in the academy.

Once aware of how metaphors organize concepts and, more importantly, how metaphors organize behaviors and values closely bound to culture, you may begin to recognize the political agenda in artificial separations of words from actions, style from logic, and, especially, public from academic discourse. Through such recognition of artificial boundaries, you may also become more conscious of your own production of language, using it more responsibly in speech and writing. These points go to the heart of this chapter and are explored not only in the discussion that follows but also throughout the thematic chapters.

Familiar Categories of Metaphor

Let's begin by looking at some common ways we understand one experience in terms of another. These ways include already familiar categories of thinking and speaking, such as slang, jargon, clichés, parables, proverbs, rituals, myths, symbols, and riddles. The first six categories are discussed here in detail.

Slang   Slang expresses our delight in making language new. It is tribute to the flexibility and richness of language and to our ingenuity as language-makers. We give a word meaning that's not found in the dictionary by making a comparison; that is, we transfer the literal meaning of a word or phrase from one conceptual domain to another with which it shares certain similarities. For example, "low wattage" in reference to a person is slang for "not smart" and is an alternative for "dim bulb," both deriving from the conventional expression, "not bright." Our understanding depends on the transferring of "power" from the conceptual domain of "electricity" to that of "human intelligence." In talking about low intelligence in terms of electrical power, we break the word "wattage" from its literal restraints. Once freed, however, most slang enjoys a short probationary life in the street. Nothing dies faster than slang. But that is in part its attraction. It's an antidote to our boredom with rules, conventions, and the rigidity we associate with the dictionary-makers.

Inventing slang expressions is one way to make language personal. We express our individuality with slang, but more often we use it to declare our membership within a group. Think of words that you share within your social group but keep secret from outsiders. Slang is one way the youth culture separates itself from adults. The word "bad," for example, has come to mean, in some instances, "good." It's slang with a hard edge, with defiance attached to it. Defiance can be seen too in some of our euphemisms for death: "croak," "kick the bucket," "buy the ranch," and others in that class. But we also use slang as a means of softening the harsher realities of life, such as these euphemisms and expressions for death: "pass away," "the big sleep," "eternal rest," "the final destination," and "the great beyond."

Applying the Idea

Either individually or as a group, consider as many slang terms as you can for a popular topic: good person/bad person, success/failure, sanity/insanity, rich/poor. What is the attraction of some of the slang terms you've recalled? Are there any particular values attached to them? Do they identify the speaker as belonging to a particular social group? In what context might an expression most likely be used? Why?

Jargon   Jargon is related to slang but springs from different motivations. It is the specialized language of a particular occupational group. Whereas slang aims at the sheer pleasure of invention, jargon aims at precision. But it can, like slang, have the effect of an insider's handshake. In that instance, people may refer to it as "lingo," as in the lingo of computer programmers. Only those in the know share the vocabulary, with one exception: If the work gains the public's interest and thus enters its consciousness as a cultural phenomenon, the special language or jargon of the insiders can quickly become a pervasive metaphor.

The most recent example of such a cultural phenomenon is computer technology. Even people who neither use nor program computers can be heard using the jargon as metaphors for other experiences. Richard Preston, in "Back to the Hot Zone," claims, "We live in a kind of biological Internet, in which viruses travel like messages, moving at a high speed from node to node, moving from city to city" (43). Marsha Norman, in "Say Amen to Somebody," explains the healing power of prayer this way:

> When I pray for you, it's like asking for a remote download from the Net. Somewhere in the universal mind, the information exists that will cure you. I'm just trying to get it copied onto your hard disk, or teach you how to access it through your browser. (119)

A *New Yorker* cartoon featured a man lying in a hammock that was strung between two trees in his backyard. The caption below: "America off-line." So pervasive is computer jargon that reality can be defined against virtual reality.

Applying the Idea

Try listing some of the computer jargon that you've heard. How have you or others used it to talk about other kinds of experiences? What values are transferred in the mapping of computer technology onto these experiences? You might also describe the ways in which your understanding of experiences has been limited by others' use of computer analogies: How do such metaphors, such as the previously mentioned examples from Preston and Norman, alienate you as a reader, if they do?

Clichés   A cliché is a comparison, usually one too easily made ("dry as toast"), that has been so overused that in some cases it no longer impresses anyone as metaphorical. In other words, people begin using the expression as if it were a direct, literal description of a thing. "Mixed metaphors" are examples of that phenomenon. Let's look at how a mixed metaphor comes about by examining two different expressions that when combined present conflicting images.

"To stick one's neck out" means "to put oneself in danger" or "to ask for trouble." The source domain (world of meaning from which the metaphor is drawn) is the physical: "to expose one's neck to the executioner's axe"; the target domain (world of meaning to which the metaphor is applied) is the psychological: "She really stuck her neck out when she contradicted the manager." "Out on a limb," another metaphor, also means to ask for trouble, and it too finds its source in the physical world: one is at risk of falling from a precarious branch,

AMERICA OFF-LINE

high on a tree. We rarely have an image of those physical dangers when we use these expressions; we use them almost synonymously with "to risk." In conversation, I heard someone say, "She really stuck her neck out on a limb with that proposal!" The speaker combined both expressions without thinking of the image they created in combination. That's a mixed metaphor.

Applying the Idea

Read yesterday's sports page and list all the worn metaphors used to describe a play in football, baseball, basketball, tennis, and so on. Why do you think many sports writers find the cliché more appealing than literal language? For another exercise, review newspaper headlines—another good place to find clichés, especially unintentionally mixed metaphors.

Parables A parable is an extended analogy with a moral meaning, a short narrative intended to teach a lesson. The most famous parables in Western culture are those recorded in the Gospels. Often the story begins with a comparison between two phenomena ("The kingdom of heaven is like a grain of mustard seed"), then continues without direct reference to the target domain ("kingdom of heaven"). Audiences are expected to derive the moral lesson by making the correspondences that are implied in the story. Fables differ only in that they feature animals, rather than people, as characters; and they close with the lesson made explicit, rather than implicit.

We mainly think of religious sermons as illustrations of parables, but within our families and other social groups, we reinforce certain principles of behavior or values through storytelling that could properly be called parables. In every family, for example, there's a lesson to be learned from the story of an uncle's failed business venture, a great aunt's courage, or a cousin's squandered youth. These stories are specific to the individual, usually full of colorful detail, yet they carry an implied message about general moral principles that the listener is expected to apply to her own life.

Applying the Idea

Tell a story that's been passed along in your family. What are the implied principles of living? Why is the story memorable to you, beyond its intended lesson? After you've listened to each other's stories, try to say what other values, beyond moral lessons, may be attached to family parables. As an alternate exercise, try writing your own fable, using as a model one of Aesop's fables, such as "The Fox and the Grapes."

Proverbs   "You can't make a silk purse from a sow's ear." "A stitch in time saves nine." "Once bitten, twice shy." "Don't judge a book by its cover." "You can lead a horse to water, but you can't make him drink." "The girl who can't dance blames the band." "People in glass houses shouldn't throw stones." "The blackest berry has the sweetest juice." "Don't put all your eggs in one basket." We read each of these specific literal statements and instantly extract generic information about human concerns. And then we use that generic information as a template to be filled by other specific cases. George Lakoff and Mark Turner fully discuss the structure of proverbs in *More Than Cool Reason*. I am drawing on their work here.

Suppose a friend in one of your classes complains that he is having trouble understanding the material and preparing for exams. You offer various suggestions, such as meeting with the peer-study group on Friday afternoons, consulting with the professor, and working with a tutor in the Learning Center to develop stronger study skills. But your friend does not follow any of this advice and once again does poorly on a test. You express your judgment by saying, "You can lead a horse to water, but you can't make him drink."

We understand a proverb first by mapping the specifics of the case onto the generic case found within it. In the proverb previously cited, we map the following information onto the concrete story of the horse:

There is a person who is in need of help.

That help is made available.

The person refuses it. And

The person can't be forced to accept it.

The generic information forms the underlying structure of the proverb. It is a template that can be filled by any number of other specific parallel situations. Using the template, we can then map the specifics of the proverb onto the specifics of another situation, as in the example of the student. The mapping works in the following way:

> The horse corresponds to a person who needs help.
>
> The water corresponds to the help that's made available to the person.
>
> The horse's refusal corresponds to the person's refusal of help.
>
> That the horse cannot be forced to drink the water corresponds to the person who can't be forced to accept help if he doesn't want it.

Applying the Idea

Give specific examples of proverbs listed on the previous pages and then list other proverbs, giving examples for them. Within groups or as a class, choose one proverb: try mapping the specifics of the case onto the generic case found within it, as illustrated in "You can lead a horse to water, but you can't make him drink."

A proverb helps us understand a broad category of experience in terms of one specific case. Proverbs are powerful metaphors but are also deceptive because they exclude qualifications on the main idea, the exceptions that show many proverbs as untrue. Some proverbs can confuse and obscure our thinking about human affairs. A popularly cited proverb in this category is "Fight fire with fire." It describes the specific case of fighting forest fires with backfires, a means of control that is the exception, not the rule. Without that qualification, the generic information extracted from the specific case is false. When we map other specific situations within the category of human conflicts onto the template, we find a justification for revenge: "Fight lies with lies," "Fight violence with violence," for example. And most of us would reject these notions as counterproductive.

Applying the Idea

Is it always the case, for example, that "haste makes waste," that "you reap what you sow," that "what goes around, comes around," or that "life is a box of chocolates"? Try to name the deceptive element in each of these proverbs. Or work with several proverbs that you can list in class. What exceptions can you think of that make the proverb not true? Why do you think proverbs exclude qualifications, and what is implied by the lack of them?

Rituals   A ritual is a stylized performance in which members of a group enact shared beliefs. It is an ordered set of specific acts that suggest by their progression the general tenets of a community in a particular place and at a particular time. Put another way, a ritual is a metaphor that is realized by performances and the series of associations implied by them. In performing a ritual, people enact a set of metaphors that lead from one to another in a chain of associations until the final scene or act. The chain of associations makes ritual a metaphoric process. Each act is important for what it suggests to performers within the whole chain of acts. A ritual is not to be confused with a habit. Habits are also repeated behaviors but do not suggest in the performance a chain of associations that imply a set of truths shared by members of a community. They are not, therefore, ceremonies in the way rituals are.

Examples of rituals are dances, prayers, parades, religious ceremonies, songs, initiation rites, and celebration of holidays. A ritual, such as an initiation rite, may include dance, song, and recitation of specific words or sentences. Rituals often designate the beginning, end, or important stage of a process. Significant events in life — birth, adulthood, marriage, and death — are marked by rituals. We can include, as well, other events, such as sports. Consider the series of acts that athletes perform before a game begins, or those their fans perform either at the stadium or at home (the Super Bowl ritual). Consider family rituals. Rituals at the workplace. The rituals of meals. Or morning, evening, and bedtime rituals. Any ordered set of behaviors to which cultural, social, or personal values are attached can be called a ritual.

To take closer look at one example, let's focus on food. It is a biological necessity for survival. Our geographical environment determines the availability of certain foods, but it is culture that defines our preferences and, conversely, our preferences define us as members of a culture or subculture. Individuals can, by openly declaring their preferences for one type of food or another, project a desired self-image.

In one of the essays in this text, "You Are What You Eat," Jill Dubisch, an anthropologist, describes the religious aspects of the health food movement. She explains that, for members of the movement, food is a system of symbols expressing a commitment to a certain worldview regarding "good" and "bad" ways to live. Membership is defined not only by the types and quality of foods consumed (yogurt, wheat germ, honey) but also by certain activities, such as exercising and organic gardening. A person is initiated into the movement by a ritualistic removal of "bad" foods from the kitchen (sugar, white bread) and through a process of change in eating and living habits. To the extent that people perceive improvement in health or another quality of life, they become converted as if to a religion and give testimony to their faith: new energy, longer life, renewed health, and, by extension, renewed spirit and peace of mind.

We wouldn't expect to encounter members of the health food movement at McDonald's, yet we would encounter those who are not just eating but are participating in a ritual that, like the health food movement, has religious associations. Conrad Kottak explores this idea in "McDonald's as Myth, Symbol, and Ritual." He asks why Americans return to McDonald's repeatedly, even seek it out when traveling abroad. The attraction lies in certain familiarities: the food, the building (golden arches, stained glass windows), the atmosphere, and certain phrases and behaviors. When people enter, they know what they'll see, eat, and pay. Employees wear the same uniform, speak the same phrases ("Fries with that?"), and prepare the food the same way. Customers know the lingo: "Big Mac with fries," "A Quarter Pounder." "Large fry," for example, does not refer to the size of the potato, but to the quantity. Anyone unfamiliar with these utterances is out of place at McDonald's.

Like performers in a ritual, customers arrive at certain times of day and for a certain period of duration. People don't linger there. McDonald's appeals to the lunch-hour crowd, to those who like breakfast on the run, and to families with young children. Most don't frequent McDonald's on holidays, for example, where "fast food" is not a priority. Eating at McDonald's is a ritual reserved for the ordinary day. Congregated there, people imply collective values as members of a social group and culture (Kottak 522–26).

Applying the Idea

Write about a ritual of your own, of your family, or your social group. It should describe some ordered set of repeated behaviors to which you attach symbolic value. In what ways do the acts you perform imply certain beliefs and values? How is a metaphor actualized by your performance of these specific acts? In other words, how do you enact a metaphoric process through your words and behavior, and therefore put into action a set of beliefs?

For example, think about the special ways your family celebrates a holiday: what repeated activities occur? Do you always eat the same meal, play the same games, decorate the house a certain way, sing the same songs? What meaning do these activities have for your family beyond their literal significance or beyond how others usually celebrate the holiday?

If you're an athlete, a dancer, an actor, or a musician, think about group ritualistic behaviors *before* a game or a performance: what repeated acts, gestures, or words occur? Why? Sometimes a series of acts carries superstitious value for the group; you play well only when you repeat such acts. What gives rise to this kind of magical thinking? What raises the sequence of acts beyond mere repetition? What special significance do these behaviors have for you beyond what they may appear to mean to others?

Or, within your social group, do you go to the same place for certain reasons known only to the group? What is this place's special attraction or meaning for you? You might think too of any set of ordered behaviors that occur at your workplace, those that have particular associations for the people there. What do they suggest about the beliefs of the community?

HOW METAPHOR STRUCTURES ORDINARY THOUGHT AND LANGUAGE

In the previous (and partial) list of metaphor categories, I've tried to show that metaphor is defined more broadly than most of us realize; that we engage metaphor frequently in speaking, thinking, and acting (as in the example of rituals); that metaphor involves thinking about one thing in terms of another; and that such transference of meaning from one conceptual domain to another includes the transference of cultural and social values (as shown in the examples for all the categories).

Now, with the help of George Lakoff and Mark Johnson, I will focus on the fundamental ways that metaphor structures our thinking in our most ordinary use of language. In "The Metaphorical Structure of the Human Conceptual System," Lakoff and Johnson explain that our conceptual system includes both metaphorical and nonmetaphorical concepts:

> Nonmetaphorical concepts are those that emerge directly from our experience and are defined in their own terms . . . [space, substance, activity]. Metaphorical concepts are those which are understood and structured not merely in their own terms, but rather in terms of other concepts. This involves conceptualizing one kind of object or experience in terms of a different kind of object or experience. (193)

For example, the nonmetaphorical concept of space includes such orientations as up/down, back/front, and in/out. The corresponding metaphorical concept includes "Happy is up" (as in "Louie's feeling up today") and "Sad is down" ("Louise has been down all week"). These expressions have their origin in nonmetaphorical concepts regarding linear orientation. In at least this case, we associate "happy" with "up" because we see physical signs of it on someone's face: smiles turn up the corners of the mouth, for example.

We need to bear in mind, however, that metaphors structure concepts only partially. Recall, for example, the illustrations of "Chill out" and the limitations of proverbs described earlier. A metaphor can be extended only so far before it creates too much complexity or it collapses; it reveals only one aspect of a concept and conceals others. If that were not the case, one concept would actually be the other. In *Metaphors We Live By,* Lakoff and Johnson provide many illustrations of those points. One popular metaphorical concept is "Argument is war." The following are my illustrations of its use in everyday language:

> You need more *ammunition* to *win* your argument.
>
> His points *hit their mark.*
>
> You can't *defend* your position.
>
> After her successful *attack* of his claims, he *retreated.*
>
> Their side was *bombed* in the debate.
>
> I've *driven the point home.*
>
> You want to *attack this ground? Fire away!*

Lakoff and Johnson explain that in structuring the concept of argument in terms of war, we are only partially defining argument since argument isn't physical but verbal battle. If it were physical, argument would really be war. And yet, it's not as if we only spoke of argument as battle; we conceptualize it that way, which in turn influences the way we engage in it: we conduct an argument as if there were defensive and offensive attacks, ground to be won and lost, and so forth. Our metaphors affect our behavior. In a very real sense, therefore, words are action. As Lakoff and Johnson say of "Argument is war," it is a metaphor "we live by in this culture." They ask readers to imagine another culture in which argument is not understood or experienced in terms of war. Imagine it is dance, they say, in which "the participants are seen as performers, and the goal is to perform in a balanced and aesthetically pleasing way." If we were to observe the verbal and behavioral performance of argument as dance, we would probably not recognize it as argument. To us, it would seem to be something else entirely. Some everyday metaphorical concepts, therefore, are grounded in cultural values (5).

While we're thinking of argument as war, and thus defining and revealing it as conflict to be won or lost, we conceal other goals of argument, such as mutual understanding. Sometimes we argue not to do battle with an opponent but to understand each other's beliefs. We aren't trying to win or fearing to lose. We are hoping to see more clearly another point of view and to represent more clearly our own.

An Accounting of War Metaphors

War, as a way of conceptualizing and talking about other phenomena, is a popular source domain. That is, we draw from the world of armed conflict to think and talk about other experiences. As Lakoff and Johnson emphasize in the previous discussion about the language of argument as war, "The metaphor is not merely in the words we use—it is in our very concept of an argument. The language of argument is not poetic, fanciful, or rhetorical; it is literal. We talk about arguments that way because we conceive of them that way—and we act according to the way we conceive of things" (5). We commonly structure other concepts and experiences in terms of battle. The following examples extend Lakoff and Johnson's point by listing other target domains (areas of experience to which terms of war are applied).

Trade and Marketing   International trade is defined in economics textbooks as a means to achieving peace based on mutually beneficial transactions between countries. If transactions were not mutually beneficial, the parties would not agree to trade. However, we commonly find "war," not "peace," as the operating metaphor. For example, "The Great Ice Cream Wars" referred to the 1988 dispute over the dairy quotas used to suppress foreign competition so American farmers could earn more than market value for milk.

National competition in marketing is also described in terms of war. Jack M. Greenberg, the vice chairman of McDonald's USA, sent a memorandum to McDonald's franchise owners in the winter of 1997, after Burger King began a $70 million campaign to promote its new french fries. Here is an excerpt:

> Burger King will launch a full frontal assault on one of our greatest assets—America's Favorite Fries. We are allocating a significant portion of our marketing firepower to aggressively promote our fries and neutralize Burger King's.... We need to work together to affirm our fries' superiority on the front lines. The most powerful weapon we have in our arsenal is for our restaurants to consistently deliver hot, fresh, great-tasting fries.... There is no better time to show our competition that we have the will and ability to crush any challenges. We will win this battle if we keep our eyes on our fries. (24)

Another example is the cola wars. Roger Enrico, Pepsi executive, recounts the history of competition between Pepsi and Coke in *The Other Guy Blinked: How Pepsi Won the Cola Wars.* Enrico says,

> A lot of executives I know like to read about naval warfare. Having seen how long it takes for battleships to turn, I understand their interest. For most of these men [sic], running a business is very much like turning a battleship—once strategic decisions in slow-moving, machinery-driven businesses are made, they're hard to adjust. (262)

As for his choice of battle books, Enrico finds that *The Art of War* is a "constant reminder that good ideas, properly utilized, are worth as much as heavy weapons" (262). For Enrico, as well as for Greenberg, marketing strategies are battle strategies.

Illness   In describing the heroic efforts of scientists and doctors to halt the spread of disease, Sharon Begley and co-authors of "Commandos of Viral Combat" use war as the controlling metaphor. "Epidemic aid," they say, "is the medical equivalent of parachuting into a war zone. Once the virus jocks get the call . . . they grab their bags and hop the first commercial flight that will drop them within striking distance of the outbreak" (50).

Susan Sontag, in *Illness as Metaphor,* states that the "controlling metaphors in descriptions of cancer are . . . drawn . . . from the language of warfare" (64). Sontag offers these examples:

Cancer cells do not simply multiply, they are "invasive."

Cancer cells "colonize" from the original tumor to far sites in the body, first setting up tiny "outposts."

Rarely are the body's "defenses" vigorous enough to obliterate a tumor. (64)

She also gives examples of how doctors use war to talk about treatment:

Patients are "bombarded" with toxic rays.

Chemotherapy is chemical "warfare" using poisons.

Treatment aims to "kill" cancer cells. (65)

Sontag argues that military language about cancer has distorted our thinking and our response to the disease. Politicians perpetuate the metaphor "war against cancer," reinforcing the medical establishment's need for "tirelessly hailing the imminent victory over cancer" and reinforcing the cancer specialists' habit of "talking like battle-weary officers mired down in interminable colonial war" (66–67).

The military metaphor at one time may have reflected our fatalistic view toward a mysterious condition of the body, but as we learn more about cancer, warfare becomes an inappropriate and ultimately dangerous metaphor for doctors, scientists, and patients. A new metaphor is needed that does not imply "either a fatalistic diagnosis or a rousing call to fight by any means whatever a lethal, insidious enemy" (87).

Because the linguistic structure of a metaphor is an equation ("cancer = war"), it omits "as if." Hence, we can sometimes forget that we are thinking in comparisons: one idea shares some resemblances with another but cannot be replaced by the other. Metaphors are not truly equations (cancer ≠ war). Again, although a metaphor can expand our thinking, it can also, if powerful and popular enough, seriously limit it. As medical scientists and doctors learn more about cancer, for example, it is crucial that they keep improving comparisons so that they can orient research and practice in more useful ways. All metaphors are provisional, speculative. They assist us when we discover a new phenomenon for which there has been no description. They move our thinking forward. As the war metaphor ceases to drive research and medical practice in useful ways, scientists find new comparisons. Metaphors about cancer treatment change, therefore, when we learn more about the disease. For example, the language about cancer had already begun to change in 1978 when Sontag published *Illness as Metaphor.* She acknowledges that "concepts have started to shift in certain medical circles, where doctors are concentrating on the steep buildup of the body's immunological responses to cancer" and looking for treatment "in some kind of immunotherapy" (86). According to Sontag, "the body's 'immunodefensive system' can also . . . be called the body's 'immune competence'" and thus completely avoid the military metaphor (87). As discussed later in this chapter, some metaphors have long-ranging effects and remain in the public consciousness long after they've been replaced. Sontag predicts the same fate for the "Cancer as war" metaphor, claiming that it "will be made obsolete . . . long before the problems it has reflected so vividly will be resolved" (87).

Slowly, then, as our understanding of a phenomenon evolves, one metaphor replaces another. Yet it's not that we get beyond metaphor; we find new and more metaphors for thinking about increasingly complex phenomena. No one analogy is sufficient; we need many to drive research in new and varied ways. The danger is the belief that any one analogy is perfect. Once criticism stops, alternative comparisons stop, and the process of knowledge-making stops too. One important question to ask of all metaphors is: what do we commit ourselves to when we accept a specific metaphor as a way of understanding our experience?

As the previous sampling of war metaphors illustrates, people in power get to impose their metaphors. Scientists, doctors, politicians, bureaucrats, and corporate executives can, through military language, distort other people's understanding about trade, marketing strategies, and cancer.

Conversation   Military and sports metaphors are common in the world of work, where they are expressions that reflect the experience of men more than of women. (I am speaking generally, of course; these experiences can also be unfamiliar to men and familiar to women.) Deborah Tannen, in *Talking from 9 to 5,* lists these war metaphors: "stick to your guns," "under the gun," "calling the shots," "an uphill battle," "getting flak," "deep-six it." But she says that women "are already doing things their way, using metaphors from cooking, birthing, and sewing along with those from war and sports" (121). It's not that any of these metaphors fail to convey the overall sense, even if the source is unfamiliar. It's that the metaphors we use can exclude people—men and women—if they don't experience work as the thrill of battle, for example.

When we talk about literal war, what do we talk about? Interestingly enough, we rarely talk about the horrific realities. When war is the target, not the source, domain, we reveal those aspects of war that are unconnected to death and destruction, except of course, when we're talking about the enemy.

In 1954, after a briefing session of the Strategic Air Command, someone asked General Curtis LeMay "what course he would advocate if hostilities were renewed in Korea—by then at truce. He answered that he would drop a few bombs in China, Manchuria, and southeastern Russia" (Rhodes 53). General LeMay is reported to have said, "In those 'poker games,' such as Korea and Indo-China, we . . . have never raised the ante—we have always just called the bet. We ought to try raising sometime" (53–54). As Richard Rhodes points out in "The General and World War III," "nuclear crises are not poker games." General LeMay did not know (nor did anyone else until 1989) that the Soviet forces in Cuba during the missile crisis "possessed one- to three-megaton hydrogen warheads for some twenty medium-range ballistic missiles that could have been targeted on U.S. cities as far north as Washington" (59).

The Gulf War has a history of metaphors that begins with its very name. First it was "Desert Shield," then "Desert Storm," and at its end "The Gulf War, 1991." (A hesitance to call war "war" is not limited to the Persian Gulf. The Vietnam War was called "The Vietnamese Conflict, 1961–1975.") American bombs in the Gulf War were called "Patriots"; the Iran-Iraq bombs were "Scuds." We heard about "target-rich environments"; and we heard about "friendly fire," a phrase derived from "friendlies," one's own troops or allies. "Friendly fire" is the horror of weapons being fired by accident on your own troops. Saddam Hussein's own contribution to war metaphors was "the mother of all battles." He was not simply personifying battle. He was recalling the memory of a specific battle in Arabic literature, the battle of Qadisiya in 636 CE, in which the Arabs won the first major victory for Islam. In the chapter "War and More War," you'll find many examples of war as a target domain: we map onto the concept of war many experiences that are not directly related to its literal reality. The source domains are rich and varied.

Lakoff and Johnson offer many examples of how categories of metaphorical concepts parallel categories of nonmetaphorical concepts, of how metaphors structure our use of language, our thinking, our behavior, and values. In addition to those in their co-authored essay and book as well as in Lakoff and Turner's book, all of which are cited in this chapter, you can find many more examples at *The Conceptual Metaphor Home Page* (the URL is http://cogsci.berkeley.edu/).

Applying the Idea

Locate a target domain on the Web site previously listed. Try "anger," for example. What are our metaphors for "anger"? One source domain is "heat." Under the structural metaphor "Anger is heat," list as many expressions of it as you can, such as "He was burned up" and "His criticism inflamed her."

Another target domain for "heat" is "lust." What expressions can you list that fall under the controlling metaphor "Lust is heat"? Here are two: "They were hot for each other," "He burned to see her again." What do we commit ourselves to when we accept "heat" as a metaphor for "anger"? Is there any other kind of anger, for example? What is revealed and concealed about "anger" and "lust" in these common metaphors?

You can do the same exercise by looking at the category "Source Domain" or simply "Metaphor" at *The Conceptual Metaphor Home Page.* Or you can come up with many categories on your own. For example, you can begin by just listing expressions for ways we talk about one of the following: ideas, the mind, desire, competition, or problems. Then see how individual expressions for talking about problems, for example, cluster into categories. The category is the main or controlling metaphor.

Because metaphor is so fundamental to our conceptual system — it's so conventional, so natural — we rarely notice the degree to which we comprehend metaphors as direct experience of physical or mental phenomena. We say, "He can't get started," "I'm winding down," "You need to be recharged," for example. These are all expressions linked to the controlling metaphor "People are batteries." And the battery metaphor is related closely to "Minds are machines" (more currently, "Minds are computers," as described earlier in this chapter). Lakoff and Johnson include the metaphor "Mind is a brittle object" as another model for mind: "She just fell apart," "I think he may crack," "Under cross-examination, he crumbled." These models are central to the way we talk and think about mind in this culture.

In "The Metaphorical Structure of the Human Conceptual System," Lakoff and Johnson list expressions that reveal "Time as money" in American culture. Included in that metaphor are other associations that we make to money: it's a "valuable commodity" and "a limited resource" (195). Hence, we say, "Can you spare some time?" "Use your time wisely," "I saved my vacation time so I could spend an extra week at the beach this summer." As the authors explain in *Metaphors We Live By,* it's not that we use our experience with money just to talk about time; we conceptualize time this way. It's not necessary to do so. Other cultures don't. The metaphors by which we connect and understand experiences, therefore, suggest values that are closely bound to culture (9).

For example, my colleague in sociology, H. B. Cavalcanti, grew up in Brazil where time is generally not conceptualized as money, and thus meetings do not carry with them the associations of contractual rigor and control that they do in the United States. Meetings tend to be scheduled on the hour or the half-hour, and yet, for a meeting scheduled at 8:00, people might arrive at 7:30 or 9:00, Cavalcanti remembers. It would have been inconceivable in his experience to arrange a meeting at 8:15. An 8:15 class, for example, would have been "disorienting" to him. He recalls with amusement his friend's surprise when an American invited them to a party that was scheduled two weeks away. "Who can schedule partying?" she asked. "You have a party when you're in a happy mood."

My colleague in the English department, Raymond F. Hilliard, recalls a trip to West Africa where a group of Americans complained about people arriving late to meetings. A West African expressed his protest in metaphor: "Americans are prisoners of time," he said. "You are always consulting your watches." With globalization, expressions for the conceptual metaphor "Time is money" are familiar in other cultures; they're just not commonly used because time is not typically conceived in terms of a valuable commodity or limited resource.

What Does Seeing and Understanding Metaphor Have to Do with Reading and Writing?

If you can identify the controlling metaphor and the extent to which a writer depends on it, you can often get to the assumptions or the premises on which an argument is constructed. Sometimes a writer does not state assumptions directly, but implies them. And sometimes the writer is not even aware of the degree to which she or he has relied on a particular metaphor. Readers may notice these metaphors more readily than the writer would. Once you are aware of implied assumptions, you can respond analytically and critically to the argument. In many arguments, the conclusions are valid if you accept the premises. So the premises are important to question and to evaluate: do you accept or reject them? If you reject them, the validity of the argument will not matter. Of course, not all implied premises are within the writer's metaphors. But many are.

Identifying and analyzing the metaphors you use in writing can help you understand your own thinking process. Because metaphor is fundamental to thought and language, understanding your own use of it provides a necessary tool for better explaining your own thinking in your writing. You will become more aware of assumptions you make in constructing your own arguments, assumptions that may otherwise remain hidden.

An understanding of metaphor helps you to see what is concealed when you commit yourself to a particular way of thinking about an experience. Once aware that thinking and behavior are in part determined by the direction of your gaze, you may be better able to consider other metaphors, other directions, so that you can test your own theories, see, and thus describe more than one aspect of a phenomenon in your writing.

Applying the Idea

Write a paragraph in which you describe either yourself as a writer or your practice of writing. For example: How do you start? What are the difficulties for you as a writer? What's easy? Where in the process of writing do you stop and why? How do you know when the writing is done (beyond the fact that it's due on a particular day)?

Don't be self-conscious about metaphor as you describe yourself as a writer or your writing process. For the purpose of this exercise, write as freely and as quickly as you can, without stopping to examine the particular expressions you use. The objective is for the class to notice all the ways metaphors for writing reveal assumptions and attitudes to which we may give little conscious thought, but which may affect our habits. Exchange paragraphs with another student, and try to identify the metaphorical ways you each talk about being a writer or the act of writing.

IT'S A STORY: METAPHOR IN ACADEMIC DISCOURSE

Throughout this chapter, we have seen how we use metaphor in our ordinary thought and language to connect our experiences and thus get hold of the world. We have also seen how we use metaphor to create the world: to construct reality. To think in this way is to generalize through comparison; we think of one phenomenon or cluster of phenomena in terms of the similarities and differences with others. If we did not have this ability to see resemblances among things, to categorize, our reality would be innumerable discrete experiences. We would have no unified sense of ourselves or of our world. Metaphor thus plays a crucial and necessary role in human understanding. Just as metaphor is indispensable to thought and language in our everyday experience, it is indispensable in the academy too. Research and scholarship in the disciplines — theory — is a matter of finding useful analogies. Analogies, like metaphors, are comparisons that depend on the concept "as if," and thus they are generally formed in the same way. Here is a common frame that illustrates the metaphorical structure: "Let me give you an analogy. Time is like a thief. Just as a thief quietly and quickly steals another's valuable possessions, so *time steals one's youth, beauty, and strength.*"

Narrative Knowledge in the Academy

In every domain of knowledge, metaphors provide the structural support of theory. Theorists begin with a general metaphor (a perceived similarity between two phenomena), modify the metaphor through analogical reasoning (through an analysis of the correspondences between the phenomena and the implications for the object under study), and then transform the original metaphor into a model, or theoretical framework that guides research and practice. Think of the model, or framework, as a plausible story that is then shared and tested by the larger community. Kernels of such stories in this chapter are "Weather forecasts are speculative because of the butterfly effect," "Gravity is like social attraction," "The brain is a kind of computer," "Abnormal behavior is an illness," and "Schools are marketplaces of ideas." What begins as an imagined correspondence between a known and unknown object becomes a process of exploring, explaining, and establishing support for further similarities. That is how the plot thickens, so to speak.

All theories are provisional by the very fact that they are based on analogies, that is, metaphors, which, as we've seen, are only partial definitions. Theorizing involves speculation, not certainty. It involves making probable assumptions through analogy, through the perception of great similarity between two objects. The greater the perceived similarity, the greater the probability. To get on with their work, theorists must make such assumptions. These analogies drive research and guide practice, even while they are repeatedly tested and criticized so that alternative analogies can be considered. Although truth, in the sense of absolute knowledge, may be the ideal goal, the belief that we have arrived there must be tentative. Scientists and humanists alike construct truths *for the time being.*

Certainty must be deferred because, as just explained, theories are based on analogical reasoning, a metaphor that by definition highlights some aspects of an object and conceals others. Analogies direct one's attention toward some but not all aspects of a phenomenon. Therefore, research must allow for many alternative and even conflicting metaphors so that other directions are not ignored, and so that an object or a concept is not simplified by a singular gaze representing one line of vision within one historical period and culture. William James, considered to be the father of modern psychology, says, "The final truth" cannot be grasped "until the last man [sic] has had his experience and had his say" (141).

Searching for truth is a continual process of disconnecting and reconnecting experiences in new ways. Our truths, therefore, are provisional and plausible. They are "likely stories," as Plato said, but his belief in an absolute ideal need not disparage the value of the knowledge we have constructed — probable truth — which is perhaps the only knowledge we can have. To think of theories as "likely stories" is an invitation to further discovery.

Metaphor Examples across the Disciplines

Generally, interesting cases of metaphor in the sciences and social sciences are those that, for a time, cannot be paraphrased literally. In other words, there is no unmetaphorical way to describe these cases. These metaphors are irreplaceable in the language of a theory. They assist initial descriptions of what has been previously unknown. They give it form.

Noodles, Towels, and Butterflies   "Chaos" is a shorthand term for the study of deterministic disorder in nature. The word refers to apparent disorder, but chaos theory describes order, either emerging or disappearing. In their research, scientists search for patterns of fine structure within a disorderly stream of data. Using special computer techniques and graphic images, theorists try to capture the visual structure of motion. Chaos theory has its own language for naming its discoveries, a metaphoric arena of "strange attractors," "folded-towel diffeomorphisms," and "smooth noodle maps."

James Gleick, responsible for bringing some of this theory to the public, says in *Chaos,* "These are the new elements of motion, just as, in traditional physics, quarks and gluons are the new elements of matter" (5). Some of the metaphors in chaos theory have already influenced business, astronomy, politics, and literary criticism. "The butterfly effect" — the notion that the stir of a butterfly's wings in Beijing can change storm systems next month in New York — has become part of our cultural knowledge. Once applied liberally to other domains of experience, such metaphors lose their original power of exploring great similarity between phenomena. That is, they can be used reductively, turned into an oversimplification of a concept or cluster of concepts. But metaphors, such as "the butterfly effect," have, for good or bad, affected our vision of everyday reality. Sometimes such metaphors remain in the public consciousness long after they have served their purpose for theorists. Scientists have gone on to new analogies because, as the information grows, the original story impedes rather than moves thinking forward.

Ironically, "chaos," as previously described, refers to apparent disorder while the theory describes the discovery of order, emerging or disappearing. "Chaos," then, is only the appearance, what things look like when one's gaze is undirected. In the history of the sciences and social sciences, metaphor has been vital in giving direction to one's gaze. Scientists have conceptualized natural phenomena through comparisons to the mechanical (clocks, radios, and telephone switchboards, for example) and, in particular, to social worlds.

The Social Life of Nature and the Gravity of Social Bonds   David Leary, in "Psyche's Muse," traces the history of using "social worlds" as a metaphor in science and points out an interesting irony in the development of metaphors for social science. In the natural sciences, for example, Sir Isaac Newton's theory of gravity is based on analogies to the social world. He conceptualized the tendency of physical objects to move toward each other as the "attraction" of people to each other. Darwin's theory of natural selection also draws on social metaphors to frame concepts, such as "the struggle for existence," "competition," "division of labor," and the "economy and polity of nature." Darwin's theory depended on a sustained comparison between artificial selection (as demonstrated by breeders) and natural selection. What Nature (which he capitalized, as if personified) does is analogous to what breeders do, except that for natural selection the changes made are fantastically slow, infinitesimal, and, to us, invisible (10–11).

Newton's and Darwin's use of human experience as an analog for natural phenomena soon influenced theories about social dynamics. To illustrate this point, Leary summarizes Bishop George Berkeley's social theory, partially quoting from "The Bond of Society":

> This theory is based on the simple, straightforward contention that there is a "certain correspondence" or "similitude of operation" between the natural and the human worlds. Just as natural philosophers (following Newton) agreed that natural bodies exert a "mutual attraction upon each other," so too, Berkeley asserted, can we observe a "like principle of attraction" in the moral world. In fact, the "social appetite in human souls" — that "greatest spring and source of moral actions" — is the very bond of society, just as gravity is the bond of nature. (13)

The irony, as Leary explains, is that Newton had drawn his analogy from the source domain of the social world — human attraction — because he had found no other way of describing or accounting for the object of study — gravity. Later, yet still within Newton's lifetime, the metaphor is used in reverse by social science: the social world becomes the target domain while nature becomes the source domain in an analog for understanding human attraction. We've come full circle: gravity is like human attraction. Human attraction is like gravity (13).

The Mind as Computer and Patient   In cognitive psychology, even those who dislike "machine" descriptions of cognition cannot escape the presence of computer metaphors. They have played a vital role in theory and have provided much of the basic vocabulary for articulating theoretical positions. According to research in the field, exploring resemblances between people and computers has influenced cognitive psychology more than any other factor. It is through metaphor, analogy, and empirical models that we lay claim to understanding, and through this same process we transcend current limits of understanding. To consider further the case of cognitive psychology, images of brain organization as "modular" and mental activities as "parallel," rather than "linear," have now changed the way we understand "information processing."

At one time our construction of reality included a clear separation between spiritual and earthly events. People who had visions, or strange imaginings, were demonized and subjected to punishment by religious authorities. The cause of such visions was spiritual — communication with the devil. Later, the burden of controlling such behavior shifted from religious authorities to medical practitioners. The new metaphor for violating social norms was "illness." Thus the shift in belief was from demonism and witchcraft to sickness as the cause for violating norms. Theodore Sarbin sketches the history of "Metaphors of Unwanted Conduct" and argues that the "mental illness" metaphor carries with it values about what behavior is wanted or not wanted. He argues too that these judgments are made by those whose power is far greater than that of the people being judged. Because those in power, the authorities, exercise judgment against a background of beliefs and values that are bound to one's cultural code, the "policies and prescriptions for labeling and dealing with unwanted conduct is, inevitably, a moral enterprise" (325).

Some scholars have argued that it is time to replace the mental illness metaphor with one that lessens the force of moral judgment. One such alternative has been "problems in living." But we have already seen how some metaphors, such as "Cancer is war" and "The brain is a computer," have become deeply embedded in the public consciousness and thus embedded within our culture's belief system. These metaphors are difficult and slow to change (Sarbin 325). And yet, do we want to commit ourselves to the belief, for example, that all mental processes are networked information systems? Is prayer, as Marsha Norman says, like "asking for a remote download from the Net"? Do we live, as Richard Preston suggests, "in a kind of biological Internet"? How far can any metaphor be extended until it ceases to be enlightening or useful? This last question must be asked of all metaphors.

The Ideas Market   Nowhere are there better illustrations of how people in power get to impose their metaphors than in law. Just as in the sciences and humanities, metaphors in legal discourse become integrated into reasoning that, in this instance, leads to judicial decisions affecting all of our lives. And these metaphors, like any other, can serve to mislead as well as enlighten. Some influential legal metaphors are "the marketplace of ideas," "the wall of separation between church and state," "the chilling effect" doctrine, a "color-blind Constitution," and "shedding one's rights at the schoolhouse gate." For our purposes, a discussion of one will suffice.

In 1965 Justice Brennan, concurring in the case of *Lamont v. Postmaster General*, introduced "the marketplace of ideas" to judiciary discourse. The Supreme Court had declared that it was unconstitutional for the postmaster general to detain and refuse delivery of unsealed "communist political propaganda" until the addressee sent a postcard expressing the wish to receive the materials. Brennan defended the right to receive: "The dissemination of ideas can accomplish nothing if otherwise willing addressees are not free to receive and consider them. It would be a barren marketplace of ideas that had only sellers and no buyers" (Bosmajian 49).

Since then, "the marketplace of ideas" has been invoked to protect First Amendment rights involving such cases as library censorship, the fairness doctrine, academic freedom, and flag burning. Here are some examples of its use in judicial decisions:

1. "The classroom is peculiarly the 'marketplace of ideas'" (Justice Brennan, 1967, arguing against New York teachers' loyalty oath).

2. "It is the purpose of the First Amendment to preserve an uninhibited marketplace of ideas in which truth will ultimately prevail, rather than to countenance monopolization of that market, whether it be by the Government itself or a private licensee" (Justice White, 1969, in defense of the fairness doctrine).

3. "The college classroom with its surrounding environs is peculiarly the 'marketplace of ideas,' and we break no new constitutional ground in reaffirming this Nation's dedication to safeguarding academic freedom" (Justice Powell, 1972, defending the right of Students for a Democratic Society to be recognized as a campus organization at Central Connecticut College).

4. "Public schools are major marketplaces of ideas, and the first amendment rights must be accorded all 'persons' in the market for ideas, including secondary school students . . . seeking redress of state action banning a book from the 'warehouse of ideas'" (Justice Cyr, 1982, regarding the banning of *365 Days* from a high school library in Maine). (Bosmajian 49–51)

Even though "the marketplace of ideas" is one of the most frequently cited metaphors in legal discourse, questions arise about its application and relevance to current First Amendment opinions. How valid are the assumptions on which this principle is based? In "The Marketplace of Ideas: A Legitimizing Myth," Stanley Ingber explains that today's "marketplace" is biased toward sophisticated information technology and tends to support the beliefs of those in power. Access and facilities are not equal in the market of ideas. Consequently, protecting freedom of expression does not ensure that new ideas can develop. Protecting a right and providing for it are not the same thing (quoted in Bosmajian 59).

A second argument is that the "marketplace" is based on the assumption of objective truth; that is, ideas are presented without distortion. Another is that today, unlike the times in which dissenting views led to additional metropolitan newspapers, the "marketplace" is monopolized by the few publishers able to compete in the economy (Bosmajian 58–59).

Considering the differences between literal marketplaces and the ideas market, we might question the relevance of the metaphor: can ideas be equated with consumerism? are knowledge and understanding commodities to be bought and sold like broccoli and beads? In 1959 Justice Frankfurter argued that "there is an important difference in the scope of power of a state to regulate what feeds the belly and what feeds the brain." Certain types of speech, however, have not been permitted in the marketplace, such as libel or speech that constitutes a clear and present (or probable) danger. Courts have prohibited profanity, obscenities, and "fighting words" in the "marketplace." Unlike the literal markets we recall nostalgically, where wares of little value were sold and purchased freely, the ideas market is restricted (Bosmajian 63).

In addition to the differences between literal marketplaces that may have existed long ago and the ideas market, there are inconsistencies in the application of the metaphor. For example, the courts have invoked the marketplace of ideas to both defend and not defend flag burners. In 1989 the Supreme Court protected the right of a flag burner. Justice Brennan wrote: "The First Amendment does not guarantee that other concepts virtually sacred to our Nation as a whole . . . will go unquestioned in the marketplace of ideas" (Bosmajian 51). In their dissenting opinion, however, Justices Rehnquist and Stevens argued that flag burning was not protected by the First Amendment. Rehnquist said, "The flag is not simply another 'idea' or 'point of view' competing for recognition in the marketplace of ideas. Millions and millions of Americans regard it with an almost mystical reverence regardless of what sort of social, political, or philosophical beliefs they may have" (Bosmajian 70).

Despite inconsistencies in the application of this metaphor, the Supreme Court "steadfastly relies upon a marketplace of ideas theory in determining what speech is protected. Marketplace imagery (competition of ideas, the value of debate) pervades the Court opinions and provides justification for their first amendment 'tests'" (Bosmajian 69). In the conclusion of his book, Haig Bosmajian states that it is important to recognize and analyze judicial metaphors, "for the acceptance or rejection of [them] will determine the legal principles and doctrines by which we will be guided and ruled" (205).

Applying the Idea

Either individually or as a team, interview a professor in your major (or in one you're considering), asking her or him to identify an important metaphor in the discipline. What analogy guides some of the research and practice in the field? Ask for some examples. You might also ask to borrow a textbook intended to introduce students to the discipline. Read the introduction and see if you can locate any metaphors that suggest a way of looking at the world through a particular comparison. (Remember that the governing metaphor in a passage will not be stated directly as, for example, "The mind is a computer." The governing or controlling metaphor is usually derived from verbs, nouns, and adjectives that imply it: "information processing," "neural network," "hardwiring," and so forth.)

Bring your findings to class and share these with each other.

READING FOR METAPHOR:
THE PRINCIPLES MODELED

The following sections include an excerpt from a reading in chapter 5, "Mind and Body," a sample annotation of the excerpt to show the pattern of metaphors and their implications, and an analysis to show one possible interpretation of meaning.

Sample Passage

In Marjorie Rosen's "New Face, New Body, New Self," several teenagers "determined to change their lives through cosmetic surgery" tell their stories. This is one.

> Ever since she was three, Stacy Hirsch had her heart set on becoming an actress. Singing and dancing lessons were part of the plan. So, too, after she turned fourteen, was a nose job. "I had made a real commitment to the profession," says Stacy, sixteen. "I thought having my nose done would give me a new look that would increase my <u>marketability</u>."
>
> Before her surgery, says Stacy, "people weren't really seeing me; they were speaking to me and thinking, 'She's got a big nose.'" Because of Stacy's unhappiness about her appearance, her parents, Larry, a manufacturer's representative, and Linda, a preschool teacher, backed Stacy's decision. "I'd had a nose job myself at sixteen," says Linda. "I never said anything to Stacy about her nose, but she knew I'd had mine done, and maybe that stuck in her mind."
>
> Still, Stacy worried that friends would perceive her as <u>vain</u> and only told those closest to her. "I asked myself, 'Should I not do this because it's not the *good* thing to do?'" she admits. "But I decided I didn't want to ask, 'What if? Would I have gotten that job if I looked different?'"
>
> In July 1991, after her freshman year at Glenbrook North High School in Northbrook, Illinois, Stacy scheduled surgery with Dr. Jack Kerth, who asked Stacy to bring in pictures of noses that she liked. "I looked through my teen magazines and tore off the noses of Julia Roberts and Cindy Crawford," says Stacy. "But I asked Dr. Kerth for a nose that fits my face, that looks natural." And, she believes, she got one. "It was the nose I was born to have and didn't get," she says.
>
> When Hirsch returned to school in September, she says, "boys noticed me." What's more, she got a part on *Energy Express,* a Chicago TV show for teens about sports, which has been picked up nationally for syndication. "I would never have had this response if I had looked a different

way," says Hirsch. "When your outside equals your inside, you're going to get twice as much as you already have."

Annotation

Reading Stacy Hirsch's story, I underlined words, phrases, or clauses that seemed to imply her assumptions. Most of those, you'll see, are expressed in metaphors. Embedded within them are personal, social, and cultural values that for Stacy occasionally conflict. My comments reflect one reading of implied assumptions.

The self is a commodity to be bought and sold in the marketplace.

The body is a container; inside is the self.

Modifying the body is a matter of ethics.

Two opposing values here—one regarding the appearance of marketable goods and the other, good behavior.

Body parts are consumer goods to be bought, or in this case, "ripped off." Like a designer ripoff?

But she implies by "fits my face" and "looks natural" that "natural" and "fitting" are that which conform to an aesthetic ideal.

Body parts are goods distributed at birth; we are deserving of particular types, yet sometimes these are withheld from us.

Ever since she was three, Stacy Hirsch had her heart set on becoming an actress. Singing and dancing lessons were part of the plan. So, too, after she turned fourteen, was a nose job. "I had made a real commitment to the profession," says Stacy, sixteen. "I thought having my nose done would give me a new look that would increase my <u>marketability</u>."

Before her surgery, says Stacy, "<u>people weren't really seeing me; they were speaking to me and thinking, 'She's got a big nose.'</u>" Because of Stacy's unhappiness about her appearance, her parents, Larry, a manufacturer's representative, and Linda, a preschool teacher, backed Stacy's decision. "I'd had a nose job myself at sixteen," says Linda. "I never said anything to Stacy about her nose, but she knew I'd had mine done, and maybe that stuck in her mind."

Still, Stacy worried that friends would perceive her as vain and only told those closest to her. "I asked myself, 'Should I not do this because <u>it's not the *good* thing to do</u>?'" she admits. "But I decided I didn't want to ask, 'What if? Would I have gotten that job if I looked different?'"

In July 1991, after her freshman year at Glenbrook North High School in Northbrook, Illinois, Stacy scheduled surgery with Dr. Jack Kerth, who asked Stacy to bring in pictures of noses that she liked. "I looked through my teen magazines and <u>tore off the noses of Julia Roberts and Cindy Crawford</u>," says Stacy. "But I asked Dr. Kerth <u>for a nose that fits my face, that looks natural.</u>" And, she believes, she got one. "<u>It was the nose I was born to have and didn't get</u>," she says.

When Hirsch returned to school in September, she says, "boys noticed me." What's more, she got a part on *Energy Express,* a Chicago TV show for teens about sports, which has been picked up nationally for syndication. "I would never have had this response if I had looked a different way," says Hirsch. "When your outside equals your inside, you're going to get twice as much as you already have."

The body and the self are separate locations relative to each other: body is outside; it is the container. Self is inside. Ideally, the body and the self are an equation: the body is the self, and vice versa. If the two are equal, the whole is a valuable package, or commodity, that can be traded in the marketplace of the self.

Interpretation of the Story

To accept Stacy Hirsch's argument for the value of a nose job, a reader must accept the premises on which Hirsch builds her case. Because the premises are implied, as premises often are, and are expressed in metaphor, readers may disagree about their pattern of significance. My response, therefore, is not definitive. Here, then, is one possible interpretation of her assumptions as I follow them along in her story:

For Hirsch, the self is a precious commodity, but it is invisible because it is hidden within the body. Goods to be sold in the marketplace have to be seen, or how do we know their value? Appearance, therefore, is important. What you see is what you get, people say. Therefore, in the marketplace of the self, according to Hirsch, we have to make the container, the body, reflect the quality of the inside, the self. The assumption, of course, is that the inside is already good. To make the container and the inside match, we modify the body to conform to aesthetic ideals that are particular to our culture and era. The more the body conforms to the ideal, the more valuable it is in the self market. "You're going to get twice as much as you already have," Hirsch claims. In her argument, the book can be judged by its cover because the container (body) and the contained (self) are "equal," or should be, she thinks.

The premises above create an ethical dilemma for Hirsch because two kinds of values conflict for her. Market value (appearance of the body) and human virtue (quality of self) are not the same thing. What's valued in the market is the "right look," but what's valued in life is "right behavior." The "goods" are not necessarily the "good." One concerns consumerism; the other concerns character. Hirsch worries that her behavior will be perceived as vanity. "Should I not do this because it's not the good thing to do?" Hirsch asks. Her answer is not to ask that question, but to ask a different one: "Would I have gotten that job if I looked different?" Given her assumptions, she can safely answer "no."

It's easy enough to show Hirsch examples of actors whose noses do not measure up, but whose talents do. Two who got the job without a nose job are Barbra Streisand and Meryl Streep. Are we "not really seeing" them, but thinking, "She's got a big nose," as Hirsch imagines her former "self" as perceived by others? And conversely, it's easy enough to show examples of people whose faces and bodies measure up to an ideal, but whose "selves" don't. Maybe they don't worry about matching the "inside" to the "outside" for the same reason that Hirsch does worry about matching the "outside" to the "inside": in a postmodern culture they assume that life is conducted entirely in a world of surfaces. Nonetheless, "The body is the self" and "The self is a precious commodity" can be dangerous metaphors because of what they conceal about the nature of human character.

Stacy Hirsch lives by her metaphors, as Lakoff and Johnson would say. It's not that she just talks about the self in terms of body image and the marketplace. She conceives of it that way and elected to modify her body rather than her thinking.

By uncovering the metaphors in Hirsch's story, we can see some of the premises from which she argues the benefits of cosmetic surgery. Once we see the premises, we can better understand the reasoning that led to her decision, and thus have a more informed response to her views.

A PRACTICE READING: APPLYING THE PRINCIPLES YOURSELF

Now that I have illustrated a reading of metaphors and a possible interpretation based on their pattern or meaning, here is an opportunity to try your hand at a similar exercise. Following, Robert J. Sternberg explains how our metaphors for love affect our relationships with others, and he provides a table of twenty-four love stories that includes advantages, disadvantages, and potential success for each metaphor. The assignment following "Love Is a Story" invites you to write your own story, applying Sternberg's methods of analysis.

Love Is a Story

Robert J. Sternberg

Robert J. Sternberg is a psychologist at Yale University and the author of a number of books, including The Triangle of Love (1988) and Successful Intelligence: How Practical and Creative Intelligence Determine Success in Life (1997). "Love Is a Story" appeared in the Spring 1994 issue of The General Psychologist. In 1998 Sternberg published Love Is a Story: A New Theory of Relationships.

Everyone knows a love story. These stories have been around for ages entertaining and sometimes instructing us. Erich Segal wrote a best-selling one and simply called it Love Story. But then there is real life, in which love is not a story at all, but the "real thing." To survive, we're told, we have to separate the stories we tell ourselves from what's actually going on — to distinguish fact from fiction. The whole point of getting to know someone better is to find out what they're "really like," and not just what we perceive or imagine them to be. A clean separation of fact from fiction, however, simply isn't possible in the context of personal relationships. Instead, we shape the facts to conform to our personal fictions.

Love really is a story, only we, rather than William Shakespeare or Gabriel Garcia Marquez or Erich Segal or Barbara Cartland, are the authors. We relate better to love stories — whether in books, plays, soap operas, or elsewhere — than we do to the lists containing generic steps to take in "understanding and improving your relationship." We should therefore be paying more attention to the love stories in our lives and less to these rational step-by-step lists. The love story underlying our relationship determines our state of mind concerning that relationship. Conventional therapies to improve peoples' love-lives don't work if they address the effects of the stories we tell ourselves (our understanding of why the relationship failed, for example) rather than the stories themselves, which cause these effects (see McAdams, 1993).

The movie, When Harry Met Sally, one of the most popular love stories of recent times, succeeded largely because it explored the idea of a love story itself and particularly how stories about love differ from those concerning friendship. Harry's relationship with Sally and his perceptions of her fit into his preconceived notion of a story about friendship. Despite their close relationship, Harry seeks romance from other women for years. He ultimately changes his story about love, in part because of his relationship with Sally. But until this story changes, Harry can't view Sally in a romantic way, no matter what either of them does.

As long as there are people who are romantically involved (presumably always!), there will be people trying to understand and improve their intimate relations. People go to great lengths to do this: They talk avidly to one another, to friends outside the relationship, to family members and therapists. They buy books, attend courses, and watch videos. People often mention the divorce rate of almost 50% in this country. And we can all think of relationships which, although they might not break up, are nevertheless unhappy. Many can count on one hand (if at all!) the relationships they know of which *are* happy. Either relationships are impossibly difficult, or, somehow, our attempts at understanding and improvement are fundamentally misguided. Here I adopt the latter perspective. Basically, our current attempts to understand and improve relationships are misconceived. This viewpoint therefore turns current conceptions of love and close relationships on their head.

RELATIONSHIPS AS STORIES

5   When we first meet someone, we sometimes feel that we need to get to know that person better so as to match up our first impressions with realities, to substitute fact for fiction, truths for stories. We imagine, in getting to know someone, that we replace a "fiction" with the "reality" of nonfiction. Forget it. We simply replace one story with another. The story may (or may not) be based on more facts; but it is a story nevertheless. Stories are not right or wrong in themselves, although they may be more or less adaptive. The story gives the relationship meaning in the context of our lives.

Just as in science any one of an infinite number of theories could describe a set of data, so there are always an infinite number of stories consistent with a set of given inferences or facts. There is no absolute way of determining what is right. Scientists never reach any absolute truth; we never reach absolute truth in our relationships either. Instead, we create stories, and over time either continue them, or replace them with others.

Consider, for example, a common problem in male-female relationships. Dan's idea of a loving relationship is that it is smooth, tranquil, and relatively conflict-free. If two people genuinely love each other, they accept each other as they are, meaning that they are non-confrontational and don't attack one another verbally. What Dan views as an attack, Susan views as a discussion. For her, two people in love confront their differences and together forge a common path. Without engaging in communication, according to Susan, especially communication about their differences, the couple cannot even begin to forge such a path. The result is that Susan confronts Dan when she sees problems. Dan views these confrontations as attacks, which, to his mind, are precisely what people who love each other should not initiate. He withdraws. Susan, frustrated by his withdrawal, becomes more assertive, resulting in further withdrawal, and so on. The relationship is deteriorating, not because the two people see different facts or even because they don't love each other. Rather, they have different stories about love, which lead them to interpret events in opposite ways. The relationship may fall apart simply because neither partner has understood the other partner's story about love.

Your story about your partner is only a part of your story about your intimate relationship. It is important to distinguish between the two. You may feel positively about your partner, for example, but much less positively about how you are relating to your partner or vice versa within the relationship. We can feel someone is a wonderful person but also feel at the same time that we couldn't make things work with that person in an intimate context.

Our story about a relationship may change, but it is always our story. Even if a partner helps us "write" the story, it is our creation, and the partner is likely never fully to understand what our story involves. The partner will almost inevitably have a story that differs to a greater or lesser degree, as will others who know the couple. We need to realize that we never reach some kind of ultimate truth. Rather, we endlessly replace old stories with new ones, which may be better or worse, but remain as stories nonetheless. We develop our stories as we go along, adding chapters as unanticipated events and new directions enter our lives. Retrospective stories—those we create after relationships end—may be quite different from prospective ones—those we create before a relationship begins—reflecting our attempts to incorporate hindsight into our understanding of what was going on in the relationship.

These stories are all we have. They are the reality we create. There is no 10 truth that we can know beyond them. This view may sound solipsistic, as though each of us lives utterly alone in the world, but it is not. We do not live each in our own isolated reality but in the company of others, who constantly challenge and modify our stories. We need to create stories which function in the context of daily life. People who are unable to do so often collapse under the mental and emotional strain caused by this lack.

WHAT ARE OUR STORIES LIKE?

Stories about our relationships are like all other stories: They have beginnings, middles, and—if the relationship concludes—they have endings. Even if our relationship hasn't ended, most of us supply an imagined ending to our present love story. Love stories have plots, themes, and characters. The characters are givens, but the plots and the themes, which combine aspects of the relationship with elements of our personal history (as do the plots and themes of all story writers), are generally of our own creation. Plot is a summary account of what is happening in a relationship; a theme, on the other hand, is a characterization of what these happenings mean. Attempts to understand relationships will fail unless one takes their storylike elements into account.

Stories, like love itself, function primarily at the experiential or intuitive level. People who are really trying to improve their relationships often turn to psychologists for help. But psychologists often fail to appreciate how much love has to do with stories rather than with scientific analysis. Freudian attempts to understand relationships, for instance, reconstruct unconscious childhood traumas rather than bringing current but subconscious stories to light. Freudians emphasize what happened to us long ago, instead of what we encounter here and now. Behaviorists often see things in terms of isolated stimuli and responses: You can discourage your lover's unacceptable habits by responding negatively to them. The same negative stimulus is supposed to correct bad behavior in anyone. People don't feel comfortable with behaviorist prescriptions because they treat a person more like a robot than a human being. Recent cognitive attempts to understand love, much in vogue today, assume that all we need to do is to get people to think rationally about love and to be wary of the irrational thoughts that may impinge upon their intimate relationships. But the stories we have are not "rationally" generated.

Love is synthetic rather than analytic — literally synthetic in the sense that we synthesize a story in the course of our experiences. Stories conform to intuitive and experiential rules, not logical and rational ones. We need to understand relationships as narratives, not logical theorems. Seymour Epstein (1993) has compared the characteristics of experiential thinking to those of rational thinking. Experiential thinking tends to be holistic, emotional, controlled by "vibes," heavily encoded in terms of images and metaphors, rapidly accomplished, slow to change, crudely differentiated and integrated, preconscious, and self-evidently valid ("experiencing is believing"). Rational thinking, in contrast, tends to be analytic, logical, conscious, abstract, more slowly accomplished, rapidly changed, symbolic, highly differentiated and integrated, conscious, and requiring justification via logic and evidence for belief.

When Brian asks Sylvia why she left him, Sylvia is able to give Brian reasons. But the reasons are only clear in retrospect. They give Brian, and to some extent Sylvia, a set of seemingly rational explanations as to why the relationship didn't work from Sylvia's point of view. Communication was increasingly poor; love-making had become unsatisfying; the time spent together was inadequate. But those reasons were just symptoms of some underlying problem, and intuitively, Sylvia knew as much. Why was communication increasingly poor? Why had love-making become unsatisfying? The real reason was that, to Sylvia, as both of their careers took off, the relationship between the two of them had become more like a business story than a romance. Their relationship, like her job, was a business. For Sylvia, the story of a love relationship did not resemble that of a business. As a result, she found herself less able to communicate with Brian and less interested in making love. The story had changed from one she liked to one she didn't. The relationship was failing, because at an intuitive level, Sylvia no longer felt herself to be in a love situation.

Often, the problem in a relationship is not the actual thinking that people do, but the presuppositions of that thinking — the stories people bring to relationships about what love should be and how it should work. The reasons by which we explain our actions and motivations are often based on these stories. Treating the symptoms of an ailing relationship can help, but one is more likely to be successful in addressing the causes of those symptoms as well. These causes lie in an individual's love story. 15

KINDS OF STORIES

All our lives we have heard stories of various kinds, many with love as a leitmotif. We thus have an array of stories (expanded versions of what Schank and Abelson, 1977, have called scripts) that we can modify and then fit into our lives. Multiple scripts (called themes here) combine to form stories.

What are the kinds of stories we have? The kinds of stories we have reflect the kinds of interests we have — as applied to close relationships. Because stories represent interests, and so do the various sections of a bookstore, the kinds of stories we have correspond loosely to the various interest sections of a bookstore. Simply having an interest does not mean you will transfer that interest to your love relationships. But if the interest is consuming, you well might. Table 1 shows many of the kinds of stories people have, and how people with each of these kinds of stories think about relationships. These kinds of stories form the heart of the love-is-a-story framework. Relationships work best when people have compatible kinds of stories. For example, a cookbook and a gardening story might work well together, but neither would work well with a police story.

Jane has become very unhappy in her relationship with Don. For Jane, the story of her relationship with Don is a police story. If he doesn't like Jane's clothes, he expects Jane to change. He'll tell her she looks dumpy, or frumpy, or sloppy. Don watches what she eats, and will even countermand her order at a restaurant if he doesn't approve. Jane finally convinced Don to let her work, but Don won't let her take a job with any remote possibility of a career track. Don's need for control is destroying the relationship, because Jane does not want to live the rest of her life like a convicted felon out on parole.

TABLE 1

Kind ("Love is . . .")	Modes of Thought and Behavior	Typical Views of Relationships	Complementary Roles	Possible Advantages	Possible Disadvantages	Potential for Success
1. Addiction	Strong, anxious attachment. Clinging behavior. Anxiety at thought of losing partner.	"I just couldn't survive without. . . ."	1. Addict 2. Co-dependent	Partner feels wanted.	Other person feels suffocated; may become co-dependent.	Low-moderate. Higher if partner is co-dependent.
2. Art	Love of partner for physical attractiveness. Importance to person of partner's always "looking good." Treating partner as a museum piece.	"— is the most [beautiful/ handsome] partner I could ever find."	1. Admirer of art 2. "Work of Art"	Intense physical attraction. Concern for partner's physical well-being.	When a person's looks start to go, uh-oh! Partner is loved for appearance, not self.	Low if partner loses attractive physical appearance. Moderate while partner retains attractive physical appearance.
3. Business	Relationships are a business proposition. Money is power. Each partner has [his/her] place.	"We're in this business together."	1.–2. Partners in business 1. Proprietor 2. Customer	Bills get paid. Partners have clearly defined roles (jobs). Partners unite against outside threats to the "firm."	A disaster if your partner is a romantic. Partner's roles may become too static. Cold and potentially dull over time.	Low to moderate because of insufficient attention to intimacy and passion. High if partner shares the story.
4. Collectibles (Antiques, rare coins, rare stamps, etc.)	Partner is viewed as "fitting in" to some overall collection scheme. Partner is viewed in a detached way. Partner, like a piece of furniture, has his or her place.	"— fits perfectly into my life."	1. Collector 2. Collectible	Concern for partner's physical well-being.	Possible desire to "add" to the collection via search for other partners. Treating partner like a collector's piece rather than like a person. Psychological distancing from partner.	Low if person wants to add to collection. Low if person decides to collect something else. Low to moderate if collector is satisfied with just one item in the collection.

Metaphor	Core belief	Quote	Roles	Advantages	Disadvantages	Prognosis
5. Cookbook	If you do things a certain way (recipe), relationship is sure to work out. As you depart from recipe for success, relationship is viewed as more likely to fail.	"We succeed because we always...."	1. Cook 2. Restaurant patron	Desire to find activities that "work." Belief that with the right recipe, the relationship will be a good story.	Rigidity. Incomprehension that no recipe truly guarantees success.	Moderate if couple is rigid. High if couple is flexible and willing to modify the recipe over time.
6. Fantasy	Often expects to be saved by a knight in shining armor or to marry a princess.	"He's my knight in shining armor." "She's my dream come true."	1. Person in need of salvation 2. Imagined savior	Admiration and respect for partner. Willingness to do a great deal to keep partner happy.	Lack of realism. Expectations that no one or no relationship could fulfill.	Poor if person expects fantasy to continue forever, and is thus disappointed. Good if tempered with realism.
7. Games and Sports	Love is a game.	"I play to win."	1. Winner 2. Loser	Excitement. Sense of fun. Recognition that life should not always be taken seriously.	May not take relationship seriously. Goal may be to "win." May be competitive in relationship.	Variable— Not so good if gamelike aspects predominate. OK if gamelike aspects are just part of the relationship.
8. Gardening	Relationship needs to be continually nurtured and tended to. Relationships that are ignored will die.	"I tend to my relationship the way I would to a beautiful rose."	1. Gardener 2. Garden	Partner is cared for. Relationship is "watered" continually.	"Overwatering." Lack of spontaneity.	Generally excellent.
9. Government	Relationships are about power. In relationships, as in all else, there are those who control and those who are controlled.	"I [my partner] is the one who makes the decisions in this relationship."	1. Governor 2. Governed	Recognition of importance of power in relationships. If democratic, concern with sharing of power.	If autocratic, one partner seeks all real power for him- or herself. Potential for becoming either a tyrant or a slave.	Variable— Depends on whether person is democratic (excellent), autocratic (poor), or anarchic (poor).

(continued)

TABLE 1 (CONTINUED)

Kind ("Love is . . .")	Modes of Thought and Behavior	Typical Views of Relationships	Complementary Roles	Possible Advantages	Possible Disadvantages	Potential for Success
10. History	Events of relationship form an indelible record. Keeps a lot of records—mental or physical (photo albums, family history, etc.).	"All our past has become a part of us."	1. Historian 2. Historical character	Remembering of happy moments, sometimes using such memories to get through hard times. Sense of context in relationships, understanding present in terms of past.	Remembers partner's every misstep and failure. Inability to let go of the past, possibly holding grudges.	Variable—Depends on whether person focuses on negative events (poor potential), positive events (good potential), or keeps balanced records (very good potential).
11. Horror	Relationships become interesting when you terrorize (or are terrorized by) your partner.	"He's/She's scared of me and I like it that way."	1. Terrorizer 2. Victim		Relationship is often maintained by fear of partner—"What would happen if he/she left?"	Poor.
12. House and Home	Center of relationship is the home; emphasis on comfortable living.	"Our home is the center of our life."	1. Caretaker 2. Person who lives with caretaker but is not recipient of care.	Recognition of the importance of having a comfortable living environment.	Maintenance of pretty home can become a substitute for a strong relationship. Too much emphasis on decoration.	Generally good.
13. Humor	Love is strange and funny.	"My wife ran away with my best friend, and I really miss him" (and other funnies).	1. Comedian 2. Audience	Sense of fun. Recognition that life has a funny side. Ability to see humor in tense situations.	May not take relationship seriously, or not know how it should be taken seriously. May use humor to cover up problems.	Not so good if relationship is seen as or becomes a joke. Good if humor is just part of the relationship.

14. Mystery	Love is a mystery and you shouldn't let too much of yourself be known.	"I have lots of secrets and I like it that way. It keeps him/her guessing."	1. Sleuth 2. Mystery figure	Excitement and sense of constant need to know more about your partner. Adventure.	Partner never really gets to know you. Mystery may hide "double life." Lack of communication.	Good up to a point; not good if mystery hides fundamental facts about person or his/her activities.
15. Police	You've got to keep close tabs on your partner to make sure he/she toes the line.	"I want to know everything you do."	1. Police officer 2. Suspect	Strong interest in life of partner.	Partner's feeling confined, jailed in. Possible paranoid fantasies.	Poor; paranoid concern masking interest in partner.
16. Pornography	Love is dirty. To love is to degrade or be degraded.	"Get out the chains."	1. Pornography addict 2. Object	———	Titillation may replace love. Excitement is through degradation. Need to debase or be debased may keep escalating, resulting in disaster.	Very poor.
17. Recovery	Survivor mentality. View that after past traumas, person can get through practically anything.	"I've survived [drugs, alcohol, disastrous relationships] and I'm ready to start my life over."	1. Survivor 1 2. Survivor 2	Willingness to undertake challenge. Recognition that nothing in life always goes smoothly.	Danger of slipping back into addictive or destructive lifestyle. Danger of partner becoming a "transitional figure."	Variable— Good if person does not slip back into past habits, and has learned from them
18. Religion	Either views love as a religion, or love as a set of feelings and activities dictated by religion.	"Love is my salvation."	1. Person in need of salvation 2. Savior	Intense devotion to partner. Love has important place in person's life.	Unrealistic expectations for what love can provide. Dogmatic views about what love is and can be.	Variable, depending on intensity. Poor if fanatical.

(continued)

TABLE 1 (CONTINUED)

Kind ("Love is . . .")	Modes of Thought and Behavior	Typical Views of Relationships	Complementary Roles	Possible Advantages	Possible Disadvantages	Potential for Success
19. Science	Love can be understood, analyzed, and dissected, just like any other natural phenomenon.	"I know exactly how he/she will respond if I. . . ."	1. Scientist 2. Object of study	Seeking understanding of partner and relationship. Recognition that many problems are soluble through rational discussion.	Over-intellectualization of relationship. Lack of romance and spontaneity. Failure to recognize limits of rational thinking. Need for very high level of predictability in partner.	Good up to a point, but poor if person truly believes that everything, or almost everything, about relationships can be understood rationally.
20. Science Fiction	Feeling that partner is like an alien — incomprehensible and very strange.	"He/She must be from a different planet." "He/She never makes any sense."	1. Human 2. Alien	Many surprises.	Lack of understanding and communication. Sense of alienation. Fear for lack of predictability of partner.	Not good.
21. Sewing and Knitting	Love is whatever you make it.	"We've created our own unique relationship."	1. Tailor or seamstress 2. Sewed object	Creativity. Recognition of options in relationship.	Danger of disagreement of what pattern should be sewn.	Usually excellent if partners agree on pattern.
22. Theater	Love is scripted, with predictable acts, scenes, and lines.	"For my next act, . . ."	1. Actor/Actress 2. Audience	Sense of drama.	Lack of spontaneity. Scripted performances. Tendency toward theatricality. Sense of play-acting.	Not so good when partner discovers it's all (a probably repeated) act.

23. Travel	Love is a journey.	"We're always in the process of becoming."	1. Traveler 1 2. Traveler 2	Dynamism in relationships. Focus on the future. Planning for tomorrow.	In extreme, need for too much change.	Excellent.
24. War	Love is a series of battles in a devastating war.	"I'm ready to fight for what I know is right."	1. Victim 2. Vanquished	——	Intense and sustained conflict.	Usually poor unless story is shared.

WHERE DO STORIES COME FROM?

Even if all we have is a set of stories about people, we like to believe that they are based exclusively on inductions from our relationships. Our view is both naive and scientific: we collect facts, and then put them together into a basically accurate story. But this isn't true. Instead, we bring to relationships tremendously variable experiences, emotions, motives, and cognitions. Our individual personality traits may also lead us to perceive things in different ways. This background serves as the basis for the themes in our stories, and very much affects the kind of story (happy-sad, long-short, heroic-villainous, etc.) that we put together. New stories are often selective combinations of portions of old ones, plus new material stemming from new relationships. If we have a history of feeling rejected, we are likely to be highly sensitive about rejections, and to interpret behavior as rejecting, even if it is not intended that way. Rejection is thus likely to become a major theme of our love stories and to be woven into every plot. If we have historically mistrusted loved ones, we will be looking for signs that our loved one is not worthy of our trust, and are likely to fashion themes of deception into our stories, because any behavior can be interpreted in an infinite variety of ways, including devious ones. We often create what's not there.

20   Allan is an example of a man who finds the theme of rejection in almost every plot. As an adolescent, Allan really did endure painful rejections from female peers. Now he is 28, but his high-school days live on inside him. If his live-in lover, Dale, is distracted one day, Allan views that as a sign that she is losing interest. If she makes plans that don't involve him, Allan feels he has been purposely excluded. If Dale rejects Allan's choice of a restaurant, Allan takes it as a personal rejection of himself. An intelligent individual, Allan often recognizes that he is responding in a less than rational manner. But the recognition usually doesn't help: He feels the rejection as painfully as if Dale actually meant to reject him. Allan's own fearful story about what their love could become disrupts his perceptions of what's actually going on.

We all say to ourselves, from time to time, "Now I see things clearly." We never see things independently of our stories, though. We are always influenced by their themes, and are better off realizing this than believing that we can somehow disregard or ignore them. The themes stem from our childhoods, from interactions with parents, siblings, and friends. They come from our adolescent interactions, often among the most painful. But they never leave us. Without knowing what they are, we cannot pinpoint their influence, for example, in altering our perceptions of events. Thus, an important task for a person is to understand the themes that contribute to his or her stories (such as vulnerability, entitlement, loss of control, unlovability, and so on). If we know, for example, that we have a tendency to feel vulnerable in front of others, and one day experience feelings of vulnerability, we are more likely to recognize it as our own predisposition to feel this way rather than as an injury that the other person meant to cause (Young, 1987).

STORIES CONTROL HOW RELATIONSHIPS DEVELOP

Our stories, as much determined by our past as by the people with whom we are involved, shape our relationships. Once we have created a story about someone and about our relationship with that person, we do what the author of any good story does: We try to continue it in a consistent way. No one likes to read a book which blatantly contradicts itself. No one likes to be in a love-situation which doesn't make sense in the context of what has happened previously—therefore, we perceive new events in terms of old stories. If a wife wants an expensive orthopedic bed, the husband's understanding of it might be that she is extremely health-conscious, or that she always wants the latest fad, or is spending him into the grave, or is a hypochondriac, or any of an infinite number of reasons. The husband's understanding of his wife's actions depends upon his current story. Our story controls the way we perceive the actions of others, which then, in turn, confirm that story. In fact, the same action or set of actions could "confirm" any number of stories. Our stories do not necessarily become more accurate over time, but they do become more elaborate. They influence the way we perceive everything our partner does, and how we react in turn.

Stories not only control the development of relationships, but dictate which relationships we choose to develop at all. Some would like us to believe that when we choose a lover or spouse from among potential candidates, we begin with a list of attributes and assign values to each potential partner. We often find ourselves, on the contrary, choosing the person who would lose such a contest. Someone possessing the optimum balance of attributes is often no more likely to be chosen than anyone else. Sometimes we go after a person whom on any rational basis we would reject straightaway. The reason is that in most cases, the story, not the numbers, influences us. Each relationship is a different story. We choose the person who presents us with the love story we like best, even though that person might not be the most compatible partner for us.

This is not to say that rational considerations aren't a factor. Some of us prefer stories about eternal love, others about money, others about friendship, control, or punishment. The themes we prefer may be rational or irrational, socially desirable or not. But ultimately, we are attracted to potential partners who enable us to weave stories fitting our notion of what we *want* love to be, regardless of what we are told it *should* be. Those who ensnare others don't do it with love, money or power, but by offering a love story about money, or power or whatever the other person wants. The reason we may not fall in love with our best friend of the opposite sex is not because that friend has anything wrong with him or her

("Why can't I love him when I like him so damn much?") but because that friend doesn't give us a story about what we want love to be, only about what we want friendship to be. The friend may in fact be perfect according to the list of attributes that we "should" look for, but it doesn't matter: The story is wrong.

25   A common problem in life, and the theme of many love stories and love songs, is emotional involvement with two people simultaneously. One partner is paper perfect. He or she has all the attributes one imagines oneself to want in a spouse. The other partner can't hold a candle to the first in terms of meeting the qualifications on the mental checklist. Yet, one is in love with the second but not the first. In an age where marriage is supposed to be a love story, people will often go for the second person, irrational though it may seem.

Maria is being courted simultaneously by two men. Sam is everything she's always wanted — intelligent, attractive, successful, considerate, stable. Maria's friends see Sam as a wonderful catch. Kurt looks terrible on paper. He's intelligent, but in a cunning sort of way. He's attractive, but not very successful at work. He blows hot and cold with Maria, paying attention to her for a while, then seeing other women on the weakest of pretexts. Kurt is about as unstable as they come. Yet, Maria loves him. She doesn't know why; she only knows it's true. She knows that she should prefer Sam. But it's Kurt she wants. He fits her story of what love is about. Indeed, Maria grew up watching stories of love that were more similar to her relationship with Kurt than to her relationship with Sam.

STORIES ARE HARD TO CHANGE

It is an established fact that people seek to confirm, rather than disconfirm, what they already believe. They will go to great lengths to ignore inconsistent information. Not surprisingly then, we avoid changing our story as long as we possibly can. Changing a story is very uncomfortable. It involves reorganizing a tremendous amount of information, admitting to ourselves that we were wrong, realizing that we are now uncertain about the relationship and understanding that our new story may also have to be changed.

Why is it often so hard for a partner to get over his or her spouse's affair? Five years ago, Jim had a brief affair. Ellen found out from what had been a mutual friend. After an initial denial, Jim admitted to the affair, broke it off, and has not had another since. But for Ellen, the relationship was fundamentally changed. Her love story is altogether different now from what it had been: Jim used to be her Rhett Butler, but now he's turned into Don Juan. Whereas Jim formerly swept Ellen off her feet, she now fears that he could seduce other women this easily as well. Jim's behavior is basically the same as it was before the affair. Ellen had previously assumed that Jim's attentions could only revolve around her; now she sees him as trying to be attractive to other women too.

How could he show her to be wrong? Ellen is trapped within this *Don Juan* story. She can't put her heart into changing back to *Gone with the Wind,* but can't move herself forward to a more workable storyline either.

It's difficult to change other people's stories because if we attempt to do so, they will often use our attempt to confirm whatever story they have (e.g., that we try to manipulate them, that we try to control them, that we only believe in our own point of view). Thus, our efforts are likely to backfire, more firmly entrenching the old, undesirable story, instead of inaugurating a new one. Most attempts to change relationships do not work because they attempt to modify cognitions, feelings, or behavior, without addressing the story that determines these. Until the story changes, the relationship cannot change fundamentally. Attempts to adjust relationships virtually never address the story as a whole, but only isolated themes or fragments of it. Even if one manages to alter these parts of a love story, the new elements are still likely to be incorporated into the old one. Nothing really changes, or, at least, not very easily.

Consider an example: In one of my classes, I ask students to commit them-   30 selves on paper to a belief which they hold strongly (it might be a belief about love, or about politics or ethics, or religion). I then ask them to think for a few minutes about how they would argue rationally and persuasively for the diametrically opposed point of view. They present the argument for the opposite point of view. Finally, I ask them to argue for what they really believe. Almost without exception, people argue better (as judged by other members of the class) for the opposite point of view. Why? Because they organize information about the opposing point of view in terms of logical arguments but organize the defense of their own point of view in terms of a story, which does not make for a persuasive logical argument. Most of them don't really know exactly why they believe what they believe, but they believe it nonetheless, often fervently. I've conducted this exercise repeatedly over several years, but no one has ever changed their opinions, despite being able to argue more effectively for the opposite standpoint. As far as personal matters are concerned, it is the story, not the logical-rational arguments, that counts. Analytical arguments don't change the story: People stick to their stories even when they know themselves to be more convincing as advocates for the contrary point of view!

WHEN STORIES DO CHANGE, IT IS OFTEN FOR THE WORSE

Stories change over time, and usually for the worse. To understand why, we need to know about two psychological phenomena.

The first phenomenon is called the "negative information effect." Negative information is much more powerful than positive information. For example, if we read a letter of recommendation for a job candidate, a single negative statement can devastate the candidate's prospects, no matter how many positive statements there are. One piece of negative information can do more harm than a hundred pieces of positive information can do good. Negative information influences our evaluation more significantly than positive information does. And of course, the negative information may not be negative at all in any objective sense, but only from the standpoint of the story which we bring to the information.

The second phenomenon is called the "fundamental attribution error" (Ross, 1977). We tend to view unfavorable behavior in others as dispositionally caused, whereas we view unfavorable behavior in ourselves as situationally caused. If our partner shouts, it is because he or she is an inherently ill-tempered person; whereas if we shout, it is because we were provoked, or in a temporary bad mood. In short, others act badly because they are bad, whereas we act badly because we are temporarily out of sorts, or because the situation compels us to do so.

Jack and Sandy seem compatible, if one believes that similarity breeds compatibility. Similarity can sometimes lead to mutual understanding. But not in this situation. Jack and Sandy both have quick tempers. Jack tends to view his flashes of temper as justified by Sandy's frequently unacceptable behavior, whereas he views her temper, ironically, as a basic character flaw. Unfortunately, Sandy's view of the situation is the mirror image of Jack's. The result is a pattern of constantly escalating conflict. Their relationship would be significantly improved if they applied to themselves the same standards they each apply to the other.

35   Over time, the negative information effect and the fundamental attribution error will often render stories less and less favorable. The change is usually very slow; often we are only vaguely aware of its happening. Eventually, though, we realize that with the story we now have, we might not have decided to enter into a partnership with the person in the first place. Because it is so difficult to change a story consciously, the change is likely to be not only gradual but pre-conscious: We don't even realize that it is happening. Over time, what began as a pleasant story has become an unpleasant one. Eventually, the preconscious story becomes conscious; this is the moment when we realize that we are unhappy. The story is no longer what we want it to be. And, having reached this point, whatever our partner does will only fit into a less favorable, rather than a more favorable, understanding of the situation.

Stories can change positively, however, if we are aware of our themes and of how we process information. In such a case, for example, we would understand how the fundamental attribution error can mislead us. We need to realize that not only do relationships affect stories, but also that stories in turn affect relationships. We thus can take a step toward improving relationships by changing our story, and then working to achieve that change in the relationship.

CONVENTIONAL ATTEMPTS TO UNDERSTAND AND CHANGE RELATIONSHIPS FAIL BECAUSE THEY IGNORE THE PROBLEM — THE STORY

Why do attempts to change relationships, whether through the couple's own efforts or through marital therapy, fail so often? They fail because they ignore the stories that control each person's view of and approach to the relationship.

Almost all of us have been involved in one or more relationships that didn't work. Often, the decision to break up is not mutual, and the person who is left behind seeks to know why, from the other person's point of view, the relationship fell apart. The person who has broken matters off often feels that he or she is contriving reasons to provide an answer to why the relationship failed, not only for the partner, but for him- or herself. The person who was left behind may also feel this way. They are both right. What they believe to be causes of the dissolution of the relationship are actually effects. We *create* reasons for the break-up, just as we once created reasons for getting together. The reasons are epiphenomenal. They may be that the partner was too demanding, or communication was not all it could be, or the relationship was not progressing, or any of a multitude of other reasons.

I do not believe that these "reasons" are the "causes" of the breakdown. Relationship counselors do, though, in helping couples figure out why they are failing or have failed. But we make up these reasons in order to justify to ourselves and others what we have done. The real reason for the breakup is that we no longer like our story. Stories are hard to change, but they do change over time. What started out as a story we liked has become one we don't like.

The behavior which we tolerated before, we now no longer tolerate, not 40 because the behavior has changed, but because it is now part of a bad story. The very things we used to like about the person we no longer like, because they now remind us of the bad story. To change the relationship, we need to change the story. And this means that we need "story therapy," not Freudian, or behaviorist, or cognitive therapy. We need to understand the story and address it. And we also need to understand our own and our partner's ideal story, which is probably what got us together in the first place.

When he was trying to recover from an alcohol problem, Gary was enchanted by Carla's nurturance. She couldn't do enough for him; she was always there when he needed her, and she was selfless in her devotion to Gary's recovery. Carla hasn't changed, but Gary's attitude toward her has. Gary now feels smothered by Carla. He needs space and feels that Carla won't give it to him. He knows she means well, but she is now part of his story of recovery from addiction, a story that he would like, by and large, to forget. The very behaviors he once admired so much are now a source of smoldering resentment.

UNDERSTANDING IDEAL STORIES

In order to understand our partner's story about us, we need to understand our partner's story about ideal relationships. Often, because the story is preconscious, our partner is not him- or herself entirely aware of it.

The particular stories we develop are, I believe, very much a function of the internalization of attributes of persons in our past whom we have wanted in some way but have been unable to have. We lose a parent, we are rejected as kids by children of the opposite sex who make fun of us, we have teenage heartthrobs and heartbreaks. Each time we lose someone, we internalize those attributes that appealed to us, and eventually build up, usually unconsciously, a composite of the attributes of which we have been deprived in the past.

Our research at Yale has shown that people have ideals for relationships, and that these ideals are every bit as important as the actual relationship itself. The ideals control not only how we form our actual story, but how happy we are with it. Furthermore, we feel emotion when we sense a match between an actual or potential story and our ideal one. The cognition of a match thus generates positive emotions. Negative emotions may come about when we expect or hope for a match and it doesn't occur. The reason for this is that when we meet people, we determine how close they are to our ideal. If they don't match at all, then we can simply dismiss them. If they are close, however, then we are likely to try to remake them into our ideal. In other words, we will interpret the actions of the other in order to fit our rosiest imaginings. We want our ideal story to come true. But we can now appreciate yet another reason why relationships stumble: We eventually realize that the actual story is not the ideal story, and we feel disappointment as the discrepancies become more obvious. To make a relationship work, we have to help a person understand his or her own ideal story, understand that this ideal can never be truly realized, and then accept the differences between the actual story and the ideal one.

45   Liz was always attracted to the strong and silent type. When she met Tim, she used to spend hours trying to puzzle out what he was thinking. Tim was not big on giving compliments, but when he did give one, Liz felt like she was on Cloud 9. The relationship was an exciting one, because for Liz, the ideal story was one in which most of what happened was inside—beneath the surface. Now Tim and Liz have been married for three years. Liz has come to a terrible realization. Underneath Tim's silence is a void. He's not like an artichoke, with a hidden core, but like an onion instead: When you peel away the layers of Tim's reticence, you find nothing left underneath. He was silent for all those years, because actually he had nothing to say. Liz now realizes that she imagined Tim to be something he was not.

Ideal stories are changeable, but not easily so. Some potential partners immediately fit into our ideal stories, leading to feelings of infatuation, while other potential partners do not. If love develops slowly out of friendship, we may sense a slow change in our ideal story to fit our current relationship. The new ideal story does not necessarily replace the old one, but may exist side by side with it. In this event, there is always the possibility that we may later meet someone who is more compatible with our original ideal. If that story has retained its hold on us, we may find ourselves wanting either to switch relationships or to be involved in both simultaneously.

STORIES WE'RE SUPPOSED TO TELL

The stories we tell, as implied above, are embedded in a cultural matrix. They are the unique stories of a peculiar time and place. Cultures approve of certain stories, and disapprove of others. For example, in the United States today marriage is supposed to be a story of true love. Historically, this is a rarity. It is considered gauche by many to marry simply for money or status, whereas such a status story would have been considered acceptable and even desirable throughout most of history. Thus, although we create our own stories, we do so within the context of our cultural mores. We are under continual, although usually subtle, pressure to create only those stories which are socio-culturally acceptable. People may be executed in one time or place for a story — about adultery, for example — that in another time or place would scarcely raise an eyebrow.

Moreover, our love story is only one of many stories we create. We create stories about other topics as well, such as jobs and family. We think of how we prefer to envision ourselves at work and with other members of our family. These stories are sometimes complementary, but may also compete with our love stories. Thus, some people have difficulty making their love and work stories mesh, with the result that they are in a constant state of tension. Some people actually prefer to combine the various stories of their lives into a single story, while others keep them more separate. But most people strive for cognitive consistency — a neat fitting of the stories to one another. To understand our love story fully, we need to appreciate how it fits into the total context of our lives.

Ben loves Lisa, but unbeknownst to Lisa, he will never marry her. Even Ben doesn't like to admit it to himself. Ben is an assistant vice-president of a large bank. No one talks about it, but everyone knows that to work your way up the ladder at the bank, you can only marry a certain type of partner. She's got to be someone who makes you look good at the bank's social functions. She has to look right, speak right, and know how to entertain. She has to be from the right kind of background. No one talks about it, because life in the modern age isn't supposed to be this way. But it is that way at the bank. Lisa's great, but marrying her would be a ticket to oblivion for Ben's career. So he waits, knowing he will have to move on to a different relationship, but not having it in his heart to do so. The story of Lisa simply doesn't fit the story Ben needs to succeed at work.

FINDING A NEW PARTNER, OR REMAKING AN OLD ONE, BY UNDERSTANDING STORIES

50   Understanding our own stories is critically important in the formation of a relationship as well as in changing it. This understanding helps us enormously in finding the right partner from the outset. Changing a relationship is best accomplished by helping a partner (or oneself) generate a revised or completely new story to use in interpreting actions or events, in much the way that "twelve-step" programs operate to change relationships between alcoholics or addicts and their loved ones.

Two years ago, Karen realized that she was looking for Mr. Goodbar. She frequented singles bars, was involved in drugs, and found the most destructive men to be the most attractive. Her life was on a fast track — in the downward direction. Then Karen understood her story, realizing that she was reliving her mother's past life. Her mother had married an abusive and violent man, and now in spite of her own protestations to the contrary, Karen was on track to do the same. She hoped to relive the process, but change the product, of her mother's past life. Casting off her old story has not been easy, but Karen now realizes that she was heading for disaster. When Karen meets a Goodbar type these days, she makes tracks — in the opposite direction.

Most "wish lists" that people carry around are not worth much. They are as likely to be based on what we feel we *should* want as on what we *really* want. But we can figure out what we really want only if we understand our ideal story. Even relationship books and guides are not optimally useful, because they list attributes people should look for if everyone were perfect and the same, rather than lists of what people actually want, based on who they are. To figure out what we want, we need to consider all of our past relationships. We need to ask ourselves what attributes the people to whom we feel most attracted have in common, and what attributes are shared by those to whom we were once attracted but are no longer. These attributes are different for different people. We can use Kelly's Q-sort technique to understand our ideals better. This technique involves generating our own set of attributes for the people in our lives so that we can understand what is important to us, as opposed to using some abstract, idealized list that may or may not be relevant to others, but probably won't be relevant to us. Whether or not we are in the "looking" mode, understanding our ideal story will help us better understand what is not working in our relationship, and what we can do to make it work. Sometimes, the ingredients are all there in our partner. Our old partner can come to be our new one (as in the "Pina Colada" song of some years ago). To change our relationships fundamentally, we need to replot our story line.

REPLOTTING

Once we understand the concepts of the various kinds of stories we tell, we are then in a position to do some replotting. We can ask ourselves what we like and don't like about our current (or past) story, and how we would like to change it. We then ask ourselves what we could do to replot the story. In doing this, we need to recognize our own background factors that affect how we plot and set the themes for our stories. At the same time, we need to understand our partner's story and how he or she would like it to change. Sometimes, we need to get outside our own or our partner's story temporarily in order to understand it better. Thus, repairing relationships requires more than rational "do-it" lists. It requires story telling and story replotting. We often need to try out new stories piece by piece, discovering which stories can work for us, and which cannot. Sometimes we need to become receptive to the help of others in replotting our stories, rather than going it on our own.

Louise and John have been committed to improving their relationship for a long time. They tried books, they tried counseling, they tried encounter groups. Nothing seemed to work. Then, almost by chance, Louise told John a fable. It was one she made up about a prince and a princess who defied all expectations — they didn't live happily ever after. Of course, the story was about Louise and John. John replied, several days later, with a story of his own. It was about a prince and a princess who did live happily ever after, following a period of discontent. The story exchange continued. It enabled both Louise and John to understand their stories, without direct confrontation, without threat, without anxiety. Soon, they started trying to live the stories they created that they liked. Today, they are these stories. They are the prince and princess who are living happily ever after.

We don't always need to be rational. Relationships at their core are not rational: They are stories. Accepting this fact means moving away from notions of who's right and who's wrong, and toward notions of understanding and changing stories that are neither right nor wrong, but very, very real. We can only understand and change relationships if we accept them for what they are, rather than what some, in a hypothetical world, might wish them to be.

RELATION TO THEORIES OF LOVE

The notion of love as a story obviously is not a theory of love, but rather a metatheory for understanding love and various theories of it. As a metatheory, the notion is not, strictly speaking, disconfirmable. But it does help us put theories of love, as well as the phenomena of love itself, into a certain context.

For example, in my own triangular theory of love, I speak of different kinds of love based on different combinations of three components: intimacy, passion, and commitment (Sternberg, 1988). Some of the kinds of love are romantic love, comprising intimacy and passion; fatuous love, comprising passion and commitment without intimacy; empty love, involving only commitment; consummate love, comprising intimacy, passion, and commitment; and so on. The love-as-a-story notion leads us to understand these differing kinds of love as differing stories about love. For some people in some relationships, love may be a romance; but for different people, or the same people in other relationships, love may be empty, with all the intimacy and passion of the past having flown. Thus, people actively participate in defining the kinds of love they have — they are not just victims of fate. And to a large extent, they can create the same kinds of stories again and again, and repeat the same patterns of love.

Similarly, in a theory such as Lee's theory (1977) of the colors of love, erotic, manic, ludic, and other styles of loving represent stories we create for ourselves and our partners. Indeed, the whole notion of ludic love is largely based on stories originally written by Ovid, just as many of our notions about romantic love stem from stories such as *Tristan and Isolde* or *Romeo and Juliet*.

Of course, there are many other theories of love as well. The basic point here is that, from the standpoint of love as a story, any theory could actually be right, although incomplete, for someone, somewhere. Theories of love deal with the nomothetic or shared parts of love, probably more within than between cultures. But the idiographic parts of love — those that give love its richness and uniqueness in each relationship — can only be captured when we understand that love is a story.

REFERENCES

Epstein, S. (1993). *You're smarter than you think*. New York: Simon and Schuster.

Lee, J. A. (1977). A typology of styles of loving. *Personality and Social Psychology Bulletin, 49*, 1589–96.

McAdams, D. P. (1993). *Stories we live by*. New York: Morrow.

Ross, L. D. (1977). The intuitive psychologist and his shortcomings: Distortions in the attribution process. In L. Berkowitz (Ed.), *Advances in experimental social psychology* (Vol. 10). New York: Academic Press.

Schank, R. C., & Abelson, R. (1977). *Scripts, plans and understanding*. Hillsdale, NJ: Erlbaum.

Sternberg, R. J. (1988). *The triangle of love*. New York: Basic Books.

Young, J. E. (1987). Schema-focused cognitive therapy for personality disorders. Unpublished manuscript.

TALKING ABOUT IT

1. Where do our love stories come from?

2. How do our metaphors for love change?

3. What happens when our metaphors for love change?

4. How can we predict whether individuals, each with a very different story, will be compatible?

WRITING ABOUT IT

1. What is your first, perhaps idealized, love story that you can find from among the twenty-four stories that Sternberg lists in his table? Where did it come from? What is your story now? How did it change? What happened when it did?

   The first part of your essay should be narrative; the second part, analysis. In your analysis, ask yourself the questions posed in "Love Is a Story" and offer your interpretation of the themes illustrated in the story you tell (the theme is what the writer makes of the story, what it means to her or him).

2. Tell the idealized story of what you hoped would be your first semester in college. Then tell the actual story of your first semester in college. Interpret your stories, using the framework of ideas in "Love Is a Story."

   Here are some questions to help you develop your interpretations of the stories you tell: do not try to answer all of these questions, nor answer them in a mechanical way as if you are taking a test. Choose the questions that seem most relevant to you as a writer.

   - What themes are revealed in your narrative(s)?
   - How does the first story influence the second?
   - How do the stories you tell limit your experience?
   - What in your experience affects the stories you tell?
   - How does your current story (the second one you tell) affect the way you perceive others?
   - How then does your perception "confirm" your story?
   - How do you live the pattern of the story you tell?
   - How could you work to change your story?
   - How does the story compete with other stories about your life?

■ ■ ■

In the next chapter, "A Writing Life," authors both explore conventional metaphors and invent their own for the writing process. Having read the previous introduction to the nature and use of metaphor, you might be better able to understand how metaphor partially structures writers' thinking and thus their experience of writing. You might also find helpful metaphors for thinking about your own writing. Better yet, you might invent your own. Ideally, these would be metaphors that assist, rather than impede, your process. They'd be metaphors you write by.

The thematic chapters that follow chapter 2 explore six topics of interest in both popular and academic culture. The authors represent a variety of educational and living experience that affects their line of vision and thus their metaphors for comprehending as well as creating the world in which they live. As you read and write, I hope you too will see the important role that metaphor plays in the way you think, talk about, and experience life.

WORKS CITED

Begley, Sharon, et al. "Commandos of Viral Combat." *Newsweek* 22 May 1995: 50–51.

Bosmajian, Haig. *Metaphor and Reason in Judicial Opinions.* Carbondale: Southern Illinois UP, 1992.

Dubisch, Jill. "You Are What You Eat: Religious Aspects of the Health Food Movement." *Applying Cultural Anthropology.* Ed. Aaron Podolefsky and Peter J. Brown. Mountain View: Mayfield, 1994. 90–97.

Enrico, Roger, and Jesse Kornbluth. *The Other Guy Blinked: How Pepsi Won the Cola Wars.* New York: Bantam, 1986.

Gleick, James. *Chaos.* New York: Penguin, 1987.

Greenberg, Jack M. "Man Your Frying Stations." *Harper's Magazine* April 1998: 24.

James, William. "The Moral Philosopher and the Moral Life." *The Will to Believe and Other Essays in Popular Philosophy.* Cambridge: Harvard UP, 1979. 141.

Kottak, Conrad. "McDonald's as Myth, Symbol, and Ritual." *Anthropology: The Exploration of Human Diversity.* New York: Random House, 1978. 522–26.

Lakoff, George, and Mark Johnson. "The Metaphorical Structure of the Human Conceptual System." *Perspectives on Cognitive Science.* Ed. Donald A. Norman. Norwood: Ablex, 1981. 193–206.

———. *Metaphors We Live By.* Chicago: U of Chicago P, 1980.

———, and Mark Turner. *More Than Cool Reason.* Chicago: U of Chicago P, 1989.

Leary, David E. "Psyche's Muse." *Metaphors in the History of Psychology.* Ed. David E. Leary. Cambridge: Cambridge UP, 1990. 1–78.

Norman, Marsha. "Say Amen to Somebody." *Mirabella* Sept.-Oct. 1995: 117–19.

Preston, Richard. "Back to the Hot Zone." *The New Yorker* 22 May 1995: 43–45.

Rhodes, Richard. "The General and World War III." *The New Yorker* 19 June 1995: 47–59.

Sarbin, Theodore. "Metaphors of Unwanted Conduct." *Metaphors in the History of Psychology.* Ed. David E. Leary. Cambridge: Cambridge UP, 1990. 300–30.

Sontag, Susan. *Illness as Metaphor and AIDS and Its Metaphors.* New York: Doubleday, 1989.

Tannen, Deborah. *Talking from 9 to 5.* New York: William Morrow, 1994.

Chapter 2

A Writing Life

The first project for a writer is that of constructing a writing life.
—David Huddle

For the authors in this chapter, writing is an integral part of their lives. It is a way of ordering and connecting experiences. It is a process of discovering the self, the other, and the world we inhabit and try to understand. The world can be understood literally as geographical locations and metaphorically as imagined locations, that is, the places we create in our minds and talk about as if these places too are bounded land areas to be identified, categorized, and quantified. For example, we talk about "making space" in our lives for certain activities, events, feelings, and ideas. We talk about boundaries: "She needs to set boundaries," or "He crossed the line," as if behavior is a physical entity like our bodies. We try to order these metaphorical spaces, mark out their territory, so that we can identify them as objects, refer to them, and thus reason about them.

"Place" could be said to draw all the authors together. To make the obvious literal point, their writing and ideas are collected within the physical space of this chapter. Less obviously, their ideas about writing and about themselves as writers occupy some of the same territory. For James D. Houston, in "A Writer's Sense of Place," place is a geographical locale that we inhabit as well as a locale that metaphorically inhabits our dreams and shapes our conscious life. We carry places with us that inform our thinking and writing. Natalie Goldberg agrees: "It's hard to write about a city we just moved into; it's not yet in our body." For David Huddle, place is a bounded area of time and prescribed set of activities. We must make space in our lives for writing; writing is a habit to cultivate for the order it can bring to life. Peter Elbow describes the power of voice, and he offers strategies for finding places in our writing where the reader stumbles, where we may need to guide our readers more easily and naturally to pauses and stops.

Bonnie Friedman explores the place that control and anxiety occupy in our struggles as writers. She describes writer's block (the sudden inability to write) as the fear that silence evokes: "You will be a person shut up inside yourself, shut up like an old apartment building with windows of brick and doors of cinderblock." Anne Lamott has had her share of writer's anxiety too. One of her strategies for breaking her silence is to impose silence on the critical voices that keep her from writing. She imagines each negative voice belonging to a mouse that she picks up by the tail and drops into a jar. "Then put the lid on," Lamott advises.

Natalia Rachel Singer argues for restoring "I" to its rightful place in the education of writers. Alan Cheuse describes the place of reading in his life as he remembers the joy of his own literacy. The pleasure of learning to read is a story that he writes down for James, and, secondarily, for us.

STARTING TO THINK ABOUT IT

1. Where do you write? Describe the setting in detail. Why do you choose that place? What associations does it have for you that aid your writing?

2. Apart from writing, what habits have you cultivated that are important to your sense of order in your life?

3. Describe a time in which you suddenly couldn't do something that you've done well and easily many times before. What did that experience feel like?

4. What does "finding your voice" mean to you as a writer?

5. Have you ever heard not to use "I" when you write? Why were you told that?

6. What is your earliest memory of reading pleasure?

A Writer's Sense of Place

James D. Houston

James D. Houston's works of fiction and nonfiction include Continental Drift *(1978),* Californians: Searching for the Golden State *(1982),* In the Ring of Fire: A Pacific Basin Journey *(1997), and* The Last Paradise *(1998). In 1973, he cowrote* Farewell to Manzanar *with his wife, Jeanne Wakatsuki Houston. "A Writer's Sense of Place," published in* The True Subject: Writers on Life and Craft *in 1993, is a lecture Houston delivered at The Squaw Valley Community of Writers Workshops.*

In writing workshops, a large part of the conversation focuses on personal relationships and matters of kinship—the husband and the wife, the mother and the daughter, the father and the son, or the absent father, or the missing lover, or the seducer, the seducee. There are good and necessary reasons for this, since this is the basic stuff of fiction: what we do to each other, and with each other.

For a few minutes today I want to talk about another kind of kinship. Each time I drive up into these mountains, climb from sea-level to six thousand feet and see the bowl of peaks rising all around us, I get reawakened to the power and the magic of landscape and open country and to the many ways that certain places can work on us. When Oakley Hall asked, "If you had to give a talk at the conference this year, what would it be?", I said that by Sunday afternoon I would probably be ready to free-associate about The Sense of Place.

By *place* I don't mean simply names and points of interest as identified on a map. What has fascinated me for a long time now is the relationship between a locale and the lives lived there, the relationship between terrain and the feelings it can call out of us, the way a certain place can provide us with grounding, location, meaning, can bear upon the dreams we dream, can sometimes shape our view of history.

The idea of place is nothing new, of course. It has been a constant in human life from day one. You can't avoid it. You have to park somewhere and get a roof over your head, and wherever this happens has to be a place of one kind or another. But we're not always aware of it as such. At some point, place moves into the conscious life. When that occurs we begin to have a sense of it, an awareness of it and our relationship to it.

I have lived most of my life on the West Coast, between San Francisco, where I was born, and Monterey Bay, where we've been based for the past thirty years. It is clearly my home region, a stretch of coastline and coastal mountain ranges I now think of as my natural habitat. But I did not always see it this way.

5

57

For many years I did not see it at all. I had to leave home and travel around the country, see a lot of other places, go out to the Hawaiian Islands, go to Mexico and to Europe. Looking back, I think I can now isolate my own moment of awakening, when I finally began to see and to contemplate my habitat.

This was in the mid-1960s, a couple of years after we moved to Santa Cruz and I was trying to get started as a writer — which involved a lot of pacing and staring out the window.

In an interview once, someone asked Bruce Jay Friedman why he had chosen this particular career, and he said, "Because it allows me to use the word *work* to describe my greatest pleasure in life."

"You mean writing," the interviewer said.

"I mean brooding," Friedman said, "and pacing back and forth and staring out the window."

10   Early in 1964, soon after I had finished graduate work at Stanford and we had moved from the Peninsula over the hill to the coast, I was brooding and pacing back and forth, trying to finish a short story about Sweden that I had started during my Air Force time in England, five years earlier. As I paused to stare out the window, I noticed a candy store that stood on a corner about a block away, on the far side of a large open lot, empty except for a few neglected fruit trees. We had been living in that house for a couple of years, and I had been visiting the town of Santa Cruz off and on since high school, so I had seen this candy store a hundred times, maybe a thousand times. Yet I had not seen it. I had never looked at it, a fixture in my daily life so familiar it had gone entirely unnoticed.

As I studied the details — the whitewashed walls, the corny Dutch windmill with its tiny window flashing in the sun — something began to buzz, the tingling across my scalp that I refer to as the literary buzz, a little signal from the top of my head that there is some mystery here, or some unrevealed linkage that will have to be explored with words.

I sat down at my typing machine and began to describe the candy store. By the time I finished, fifteen pages later, I had described the stream of cars along the shoreline road that runs through the neighborhood, I had described the town, and where I thought it fit into some larger patterns of northern California and the West. I had begun to examine, as well, why I had chosen this town and this stretch of coast, and the elderly, windblown house we still occupy.

The result was an essay both regional and personal. In terms of my perception of myself as a writer and what I could write about, it was a small but crucial turning point. It was my first attempt to write not only *about* this part of the world, but to write *from* this part of the world. This also turned out to be the first piece I sold to a national magazine, which seemed at the time to validate the impulses that had propelled the writing. It came out in the now-defunct *Holiday,* making it the first piece to earn anything like a significant amount of money, six hundred dollars—a decent fee for an essay back in the mid-1960s, and a bonanza for us, in the days when four hundred was our monthly budget.

Since then the sense of region and place has played an ever larger role in what I've chosen to write about, both in nonfiction and in fiction. As far as storytelling goes, in the most general terms, I think there are two ways it can work. Sometimes a character in the story has a conscious sense of place. More often it is the writer who has the sense of place, or who grasps the relationship between a life and a locale. In *The Grapes of Wrath,* to take a famous example, John Steinbeck knows the layout of the San Joaquin Valley. He knows the water systems, the fertility of the soil, the appeal of the soil, and the role of agriculture in the region's history. He also knows the power of the legend that has drawn the Joad family west from Oklahoma. He knows a lot more about this than the Joads themselves know or have time to think about, since they have so recently arrived and their full attention is on survival. A large part of the novel's concern might be described as a dialogue between their struggle and the magnetic power of the place they've been drawn to—the natural endowments of that place, the dream that has attached to it, and the irony or the underside of that dream.

In recent years I've been working on a sequence of novels tied to the terrain of northern California, in which the lives of one family have been much affected by this terrain. In these novels there is always a character whose personal sense of place is central to the story. The first of these was *Continental Drift,* published by Knopf in 1978. It's set in the coast range near Monterey Bay. It's a family saga, a love story, a murder story, an exploration of the geography and the geology. The title, of course, refers to the global pattern of tectonic plates and fracture lines that has helped us to understand the profound feature of the continent's western edge we call the San Andreas fault. It also provides the novel's metaphor. Via the fault line, the landscape of California has its built-in disaster factor; and yet this same landscape, due to the same forces that created the fault line, continues to be a source of nourishment and even spiritual sustenance. Call it the yin and yang of coastal geology.

The central character is a fellow named Montrose Doyle. He is forty-six. With his wife and two sons he presides over fifty-five acres of orchard and grazing land that borders the San Andreas, which has given him a way of thinking about where he lives and—in this passage from the novel's early pages—thinking about The Big One:

> Is Montrose a fatalist? Yes. And no. He anticipates. Yet he does not anticipate. What he loves to dwell on is that steady creep which, a few million years hence, will put his ranch on a latitude with Juneau, Alaska. He admires the foresight of the Spanish cartographers who, in their earliest maps, pictured California as an island. Sometimes late at night, after he

has been drinking heavily, he will hike out to his fence line and imagine that he can feel beneath his feet the dragging of the continental plates, and imagine that he is standing on his own private raft, a New World Noah, heading north, at two inches per year.

Most of the time he doesn't think about it at all. It is simply there, a presence beneath his land. If it ever comes to mind during his waking hours he thinks of it as just that, a presence, a force, you might even say a certainty, one thing he knows he can count on — this relentless grinding of two great slabs which have been butting head-on now for millennia and are now about to relax.

There is a companion novel to *Continental Drift*. It's called *Love Life* and it came out in 1985, also from Knopf. It's not a sequel. But maybe it qualifies as a spin-off, since it deals with the same territory, the Santa Cruz Mountains, and members of the same family, in this case the older son of Montrose Doyle, and this son's wife, Holly. They are both thirty-two, married ten years, with two kids. *Love Life* is the wife's story, Holly's story, told in her voice, and it begins on the day she discovers that her husband, Grover, is involved with a younger woman. So this too is a family drama, but with quite a bit of geography mixed in.

The crisis in their relationship is linked to a crisis in the environment. The story is set during a devastating winter storm that comes in off the Pacific and leaves them isolated at the end of their river valley road. The bridges are out, hillsides crumble, phone lines and power lines are down. At a time when they both want nothing more than to get away from each other, they are in fact trapped by the mud and the water and tree trunks that come crashing across their road.

Part of what gets Holly through it is her sense of place. As narrator and as a central character, she is attuned to the features of her region, her habitat — the light, the creek, the trees, the nearest hills. I wanted to get this established right at the outset. In the opening pages, before we meet her husband or her kids, we are looking out her early morning window:

> An orange light had set our bedroom curtains smoldering. The cur-
> tains were orange. When it wasn't raining they smoldered most of the
> time, which is what I had hoped for when I bought them at Macy's. But
> this light passing through the window seemed about to burst them into
> flame. I drew them back and saw the sun filling a low notch in the east-
> ern hills, the sun's most southerly point, only rising through that notch
> for a couple of weeks before starting north again. If I had been asleep for
> twenty years and had awakened that morning, I would have known the
> season in an instant, the month, perhaps the week, by the sun's angle and
> the winter clarity of its flame, igniting curtains, backlighting the camelia

bushes and the spindly saplings I had planted on the slope behind the house, backlighting the creek whose waters then were high enough and full enough to make a glossy surface under the trees, and backlighting the light itself, so that all the air around the house and above the creek and all the air between the window and the farthest ridge seemed polished by this ball of new fire.

I'd like to move away from works of fiction now and make a few, more general comments. The idea that a place can have holding power or be some kind of sustaining factor in a person's life is not widely agreed upon. In fact, it is an idea most Americans nowadays are out of touch with. There are a lot of reasons for this: the concept of private property, for example. It's a useful concept, up to a point. But if you're not careful, it leads to the idea of real estate, which in turn tends to promote the view of land or property as a commodity, as something to be bought and sold, rather than a place to be inhabited and respected. In this country we are also extremely mobile. It's not unusual to move five, six, seven times. We are a restless nation, and from this mobility and restlessness has come a whole fiction of *dis*placement, which accounts for a great deal of what is being written these days — a vast literary subject unto itself.

Meanwhile, there are still places you can visit in the United States that have been inhabited for centuries by people who have more or less stayed put. At Taos Pueblo, north of Santa Fe, people have been a continuous presence for more than eight hundred years. On the north shore of the Big Island of Hawaii there is a temple site called Mo'okini, laid out fifteen hundred years ago. According to their genealogy chart, one Hawaiian family has provided the guardians for this site, in unbroken lineage, since 500 AD.

Luckily for the rest of us, histories like these have kept alive the idea that a place can have power, sustaining power, shaping power, sometimes sacred power. When voices in touch with these places and their traditions speak to us, more and more of us tend to listen, because there is a yearning now to reconnect with the power that resides in the places of earth, to remember things we have forgotten. No matter where you live these days, some feature of the nearby landscape is under siege — the river, the forest, the seashore, something. This in itself forces us to become better informed, pay closer attention, look at what's right around us before it's changed too drastically or perhaps gone forever. The knowledge that we can lose our places has quickened our sense of place. The knowledge that the entire planet is now endangered has quickened our sense of the precariousness of the Earth and the need to honor and respect all its systems and its habits.

A while back I was talking with my friend, Frank La Pena, who heads the Native American Studies program at Sacramento State University. He grew up farther north, in a region bounded by the McCloud River, Redding, and Mount

Shasta, traditionally the home territory of his people, the Wintu. They have called that region home for more than ten thousand years.

Frank is a man so deeply rooted you can almost think the Western earth speaks through him. He likes to talk about Shasta, which dominates the landscape in Wintu country. For him this fourteen-thousand-foot volcanic peak is much more than a dramatic landmark and photographer's delight, much more than a challenge for climbers and skiers. It is a holy place he approaches with reverence. For him the mountain can be a kind of mentor. It can also serve as chapel and sanctuary. He told me about a pilgrimage he made to the mountain when a favorite uncle passed away. Frank went on foot and left behind a lock of his own hair as he expressed his grief and prayed for safe passage. For the Wintu, who call themselves "the mountain/river people," Shasta is the final point of contact with this world, and the gateway to the next.

25   When I heard that story I envied Frank, and I told him so. I told him that after the Loma Prieta quake in October of 1989 — with its epicenter just eight miles from our home — I had been filled with fear and runaway anxiety and, for a while, a sense of betrayal. I longed then for a place I could go and stand and voice my fear and release my anxiety and make some kind of peace with the powers residing in the earth.

"As you tell me about your pilgrimage to the mountain," I said, "I realize what a yearning I have in my life for that kind of ritual or for that kind of relationship. I wish my culture provided me with more guidance in this area, but it doesn't."

I was astounded by his reply. "You don't have to deprive yourself of that," he said. "It is really up to you. It is always available. You can awaken that aspect of a place, if you make your own connection with it."

It is really up to you. This was a truly liberating idea — that I could awaken the sacred aspect of a place, or at least open the way to this possibility. What it means is being awakened to that place in myself, that possibility in myself, and allowing the openness to such a dialogue.

The key word here, I think, is dialogue. And maybe this is what can bring my rambling digression back to fiction-making and storytelling. Very often *place* functions primarily as setting, as background for the action. That is its role, and that's okay; the emphasis in the piece is located somewhere else. But from time to time you come across a story where the place is profoundly felt, as a feature of the narrative that is working on the characters or through the characters or is somehow bearing upon their lives. I think of works by Wallace Stegner, Willa Cather, Eudora Welty, Edward Abbey, James Welch, William Kittredge, Leslie Marmon Silko, Rudolfo Anaya. Our literature is rich with such works, stories wherein at least part of what's going on is some form of dialogue between a place — whether it be an island or a mountain or a city or a shoreline or a subregion of the continent — and the lives being lived. I look upon this as one more version of the endless dialogue we're all involved in, between the human imagination and the world we find ourselves inhabiting and continually trying to understand.

TALKING ABOUT IT

Seeing Metaphor: Revealing and Concealing

1. Both in paragraph 5 and paragraphs 27–28, Houston refers to the idea of an "awakening." What has he been awakened to in each case? How are the two awakenings connected? Does the metaphor work the same way in both places, or is it essentially different?

2. Houston describes his use of landscape as metaphor in two of his novels: In *Continental Drift* the San Andreas fault represents both the potential for disaster and a sense of spiritual nourishment in its characters' lives, while in *Love Life* a devastating winter storm forms the backdrop of a stormy personal relationship. Think of some ways that a landscape or physical place can assume the quality of metaphor in real life.

Seeing Composition: Frame, Line, Texture, Tone

1. This essay began as a public address to other members of a writers' workshop. Point out places where the prose has much of the informality of speech. How do you respond to this relatively informal tone?

2. Paragraph 20 begins with a transition, essentially dividing the essay into two parts: "I'd like to move away from works of fiction now and make a few, more general comments." Do you find the connection between these two parts clear? Why or why not?

Seeing Meaning: Navigating and Negotiating

1. In paragraph 20 Houston suggests that the concept of private property leads to "the idea of real estate, which in turn tends to promote the view of land or property as a commodity, as something to be bought and sold, rather than a place to be inhabited and respected." How is this statement related to his larger argument? Does your experience support or contradict Houston's view?

2. Houston concludes by encouraging a "dialogue" between individuals and the landscape they occupy. Do you think he is speaking metaphorically here, or does he intend such a dialogue to be "real"? How would you describe such a dialogue? If you find such a description impossible, explain why.

WRITING ABOUT IT

1. Consider the particular locale where you have lived most of your life. How has this place become more than a geographical location and "moved into [your] conscious life"? In other words, how do you carry this place with you such that it bears on your dreams, shapes your views, and provides meaning in your life? Try to describe what Houston calls the relationship between a "terrain and the feelings it can call out of [you]."

2. Write about a place that has served as a "chapel" or "sanctuary" for you, a place where you have gone as if on a pilgrimage. What yearning has that place satisfied for you? How might you have "awakened the sacred aspect of [that] place," or, in other words, made a deeply personal connection with it?

   In your writing group, read each other's description of such a place and the special meaning it has for her or him. Then try writing collaboratively about how all your descriptions could be understood, according to Houston, as versions of one dialogue "between the human imagination and the world we find ourselves inhabiting and continually trying to understand."

Composting

Natalie Goldberg

Natalie Goldberg has written three books about writing as well as a novel (Banana Rose, 1996) and essays. She teaches writing workshops based on the methods in Writing Down the Bones: Freeing the Writer Within *(1986), from which the following selection is taken.*

It takes a while for our experience to sift through our consciousness. For instance, it is hard to write about being in love in the midst of a mad love affair. We have no perspective. All we can say is, "I'm madly in love," over and over again. It is also hard to write about a city we just moved to; it's not yet in our body. We don't know our new home, even if we can drive to the drugstore without getting lost. We have not lived through three winters there or seen the ducks leave in fall and return to the lakes in spring. Hemingway wrote about Michigan while sitting in a café in Paris. "Maybe away from Paris I could write about Paris as in Paris I could write about Michigan. I did not know it was too early for that because I did not know Paris well enough."

Our senses by themselves are dumb. They take in experience, but they need the richness of sifting for a while through our consciousness and through our whole bodies. I call this "composting." Our bodies are garbage heaps: we collect experience, and from the decomposition of the thrown-out eggshells, spinach leaves, coffee grinds, and old steak bones of our minds come nitrogen, heat, and very fertile soil. Out of this fertile soil bloom our poems and stories. But this does not come all at once. It takes time. Continue to turn over and over the organic details of your life until some of them fall through the garbage of discursive thoughts to the solid ground of black soil.

When I have students who have written many pages and read them in class, and the writing is not all necessarily good but I see that they are exploring their minds for material, I am glad. I know those people will continue and are not just obsessed with "hot" writing, but are in the process of practice. They are raking their minds and taking their shallow thinking and turning it over. If we continue to work with this raw matter, it will draw us deeper and deeper into ourselves, but not in a neurotic way. We will begin to see the rich garden we have inside us and use that for writing.

Often I will stab many times at something I want to say. For instance, you can look in my notebooks from August through December 1983 and see that I attempted several times a month to write about my father dying. I was exploring and composting the material. Then suddenly, and I can't say how, in December I sat transfixed at the Croissant Express in Minneapolis and a long poem about that subject poured out of me. All the disparate things I had to say were suddenly fused with energy and unity — a bright red tulip shot out of the compost. Katagiri Roshi said: "Your little will can't do anything. It takes Great Determination. Great Determination doesn't mean just you making an effort. It means the whole universe is behind you and with you — the birds, trees, sky, moon, and ten directions." Suddenly, after much composting, you are in alignment with the stars or the moment or the dining-room chandelier above your head, and your body opens and speaks.

5   Understanding this process cultivates patience and produces less anxiety. We aren't running everything, not even the writing we do. At the same time, we must keep practicing. It is not an excuse to not write and sit on the couch eating bonbons. We must continue to work the compost pile, enriching it and making it fertile so that something beautiful may bloom and so that our writing muscles are in good shape to ride the universe when it moves through us.

This understanding also helps us to accept someone else's success and not to be too greedy. It is simply that person's time. Ours will come in this lifetime or the next. No matter. Continue to practice.

TALKING ABOUT IT

Seeing Metaphor: Revealing and Concealing

1. Explain Goldberg's central metaphor in "Composting." She applies the idea specifically to writers, but how can you connect the metaphor to other areas of life as well?

2. Goldberg works out her metaphor in abundant detail. What, however, might the metaphor of composting conceal about the writing process based on your own experience as a writer?

Seeing Composition: Frame, Line, Texture, Tone

1. Goldberg's brief essay is characterized by highly specific, concrete language. Point out examples you find especially striking. How does this language affect your response?

2. What do you think of Goldberg's final paragraph, with its reference to greed and patience? Do you find that it brings the essay to a graceful close? Why or why not?

Seeing Meaning: Navigating and Negotiating

1. When you have a writing assignment, do you find yourself "composting" in the way Goldberg describes? Does the idea appeal to you as a writer? Why or why not?

2. What do you make of Goldberg's final words: "Continue to practice"? Do you think this is good advice?

WRITING ABOUT IT

1. Natalie Goldberg describes the process of collecting experience and turning it over in our minds as "composting." She imagines a garbage heap that writers rake over, working with raw material, sifting and cultivating it until it becomes fertile soil and, later, a rich garden. Invent your own metaphor for the process of developing ideas for writing. Try to extend the metaphor the way Goldberg does so that, in describing the experience, you draw on the terms related to the metaphor. For example, Goldberg uses many words related to "composting" as she explains the movement from "raw" material to "rich garden." She mentions "cultivating" patience so that ideas can "bloom" and so forth.

2. Instead of inventing a new metaphor, use Goldberg's "composting" metaphor to describe your own writing process. Extend her metaphor in ways that are suited to your own "gardening" practice. Maybe you don't "cultivate" patience, for example, but become exasperated if nothing "blooms" when you expect it to. In other words, you could use the "composting" metaphor to describe a positive or negative experience. After a page of description, write a short reflective analysis of the metaphor's usefulness for you.

The Writing Habit

Daᴠɪᴅ Hᴜᴅᴅʟᴇ

David Huddle teaches at the University of Vermont and at the Bread Loaf School of English and is the author of several collections of poetry, short stories, and essays. Recent books include Intimates: A Book of Stories *(1993) and* Tenorman: A Novella *(1995). The following selection is from* The Writing Habit: Essays *(1991).*

The major difficulty a writer must face has nothing to do with language: it is finding or making the circumstances that make writing possible. The first project for a writer is that of constructing a writing life.

Achievement in writing requires many hours and many pages of concentrated effort. That work must be carried out in a sustained fashion: a writer must be able to carry what has been learned from one day's writing into the next, from one week's writing into the next, and so on. Significant accomplishment in writing depends on growth. A writer's development depends on being able to write regularly and without distraction.

The actual details of writing lives differ with the personalities of individual writers. I remember a lecture given by the novelist Don Bredes, a very down-to-earth man, in which he set forth what he thought were the requirements of a writing circumstance. Shelves, he said, were necessary, in order to set out one's manuscripts, supplies, and reference materials. A phone immediately at hand was necessary so that one would not be ripped away from one's desk when the phone rang in another part of the house. A window with a view was necessary, but I don't remember if Don thought one's desk should face toward the window or away from it. And a plant, preferably a cactus, was necessary. I haven't remembered why Don thought one needed a plant — probably something to do with the benign influence of a low-profile living presence.

In her memoir of her father, Susan Cheever describes the young John Cheever putting on a suit and tie each morning, riding the elevator down to a basement storage room of their Manhattan apartment building, taking off his trousers and hanging them up with his coat to prevent wrinkling, and in his boxer shorts sitting down to his writing desk for his day's work. The established Cheever claimed to have written each of his later books in a different room of his Ossining, New York, home.

5 Eleanor Ross Taylor has written an intriguing description of the poet Randall Jarrell, apparently a very sociable man, keeping a writing pad and pen with him in his home, and writing intermittently all through his day, while entertaining visitors and tending to domestic duties.

I have had various writing circumstances, some of them refined to a state of high peculiarity. The most productive of them came together in the winter of 1978 when I lived alone in a cottage beside a small lake. I rose at sun-up, did fifteen minutes of calisthenics, showered, made coffee and ate a light breakfast. Then I worked at "fresh" writing, beginning around seven or seven-thirty. I tried not to excuse myself before eleven, though if momentum was with me, it was o.k. to stay later. My output for those hours was three to six pages of fresh prose each morning. I composed on a portable electric typewriter, the humming of which always seemed to me like very good company. I used canary yellow "second sheets" for that first draft material. My desk faced a large window that overlooked a woodsy hillside where I had set out bird food. For some reason I took to lighting a large "patio lantern" candle when I sat down to work and to blowing it out when I felt I had finished for the morning.

Those months of living beside Lake St. Clair were the one period of my life when I have been a runner, or more accurately a jogger. My run was my reward for having worked through my morning hours. Just as I had had to work up to my three or four hours of fresh writing a day, I had gradually to increase my running distance. The road around Lake St. Clair is a very hilly 2.3 miles long. When I began running in early February, I could trot only about a quarter of the way around it without stopping to walk — and I would always walk the rest of the way around, often picking up my pace again after I'd caught my breath. When I left Lake St. Clair in mid-May I was jogging (vigorously) around it twice without stopping. On the run I occasionally saw a pileated woodpecker, a blue heron, wild turkeys, and various other birds.

When I returned from jogging, I did some stretching, took a shower, and fixed myself a light lunch. For the first time in the day, I listened to the radio; I neither read, nor was I tempted to read, any newspapers during my lakeside tenure. After washing my lunch and breakfast dishes, I was in my "free period." I could do whatever I wanted. Whatever I wanted was almost always to read for a while and then to take a nap.

A few words here about naps: I'm convinced that naps are an essential part of a writing life, that they "clean" the brain by discharging the clutter and allowing the subconscious to address some of the central issues of the morning's writing. If I know I want to do some more writing in the afternoon, I'll always try to schedule that session immediately after a nap. It's rare for me to try to accomplish fresh writing in the afternoon, but I often try to carry out revisions if I have at least an hour or more of afternoon time available to me.

When I woke from a nap at Lake St. Clair, I had the delicious sensation of 10 having nothing pressing to do and not having to hurry with whatever I chose to do. Most often I simply lay in bed, letting my mind wander as it would. Because I had minimum distraction there, whatever I was writing was what I thought about most of the time. It wasn't long after I awaked from my nap that I would turn to my manuscript; usually I'd be curious about the pages I'd written that morning and want to check them out. Of course, as I read, I reached for a pen to make corrections, changes, notes, and it wasn't uncommon for me to find myself again sitting before the typewriter, relighting my candle, retyping the morning's pages, perhaps even proceeding into a page of "fresh writing" without consciously deciding to do so. These afternoon writing sessions usually lasted only an hour or two, but I always considered them a bonus. Because my writing days became so productive, I felt more and more virtuous while I lived at Lake St. Clair.

At the end of an afternoon work session, I rewarded myself with a walk around the lake. I made myself walk slowly and try to observe my surroundings as carefully as I could. The world itself seemed especially charged with energy; it became an intense presence in my life. I was primarily interested in birds—I'd bought a field guide and begun keeping a list of the birds I saw—but I also became a student of the landscape, the variety and quality of light in different weathers and at different times of day. I suspect that the attention I paid to the world of my 2.3 mile walks around Lake St. Clair was of benefit to me in my writing. The fiction I wrote during those months seems to me informed by the world's presence and to articulate an intense connection between my characters and the world around them.

In the evenings I listened to the radio—jazz or classical music. Sometimes I worked on my writing. Evening work sessions were rare and likely to come about only if I was trying to complete a finished draft of a story and what had to be done was merely typing clean copy. Mostly I read, because reading had become unusually exciting to me: I felt as if I were reading on two levels, for the usual pleasure of poetry and narrative and also for my writerly education. In the works of other authors, I was able to observe technical achievement that I thought would be of eventual use in my own work.

I got sleepy early. It was rare that I didn't turn out my bedside light by ten or ten thirty. I went to sleep thinking about the writing I'd accomplished and about the work I meant to do the next morning. The telephone did ring now and then, and I had visitors, visitors I wanted and ones I didn't want. But what I had most of the time at Lake St. Clair was solitude, which instructed me: the more of it I had, the more I learned to make use of it. When a writing life is in good order, as mine was then, everything is relevant to it; every detail of one's day has a connection to one's writing.

I have been a resident of artists' colonies at Yaddo and the Virginia Center for the Creative Arts; on some occasions I have been able to work better at those places than at home, but in my best colony experience I've been only about fifty percent as productive as I was at Lake St. Clair. The obvious difference is that colonies have a social life that I felt I had to attend; I was guaranteed solitude during the day, but in the evenings I ate with the other colonists, I chatted after dinner, I made friends, and so on. This social life can be a healthy influence in a writing life, especially if two writers begin exchanging manuscripts and criticism. Along with valuable friendship, a writer can also find inspiration and illumination from visual artists and composers. But finally a social life is a distraction. Instead of having the evening hours to compose yourself, to let your mind wander back to the writing, you become involved with others. In the morning, when there should be no obstacles between self and work, you find you're reviewing last night's conversation.

Lake St. Clair was a temporary situation for me brought about by the luck- 15 ily converging circumstances of a sabbatical leave from teaching at the University of Vermont, an NEA Fellowship that paid the bills for it, and a wife who for those months was willing to look after herself and our daughter. I have often wondered how different things would have been if I had thought of it as my permanent circumstance. Would all that solitude have seemed so luxurious then, or would it have seemed a punishment, a burden, an entrapment? Would I have found my work so fulfilling if I had believed it must take the place of my family? I don't think my writing would be helped by being permanently without the company of family and friends. Most likely I was able to put my solitude to such excellent use because I knew there would be an end to it.

When I left the lake, I had come to think of myself as a kind of esthetic saint. I had lost weight. I was in excellent physical condition. I had stripped my life down to what was essential to me. I had accomplished a greater quantity and a higher quality of writing than I ever had before. I had established a meaningful connection between myself and the natural world. I felt this exhilarating rightness to my life. I felt certain that I would be able to transport the habits I had formed into my "regular life," which now (from my saintly viewpoint) seemed cluttered, distracting, piggish, physically and esthetically unhealthy.

The disintegration took about a week. If I did my early morning calisthenics anywhere in the house, I made such a clatter that I woke my wife and daughter. My wife had to go to work and my daughter had to go to day-care; their preparations necessarily disturbed my concentration on my work. Near my house there was nowhere to run or walk without encountering traffic and carbon monoxide. In the house, everywhere I looked, there were little chores that needed doing, dishes to be washed, toys to be picked up, stacks of magazines to straighten, bills to pay, a screen with a hole in it, a borrowed book that needed to be returned. The phone rang more often now that I was back in my own community. I played tennis, I met a friend for lunch, I attended a surprise birthday party. I snacked between meals. I watched TV. In short, I drifted away from my writing life. My Lake St. Clair habits were not transportable.

Before and after my tenure at Lake St. Clair, I was a sporadic writer—if I had something I was working on, I worked at it until I finished it; then I didn't write again until something else pressed me urgently enough to begin it and pursue it. For periods of as long as a year, I wrote nothing. I had a rationale worked out about being a sporadic writer: I wasn't a factory, and it was only because of a national assembly-line mentality that American writers felt obligated to churn out books. Who needed another piece of writing anyway? If I wasn't writing, it probably meant I had nothing worthwhile to say. And so on. But my Lake St. Clair experience demonstrated to me what it felt like to have a real writing life, to have something that held my attention over a period of time, to have ongoing, deeply fulfilling work. I have never been able to duplicate that experience, but because I had it that once, it gave me something to aspire to again. I've gotten better and better at constructing a writing life for myself in the midst of my "regular life." I don't have any remarkable secrets about it, but I do have what I think are a few useful concepts.

To write well one must use one's "good hours" for one's writing. My good hours are the first three or four of my day. If I want to use them for my writing, that means I have to get up early and start writing before other demands are made on me. A few people I know have their good hours late at night, and that's when they should be writing. A poet I know warms up slowly; she finds her good hours to begin around mid- or late-morning.

20   Since I teach school for a living and since much of the work of my teaching involves reading and responding to student manuscripts, I find that I have to use my "next-best hours" (late morning or afternoons) for that work. But responding to student manuscripts is almost always in direct competition with my own writing for my good hours; I have to be clever to manage a heavy teaching load with a productive writing schedule. On a day when I teach my first class at 9:25 and I have a dozen student stories to respond to, I'll need to get up at 4:00, be at the writing desk by 4:45, work on my own writing until 6:00, write my responses until 8:30, and get to my office by 9:15.

Along with using my good hours for my writing, I've learned more about how to use my less-good hours for clearing the way for efficient use of my writing time. I'm a house-husband, which means that I have cooking, laundry, cleaning, and child-care duties to attend to, and like most writers I am very distractable; house-husbanding can devour my good writing hours if I let it. But nowadays my motto is that everything has to get done sometime, and the trick is to make sure that my writing always comes first. Taking a break from my writing, I can wash the dishes because doing that little task is just distracting enough to give me a new "take" on whatever it is I'm working on. Putting away laundry can often be a very useful fifteen-minute writing break. I can pay my bills while my printer is typing up a manuscript. What I understand better and better is how to clear the way to my good hours with my writing. Before I go to bed I try to have my little computer, with its battery charged, waiting for me, preferably with the document I'm working on ready to come up on the screen when I switch it on. I want my reading glasses right where I can find them, my coffee thermos clean, and the room straightened up. If I have bills to pay or letters that need to be answered, I want them neatly stashed where they won't catch my eye first thing when I sit down to write.

Robert Hass's poem "Measure" uses the phrase "the peace of the writing desk." These words accurately describe my own experience. My writing time is when I set my life in order. I examine my life through the act of writing. Although I try to sell most of my writing, my first desire for it is that it be as truthful and beautiful as I can make it out of what I know and think and feel. Therefore writing is to me a kind of meditation. It isn't a purely spiritual activity, but it is one in which my spirit is nourished. Writing has become so essential for my daily life that I feel denied if I miss a day of "the peace of the writing desk."

When I tell people that I get up at 4:30 or 5:00 to do my writing, they often praise my discipline, but now that my writing life has been established, discipline has nothing to do with it. Getting up to do my writing requires no more discipline than sitting down to eat a meal or going to bed at night to get some sleep. It's natural and necessary.

Flux has never been an easy principle for me to understand or to incorporate into my life. My make-up is conservative. My instinctive way of doing things is to try to get them just right and then to keep them that way. Some nasty lessons have taught me that I had better give flux its due. Thus it was silly of me to try to import my Lake St. Clair writing habits into the life I lived in my home with my family. Instead of becoming frustrated because I couldn't repeat my successful methods, a more intelligent course of action would have been to try to discover the different writing habits that would work in that different situation.

Cheever needed different rooms of his house because at different times of his life, he was a different writer and was writing different books. Learning to understand and monitor one's own writerly needs is the main project of a writer's education. Beginning writers almost always feel that they have to learn the secrets that all successful writers have mastered. They think they need to take possession of something outside themselves. Writing teachers are often frustrated because they can't make students see how they're looking away from the place where the real secrets are located. The elements of a writer's making are within the individual, and they are different with each individual. Each writer makes his own habit.

I write well at 5:30 a.m. sitting in an easy chair with a portable computer in my lap, a coffee thermos and a cup by my chair, and Glenn Gould playing Bach's "Well-Tempered Klavier" on the stereo. Across town, a little later, Alan Broughton will be sitting at his desk in his study using a pencil and a legal pad for his first draft, which he will later in the day type into his word processor because he can't read his handwriting if he lets it sit "untranslated" more than a few hours. And even later, between classes, in his office at St. Michael's College, John Engels will be furiously annotating the manuscript of a poem he printed out yesterday. He will completely dismantle and reassemble his poem in the minutes available to him between conversations with students and colleagues who drop by to see him.

The options are various. If you're a would-be writer, what you need to find out is not how someone else works but how you are inclined to work. You have to determine your good hours, the writing tools and writing environment that best suit you, the limitations you can overcome and the best methods for dealing with the limitations you can't overcome.

You also have to become aware of your inclinations toward laziness, dishonesty, glibness, and other personal foibles. You have to become skillful at outwitting those negative aspects of your character. For instance, I know I am inclined to send manuscripts out before they're really ready to be submitted any place — before they're finished. I haven't been able to correct this failure, but I've gotten so I can delay my sending out a manuscript by giving copies of it to certain friends of mine to read and respond to it before I make up a "final copy." The more friends who give me responses to a manuscript, the more drafts I'll run it through. The help of peers is essential to most of the writers I know. To discuss our work, I meet with two other writers about every three weeks; we try to bring fresh writing or significant revisions to our meetings. We try to be very tough-minded in our responses to each other's work. Not only are these other two writers helpful to me as critics; they also inspire me to work regularly in hopes of producing something they will appreciate.

Like most writers, I'm a highly skilled procrastinator. I've had to develop the appropriate counter-skills. One of my more successful counter-procrastinating techniques is the bend-and-snap-back move: I'll tell myself yes, I really do need a break right now, but the only way I can justify it is by using it to accomplish some little task that might distract me from writing tomorrow morning.

30   These maneuvers of self against self for the good of getting my work done are not unlike similar moves I've learned for improving the writing itself. For instance, I have come to understand that I am weak when it comes to portraying female characters as whole human beings. My natural, porcine inclination is toward second-rate versions of characters like Hemingway's Maria, Faulkner's Eula Varner Snopes, Nabokov's Lolita, and Terry Southern's Candy. My more responsible writing self must always be questioning and arguing with this lesser Huddle. The tension is a healthy one for my writing; my female characters get so much of both the porcine and the responsible varieties of my attention, that in a few instances I've been able to create portraits of women who have both sexual force and emotional-intellectual complexity. And I count myself lucky that I'm able to write across gender even as well as I have been able to do so far.

Managing contraries within the self is an ability that must be cultivated by a writer, both in and out of the work. Your natural inclinations are often less than admirable, but rather than trying to eliminate them from your personality, you can learn how to change them into positive elements of your writing. Thus you can convert your inclination toward distraction and procrastination into habits that will clear the way toward using your good hours for concentrated writing. Thus you can transform your inclination toward fantasizing about wish-fulfilling female characters into the creation of appealingly whole human beings. Such alchemy is still possible in a well-constructed writing life.

Once you understand that your negative qualities can be put to use both inside and outside your writing, you can begin to be kind to yourself. No longer necessary are those lectures, "You lazy such and such, you took a nap when you should have been writing, you can't write about women, you sent out that story too soon, you . . ." Instead of flailing away like that, you can become crafty, learn how to use your whole self in your writing.

Hemingway had a rule that has been especially useful for my work. He thought you ought to stop writing for the day at a point where you knew what you were going to do next. I like that notion just as it stands — often at the end of my morning's writing session, I will make a few notes about what I think ought to come next. I also think a writer needs to stop work with a little bit of energy left. I feel good when I've written enough to be tired, but if I've written myself into a state of exhaustion, I don't feel so eager to get back to work the next day.

Hemingway's quitting-time axiom is one version of what seems to me a basic principle of the writing life: you must nourish the "ongoingness" of your work. Sometimes I convince myself that what is crucial is to finish this piece or that piece of writing, that the only thing that matters is to get this manuscript in the mail. But a real writing life is nothing so desperate as all that, not something you do merely for a day or a month or a year. Stories, poems, essays, and books are the by-product of a writing life; they are to be cherished, but they separate themselves from their creators and become the property of editors, reviewers, and readers. For a writer, the only truly valuable possession is the ongoing work — the writing habit, which may take some getting used to, but which soon becomes so natural as to be almost inevitable.

TALKING ABOUT IT

Seeing Metaphor: Revealing and Concealing

1. Huddle writes in his first paragraph about "constructing a writing life." What does he mean? How does he elaborate on this metaphor throughout his essay? Do you find it illuminating? Does it limit your understanding any way?

2. Huddle also writes metaphorically about jogging, taking naps, sainthood, and assembly lines. Locate these examples in his text and explain what each represents, as well as its relation to his central metaphor.

Seeing Composition: Frame, Line, Texture, Tone

1. Is Huddle's essay as "structured" as his writing life? That is, do you find it carefully ordered and organized, or does it ever seem to ramble or jump suddenly to new topics? Point to specifics in the essay to explain your view.

2. How would you describe Huddle's tone in this essay? What kind of persona does he create for you? Do you respond to his voice positively, or are there elements of the personality he projects that strike you as negative? Do you think he would make a good writing teacher?

Seeing Meaning: Navigating and Negotiating

1. What do you think of Huddle's advice about constructing a writing life within one's "regular" life? Even if you're not an aspiring writer, could you apply this advice to your writing as a student or for your job? Would you ever find that the writing habit is its own reward, as he suggests in his final paragraph?

2. Compare Huddle's thoughts about writing with those of Natalie Goldberg in the previous essay. Is there a fundamental difference between seeing the process as "constructed" and seeing it through the metaphor of composting? Or are the two writers giving essentially the same advice? Why do you think so?

WRITING ABOUT IT

1. David Huddle claims, "My writing time is when I set my life in order. I examine my life through the act of writing. . . . Writing is to me a kind of meditation. It isn't purely spiritual activity, but is one in which my spirit is nourished." Other activities can serve in similar ways. Write about an activity through which you examine your life and perhaps set it in order. How might this activity be for you a kind of meditation, a way to nourish your spirit? Then compare that activity with the act of writing: How does writing serve or not serve these purposes for you? Why or why not?

2. Huddle speaks of "managing the contraries within the self" and putting negative qualities to use. How have you tried to manage contraries within yourself and put your negative qualities to use in life? How might you apply those strategies to your writing?

How to Get Power through Voice

PETER ELBOW

Peter Elbow is a professor of English at the University of Massachusetts at Amherst and has written many essays and books on writing and teaching. "How to Get Power through Voice" is from Writing with Power: Techniques for Mastering the Writing Process *(1981).*

People often lack any voice at all in their writing, even fake voice, because they stop so often in the act of writing a sentence and worry and change their minds about which words to use. They have none of the natural breath in their writing that they have in speaking because the conditions for writing are so different from the conditions for speaking. The list of conditions is awesome: we have so little practice in writing, but so much more time to stop and fiddle as we write each sentence; we have additional rules of spelling and usage to follow in writing that we don't have in speaking; we feel more culpable for our written foolishness than for what we say; we have been so fully graded, corrected, and given feedback on our mistakes in writing; and we are usually trying to get our words to conform to some (ill-understood) model of "good writing" as we write.

Frequent and regular freewriting exercises are the best way to overcome these conditions of writing and get voice into your words. These exercises should perhaps be called compulsory writing exercises since they are really a way to *compel* yourself to keep putting words down on paper no matter how lost or frustrated you feel. To get voice into your words you need to learn to get each word chosen, as it were, not by you but by the preceding word. Freewriting exercises help you learn to stand out of the way.

In addition to actual exercises in nonstop writing — since it's hard to keep writing *no matter what* for more than fifteen minutes — force yourself simply to write enormous quantities. Try to make up for all the writing you haven't done. Use writing for as many different tasks as you can. Keep a notebook or journal, explore thoughts for yourself, write to yourself when you feel frustrated or want to figure something out.

Practice revising for voice. A powerful exercise is to write short pieces of prose or poetry that work without any punctuation at all. Get the words so well ordered that punctuation is never missed. The reader must never stumble or have to reread a phrase, not even on first reading — and all without benefit of punctuation. This is really an exercise in adjusting the breath in the words till it guides the reader's voice naturally to each pause and full stop.

Read out loud. This is a good way to exercise the muscle involved in voice and even in real voice. Good reading out loud is not necessarily dramatic. I'm struck with how some good poets or readers get real voice into a monotone or 5 chant. They are trying to let the words' inner resonance come through, not trying to "perform" the words. (Dylan Thomas reads so splendidly that we may make the mistake of calling his technique "dramatic." Really it is a kind of chant or incantation he uses.) But there is no right way. It's a question of steering a path between being too timid and being falsely dramatic. The presence of listeners can sharpen your ear and help you hear when you chicken out or overdramatize.

Real voice. People often avoid it and drift into fake voices because of the need to face an audience. I have to go to work, I have to make a presentation, I have to teach, I have to go to a party, I have to have dinner with friends. Perhaps I feel lost, uncertain, baffled—or else angry—or else uncaring—or else hysterical. I can't sound that way with all these people. They won't understand, they won't know how to deal with me, and I won't accomplish what I need to accomplish. Besides, perhaps I don't even know *how* to sound the way I feel. (When we were little we had no difficulty sounding the way we felt; thus most little children speak and write with real voice.) Therefore I will use some of the voices I have at my disposal that will serve the audience and the situation— voices I've learned by imitation or made up out of desperation or out of my sense of humor. I might as well. By now, those people think those voices are me. If I used my real voice, they might think I was crazy.

For real voice, write a lot without an audience. Do freewritings and throw them away. Remove yourself from the expectations of an audience, the demands of a particular task, the needs of a particular interaction. As you do this, try out many different ways of speaking.

But a certain *kind* of audience can help you toward real voice even though it was probably the pressures of audience that led you to unreal voices in the first place. Find an audience of people also committed to getting power in their writing. Find times when you can write in each other's presence, each working on your own work. Your shared presence and commitment to helping each other will make you more powerful in what you write. Then read your rough writing to each other. No feedback: just welcoming each other to try out anything.

Because you often don't even know what your power or your inner self sounds like, you have to try many different tones and voices. Fool around, jump from one mood or voice to another, mimic, play-act, dramatize and exaggerate. Let your writing be outrageous. Practice relinquishing control. It can help to write in settings where you never write (on the bus? in the bathtub?) or in modes you never use. And if, as sometimes happens, you know you are angry but somehow cannot really feel or inhabit that feeling, play-act and exaggerate it. Write artificially. Sometimes "going through the motions" is the quickest way to "the real thing."

10   Realize that in the short run there is probably a conflict between developing real voice and producing successful, pragmatic writing—polished pieces that work for specific audiences and situations. Keeping an appropriate stance

or tone for an audience may prevent you from getting real voice into that piece of writing. Deep personal outrage, for example, may be the only authentic tone of voice you can use in writing to a particular person, yet that voice is neither appropriate nor useful for the actual document you have to write — perhaps an official agency memo or a report to that person about his child. Feedback on whether something works as a finished piece of writing for an audience is often not good feedback on real voice. It is probably important to work on both goals. Work on polishing things and making sure they have the right tone or stance for that audience. Or at least not the wrong one: you may well have to play it safe. But make sure you also work on writing that *doesn't* have to work and doesn't have to be revised and polished for an audience.

And yet you needn't give up on power just because a particular writing situation is very tricky for you. Perhaps you must write an essay for a teacher who never seems to understand you; or a report for a supervisor who never seems able to see things the way you do; or a research report on a topic that has always scared and confused you. If you try to write in the most useful voice for this situation — perhaps cheerful politeness or down-to-business impersonality — the anger will probably show through anyway. It might not show clearly, readers might be unaware of it, yet they will turn out to have the kind of responses they have to angry writing. That is, they will become annoyed with many of the ideas you present, or continually think of arguments against you (which they wouldn't have done to a different voice), or they will turn off, or they will react condescendingly.

To the degree that you keep your anger hidden, you are likely to write words especially lacking in voice — especially dead, fishy, fake-feeling. Or the process of trying to write in a non-angry, down-to-business, impersonal way is so deadening to you that you simply get bored and sleepy and devoid of energy. Your mind shuts off. You cannot think of anything to say.

In a situation like this it helps to take a roundabout approach. First do lots of freewriting where you are angry and tell your reader all your feelings in whatever voices come. Then get back to the real topic. Do lots of freewriting and raw writing and exploration of the topic — writing still in whatever style comes out. Put all your effort into finding the best ideas and arguments you can, and don't worry about your tone. After you express the feelings and voices swirling around in you, and after you get all the insights you can while not having to worry about the audience and the tone, then you will find it relatively easy to revise and rewrite something powerful and effective for that reader. That is, you can get past the anger and confusion, but keep the good ideas and the energy. As you rewrite for the real audience, you can generally use large chunks of what you have already written with only minor cosmetic changes. (You don't necessarily have to write out *all* the anger you have. It may be that you have three hundred pages of angry words you need to say to someone, but if you can get *one* page that really opens the door all the way, that can be enough. But if this is something new to you, you may find you cannot do it in one page—you need to rant and rave for five or ten pages. It may seem like a waste of time, but it isn't. Gradually you will get more economical.)

By taking this roundabout path, you will find more energy and better thinking. And through the process of starting with the voices that just happen and seeing where they lead, often you will come to a *new* voice which is appropriate to this reader but also rings deeply. You won't have to choose between something self-defeatingly angry that will simply turn off the reader or something pussyfooting, polite, and full of fog—and boring for you to write.

15   A long and messy path is common and beneficial, but you can get some of the benefits quicker if you are in a hurry. Just set yourself strict time limits for the early writing and force yourself to write without stopping throughout the early stages. When I have to write an evaluation of a student I am annoyed at, I force myself to write a quick freewriting letter to the student telling him everything on my mind. I make this uncensored, extreme, exaggerated, sometimes even deliberately unfair—but very short. And it's for the wastepaper basket. Having done this, I can turn to my official evaluation and find it much easier to write something fair in a suitable tone of voice (for a document that becomes part of the student's transcript). I finish these two pieces of writing much more quickly than if I just tried to write the official document and pick my way gingerly through my feelings.

Another reason people don't use real voice is that it makes them feel exposed and vulnerable. I don't so much mind if someone dislikes my writing when I am merely using an acceptable voice, but if I use my real voice and they don't like it—which of course is very possible—that hurts. The more criticism people get on their writing, the more they tend to use fake voices. To use real voice feels like bringing yourself into contact with the reader. It's the same kind of phenomenon that happens when there is real eye contact and each person experiences the presence of the other; or when two or more people stop talking and wait in silence while something in the air gets itself clear. Writing of almost any kind is exhibitionistic; writing with real voice is more so. Many professional writers feel a special need for privacy. It will help you, then, to get together with one or more others who are interested in recovering their power. Feeling vulnerable or exposed with them is not so difficult.

Another reason people don't use their real voice is that it means having feelings and memories they would rather not have. When you write in your real voice, it often brings tears or shaking—though laughter too. Using real voice may even mean finding you *believe* things you don't wish to believe. For all these reasons, you need to write for no audience and to write for an audience that's safe. And you need faith in yourself that you will gradually sort things out and that it doesn't matter if it takes time.

Most children have real voice but then lose it. It is often just plain loud: like screeching or banging a drum. It can be annoying or wearing for others. "Shhh" is the response we often get to the power of our real voice. But, in addition, much of what we say with real voice is difficult for those around us to deal with: anger, grief, self-pity, even love for the wrong people. When we are hushed up from those expressions, we lose real voice.

In addition, we lose real voice when we are persuaded to give up some of our natural responses to inauthenticity and injustice. Almost any child can feel inauthenticity in the voices of many TV figures or politicians. Many grown-ups can't hear it so well — or drown out their distrust. It is difficult to get along in the world if you hear all the inauthenticity: it makes you feel alone, depressed, hopeless. We need to belong, and society offers us membership if we stop hearing inauthenticity.

Children can usually feel when things are unfair, but they are often persuaded to go along because they need to belong and to be loved. To get back to those feelings in later life leads to rage, grief, aloneness and — since one has gone along — guilt. Real voice is often buried in all of that. If you want to recover it, you do well to build in special support from people you can trust so you don't feel so alone or threatened by all these feelings.

Another reason people don't use real voice is that they run away from their power. There's something scary about being as strong as you are, about wielding the force you actually have. It means taking a lot more responsibility and credit than you are used to. If you write with real voice, people will say "You did this to me" and try to make you feel responsible for some of their actions. Besides, the effect of your power is liable to be different from what you intended. Especially at first. You cause explosions when you thought you were just asking for the salt or saying hello. In effect I'm saying, "Why don't you shoot that gun you have? Oh yes, by the way, I can't tell you how to aim it." The standard approach in writing is to say you mustn't pull the trigger until you can aim it well. But how can you learn to aim well till you start pulling the trigger? If you start letting your writing lead you to real voice you'll discover some thoughts and feelings you didn't know you had.

Therefore, practice shooting the gun off in safe places. First with no one around. Then with people you know and trust deeply. Find people who are willing to be in the same room with you while you pull the trigger. Try using the power in ways where the results don't matter. Write letters to people that don't matter to you. You'll discover that the gun doesn't kill but that you have more power than you are comfortable with.

Of course you may accept your power but still want to disguise it. That is, you may find it convenient, if you are in a large organization, to be able to write about an event in a fuzzy, passive "It has come to our attention that . . ." kind of language, so you disguise not only the fact that it was an action performed by a human being with a free will but indeed that *you did it.* But it would be incorrect to conclude, as some people do, that all bureaucratic, organizational, and governmental writing needs to lack the resonance of real voice. Most often it could do its work perfectly well even if it were strong and clear. It is the *personal, individualistic,* or *personality-filled* voice that is inappropriate in much organizational writing, but you can write with power in the impersonal, public, and corporate voice. You can avoid "I" and its flavor, and talk entirely in terms of "we" and "they" and even "it," and still achieve the resonance of real voice. Real voice is not the sound of an *individual personality* redolent with vibes, it is the sound of *a meaning* resonating because the individual consciousness of the writer is somehow fully behind or in tune with or in participation with that meaning.

I have stressed the importance of sharing writing without any feedback at all. What about asking people to give you feedback specifically on real voice? I think that such feedback can be useful, but I am leery of it. It's so hard to know whether someone's perception of real voice is accurate. If you want this feedback, don't get it early in your writing development, make sure you get it from very different kinds of people, and make sure not to put too much trust in it. The safest method is to get them to read a piece and then ask them a week later what they remember. Passages they *dislike* often have the most real voice.

25   But here is a specific exercise for getting feedback on real voice. It grows out of one of the first experiences that made me think consciously about this matter. As an applicant for conscientious objector status, and then later as a draft counselor, I discovered that the writing task set by Selective Service was very interesting and perplexing. An applicant had to write why he was opposed to fighting in wars, but there was no right or wrong answer. The draft board would accept any reasons (within certain broad limits); they would accept any style, any level of skill. Their only criterion was whether *they* believed that the *writer* believed his own words. (I am describing how it worked when board members were in good faith.)

Applicants, especially college students, often started with writing that didn't work. I could infer from all the arguments and commotion and from conversations with them that they were sincere but as they wrote they got so preoccupied with theories, argument, and reasoning that in the end there was no conviction on paper. When I gave someone this feedback and he was willing to try and try again till at last the words began to ring true, all of a sudden the writing got powerful and even skillful in other ways.

The exercise I suggest to anybody, then, is simply to write about some belief you have — or even some experience or perception — but to get readers to give you this limited, peculiar, draft-board-like feedback: where do they really believe that you believe it, and where do they have doubts? The useful thing about this exercise is discovering how often words that ring true are not especially full of feeling, not heavy with conviction. Too much "sincerity" and quivering often sounds fake and makes readers doubt that you really believe what you are saying. I stress this because I fear I have made real voice sound as though it is always full of loud emotion. It is often quiet.

In the end, what may be as important as these specific exercises is adopting the right frame of mind.

Look for real voice and realize it is there in everyone waiting to be used. Yet remember, too, that you are looking for something mysterious and hidden. There are no outward linguistic characteristics to point to in writing with real voice. Resonance or impact on readers is all there is. But you can't count on readers to notice it or to agree about whether it is there because of all the other criteria they use in evaluating writing (e.g., polished style, correct reasoning, good insights, truth-to-life, deep feelings), and because of the negative qualities that sometimes accompany real voice as it is emerging. And you, as writer, may be wrong about the presence or absence of real voice in your writing — at least until you finally develop a trustworthy sense of it. You have to be willing to work in the dark, not be in a hurry, and have faith. The best clue I know is that as you begin to develop real voice, your writing will probably cause more comment from readers than before (though not necessarily more favorable comment).

If you seek real voice you should realize that you probably face a dilemma. 30 You probably have only one real voice — at first anyway — and it is likely to feel childish or distasteful or ugly to you. But you are stuck. You can either use voices you like or you can be heard. For a while, you can't have it both ways.

But if you do have the courage to use and inhabit that real voice, you will get the knack of resonance, you will learn to expand its range and eventually make more voices real. This of course is the skill of great literary artists: the ability to give resonance to many voices.

It's important to stress, at the end, this fact of many voices. Partly to reassure you that you are not ultimately stuck with just one voice forever. But also because it highlights the mystery. Real voice is not necessarily personal or sincere. Writing about your own personal concerns is only one way and not necessarily the best. Such writing can lead to gushy or analytical words about how angry you are today: useful to write, an expression of strong feelings, a possible *source* of future powerful writing, but not resonant or powerful for readers as it stands. Real voice is whatever yields resonance, whatever makes the words bore through. Some writers get real voice through pure fantasy, lies, imitation of utterly different writers, or trance-writing. It may be possible to get real voice by merging in your mind with another personality, pretending to be someone else. *Shedding* the self's concerns and point of view can be a good way to get real voice — thus writing fiction and playing roles are powerful tools. Many good literary artists sound least convincing when they speak for themselves. The important thing is simply to know that power is available and to figure out through experimentation the best way for you to attain it.

TALKING ABOUT IT

Seeing Metaphor: Revealing and Concealing

1. Elbow suggests that achieving "real voice" as a writer can be a "long and messy path" (paragraph 15). What does he mean literally? That is, what does pursuing this "path" actually involve? How well do you think the metaphor of a path illuminates the point Elbow is making?

2. In paragraphs 21 and 22, Elbow likens the practice involved in finding one's voice to shooting a gun before one has learned to aim it well. What is his point? Do you agree with him that "people don't use real voice [because] they run away from their power"? Can you see this connection at all in your own voice as a writer? Why or why not?

Seeing Composition: Frame, Line, Texture, Tone

1. The central subject of Elbow's essay is what he sees as the distinction between the "fake voices" writers generally use and the "real voice" they should try to develop. How well do you think he defines this distinction? Do his remarks convince you that much of your own writing reflects a "fake" voice and that you would benefit from pursuing the exercises he suggests for developing a "real" voice? Explain.

2. Does Elbow's own voice seem "real"? Point to specific passages in the essay that support your conclusions.

Seeing Meaning: Navigating and Negotiating

1. Elbow offers a number of suggestions for writers attempting to develop a "real" voice: writing short pieces without using punctuation, writing often without an audience, taking a roundabout approach, and writing about some belief or perception and asking readers to tell you where they believe and where they doubt you, among others. Which of these suggestions do you think you would find most personally helpful? Or do you not see them as likely to be helpful at all? Explain your response.

2. Elbow also offers a number of reasons that writers avoid a "real" voice and admits that "in the short run there is probably a conflict between developing real voice and producing successful, pragmatic writing" (paragraph 10).

What do you think are the best reasons for developing the kind of "real" voice Elbow advocates? Do you think it's worth the effort and the short-run conflict?

WRITING ABOUT IT

1. Write a short piece (a substantially developed paragraph) without any punctuation, as Peter Elbow suggests. Try to "get the words so well ordered that punctuation is never missed." Exchange paragraphs within your writing group. Read each other's out loud. Listen for places where a reader stumbles or has to reread. These are places where the writer needs to revise so that the reader is guided more easily and naturally to pauses and stops.

2. Find an example from your own writing that could be called "fake," as Peter Elbow defines it. This is writing during which you feared your audience and tried to imitate the sound of a voice that you believed your audience would accept. Exchange samples of "fake" writing with members of your writing group. First, talk with each other about how your audience seemed to motivate a "fake" voice: what did each of you imagine your audience to be like? how had it "hushed you up"?

   Second, after discussing these matters, write to the members of your group about some belief you have. (A page or two should be sufficient for the exercise.) When they have read the piece, ask them to give you the same limited "draft-board-like feedback" that Elbow describes: "Where do they really believe that you believe it, and where do they have doubts"? Where do you sound "real"? As listeners, they can help you hear when you are either "too timid" or "falsely dramatic." They can also tell you when they hear the "sound of a meaning resonating because the individual consciousness of the writer is somehow fully behind or in tune with . . . that meaning."

Anorexia of Language: Why We Can't Write

BONNIE FRIEDMAN

Bonnie Friedman's work has appeared in many magazines and newspapers, including Ladies' Home Journal, Redbook, *and the* New York Times. *She is also the author of* Writing Past Dark: Envy, Fear, Distraction, and Other Dilemmas in the Writer's Life *(1993), from which this selection comes.*

I have been staring into silence's blank face all month, and I want to rattle it, to shake it, to force it to confess what's at its obsessive, fanatic core.

This is our first real encounter. Before this, I'd hardly met with silence at all. When I came across others who suffered with it, who could not write and yearned to, I was mystified. What was the big deal? It was like watching someone writhe in an invisible straitjacket. What are you doing? you ask. Don't you know you are free? I'd written for so many years without being blocked that I thought I was immune. And I was full of advice, the advice of one who has an answer while scarcely understanding the question.

Now I am amazed at the power of silence's chill presence. The air is so brittle it feels it will crack. How hard it is to breathe! I feel so unwell, so bizarrely estranged from myself. Some key part of me has been kidnapped, stolen, swallowed by silence. "Spit it out!" I want to cry, but I know it won't spit.

If silence is anything, it's decorous. Its face opposite me is flawlessly made up. Its hands are folded neatly on its knees, and it is good as any schoolchild, slim to the point of vanishing, with not a hair out of place as it gazes at me with lucid blue eyes. It is stronger than I, I fear. I feel like a bad psychiatrist, judgmental and punishing. I have an urge to slam the desk and shout, "Why are you doing this to me? You're ruining my career! Be good! Speak, goddam it!"

5 Silence swallows. She stares at me in pain as if to say she cannot help herself. If she could — oh, the volumes she'd say! There'd be no stopping her. But —

"But what? Say it! *But What?*"

Her eyes break from mine and roam the room as if searching for a correlative to point to, something that will illustrate what she means. She finds nothing, and shrugs. Her restraint is perfect, virginal, absolute. In all this time she has said nothing for which she could be blamed. Yet her eyes shine with desire! "If only, if only — " her whole body seems to say, her hands twisted, her legs crossed.

Her presence makes me frantic. Alone with silence, I want to eat, dash from the house, wash the dishes, sleep. Panic fills me. I feel sick. I feel I will dissolve in the face of silence, and then it will have triumphed. I will be infected by it and grow mute. What would I be? A petrified woman, calcified, stone-hard.

Knock on it—no resonance. Touch it—it is cold as granite, drawing heat from your hand.

Here is the fear silence breeds: you will be a person shut up inside yourself, shut up like an old apartment building with windows of brick and doors of cinderblock.

Since I have sat with silence, friends have entrusted stories to me. The 10
same thing sometimes happens to pregnant women or people who have been in accidents—horror stories arrive. Even relative strangers stop to impart the tale of a particularly gruesome delivery or of a paralyzing whiplash that manifested all of a sudden a full month later, when the person in the car crash thought everything was okay ("One moment he was sitting there eating his coleslaw, the next—*bam!*—his neck had turned to iron!").

"I knew a woman who won a Radcliffe Bunting Fellowship," my friend Stacia says. "Suddenly she couldn't write. Every day she went to the office they provided and just sat there. Five months went by like this, and then she could write again."

Five months! What a torture!

"What changed for her?"

Over the phone, I practically hear Stacia shrug. "I don't know, actually. I don't think she ever said."

My friend Joel says, "It can take years to get over a block. It's been three years 15
since I signed my book contract, and I haven't written a chapter since then."

Joel, my dear friend Joel! It never occurred to me that he might be blocked about his book. I thought he merely chose to write other things or not to write at all, he seems to live with such easy grace. But my silence has let him tell about his.

"Years?" I say.

"Yes, years to forget there is an editor waiting for your work, years until you are sure the editor has forgotten your name."

Ah: one must be sure one's editor has forgotten one's name.

In Joel's desk lies an embossed document bearing the imprint of a distant 20
company and below it Joel's name signed in his own hand promising to deliver his entire book by a certain specific date. Now Joel can visualize an editor outside himself, an editor with a face that is not Joel's own. He hardly knows this man. He has met him once or twice. How can he be sure to please him? Joel is free to project onto this man all the astringent disapproval he himself often feels about his own work. Now he has a contract and editor outside himself to reinforce the ones within.

I call my friend Alice, who dropped out of graduate school with seven incompletes because she couldn't do her papers. Certainly she triumphed over her block—she works for a computer company now, writing software manuals. What's her solution?

"Computer stuff is a game," she says. "It doesn't really matter to me. I write about what I do not passionately care about. You'll notice I don't write about art history," she says, which was her field of study.

And now it occurs to me that I myself worked for a professor who was blocked. I just didn't recognize it. He had been awarded permission to write the official biography of a certain towering literary critic, a man this professor had devoted his entire life to studying. How many years have elapsed since then! And still his book has not appeared (oh, "appeared"! — as if we wrote in closets, as if our writing was a personal delusion until it erupted, Athena-like, sporelike, into bookstores!). This professor labored over his paragraphs, stuffing them fuller and fuller of gratuitous erudition, references for their own sake (or, rather, for *his* own sake), refusing to let them split into other paragraphs — perhaps because his subject, the eminent literary critic, had a quirk of long paragraphs — until each paragraph was at least two pages and so crammed it was virtually unreadable. Flow? The poor man himself could hardly breathe under the pressure of it all!

At the time he seemed silly to me, a buffoonish creature, red-faced, sweat flying off him, gasping from his run up my stairs at one o'clock, starved, scavenging for a slice of bread I begrudged him, ripping open a packet of Vitamin C powder ("Bursting with the power of Citrus!" it said in neon orange on a blue field) from a box he left in my kitchen like a claim on me — a lover's memento, and I resented that too — desperate to show me the paragraphs he'd corrected and recorrected, adding and erasing, and adding, always adding more with his exquisitely sharpened pencils (those flanks of pencils!) with their neatly beveled pink rubber caps, adding until his paragraphs seized up like an engine without oil, impenetrable.

25   "What do you think?" he asked.

"Um, it's fine. It's just terrific. I think you can move on now."

"You really think so? You think it's terrific?"

"Yes, I do. Although, you know" — what imp prodded me? — "I think you might be able to cut a bit. But you can do that later, when you're all done, when it's time to edit."

"Cut? Where?" And he seized the sheet and stared at it, but instead of cutting he added even more.

30   I regarded him from my station behind the hulking gray IBM typewriter he had brought me. It was as heavy as a stove, consumed more than half my kitchen table, and seemed capable of typing *Ulysses* a couple of dozen times before it would need servicing. I sighed and glowered and tapped my foot, and did not offer him cheese or butter to go with the bread he wolfed from my fridge.

And yet he returned. I was hired merely to type his manuscript, but had myself become magically endowed with the power to help, to *help* — until at last he traveled a thousand miles, lugging valises full of reference books, and going to the expense of a hotel so I could type for him and talk a bit. At the time it seemed merely strange and comic (it was too odd to be flattering), although I was grateful for the money and the interesting work—but now it seems poignant.

Here was a man struggling for his life. How could he construct a book so firm and big and steady he could pile his whole life on top and not sink? How could he write a book so masculine and intelligent, so extraordinarily intelligent, it would be worthy of his terrifying, Freudian-freighted, large-craniumed subject? This man, this professor, did not even have his own name! Or, rather, the name he had was the same name his father and grandfather had had and that his son now bore, too. Each of them, to commemorate the fact of their separate identity, had been given a Roman numeral—an I—to accrue to the family moniker, and they had all graduated from the same Ivy League school ("My father's father, my father, and I all attended Yale," he announced, as if they went as a group. To his discomfort, his son was toying with the idea of Swarthmore), and it was as if now this man must salvage them all, must show he deserves to be one, must, must—what? Do something that will endure the scrutiny of that gathering of namesakes, an ancestral corridor of portraits all bearing his own face. Struggling for his life? Oh, yes. Struggling at the age of about fifty to prove that his own separate I has not been in vain.

The trick, obviously, to writing such a book is to give up on oneself. It is to evade oneself, to push one's own resistant ego down into the hot close darkness and hope to get some work done before the thing springs out of its jack-in-the-box again. It is to take a leap of faith.

When Kierkegaard writes about the leap of faith, he means an act that makes no sense, a bargain that is no bargain—one makes the ultimate sacrifice, gives up that which is at one's core, that which one understood perhaps to be the very purpose of one's life—and at that very instant of relinquishment, "by virtue of the absurd," one gets it back, redeemed. But the key point is you don't know you will get it back. When you make the sacrifice, you *really* make it.

Kierkegaard takes as his text Abraham and Isaac. God asked for the sacrifice of Isaac, specifying to Abraham that He wanted "your son, your favored one, Isaac, whom you love." Why put it like this? It is as if God wanted Abraham to know He was acutely aware of just what He was asking. And the very next sentence of the story says Abraham saddled his ass and split the wood. When the time came he bound Isaac, laid him on the altar, and "picked up his knife to slay his son." He was going to do it. He was doing it. He did not hold back. His faith was so true—the way a bird's flight is said to be true—that he would sacrifice, bloodily, with his own sweating hands, the child he loved.

A dazzling story. And, like the story of Job, it is so dangerous it is preceded by the reassurance that this devout man is just being put "to the test," so that the reader is spared from being in Abraham's or Job's position even in imagination. Who but they wouldn't lose faith when confronted with this infinite demand?

Kierkegaard tells the story over and over in *Fear and Trembling* as if he could not pull his mind from it, as if, always, the story itself had even more latent power.

For, according to Kierkegaard, the contradiction is that Abraham felt that God was asking him to murder his son *and* that He was good. That was the leap of faith. Not bitterly, not renouncing the joys of this earth like some sort of abstracted glaze-eyed monk, but with his eyes clear and love in his veins, Abraham lifted the knife. He gave up his reason. He leapt. "To be able to lose one's reason, and therefore the whole of finiteness of which reason is the broker," Kierkegaard writes, "and then by virtue of the absurd to gain precisely the same finiteness — that appalls my soul, but I do not for this cause say that it is something lowly, since on the contrary it is the only prodigy . . . The dialectic of faith is the finest and most remarkable of all."

To gain the book, one must give up all hope for the book. It is the only way the book can get written. While one writes one cannot simultaneously be gazing up at a glorious, abstract painting of what the book should be, a painting that is all golden glow and admirable wordless heft conveying a sense of a book like a bible, like your very own bible, penned by you — and at the same time expect to be advancing into the body of this particular earthly book. It won't work. You may gaze and gaze, but you may be sure that when you begin to write, that gorgeous ineffable volume will not coalesce on the page. Something else will appear. And then you have a choice. You can accept it, and get on with your writing, or you can throw it away, and pine for the painting. It is so beautiful! When you're not actually writing, you have the feeling it would be so simple to get it down on paper. Yet when the time comes, your sentences tangle you. They knot and seethe, grasping like desperate children, hampering you and making you fall so that the beautiful book, the infinite book, is forever out of reach.

The only way is to set the unbook — the gilt-framed painting of the book — right there on the altar and sacrifice it, truly sacrifice it. Only then may the book, the real live flawed finite book, slowly, sentence by carnal sentence, appear. Leopold Bloom starts his day by eating a slightly burnt grilled kidney which imparts "to his palate a fine tang of faintly scented urine." Even from here literature may begin.

■ ■ ■

40   All of which is easily said.

The *Tao Te Ching*, says, "Care about people's approval / and you will be their prisoner." I nod my head and copy it into my notebook. This does not free me from caring about people's approval.

Well, I can read the words over and over. I can plaster them to every square inch of my room. I can quote them and expound on them and tattoo them onto my flesh. It would be like a fetish, though: I almost expect the words to perform the transformation for me. It is as though I hope to hypnotize myself with them.

It is as though I want to mesmerize myself with them through a ritual rhythm the way the Bushmen were said to mesmerize themselves, to enchant themselves, to induce a trance state for themselves so that a vision could come, an ecstatic experience beyond what they could reach with their ordinary minds. How does one change?

The Bushmen had visions of being what they hunted, what gave them life: an eland. They had visions of being dead, of being under water — a fish — and they returned from the trance swimming back toward life, their arms gliding, swimming back into the rhythmic pounding of stamping feet. People in the community had to touch them, had to welcome their bodies with their own patting hands so that they could fully return, so that they could be here now.

This was where wisdom came from: surrendering to what is beyond yourself, where your self is not. Discovering that you are part of an existence that is greater than you, that is greater than even your humanity, although you may experience this only when your thinking self is quenched. How not to eat humbly, to walk lightly, with gratitude, afterward? On the mountain where Abraham lifted the knife to slay Isaac, he also had a vision. "And Abraham named that site Adonai-yireh," the Bible says, "whence the present saying, 'On the mount of the LORD there is vision.'" What vision? That relinquishment will bring plenty; that faith returns what you love to you, dazzling, redeemed.

Most of us must go on without a vision, though. We are bereft of the experience that ravishes and transforms. We cling to what is dear to us; we safeguard it under lock and key. We are leery of the surrender that it takes to write. We want to have our vision before we begin, before we lift the knife to slay what we love, our cherished egos, our desire to be excellent. We want them back before we give them up. Not later, but now we want our vision. Not as reward but as guarantee.

If only the knowledge that one must have faith provided faith! If only advice transformed us, instead of remaining something external if correct, something easy to agree with but remote as someone talking on TV.

So far I have tried to say everything in this essay well. I have tried to say it beautifully, and that is a sort of strain. What I've really meant to say, what I really care about saying, I have not said. If I say enough beautiful things, I feel, I will earn the right to say what I really mean. Then I can take that risk.

It is possible to write whole novels this way. I have written a few this way myself, the whole thing one gigantic preamble to what I really mean to write about. One novel about a ménage à trois starts a full year earlier, in a different country altogether, where the two women in the triangle meet. Oh, the pleasure of writing about fields of withering sunflowers and women in black trudging up rocky streets, and shops the size of closets devoted solely to three- and five-cent rolls, and gaunt, writhing images of Jesus with eyes like steel darts — hundreds of pages can be spent on this, while in the back of her mind the writer cries, "Wait! Wait! The good part is about to come! Just a few more chapters!" so that when the reader at last arrives at the ménage, it is with predictable fatigue, and the writer rushes the crucial scenes. It is like a person who waits until the whole room is nodding on the verge of sleep before producing from her purse the pages she waited all evening to share, or like a student giving an oral report and dutifully enumerating the mineral and agricultural endowments of the assigned country while her face pounds with the marvelous anecdote she can hardly wait to tell, the shocking anecdote that brought the whole country alive to her (she wants to say, "Chile is shaped like a woman's leg! It's like the leg of a woman in a chorus line, which reminds me of something that happened in Santiago once . . .") but which she suppresses, hoping there's time for it in the end. If there's time, it will probably be the one thing the class remembers about Chile. If there's not time, she will have delivered an organized, thorough report of no real importance to her or probably anyone else. And yet, even as an adult, how hard it is to trust that what you care about really matters! How much easier it is to spend one's time doing what the schoolteacher inside oneself would think is good. One hoards what matters, unwilling to risk ridicule. One tries to say things beautifully — I try to say things beautifully — and puts off saying what one really means.

I am not sure that what I really mean to say is beautiful or extraordinary. I identify with it, and not with the more formal things I've already said. The somewhat "strained" things I've written (I think of a strainer holding back the irregular, hard-to-digest clumps and seeds and allowing the smooth sauce of style to slide through) serve the purpose of telling me that I can write decently: they remind me of things I've written that people liked. And I need that.

50   Every day I must prove to myself I am a writer. The knowledge goes away in my sleep. What I wrote yesterday was paltry, meager, so flawed it is barely anything. Or, if it is good, I am no longer the person who could write it. In either case — shame or approval — it is utterly separate from me, that piece of writing, as if a skin formed on it like the skin on pudding when it chills, a thin, rubbery, albumenlike skin separating it from me. I am insufficient again.

And every day I must reach down into myself and see if the place that makes writing exists. Is it still there? The only way to know is to write, but before I write, and while I am at the beginning of writing, and before I hear the voice of the piece, before it speaks through me, there is this anxiety, this panic, this lack of belief. I don't feel it! It's gone! In my sleep an operation must have happened, an amputation, and now I am hollow. Or I've been anesthetized, and now the part of me that writes is asleep, a sort of exquisite, morbid Snow White sleep, the waking voice irrecoverable for 100 years.

Why should this be? Why this perpetual sense of doubt and loss?

A friend of mine who has a young daughter wakes up at four-thirty in the morning to write. She says she does it not so much for the writing, but because if she doesn't do it she feels like an aspirin tablet in water: dissolving. "I am that tablet," she says, and I hear in that the strength of her being a writing tablet and the terror that she will dissolve and disappear.

Is this terror more common to some of us? Are some of us prone to dissolving, like the witch in *The Wizard of Oz?* (How sorry I felt for her just at that moment when she cried in anguish, "I'm mellllllting!" As much as I'd hated her before, suddenly I was overwhelmed by such remorse, such shocking guilt and sympathy! She was my own mother, then! At the last instant I recognized her!) Some of us seem actually *designed* to give way. Women especially are raised to be so extremely sensitive to others we feel permeable; we are so accustomed to swallowing our wants before they even reach consciousness that a bewildering, uneasy passivity often persists in us. At worst, we even resent our own feelings. We experience them as intrusive. It is as if the emotional part of ourselves is a stubborn, fleshy, disruptive, and even aggressive appendage (aggressive because it causes such wrenching disharmonies between ourselves and those we love), and we resent it so intensely that we half wish to amputate it, to carve it out of ourselves and toss it in the garbage, this lump of self like an inflamed tonsil or hermaphroditic, mistaken penis — half wish to amputate it even though it is the very thing that keeps us *from* dissolving — and half wish to annihilate the Other, the beloved, who has made such an enemy out of what we know to be most absolutely essential to our self, and without which no true pleasure, no true anything, is possible.

The fear of anaesthesia is related to the wish for anaesthesia. The terror of 55 a midnight amputation is connected to a devout wish for just such an event, as well as to the actual sense-memory of amputations, experiences of dissociating from a part of oneself because it is too frighteningly disruptive.

But where do we imagine real writing comes from? Can we suppose that we may be missing a vital organ or two and yet write? Or that we may be internally bound and gagged, and yet still wield a pen? So many of us would prefer to dissolve ourselves and reconvene elsewhere. So many of us, practiced in administering our own internal morphine, wish to preserve harmony at all cost, to be good wives and virtuous daughters, yet write. We disregard the fugitive emotion we are not supposed to feel, and whose presence we do not understand.

I phoned a friend to tell her something I had said only once or twice before in my life. My throat clenched, my heart banging, I said that I was hurt and even angry about something she'd done. Within five minutes I was holding the phone to my ear, listening to her sob. The reason she'd hurt me, she explained, had to do with her own suffering, of which my complaint reminded her. Through her tears she told me how hard things were for her these days. Yet how familiar they were, her tears! I felt quite distant suddenly, as if something in me had been short-circuited, or as if I'd forgotten something important, pressing her sobs to my ear sitting on the hard, grimy kitchen floor.

I tried to accept her tears as a gift, as intimate self-revelation, as the nonaggressive reason for her earlier hurtful behavior. Why did part of me feel left out? Her tears again! How often I had sat with the phone crammed against my ear, held hostage by her tears. I felt far away, and even bored while she wept, as if this were something I had no choice but to wait out if I was going to be a decent human being—and at the same time I felt monstrous for my cold reaction to her tears. What was wrong with me? Of course I didn't mention my feeling. It was nonsensical to me, and I tried not to see it. After we said good-bye, I drifted away from the phone, drifted into the living room, a benign emotion surrounding me like fog.

"How was your phone call?" my husband asked.

60   "Oh, fine, fine." I blinked, and sighed.

Only the next day, when a friend suggested a new analysis, did I understand what the nonsensical emotion meant. I would rather not have known. I would have preferred to go on feeling that vague, drifty, blissful intimacy with my friend rather than the renewed blaze of anger. I had been, I felt, at peace.

How tempting it is to choose this apparent peace! And because so many of us are trained to do so, how evanescent is our sense of self.

Time and again my students tell me, "I am here to find my voice." I want to say, "When did you lose it, and how? Where did you hear it last? Try to remember every place you have been since then and maybe it will occur to you where you lost it." Some of us are like deaf people who need someone to place our hands on our throats. Feel this? This is you, speaking. Some of us need it pointed out: this is your arm, this is your leg, this is your voice. Yes, here. Right here. Can you hear it? It sounds like you.

And some of us, even able to hear our own voice, are overwhelmed by a sense of unimportance.

65   "I am paralyzed by the conviction that no one would be interested in what I have to say, or how I say it," wrote a friend in a letter a few years ago.

"I no longer feel special enough to write anything but facile responses to assigned exercises," another woman, a student of mine, said.

A third reported, "I feel petrified by the pressure." In a ten-minute freewrite, this student produced just one sentence. It was the only writing she offered all semester long, although she routinely provided lacerating critiques of the novels we read.

The feeling of nullity, the suspicion of internal anaesthesia—these were not strangers to me. They were familiar phantoms I'd lived in the company of my whole life without ever really noticing. I did not notice because as long as I could work, my life was by definition okay. Only when these emotions became a paralyzing constant and the writing would not come—only then did I fully perceive these feelings and question them.

My silence was an anorexic, I began to see. Over the weeks we were together, this trait became more and more apparent. She refused to open her mouth for any purpose. She presided over herself with an iron tyranny. Her bones sought the surface as if she were proud of them. Her blue eyes, burning fiercely, sank into her skull, and her legs grew spindly, yellowish, like stilts, as if — if she rose — she would be balanced above her body, as if only her face was really her self. Her face loomed now above her dwindling body as if trying to break free.

And then, late one tense but tedious afternoon, an afternoon when we had   70
sat across from each other so long, so rigidly, it seemed we would always be locked like this, I realized that perhaps she *was* trying to communicate. She seemed to be X-raying herself. She seemed to be burning the opaque flesh from herself. She seemed to be unwrapping herself, paring the bark off herself, pressing some horrible, intolerable thought out of the core of herself. Her whole body was an Adam's apple about to spring through the skin. Why, that was it! That's all it was! She was showing the structure of herself, exposing the very composition of herself, making visible to the world the most basic anatomical unit of a self that would not be compromised, that possessed an inherent unbudging rigidity.

Look, each rib and joint seemed to say, I am real. I exist. Unlikely as it seems in this girl who has been so compliant for so very long — momma's angel, daddy's special darling (you could see it in the Peter Pan collar, the dainty pearl earrings, the hands so scrubbed they looked chapped, the nails bitten to the point of extinction) — there is a hard spine, a pith of rock, a blazing brick-hard calcareous stick.

"Perfectionist behavior elicits approval from parents and teachers, who think of the potentially anorexic child as unusually good and competent," reports Hilda Bruch. I read her work with rapt attention. Because even without personifying silence, it would still be clear that writer's block is a form of anorexia. Reading Bruch, I was astonished at how much I saw myself in her description of the anorexic's childhood, and how thoroughly it related to my battle with silence. "Some of the more serious conceptual disturbances can be traced to this pseudosuccess of being praised and recognized for fake good behavior," she says. "This praise reinforces the anorexic's fear of being spontaneous and natural, and interferes with her developing concepts, especially a vocabulary for her true feelings, or even her ability to identify feelings . . .

"Future anorexics are described as serious, precocious in their sense of responsibility, trustworthy, and capable of having adult conversations . . . When maintaining this facade becomes too strenuous, they finally protest and express their underlying frustration by giving up the behavior that they themselves call 'fake.'

"Superficially the relationship to the parents appears to be congenial: actually it is too close, with too much involvement, without necessary separation and individuation. This harmony . . . is achieved through excessive conformity on the part of the child. After the illness has existed for some time, glaring hostility becomes evident."

75   Here is the rebellion of pent-up girlhood. Here is the onslaught of the virtuous. Here is the revolt of the good by means of excessive goodness. Here is the break with the mother by means of breaking with oneself, denying one's own needs more and more ruthlessly. One girl, Bruch reports, saw her shadow on the beach and vowed to get as thin as it. Perfection is being a gaunt substanceless figure projected on the earth. It must be what the mother unwittingly taught: that this girl should be a specter riveted to her creator, inseparable from her, echoing and mirroring and forever called to heel, racing over the sands to keep pace, able to tolerate her own self only if it displayed the utmost pleasant obedience.

The rebellion, when it comes, baffles the rebel. Her reasons, her own history in fact, are cloudy to her. Bruch reports: "It is quite difficult for most anorexics to present the facts as they have taken place, because their upbringing did not foster clear and independent observation and thinking."

Happiness for this child is pleasing the mother, bringing home an A, several A's, on which to feed her. It is walking, mother and daughter, with arms wrapped around each other, a few feet ahead of everyone else at the girls' camp open house. The girl, myself, is fifteen already, wearing a beige Huckapoo blouse that snaps at the crotch, blue jeans, and long brown hair flooding from a central part, leaving visible just a narrow plank of her face like someone peering through a scarcely open door. Her hips bump her mother's awkwardly, embarrassingly from time to time. What a superlative relationship I have with my mother, she thinks proudly, noticing another girl who maintains from that girl's mother a surly distance of at least two feet. How can she? Isn't the mother hurt? What a horrible, brutish, sloppy daughter that is! — like her very own sister, in fact, who in a rage heaves the bedroom door shut so it booms like a cannon and plaster clatters down. The plaster seems to fall within their own fragile mother.

This daughter, the pleasant one, never plays rock music at home: she doesn't own a record although there is a record player in the living room and dozens of classical recordings. The loud noise would bother her mother, or else her mother would sit tensely waiting it out: what was the pleasure there? Once when she was thirteen a girlfriend had given her the album to *Hair* with its greenish yellow psychedelic boy on the cover. At the girlfriend's house she'd love to lie down right beside the speaker turned on high: it was thrilling! A teenage virgin, LBJ, dropping out, Timothy Leary — and the syncopation made her smile. But when her friend gave her a copy for her birthday — what a great friend she was! how she loved her for this — she had given it back after a few days. She couldn't imagine playing it in her parents' apartment. She couldn't bear even to have it in the apartment, couldn't bear to have her parents' eyes even see it.

She doesn't drink Pepsi, this daughter, only Coke. In fact, she is angry at Pepsi. What's wrong with the drink of the older generation? Why does the new generation need its own drink? The commercials actually hurt her, fill her with a painful wistfulness like seeing gray in her father's hair. Most special are the evenings at Daffodil Hill in the Botanical Gardens, listening to opera, her contented parents gazing at the lit-up orchestra. The only bad part is the walk back to the car through the park, stumbling in the night with just her father's wobbly small yellow flashlight beam to find their way, the dark figures of other people brushing past them, vaguely hostile, so uncaring of her parents' uneasy progress. What a relief when they find their own car! They lock the doors, keeping the rushing unstoppable distended aggressive figures out. Inside the small space of the car all is peaceful. Threats come only from outside.

Which is to say that although the eventual anorexia is a rebellion, it is impossible for the daughter to know this. She is doing what she had been taught to do, with a vengeance.   80

The poet Louise Glück writes, "In mid-adolescence, I developed a symptom perfectly congenial to the demands of my spirit. I had great resources of will and no self . . . I couldn't say what I was, what I wanted, in any day-to-day, practical way. What I could say was *no:* the way I saw to separate myself, to establish a self with clear boundaries, was to oppose myself to the declared desire of others, utilizing their wills to give a shape to my own . . . The tragedy of anorexia seems to me that its intent is not self-destructive, though its outcome so often is. Its intent is to construct, in the only way possible when means are so limited, a plausible self."

The conviction of internal emptiness, the fear of being spontaneous, the rigid barrier between oneself and one's emotions — all this pertains to silence, which orders one to prove one's worth day by day.

I became unable to write at the moment of my success. On the basis of a proposal, I had at last sold a book. When I sat down to write it, though, I found myself paralyzed.

It was not that I could not think. I could think. It was not that I'd forgotten what I wanted to say. I knew exactly what I wanted to say. I merely could not grab hold of the words and stick them to the page. They seemed to float away from me into shadowy depths. It was exactly the same sensation as being unable to remember a word: you can heft the precise length of the word in your mind, you know that it starts with a *b* perhaps or a *p*, and maybe even where on a certain page of *Love in the Time of Cholera* you read this word — but the word itself won't come. It resists you. It is like a cloaked figure you encounter, whose body you *know* — why, the instant you see who it is you will cry, "Of course! I knew it all along!" — but who won't throw off his hood. How tantalizing, this information held just out of reach! Not being able to think of a word duplicates writer's block exactly, except that writer's block is more protracted, and envelops one's whole vocabulary.

85   Being unable to write also felt like having the key to me stolen. I had not even known there was a key to me, and now I found it gone! It was as if I had been secured in a sort of invisible chastity belt, my most intimate parts locked behind an iron gate (again, I did not imagine these parts were not there; I simply no longer had access to them), my master having vanished with the key. It was an eerie and frightening experience. I believed I was self-possessed. One day the key was turned, and I found I'd been living my life in a see-through cage.

I sat bolt upright at the desk in a sort of rigid agony, unable to do more than put one or two meager words on the page which I instantly discarded before casting about for more slow minutes for some more words. My mind swam in a haze while my body was stiff, contracted, as if all the space between my bones had vanished, and they were stuck against one another. At last I stood, yawned, and burst into tears.

I was not surprised. I had entered a time when I cried every day at some time or another. I had never in my life been a crier; now my heart was a great big bloated painful thing like an infected foot, and the least pressure on it made it burst. I learned to drive crying, and pee crying, and even read a book crying, stopping only occasionally to wipe my eyes so the words didn't meld. Often I didn't wipe my eyes, though. I liked the feeling of my face slick with tears — it stung, and felt shiny — because at least these tears were something real, something that came spontaneously from within me at a time when nothing else would. They meant that something was going on even if I didn't know what.

I imagined that the missing key to me was something very ordinary. It was, I supposed, something small and cheap as the key to a diary, inconsequential as a flip-top. It was dull silver as the key to a tin of sardines whose lid curls stiffly back to reveal multiple flattened twin-eyed faces numberless as a pack of sperm, each one shaped like a slimy key.

A thousand keys, a million keys, the key of C, of A and B, the key to the city, to the riddle, to the silver skates, and to the whole cascade of typewriter keys, those keys like *Ziegfeld Follies,* in tiers, or like the Palisades, a glacial ebb: QAZ, WSX. There was a whole kingdom of keys locked away from me. It was multitudinous as the bevy of keys in my mother's drawer, keys to places where we had not lived for decades, to forgotten neighbors' apartments and lost jewelry boxes, to underground storage rooms holding childhood Flexible Flyers and one-speed bikes, keys with dust clinging to them and smelling so strongly of steel your mouth filled with the taste, keys with ragged teeth that looked random and nonsensical now that the doors for them were gone. All lost to me. To be able to write is to unlock imaginary rooms that contain real keys, to adapt Marianne Moore's statement. My master key was gone. It was an object so obvious that it was invisible, like something you lose in your own house, and which only someone else can find.

Who had found my key?   90

The publisher, I assumed. My writing had always been the one thing that was all my own. I'd sold it, and now it avoided me.

I phoned the editor and told her not to expect the manuscript for a long, long time.

But I still felt spooked. One day someone was standing in the room with me. My back and neck prickled. I spun my head and stared at the empty gray space behind me, the mound of laundry near the door. I had the urge, like a child, to glance in the closets. Someone was stealing from me, someone was watching me, someone was doing a terrible thing to me. I had no defense against it.

This was the worst. It was even worse than not writing: the feeling of being absolutely porous, without barriers, as if anyone at any time of day or night could open the door and walk in, as if the key to me had been duplicated a million times and strewn all over the world, and now anyone could come and take.

I had begun to write a little bit, and the crying had stopped. But if a foot 95 thumped upstairs, I froze. I dared not try another word. I felt, if I lose myself in my writing, and another thump comes, it will be excruciating. My good idea will vanish. While writing, I was continually reaching for and just barely seizing things being thrown to me. If a thump happened just when I was about to catch a thought, it would sail into the irretrievable beyond. So I sat suspended, waiting for a thump. It benefits my neighbor nothing to take my writing, I thought, and it costs me everything, my whole life, my mind, my creativity — everything. How *dare* she make my writing worth so little!

Similarly my sister-in-law and a friend's mother who happened to be in town and innumerable close friends haunted me. This one had said many pissy things at dinner; that other demanded too much. "Call soon," a friend said, and I had to call right away. If I suspected someone was angry at me — and my newly confrontational behavior seemed practically designed to provoke anger — I must force that anger into the open. I couldn't bear for anything to happen soon. It must happen *now,* so that it could be done with, and then I could immerse myself in my book with a feeling of safety.

All the danger I felt between me and the unwritten book was being forced out into the world, where I could contend with it.

"You are looking for tyrants," my friend Carole said.

I found them everywhere.

I noticed the tiny but constant ways I compromised myself. These used to 100 be invisible, like paper cuts. Now the least artificial compliance on my part cost too much. It was as if a friend asked, "May I drink just a little bit of your blood? Just an eighth of a cup?" I could not sacrifice any part of myself for the sake of false harmony.

Faced with the extreme devaluation of my work which I projected out into the world, I at last had to be my work's champion, or the work would not exist. My voracious, devouring sister, whom I had grown up accommodating, had been unleashed. She was in me, and still punishing me now, twenty years later, for wanting to put my book out in the world because in the perpetually frozen era of our childhood it threatened her. How did it threaten her? It incited her envy. It was something entirely my own, an independent source of pleasure that seemed to enlarge me, and to make her more ordinary, more likely to be left behind. In response I felt furious. Rage was everywhere.

My landlady, a high-strung woman with chopped dyed-white hair, sawed and slammed under my floorboards every afternoon for a week. That week I could not write even in the mornings because the anticipation of her intrusion called up an answering rage in me so strong the red veins in my eyes seemed to have swollen and I could not see the computer screen. When the landlady left, the red drained to my cheeks; they blazed with embarrassment. And then the old depression overtook me, the tears and sense of futility. I felt like the internal air shaft of an apartment building. All around it plants thrive and children grow from nursery school to college. It, however, remains static, a mute column of dust, the trapped shadow just as it was when the building was first erected.

All this was occasioned by the moment of my success. Approval came for past accomplishments, but they did not match what was inside me, which was inchoate, scattered, obsessed, contradictory, a column of electrified dust—yet all that mattered. I had no faith that I could produce a book from it.

The everyday key which I was missing was of course the gleam of confidence: the sense that one's instinctive way is valuable. It is the magic possession. Wanting it, I cluttered the windowsill with amethysts and blue origami cranes and inspirational quotes from Rilke, and a playing card that said EXTRA JOKER, which I had discovered face down on the street, and which my friend Mary said meant "a chance beyond chance. Why," she'd added, "it's even better than the Queen of Hearts!" A desperate hoard meant to remind me of what I had inside that was magical. Mute keys cluttering a windowsill.

105   Writing returned to me when I thought, Even my experience of this hollow feeling is valuable. Even this is real, and is my own. When I thought, My valuable book may begin even here.

I had entered therapy when I could not write. I discovered that I made sense even when I felt my worst. I did not have to strain. Wild riches were packed into even my bad feelings, like wild onion in dark grass. Here were long-abandoned clumps of meaning: sources of strength. This therapist took me at my word. She heard the truth—the meaningful voice speaking—in even the most frenetic emotions. She was skeptical of nothing in me. I had been accustomed to regarding my own thoughts as exaggerated, erratic, untrustworthy.

Therapy started to cure me of this. Experiencing my own coherence brought my writing back to me.

A paradox happened. While I learned to give up my enchanting dream of the ideal book and accept the particular imperfect book that appeared, I felt as if I were building a stronger and stronger, or rather a bigger and bigger, inner self. I suppose this is because I accepted more of my split-off aspects. Parts of myself I'd estranged decades ago began to pulse with life, even the part of me that was my sister Anita. I tolerated more ambiguity in myself. My old way was to be like the Abraham who is abstract, glaze-eyed. What was ugly, anomalous, frightening, inconceivable — went into soft focus. All those tears that season I refused to write — didn't they keep the world a blur, a watercolor, dreamy and vague? They were like my friend's tears the day I sat on the hard, grimy kitchen floor — because of course I was my angry, tearful friend too — mournful and furious at the loss of the old dispensation, pining for the old way, the old closeness in which the phone didn't ring with a message of accusation, the old coherence during which I was solicitous, generous, nice. The world dissolved and dissolved in my tears, the season I sat bolt upright at my desk. I refused to be the ugly woman, the Wicked Witch who dissolves like an aspirin tablet. I refused to disintegrate into the various greedy, unseemly parts of myself by writing my book. Instead, I made the world drench and drain away. That was my protest. I was like my friend who wept because she couldn't stand to be the person who'd been hurtful and greedy. I wanted only to be beautiful and loved. I could not write until I could risk appearing ugly. Tears are the last resort of the dream. After the flood, a new spangled coherence emerges whose emblem is the rainbow, a whole spectrum. Writing this new, riskier way, I felt more substantial, more solid in the world, more real.

To surrender takes faith, and first of all one must have faith *in something* to leap. Abraham had faith in God, the Bushmen have faith in their religious passage and in the strength of the community to receive them back. Writers need faith that a kingdom of significance stands within. Faith is also the key to the kingdom. Experience teaches it. It is learned through the body and the spirit, not the mind, which is why advice helps so little. One must allow oneself an education of experience.

Silence departed when I embraced fragment imperfection, the roses of the bush I discovered all overgrown in my yard. It had been an indeterminate tangled heap all through the first dank autumn we lived here, a prostrate sodden mass that winter. I assumed we had a yard of weeds. Only at the beginning of June did I notice the first blossom, a blush white. Soon there were dollops of cream all over the bush, each one plush as a satin cushion, the petals dusted with powder and turning a bruised translucent blue if held. I rarely touched them, though, merely watched them open more each day.

110   They opened past reason. They budded and bloomed and opened — more and more of them — until several branches sagged and at last lay on the ground, the big blush roses pressing open until their petals scattered in an opulent surge of scent. The rosebush taught me how winter rosebushes look, just as good ideas teach you to see other ideas that are not yet ripe, and to trust in them.

When I embraced imperfection, silence dissolved. The inner absolutist, the fanatic mistress of restraint who, suffering, defines herself through refusal, at last departed, or rather receded into me, which is of course where she'd come from in the first place. She had finally disclosed what was at her core: a hunger for faith.

TALKING ABOUT IT

Seeing Metaphor: Revealing and Concealing

1. Friedman opens her essay by describing her encounter with a personification of silence, a metaphor for her inability to write. What do you make of this image? In what ways can it be seen as a mirror of the writer herself? Later she begins to see her silence as an anorexic. How does this realization set Friedman to thinking of her own childhood and eventually lead to the departure of silence?

2. In the final part of her essay, Friedman's central image is that of the key to herself which has been stolen. Trace her use of this image. Does she manage to keep what could be a fairly clichéd image from seeming trite? What, in the end, does that key turn out to be, and how does Friedman find it?

Seeing Composition: Frame, Line, Texture, Tone

1. How would you describe Friedman's tone in the essay? Look for shifts in intensity, from colloquial to more formal, from serious to ironic. What general persona do these shifts add up to for you, and how does this persona affect your reading of the essay?

2. In her final five paragraphs, Friedman brings together many of the themes and images she has referred to throughout earlier parts of the essay. Identify these, and examine the importance of each to the essay's overall effect.

Seeing Meaning: Navigating and Negotiating

1. Friedman suggests that part of what kept her from writing was "the enchanting dream of the ideal book." Do you think that the goal of the perfect paper has ever kept you from being able to write? Can such stifling dreams of perfection also stymie one's performance or creativity in other areas of life?

2. Look at Friedman's use of the story of Abraham and Isaac and Kierkegaard's interpretation. How is this story essential to her themes?

WRITING ABOUT IT

1. Bonnie Friedman describes her experience of writer's block as an "anorexic." What metaphor would you use to express your own bad feelings about writing? Write that story. Then explain how you moved beyond this feeling in order to write. Within your writing group, list the strategies each writer found for breaking the silence, for getting the writing done. Then, as a class, collect the strategies from each group and make a master list. Refer to it whenever you come face to face with silence.

2. Consider the various ways Friedman talks about writing. How would you characterize Friedman's stories of herself as a writer? To which story do you respond most positively? To which do you respond most negatively? Why?

Shitty First Drafts

ANNE LAMOTT

Anne Lamott is the author of the memoir Operating Instructions: A Journal of My Son's First Year *(1993) and* Bird by Bird: Some Instructions on Writing and Life *(1994), from which the following selection is taken. She is also a novelist (*Crooked Little Heart, *1997, is her most recent book) and has been a book review columnist for* Mademoiselle, *a restaurant critic for* California *magazine, and a teacher at the University of California at Davis.*

Now, practically even better news than that of short assignments is the idea of shitty first drafts. All good writers write them. This is how they end up with good second drafts and terrific third drafts. People tend to look at successful writers, writers who are getting their books published and maybe even doing well financially, and think that they sit down at their desks every morning feeling like a million dollars, feeling great about who they are and how much talent they have and what a great story they have to tell; that they take in a few deep breaths, push back their sleeves, roll their necks a few times to get all the cricks out, and dive in, typing fully formed passages as fast as a court reporter. But this is just the fantasy of the uninitiated. I know some very great writers, writers you love who write beautifully and have made a great deal of money, and not *one* of them sits down routinely feeling wildly enthusiastic and confident. Not one of them writes elegant first drafts. All right, one of them does, but we do not like her very much. We do not think that she has a rich inner life or that God likes her or can even stand her. (Although when I mentioned this to my priest friend Tom, he said you can safely assume you've created God in your own image when it turns out that God hates all the same people you do.)

Very few writers really know what they are doing until they've done it. Nor do they go about their business feeling dewy and thrilled. They do not type a few stiff warm-up sentences and then find themselves bounding along like huskies across the snow. One writer I know tells me that he sits down every morning and says to himself nicely, "It's not like you don't have a choice, because you do — you can either type or kill yourself." We all often feel like we are pulling teeth, even those writers whose prose ends up being the most natural and fluid. The right words and sentences just do not come pouring out like ticker tape most of the time. Now, Muriel Spark is said to have felt that she was taking dictation from God every morning — sitting there, one supposes, plugged into a Dicta-phone, typing away, humming. But this is a very hostile and aggressive position. One might hope for bad things to rain down on a person like this.

For me and most of the other writers I know, writing is not rapturous. In fact, the only way I can get anything written at all is to write really, really shitty first drafts.

The first draft is the child's draft, where you let it all pour out and then let it romp all over the place, knowing that no one is going to see it and that you can shape it later. You just let this childlike part of you channel whatever voices and visions come through and onto the page. If one of the characters wants to say, "Well, so what, Mr. Poopy Pants?," you let her. No one is going to see it. If the kid wants to get into really sentimental, weepy, emotional territory, you let him. Just get it all down on paper, because there may be something great in those six crazy pages that you would never have gotten to by more rational, grown-up means. There may be something in the very last line of the very last paragraph on page six that you just love, that is so beautiful or wild that you now know what you're supposed to be writing about, more or less, or in what direction you might go — but there was no way to get to this without first getting through the first five and a half pages.

I used to write food reviews for *California* magazine before it folded. (My writing food reviews had nothing to do with the magazine folding, although every single review did cause a couple of canceled subscriptions. Some readers took umbrage at my comparing mounds of vegetable puree with various ex-presidents' brains.) These reviews always took two days to write. First I'd go to a restaurant several times with a few opinionated, articulate friends in tow. I'd sit there writing down everything anyone said that was at all interesting or funny. Then on the following Monday I'd sit down at my desk with my notes, and try to write the review. Even after I'd been doing this for years, panic would set in. I'd try to write a lead, but instead I'd write a couple of dreadful sentences, xx them out, try again, xx everything out, and then feel despair and worry settle on my chest like an x-ray apron. It's over, I'd think, calmly. I'm not going to be able to get the magic to work this time. I'm ruined. I'm through. I'm toast. Maybe, I'd think, I can get my old job back as a clerk-typist. But probably not. I'd get up and study my teeth in the mirror for a while. Then I'd stop, remember to breathe, make a few phone calls, hit the kitchen and chow down. Eventually I'd go back and sit down at my desk, and sigh for the next ten minutes. Finally I would pick up my one-inch picture frame, stare into it as if for the answer, and every time the answer would come: all I had to do was to write a really shitty first draft of, say, the opening paragraph. And no one was going to see it.

So I'd start writing without reining myself in. It was almost just typing, just making my fingers move. And the writing would be *terrible*. I'd write a lead paragraph that was a whole page, even though the entire review could only be three pages long, and then I'd start writing up descriptions of the food, one dish at a time, bird by bird, and the critics would be sitting on my shoulders, commenting like cartoon characters. They'd be pretending to snore, or rolling their eyes at my overwrought descriptions, no matter how hard I tried to tone those descriptions down, no matter how conscious I was of what a friend said to me gently in my early days of restaurant reviewing. "Annie," she said, "it is just a piece of *chick*en. It is just a bit of *cake*."

But because by then I had been writing for so long, I would eventually let myself trust the process—sort of, more or less. I'd write a first draft that was maybe twice as long as it should be, with a self-indulgent and boring beginning, stupefying descriptions of the meal, lots of quotes from my black-humored friends that made them sound more like the Manson girls than food lovers, and no ending to speak of. The whole thing would be so long and incoherent and hideous that for the rest of the day I'd obsess about getting creamed by a car before I could write a decent second draft. I'd worry that people would read what I'd written and believe that the accident had really been a suicide, that I had panicked because my talent was waning and my mind was shot.

The next day, though, I'd sit down, go through it all with a colored pen, take out everything I possibly could, find a new lead somewhere on the second page, figure out a kicky place to end it, and then write a second draft. It always turned out fine, sometimes even funny and weird and helpful. I'd go over it one more time and mail it in.

Then, a month later, when it was time for another review, the whole process would start again, complete with the fears that people would find my first draft before I could rewrite it.

10   Almost all good writing begins with terrible first efforts. You need to start somewhere. Start by getting something—anything—down on paper. A friend of mine says that the first draft is the down draft—you just get it down. The second draft is the up draft—you fix it up. You try to say what you have to say more accurately. And the third draft is the dental draft, where you check every tooth, to see if it's loose or cramped or decayed, or even, God help us, healthy.

What I've learned to do when I sit down to work on a shitty first draft is to quiet the voices in my head. First there's the vinegar-lipped Reader Lady, who says primly, "Well, *that's* not very interesting, is it?" And there's the emaciated German male who writes these Orwellian memos detailing your thought crimes. And there are your parents, agonizing over your lack of loyalty and discretion; and there's William Burroughs, dozing off or shooting up because he finds you as bold and articulate as a houseplant; and so on. And there are also the dogs: let's not forget the dogs, the dogs in their pen who will surely hurtle and snarl their way out if you ever *stop* writing, because writing is, for some of us, the latch that keeps the door of the pen closed, keeps those crazy ravenous dogs contained.

Quieting these voices is at least half the battle I fight daily. But this is better than it used to be. It used to be 87 percent. Left to its own devices, my mind spends much of its time having conversations with people who aren't there. I walk along defending myself to people, or exchanging repartee with them, or rationalizing my behavior, or seducing them with gossip, or pretending I'm on their TV talk show or whatever. I speed or run an aging yellow light or don't come to a full stop, and one nanosecond later am explaining to imaginary cops exactly why I had to do what I did, or insisting that I did not in fact do it.

I happened to mention this to a hypnotist I saw many years ago, and he looked at me very nicely. At first I thought he was feeling around on the floor for the silent alarm button, but then he gave me the following exercise, which I still use to this day.

Close your eyes and get quiet for a minute, until the chatter starts up. Then isolate one of the voices and imagine the person speaking as a mouse. Pick it up by the tail and drop it into a mason jar. Then isolate another voice, pick it up by the tail, drop it in the jar. And so on. Drop in any high-maintenance parental units, drop in any contractors, lawyers, colleagues, children, anyone who is whining in your head. Then put the lid on, and watch all these mouse people clawing at the glass, jabbering away, trying to make you feel like shit because you won't do what they want—won't give them more money, won't be more successful, won't see them more often. Then imagine that there is a volume-control button on the bottle. Turn it all the way up for a minute, and listen to the stream of angry, neglected, guilt-mongering voices. Then turn it all the way down and watch the frantic mice lunge at the glass, trying to get to you. Leave it down, and get back to your shitty first draft.

A writer friend of mine suggests opening the jar and shooting them all in   15
the head. But I think he's a little angry, and I'm sure nothing like this would ever occur to you.

TALKING ABOUT IT

Seeing Metaphor: Revealing and Concealing

1. Is it helpful for you to see a first draft as, in Lamott's words, "the child's draft"? Lamott also quotes a friend who refers to the first "down" draft, the second "up" draft, and the final "dental" draft. What do these images suggest about the act of writing?

2. Consider the advice Lamott offers in her next to last paragraph for getting rid of the negative voices in one's head. In what ways is she suggesting a larger metaphor for living here?

Seeing Composition: Frame, Line, Texture, Tone

1. Why do you suppose Lamott chose to use the phrase "shitty first drafts," rather than "crummy first drafts" or "lousy first drafts"? How do you respond to her language?

2. Compare Lamott's tone with Peter Elbow's, or David Huddle's, or Natalie Goldberg's—writers who also offer advice to writers in essays earlier in this chapter. How does the writer's tone affect your response to the writer's advice?

Seeing Meaning: Navigating and Negotiating

1. In telling of her monthly restaurant reviewing, Lamott says that, even after years of writing to assignment, panic would set in when she sat down to draft. What does this suggest about the nature of writing? How might you apply Lamott's lessons to your own work?

2. Have you ever had the kind of experience Lamott describes when she writes of the critical voices in her head? What do you think of her advice for getting rid of them?

WRITING ABOUT IT

1. "What I've learned to do when I sit down to work . . . is to quiet the voices in my head," Anne Lamott says. She then names and describes the critical voices that she hears. Afterward, she describes a strategy, learned from a hypnotist, for silencing these voices: she imagines them to be mice that she drops into a mason jar.

    Write your own description of the critical voices that interfere with your writing. Give them names and describe what they say, as Lamott does. Then invent a revenge story that serves as a strategy for quieting those voices. Like Lamott, stop short of "shooting them all in the head." Of course, as she says, "I'm sure nothing like this would ever occur to you."

2. Anne Lamott tries to dispel the myth that good writers sit down to write and, "after a few stiff warm-up sentences, . . . find themselves bounding along like huskies across the snow." She then describes her strategies for writing a first draft. Write an essay describing your own process of "getting something—anything—down on paper." How do you then proceed from the "down draft" to the "up draft" to the "dental draft"?

Nonfiction in First Person, without Apology

NATALIA RACHEL SINGER

Natalia Rachel Singer is an associate professor of English at St. Lawrence University. The selection here is a version of a talk she gave at St. Lawrence when she was applying for the job. Her non-fiction and fiction have been published in Ms., Helicon Nine, Sundog, Harper's *and the* North American Review, *where she is a contributing editor.*

In his introduction to the 1989 "The Best American Essays," Geoffrey Wolff tells a story about how, in writing an essay on "King Lear" as a young boarding school boy, he could not help but narrate some of his own misunderstandings with his Duke of Deception father to illustrate his sympathy with Cordelia. Wolff's teacher wrote the customary "Who cares?" in red ink on his essay, insisting, as we were all taught, that when one writes nonfiction, it is necessary to "take facts in, quietly manipulate them behind an opaque scrim, and display them as though the arranger never arranged." Reading Wolff's story made me think of my childhood in Cleveland, and my decision, at the ripe age of five, to devote my life to becoming a writer. I remember thinking, as I watched my parents' marriage dissolve, and I stayed up late staring out the window at the oak tree in the yard and listening to the cranes at the city dump two blocks away scoop up crushed aluminum, that if I could record "this": parents fighting, squirrels crunching acorns, garbage sorted like bad memories, that if I could find words to make sense of my own life, I could write anything. But in the neighborhood I grew up in, to be a writer meant to be a dead English novelist, like Charles Dickens. It simply wasn't done. Some people had heard of Ernest Hemingway, but you had to know something about fishing and bullfighting. Women writers usually went mad or changed their names to George. I wanted to continue to be a female person, and I wanted to tell "the truth." I wanted to explore "real life." Mine, at least for starters. I would have liked to have written my memoirs, but only famous people wrote their memoirs. To my teachers, writing about "real life" meant only one thing, and I was tracked early on to write for newspapers.

By the time I got to high school I was writing most of the feature stories on our school paper. I was often asked to go after "difficult and sensitive" subjects which required intimate self-disclosures from the interviewees. My portfolio is filled with family tales of woe and grief. Picture me at 15, asking a laid-off worker from the Acorn Chemical Corporation plant, the father of eight, what it feels like now that his house has just burned down and all of his family's possessions have been destroyed. Imagine me interviewing the pastor's wife after her son, who was in my homeroom on the rare days he showed up, has just fatally overdosed on *windowpane*. It is no wonder that I was soon nicknamed "The Sob Story Queen."

I did not know that I would someday decide I had exploited the people I wrote about. It never occurred to me to question why these stories did not satisfy my burning desire to write, or why, after writing them quickly and easily, I would hop on the back of Gary Pritchik's big black motorcycle and ride to the river where we tried again and again, beneath the blinking yellow factory lights, to set the Cuyahoga on fire. As a highschooler, I did not aim to achieve High Art; I wanted to pile up enough extra-curricular activities on my record to get into a decent college as far away from Cleveland as possible.

When I was asked to write a feature story on a friend of mine named Sharon who was suffering from Lupus, I realized that I was getting uncomfortable with this form of writing. I did it anyway, and the story won me a major journalism prize in Ohio, plus a scholarship to the Medill School of Journalism at Northwestern University, but it cost me a friend. After I wrote the story, Sharon and I simply never felt comfortable with one another again. It was as though, as Native Americans once said about their photographers, that I had *stolen her soul*. What interests me now about this incident is that out of all the people who might have written the article, I was truly the most familiar with Sharon's "before and after story," because I knew her body like I knew my own. Sharon and I had gone on our first diet together back in eighth grade. We had taken each other's measurements week after week and finally, one spring morning, had pronounced each other beautiful. We had coached each other on what to expect from boys. None of that was in the story because my hard-nosed editor would have written "Who cares?" across the front with his favorite grease pencil. Sharon remained *other* and her situation was simply *tragic*. Stripped of the noisy, meddling, "I," the writer whose observations affect and interact with and ultimately bring life to the observed, Sharon as subject was now reduced to an object; she was not that living, wisecracking teen-age girl with whom I'd once compared bellies and thighs.

5   Our first year in journalism school we had to take a course called Basic Writing; 50% of our grade was based on our final feature story which would be read in front of the class. I had not written a feature since the one I wrote on Sharon, and I was gun-shy. I searched the campus desperately for story ideas until one day, in the middle of Sex Role Socialization Class, my professor told us about a fascinating woman she'd met at a party the night before who was a preschool teacher by day, and madam for the most elite massage parlor in Chicago by night. This was before the time when we began to have suspicions about some of our preschool teachers. The madam — whose name I've since forgotten but it was something very unexotic, like Doris — would be coming to the next class, and was eager to talk to any of us in private.

The next Saturday the madam drove out to Evanston in her beat-up orange Opal and sat across from me in my dorm room beneath my Arthur Rackham poster of Alice in Wonderland, eating the cookies and milk I'd bought at the campus snack shop. She reminded me of Mama Cass turned bombshell in her flowing Indian skirts and her low-cut blouse with the shiny red heart she'd lip-sticked onto her considerable cleavage. When she laughed her whole body shook, and the heart bobbed up and down like a fish. Outside the window there were kids playing Frisbee while she told me everything I wanted to know, and more. Finally, after we'd talked for hours, she picked up my stuffed koala bear with its N.U. garter belt looped around its waist like a goofy satin hoola hoop, and she set it down again on top of the tape recorder. "You aren't going to get the real story inside your sweet little ivory tower over here," she said. "If you really want to know your material, you have to spend a day at 'the house.'"

"The house" was not as seedy as I'd imagined. The "waiting area" was furnished discreetly with beige couches and chairs, Impressionist prints, potted plants, and a stereo that was playing the Brandenburg Concertos. I would have thought I was in an upscale dentist's office if not for the two women posing at the window in fancy lingerie. One of these women told me that before she'd started hooking six months before she'd only slept with one man in her life, her abusive ex-husband. She was 27. She looked at me with anger, imagining condemnation in my eyes. The other woman was 18, just my age, and I took to her immediately. Both were black, although the madam assured me that the massage parlor was a veritable melting pot of colors and Chicago neighborhoods, and that white girls who looked like junior varsity cheerleaders were in high demand.

As the madam had promised, the house catered to men's fantasies, and women were hired on the basis of whether or not they fit a "type." There was also a room full of costumes and make-up which could have serviced a theater's full repertory season, from *Macbeth* to *A Streetcar Named Desire.* My new friend, the 18-year-old, was six feet tall, and she'd been hired to deal specifically with men who needed women to be big. Her most frequent client was a prosecuting attorney who happened to be nearly seven feet tall. When he appeared socially with his wife, who was not quite five feet, people called them Mutt and Jeff. When the prosecutor visited the house, his lady for hire donned boxing gloves, duked it out with him in their imaginary ring, and knocked him down. Afterwards he would leap up unharmed, take off his gloves and hers, measure all 72 inches of her against the bedroom door with a yardstick, and then promptly carry her to bed, a redeemed slugger.

Then there was the pediatric prof at the medical school who wrote medical books by day and kinky fairy tales at night. The management required its women to be 18-and-over but they had no trouble finding voting-age gals who *looked* undeveloped, ponytailed and girly-girlish enough to play Little Red Riding

Hood to his Big Bad Wolf in those alliterative scripts he brought with him. And then there was the tax accountant necrophiliac.

10   The only client I talked to was the priest, who went there every Sunday after church and stayed all day. He loved to bake for his women and today he brought a loaf of bread which we all broke together and washed down with Diet Pepsi instead of wine. He was a lonely, inarticulate man with a voice that sighed instead of sang, and I could not imagine him inspiring fervor and faith from behind his pulpit. Nor, for that matter, could I — or did I want to — picture him naked and panting with one of these women, but that's exactly what I ultimately saw. Just as I was getting ready to leave, the 27-year-old insisted that if I were a true journalist and not a princess from the suburbs that I'd complete my research from behind the bedroom door. Before I could think about it I was in the same room with them, watching, notebook in hand, while they oiled, massaged, and stroked the priest to transcendence, all "on the house."

That night, tucked safely inside my dorm room, I began to wade through all this rich material. Immediately I was pressed with many writerly problems. How was I to deal with point of view? Whose story was it? The working women's? The clients'? My original goal had been to profile the madam, but she was swiftly being eclipsed by the prosecutor, the pediatrician, the necrophiliac, and the priest, who were all far stranger than she was. How much of the dirt should I put in? What should I leave to the imagination? What about what I'd seen with my own eyes inside that room?

I finally chose to make the place and its strange characters the subject of my article, and to do this I took myself entirely out of the story. I wrote it as though I were a bug on the wall watching a typical day in the house, but I tried to use the voice of the madam as much as I could.

As it turned out, the teaching assistant took me aside later and told me he thought I could publish it in *The Chicago Reader*. Other students in the class had interviewed the Chicago journalists they hoped to line up internships with for the summer and he and the prof were thankful that I'd gone for something with "grit." There was only one problem, he said, and that was the style. It was simply too literary. If I cut out all the adjectives, he said, I would be on my way to becoming a journalist.

I turned down his generous offer, as flattered as I was, because I'd promised the women I wouldn't publish the piece. Now that I look back, it seems that there were other reasons why I didn't want to sell this story to the *Reader*. One was that I wasn't interested in developing the dry, "just the facts" style that the t.a. thought I needed to master in order to become a valid journalist. The other reason was that the real story for me was not, as everyone supposed, that respectable professional men can be sleazy but simply that an 18-year-old girl/woman with Arthur Rackham posters and a stuffed koala bear with a Northwestern garter belt had been in this place and talked to these people and seen what she'd seen, and that she had somehow been changed by having told this story. My problem, in 1976, was that I didn't know of a journalistic form that would allow me to tell it the way it wanted to be told; those new literary journalists were not yet being taught. But neither, I discovered when I switched into creative writing, could it be told in a poem or short story.

Poetry writing was a two-quarter sequence taught by a woman who was   15 writing her doctoral dissertation on the Modernist poets. Each week she had us read several volumes of the poet of the week—Eliot, Pound, Moore, Bogan, Stevens, Williams, and others—and then write two poems, the first a "pastiche" for which we obviously stole not only the poet's technical bag of tricks but his or her material as well, and the other an "imitation" for which we borrowed a technique but still tried to write our own poem. By the end of the first semester, whatever "voice" we'd all had before had been consumed by the tones and postures of our Modernist mentors. We would call each other on the phone and say, "How do you write a poem?"

The summer after that workshop I went to Wesleyan College and attended my first writers' conference. My workshop teacher read my poems and was kind enough to point out the origins of each line in my work. "That's from Shakespeare's Sonnet 18," he said, "and that's from 'Love Song of J. Alfred Prufrock,'" and "that's one of Louise Bogan's metaphors for depression. Where are *you* in these poems?"

A year or so later I went to one of my old poetry teacher's readings. She closed with a poem about the town where she'd grown up, which was somewhere—I couldn't believe it—in the South. I'd always assumed, given her diction, that she'd spent much of her life in English boarding schools. Maybe she had. Then it dawned on me. On a certain level, my teacher's aspirations to literary academia may have been spawned by a profound self-hatred. As mine had. Along with the dreams of countless other girl-women I knew skulking around miserably in the library. If my teacher had exerted so much energy trying to transform herself from the "down home" girl to the Oxford poet scholar, then how could she help me go deep into myself to find my authentic voice and material and story? I signed up for fiction writing and hoped for the best.

The fiction writing class was taught by a tall, trim, blue-jeaned, very hip late-30'ish fellow who was nicknamed "The Marlboro Man" by the circle of female students who had crushes on him. He had a slight Western twang and wore cowboy boots. When he came to our parties he smoked pot with us and told humorous anecdotes about the famous writers he'd met. His class was entertaining and lively. We got to write about subjects closer to our own life, but there was still a lot of stigma against being "self-indulgent" and "autobiographical." Style was more important than content—you had to be slick and exude a certain daring razzmatazz. You couldn't be political or direct. Processing personal experience was only okay if you applied heavy irony. Think of the times. It was now 1978, and people everywhere were trying to numb their pain from the previous decade by wearing shiny half-buttoned shirts and jumping into vats of hot water with near strangers to the beat of the Bee Gees.

Although there was some lip service paid to the original "voice" and "place" in my writing training, the fashionable voices were usually male back then: Bellow, Nabokov, Gass, excerpts from Pynchon, and a smattering of Ishmael Reed for color. I felt pressure to rev up my narrative engine, just as, when the Carver school made the grade soon thereafter, I felt pressure to edit everything back out except for the name brand products. And as far as place was concerned, it seemed to me you had only two choices. You could write about rural New England, of course, or you could write about the gritty "mean streets" of a Chicago, L.A., or New York. But what about a place as modest and chintzy as Cleveland, nicknamed "The Mistake by the Lake"? When I looked out the window I saw not Mt. Monadnock, not the pushers at the subway, but a few scrappy trees and a mechanical crane devouring crushed cars. I wrote stories, back then, set in places I'd never been, like Paris and Barcelona and San Francisco, because, it seemed, my own eyes had never seen anything worth mentioning.

20   I've heard that when Annie Dillard first began writing what became "Pilgrim at Tinker Creek," she intended to set it in Acadia National Park in Maine and write it in third person, in the voice of a *50-year-old male academic metaphysician*. After a time she realized that she didn't know Acadia the way she knew her home in Virginia, but it took a great deal of coaxing on the part of an enlightened editor to get her to write it in her own young female voice. This book, published just a year before I started college, points to a problem that women and people of color have always had in this country. Many of us have gotten one too many "Who cares?" written in red ink on our work. I think it is very common for the writer, especially the student writer, to approach a writing project with the feeling I am not worthy, as I am, with what I know now, to tell this story as I see it in my own words. To be an authority on this subject I have to hide behind the voice of someone else, perhaps someone whiter, with more Y chromosomes; to sound like I've "been around" I have to be from New York, or London, or Paris, or a charming old farm in New England with a ghost in the apple orchard who recites Robert Frost. It was not until I was nearly 30 — just as memoir and the whole genre of creative nonfiction began to flower — that the stories from my life I'd tried to disguise and romanticize in fiction came exploding, honestly and urgently, onto the page. As a writer, a teacher, and a reader myself, I have come to see that today's readers are hungering for I-as-eye-witness truth, perhaps because we live in an age where it is now commonly known that our political leaders are liars and thieves. People are choosing to learn about Vietnamese war brides, the years of Stalin, and the American 1950s not from the so-called expert historians or the ruling patriarchs who led from inside their offices, but from "real people" whose solitary landscapes and single voices have a power which illuminates the larger humanity we all share — which makes, as the short story once did, the strange familiar and the familiar strange.

Just as readers are hungry to learn the truth in a language that is more lively than they find in the daily papers, our students yearn to tell their own truths and to come to understand themselves and their connection to the world better in the process. Creative nonfiction is a genre in which student writers can use their authentic voices and make no bones about their presence in the work. They can write about places they know well. They can feel that what they have seen with their own eyes is of literary value, and of human value to others.

It is my belief that education should be a nourishing place for the heart and soul as well as the mind, and it should build confidence, not destroy it. How do we help our students draw on their own resources, not just their acquired knowledge? The teaching of creative nonfiction can validate the students' current lives, and strengthen their writing skills. Nonfiction writing in first person teaches the young writer to sharpen her powers of observation and use of memory, to hone his specificity and finesse for naming concrete things, and to create an honest, living voice. For the student writer, the permission to write about something he or she passionately cares about is what motivates that writer to go the extra mile to make the prose vivid and clear, rather than flat, empty, and vague. To write first-person nonfiction well, one must make contact with what Brenda Ueland calls "our True Self, the very Center, for . . . here lies all originality, talent, honor, truthfulness, courage and cheerfulness."

I suspect that had courses in creative nonfiction been available to me back in Cleveland, I could have saved myself about 15 years' worth of writing mistakes.

Perhaps one day when encouraging a student to seek her "True Self" in nonfiction prose is a basic component of writing pedagogy and not some retrograde 1960s concept, it will be customary to write "Why do *you* care about this?" on student essays, instead of "Who cares?" Perhaps helping our students search for "the very Center" right from the start will save them several years of writing mistakes. Whereas William Gass, in his introduction to "In the Heart of the Heart of Country" advises the aspiring young fiction writer always to "wait five years," the young nonfiction writer who has found his or her voice can often master a particular piece of memoir well enough to create something worthwhile and even publishable right now.

TALKING ABOUT IT

Seeing Metaphor: Revealing and Concealing

1. When Singer was a student, what different requirements were presented to her for journalistic writing, for poetry writing, and for fiction writing? How did the standard image of the work of the journalist, the poet, and the fiction writer act to limit her own development as a writer?

2. How do the comments "Who cares?" and "Why do *you* care about this?" represent for Singer two very different approaches to teaching writing?

Seeing Composition: Frame, Line, Texture, Tone

1. Singer tells a number of personal stories in this essay: about writing a feature profiling a friend suffering from lupus, about researching and writing a story about a madam and her establishment, about writing poetry and fiction in college courses. What do each of these stories contribute to Singer's central point about her difficulty in finding a personal voice?

2. In the final few paragraphs of the essay, Singer shifts from exploring her own experiences to offering more general thoughts about the teaching of writing. Do you detect any shift in style and tone here as well? Point to specific examples.

Seeing Meaning: Navigating and Negotiating

1. When, as a young child, Singer decided she wanted to be a writer, what was her goal? Why did it take her "about 15 years' worth of writing mistakes" to write as she wanted?

2. Based on your own experience in writing classes, has the teaching of writing changed much since Singer was in school in the 1970s and 1980s? Note that Singer doesn't discuss strictly academic writing. Do you think that using the first person "I" would be accepted in papers for courses beyond composition?

WRITING ABOUT IT

1. In your writer's journal, collect notes and memories about a story from your life. Then write the story as a journalistic, factual account in third person. Next, write the same story in first person. Finally, explain how the experiences of telling the story in these ways differ for you as writer and owner of the story.

2. In many college courses, you are not, as Singer wishes, given permission to write about something you care passionately about. The subject matter is given to you. Nevertheless, in response to your writing, a reader may well ask, "Why do *you* care about this?" When we are not writing from what we know well in our personal lives, how can we still motivate ourselves "to go the extra mile to make the prose vivid and clear, rather than flat, empty, and vague"?

   Write about a time you discovered a strategy for making an assignment your own, one that you cared about. Share this writing with members of your group. Then, collaboratively, write a list of these strategies for the rest of the class. Finally, as a class, make a master list.

Writing It Down for James: Some Thoughts on Reading towards the Millennium

ALAN CHEUSE

Alan Cheuse is a professor of English at George Mason University and book critic for National Public Radio's newsmagazine, All Things Considered. *His writing includes the novel* The Light Possessed *(1998), the short story collection* The Tennessee Waltz *(1992), and the memoir* Fall Out of Heaven: An Autobiographical Journey Across Russia *(1987). The selection here appeared in the Fall 1993 issue of the* Antioch Review.

On a cold, rainy Washington night this past December, this traveler drove over to the Congressional Office Building on Capitol Hill to attend the Christmas party of a local literary council. A group of young professionals, many of them lawyers and college teachers, who serve as tutors for the District's largest adult literary project — not an official part of either the D.C. or federal government but rather a nonprofit organization that belongs to a national umbrella group that fosters the teaching of reading to adults — served plates of roast turkey and baked ham and many side dishes to a couple of dozen adults and a few teenagers, almost all of them black, who all share the desire to learn how to read.

One of these late bloomers was a fifty-three-year-old truck driver from South Carolina named James. James picked up a newspaper only about a year and a half ago after a lifetime of work and raising a family. He had dropped out of school at the age of six to pick crops at nearby farms and never went back. Though unable to read a word, he'd performed such tasks as stevedore and foreman at a shipping company; for the last two decades he has been working as a teamster, in some instances hauling his load as far away as the Canadian border without knowing how to read the road signs.

When I expressed my astonishment at this feat, James laughed and said, "Hey, once you pass the driver's test, the rest ain't all that hard. It's usually just a matter of counting. Counting the stop signs, things like that. You recognize landmarks in town or out on the road and you sort of steer by them."

But after a lifetime of living in his own country as though it were a foreign land where he didn't know the language, James decided that since all his children had learned to read and had gone on to good jobs, he could take the time out to learn how to read himself. This he told me over a plate of food, his right leg moving up and down, up and down, his plate shaking on his lap.

"I wanted to learn to read a newspaper, see? I wanted to *read* about life, not just live it. So I can just about do that now. And now I want to read a whole 5 book. I want to read a story. A good story." The desire for a good story—that had been on my own mind ever since I could remember. And for the last three decades reading and writing had become a large portion of my daily life. I write, usually, into the early afternoon, and the rest of the day, when I'm not leading a workshop or at the gym or the supermarket or the movies, I give over to reading. Read, read, read, a rage to read. It's an appetite as great as that for sex and food and even for the air we breathe. Death will be a great disappointment if no love or family or friends come with it, but I'd even forgo food in the next life (if there is one) if I could go on reading the good new novels as they come out. In the last ten years I've reviewed nearly five hundred books for National Public Radio's evening newsmagazine *All Things Considered* and, like most people who love narrative, whether fiction or history or politics or science (though fiction is the best narrative of them all), I've read a lot more than those I've reviewed during this past decade, rereading books as I teach them to my writing students (because as I explain to them, thinking that at the same time if I have to explain it to them then perhaps they are already lost, good writers are good readers and great writers are great readers), rereading as I write essays and articles as well as reviews.

But a lifetime—yours, mine—with books has to begin somewhere. And while talking with James over our plates of turkey at the literacy party, I kept on trying to recall exactly when it was I first learned how to read. James could pinpoint his own beginning with the printed word: on a certain night in June, in Washington, at a restaurant where he had first met his tutor. Before that time, the printed language was a mystery to him, a cipher used by the rest of the world to keep him constantly on his toes. On the job he devised elaborate formulas to keep up with his work. In the supermarket he often depended on the kindness of strangers to tell him where certain foods were located. And as he was talking about his own pre-literate life as an adult, I got carried back to one of the few pre-literate scenes in my own memory.

Once upon a time a young boy—he must have been about three years old—crawled into bed with his mother and father. It was a Sunday morning, in spring, probably, because even though it was light outside the window, his father still lay in bed rather than having gone to work. While his mother created a space between them where the boy might burrow beneath the covers, his father reached over to the night table and picked up a rectangular object about six by nine inches—it had an orange and sepia cover, an abstract design that suggested not quite formed stars and crescents—that he said he had just found in his old trunk from a place he called *Roosh*-a. The boy loved the sound of the word and asked his father to say it again: *Roosh*-a. There was a smell to the object too, this thing made of paper and bound in stiff board, the odor of dust and oranges that had been lying long in the hot sun.

When his father opened the front of it, the boy noticed strange designs stretched out in rows. The only thing he recognized was a drawing, that of a golden rooster-like bird. *The tale of the golden cockerel,* his father announced as he fixed his eye on the page and began to speak in a strange and incomprehensible fashion, making a series of globlike and skidding sounds, with a lot of phushes and ticks and bubblelike slurs and pauses.

The boy was me, of course, and the man was my father reading to me in Russian, a language I've never learned, from a book of fairy tales that has long ago been lost in the flood of years that rushes through a family's life. And he of course is gone, too, and I'm old enough now to have a while ago put aside such fairy tales and think instead about what novels to give as gifts to my children for Christmas and other occasions. But I still recall the way my father opened to the first page of that now lost volume and began to make those sounds with his mouth and tongue, interpreting the odd designs in front of him as if it were the easiest thing in the world. It was from this day on that I decided, I believe — if "deciding" is what children at that age I was then ever do — that I would learn to read for myself.

I don't actually remember when I first mastered this basic intellectual ap- 10 titude. As Roger Shattuck has pointed out in a recent essay, few of us do. "Most minds," he says, "bury those early faltering steps under recollections of later rewards — the fairy tales or comic books on which we perfected our new skill." But some writers have tried to remember. Novelist Nicholas Delbanco describes a wonderful example of this when he writes of a transatlantic crossing, from England to America, at the age of six. On the third day out, he recalls, he received his first pair of long pants and he taught himself to read using a book about boats. Suddenly "the alphabet's tumblers went 'click', I remember the feel of it, the pride in it, the pleasure, the way the world made sense." Only as a middle-aged adult did he find a copy of a book called *Henry's Green Wagon,* inscribed to him from his kindergarten teacher in London for being "the best reader in Miss Jamaica's Kindergarten Class" in the year before his voyage.

I don't recollect beyond my one tantalizing session with the book of Russian fairy tales that my father ever read to me again. Or my mother. Though I suppose they must have. I certainly hope that my children recall the time that I read to them. If Delbanco can't recall winning his award from Miss Jamaica's kindergarten class, I probably shouldn't expect my son or daughters to keep in mind the hours we spent going over *The Little Engine That Could* or the "Ant and Bee" stories. If we do teach our children to read we can never forget the first few times that they skate off across the page on their own, a thrill in life something like the first time we sail away on our bikes without the use of training wheels.

An industry now supports this hope-filled activity. The middle class is urged to prep its children in advance of school. "Improved reading skills begin at home," say headlines in the "Parent and Child" columns of the *New York Times.* You can buy books, take courses. And you can hook your child up to your computer and plug in such programs as the Disney-made "Mickey's ABCs" and

"Follow the Reader." You can learn tips about how to encourage your children to read. And read to them yourself. In a statement of what seems to be the Original Sin of illiteracy Dr. Michael Pressley, a professor of educational psychology at the University of Maryland, is quoted as saying, "The kids who have the most trouble tend to have parents who didn't read to them when they were younger . . . and didn't see their parents or other people reading and writing."

But just as I have only that single memory of being read to, and in Russian besides, I don't recall seeing my parents read much at all. I do have the faint recollection of watching my father sit in a small alcove of a second-floor apartment on lower State Street in Perth Amboy, New Jersey, tapping on the keys of a small black typewriter, trying to write stories in English in the manner of the Russian satirists Ilf and Petrov. But I never saw him read anything other than the newspaper or a beat-up old copy of Richard Halliburton's *The Nine Wonders of the World*, the texture of whose cover and quality of photographs — waterfalls, drawings of statues — I recall rather than any text. My mother might have read the front page of the newspaper. I never saw her hold any book in her hand.

But I grew up reading, reading like a bandit. And no fairy tales for me. I went straight to comic books, *Archie Comics* at first, and then the superheros, *Superman* and *Batman, Plastic Man, Wonder Woman,* and then on to the horror comics, *EC Stories,* and *The Heap,* building a collection that rivalled just about any in the neighborhood. Of a Saturday you could see us comic fans, pushing baby carriages left over from our younger siblings' infancies filled with our collections on our way to trade meets at someone's house. After a while a quest for something more than *Archie,* etc. sent me onward to better reading, which meant, of course, *Classics Illustrated.* The Western world's greatest poems and stories turned into comic books, from *The Iliad* and *The Odyssey* on through the centuries all the way to Poe, that was my reading for years of adolescence.

15   Some educators these days are encouraging parents to allow their kids to cut their first reading teeth on *Classics Illustrated,* then watch them go on to more complicated books. I watched myself graduate to the serialized Christmas story that appeared in our local newspaper each December, and then to the sea adventures of C. S. Forrester, his Captain Horatio Hornblower series, to years and years of science-fiction novels and short stories. Although we "read" *Silas Marner* in junior high school I don't remember a thing about it. It was always the adventure stories and speculative fiction that captured me. Proust's Marcel writes of his afternoons with novels in the fabled Combray:

> On the sort of screen dappled with different states and impressions which my consciousness would simultaneously unfold while I was reading, my innermost impulse, the lever whose incessant movements controlled everything else, was my belief in the philosophic richness and beauty of the book I was reading, and my desire to appropriate them for

myself, whatever the book might be. . . . Next to this central belief which, while I was reading, would be constantly reaching out from my inner self to the outer world, towards the discovery of truth, came the emotions roused in me by the action in which I was taking part, for these afternoons were crammed with more dramatic events than occur, often, in a whole lifetime. These were the events taking place in the book I was reading. . . .

How many summer afternoons and long winter evenings this Jersey Marcel, yours truly, spent lost in this fashion! As you all have been lost, discovering and deepening your imaginative life in such a way as to change your ordinary waking physical life forever.

Except for those math geniuses who are probably anomalies when it comes to the quality of their minds, most of us find this period in which we encounter the mental adventures of reading the most important part of our maturation. Though to try and watch it happen is to see nothing. Last spring, for example, I spent a few days behind one-way glass observing an eighth-grade reading class at a middle school in Huntsville, Texas. I'm not sure what I expected to find, but this was what I saw: several dozen kids from around ages eleven to thirteen seated at their desks or sprawled on large cushions on the floor holding books open in front of them. They moved their limbs and twitched their eyes as they might have in sleep. Scarcely any of them did more than change position on the cushions or cross or extend their legs beneath their desks. Yet the internal processes in their minds, no more visible than coal changing under pressure into diamond, would change their lives. It will help them discover the world in a way like no other, to learn of history and philosophy and science and art, to acquire an awareness of God and insects, of water and the nature of life in a mining town in Belgium in 1900, to study Buddhism and physics, or merely to keep boredom at arm's length on an autumn evening in Great Falls, Montana; to become army captains and sales managers and priests and cotton farmers, and to ponder, if they are so inclined, the relation between their hometown, in this case, Huntsville, Texas, and the rest of the state, the country, the continent, the world, the solar system, galaxy, and cosmos.

However, you have only to observe a lower-level reading class in order to be reminded, if you need such an elemental tip, that this skill is not part of what we would call human nature. Kids study the shape of the letters and learn to sound each letter, group of letters, then make words. We've sounded letters, vowels and consonants resounding and popping for our own kids. To watch a whole batch of them at once get this training is like witnessing the first hatch of tree frogs in a warm climate in early spring. The entire air fairly sings and squeaks with the wondering noise of it all. But despite the illusion of the naturalness of reading, an activity as everyday as breathing, this skill is, in the history of western culture, a relatively new invention. For the majority of humanity in Europe and the West

verbal art was spoken or sung. And what we now call illiteracy was once the normal condition of culture in what we also name the Golden Age of Greece.

The thousand years or more prior to the sixth century BC in Athens was
the time of the Homeric rhetors or rhapsodes, who chanted and sang the great
poems of the culture to devoted audiences. It was only with the faltering of the
Homeric tradition, when it seemed as though the transmission of the poems in
memory from one generation to the next was in danger of dying out, that Pisis-
tratus, the Greek tyrant, ordered that scribes record the performance of the two
great epics, *The Iliad* and *The Odyssey,* on papyrus lest they be lost for all time.

Maybe that's when Paradise was truly lost, when it became necessary to
read the great songs that had formerly been sung. Is it C. M. Ciorian who describes this transition as the culture's "fall into language"? Prior to this time no
one read because there was no written language, but a hunger was present—
present, it seems, from the beginnings of human culture—the hunger for story,
for narrative, for the arrangement of incidents into an action, even an action that
might move the listener to feel pity and fear. This craving for order with emotional
resonance was satisfied during the pre-classical period in the Mediterranean only
by oral epic.

20 Drama arose during the fifth century BC and filled, among its other functions, the traditional need for a public gathering at which poetry was performed
over an extended period of time. But by the first century AD poetry and drama
were as often as not read on papyrus as performed. Prose narratives were composed as well, but these, like the *Satyricon,* seemed to take second place to the
more engaging works of history in the mind of an audience looking, apparently,
for a way both to restore a certain order to a life from which the formerly awesome power of the old gods had faded and for exciting and interesting stories
that spoke to their own daily round.

Between the decline of Greece and Rome and the withering away of the
Christendom that arose to take their place most westerners had to settle for one
book, the Bible, with its multitudes of stories, as the storehouse of narrative. It
wasn't really until the fourteenth century and the creation of *The Decameron*
that secular stories came to prominence as literary art—folk narratives were as
plentiful as trees—in Europe. As every school kid used to know, the invention
of movable type eventually made it possible for the wide dissemination of texts
of all varieties, not just the Bible for which the printing press was first widely
used. After Luther's revolt against Rome's authority as the prime interpreter of
the Holy Book, literacy became a necessity in his part of Europe for the religious
man, and soon evolved into a means of power among the rising merchant class,
and reading became a sign that a person was wholly civilized.

Consider for a moment what this meant in existential terms for European
society. In the great Homeric age of Greece, any citizen of Athens who could attend the performances of the epics—at four seasonal renderings each year in

the great amphitheater of the city — could apprehend them merely by listening attentively. To be a citizen thus meant among other things to be a listener, collectively, with all the other citizens of Athens. You listened and the words of the gods, through the conduit of the poet, went directly to your ears, telling of the great heroes and heroines, gods and goddesses, engaged in the straightening out, or messing up, of epic affairs in heaven, earth, and the underworld.

With the breakup of this oral culture and the rise of scriptural authority, reading became a prized activity, not just for the priesthood but for the elite of the continent's court and fief. The book became a metaphor for the world, and reading emerged as a method for interpreting God's creation. To be illiterate meant one stood several stages removed from a knowledge of sacred reality. The idea that one listened to the words of the epic poet and thus heard the language of the muses directly in one's ears became, in this thousand-year interregnum between the demise of oral poetry and the establishment of a secular reading culture, static and sterile when the priest, rather than the poet, served as conduit between holy work and worshipper. With the secularization of storytelling, from Boccaccio forward, the printed word became even further detached from its sacred origins in theodicic poetry, telling stories of the death of kings and then barons and then squires, so that by the time of Balzac, say, readers learned of the lives, loves, and sorrows of the denizens of a great secular city, which is to say, themselves.

As the story evolves — some might want to say descends — from scripture to secular tales of middle-class life, the relation of text to reader evolves as well. Christian theology demanded a singular oath from its worshippers, the acceptance of Christ on the part of the individual as his savior. Eighteen hundred years later the individual picks up a copy of *Tom Jones* and finds that the story illuminates part of his or her daily round, a far cry from any hint of salvation. In fact, quite the opposite, if you consider the distance between the hope of heaven and the worlds in contemporary fiction. To pass one's eyes across the lines of the Holy Writ was an act of prayer. What is it then to read modern fiction?

Proust's Marcel has — again — a pretty good way of seeing it. A real person, he asserts, because he is known to us only through our senses, remains opaque to us: 25

> If some misfortune comes to him, it is only in one small section of the complete idea we have of him that we are capable of feeling any emotion; indeed it is only in one small section of the complete idea he has of himself that he is capable of feeling any emotion either. The novelist's happy discovery was to think of substituting for those opaque sections, impenetrable to the human soul, their equivalent in immaterial sections, things, that is, which one's soul can assimilate. After which it matters not that the actions, the feelings of this new order of creatures appears to us in the guise of truth, since we have made them our own, since it is in ourselves

that they are happening, that they are holding in thrall, as we feverishly turn over the pages of the book, our quickened breath and staring eyes. And once the novelist has brought us to this state, in which, as in all purely mental states, every emotion is multiplied tenfold, into which his book comes to disturb us as might a dream, but a dream more lucid and more abiding than those which come to us in sleep, why then, for the space of an hour he sets free within us all the joys and sorrows in the world, a few of which only we should have to spend years of our actual life in getting to know, and the most intense of which would never be revealed to us because the slow course of their development prevents us from perceiving them. . . .

So we read for pleasure? and for a glimpse of what a coherent vision of the world might be like? It may well be that putting together in our own minds a lifetime of novel reading is close to knowing what it must be like in the mind of God. From these simple stories, of a foolish hidalgo in search of a phantom lover, of the way the past rises up against the present in an English village called Middlemarch, of a Jewish advertising salesman wandering about Dublin looking for sympathy, of a Mississippi family plagued by alcoholism, madness, and imagined incest, of a woman named Maria who aimlessly drives the L.A. freeways, we make up a cosmos.

Think of reading then as an act of praise, of prayer, even, in which individuals reassert their devotion to creation and to the immanent world in which we reside, a world in which every aspect of life, from old used tires piled high in a trash heap to the multiform patterns of snowflakes on a day in high winter, from the sickness of murder to the charity of parenthood, all make up part of a larger pattern. And when we read, we reenact that pattern, an activity that may be as close to serious prayer as most of us will get. Or want to. The organized modern religions hold no patent on expressing devotion to the universe. In fact, the pagan poets, the epic Homers of the oldest stories of the western Mediterranean, show a lot more imagination when it comes to creating great characters and overarching plots than the lyricists and lamenters of the Old and New Testaments. Some great poetry in the former, but nothing much in the latter unless you're spiritually bound to the text. Apply the test of narrative coherence and the pagan epics win hands down. And if the response of the reader, the immersion into a story that delights and instructs in the deepest fashion we know, is any test of the presence of godliness, there's no doubt in my mind which stories show the mark of real deity.

If there is such a thing. The great hype about our present epoch is that we've moved into a period of technology with exponential possibility. The computer has become the metaphor for God. Fine with me. I'm an old science-fiction fan from way back when I first started reading. Let's fly to Jupiter, let's shine our pen-lights into black holes. But on those long flights to the outer planets, or even the short hyperspace commuter hops between galaxies, there's going to be time that's free. Maybe some techno-hotshots will want to use those hours, or months or years, to play computer games or speak with voice-activated viewer-integrated videos. But most of the crew and/or passengers will probably want to read. And what will we do with our spare time once we move out beyond this current pioneering age of space exploration?

Imagine an engineer lying in his bunk in a space station at the outer reaches of our solar system with a peerless view of stars, to borrow a phrase, like dust. As people such as this have done for — what's the phrase here? — countless eons, he picks up a copy of a book, or punches out the text on his computer screen, and begins to read, or, if you will, scan the text. And what might it be? Anything from the stories of Louis L'Amour to *Paradise Lost* or *Moby-Dick,* no doubt. Consider how the poetry of Milton or the ocean scenes of Melville or the cowpokes and bandits of L'Amour would carry him back to earth-themes and earth-places. Even if he's never set foot on Earth, these are still the stories of the species' home place.

Reading — reading is home itself, the place where we go when we wish to be 30 with ourselves and our own minds and our own hearts. It is an act of the eye which, unlike the viewing of painting or film, has little to do with what the eye perceives before it. Theater and film are the imagination externalized, the created images of the mind or minds of other parties performed objectively before us. While viewing a dance or a play, our eye is captive. Narrative prose or poetry, like music, is a different and, I believe, higher form of representation. The words, like musical notations, are mere potential art, waiting to be performed by the reader on the interior stage of the imagination. And just as nothing could be more public than the performance of a play, nothing could be more private than reading a novel or story. As novelist Laura Furman recently suggested, reading may in fact be the last private activity of merit in our culture.

Neurologically one can distinguish the act of reading from the perception of other art forms, such as dance and drama, and one can see how it has a social reality distinct from the external performance, and perception, of ancient oral poetry, medieval drama, and all the other theatrical and visual art that has come after. Unlike oral poetry, which presumed the presence of a community ethos and the absence of what we would call individual ego, prose on the page demands individual participation and, ever since the advent of the age of symbolism, individual interpretation. Everyone in the Homeric audience understood the explicit meaning of the poems — there was no *im*plicit meaning — and celebrated these values and beliefs by means of listening. Since the middle of the eighteenth century, readers have pondered the implicit values of a work within the confines of their own imaginations, and sometimes despaired of a world in which such solitariness is the norm and values are determined by the situation of the individual.

It's no wonder then that we all know so many people who never dare venture seriously into the world of reading. For most people a functioning imagination can be a treacherous and even frightening possession, generating such trivial but annoying conditions as hypochondria on the one hand and much more dangerous situations such as jealousy, paranoia, and megalomania on the other. In this regard, we read *Don Quixote,* the first modern novel, as a book about the dangers of taking books literally. Logos detached from its divine origins is a symbol awaiting interpretation by the god within us, which is to say, our imaginative powers. Woe to him — look at poor Quixote — who takes it at face value.

But that woe, the woe of literalism in an age of symbolic interpretation, is exactly what many Americans rush to embrace, cheered on by McLuhanite theoreticians of the new media. The flat screen, the so-called interactive game, has become the new repository for the faith of tens of millions, the perfect altar for our neo-Puritanical faith in which efficacy is next to godliness, and poetry (which as Auden puts it in his elegy for Yeats) "makes nothing happen," and fiction is relegated to the dust-bin of the new age. There seem to be two kinds of citizens in this nation that produced *Moby-Dick,* either Ahabs or Ishmaels, and the former appear to be growing in direct proportion to the growth in population while the latter may be diminishing in number.

The figures on readership in America and the reading aptitude seem to suggest that this is so. More Ahabs, fewer Ishmaels. American students are reading less and less and watching more and more television every year. The majority of American students, it seems, read only to get along, most of them having been taken over by the games mentality of the new high-tech sales culture. So-called computer literacy has led to what we can only hope is a temporary rise in a new variety of illiteracy, the willful avoidance of narrative fiction and poetry as a means of knowledge and awareness. For the new exploding ranks of American students it seems to be Gameboy over C. S. Forrester, and coming right up behind Gameboy, and as far and away from computer games today as they are from pinball, is the burgeoning new industry of virtual reality or VR. Probably within the next five years and certainly within the next ten, VR will become the distraction of choice for the majority of school kids and reading will be demoted even further down the line than where it is now, somewhere between violin lessons and learning a foreign language. In other words, it will become an activity for the few and elite, just as it was in Goethe's Germany where out of sixty million inhabitants only about sixty thousand could read.

35   That's one scenario, anyway, and not an impossible one, considering the current state of popular culture in which trash seems to have driven out the good. From Emerson to Donahue, from Twain to Robert Fulgham, it's been a bad long slide downward. There are some areas, of course, where we can see actual evolutionary forces at work to good ends, particularly in music. When you consider the

way in which jazz has worked its way into the majority consciousness—and radio programming—or the rise of bluegrass, there's cause for celebration.

But in literary culture, things look bleak. For a century that started out with such wise and valuable critics as Van Wyck Brooks and Edmund Wilson and Suzanne Langer and saw its mid-age in the wonderful company of Alfred Kazin and John W. Aldridge, the prospects for the next century seem less plausible. Great literature demands great critics, and though it may well be that all of us who are writing fiction today truly deserve the company of the myopic—and at the same time megalomaniac—crew of neo-Marxists and femsters and post-post-modern academic culture vultures, to have to live with them is not thrilling, to say the least.

On the one hand they puff up second- and third-rate work because it serves their theses, rather than, as the great critics have always done, discovering their values in the great work of the time. On the other, they ignore entire areas of creation because it does not suit their already decided upon values. But more important for the situation of the reader is the fact that none of these critics writes well enough to have much appeal for the lay person. This leaves the playing field to the contest between the reviewers and the publicists. And since many of the best reviewers are novelists (the best of these is John Updike), and put their best efforts as they should into writing fiction rather than just writing about it, the formation of public taste is usually worked on full-time only by the publicists.

I don't mean to attack publicists. They do what they're supposed to do, which is bring the books to the public attention. God help writers these days who don't have a good one working on their behalf. But with hundreds of novels published each year and a limited number of dollars in the pockets of potential readers, someone has to try and do more than merely assert that whatever book they're touting at the moment is the best book of the moment. Yet fewer and fewer voices are speaking with critical authority, style, and intelligence in an effort to help the reading public sort things out.

The results are paradoxical and, for serious readers, not to mention serious writers, somewhat demoralizing. On the one hand we have limited, what we might call "pocket," successes, American versions of the European art novel, that find a small but devoted audience—novels by, say, Joyce Carol Oates or Jayne Anne Phillips. And then there is the work put forward in certain academic circles because it stands as evidence of a particular presentation of American culture (I'm using the word *culture* rather than *life* because this sort of book, for me, at least, never really lives except as part of a larger argument about society), the work of Don DeLillo and Paul Auster coming to mind here. At the other extreme is the big-seller list, which is by and large pretty awful stuff, with Stephen King and Tom Clancy standing at the top of the pile. Now and then a movie tie-in or some ethnic predilection will kick a serious book up on the list, a novel by

Doctorow or Edith Wharton or Amy Tan or Toni Morrison. But for the most part mainstream readers elevate the awful to stardom. It's been that way since the creation of the best-seller list just before World War One and it will certainly not get better for a while, if at all.

40   For the past few seasons, for example, the novels of Mississippi lawyer John Grisham have been all the rage. When I picked up a copy of *The Firm* — having been surrounded at family occasions by relatives urging me to do it — out of the hope for some fast-paced reading pleasure, the kind I used to look for in those sea stories of Forrester and in science fiction and for the past few decades have found in a select band of spy novelists and thriller writers from John Le Carré to Thomas Harris, I was terribly disappointed. But not surprised. The same thing happened years before when I tried out of desperation to fend off the Robert Ludlum crowd. It's all mediocre fare, with no real sense of language or psychology or plot beyond the melodramatic. Danielle Steel and the other romance writers are no better. "He entered her and they made love all night." That sentence of Steel's has stayed with me since I first read it. You can't get much worse and still be writing published fiction. But anything this woman touches turns to money. So that's the good news and bad news about the American reading public, as John Gardner used to say: "The good news is that in actual numbers more people are reading today than ever before in the history of the planet. The bad news is that they're reading mostly shit."

Commercial publishers don't offer all that much optimism. Even as they produce sales figures slightly above last year's, you notice that the dreck makes up most of the sales. Perhaps it's always been so, but lately it seems more so than usual. As the late publisher Sol Stein once put it so ironically and truly, "It's only those books that transmit the culture from one generation to the next" that are being left off the lists these days. And so called "midlist" writers, wonderfully entertaining and serious all in one, find themselves driven out of the marketplace for — where? If the trend keeps moving in this direction, an entire generation of gifted but non-best-selling American fiction writers are headed towards oblivion long before death.

"But look at all the book clubs just here in Washington," a friend pointed out to me the other day when I presented him with this portrait of literary culture and readership in chaos. "There are readers all over the place." And it's true. This is a city of book clubs, and I'm sure there are many, many cities like it across the country. And in the schools across the country there's no dearth of bright readers. Those kids lying on cushions in that classroom in Huntsville, Texas, for example. Or the Jane Austen fans at the private girls' school in Troy, New York, where I visited one afternoon to witness a discussion of *Mansfield Park* that was as heated and intense as any gents' squash game. Or the Washington, D.C., public school classes where the PEN/Faulkner Foundation sends visiting fiction writers to discuss their work with interested students.

It's not that we're sliding back into some dark age of total illiteracy. But as we lurch towards the millennium the news for the future of the American readership is growing exceedingly strange. McLuhanite doomsayers are appearing on all sides. Ivan Illich, for example, argues in his new book(!) *In the Vineyard of the Text* that "the age of the bookish text seems to be passing." The advent of the personal computer and the electronics era, Illich goes on, has irrevocably undermined the primacy of the book and altered our way of pursuing knowledge. Such faddish visions make the writer's heart sink.

But it's the reader in me more than the writer that takes the greatest offense. Having grown up in the time of the Big Talk about the Death of the Novel and now finding myself on the verge of an epoch in which the Big Talk focuses on the Death of Literature and possibly even the Death of the Book itself, all the Jersey rises up in me and wants to spit on the Reeboks of whatever current theologian of culture makes this argument. And there's no help from the academy either. In exactly that quarter where you'd think you might find people professing their love of literature and the importance, if not the primacy, of the art of fiction and poetry, you meet instead theory-fraught ideologues, waving foreign paradigms about in place of scripture, telling us of every reason under the sun for spending time with a book except the necessary ones.

To know another mind. To know another life. To feel oneself in the heart 45 of another age, in the heart of another human being. To live out the entire trajectory of a human motivation and understand its fullness in time. To move out of ourselves, lifted into another scene, another action, another destiny, so that we might gain a better sense of our own. To warm our spirits by the heat of a fine story, to help us keep the vision (even if illusion) of order in a world constantly on the verge of chaos. Bored theoreticians, losing hold of their own humanity, turn away from these blessings that the novel offers in order to further their own pallid fantasies of the modern spirit. And by shirking their responsibility towards the very humanist tradition that spawned them, they show their contempt not only for their own best (now sadly blighted) tendencies as readers but also for the new generations of potential readers to come who even now in the elementary schools of urban America are doing their best to prepare themselves — sounding their vowels, making out their letters, clumping them together into stumbling words on the page — to partake of the riches of our culture from Homer to Virginia Woolf to John Edgar Wideman. And for the potential new readers among our immigrant populations. And for the newly educated adults, born here but not born free enough to learn to read as children, new readers such as James the truck driver, my companion at the literacy council Christmas supper.

"TV gets to you after a while," James said to me as we were finishing up our turkey. "And let me tell you, life is tough enough without finding out a way to see it a little better. I learned the hard way, by not learning until now. My

Mama told us good stories when we were children, but she couldn't write them down. I'm missing a good story like in the old days. So when I get good enough with my reading, that's what I'm going to do."

"Write them down?" I said.

James laughed and chewed a bite of food.

"I don't know if I'd ever get that good. But I could like to read one."

50   "Talking here with you," I told him, "made me remember the first time I ever heard a story, the first time I ever thought about learning how to read."

"Tell me the story," he said.

I explained that I couldn't because it had been in Russian and all these years I had never found the English version of that tale.

"Well, that's a story by itself," he said. "Remembering it, trying to find it, not finding it. Write that one down. And maybe sometime when I get good enough I'll see it on a page."

So this is what I've done.

TALKING ABOUT IT

Seeing Metaphor: Revealing and Concealing

1. The book, writes Cheuse, has become "a metaphor for the world," and "putting together in our own minds a lifetime of novel reading is close to knowing what it must be like in the mind of God." Why do you think Cheuse presents such an all-encompassing view of books and reading? Do you find his ideas compelling? Why or why not?

2. In a later passage, Cheuse suggests that increasingly the computer "has become the metaphor for God." What does he mean, and what further metaphor does he use to posit that computers will never replace reading?

Seeing Composition: Frame, Line, Texture, Tone

1. Cheuse opens and closes his essay by relating his conversation with James, the truck driver in the Washington literacy program. In paragraphs 6–8, he also tells the story of his own first encounter with literacy, an incident he shares with James at the conclusion. What do these stories contribute to your overall response to the essay?

2. Cheuse alludes to a wide variety of novels and novelists that he assumes his readers will be familiar with. How many did you recognize, and which were unfamiliar? How did your familiarity and lack of familiarity influence your reading?

Seeing Meaning: Navigating and Negotiating

1. "The majority of American students," Cheuse writes, "read only to get along" and exhibit "the willful avoidance of narrative fiction and poetry as a means of knowledge and awareness." How do you respond to his characterization? Why do you think the matter so concerns him?

2. Near the end of his essay, Cheuse dismisses best-selling novelists like John Grisham and Danielle Steel. Yet, at the end, he seems to endorse James's desire to read "a good story." Why do you think he sees such best-sellers as something less than good stories?

WRITING ABOUT IT

1. Alan Cheuse describes his reading pleasure as "an act of praise, of prayer," as "home itself." Near the end of his essay, he lists many reasons for spending time with a book: "To know another mind. To know another life. . . . To move out of ourselves. . . . To warm our spirits by the heat of a fine story, to help us keep the vision (even if illusion) of order in a world constantly on the verge of chaos." Write an essay in which you describe your own reading pleasure, and give examples of the books that support your reasons for spending time with them. How do you imagine that Cheuse would respond to your reasons? Why?

2. Try to recall your earliest memory of hearing a story, the first time you ever thought about learning to read. Write it down for someone you know. Call it "Writing It Down for _____." Then go back to the beginning of your essay and tell your secondary audience, as Cheuse tells us, who the person is and why this story might be important for her or him.

PERMEABLE BOUNDARIES: WRITING WHERE THE READINGS MEET

1. How might David Huddle respond to Bonnie Friedman's stories about her writing struggles? For example, could he see them as one writer's "way of managing contraries within the self" or of putting negative qualities to good use? Why or why not?

2. Imagine that Natalia Singer and Peter Elbow are co-authors for an essay on the concept of voice. How might some of Singer's personal experiences serve as illustrations for Elbow's ideas about audience and the writer's relationship to it? How might Singer's advice for writers enrich Elbow's ideas about voice?

3. How does what James Houston says about writing and sense of place tie into Huddle's discussion of "the writing habit"? What new insights might you have about the writing process from exploring the connection between these two essays?

4. Anne Lamott, like Bonnie Friedman, describes writer's panic: "I'd write a couple of dreadful sentences . . . and then feel despair and worry settle on my chest like an x-ray apron. It's over, I'd think, calmly. I'm not going to be able to get the magic to work this time. I'm ruined." While Lamott may share Friedman's panic of not being able to write, Lamott's tone is considerably lighter.

   Within your writing group, try to account for the differences in tone. Are the differences a matter of image or a matter of the stories the writers tell? Are the differences a matter of sentence style? Of voice?

   As an exercise in tone, tell one story of your own writer's panic: write it first the way you imagine Bonnie Friedman would tell it; write it a second time the way you imagine Anne Lamott would tell it. Exchange these stories with members of your group. Ask them to tell you which imitation is of which author.

Chapter 3

Naming and Claiming

Not all big ones eating the meadow are horses. Some are cows.
—Reg Saner

Since a primary goal of metaphor is to name by claiming connections between two conceptual domains, all the chapters could collapse into this one. Here, however, the issue of naming is explicitly addressed: names for scientific events, names for plants and animals, and names for people. Why do names matter? How do they influence the way we perceive the world and ourselves? To what extent do we make the world in which we live through the habit of naming and of seeing likenesses between things? And finally, how might names limit our vision, even blind us?

The name "black hole," as Kip Thorne explains, is a metaphor invented by physicist John Wheeler to describe the object created by stellar implosion. Replacing "frozen star" and "collapsed star," the new image redirected physicists' attention in important ways. In "The Ink of Night," Chet Raymo argues, "Metaphors have a way of exploding the bounds of perception. . . . Great science often happens when likenesses are perceived where none were thought to exist."

The name "black hole" not only furthered implosion research but also made a dramatic impact on the general public. "Calling these things black holes was a masterstroke," says Stephen Hawking, famous for his discoveries in theoretical physics, especially cosmology. "The name," he explains, "conjures up a lot of human neuroses." While it may be true that this particular image became a cultural phenomenon in the 1970s, many scientific names make no impact on the public consciousness and, in fact, seem downright boring. Yet Ray Conniff describes taxonomy, the system of classifying plants and animals, as something more than a Latin or Greek vocabulary test. Hidden within those dusty phrases for the genus and species of bugs (millions of them still to be named) are jokes, puns, and insults. Who says taxonomists don't have fun, at least among themselves?

Reg Saner, in "Naming Nature," asks what escapes us when we're naming. What do we know when we know the name of a plant or an animal? He insists that there is finally a presence beyond language and quotes Taoism: "The name you can name is not the name." He explains that "in answering to the aptest word we can give it, each thing in creation asks to be seen, thus known, even more truly."

The names parents give to children can also evoke Saner's question: What escapes us when we're naming? To what degree does a name negatively influence someone's self-image or the image others have of her or him? Some people, like Itabari Njeri, choose to change their names to reflect their own sense of self and culture. Through a sequence of dialogues, Njeri reveals the false assumptions people make upon hearing only her name. Like Louise Erdrich in the poem "Birth," she invites us to consider how a name can be a "net." Toward the end of this chapter, Ursula K. Le Guin tells us a fairy tale, "The Rule of Names," in which no one is allowed to ask another's true name or to tell one's own. Finally, Khuankaew Anantachart, a student writer from Thailand, describes the negative impact of a name that anthropologists gave to a small tribe newly discovered.

STARTING TO THINK ABOUT IT

1. Why do you think some people don't care about the names of plants and animals? And, conversely, why do you think some care only to know the name but don't appreciate the plant or animal itself?

2. Why might Latin and Greek be the languages of choice for scientists naming the universe? What are they trying to do when they name a new species? Why do pharmaceutical companies often use Latin-like names for drugs, even the most simple, over-the-counter medications?

3. Have you ever seen something that you didn't have a name for? If so, how did you make sense of it, or, if you didn't, why did you hold on to the memory? What did learning the name accomplish?

4. To what extent has your name influenced you as a person, and to what extent do you believe that you have influenced the impact of your name on others?

Black Hole Birth

KIP THORNE

Kip Thorne is the Feynman Professor of Theoretical Physics at the California Institute of Technology and the 1994 recipient of the American Institute of Physics Science Writing Award. His books include Gravitation *(1973; with John Wheeler and Charles Misner) and* Black Holes and Time Warps: Einstein's Outrageous Legacy *(1994), the source of the selection here.*

The names that we give to things are important. The agents of movie stars, who change their clients' names from Norma Jean Baker to Marilyn Monroe and from Béla Blasko to Béla Lugosi, know this well. So do physicists. In the movie industry a name helps set the tone, the frame of mind with which the viewer regards the star — glamour for Marilyn Monroe, horror for Béla Lugosi. In physics a name helps set the frame of mind with which we view a physical concept. A good name will conjure up a mental image that emphasizes the concept's most important properties, and thereby it will help trigger, in a subconscious, intuitive sort of a way, good research. A bad name can produce mental blocks that hinder research.

Perhaps nothing was more influential in preventing physicists, between 1939 and 1958, from understanding the implosion of a star than the name they used for the critical circumference: "Schwarzschild singularity." The word "singularity" conjured up an image of a region where gravity becomes infinitely strong, causing the laws of physics as we know them to break down — an image that we now understand is correct for the object at the center of a black hole, but not for the critical circumference. This image made it difficult for physicists to accept the Oppenheimer–Snyder conclusion that a person who rides through the Schwarzschild singularity (the critical circumference) on an imploding star will feel *no* infinite gravity and see *no* breakdown of physical law.

How truly *nonsingular* the Schwarzschild singularity (critical circumference) is did not become fully clear until David Finkelstein discovered his new reference frame and used it to show that the Schwarzschild singularity is nothing but a location into which things can fall but out of which nothing can come — and a location, therefore, into which we on the outside can never see. An imploding star continues to exist after it sinks through the Schwarzschild singularity, Finkelstein's reference frame showed, just as the Sun continues to exist after it sinks below the horizon on Earth. But just as we, sitting on Earth, cannot see the Sun beyond our horizon, so observers far from an imploding star cannot see the star after it implodes through the Schwarzschild singularity. This analogy motivated Wolfgang Rindler, a physicist at Cornell University in the

1950s, to give the Schwarzschild singularity (critical circumference) a new name, a name that has since stuck: He called it the *horizon*.

There remained the issue of what to call the object created by the stellar implosion. From 1958 to 1968 different names were used in East and West: Soviet physicists used a name that emphasized a distant astronomer's vision of the implosion. Recall that because of the enormous difficulty light has escaping gravity's grip, as seen from afar the implosion seems to take forever; the star's surface seems never quite to reach the critical circumference, and the horizon never quite forms. It looks to astronomers (or would if their telescopes were powerful enough to see the imploding star) as though the star becomes frozen just outside the critical circumference. For this reason, Soviet physicists called the object produced by implosion a *frozen star*—and this name helped set the tone and frame of mind for their implosion research in the 1960s.

5   In the West, by contrast, the emphasis was on the viewpoint of the person who rides inward on the imploding star's surface, through the horizon and into the true singularity; and, accordingly, the object thereby created was called a *collapsed star*. This name helped focus physicists' minds on the issue that became of greatest concern to John Wheeler: the nature of the singularity in which quantum physics and spacetime curvature would be married.

Neither name was satisfactory. Neither paid particular attention to the horizon which surrounds the collapsed star and which is responsible for the optical illusion of stellar "freezing." During the 1960s, physicists' calculations gradually revealed the enormous importance of the horizon, and gradually John Wheeler—the person who, more than anyone else, worries about using optimal names—became more and more dissatisfied.

It is Wheeler's habit to meditate about the names we call things when relaxing in the bathtub or lying in bed at night. He sometimes will search for months in this way for just the right name for something. Such was his search for a replacement for "frozen star"/"collapsed star." Finally, in late 1967, he found the perfect name.

In typical Wheeler style, he did not go to his colleagues and say, "I've got a great new name for these things; let's call them da-de-da-de-da." Rather, he simply started to use the name as though no other name had ever existed, as though everyone had already agreed that this was the right name. He tried it out at a conference on pulsars in New York City in the late fall of 1967, and he then firmly adopted it in a lecture in December 1967 to the American Association for the Advancement of Science, entitled "Our Universe, the Known and the Unknown." Those of us not there encountered it first in the written version of his lecture: "[B]y reason of its faster and faster infall [the surface of the imploding star] moves away from the [distant] observer more and more rapidly. The light is shifted to the red. It becomes dimmer millisecond by millisecond, and in less than a second is too dark to see . . . [The star,] like the Cheshire cat, fades from view. One leaves behind only its grin, the other, only its gravitational attraction. Gravitational attraction, yes; light, no. No more than light do any particles emerge. Moreover, light and particles incident from outside . . . [and] going down the black hole only add to its mass and increase its gravitational attraction."

Black hole was Wheeler's new name. Within months it was adopted enthusiastically by relativity physicists, astrophysicists, and the general public, in East as well as West — with one exception: In France, where the phrase *trou noir* (black hole) has obscene connotations, there was resistance for several years.

TALKING ABOUT IT

Seeing Metaphor: Revealing and Concealing

1. Why did using the term "singularity" prevent physicists up through the late 1950s from understanding what happens when a star implodes? How did David Finkelstein's "new reference frame" — and his new term, "horizon" — represent a breakthrough? Do you see both terms as essentially metaphors, only one of them, or neither?

2. Equally important, according to Thorne, was John Wheeler's new term — "black hole" — to replace the terms "frozen star" and "collapsed star." Consider the implications of each of these terms. How did Wheeler's term suggest a whole new way of thinking about star implosion?

Seeing Composition: Frame, Line, Texture, Tone

1. How well do you think Thorne succeeds in explaining abstract scientific concepts for general readers? Point out specific passages that you find particularly clear, as well as any that may have given you difficulty. What do you think makes some passages clear and others not?

2. Thorne starts off with the example of movie stars assuming new names to help "set the tone, the frame of mind with which the viewer regards the star." How effective do you find this opening? Does the analogy between movie stars and imploding stars strike you as apt?

Seeing Meaning: Navigating and Negotiating

1. Thorne emphasizes the importance of naming in physics: "A good name will conjure up a mental image that emphasizes the concept's most important properties, and thereby it will help trigger . . . good research. A bad name can produce mental blocks that hinder research." How did the evolution of the terms "singularity"/"horizon" and "frozen star"/"collapsed star"/"black

hole" inspire a new way of perceiving these phenomena? Does it seem to you that the new terms were themselves inspired by someone seeing star implosion in a new way?

2. Consider an area of interest in which you feel you have some expertise, and choose some terms that are crucial to understanding that subject. Can you come up with any new terms that would better emphasize each concept's most important qualities?

WRITING ABOUT IT

1. Extend Kip Thorne's point and offer another illustration for his opening statement "The names that we give to things are important." Consider a name that has significance because it affects the way you perceive the concept, the object, the person, the animal, or whatever. Some possibilities include family names or nicknames; commercial products; specialized terms from courses of study or from sports and games; special terms within your social group or family; names you've given to pets. Try to say what the name reveals about ＿＿ and what it conceals. What are the advantages and disadvantages of the name?

2. Extend Kip Thorne's point and offer another illustration for his opening statement "The names that we give to things are important." Consider a class of names for a particular object or product, such as cars or perfume or breakfast cereal. What's significant, say, about the recent trend in naming perfumes simply "Happy," or "Cool Water," or "Pleasure," compared to names in the past decade or an earlier one? Or what's culturally significant about the names of currently popular breakfast cereals compared to the names of earlier popular ones? Try to say what the trend in naming reveals about our changing cultural values.

Black-Hole Encounter

JOHN BOSLOUGH

John Boslough is the author of Stephen Hawking's Universe *(1985), which is the source of the selection here, and former science editor of* U.S. News & World Report. *He has also published articles in* National Geographic, Smithsonian, Psychology Today, *and the* Washington Post.

The publication of a cover story on black holes by *Time* magazine on September 4, 1978, was the culmination of popular intrigue with these unseen and often misunderstood objects. Hawking was mentioned prominently in a sidebar to the article, and referred to as "one of the premier scientific theorists of the century, perhaps an equal of Einstein."

Hawking laughed when I asked him about the comparison. "It's never valid to compare two different people — much less two different physicists," he said. Closing the subject, he added, "People are not quantifiable."

Hawking doesn't dispute the notion that he is a master of black holes, and although his attention is now focused elsewhere — mainly on the very early universe — he still looks on black holes with awe and amusement. He is always ready to talk about them.

"You can't get there from here," he said with a grin when I asked him what an encounter with one would be like. Then, with a barely detectable shrug of his slight shoulders, he asked how deeply I wanted to go into the mathematics as he started explaining in detail his work with black holes.

Black holes, as Hawking tells it, are rips in the fabric of space and time so 5 dense and distorted by unimaginable gravitational forces that for years physicists believed nothing could escape from one, including light. They are thus, by definition, invisible. No one has seen or ever will see one, no matter how powerful the telescope.

Hawking is certain they exist. "There may be as many as a thousand million in our galaxy alone," he said. I asked him for the evidence, and he conceded that for the moment their existence can be confirmed only as special solutions of the equations of general relativity and by a few scanty parcels of indirect physical data.

Despite the mystery, physicists in recent years have begun calling on black holes, largely as a result of Hawking's work, to explain everything from the creation of galaxies and quasars to the ultimate fate of the universe itself.

"It's a little like using the unexplainable to explain the unexplainable," Hawking told me. As much as anybody else, he delights in the enigma and mystery of these most mysterious of all celestial bodies. "Within black holes, space and time as we normally perceive them come to an end. It's a disturbing thought."

An object like an asteroid or astronaut coming too near the edge of a black hole would first be stretched out of shape like a rubber band—then vanish into the hole without a trace. In that sense, black holes are cosmic vacuum cleaners that suck up everything they encounter, from giant stars to particles of space dust and the photons that make up light. There is no escape from a black hole.

10 Hawking and other theorists are convinced that the long-sought unifying concept in physics—the theory that would explain the central interaction of the universe—lies at the periphery of black holes or similar peculiar constructions arising at one point or another in the evolution of the cosmos.

Such a mathematical construction should, at least in theory, be able to explain the construction of every bit of matter in the universe as well as all the forces that interact between this matter—somewhat akin to concocting a single recipe that would work for soup and cement and everything in between, all expressed mathematically. Farfetched as it sounds, Hawking assures me that physics is within twenty years or less of such an all-encompassing concept.

When I asked Hawking how he first became interested in black holes, he told me, "It was in black holes that it first became apparent to me that strong forces that bind the elementary particles could come together with the weaker forces of gravitation. And of course, black holes have a certain appeal all their own, in their mystery and the images they convey to the human mind."

Black holes are the natural consequences of the death of stars. If the collapse of a star may lead ultimately to a singularity, a black hole might be described as the final stage in the death of a star before the point of singularity is reached. And it is the black hole that finally masks the singularity from the rest of the universe, creating a break with the ordinary space-time around it.

Using only Newtonian ideas about gravity and light, the French scientist Pierre Simon Laplace first suggested in 1796 what might happen if a star were large enough. He theorized that there could be a strong enough gravitational attraction to recapture all the star's radiation, including light.

15 "It is possible that the largest luminous bodies in the universe may actually be invisible," wrote Laplace, nearly two centuries ahead of his time.

In the case of the sun, there has been a standoff between the contending forces for close to 5 billion years. Astronomers think it will continue in equilibrium for at least that much longer. At that time, it is theorized, gravity will at last begin winning the tug-of-war as the sun's nuclear fuel is spent. The mass of the sun, a ball of dense, hot gas 865,000 miles across, will then begin to collapse.

When the sun's matter has become condensed enough, it will become what astronomers call a "white dwarf," a figurative name that refers to a seething ball of atomic nuclei and loose electrons that, in the case of the sun, would be only about four times as large as the earth, minuscule in cosmic terms.

Its mass would remain about the same as it is now, however. As a result, the gravitational pull on the atomic matter at its surface would be far stronger than it is today. The velocity required for an object like a rocketship to escape from the sun's surface would have increased from 380 miles per second today to over 2,100 miles per second.

The collapse can continue. Physicists are certain that a star can collapse indefinitely. To get to that point of permanent self-annihilation, the star has to be massive indeed. In the case of the sun, with only average initial mass, it will collapse no further once it becomes a white dwarf. A law of physics called the exclusion principle intervenes at that point.

This law states that two electrons cannot occupy the same energy space, meaning there is a limit to how tightly matter can be packed together. This limit is high by ordinary standards: at the white dwarf stage, a thimbleful of the sun would weigh tons.   20

If the original star has a greater mass — estimated to be 1.4 times or more that of the sun — the exclusion principle will be overpowered by gravitation. Such a star going through the throes of gravitational collapse would be drawn down further, breaking atomic nuclei apart, destroying atoms.

It eventually becomes a "neutron star," a heavy mass of neutrons just a few miles across. Escape velocity at the surface would be 120,000 miles per second. If the star is more than about 3.6 times the mass of the sun, it will not stop contracting at the neutron star stage. Gravity is clearly in charge now, and it shows no mercy. It draws the star down into itself, a victim of its own weight. Finally it reaches the point where the escape velocity at the surface is so great it reaches 186,282 miles per second — the speed of light. If you watched a star at that exact instant, its already dim glow, not much more than a weak electromagnetic shadow, would flicker out.

Gravity claims light as its final victim. The former star, now a black hole, has become absolutely and perfectly invisible and will remain so for a very, very long time.

Astronomers have been able to pick up traces of white dwarfs that still radiate enough light to be photographed by large telescopes, and the electromagnetic squawks of neutron stars can be detected by radio telescopes. By their nature, however, black holes are poor correspondents. There is general agreement that they exist, but astrophysicists — and even theoretical physicists — would dearly like to have a look.

As for Hawking himself, does he really believe that black holes exist beyond the figment of an equation? In fact, he has become convinced, along with some other physicists, that at least one has been found.   25

"If you look at the constellation Cygnus, there is a good chance that you will be looking in the direction of a black hole," he maintains.

Some stars travel in pairs. They are called binaries and orbit a common center of gravity. Astronomers reason that if one of the stars in a binary system has collapsed into a black hole, the invisible black star would still hold its gravitational embrace on its visible mate. Hawking is certain astronomers have found one such mixed marriage in the constellation Cygnus, 6,000 light-years from earth. "The visible star, a blue one, is stretched and distorted," he says. The reason: its mate, a black hole, is exerting tremendous gravitational force on it, pulling it into the shape of an egg.

The discovery in 1973 of this apparent black hole in the binary system called Cygnus X-1 has excited theoretical astrophysicists far more than if another planet had suddenly drifted into sight beyond Neptune (which now, by a temporary quirk in orbit, is the most distant planet from the sun). Its origins are the subject of endless speculation.

Hawking has made a bet with one of his best friends, Kip Thorne, a respected theorist at the California Institute of Technology, about the ancestry of the mysterious object in Cygnus X-1. If it turns out that the binary system does not contain a black hole—breaking many a physicist's heart—Hawking will win a four-year subscription to the British humor magazine *Private Eye*. If it is a black hole, Thorne wins a one-year subscription to *Penthouse*.

This odd four-to-one bet has become rather notorious in physics circles. Why would Hawking, whose work virtually requires the existence of black holes, bet against them? "It really is a statement about my own psychology," he told me one day as we talked about the probability that Cygnus X-1 contains a black hole. "Actually I could win easier than Kip. Any number of observations—such as the emission of pulses—could disprove a black hole."

However, he is certain that Cygnus X-1 will turn out to be the real thing. "If it isn't a black hole, it really has to be something exotic," he said.

Astronomers may have found more than one. A team of Canadians and Americans announced in 1983 that they had discovered a second black hole, this one outside our own galaxy. They found it, by its emission of powerful X-rays, in the Large Magellanic Cloud, a satellite galaxy of the Milky Way visible only in the Southern Hemisphere.

Using the 158-inch telescope at the Inter-American Observatory at Cerro Tololo, Chile, they estimated the black hole's distance from earth at 180,000 light-years, its weight about ten times that of the sun, and its distance from its binary mate a mere 11 million miles.

Within Cygnus or the Large Magellanic Cloud or elsewhere, a black hole by any definition is a weird resident of the universe. Its existence strains the laws of physics. Moreover, what is to prevent a black hole from collapsing even more—in fact, down to a singularity, an infinitesimal speck of infinite density like the one at the outset of the Big Bang?

Hawking and Penrose demonstrated in their early work that this is precisely 35 what could be expected to happen in the case of some burned-out stars. Later, Hawking, working with other colleagues, was able to show that a black hole probably would settle down into a fairly stationary state that was no longer related to the star from which it had collapsed. In fact, such black holes would be possessed of only three measurable parameters: mass, rate of rotation, and electrical charge.

"This turned out to be of actual practical importance," Hawking said. I had asked him what difference it made if an object that could not be seen nor measured did have actual parameters.

"Well," he explained, "it meant, for one thing, that the structure of the gravitational field of any black hole could be accurately predicted. And that meant that one could construct models of astrophysical objects — such as Cygnus X-1 — thought to contain black holes. The properties of the model could then be compared with actual observations."

In the 1970s black holes began making an appearance as a cultural phenomenon. Bumper stickers and T-shirts assured us that "black holes are outta sight." They were a common topic on talk shows, and the subject of endless gags and jokes. The public passion of the mid-1970s for black holes was perhaps just a fad. In that sense black holes were a sort of Bermuda Triangle of space, something lying somewhere between parapsychology, the occult, UFOs, and astrology.

The image of a black hole or the Big Bang both confuses and delights our subconscious. Black holes might be a metaphor for our own fate or for the fate of the universe. If a star can crash down in upon itself, why not the entire universe?

"Calling these things black holes was a masterstroke by John Wheeler," said 40 Hawking. "The name conjures up a lot of human neuroses. There is undoubtedly a psychological connection between the naming of black holes and their popularization.

"It is important to have a good name for a concept," he said, speculating for a moment on the psychology of scientific terms. "It means that people's attention will be focused on it. I suppose that the name 'black hole' does have a rather dramatic overtone, but it also is very descriptive. It has a strong psychological impact. It could be a good image for human fears of the universe."

Just as there was utter oblivion before the Big Bang, there is utter oblivion at the center of a black hole. Normal time ceases to exist just as surely as it did not exist before the Big Bang. Therein lies much of the appeal of black holes and the Big Bang for Hawking. Moreover, in both concepts come together the twin pillars of twentieth-century physics: Einstein's theory of general relativity and Max Planck's quantum theory. In 1974 Stephen Hawking, in a bold and risky theoretical gambit, proposed a startling new idea about black holes that hinted for the first time that quarks and quasars actually might operate within the confines of a single, although deeply hidden, law of physics.

TALKING ABOUT IT

Seeing Metaphor: Revealing and Concealing

1. Black holes, Boslough writes, are being called on "to explain everything from the creation of galaxies and quasars to the ultimate fate of the universe itself," which Stephen Hawking refers to as "a little like using the unexplainable to explain the unexplainable." What do these statements suggest to you about the way physicists think about the universe?

2. Near the end of the selection, Hawking talks about the name "black holes." Why does he think the name caught on so with the public? What associations does the name conjure up for you? Do you agree that it is "a good image for human fears of the universe"?

Seeing Composition: Frame, Line, Texture, Tone

1. How effectively do you think Boslough has explained the concept of black holes for general readers? Did he help add to your own understanding? If so, how? If not, why? Compare Boslough's treatment of the subject with Kip Thorne's in the previous reading. Do you think one writer does a better job than the other of reaching a general audience?

2. Boslough quotes from Hawking throughout the selection. What do the quotations contribute to the tone here? How would the reading be different without them?

Seeing Meaning: Navigating and Negotiating

1. Boslough asks Hawking if "he really believes that black holes exist beyond the figment of an equation." What are the implications of such a question? Do you find Hawking's response convincing? Why or why not?

2. When asked about his work being compared to Einstein's, Hawking responds, "It's never valid to compare two different people — much less two different physicists. . . . People are not quantifiable." How do you respond to this statement? What does it suggest to you about Hawking the scientist?

WRITING ABOUT IT

1. Write about the name of another natural event or scientific concept that has made "an appearance as a cultural phenomenon." What might explain the strong impact of the name on the general public? What images might the name conjure up that could account for its popular appeal?

2. Boslough sometimes talks about stars and gravity as if they were people; that is, he personifies natural phenomena. Write a paragraph in which you define or describe an object or a natural force as if it were a person. Choose a subject you know well, and write about it for someone who doesn't have your knowledge.

    Next, write another paragraph about the object or natural force as literally as you can. What is gained and lost in each of your definitions from the point of view of someone who knows the subject well — yourself? Then, ask your reader (or a classmate who doesn't have your understanding of the subject) to answer the same question: what is gained and lost in each of your definitions? Finally, incorporate both paragraphs and the double analysis (yours and your reader's) into a coherent essay that concludes with what you understand about this particular process of naming and connecting for the writer and for the reader.

The Ink of Night

CHET RAYMO

*Chet Raymo is a science writer (*Honey from a Stone: A Naturalist's Search for God, *1987;* Skeptics and True Believers: The Exhilarating Connection Between Science and Religion, *1998) and a novelist (*In the Falcon's Claw: A Novel of the Year 1000, *1990). He also writes a science column for the* Boston Globe. *The selection here is from* The Virgin and the Mousetrap: Essays in Search of the Soul of Science *(1991).*

A *New Yorker* cover by Eugene Mihaesco is tacked on the wall above my desk. The drawing on the cover is simple. A pen lies on a white table, its nib dark with ink. An ink bottle stands open. The ink in the bottle is a map of constellations of the northern sky — Ursa Major, Ursa Minor, and Draco — including the stars Dubhe, Merak, and Mizar. Simple, yet hauntingly provocative. Again and again I pause in my work to look at the drawing. It seems to suggest that the possessor of the pen (Who? A poet? An artist? An astronomer?) draws inspiration from the ink of night. But the star map in the bottle, with its thin white lines defining constellations and star names, is itself a work of creative imagination. So the ink is both night and an image of night. Ambiguous? Certainly. Precisely this ambiguity lies at the heart of science.

Does science describe reality, or does science invent reality? The question is as old as Parmenides and shows no sign of resolution. I suspect that most scientists are willing to live with the ambiguity. They are confident that their theories describe reality, but they also know that theories are creations of the human mind. Consider that little patch of night in the ink bottle, the constellations near the northern pole. Few star groups have so excited the human imagination as Ursa Major, the Great Bear. The seven brightest stars of the constellation — the stars we know as the Big Dipper — are so instantly recognizable that sometimes I wonder if the pattern might not be genetically encoded in the human brain, the way some birds are endowed with an ability to navigate by stars. Those seven gorgeous presences demand recognition. The Greeks provided a charming legend. The nymph Callisto was loved by Zeus, who transformed her into a bear to protect her from the wrath of Hera, his jealous spouse. One day Callisto's son Arcas was out hunting in the forest and raised his bow to shoot the bear, not recognizing his mother in altered form. Zeus observed the impending tragedy from Mount Olympus, and speedily intervened. He changed Arcas into a little bear, and placed mother and son into the heavens where they remain today, the Great Bear and the Little Bear, arched poignantly toward each other, eternal victims of Zeus' wandering eye. But Hera had the last laugh; she moved the two bears into

the part of the sky near the celestial pole, where they never set and therefore never rest.

There was a time when images of bears and the story of Callisto and Arcas might have satisfied our curiosity about the polar stars, but the tension between experience and story has become too slack for the story to any longer have currency as science. Today we require new stories, stories more closely tied to our experience of the stars and more consistent with our other knowledge of the world. Let me dip my pen into Mihaesco's ink of night and tell the astronomer's story of Dubhe, Merak, and Mizar, the three stars that are named on the map in the bottle. Dubhe, the star at the lip of the Dipper, is a yellow-orange giant star ten times larger than the sun and a hundred times more luminous. It lies one hundred light years from Earth, a distance so vast that it would take a Voyager spacecraft, such as the craft we sent to Jupiter, Saturn, Uranus, and Neptune, a million years to get there. Dubhe was once a star very much like the sun, but it has depleted its energy resources and entered its death throes, swelling up to devour its inner planets and boiling away whatever oceans and atmospheres those planets might have had. Dubhe's fate will someday be the fate of our sun. Merak and Mizar, at the bottom front of the Dipper's bowl and at the bend of the handle respectively, are sibling stars, born from the same great gassy nebula and streaming together through space from the place of their birth. They are stars in the prime of life, many times brighter than the sun, and almost certainly accompanied in their travels by families of planets. Mizar is a wonderful thing to behold through a telescope. It is actually a system of two great suns, bound together by gravity, circling about a common center of attraction once every ten thousand years.

How is it that astronomers can tell such stories, stories more fabulous than any myth of gods and nymphs, when the ink of night offers to the eye only pinpricks of light? The answer is both simple and complex. *We look, we invent, we look again.* We test our inventions against what we see, and we insist that our inventions be consistent with one another, that our stories of the stars be consistent with our stories of the earth, of life, and of matter and energy. And tension! Always we are testing the tension of the instrument that is science, observing that the strings of theory are taut and resonant, and that every ear hears an identical note when the strings are bowed. The same theories of gravity and dynamics describe the fall of an apple from a tree and the streaming of stars through space. The story of the falling apple and the story of the stars must resonate together. Only then, when our stories of the world vibrate with a symphonic harmony, are we confident that our inventions partake of reality.

5   The starry night is both the ink of invention *and* the invention; it is an ambiguity we have learned to live with. We are confident (or we wouldn't do science at all) that out there in space, six hundred trillion miles from Earth, the dying star Dubhe burns with the brilliance of a hundred suns, and Merak and Mizar stream together from a common point of origin. But we also know that the astronomer's stars, like the stars of the Greek storytellers, are constructed of the frail stuff of likeness. Even the sturdiest of scientific concepts is rooted in metaphor.

■   ■   ■

Reaching for a book on a high shelf I tipped down *Season Songs* by poet Ted Hughes, which attracted attention to itself by delivering a lump on the head. I sat on the floor and read again those nature poems written twenty years ago by Britain's present poet laureate.

> Fifteenth of May. Cherry blossoms. The swifts
> Materialize at the tip of a long scream
> Of needle — "Look! They're back! Look!"

At Hughes's invitation I watched the swifts, those quickest of birds, watched their "too-much power, their arrow-thwack into the eaves." Arrow-thwack! Yes, I thought, that's exactly right. That's exactly the way swifts zip into the eaves of the old barn on their evening high-speed revels. As if shot from a bow. Too quick to be animate. Then, at poem's end, a lifeless young swift is cupped in the poet's hand in "balsa death." What a phrase! By it we are made to feel the surprising un-heaviness of the bird in the hand, the hollowed-out bones and wire-thin struts beneath the skin of feathers, a tiny machine perfected by one hundred million years of evolution to skim on air, as light as balsa. Hughes's delightful images reminded me how much scientists need poets to teach us how to see.

Scientists are trained in a very un-metaphorical way of seeing. We are taught to look for *immediate* connections: X causes Y, Y causes Z. We strip away the superfluous, the noncausal. We isolate. We weigh and measure. The average density of a bird is significantly less than the average density of a mammal of comparable size. That's one reason birds fly. Balsa wood has nothing to do with it. But anyone who has held a bird in the hand will recognize the aptness of Hughes's balsa wood image, the curious absence of expected heft. The metaphor is instructive. We learn something about birds that no ornithological text quite so vividly conveys. Make no mistake. I am not dismissing the scientific way of seeing. Weighing, measuring, abstraction, and dissection have proved their worth as royal roads to truth. But the poet's eye guides us to truths of another kind. No field biologist has seen "hares hobbling on their square wheels," yet Ted Hughes's metaphor is so perfectly truthful we can't help but laugh. No ichthyologist has recorded the mackerel's "stub scissors head," but we readily imagine the blunt jaws of the fish shearing open and shut as if operated by a child's deliberate hand. No astronomer has watched a full moon that "sinks upward / To lie at the bottom of the sky, like a gold doubloon," but Hughes's lunar image truthfully reminds us that there's no up or down to the bowl of night.

Philosophers of science insist that science is metaphorical. They cite, for example, Newton's "clockwork" solar system and Robert Boyle's elastic "spring" of air. Christian Huygens, a Dutchman who lived by water, first thought of light as a "wave." Alfred Wegener, a meteorologist who traveled in the frozen arctic, conceived of continents drifting like "rafts" of ice. The philosophers are right: At root, all scientific knowledge is metaphorical. The stars of the astronomers (colossal suns, hugely distant fires, furiously blazing globes of gas) are as unlike the objects of actual experience (pinpricks of cold light in the dome of night) as are the nymphs and randy gods of Greek myth — and no less metaphorical. But young scientists are not trained to think (or to see) metaphorically and we may be poorer for it. Metaphor is a way of seeing noncausal connections, as when Ted Hughes speaks of April "struggling in soft excitements / Like a woman hurrying into her silks." On the face of it, there's nothing in the metaphor of use to a scientific student of the seasons, yet the words significantly alter our perception of spring. "Struggle," "soft," "excite," "hurry," and "silk" force us to think about spring in layers and levels of meaning.

10   Scientists, especially those working in narrow areas of specialization, are often trapped by tunnel vision. Metaphors have a way of exploding the bounds of perception, of making plain the essential unity of nature. Great science often happens when likenesses are perceived where none were thought to exist: Life is a "tree." The electron is a "wave." Thermodynamic systems are "information." In his best-selling book *Chaos: Making a New Science,* James Gleick describes how people working in widely different areas of science came to understand that certain apparently diverse phenomena had much in common. A dripping faucet, a rising column of cigarette smoke, a flag flapping in the wind, traffic on an expressway, the weather, the shape of a shoreline, fluctuations in animal populations, and the price of cotton: All these things, it turns out, can be described by a new kind of mathematics — fractal geometry and its variations — based on randomness and feedback. The new chaos scientists, says Gleick, are reversing the reductionist trend toward explaining systems in terms of their constituent parts, and instead are looking at the behavior of whole systems. Their ability to see likenesses between systems is the key to their success.

And that's what poets can teach scientists. Perhaps a course in metaphor should be as important a part of a scientist's training as a course in mathematics. When Ted Hughes writes . . .

The chestnut splits its padded cell.
It opens an African eye.
A cabinet-maker, an old master
In the root of things, has done it again.

. . . he may be on to more than he knows. The old master at the root of things is metaphor.

Science and poetry are both metaphorical, but science is not poetry. Robert Frost once said that writing free verse is like playing tennis with the net down; it is not a sentiment I happen to agree with, but if Frost's simile is accepted, then doing science is like playing tennis on a court thick with nets and white lines, constrained by hugely complicated rules. Profound strictures on the language of science are imposed by the requirement that science be public knowledge, internally consistent, reproducible, and (in its expression) as unambiguous as possible. Metaphor may be the spark that ignites scientific understanding, but the expression of the flame soon leads into a fractured maze of specialized vocabularies.

In his *Field Guide to the Birds*, Roger Tory Peterson gives this characterization of the purple finch: "Male: About the size of a House Sparrow, rosy-red, brightest on head and rump." And then he adds a traditional description: "a sparrow dipped in raspberry juice." That's it. Decisive. The perfect fit. Anyone who has ever seen a purple finch will recognize the aptness of that final phrase. The raspberry juice image is perfect — for the poet or amateur birdwatcher — but it hardly qualifies as science. Science has as its task elucidation of the real, unarbitrary connections between things, and "sparrow dipped in raspberry juice" isn't terribly helpful. Sparrows and finches do belong to the same family (Fringillidae) of the perching birds (order Passeriformes, class Aves), but they are different enough in subtle anatomical ways to be classified in separate genuses. The genus and species designations of the purple finch (*Carpodacus purpureus*) tell us more about the bird's proper place in the tree of life than Peterson's evocative metaphor.

Popular speech often muddies the water of understanding. Consider these examples from botany: The asparagus fern that grows at our kitchen window is not a fern at all. It is a seed-bearing plant of the lily family, although, superficially, it certainly looks more like a fern than a lily. The strawberry begonia, also called strawberry geranium, is not a strawberry, nor a begonia, nor a geranium, and is not in any of those plant families. It is instead *Saxifraga*, a genus closely related to the roses. It is the technical designations of the plants, not their popular names, that convey reality to the botanist. And here, in the forced retreat into specialized vocabularies, science begins to take on a cold and distant aura, and here also many people desert science for the easily accessible, anthropocentric metaphors of pseudoscience.

Ordinary language is so steeped in misconceptions that scientists often find it best to start from scratch, inventing purpose-made languages. In the introduction to his *Wildflower Guide*, Peterson lists sixty ways that a botanist can say that a plant is not smooth: aculeate, aculeolate, asperous, bristly, bullate, canescent, chaffy, ciliate, ciliolate, coriaceous, corrugated, downy, echinate, floccose, flocculent, glandular, glanduliferous, glumaceous, glutinous, hairy, hispid, hispidulous, and so on. The dictionary defines both "aculeate" and "echinate" as prickly, and one might reasonably ask why a good English word like prickly won't serve the purpose. The botanist, I am sure, has an answer, presumably involving subtle

shades of difference. Those shades of difference are the basis of the botanist's superior knowledge of plants. We can only know something if we can say it, so it is
perhaps inevitable that the language of science becomes more specialized as we
understand the world in ever greater detail. The Eskimos have a dozen words for
snow, and in the Arabic language there are thousands of words associated with
camels. If you live all of your life on snow or with camels, then a dozen, or even a
thousand words, are barely sufficient to describe your experience. And if your life
is devoted to the study of plants, then a stem that is aculeate or echinate may appear significantly different from one that is merely prickly.

Some linguists insist that the language we speak actually determines what
we see. This remarkable idea was first suggested by the nineteenth-century German philologist Wilhelm von Humboldt, who said, "Man lives with the world
about him, principally, indeed exclusively, as language presents it." In other
words, if you have a word for it, then it exists; if you don't have a word for it, it
doesn't exist. This idea was taken up in our own century by the linguist Edward
Sapir and his student Benjamin Lee Whorf, and has come to be known as the
Sapir-Whorf hypothesis. According to this school of thought, the vocabulary
and grammatical structure of a language place powerful constraints on how the
speaker perceives the world. Whorf's own work was primarily with the language
of the Hopi Indians of the American Southwest; he offered many examples of
how Hopi language and Hopi science go hand in hand, and how they differ in
significant ways from European languages and science.

Of course, the problem with the Sapir-Whorf hypothesis is the problem of
the chicken and the egg. Does language determine experience, or does experience determine language? (Which is another way of expressing the question
which began this essay: Does science describe reality, or does science invent reality?) In recent years the Sapir-Whorf hypothesis has gone rather out of fashion; nevertheless, the two linguists and their followers clearly demonstrated a
close connection between language and perception. All of which helps explain
why scientists find the need to invent specialized vocabularies. Words like bullate, glanduliferous, and hispid do not trip lightly from the tongue, but they are
well suited for their purpose. Each word gives precise expression to something
seen, and helps free perception from the muddy imprecisions of popular speech.

Philosopher of science John Ziman says this of scientific communication:
"Vivid phrases and literary elegances are frowned upon; they smell of bogus
rhetoric, or an appeal to the emotions rather than to reason. Public knowledge
can make its way in the world in sober, puritan garb; it needs no peacock feathers to cut a dash in." It is easy, even for the scientist, to regret the brusque in-
elegance of specialized scientific languages, and long for the graceful poet's
metaphor ("struggling in soft excitements"), but that is the price we pay for clarity of thought. Truth is not served by making the world conform to the soft con-

tours of our tongue. Language must be made to serve reality, rather than the other way around. Calling the asparagus fern a lily ("Perianth usually conspicuous, not chaffy, regular or nearly so, 6-parted; stamens hypogynous or adnate to the perianth; pistil 1; ovary 3-celled, usually superior") may offend common sense, but it makes perfect sense as science. And calling the purple finch "a sparrow dipped in raspberry juice" may be deliciously poetic, but — scientifically speaking — *Carpodacus purpureus* is the bird's real name.

TALKING ABOUT IT

Seeing Metaphor: Revealing and Concealing

1. Raymo writes that "[e]ven the sturdiest of scientific concepts is rooted in metaphor," and he goes on to list examples such as Newton's "clockwork" solar system and Boyle's elastic "spring" of air. He also writes, "Perhaps a course in metaphor should be as important a part of a scientist's training as a course in mathematics." Yet in his conclusion he suggests that scientists must avoid "the graceful poet's metaphor" in order to achieve "clarity of thought." Is there a contradiction here? What is Raymo ultimately saying about the place of metaphor in scientific thinking?

2. Raymo quotes a number of passages from Ted Hughes's collection of poems *Season Songs*. Choose one or two of these to "translate" into more straightforward prose such as a scientist might write. What happens to the metaphor? Does it get lost, or is it somehow embedded in the new prose?

Seeing Composition: Frame, Line, Texture, Tone

1. In paragraphs 2 and 3, Raymo relates the ancient Greek legend explaining the origin of the constellation Ursa Major and then his own "scientific" story of three of its stars. Do you find Raymo's own story "more fabulous than any myth of gods and nymphs," as he suggests?

2. How would you describe Raymo's voice here? Does he seem to be writing to other scientists, to general readers, or perhaps to both? What makes you think so?

Seeing Meaning: Navigating and Negotiating

1. At the beginning of his essay, Raymo poses the question "Does science describe reality, or does science invent reality?" How does he answer this question? What does it have to do with the points he makes about science and metaphor?

2. Raymo describes the Sapir-Whorf hypothesis as suggesting that "the vocabulary and grammatical structure of a language place powerful constraints on how the speaker perceives the world." What does this mean to you? What point does Raymo make with regard to this hypothesis?

WRITING ABOUT IT

1. Chet Raymo quotes Wilhelm von Humboldt who said "Man lives with the world about him, principally, indeed exclusively, as language presents it." "In other words," Raymo explains, "if you have a word for it, then it exists; if you don't have a word for it, it doesn't exist." To what extent can you support Raymo's assertion from your own experience with language? Offer an illustration of how learning a name affected your perception of the world. How does your story resonate with what Humboldt and Raymo are saying?

2. Raymo claims that scientists "are often trapped by tunnel vision." "Metaphors," he continues, "have a way of exploding the bounds of perception. . . . Great science often happens when likenesses are perceived where none were thought to exist." What he says can be true for nonscientists as well. Sometimes we see a striking likeness between two things, and we realize that we too had been trapped in a tunnel. Write about such an experience of your own, and describe how the boundaries of your perception expanded as a result of your ability to see likenesses.

What's in a Name? Sometimes More Than Meets the Eye

RICHARD CONNIFF

Richard Conniff is a natural history writer; his books include Spineless Wonders: Strange Tales from the Invertebrate World *(1996) and* Every Creeping Thing: A Book of Beasts *(1998). His writing has also been published in many periodicals, including* Architectural Digest, Audubon, Time, *and* Smithsonian, *where this selection appeared in December 1996.*

People who become zoologists generally do so in the face of sober parental warnings that their earthly rewards will be few and mostly of a dubious nature. And the parents, bless them, are dead right. You get a hint of this over lunch one day at the National Museum of Natural History (NMNH) when a researcher remarks with pride and ruefulness, "I've had two dung beetles named after me. And a louse."

It isn't the sort of thing a proud mother can hang on her wall, is it?

Among zoologists, having colleagues name a new species after you is what passes for immortality. But it can be an occasion for dread more than joy. Entomologist May Berenbaum became apprehensive after she discovered a new species and passed it on to an expert at the Smithsonian. "The last thing I need," Berenbaum fretted, "is for a beetle whose distinguishing feature is a proboscis fully half the length of its body to be known as Berenbaum's weevil."

The sort of animals most people would dream about having for namesakes — a gazelle, say, or a mountain bluebird — were taken long ago. New species nowadays tend to be invertebrates. In other words, you can still get your name put up in scientific lights, but mostly on the backs of strange, small creatures that the unenlightened public regards as, well, vermin. The good news is that, at least for now, there are lots of these creatures to go around. A Smithsonian researcher named Terry Erwin has taken extensive samples of ants, beetles and other life in the tropical rain forest canopy and demolished the old estimate that there are 1.5 million species on earth. He figures that there are actually more like 30 million, almost all of them insects in need of names.

This is a daunting nomenclatural challenge. Erwin has 1,500 species ready to 5 be named just in his narrow specialty of ground beetles of the genus *Agra*. He once called a difficult species *Agra vation* and another *Agra phobia*. A colleague, Arnold Menke, gave a genus a name giddy with the elixir of discovery, *Aha*. (One of the first species was even giddier, *Aha ha*.) But since there were already 8,000 known species in his specialty, the sphecid wasps, Menke also threatened to name his next such discovery in a scientific paper titled "*Ohno*, another new genus of sphecid wasp . . ."

Menke is the recording angel of offbeat zoological nomenclature. Until his recent retirement, he worked for the U.S. Department of Agriculture (USDA) in a fourth-floor office at NMNH and kept what appeared to be the business card of a Bulgarian rug merchant on the door:

Vyizder Zomenimor

Orziz Assiz

Zanzer R. Orziz

Repeat this two or three times. If you get the joke, you may have missed your true calling: creating the sort of bizarre scientific names Menke has collected over the years. Among them are a fly named *Phthiria relativitae* and a spider named *Draculoides bramstokeri*, a pair of musical chiggers in the genus *Trombicula* named *doremi* and *fasolla*. (OK, you didn't get the joke. It's actually one of the world's last great unsolved zoological and philosophical mysteries: "Vy iz der zo many more horse's azziz . . .")

Naming a new species is a serious business, of course, and the rules are complicated enough to fill 338 pages of the *International Code of Zoological Nomenclature*. But they boil down to just about the same system of scientific classification that the Swedish botanist Carolus Linnaeus first devised in the 1750s. Every plant or animal must have two names, a genus identifying the group to which it belongs and a species to distinguish it from other members of the same genus. These names are usually constructed on Greek or Latin lines. But Linnaeus wasn't trying to turn the biological world into an outpost of Eurocentric cultural imperialism. He merely wanted scientists to agree on one universally accepted name for every species to avoid befuddling one another with a vast array of different local names.

Linnaeus left plenty of room in his system for scientists to coin names from almost any multicultural phenomenon. Menke and his colleague David Vincent have named wasps *Polemistus chewbacca* and *P. yoda*, in honor of two well-known extraterrestrials. Likewise, there is a fish called *Zappa confluentus* named after Frank Zappa; a fossil turtle genus *Ninjemys*, named after that totally rad, fearsome foursome, the Teenage Mutant Ninja Turtles; and a crustacean genus *Godzillius*, named after Godzilla.

10   Smithsonian biologist Clyde Roper (*Smithsonian*, May 1996) once named a whole family of squid Batoteuthis, from the Greek *batos*, meaning "thornbush," because the squid has a long, thornlike tail and large, bushy clubs. But this was also the middle of the Batman craze, and if you look closely at the illustrations accompanying Roper's article in a learned oceanographic journal, you may notice a tiny bat of unknown species flying out of the squid's oviduct. (Roper protests that he thought the editors would white it out.)

"Scientific names have much in common with crossword puzzles," a lepidopterist writes, and if the person coining a name "can mystify his fellow entomologists, he will derive sadistic pleasure in so doing." Hidden meanings are commonplace. For example, the formidable *Brachyanax thelestrephones* translates as "little chief nipple twister." The originator, Neal Evenhuis of Hawaii's Bishop Museum, says it has something to do with the shape of this bee fly's antennae.

The fly called *Dicrotendipes thanatogratus* comes from the Greek word for "dead" and the Latin word for "grateful" and was coined in 1987, by an entomological Deadhead. Other names damn while seeming to praise. *Dinohyus hollandi,* for example, is a small extinct species named for W. J. Holland, who was director of the Carnegie Museum and a popular writer on moths and butterflies. But Holland apparently made some enemies, because the name, loosely translated, means "Holland is a terrible pig." A more broadly misanthropic urge also sometimes seems to take hold of a scientist, as when Menke named a wasp species *Pison eu.* There is also a snail called *Ba humbugi* and a chigger named *Trombicula fujigmo,* the latter to commemorate a slang term once common among American soldiers being sent home at the end of World War II. If you had never heard how G.I.'s really talk, you could translate the acronym "fujigmo" as "Fie on you, Jack, I got my orders."

There are scientists who frown on such shenanigans. As Menke stepped out of the elevator one day recently, a colleague remarked that in his days as a journal editor he never allowed odd scientific names. "I thought they lent taxonomy to ridicule," he added dourly. Menke shrugged and said, "Some people don't have any fun."

People like Menke, a boyish 62-year-old with a gray beard and long hair swept back over his collar, spend most of their careers hunched over microscopes. Their job is to distinguish between obscure but almost identical insect species on the basis of body parts most people have never even heard of—the clypeus on a wasp's face, say, or the epandrium on a horsefly's behind. For the most part, they confer dutifully descriptive names, like *longicornis* (long antennae) or *megacephalus* (big- or maybe fat-headed). They publish their results in respectable scientific journals to be duly noted by the world's three or four other experts on bees' knees.

Yet they love their work, these humble taxonomists, and every once in a 15 while a wild impulse of delight drives one of them to fling off the fetters of convention. On the brink of his retirement, for instance, a USDA wasp guy and Menke pal named Paul Marsh published a paper naming one species *Verae peculya,* another species *Heerz tooya* and another *Heerz lukenatcha.*

Sometimes thoughts of love inspire a taxonomist, as when the English entomologist George Kirkaldy named several genera of bugs *Peggichisme* (or "Peggy kiss me"), *Polychisme, Dolichisme* and, a little too ardently, *Ochisme.* Carl Heinrich, who was a USDA lepidopterist in the first half of the century, once told an entire short story in scientific names. In 1923, he called a genus *Gretchena*, after a woman with whom he presumably was involved. Heinrich went on to name species *Gretchena delicatana* (delicate), *dulciana* (sweet), *amatana* (beloved) and *concubitana* (possessed). The tale ended sadly with *Gretchena deludana* (deceived).

Curious scientific names also played a role in some sleuthing undertaken recently by Marc Epstein, a lepidopterist at the Smithsonian, and Pamela Henson, who is the Institution's historian. They were researching the life of Harrison G. Dyar jr., a Smithsonian entomologist early in this century. Dyar is remembered, officially, for having propounded something called "Dyar's law of geometric growth" and for bringing more precise standards to entomological taxonomy. Unofficially, he is celebrated for a life of bugs, bickering and bigamy. Epstein and Henson first tracked down one of the most celebrated myths in zoological nomenclature, that the quarrelsome Dyar named a species *corpulentis* after an obese rival, and that the rival in turn retaliated by naming a moth species, in his honor, *dyaria*. Sadly, the tale is false: Dyar seems to have done plenty of nasty things to the rival in question, but he never named a species *corpulentis* after him. The genus name *Dyaria* was coined by a New York banker who simply suffered from a tin ear. He was an amateur lepidopterist and cited Dyar as his "faithful co-labourer and friend," apparently under the impression that he was paying him an honor.

But as Epstein and Henson researched Dyar's life, they began to discuss another moth species that Dyar had named *P. wellesca*. It reminded them of "tales more lurid in nature." For years odd rumors had circulated around the Smithsonian that Dyar had a second family, that mysterious tunnels connected his two homes and that his bigamous deception fell apart when his children from both families discovered at a high school function that they shared a father with a passion for insects.

According to Epstein and Henson, Dyar did indeed own the house next door to the one where he lived with his first wife, Zella, and their children, but he used it mainly for rearing moth and mosquito larvae (and possibly also for getting away from his mother-in-law). His third house, however, was home to his spiritual adviser, Wellesca Pollock, whom he married in 1906, apparently under an assumed name. But this house was blocks from Zella's and no tunnels connected the dwellings. According to Epstein and Henson, digging tunnels aimlessly was merely "an eccentric hobby" for Dyar, who seems to have enjoyed a superabundance of energy. Oddly, considering his ability to quarrel with almost everyone else, Dyar seems to have maintained warm relations with both women and their five children. He came up with the name *P. wellesca* in 1900. In 1927, perhaps in the interests of taxonomic and romantic balance, he named a species *zellans* after his first wife, whom he didn't divorce until 1916. Epstein says Dyar also named species for "zillions" of other women along the way.

None of this seems terribly surprising, when you remember that scientists,   20
too, belong to that most hapless of species, *Homo sapiens.*

Linnaeus himself seems to have understood the human knack for folly. He
created the Linnaean system to bring order and harmony to the biological
world — but one of the first species he named was *Chaos chaos.*

TALKING ABOUT IT

Seeing Metaphor: Revealing and Concealing

1. There's a certain power involved in being able to name a new species. According to the examples given here, in what different ways do scientists seem
   to regard that power?

2. One scientist whom Conniff quotes likens scientific names to crossword
   puzzles. What does this scientist mean? What else does scientific naming
   seem like to you?

Seeing Composition: Frame, Line, Texture, Tone

1. Notice how Conniff structures his essay. Why do you think he waits until
   his fifth paragraph to introduce his first example of a humorous scientific
   name and his eighth to explain the Linnaean system of naming? Why does
   his point that some scientists "frown on such shenanigans" come in the
   middle of the essay? And why do you think the long story about Harrison
   Dyar comes just before his conclusion?

2. Conniff translates or explains most of the names he mentions, but there are
   a number that readers must figure out for themselves. Why do you think he
   doesn't explain these? Are there any for which you couldn't figure out the joke?

Seeing Meaning: Navigating and Negotiating

1. What does this essay suggest to you about how zoologists work together
   and about how they view their work?

2. If you had the opportunity to name a new genus and species, how would
   you go about choosing that name?

WRITING ABOUT IT

1. Pretend you are a taxonomist who has the pleasure of naming some new
   species belonging to a genus. You could be someone like Terry Erwin, who
   had many species ready to be named within the genus *Agra.* Two names he

invented were *Agra vation* and *Agra phobia.* Or you could be another Arnold Menke, giddy over discovering a new genus, which he named *Aha,* and then naming the first species *Aha ha.*

Coin names for your discoveries, following the system of identifying the genus (the group to which the plant or animal belongs) and species (the name that distinguishes one member of the group from another). As is the case for some taxonomists, your inspiration could derive from any multicultural phenomenon: popular musicians, cartoons, movie monsters or superheroes; or you could follow some impulse of your own. Whichever source you use, try to mystify your fellow scientists with unusual spelling, inventing fake Latin names for the little creatures. You might even draw the animals next to their names. Then follow your list of discoveries and illustrations with the history of your naming process. In class, you could exchange only the illustrations and names to see if others can guess the "hidden meanings."

2. Consider the names of streets where you live now or where you grew up, or consider the names of particular buildings in a town (its banks, for example, or its campus buildings), or consider names in a family. After you have listed them, look for patterns and try to get at the logic of the names, the principle behind the naming.

Naming Nature

REG SANER

Reg Saner, poet and essayist, is the author of Climbing into the Roots
(1976), So This Is the Map *(1981),* Essay on Air *(1984), and* Reaching Keet Seel: Ruins' Echo and the Anasazi *(1998). He teaches
English and creative writing at the University of Colorado. The following piece is from his nonfiction collection,* The Four-Cornered
Falcon: Essays on the Interior West and the Natural Scene *(1993).*

Why do we care to know a plant's or animal's right name? And what do
we know when we know it? Syllables?

In the Swiss Alps one July afternoon I was aboard a cog-rail train gearing
itself steeply up from the great, green, glacial valley at Lauterbrunnen toward
Kleine Scheidegg. There, between the Eiger and the Jungfrau, I overheard a sort
of primal phase in naming nature. At a half-open window of the train, and with
her dark curls breezing across her eyes, a French toddler squinted into the sun at
some grazing cattle, Swiss browns, a whole herd of them. Because she was just
learning the world, she pointed her tiny index finger out the window, "*Oh-h-h,*"
she said, with the rising note of discovery that toddlers have, "*les chevaux!*"

Five-second pause.

Then, murmuring it almost inaudibly, that toddler's barely older sister
said, "*les vaches . . . les vaches.*"

It sounded like both a correction and a memo to herself: "Not all big ones   5
eating the meadow are horses. Some are cows."

Soon her baby sister would also see that. Because she would *want* to. We
name this spontaneous desire "coming into language," and we marvel that no
grown-up, however ravenous, can match a child's hunger for names; but since a
toddler's word-hunger is her gusto for this manifold earth, we might as well call
it "coming into the world."

So far as I could tell, though, this particular little one hadn't quite come
into the world's bovine phase yet. A shadow of puzzlement crossed her expression. "Not horses? But they are big, they go slow on lots of legs, and they are eating the grass up." She saw, kind of. In the cow/horse blur, distinctions gross
enough to us just weren't out there for her. The impulse to say a name, however,
was as eager as her openness to language — and therefore to the world — was
wide. "*Oh-h-h! Les chevaux!*" So, ever since, that herd of misnomered cows has
gone on browsing for me in a child's eye, the most memorable blur I've ever
heard spoken.

Several summers later, back in Colorado, I groped for a name out of a frustrated impulse far from any childlike innocence. Wanting to identify roadside

stalks whose sky-blue blossoms I'd been jogging past for years, I couldn't. Nobody I asked knew what to call them. Nobody I asked seemed to mind not knowing. I minded a lot. "What *is* the name of that stuff?" Its pithy stalks and blue petals had brushed against my socks and calves by the half mile. "Inconceivable," I said to myself, "that nobody around here can say what it is." Were the blooms any less beautiful for being dirt common?

My botanist friend, William Weber, could have immediately told me the plant's names in English and Latin, and much more. But why bother him, formidable taxonomist, with an identification so easy? After all, I owned a thumb-soiled copy of his field guide, *Rocky Mountain Flora*. He knew I owned it. And in improving on a system of naming begun in the eighteenth century by a young Swede named Carl Linnaeus, hadn't Weber planned every least particular of its nearly five hundred pages — dense with detail — to make the book useful to people like me? He had. Was I going to admit, despite all that tradition and care behind it, his guide resisted my powers? I wasn't, till I did. "Oh," he said, "that's chicory."

10   Later I looked it up in his *Rocky Mountain Flora*: "*Cichorium intybus.* Introduced and locally established as a roadside weed on the plains and piedmont valleys." In learning its name was I really the wiser? Field guides aren't encyclopedias. What surface had I scratched in gratifying the trivial itch of curiosity? True, ever since, in passing those gawky, angular stalks of cerulean blossom, it has felt good to say "chicory . . . chicory." But why? What had those syllables given me? What did I know now, that I hadn't known, except for their sound? Nothing I knew how to name.

Perhaps a *Field Guide to Human Curiosity* would identify these questions as "roadside weeds of the mind." Nonetheless, with the acquisition of *chicory* my vague sense of what we know when we know a name began to sharpen focus: we know a satisfaction. Though true, perhaps primevally so, it's an answer that at once begets the next question, "Why?" Am I lying to myself when I say I had felt indebted as I ran, had felt I *owed* it to the intense chicory-blue of those petals, often backlit by sunrise, to learn their right name?

We do well to be suspicious of noble motives, especially our own. Our impulses aren't often unalloyed. Mine may have been low as pride, even lower: mere vanity, which, etymologically speaking, means "empty." Had empty conceit that *I* should know, even if no one around me did — had that impelled me to acquire *chicory*? I'd sag a little and confess, "Guilty as charged, as usual," if it hadn't been for the passionate, sunfire blue of those petals. In decency, I did seem to *owe* them their name, however arbitrary I know names to be.

"Come off it," cool reason mutters. "Indebted to petals? Hogwash!" The analytic mind doesn't admit of petals being *owed* anything. They're just bee-bait contrived by scheming vegetation. From reason, of course, there is no appeal. All the same, the day we don't feel we owe this world a grace note of response, we ought to be wrapped in graph paper and mailed fourth class to the Bureau of Statistics.

Without bowing to reason on what we might owe even to "weeds," I do confess that pride has its share in wanting to know plant names. Which of our acquisitions isn't it part of? Nonetheless, before considering that pride might itself be alloyed with urges less trivial, it may be well to face that seamy side of expertise open-eyed and unblinking.

Whether in the woods or a public garden we've all met sharks among the   15 botanicals. These are the people who vent aggressive relish in bandying names of, say, wild grasses which—as they rightly suppose—are to us quite anonymous. Lacking a window into souls, I can't be sure; yet it does seem that anyone tossing off names such as "sloughgrass," "brome," "three-awn," "tufted hairgrass," "muhly," "false melic," or "little bluestem," and doing so with nonchalance, may be less a friend of the earth than of the performing arts.

My sister Rose Marie isn't really a shark. She likes flowering plants wholeheartedly. She also likes to be good at things. Long ago our family recognized her as the brainy one. No vote was needed, nor were her straight As and scholarships the least surprising. Once, having driven from St. Louis to visit me for a tour in western Colorado, no sooner had her tires stopped rolling then she was out of the car naming flora all over the place. She was strongest on blossoms, none of which had she ever seen except in her wildflower book.

Pacing ahead of me along a trail leading south from Mesa Verde, she kept scoring well and aloud, her extended index finger indicating "Fireweed?"—at which cue I would nod, or say "Yes." Then a few meters further, "Broomrape?" Yes, again. Within minutes, my own seminative acquaintance with Western plants had thus come into play. And into question. Under the fragrant shade of cliff rose she would pause, sniff at its pale yellow blossoms, pleased yet baffled, then deter to my years in the West: "This must be . . . oh, it's on the tip of my tongue, it just has to be a . . ." Frustrated shrug. "Help me out here, Reg. *You* know." Often I did, not always. Her joy in seeing live blooms previously met only in books kept our stroll from becoming a wildflower *mano-a-mano*. Then too, aside from liking to be good at things, a sister named Rose Marie may well have felt that she, especially, owed our flora its names.

Pride leading to a literal indebtedness revealed itself one desert morning at Joshua Tree National Monument. There, not much east of Indio, California, with frond-splashes of date trees dangling clustered fruit, I inhaled cool dawn while drawing water into canteens. At the campground spigot another early bird arrived with her water jugs.

"Do you know what that plant is?" I asked her, nodding toward what looked like a somewhat cousin to tamarisk. It grew languid and wispy everywhere about us, in bushes up to eight feet high.

She was pretty, about thirty-five, with lively, intelligent eyes. "I know to my   20 cost, literally. I bet my husband $20 it was cottonwood. But it's creosote."

"Cottonwood! You were really dumb," I said. And she laughed.

Neither of us would've done well in Eden. There, without resort to field guides, Adam—perhaps seated on the greensward under the Tree of Knowledge—casually named all the animals. Did Adam, Eve, and the Creator speak the same language? Presumably our first parents uttered a language which, like everything else in Eden, was created word perfect. A charming implication of the accounts in Genesis, therefore, is that Adam's prelapsarian intellect required the merest glimpse of any animal to say not just *a* name. Each oracular guess conferred that animal's *right* name. This gift even has a fancy name of its own: onomathesia. With the Fall, however, Adam and Eve lost more than the Garden's ideal ecology; the right names of everything were effaced from their sin-dimmed intellects. Those angels who evicted them while brandishing flames for swords might as well have put a road sign over the gate leading forever outward from Eden: "Exit Spoken Perfection."

And enter confusion with the Tower of Babel, our planet. In its linguistic history since Eden, how many different bits of shaped air have human tongues coined for the kind of creature Adam and Eve thought they were? How many names for the moon? How many different moon-names are being spoken over the globe right now?

If our own minds were as rich in right words as Eve's vocabulary unfallen, if we her sons and daughters could speak rightly of each plant, animal, and mineral variant to every species within every genus, how many names would we know? At the threshold of the twenty-first century, those best informed still haven't any idea. The two-volume *Synopsis and Classification of Living Organisms* edited by S. P. Parker draws on the global expertise of other biologists to list some 1.4 million living species already described. To name insects alone would call for half that total. But once we got all those insects by heart, naming known plants would seem easy—a quarter million. Beetle species, for example, if fully inventoried, might number nearly a million, since well over 250,000 kinds have been cataloged. Then there'd be the spineless animals—protozoans, worms, jellyfish, corals, mollusks. We vertebrates amount to a mere 40,000.

25   But if like our ancestor Adam we're going to name *all* the animals, micro and macro, protozoan to elephant, the known and the yet-to-be-discovered, how many names will we need? Using selected habitats on which extensive field studies have been done, E. O. Wilson, a specialist in social insects, supposes that the full inventory *of insects alone* "is likely to exceed 5 million." Wilson admits to be guessing, admits no one has more than a rough estimate. Recently, at a conference on biodiversity, in underlining the wildness of our present surmise, he claimed that there's really no telling. Earth could have 5, 10, or 30 million different species. "There is no theory," according to Wilson, "that can predict what this number might turn out to be." Despite our expensive itch to colonize the red sterilities of Mars, any child can name every single life form on Mars with closed lips. Earth is far more truly the unexplored planet.

Our Anglo-Saxon forebears, on whose lips Old English evolved, knew nothing of such abundance, of course, nor were they sticklers in nomenclature. "Worm," for example, they applied to whatever crept or looked like it wanted to, whether serpent, tapeworm, nightcrawler, or Northumbria's specialty, dragons. Similarly, the countrymen of Aethelstan and Aelfric might call "fish" any swimming or water-dwelling thing: whale, shark, sea otter, herring, starfish, crayfish, or clam. Anatomically, of course, the gap between mollusk and crab—both "shellfish" even today—is wider than that separating a trout from Cleopatra.

Obviously, more sharply focused names imply the distinctions of closer knowledge. One assumes the Anglo-Saxon eye could see particulars its vague naming doesn't signal, but how vague can labeling become without betraying fuzziness in our view of the world?

Recently I did a wholly unscientific survey among university students to learn how many of them could name aspects of Colorado's natural environment, including things seen almost daily. My sole "method" was to choose questions as simple and as general as possible; and to choose for subjects students who had said they wanted to write about nature. Next to biology majors, you'd expect such a group to be especially keen on naming things.

My one-sheet questionnaire began with Boulder's celebrated "Flatirons," mountainous rock formations rising abruptly as cliffs just a few minutes west of where my students were gathered, and as distinctive to Boulder as Vesuvius is to Naples. "Do you know what the Flatirons formations are made of?" (The answer is sandstone; more specifically, conglomerate sandstone.) Though each student had scrambled among those rocks, sunning, climbing, or just chatting atop great hunks of the stuff, few had looked closely. Here is a fair sample of their answers: "granite?", "slate!", "Big ones," "I suppose maybe slate," "granite," "granite," "sandstone," "don't know," "granite, slate," "red rock," "?", "sandstone?", "sandstone," "granite?", "sedimentary."

Next I asked each person, "What's the name of that big black-and-white bird 30 with the long black tail?" (Because magpies are omnipresent in Boulder, I was able to point out the window at one.) More than half knew its name, the others groped. Responses like "lark bunting," "I've often wondered," "?", or "not real sure" were typical. Though magpie plumage is an everyday sight, 40 percent of my group were content to let our gaudiest bird fly anonymously through their lives.

So much for ornithology. I then tried mule deer. Boulder's western edges abound in them. They poke around neighborhoods, gourmandize from lawn to lawn, nibble tree bark, browse on expensive bushes, nip our roses in the bud, lounge by the half-dozen in backyards, and savor the best that town and country munching can offer. To use a medieval expression for tame, they've become man-sweet. Did my would-be writers know what *kind* of deer? Not really. Oh, three students correctly said "mule deer," while most said "white tail," and one or two admitted "no idea," "not sure."

In every time and clime, I realize, students have had keener eyes for wildlife in each other than for local fauna. So be it. Aside from sparrows, squirrels, and ambling dogs, however, few Boulder animals could be more common than magpies or mule deer. One would have thought *not* knowing would nag at "I've often wondered" until it felt like privation. Doesn't curiosity aim at satisfying *feeling*? After all, the moment a girl sees a boy she likes the look of, doesn't she ask, "What's his name?" Every time. Though her conscious motives may feel intensely practical, her question comes of an urge older than she dreams.

While I'm unclear on linkage between feeling, seeing, and naming, clearly there is one. My itch to learn *chicory* was somehow involved in it, to the extent that I took sharper, better informed looks at its structure after each fruitless search in my guidebook. Even learning to distinguish evergreens can involve an interaction between the eye and desire — as I discovered one summer.

When I was a boy, anything but the grossest conifer distinctions summed up that particular vanishing point in my knowledge. To me they were either "evergreens" or "pines." Same difference. Then one day a couple of decades ago while hiking under Avery Peak near Gothic, Colorado, I was determined to see better. Perhaps because the July morning felt as buoyant as its cumulus puffs scudding west to east overhead, and because it felt — at nine thousand feet — just comfortably warm, even in shadow, I had resolved to walk along consulting tall trunk after trunk until I could *see* why "blue spruce," "white spruce," "white fir," "subalpine fir," "Engelmann spruce," "one-seed juniper," and "Rocky Mountain juniper" were needed in the tree lexicon. But to see minor distinctions in conifers takes energy we may not recognize for what it really is: a form of desire.

35   My way led up a steep mining road built and abandoned in the last century. Its sole traffic that morning were shade-tolerant wildflowers and me. And thistles. On one thistle a little higher than my head I counted, in its opulence of prickled leaves, 103 buds. What ambition! So amid the agreeable evergreen glooms of forest, and blossoms repossessing a rock road whose patches of high-country sunlight made its mica facets dazzle, I stepped slowly along — hoping to note instant difference. I wanted to murmur "white spruce" or "blue spruce," "white fir" or "Douglas fir" at first glance.

Fools do rush in. Little did I realize, then, a trained botanist might well have said, "Good luck." I've since learned that even an adept can't always tell a conifer's species on sight.

Any other morning, the seed-catalog lavishness of July's high-country flowers would have distracted me. There were subalpine Jacob's ladder, lousewort; and marsh marigolds pale as winter butter, growing low in their microbogs. And lavender daisies, called — among other things — fleabane. Then too, purple loco weed not quite the blue-purple of Wyeth's lupine in ditches, nor yet the midnight purple of larkspur or monkshood. And of course the incendiary red of Indian paintbrush, the hot magenta of fireweed. All of them consorting to

produce the kind of a morning that memory likes to build on. But my tree identifying made blossoms just a fringe benefit.

I'd long since noticed that two fir seedlings, for example, from virtually the
same cone may grow so much unlike each other as to seem different species.
Where it takes root can and does greatly alter a tree's character, which can be
virtually disguised by conditions its seed chanced to light among. All that
forenoon, therefore, I consulted my botanical guide with its "keys," a garden of
printed synapses that fork, fork further, fork again, and keep forking, like the
Tree of Life itself. Take one wrong turn looking up a conifer, you may end lost in
pages devoted to *umbelliferae,* staring at a drawing of "Alpine parsley." Guidebook? It can be a jungle in there.

Meanwhile I tried very hard to learn every which way a Douglas fir might
grow that a white fir couldn't mimic. And vice versa. It was a process teaching
me how much of what we call eyesight is *wanting* to see. Small wonder that, cytologically speaking, retinal tissue and brain tissue are cousins. Eyes seem to be
the mind leaning forward.

The trees I conversed with and sampled! From spruce twigs I plucked nee-   40
dles for examining under my magnifier, and winced each time like a small
brother pulling his sister's hair. Did I really believe those spruce boughs felt
pain? Ever so remotely. Being wood didn't mean they were wooden. Their
chloroplasts and phloem cells and photosynthetic sugars, their rows of leaf pores
fine as dust on a bug, their root-imbibed minerals were alive and breathing, as I
was. Same era, same season, same hour. Under the blue sky's wisps of cloud I
knew that soon the morning and I would have already happened. Soon "today"
would become "long ago." As a spruce cone fell toward the half repossessed road,
I knew that soon it would have hit and rotted away in a distant century, which
was this one, mine while I lasted. Knee-high fir seedlings whose as yet unhard-
ened needles I stroked for their suppleness would rise to be great-hearted trunks
still here three hundred years from the moment I bent to touch them. Impossible not to be touched, in turn, by all the chances any great tree must run, growing toward its long continuance.

How many times did I stuff the guidebook back into my pack "once and
for all" — then fifty yards further along pluck it with a resigned sigh back out
again? Ever so slowly, however, distinctions began coming clear. Or clearer. *I
began to see difference in sameness.*

Wouldn't the earliest language have had to grow its store of thing-words
the same way? For example, "that!" in post-Edenic proto-Indo-European must
have narrowed through millennia past numbering to something like "tree," which
in turn would have split — whatever their actual sounds — into versions of
"cone tree" and "tree of no cones," with each of those splitting — again, however
crudely — into practicalities simple as "edible" and "not edible" or "good wood"
and "wood not so good." It might be a long time before the earliest speakers

needed to see any difference not related to use. But the word hoard would grow with that need, *as difference got spoken*. It might require 500,000 years for a word like *tree* to beget the syllabic differences needed for naming kinds of trees in a forest; nonetheless, even if the very first vocal noise for tree begot and gave birth to its offspring unimaginably more slowly than an actual forest ramifies from one cone, it would, at last, reproduce the forest in words. The longer our species carefully looked into it, the more our language would receive in return.

We may weary of hearing that Inuits have lots of names for snow — certainly I myself find it wearisome — but not of realizing how needed those names are. For seeing by. For finding our way. In a whiteout, in level terrain so very near the magnetic pole, snow's texture, direction, granulation, incrustations, may be the only workable compass. Desire to see difference in sameness could hardly be stronger. Similarly, rain-forest dwellers have a wealth of ways to say more than just "tree," but know only one or two sky words.

Thus in trying to coax differences from my generic sense of "evergreen" or "conifer," in trying to see ways "firs" have taken that "pines" haven't, in matching the syllables "white fir" to its distinction from "Douglas fir" and "subalpine fir," I felt myself crudely rehearsing the invention of speech, which is as much as to say the birth of my species. Whatever the truth of that conjecture may be, features under my nose also conspired to make me feel like a tree dunce. "Oh," I kept saying to myself as one or another hitherto invisible variant in cone shape or twig pattern declared itself, "how obvious!" Not all such distinctions were. Some required squinting through a pocket lens. I could just hear my friend Hal asking, "Is it worth all that bother?" To me, yes. But the more interesting question remains. Why?

45   Beyond utility, beyond the satisfaction of seeing more clearly, the deepest urge may, I suspect, be primeval. Not the urge to dawdle along the gash of a wagon road being healed by forest. Instead, toward naming. I further suspect that our other motives grow like trunk and branches out of that taproot. In saying some names have "charm" we use a syllable derived from chants and spells rooted in magic; so remarking a thing has charm doesn't go far enough. Once upon a time, certain names *were* charms.

In special cases, to name was to cause, to cause to befall, even to create. The history of religion teems with examples of sacral names that contained or conferred real power, power devoutly believed in as real, just as anthropology has yet to discover primitives who consider names arbitrary. Whereas *we* know that a rose by any other word would smell as sweet, it's highly unlikely that humankind's earliest speakers believed it would.

Twentieth-century children of technology reflect traces of that ancient attitude especially when they begin study of a foreign language. Annually, every high school French teacher sees primitive behavior reenacted. Like Sisyphus, he or she must once again struggle uphill against heavy resistance to the idea that

English names are somehow true to their objects, whereas French names for the same things are unnatural. Students *know* better. Exchanging students with schools in France, however, leaves untouched their deepest levels, where the primitive feeling that a thing *is* its name still resides. Annually, therefore, that language teacher's more callow students will feel in their bones that the French way of talking goes against reality. No matter how many million French kids call trees and snow "*les arbres*" and "*la neige,*" calling those things by those names is worse than effeminate, worse than absurd. It's wrong.

In fact, there is the story of the sixteenth-century Englishman arguing that French and Spanish are less logical than English: "The French call a fish *poisson,* and the Spanish call it *pescado,* whereas we call it what it really is, a *fish.*"

The most naive present-day speaker, however, will scarcely feel that naming brings a thing into being. Our talking avatars seem to have felt otherwise. And more. Felt that without its right name a thing couldn't fully exist as itself. An obvious vestige of that feeling appears in the first dozen lines of Genesis: "And God said, Let there be light: and there was light. . . . And God called the light Day, and the darkness he called Night." The sequence of creating and naming then proceeds through the firmament, named "Heaven," dry land called "Earth," the waters called "the Seas," and so forth. This link between word and words pervades the Old Testament. Psalm 30 offers merely one instance among dozens: "By the word of the Lord were the heavens made; and all the host of them by the breath of his mouth. . . . For he spake, and it was done." In the beginning was the name.

On the other hand, though God created the animals, it was Adam who   50 named them: "And out of the ground the Lord God formed every beast of the field, and every fowl of the air; and brought them to Adam to see what he would call them: and whatsoever Adam called every living creature, that was the name thereof. And Adam gave names to all cattle, and to the fowl of the air, and to every beast of the field." Here the relation between creating and naming modulates to naming as charm or empowerment. God's naming of elements in the cosmos implies that He alone controlled those elements; similarly, Adam's naming the animals implies the power humankind was to have over earth's creatures.

Some of our ancestors either misliked or ignored that distinction, and backslid into the more primitive view. Mythic variants preserved in the Midrash, the Cabbala, and in gnostic lore credit Adam the namer of animals with having created the cosmos itself! These underground variants make Adam the source and origin of the universe. Before it existed, he was. And was hugely good looking. His colossal stature filled up the whole world.

Earlier but still within what is now the Near East, passages in the Babylonian poem called the Gilgamesh epic parallel the implication in Genesis that creating the cosmos goes hand in hand with naming sky, earth, and water. Their nebulous existences may precede naming, but they can't be fully present in the world till their right names are assigned. Gods too. One verse in the Gilgamesh poem speaks of a time when "none of the gods were created, and as yet had no names."

Worldwide, in fact, various myths reflect the feeling that a thing can't fully and properly exist without its name. From skies far greyer and chillier than Eden's, the Norse Eddic poem *Völuspa* illustrates this sense of nameless things not yet fully themselves:

> From the south the sun, the moon's mate,
> Passed its right hand along the sky's edges
> Not knowing where it should dwell;
> Neither did the stars know their own places
> Nor the moon, how strong her own light.
>
> Then all the spirits gathered in council
> The sacred gods and discussed the matter:
> Night they gave a name to, and to the new moon,
> Named both the morn and midday, then sundown
> And twilight, so the years might be counted.

If names can translate, charm, empower, and create, they may also invoke. The annals of our human past abound with instances. Through a name's invocation, the named reveals its nature. Five years ago I was surprised to find myself at the spoken center of just such an occurrence. It was a snowy evening, late March — the thirty-first in fact — but its twilight was dim and wintery. Stalled snow clouds covered the upper half of Boulder Mountain. Heading home, I had stopped out on a mesa near my house and, squinting through the slant of clumped flakes, had made out ground-feeding birds in unusual numbers. Their dark forms went flitting and hopping low over the new snow on winter-beaten field-weed which earlier snows had long since lodged. Maybe it was the murk of that overcast, saying at the very sill of April, "How about another helping of wet snow?" Whatever the cause, my mood was a touch rueful; that is, it was until I came upon those birds. Their blithe darting and pecking so lifted my spirits that I stopped in my tracks, the better to watch.

55 Sure enough, the dozens that had startled into the air from a cluster of small ponderosa pines began now to reconsider. They twittered a while among stark naked twigs they'd fled to; then, a few at a time, took wing again, back to the much cosier shelter of those pines. Which were but a step or two from me, living statue. By now quite a lot of snow had accumulated in the blue folds of my parka, on my boot tops, my hood. Gradually, by cautious hops a bird came closer, pecking into withered tufts that poked up through snow, beaking insects or seeds, cocking a wary eye at me as if considering; then hopping closer, closer yet, till within inches of my boots. I stayed budgeless. Soon others followed, a

few tentative hops at a time. Apparently I was standing amid an especially food-sown patch; but had disappeared. Had become part of the scenery. Up close, despite snowfall and dusk thickened almost to night, I finally could see to name them: "Bluebirds!"

At the word's invocation they at once revealed themselves fully — through good omens condensed in its syllables. Thus invoked, they became an apparition transforming both the weather and me. My touch of the sullens vanished. "Snow or no snow, these are bluebirds!"

Rationalizing, we admit that a name's invocatory power comes of what's already condensed within. Unlike primitives, we know that any name "reveals" only what our own prior experiences have hidden inside it. Semantically stored knowledge and feelings may, when conditions are right, thereby release like wings fluttering from a magician's hat the moment we say "white pigeons." But since context alters content, the auspicious revelations that "bluebird" summons — in containing them — may be intensified by an opposite such as "snow." That's why any particular name, differing from itself, never reveals exactly the same things twice. What's released depends on where and how that name occurs.

Altering its context can show an apparently limited syllable like *rose* to be encyclopedic. Which is to say that nature's names are both sounds and living relationships. Even as concept, words like *forest* and *ocean* stand for a deep and teeming plenitude whose highly individual many are one, and, at the same time, less a thing than a spatial experience. Pronounced alone in a low exhalation, *forest* can create what it names. Can place the pronouncer inside it.

All this is so. Nonetheless, to deny that words both name and fail to name would be dishonest. If they reveal they also conceal, and we know it. As far as that goes, don't most truths include their own opposites? On the level of folk wisdom alone, you could make an anthology of such marriages, proverbial "truths" paired antithetically, each partner contradicting its mate.

So, having learned to name "magpie," we'd be lazy to let our seeing stop at the plane of a name, which is to "see" dismissively. We need to look past language to discover, for example, what rich iridescences a magpie's "black" feathers can show: dark emeralds, dark azures, hints of deep burgundy almost not visible — their prismatic wealth refracted in preen oil. "Black-and-white" doesn't touch it. Here I must plead guilty again. Because magpies are identifiable at the most distant glance, I've often watched one after another swoop down from our foothill mountains, and failed to see past their name. So I was years in realizing how different from other corvids their wing management is in dipping and gliding. In the same way, just as we must look past *wing* to see what a wing truly is, we must look past *bird* to see the strangeness in our sky's having animals. To name is, yes, to know. But only to know better, far from completely, and never once and for all.

More important perhaps than a name's cover-up of details is its blurring of the fact that each thing is really an *event,* thus a confluence of forces still in motion; forces traceable—if we've time to reflect that far—back toward the time our solar system was fog, the sun not yet resolved to a focus with hydrogen fusion at heart. To see beyond language may be to receive flashes of a luminous whole; to feel an obsidian chip, for example, change into its molten past or vaporized future even as the sperm and egg we once were stoop to pick it up.

Because mystic experiences can't be spoken, only hinted at, and even then only after years of disciplined, humble waiting for glimpses which can neither be willed nor commanded, it's simplistic to say mysticism, too, aims at being where names can't take us. But that is at least an element in Christian as well as Taoist and Zen practice.

Chuang-Tzu, a wise and kooky Taoist of China's fourth century BC, speaks of "entering the bird cage without making the birds sing." Through wordplay on "cage" and "song" in Chinese, he hints at entering a state beyond the twittering of words. Only then would one have stepped past the plane of language into the actual. Zen Buddhism aims at the same state: getting outside any webwork of names mistaken for how things really are. To exist in the real. There, as in Taoism, one would have gone beyond the spoken ghosts enabling language to be what it is.

Other than these silences of profound meditation, the only remaining escape from illusions built into nomenclature would be to speak names truer to their things than any names those things presently have. Various sane and crazy paths lead that way. One sane version may be poetry: the poem as a single, complex word unique to what it translates, creates, or invokes, and thus names— often a particular moment. Or a feeling for which there's no word till the poem spells it out. The craziest path would be toward a total language. In it, each actual, particular leaf of sorrel, each individual stem of Canadian reed grass, each particular wing feather of every house finch, each toe pad on a gecko, each and every molar in every hippo's maw would have its own name. To make a world you need some of everything, but to make a language you need a whole lot less. Logically, therefore, as this total language grew to become coextensive with every particle of the universe, it would disappear into itself as one vast synonym for god.

65   Actual taxonomy, the science of classification, is much more a plodder's route to omniscience, yet the founding father of biology's naming seems at times to have felt that he was divinely ordained to that task. As a child in Sweden, Carl Linnaeus fell under the influence of his father's horticultural passion. Though the mother never forgave her son's choosing the life of plants instead of a life in the ministry, the father, himself a minister, proved more indulgent. By the time that son was twenty-three he had devised a taxonomic system whose essentials remain in global use to this day.

The young Linnaeus's method was to name plants in a way that contextualized each within an order of relationships; hence the title of his *Systema Natu-*

rae, which brought to the helter-skelter vocabulary of "natural philosophy" a set of widely acceptable classifying procedures which science had hitherto lacked. The result was a sort of Dewey decimal system of naming. Though many of us may find biology's Latin labels about as exciting as call numbers on library books, we can't deny their usefulness. From its first few printed pages in the edition of 1735, Linnaeus's *Systema Naturae* won quick acceptance. Successive editions expanded as nature became better known. Taxonomy itself became a science.

Prior to Linnaeus, natural history had been seriously encumbered by a sprawling nomenclature with as many "systems" as there were groups of naturalists. How could a botanist, pharmacologist, or zoologist in Strasbourg, for example, know what a naturalist writing in England means by *pole cat* or *chimney sweepers*? For that matter, how could a Virginian or Carolinian? In Warwickshire a "chimney sweeper" was what Americans call a dandelion, which in France is called a *"pis-en-lit,"* or "piss-in-the-bed." And because skunks are unique to North America, an English writer referring to a "pole cat" might be misunderstood in Pennsylvania.

Or take *kinnikinnik,* whose palindromic syllables I have loved from first hearing—before ever seeing what they named. In Colorado, as my friend William Weber has pointed out to me, this originally Algonquin word refers to a type of ground cover whose evergreen leaves are glossy as laurel. Some people, however, call the plant "bearberry," others call it "hog-crawberry," or "mountain box," "rapper dandies," and I don't know what all. Spoken in Canada, *kinnikinnik* names quite another set of leaves, *Amelanchier pumila,* which has in common with our plant only the coincidence that Indians once used it too for tobacco.

Though scientifically needed to avoid confusing the Colorado plant with one up in Canada, both *Arctostaphylos uva-ursi* and *Amelanchier pumila* do indeed stick to the palate compared with *kinnikinnik.* Nonetheless, Linneaus's system of binominal naming—akin to a person's family name and given name—stressed a plant's botanical context. Naming a plant in relation to its genus and species, Linnaeus reasoned, would summon facts about it by association. In effect, therefore, the youthful Swede who was mad about naming gave science an international code, in which names functioned neatly as shorthand.

Even if his "sexual system" of classifying plants by their reproductive organs was so far from perfect that Linnaeus himself didn't always abide by it, such a method was nonetheless perfectible. And as this "prince of plants" emphasized, "The Ariadne thread in botany is classification, without which there is chaos." Lifelong he held names to be the road to a knowledge of things, an enthusiasm going back to his childhood habit of wheedling botanical names from his father, and from reading that father's old herbal books for interesting names. Years later he indulged that passion through books of his own, as for example in his preface to *Hortus Cliffortianus,* the printed catalog of a wealthy Hollander's zoological and botanical garden, where he saw "American falcons, divers kinds

of parrots, pheasants, peacocks, guinea-fowl, American capercaillie, Indian hens
. . . American crossbills . . . orchids, cruciferae, yams, magnolias, tulip-trees, cal-
abash trees, arrow, cassias, acacias, tamarinds, pepper-plants, Anona, manicinilla,
cucurbitaceous trees . . . Hernandia, silver-gleaming species of Portea and camphor-
trees." If ever anyone loved naming nature it was Carl Linnaeus.

In Lutheran Sweden, however, there was harrumphing when it came to
Linnaeus's choice of plant genitals as the basis for classification. No sooner had
the *Systema Naturae* begun its influence than the high-toned Johann Siegesbeck
took exception to its explicitly sexual mode of plant identification: "Such loathe-
some harlotry as several males to one female would never have been permitted
in the vegetable kingdom by the Creator." The scandalized Siegesbeck despaired
to know "how anyone could teach without offence so licentious a method to studious youth."

Had Herr Siegesbeck been with me last summer, he might have felt his dis-
may confirmed. On one side of a seven-passenger van parked outside the Back-
county Office at the Grand Canyon, studious youth had stuck impromptu
lettering in yellow tape: "UNIVERSITY VAN #7, DAY 16" and on the other side, "2 PIS-
TILS, 5 STAMENS." It would seem that even today Linnaeus's system may risk titil-
lating chaste minds.

It was a risk the studious youth of eighteenth-century Sweden were eager
to run. Linnaeus's university lectures filled to overflowing. His field trips became
festivals. At the height of his career, young men and women flocked by the hundreds to join his botanical outings into summer countryside around Uppsala.
Though these excursions lasted from eight in the morning till nine in the long
Scandinavian evening, "studious youth" weren't too weary for escorting Linnaeus back home with banners, French horns, and kettledrums—then taking
their leave of him amid shouts of "*Vivat Linnaeus!*" several times repeated. Can
any professor of botany ever have been so adulated? Will any ever be so again?

Though given to bouts of depression, in his manic phases this workaholic
minister's son seems indeed to have seen himself as the Lord's own botanist. In
fact, his status as nature's "second Adam" made "Linnaeus" a household word internationally. By the end, however, the man who lifted naming to the level of science, the man who came to be called "God's registrar," had grown literally
oblivious to his renown. On good days, when well enough to be led out into the
garden, his delight in its green world—which had begun in earliest childhood—
was yet alive; but all knowledge of plants had been taken from him. A stroke saw
to that. It left his garden's flora nameless as Eden's had been prior to Adam. He
knew neither his own books—not so much as the title of his great *Systema
Naturae*—nor even who he was. By the end he didn't know his own name.

75   The Linnaeus I care to think about, however, is the young man mad about
plants, the one whose students choired him home after field trips, the one whose
boyhood wonder at the rareness, muchness, and strangeness of his father's gar-

den reached to the ends of this earth. In his prime, Carl Linnaeus, believing with Messianic fervor that names both give order to knowledge and summon it, might have grumbled plenty at the idea that any familiar thing may suddenly choose to transcend whatever we call it by, and reveal its unnameable nature. At such moments, nonetheless, reality deepens till the only really apt name is wordless.

Years ago on the Tyrrhenian coast of Italy, for example, I certainly felt that way. It was toward the end of a hot August afternoon, day's end really. The final 10-year-old vendor had traipsed past my beach chair and faded umbrella, crying up his tepid soda and limp ice cream bars. A few at a time the midafternoon crowd had long since left. Out over the becalmed Bay of Lerici a westering sun ruddied as it lowered. Already the trompled sand was cratered with shadows marking each footfall. We remaining die-hards were about to leave too, though the evening breeze was still August-warm on bare torso and legs. Having gathered up the usual odds and ends, I was shaking out my beach towel when I turned westward.

The edge of an enormous orange-red sphere was just about to kiss the sea's horizon. Everybody else seemed to be watching it also. Their casual babble lessened, fell silent. In that speaking stillness something important was about to happen. Something serious, and very strange. The placid waters had become a burning smear. We all watched a huge orb of fire taking itself away. More than the sun was slipping out of sight.

Before our eyes, it was pulling one of our days down with it. Our most recent history was being transformed from casual and mindless to something terribly precious, at the same rate that it was sinking forever into the sea. Its mystery — the mystery of what the sun really is, and consequently this world and all our days, gone and to come — now fused with one actual day made visible in disappearing. A half-moment before the great red *thing* had taken itself entirely away, a little girl called out to it. Then gone. Then afterglow off cloud banks, their red memory fading from the waters.

And voices resumed, at first only as murmur. We all — American, Italian, French I suppose, and undoubtedly German — must have had different reactions to what we had seen. I doubt that "*tramontana*" or "*coucher du soleil*," for example, or "*sonnenuntergang*" named any of them.

Later, if some of us, recalling that evening, ever tried finding words to express the inadequacy of "sundown," wouldn't we have been reenacting the rise of Homo sapiens? By pressing back against the pressure of what words can't say — isn't that how we made ourselves human? But the paradox of "the sun," "*die Sonne*," "*il sole*," "*le soleil*" both concealing and revealing isn't really a dilemma; or at least not inescapably so. If we can't be Chuang-Tzu and Carl Linnaeus, a circle and a straight line, simultaneously, it's also true that neither one of them was *always* the one and never the other. If that had been the case, neither could have been either.

Taoism never tires of reminding us that the ineffable remains beyond language: "The name you can name is not the name." That's true of more than just "the Tao." Each presence in nature may tend toward our naming, yet in answering to the aptest word we can give it, each thing in creation asks to be seen, thus known, even more truly. Just as we do.

TALKING ABOUT IT

Seeing Metaphor: Revealing and Concealing

1. What does naming represent for Saner? Why is it so important for him to learn the name of the chicory stalks? To distinguish the various evergreens on his hike? To identify the birds in the snow as bluebirds? How, for him, are "seeing" and "knowing" dependent on "naming"?

2. In his conclusion Saner writes about the inadequacy of words, "the pressure of what words can't say," and points to the paradox of a phrase like "'the sun'. . . both concealing and revealing." What does he mean? What is concealed and what is revealed? And how does this idea relate to his central reflections on naming?

Seeing Composition: Frame, Line, Texture, Tone

1. Saner opens and closes his essay with two stories about times he was traveling in Europe: in the first, a French toddler sees cows from a train window and identifies them as horses; in the second, he and others on a beach on the coast of Italy marvel at a particularly spectacular sunset. How do these two stories serve to frame the essay? What does each contribute to Saner's overall point?

2. Saner' vocabulary in this essay is particularly rich and varied. Choose several paragraphs and look closely at his choice of words. How do the words he uses contribute to the texture and tone of his essay?

Seeing Meaning: Navigating and Negotiating

1. Of his hike among the evergreens near Avery Peak, Saner writes, "I was determined to see better," and later he notes that "much of what we call eyesight is *wanting* to see. Small wonder that, cytologically speaking, retinal tissue and brain tissue are cousins. Eyes seem to be the mind leaning forward." How might you train yourself to "see better"? To what extent do you think it is a matter of "wanting to see"?

2. Saner says that beginning students of foreign languages often persist in believing that "English names are somehow true to their objects, whereas

French names of the same things are unnatural." Have you ever felt this way when trying to learn a foreign language? Why do you think people tend to cling to their native language?

WRITING ABOUT IT

1. Reg Saner ends his essay with a quotation from Taoism: "The name you can name is not the name." What escapes us when we're naming? Answer this question from your own experience by offering an illustration and explanation for the truth of his conclusion.

2. Find other names for something that you know well. Make a collection of names for that one thing. How does the thing itself change with each change in name? What does that tell you about the relationship between the sign and the thing it points to? Your final objective is to say what your own collection tells you about the nature of naming.

3. Saner begins with the questions "Why do we care to know a plant's or animal's right name? And what do we know when we know it?" From what angles does he come to answer those questions? Next, describe your own reasons for caring to know something's right name and what you know now that you know it. Connect your response to Saner's essay by showing where your reasons and his meet, and where they part company.

Birth

LOUISE ERDRICH

Louise Erdrich won the National Book Critics' Circle Award in 1984 for the novel Love Medicine *(1984). Three subsequent novels (* The Beet Queen, *1986;* Tracks, *1988;* The Bingo Palace, *1994) followed members of the same Native American family. Erdrich's most recent novel is* The Antelope Wife *(1998). She has also written two collections of poetry,* Jacklight *(1984) and* Baptism of Desire *(1989), the source of the following poem.*

When they were wild
When they were not yet human
When they could have been anything,
I was on the other side ready with milk to lure them,
5   And their father, too, each name a net in his hands.

TALKING ABOUT IT

Seeing Metaphor: Revealing and Concealing

1. What is the central metaphor of this poem? Do you find it surprising?

2. The poem ends with the phrase "each name a net in his hands." In the context of the poem, in what ways is a "name" a "net"?

Seeing Composition: Frame, Line, Texture, Tone

1. Note the line lengths in the poem. How do they contribute to its rhythm?

2. What is the effect of the repetition in the first three lines?

Seeing Meaning: Navigating and Negotiating

1. How do you interpret the line that stands at the middle of the poem: "When they could have been anything"?

2. Imagine reading this poem without first knowing its title. Would you understand it in a different way?

WRITING ABOUT IT

How can a name be considered a "net" in a parent's hands? Discuss two possibilities for defining "net" in this context, and offer illustrations for each from your experience. What is the responsibility that naming foists on us?

What's in a Name?

ITABARI NJERI

Itabari Njeri, once a professional singer and actress, is now a contributing editor of the Los Angeles Times Magazine. *She won the* Before Columbus Foundation's American Book Award *in 1990 for* Every Good-Bye Ain't Gone: Family Portraits and Personal Escapades *(1990), from which the following selection is taken. In 1997 she published* The Last Plantation: Color, Conflict, and Identity: Reflections of a New World Black.

The decade was about to end when I started my first newspaper job. The seventies might have been the disco generation for some, but it was a continuation of the Black Power, post–civil rights era for me. Of course in some parts of America it was still the pre–civil rights era. And that was the part of America I wanted to explore. As a good reporter I needed a sense of the whole country, not just the provincial Northeast Corridor in which I was raised.

I headed for Greenville ("Pearl of the Piedmont"), South Carolina.

"*Wheeere,*" some people snarled, their nostrils twitching, their mouths twisted so their top lips went slightly to the right, the bottom ones way down and to the left, "did you get *that* name from?"

Itabiddy, Etabeedy. Etabeeree. Eat a berry. Mata Hari. Theda Bara. And one secretary in the office of the Greenville Urban League told her employer: "It's Ms. Idi Amin."

Then, and now, there are a whole bunch of people who greet me with "Hi, Ita." They think "Bari" is my last name. Even when they don't, they still want to call me "Ita." When I tell them my first name is Itabari, they say, "Well, what do people call you for short?"

"They don't call me anything for short," I say. "The name is Itabari."

Sophisticated white people, upon hearing my name, approach me as would a cultural anthropologist finding a piece of exotica right in his own living room. This happens a lot, still, at cocktail parties.

"Oh, what an unusual and beautiful name. Where are you from?"

"Brooklyn," I say. I can see the disappointment in their eyes. Just another home-grown Negro.

Then there are other white people who, having heard my decidedly northeastern accent, will simply say, "What a lovely name," and smile knowingly, indicating that they saw *Roots* and understand.

Then there are others, black and white, who for different reasons take me through this number:

"What's your *real* name?"

179

"Itabari Njeri is my real, legal name," I explain.

"Okay, what's your original name?" they ask, often with eyes rolling, exasperation in their voices.

15   After Malcolm X, Muhammad Ali, Kareem Abdul-Jabbar, Ntozake Shange, and Kunta Kinte, who, I ask, should be exasperated by this question-and-answer game?

Nevertheless, I explain, "Because of slavery, black people in the Western world don't usually know their original names. What you really want to know is what my slave name was."

Now this is where things get tense. Four hundred years of bitter history, culture, and politics between blacks and whites in America is evoked by this one term, "slave name."

Some white people wince when they hear the phrase, pained and embarrassed by this reminder of their ancestors' inhumanity. Further, they quickly scrutinize me and conclude that mine was a post–Emancipation Proclamation birth. "You were never a slave."

I used to be reluctant to tell people my slave name unless I surmised that they wouldn't impose their cultural values on me and refuse to use my African name. I don't care anymore. When I changed my name, I changed my life, and I've been Itabari for more years now than I was Jill. Nonetheless, people will say: "Well, that's your *real* name, you were born in America and that's what I am going to call you." My mother tried a variation of this on me when I legalized my traditional African name. I respectfully made it clear to her that I would not tolerate it. Her behavior, and subsequently her attitude, changed.

20   But many black folks remain just as skeptical of my name as my mother was.

"You're one of those black people who changed their name, huh," they are likely to begin. "Well, I still got the old slave master's Irish name," said one man named O'Hare at a party. This man's defensive tone was a reaction to what I call the "blacker than thou" syndrome perpetrated by many black nationalists in the sixties and seventies. Those who reclaimed their African names made blacks who didn't do the same thing feel like Uncle Toms.

These so-called Uncle Toms couldn't figure out why they should use an African name when they didn't know a thing about Africa. Besides, many of them were proud of their names, no matter how they had come by them. And it should be noted that after the Emancipation Proclamation in 1863, four million black people changed their names, adopting surnames such as Freeman, Freedman, and Liberty. They eagerly gave up names that slave masters had imposed upon them as a way of identifying their human chattel.

Besides names that indicated their newly won freedom, blacks chose common English names such as Jones, Scott, and Johnson. English was their language. America was their home, and they wanted names that would allow them to assimilate as easily as possible.

Of course, many of our European surnames belong to us by birthright. We are the legal as well as "illegitimate" heirs to the names Jefferson, Franklin, Washington, et al., and in my own family, Lord.

Still, I consider most of these names to be by-products of slavery, if not actual slave names. Had we not been enslaved, we would not have been cut off from our culture, lost our indigenous languages, and been compelled to use European names.

The loss of our African culture is a tragic fact of history, and the conflict it poses is a profound one that has divided blacks many times since Emancipation: Do we accept the loss and assimilate totally or do we try to reclaim our culture and synthesize it with our present reality?

A new generation of black people in America is reexamining the issues raised by the cultural nationalists and Pan-Africanists of the sixties and seventies: What are the cultural images that appropriately convey the "new" black aesthetic in literature and art?

The young Afro-American novelist Trey Ellis has asserted that the "New Black Aesthetic shamelessly borrows and reassembles across both race and class lines." It is not afraid to embrace the full implications of our hundreds of years in the New World. We are a new people who need not be tied to externally imposed or self-inflicted cultural parochialism. Had I understood that as a teenager, I might still be singing today.

Even the fundamental issue of identity and nomenclature, raised by Baraka and others twenty years ago, is back on the agenda: Are we to call ourselves blacks or African Americans?

In reality, it's an old debate. "Only with the founding of the American Colonization Society in 1816 did blacks recoil from using the term African in referring to themselves and their institutions," the noted historian and author Sterling Stuckey pointed out in an interview with me. They feared that using the term "African" would fuel white efforts to send them back to Africa. But they felt no white person had the right to send them back when they had slaved to build America.

Many black institutions retained their African identification, most notably the African Methodist Episcopal Church. Changes in black self-identification in America have come in cycles, usually reflecting the larger dynamics of domestic and international politics.

The period after World War II, said Stuckey, "culminating in the Cold War years of Roy Wilkins's leadership of the NAACP," was a time of "frenzied integrationism." And there was "no respectable black leader on the scene evincing any sort of interest in Africa—neither the NAACP or the Urban League."

This, he said, "was an example of historical discontinuity, the likes of which we, as a people, had not seen before." Prior to that, for more than a century and a half, black leaders were Pan-Africanists, including Frederick Douglass. "He recognized," said Stuckey, "that Africa was important and that somehow one had to redeem the motherland in order to be genuinely respected in the New World."

The Reverend Jesse Jackson has, of course, placed on the national agenda the importance of blacks in America restoring their cultural, historical, and political links with Africa.

35   But what does it really mean to be called an African American?

"Black" can be viewed as a more encompassing term, referring to all people of African descent. "Afro-American" and "African American" refer to a specific ethnic group. I use the terms interchangeably, depending on the context and the point I want to emphasize.

But I wonder: As the twenty-first century breathes down our necks — prodding us to wake up to the expanding mélange of ethnic groups immigrating in record numbers to the United States, inevitably intermarrying, and to realize the eventual reshaping of the nation's political imperatives in a newly multicultural society — will the term "African American" be as much of a racial and cultural obfuscation as the term "black"? In other words, will we be the only people, in a society moving toward cultural pluralism, viewed to have no history and no culture? Will we just be a color with a new name: African American?

Or will the term be — as I think it should — an ethnic label describing people with a shared culture who descended from Africans, were transformed in (as well as transformed) America, and are genetically intertwined with myriad other groups in the United States?

Such a definition reflects the historical reality and distances us from the fallacious, unscientific concept of separate races when there is only one: *Homo sapiens.*

40   But to comprehend what should be an obvious definition requires knowledge and a willingness to accept history.

When James Baldwin wrote *Nobody Knows My Name,* the title was a metaphor — at the deepest level of the collective African-American psyche — for the blighting of black history and culture before the nadir of slavery and since.

The eradication or distortion of our place in world history and culture is most obvious in the popular media. Liz Taylor — and, for an earlier generation, Claudette Colbert — still represent what Cleopatra — a woman of color in a multiethnic society, dominated at various times by blacks — looks like.

And in American homes, thanks to reruns and cable, a new generation of black kids grow up believing that a simpleton shouting "Dy-no-mite!" is a genuine reflection of Afro-American culture, rather than a white Hollywood writer's stereotype.

More recently, *Coming to America,* starring Eddie Murphy as an African prince seeking a bride in the United States, depicted traditional African dancers in what amounted to a Las Vegas stage show, totally distorting the nature and beauty of real African dance. But with every burlesque-style pelvic thrust on the screen, I saw blacks in the audience burst into applause. They think that's African culture, too.

And what do Africans know of us, since blacks don't control the organs of communication that disseminate information about us?

"No!" screamed the mother of a Kenyan man when he announced his engagement to an African-American woman who was a friend of mine. The mother said marry a European, marry a white American. But please, not one of those low-down, ignorant, drug-dealing, murderous black people she had seen in American movies. Ultimately, the mother prevailed.

In Tanzania, the travel agent looked at me indignantly. "Njeri, that's Kikuyu. What are you doing with an African name?" he demanded.

I'd been in Dar es Salaam about a month and had learned that Africans assess in a glance the ethnic origins of the people they meet.

Without a greeting, strangers on the street in Tanzania's capital would comment, "Oh, you're an Afro-American or West Indian."

"Both."

"I knew it," they'd respond, sometimes politely, sometimes not.

Or, people I got to know while in Africa would mention, "I know another half-caste like you." Then they would call in the "mixed-race" person and say, "Please meet Itabari Njeri." The darker-complected African, presumably of unmixed ancestry, would then smile and stare at us like we were animals in the zoo.

Of course, this "half-caste" (which I suppose is a term preferable to "mulatto," which I hate, and which every person who understands its derogatory meaning — "mule" — should never use) was usually the product of a mixed marriage, not generations of ethnic intermingling. And it was clear from most "half-castes" I met that they did not like being compared to so mongrelized and stigmatized a group as Afro-Americans.

I had minored in African studies in college, worked for years with Africans in the United States, and had no romantic illusions as to how I would be received in the motherland. I wasn't going back to find my roots. The only thing that shocked me in Tanzania was being called, with great disdain, a "white woman" by an African waiter. Even if the rest of the world didn't follow the practice, I then assumed everyone understood that any known or perceptible degree of African ancestry made one "black" in America by law and social custom.

But I was pleasantly surprised by the telephone call I received two minutes after I walked into my Dar es Salaam hotel room. It was the hotel operator. "Sister, welcome to Tanzania. . . . Please tell everyone in Harlem hello for us." The year was 1978, and people in Tanzania were wearing half-foot-high platform shoes and dancing to James Brown wherever I went.

Shortly before I left, I stood on a hill surrounded by a field of endless flowers in Arusha, near the border of Tanzania and Kenya. A toothless woman with a wide smile, a staff in her hand, and two young girls at her side, came toward me on a winding path. I spoke to her in fractured Swahili and she to me in broken English.

"I know you," she said smiling. "Wa-Negro." "Wa" is a prefix in Bantu languages meaning people. "You are from the lost tribe," she told me. "Welcome," she said, touching me, then walked down a hill that lay in the shadow of Mount Kilimanjaro.

I never told her my name, but when I told other Africans, they'd say: "*Emmmm,* Itabari. Too long. How about I just call you Ita."

TALKING ABOUT IT

Seeing Metaphor: Revealing and Concealing

1. In what sense does Njeri's changing her name represent something more than a shedding of her "slave name"? What does her name reveal, and what does it conceal?

2. Njeri writes that after the Emancipation Proclamation, black people adopted surnames like Freeman and Liberty as well as "common English names . . . that would allow them to assimilate as easily as possible." What does this — and the more recent movement of African Americans like Njeri to adopt African names — suggest about the relationship between such name changes and a person's sense of identity?

Seeing Composition: Frame, Line, Texture, Tone

1. In the opening paragraphs of her essay, Njeri focuses on dialogues with people in the United States about her name, and in the final paragraphs she reproduces conversations she had with people in Africa. How do these two series of personal interactions serve to frame the essay? Do you think Njeri intends some irony here?

2. How would you describe Njeri's tone in this essay? How does her tone serve her apparent purpose in writing this?

Seeing Meaning: Navigating and Negotiating

1. Njeri notes that many people — both black and white (and including her mother) — have been skeptical of her name. Why do you think that would be the case? How do you respond to her name?

2. The term "African American," Njeri believes, should be "an ethnic label describing people with a shared culture who descended from Africans, were transformed in (as well as transformed) America, and are genetically inter-

twined with myriad other groups in the United States" (paragraph 38). Njeri was writing at a time when Jesse Jackson and others were just beginning to call for the use of "African American" rather than "black." What is the difference between these two "labels"? To what extent does a change of name here lead to a change in thinking?

WRITING ABOUT IT

1. Write about a time that you made wrong assumptions about a person upon first hearing her or his name. On what had you based your assumptions? How were they shown to be mistaken?

2. You may have an unusual name, or, if not, you probably know someone who does. Like Itabari Njeri has done, write a sequence of exchanges between the person and those who question her or his name. Let each exchange imply or make explicit the assumptions made by the questioners. Try to interweave the dialogue sequence and a discussion of more general issues related to the name.

3. If you could choose your name, would you keep the one you have or take another? Why?

The Rule of Names

Ursula K. Le Guin

Ursula K. Le Guin is a writer of highly respected science fiction (The Left Hand of Darkness, 1969; The Dispossessed, 1974; The Lathe of Heaven, 1982) poetry, and criticism (Dancing at the Edge of the World: Thoughts on Words, Women, and Places, 1989; The Language of the Night: Essays on Fantasy and Science Fiction, 1992). The following story comes from her collection The Wind's Twelve Quarters *(1975).*

Mr. Underhill came out from under his hill, smiling and breathing hard. Each breath shot out of his nostrils as a double puff of steam, snow-white in the morning sunshine. Mr. Underhill looked up at the bright December sky and smiled wider than ever, showing snow-white teeth. Then he went down to the village.

"Morning, Mr. Underhill," said the villagers as he passed them in the narrow street between houses with conical, overhanging roofs like the fat red caps of toadstools. "Morning, morning!" he replied to each. (It was of course bad luck to wish anyone a *good* morning; a simple statement of the time of day was quite enough, in a place so permeated with Influences as Sattins Island, where a careless adjective might change the weather for a week.) All of them spoke to him, some with affection, some with affectionate disdain. He was all the little island had in the way of a wizard, and so deserved respect, but how could you respect a little fat man of fifty who waddled along with his toes turned in, breathing steam and smiling? He was no great shakes as a workman either. His fireworks were fairly elaborate but his elixirs were weak. Warts he charmed off frequently reappeared after three days; tomatoes he enchanted grew no bigger than cantaloupes; and those rare times when a strange ship stopped at Sattins Harbor, Mr. Underhill always stayed under his hill — for fear, he explained, of the evil eye. He was, in other words, a wizard the way walleyed Gan was a carpenter: by default. The villagers made do with badly-hung doors and inefficient spells, for this generation, and relieved their annoyance by treating Mr. Underhill quite familiarly, as a mere fellow-villager. They even asked him to dinner. Once he asked some of them to dinner, and served a splendid repast, with silver, crystal, damask, roast goose, sparkling Andrades '639, and plum pudding with hard sauce; but he was so nervous all through the meal that it took the joy out of it, and besides, everybody was hungry again half an hour afterward. He did not like anyone to visit his cave, not even the anteroom, beyond which in fact nobody had ever got. When he saw people approaching the hill he always came trotting out to meet them. "Let's sit out here under the pine trees!" he would say, smiling and waving towards the fir grove, or if it was raining, "Let's go have a drink at the inn, eh?" though everybody knew he drank nothing stronger than well-water.

Some of the village children, teased by that locked cave, poked and pried and made raids while Mr. Underhill was away; but the small door that led into the inner chamber was spell shut, and it seemed for once to be an effective spell. Once a couple of boys, thinking the wizard was over on the West Shore curing Mrs. Ruuna's sick donkey, brought a crowbar and hatchet up there, but at the first whack of the hatchet on the door there came a roar of wrath from inside, and a cloud of purple steam. Mr. Underhill had got home early. The boys fled. He did not come out, and the boys came to no harm, though they said you couldn't believe what a huge hooting howling hissing horrible bellow that little fat man could make unless you heard it.

His business in town this day was three dozen fresh eggs and a pound of liver; also a stop at Seacaptain Fogeno's cottage to renew the seeing-charm on the old man's eyes (quite useless when applied to a case of detached retina, but Mr. Underhill kept trying), and finally a chat with old Goody Guld, the concertina-maker's widow. Mr. Underhill's friends were mostly old people. He was timid with the strong young men of the village, and the girls were shy of him. "He makes me nervous, he smiles so much," they all said, pouting, twisting silky ringlets around a finger. "Nervous" was a newfangled word, and their mothers all replied grimly, "Nervous my foot, silliness is the word for it. Mr. Underhill is a very respectable wizard!"

After leaving Goody Guld, Mr. Underhill passed by the school, which was 5 being held this day out on the common. Since no one on Sattins Island was literate, there were no books to learn to read from and no desks to carve initials on and no blackboards to erase, and in fact no schoolhouse. On rainy days the children met in the loft of the Communal Barn, and got hay in their pants; on sunny days the schoolteacher, Palani, took them anywhere she felt like. Today, surrounded by thirty interested children under twelve and forty uninterested sheep under five, she was teaching an important item on the curriculum: the Rules of Names. Mr. Underhill, smiling shyly, paused to listen and watch. Palani, a plump, pretty girl of twenty, made a charming picture there in the wintry sunlight, sheep and children around her, a leafless oak above her, and behind her the dunes and sea and clear, pale sky. She spoke earnestly, her face flushed pink by wind and words. "Now you know the Rules of Names already, children. There are two, and they're the same on every island in the world. What's one of them?"

"It ain't polite to ask anybody what his name is," shouted a fat, quick boy, interrupted by a little girl shrieking, "You can't never tell your own name to nobody my ma says!"

"Yes, Suba. Yes, Popi dear, don't screech. That's right. You never ask anybody his name. You never tell your own. Now think about that a minute and then tell me why we call our wizard Mr. Underhill." She smiled across the curly heads and the woolly backs at Mr. Underhill, who beamed, and nervously clutched his sack of eggs.

" 'Cause he lives under a hill!" said half the children.

"But is it his truename?"

10   "No!" said the fat boy, echoed by little Popi shrieking, "No!"

"How do you know it's not?"

" 'Cause he came here all alone and so there wasn't anybody knew his true-name so they couldn't tell us, and *he* couldn't — "

"Very good, Suba. Popi, don't shout. That's right. Even a wizard can't tell his truename. When you children are through school and go through the Passage, you'll leave your childnames behind and keep only your truenames, which you must never ask for and never give away. Why is that the rule?"

The children were silent. The sheep bleated gently. Mr. Underhill answered the question: "Because the name is the thing," he said in his shy, soft, husky voice, "and the truename is the true thing. To speak the name is to control the thing. Am I right, Schoolmistress?"

15   She smiled and curtseyed, evidently a little embarrassed by his participation. And he trotted off towards his hill, clutching his eggs to his bosom. Somehow the minute spent watching Palani and the children had made him very hungry. He locked his inner door behind him with a hasty incantation, but there must have been a leak or two in the spell, for soon the bare anteroom of the cave was rich with the smell of frying eggs and sizzling liver.

The wind that day was light and fresh out of the west, and on it at noon a little boat came skimming the bright waves into Sattins Harbor. Even as it rounded the point a sharp-eyed boy spotted it, and knowing, like every child on the island, every sail and spar of the forty boats of the fishing fleet, he ran down the street calling out, "A foreign boat, a foreign boat!" Very seldom was the lonely isle visited by a boat from some equally lonely isle of the East Reach, or an adventurous trader from the Archipelago. By the time the boat was at the pier half the village was there to greet it, and fishermen were following it homewards, and cowherds and clam-diggers and herb-hunters were puffing up and down all the rocky hills, heading towards the harbor.

But Mr. Underhill's door stayed shut.

There was only one man aboard the boat. Old Seacaptain Fogeno, when they told him that, drew down a bristle of white brows over his unseeing eyes. "There's only one kind of man," he said, "that sails the Outer Reach alone. A wizard, or a warlock, or a Mage . . ."

So the villagers were breathless hoping to see for once in their lives a Mage, one of the mighty White Magicians of the rich, towered, crowded inner islands of the Archipelago. They were disappointed, for the voyager was quite young, a handsome black-bearded fellow who hailed them cheerfully from his boat, and leaped ashore like any sailor glad to have made port. He introduced himself at once as a sea-peddlar. But when they told Seacaptain Fogeno that he carried an oaken walking-stick around with him, the old man nodded. "Two wizards in one town," he said. "Bad!" And his mouth snapped shut like an old carp's.

As the stranger could not give them his name, they gave him one right   20 away: Blackbeard. And they gave him plenty of attention. He had a small mixed cargo of cloth and sandals and piswi feathers for trimming cloaks and cheap incense and levity stones and fine herbs and great glass beads from Venway — the usual peddlar's lot. Everyone on Sattins Island came to look, to chat with the voyager, and perhaps to buy something — "Just to remember him by!" cackled Goody Guld, who like all the women and girls of the village was smitten with Blackbeard's bold good looks. All the boys hung round him too, to hear him tell of his voyages to far, strange islands of the Reach or describe the great rich islands of the Archipelago, the Inner Lanes, the roadsteads white with ships, and the golden roofs of Havnor. The men willingly listened to his tales; but some of them wondered why a trader should sail alone, and kept their eyes thoughtfully upon his oaken staff.

But all this time Mr. Underhill stayed under his hill.

"This is the first island I've ever seen that had no wizard," said Blackbeard one evening to Goody Guld, who had invited him and her nephew and Palani in for a cup of rushwash tea. "What do you do when you get a toothache, or the cow goes dry?"

"Why, we've got Mr. Underhill!" said the old woman.

"For what that's worth," muttered her nephew Birt, and then blushed purple and spilled his tea. Birt was a fisherman, a large, brave, wordless young man. He loved the schoolmistress, but the nearest he had come to telling her of his love was to give baskets of fresh mackerel to her father's cook.

"Oh, you do have a wizard?" Blackbeard asked. "Is he invisible?"   25

"No, he's just very shy," said Palani. "You've only been here a week, you know, and we see so few strangers here. . . ." She also blushed a little, but did not spill her tea.

Blackbeard smiled at her. "He's a good Sattinsman, then, eh?"

"No," said Goody Guld, "no more than you are. Another cup, nevvy? keep it in the cup this time. No, my dear, he came in a little bit of a boat, four years ago was it? just a day after the end of the shad run, I recall, for they was taking up the nets over in East Creek, and Pondi Cowherd broke his leg that very morning — five years ago it must be. No, four. No, five it is, 'twas the year the garlic didn't sprout. So he sails in on a bit of a sloop loaded full up with great chests and boxes and then says to Seacaptain Fogeno, who wasn't blind then, though old enough goodness knows to be blind twice over, 'I hear tell,' he says, 'you've got no wizard nor warlock at all, might you be wanting one?' 'Indeed, if the magic's white!' says the Captain, and before you could say cuttlefish Mr. Underhill had settled down in the cave under the hill and was charming the mange off Goody Beltow's cat. Though the fur grew in grey, and 'twas an orange cat. Queer-looking thing it was after that. It died last winter in the cold spell. Goody Beltow took on so at that cat's death, poor thing, worse than when her man was drowned on the Long Banks, the year of the long herring-runs, when nevvy Birt here was but a babe in petticoats." Here Birt spilled his tea again, and Blackbeard grinned, but Goody Guld proceeded undismayed, and talked on till nightfall. ⚒

Next day Blackbeard was down at the pier, seeing after the sprung board in his boat which he seemed to take a long time fixing, and as usual drawing the taciturn Sattinsmen into talk. "Now which of these is your wizard's craft?" he asked. "Or has he got one of those the Mages fold up into a walnut shell when they're not using it?" ✗

30   "Nay," said a stolid fisherman. "She's oop in his cave, under hill."

"He carried the boat he came in up to his cave?"

"Aye. Clear oop. I helped. Heavier as lead she was. Full oop with great boxes, and they full oop with books o' spells, he says. Heavier as lead she was." And the stolid fisherman turned his back, sighing stolidly. Goody Guld's nephew, mending a net nearby, looked up from his work and asked with equal stolidity, "Would ye like to meet Mr. Underhill, maybe?"

Blackbeard returned Birt's look. Clever black eyes met candid blue ones for a long moment; then Blackbeard smiled and said, "Yes. Will you take me up to the hill, Birt?"↙

"Aye, when I'm done with this," said the fisherman. And when the net was mended, he and the Archipelagan set off up the village street towards the high green hill above it. But as they crossed the common Blackbeard said, "Hold on a while, friend Birt. I have a tale to tell you, before we meet your wizard."

35   "Tell away," says Birt, sitting down in the shade of a live oak.

"It's a story that started a hundred years ago, and isn't finished yet — though it soon will be, very soon. . . . In the very heart of the Archipelago, where the islands crowd thick as flies on honey, there's a little isle called Pendor. The sealords of Pendor were mighty men, in the old days of war before the League. Loot and ransom and tribute came pouring into Pendor, and they gathered a great treasure there, long ago. Then from somewhere away out in the West Reach, where dragons breed on the lava isles, came one day a very mighty dragon. Not one of those overgrown lizards most of you Outer Reach folk call dragons, but a big, black, winged, wise, cunning monster, full of strength and subtlety, and like all dragons loving gold and precious stones above all things. He killed the Sealord and his soldiers, and the people of Pendor fled in their ships by night. They all fled away and left the dragon coiled up in Pendor Towers. And there he stayed for a hundred years, dragging his scaly belly over the emeralds and sapphires and coins of gold, coming forth only once in a year or two when he must eat. He'd raid nearby islands for his food. You know what dragons eat?"

Birt nodded and said in a whisper, "Maidens."

"Right," said Blackbeard. "Well, that couldn't be endured forever, nor the thought of him sitting on all that treasure. So after the League grew strong and the Archipelago wasn't so busy with wars and piracy, it was decided to attack Pendor, drive out the dragon, and get the gold and jewels for the treasury of the League. They're forever wanting money, the League is. So a huge fleet gathered from fifty islands, and seven Mages stood in the prows of the seven strongest ships, and they sailed towards Pendor. . . . They got there. They landed. Nothing stirred. The houses all stood empty, the dishes on the tables full of a hundred years' dust. The bones of the old Sealord and his men lay about in the castle courts and on the stairs. And the Tower rooms reeked of dragon. But there was no dragon. And no treasure, not a diamond the size of a poppyseed, not a single silver bead . . . Knowing that he couldn't stand up to seven Mages, the dragon had skipped out. They tracked him, and found he'd flown to a deserted island up north called Udrath; they followed his trail there, and what did they find? Bones again. His bones—the dragon's. But no treasure. A wizard, some unknown wizard from somewhere, must have met him singlehanded, and defeated him—and then made off with the treasure, right under the League's nose!"

The fisherman listened, attentive and expressionless.

"Now that must have been a powerful wizard and a clever one, first to kill a dragon, and second to get off without leaving a trace. The lords and Mages of the Archipelago couldn't track him at all, neither where he'd come from nor where he'd made off to. They were about to give up. That was last spring; I'd been off on a three-year voyage up in the North Reach, and got back about that time. And they asked me to help them find the unknown wizard. That was clever of them. Because I'm not only a wizard myself, as I think some of the oafs here have guessed, but I am also a descendant of the Lords of Pendor. That treasure is mine. It's mine, and knows that it's mine. Those fools of the League couldn't find it, because it's not theirs. It belongs to the House of Pendor, and the great emerald, the star of the hoard, Inalkil the Greenstone, knows its master. Behold!" Blackbeard raised his oaken staff and cried aloud, "Inalkil!" The tip of the staff began to glow green, a fiery green radiance, a dazzling haze the color of April grass, and at the same moment the staff tipped in the wizard's hand, leaning, slanting till it pointed straight at the side of the hill above them.

"It wasn't so bright a glow, far away in Havnor," Blackbeard murmured, "but the staff pointed true. Inalkil answered when I called. The jewel knows its

40

master. And I know the thief, and I shall conquer him. He's a mighty wizard, who could overcome a dragon. But I am mightier. Do you want to know why, oaf? Because I know his name!"

As Blackbeard's tone got more arrogant, Birt had looked duller and duller, blanker and blanker; but at this he gave a twitch, shut his mouth, and stared at the Archipelagan. "How did you . . . learn it?" he asked very slowly.

Blackbeard grinned, and did not answer.

"Black magic?"

45   "How else?"

Birt looked pale, and said nothing.

"I am the Sealord of Pendor, oaf, and I will have the gold my fathers won, and the jewels my mothers wore, and the Greenstone! For they are mine. — Now, you can tell your village bobbies the whole story after I have defeated this wizard and gone. Wait here. Or you can come and watch, if you're not afraid. You'll never get the chance again to see a great wizard in all his power." Blackbeard turned, and without a backward glance strode off up the hill towards the entrance to the cave.

Very slowly, Birt followed. A good distance from the cave he stopped, sat down under a hawthorn tree, and watched. The Archipelagan had stopped; a stiff, dark figure alone on the green swell of the hill before the gaping cave-mouth, he stood perfectly still. All at once he swung his staff up over his head, and the emerald radiance shone about him as he shouted, "Thief, thief of the Hoard of Pendor, come forth!"

There was a crash, as of dropped crockery, from inside the cave, and a lot of dust came spewing out. Scared, Birt ducked. When he looked again he saw Blackbeard still standing motionless, and at the mouth of the cave, dusty and disheveled, stood Mr. Underhill. He looked small and pitiful, with his toes turned in as usual, and his little bowlegs in black tights, and no staff — he never had had one, Birt suddenly thought. Mr. Underhill spoke. "Who are you?" he said in his husky little voice.

50   "I am the Sealord of Pendor, thief, come to claim my treasure!"

At that, Mr. Underhill slowly turned pink, as he always did when people were rude to him. But he then turned something else. He turned yellow. His hair bristled out, he gave a coughing roar — and was a yellow lion leaping down the hill at Blackbeard, white fangs gleaming.

But Blackbeard no longer stood there. A gigantic tiger, color of night and lightning, bounded to meet the lion. . . .

The lion was gone. Below the cave all of a sudden stood a high grove of trees, black in the winter sunshine. The tiger, checking himself in midleap just before he entered the shadow of the trees, caught fire in the air, became a tongue of flame lashing out at the dry black branches. . . .

But where the trees had stood a sudden cataract leaped from the hillside, an arch of silvery crashing water, thundering down upon the fire. But the fire was gone. . . .

For just a moment before the fisherman's staring eyes two hills rose — the green one he knew, and a new one, a bare, brown hillock ready to drink up the rushing waterfall. That passed so quickly it made Birt blink, and after blinking he blinked again, and moaned, for what he saw now was a great deal worse. Where the cataract had been there hovered a dragon. Black wings darkened all the hill, steel claws reached groping, and from the dark, scaly, gaping lips fire and steam shot out.

Beneath the monstrous creature stood Blackbeard, laughing.

"Take any shape you please, little Mr. Underhill!" he taunted. "I can match you. But the game grows tiresome. I want to look upon my treasure, upon Inalkil. Now, big dragon, little wizard, take your true shape. I command you by the power of your true name — Yevaud!"

Birt could not move at all, not even to blink. He cowered, staring whether he would or not. He saw the black dragon hang there in the air above Blackbeard. He saw the fire lick like many tongues from the scaly mouth, the steam jet from the red nostrils. He saw Blackbeard's face grow white, white as chalk, and the beard-fringed lips trembling.

"Your name is Yevaud!"

"Yes," said a great, husky, hissing voice. "My truename is Yevaud, and my true shape is this shape."

"But the dragon was killed — they found dragon-bones on Udrath Island —"

"That was another dragon," said the dragon, and then stooped like a hawk, talons outstretched. And Birt shut his eyes.

When he opened them the sky was clear, the hillside empty, except for a reddish-blackish trampled spot, and a few talon-marks in the grass.

Birt the fisherman got to his feet and ran. He ran across the common, scattering sheep to right and left, and straight down the village street to Palani's father's house. Palani was out in the garden weeding the nasturtiums. "Come with me!" Birt gasped. She stared. He grabbed her wrist and dragged her with him. She screeched a little, but did not resist. He ran with her straight to the pier, pushing her into his fishing-sloop the *Queenie,* untied the painter, took up the oars and set off rowing like a demon. The last that Sattins Island saw of him and Palani was the *Queenie*'s sail vanishing in the direction of the nearest island westward.

The villagers thought they would never stop talking about it, how Goody Guld's nephew Birt had lost his mind and sailed off with the schoolmistress on the very same day that the peddlar Blackbeard disappeared without a trace, leaving all his feathers and beads behind. But they did stop talking about it, three days later. They had other things to talk about, when Mr. Underhill finally came out of his cave.

Mr. Underhill had decided that since his truename was no longer a secret, he might as well drop his disguise. Walking was a lot harder than flying, and besides, it was a long, long time since he had had a real meal.

TALKING ABOUT IT

Seeing Metaphor: Revealing and Concealing

1. What do you think is going on in this story? Can you read it as something more than a fantastic tale? Does it represent a more general meaning?

2. Palani, the schoolteacher, elicits from the children the two rules of names: not to ask anyone his name and never to tell one's own name. The reason, Mr. Underhill explains, is that "the name is the thing, . . . and the truename is the true thing. To speak the name is to control the thing." In what sense does naming imply control?

Seeing Composition: Frame, Line, Texture, Tone

1. Reread the opening description of Mr. Underhill. In what way does that description become ironic in light of the conclusion? Can you find other such examples that foreshadow the surprising conclusion?

2. In the climatic battle between Mr. Underhill and the Sealord of Pendor, consider Le Guin's description of their various physical transformations. How do her language and sentence structure help to create a sense of epic magic in this scene?

Seeing Meaning: Navigating and Negotiating

1. How do you respond to this story? Do you find it humorous, grotesque, frightening, or what? How do you account for your response?

2. Why do you think the dragon/wizard spent so long in the guise of Mr. Underhill? Does he seem to have enjoyed his role? What might Le Guin be suggesting about "wizardry"?

WRITING ABOUT IT

1. Palani, the schoolteacher, elicits from the children the two rules of names: not to ask anyone what his or her name is and never to tell your own name. "Why is that the rule?" she asks. Mr. Underhill answers: "Because the name

is the thing . . . , and the truename is the true thing. To speak the name is to control the thing." How, then, does the ending of the story surprise us? How does the story seem to define "control"?

2. Fairy tales, like myths, are metaphorical. They are ways of transferring cultural values and beliefs to the members of a community. What values and beliefs are being transferred through "The Rule of Names"? Why might a writer choose to tell a fairy tale rather than a more modern story, or rather than write an essay that offers a more straightforward explanation of ideas?

Pee Tong Lueng: Victims of the Name

KHUANKAEW ANANTACHART

Khuankaew, nicknamed "Cookie" by her parents, grew up in Bangkok, Thailand. Some of her essays explore conceptual metaphors in Thai, such as "Thai Culture in Boxing," where she describes the cultural values attached to ways the sport is taught and practiced and explains how Thai boxing terms have become popular in everyday language and thought. In the essay below, she describes how the wrong name had disastrous effects on a small tribe in northern Thailand.

In the excerpt from *Black Holes and Time Warps,* the physicist Kip Thorne shows the negative impact of a name. He describes how the name "Schwarzschild singularity" misled scientists in their research of the phenomenon now known as "black holes." Similarly, the name "Yellow Man" or "Pee Tong Lueng" that anthropologists gave to a small tribe in Thailand had a negative impact. The tribe almost became extinct.

During the 1980s, Thai anthropologists discovered a tribe of people who live in the northern part of Thailand. The anthropologists couldn't figure out where the people came from. Communication with them was difficult because no one could understand their language. They do not look the same as other Thai people either. All their clothes are made of leaves such as banana leaves. Their skin looks more yellowish than that of other Thais. They also wander for food in the forest instead of farming. In fact, they have lived in a primitive way much as our ancestors did a thousand years ago.

Since communication was difficult, anthropologists did not know what the tribe named itself. A long scientific name was given, but anthropologists also gave them a shorter name based on the people's physical characteristics: "Pee Tong Lueng." In Thai, "Pee" means ghost, while "Tong Lueng" means "yellow." The name, then, means "Yellow Ghost." Generally, these people, both men and women, have long hair that covers their faces. They are very shy and do not want to be recognized. They tend to sneak from one place to another, trying not to make noise. Their long hair and the way they walk — in a crouch — resembled the ghosts in Thai folk tales. Hence, anthropologists called them "Pee."

The ritual belief of people in this tribe leads to the name "Tong Lueng." They believe that humans should have yellow skin color to distinguish themselves from ghosts who are white. That is why the people cover themselves with yellow substances such as yellow soil or banana leaves. Their beliefs account for their appearance. And anthropologists, not knowing their beliefs, named them for their unique appearance. Kip Thorne says that the focus of the observer is what contributes to the name (255). Soviet physicists, for example, focused on astronomers' vision of star implosion and thus named the object "frozen star." Similarly, anthropologists focused on the visual, too, and the name "Tong Lueng" was created.

As Thorne states, "A good name will conjure up a mental image that em-   5 phasizes the concept's most important properties, and thereby, it will help trigger, in a subconscious, intuitive sort of a way, good research (254–55). The name "Pee Tong Lueng" also conjures up a mental image but a negative one. The word "Pee" made some rural people think that this tribe of people were "real" ghosts. And since people are afraid of ghosts, whenever they saw "Pee Tong Lueng," they threw things and yelled at them. Pee Tong Lueng, therefore, had a difficult time finding food. They had to hide themselves in the forest and come out only at night. Moreover, some superstitious people tried to use black magic to get rid of the tribe, believing that Pee Tong Lueng brought them bad luck. And since their name indicated that they have yellow skin, it was easy to recognize, catch, and kill these people. For all these reasons, Pee Tong Lueng's population decreased. "Pee" had concealed that this tribe is human. They are not ghosts.

We can see from the example here that the names we use to identify things are very important, especially if the name hinders truth. Thorne claims that "a bad name can produce mental blocks that hinder research" (255). Even though he uses it to describe scientific research, the same idea can be applied to the names of people. In this case, the name "Pee Tong Lueng" had hindered Thai people from realizing the truth, and it almost led to the extinction of one tribe of people. What saved them is a change of name. They are now called "Manood Lueng" instead.

"Manood" means "human." Since that change in name, Thai rural people changed their views toward people in this tribe. Even though their skin color is still yellow and the way they walk and wear their hair still resembles ghosts, no one throws things or yells at Manood Lueng as in the past. Now, these characteristics belong to "human," too, so the name made all the difference. Manood Lueng can come out from the forest and wander for food. The fear that Thai people had is gone, and, at the same time, the attempts of superstitious people to get rid of this tribe have diminished. Manood Lueng's population has increased. And they can live life more happily in Thai society.

Parenthetical references in the essay are to page numbers in the original source.

PERMEABLE BOUNDARIES: WRITING WHERE THE READINGS MEET

1. In "Naming Nature," Reg Saner proposes in his conclusion that "the name you can name is not the name." There is always something ineffable about any presence in the world, something about it that's beyond language, beyond our "aptest word" for it. Consider, then, how the following quotation from his essay and another from Ursula Le Guin's "The Rule of Names" might be saying something different as well as saying the same thing: "The name you can name is not the name. . . . In answering to the aptest word we can give it, each thing in creation asks to be seen, thus known, even more truly. Just as we do" (Reg Saner). "The name is the thing . . . and the truename is the true thing" (Mr. Underhill in "The Rule of Names").

2. Itabari Njeri chose her name to reflect her self-image and her values. After considering how her name has affected the way others perceive her and the way she responds to those perceptions, connect her ideas to points made by two or three other writers in this chapter. How might these writers lend support to Njeri's argument?

3. Reg Saner spends some time describing Carl Linnaeus, the man and his work. Richard Conniff also refers to Linnaeus at the beginning and end of his essay. How do you imagine the Carl Linnaeus that Saner describes would respond to the playful taxonomists that Conniff describes in "What's in a Name? Sometimes More Than Meets the Eye"? What do these two essays seem to say together that neither says alone?

4. Read the following passage from "Naming Nature":

> So, having learned to name "magpie," we'd be lazy to let our seeing stop at the plane of a name, which is to "see" dismissively. We need to look past language to discover, for example, what rich iridescences a magpie's "black" feathers can show: dark emeralds, dark azures, hints of deep burgundy almost not visible—their prismatic wealth refracted in preen oil. "Black-and-white" doesn't touch it. . . . Just as we must look past *wing* to see what a wing truly is, we must look past *bird* to see the strangeness in our sky's having animals. To name is, yes, to know. But only to know better, far from completely, and never once and for all. (Reg Saner)

Chet Raymo acknowledges the power that poetry can lend to the scientist's gaze: "Even the sturdiest of scientific concepts is rooted in metaphor." Yet, while acknowledging that "science and poetry are both metaphorical," he argues that "science is not poetry." Raymo quotes the following description of the purple finch in *The Field Guide to Birds*: "a sparrow dipped in raspberry juice." He then claims that the image is "perfect" but that it "hardly qualifies as science."

Where do Raymo and Saner meet in their ideas about naming when it comes to the problem of "knowing the right name"? What do they mean by "knowing" or "right"? "Right" for whom, under what circumstances? What do they seem to say about the limits of knowing within one field of vision or the other — science and poetry?

Chapter 4

Illness and Health

Illness remains a wilderness beyond our grasp, strangely forbidding and forever a mystery—despite its continuing presence in our lives.

—Kat Duff

How do we define and talk about illness? How does the language we use affect not only the way we conceive of illness but also how we experience it and even how we attempt to cure it? Can illness itself be seen as a metaphor? These are the larger questions that authors in this chapter address.

Sharon Begley and Richard Preston describe the fear of the Ebola virus and other unknown viruses that may continue to threaten us as we destroy the rain forests. These authors also describe the teams of doctors and scientists who risk their lives in order to identify and halt the spread of disease in infected areas. Paul Farmer, Arthur Kleinman, and Susan Sontag discuss AIDS and the ways we have come to think about it that affect human suffering. Marjorie Gross uses humor to describe her sense of self as a result of cancer. Marsha Norman and Kat Duff call for meditation and prayer as an alternative means to restoring health. Their views assume a strong connection between mind and body and among people in general. Norman believes in the healing power of prayer, and Duff suggests that illness may be its own cure. Cindy Feltner, student writer, links Richard Preston's "Back in the Hot Zone" and Kat Duff's "Towards an Ecology of Illness" through a discussion of illness as a consequence of destructive behavior. By quoting a passage from Preston's book *The Hot Zone*, Feltner shows an interesting reversal in the concept of illness: "People are making the earth sick," she explains after quoting Preston's metaphor, "The earth is mounting an immune response against the human species." In this view, viruses are earth's attempt to cure itself.

To what degree can we claim that deviant behavior is illness? Chapter 1 included reference to psychologist Theodore Sarbin, whose essay "Metaphors of

Unwanted Conduct" traces the history of language use for "unwanted conduct" from the belief that deviant behavior was caused by demons to the current belief that it is illness. Has "mental illness" outlived its usefulness as a metaphor? What might be an alternative to reflect the evolution of psychiatric research, theory, and practice? Kay Redfield Jamison, a clinician and researcher as well as a patient diagnosed as "bipolar," or "manic-depressive," describes her experience in *An Unquiet Mind*. Susanna Kaysen, in *Girl, Interrupted*, recalls a period of her youth spent in psychiatric treatment for "borderline personality." Like Jamison, Kaysen sees "boundary" as an important metaphor for identifying states of mind and behaviors, one that has serious consequences for overstepping it.

STARTING TO THINK ABOUT IT

1. If you have read anything about the Ebola virus or have seen any of the films about it, such as *Outbreak,* starring Dustin Hoffman, how would you explain the public's fascination with the disease?

2. What has guided your thinking about AIDS? Has your thinking evolved since you first learned about it? If so, how?

3. Have you ever sought alternative methods of healing, that is, methods beyond conventional medicine? What were they, and why did you seek them?

4. In what ways do you think "mental illness" describes a disease, and in what ways does it seem not to?

Commandos of Viral Combat

Sharon Begley with Alden Cohen, Christopher Dickey, and Dana Lewis

"Commandos of Viral Combat" is a sidebar to the Newsweek article "Outbreak of Fear" (May 22, 1995), a collaborative report by journalists Sharon Begley with Alden Cohen, Christopher Dickey in Paris, and Dana Lewis in Fort Detrick, Maryland. Additional information came from bureau reports.

They call it epi-aid, short for "epidemic aid," and it's the medical equivalent of parachuting into a war zone. Once the virus jocks get the call—usually from the American ambassador in a foreign country or from an international agency like the World Health Organization (WHO)—they grab their bags and hop the first commercial flight that will drop them within striking distance of the outbreak. Staring down customs officers suspicious of the high-tech medical equipment and test tubes filled with mysterious liquids, browbeating terrified pilots to fly into the infected area, the doctors and scientists from the U.S. Centers for Disease Control, Paris's Pasteur Institute and WHO's own staff cut through daunting medical and logistical barriers. Their goal: identify the cause of the epidemic, pinpoint its source and halt its spread. In her gripping 1994 book *The Coming Plague*, Laurie Garrett aptly calls them "disease cowboys." When local docs hit the roads in a panic, as they did during the plague outbreak in India last year and the Ebola epidemic in Zaire last week, the virus hunters itch to go in.

CDC fields about 1,000 S.O.S. calls a year. Most require just over-the-phone advice, about how to contain, say, an outbreak of Lyme disease. But a CDC team heads into the field about 100 times a year, sometimes with the U.S. Army Medical Research Institute of Infectious Diseases in Fort Detrick, Md. (USAMRIID battled the Ebola outbreak described in Richard Preston's bestseller *The Hot Zone*.) Typically they take examination gloves, disposable boots, plasma, gowns with impermeable linings, syringes, needles, generators and refrigerators to store samples of blood, kidney and liver. And body bags. Once in-country, each member of a team may be ordered to take his or her temperature twice a day to catch an incipient fever that is often the first sign of a deadly infection. And they work in groups, so partners can monitor each other for fatigue that could lead to such fatal mishaps as pricking oneself with a contaminated needle. Especially with an unknown virus, "you hold your breath for a couple of weeks," says former CDC virologist Karl Johnson, who led the investigation of the 1976 Ebola outbreak in Zaire. "You never know where an epidemic will go."

PAST PLAGUES

Bubonic plague   The "Black Death" killed a full quarter of Europe's population during the 13th and 14th centuries.

Cholera   Millions died in Asia during the Dark and Middle Ages. Still resistant to all antibiotics.

Smallpox   In 1764, nearly one 10th of the Swedish population succumbed.

Typhus   More than 3 million Russians were killed during World War I.

Influenza   During the winter of 1918–19, an estimated 20 million people worldwide died.

Specialists divvy up the sleuth work. An entomologist or ecologist searches for insects or other animals that harbor the disease. In Zaire in 1979, a CDC/WHO team captured and tested several hundred animals, from mosquitoes to cows, for signs of current or past infection to discover where Ebola hides between human outbreaks (to this day, no one knows). Epidemiologists search for the "index" case, the first person to contract the disease. Then they trace the contagion to determine how it spreads (through sex? through the air?) and how long after infection symptoms appear. They seek out people who have fought off infection; their blood will contain antibodies that can identify virus in others' blood, and possibly provide serum that might save the lives of infected people. Often this requires jettisoning the impermeable suits and headgear that scare off the very people the scientists need to study. "One look at the doctors and the people would be gone, into the woods," says Johnson, now a consultant to CDC.

Primitive conditions push the epi-aid team to the breaking point. In Zaire in 1976, "we always had radios that didn't work," recalls Johnson. "Any time it rained — and that was every afternoon — the phones [in Kinshasa, their base of operations] shorted out." The sheer terror that mysterious new viruses inspire also hampers the epi-aid team. Johnson was forever persuading pilots to ferry his team into or out of the epidemic region. And when virologist Don Francis, investigating the Sudan strain of Ebola in 1976, chartered a plane in Nairobi, "the people there said they'd burn it if it came back," he recalls.

5   Once they find pilots to fly them to the outbreak, the doctors take blood and tissue samples from disease victims. USAMRIID's Aeromedical Isolation Teams whisk infected Americans — usually soldiers — back to the "Slammer," a two-bed maximum-isolation ward at Fort Detrick, where doctors take Lysol showers after checking to see if their medevaced patients are still alive. The blood and tissue samples get pigeoned out to any of the world's six biosafety level 4 (BL-4) labs, facilities that can handle the deadliest viruses. With electron microscopy, a sample of blood is examined for the presence of a new or known virus. The viruses are so deadly that scientists have to work in the equivalent of

spacesuits. "I'm the thickness of a glove away from certain disease and possible death at any point," says USAMRIID's Peter Jahrling. "From time to time, I get a reality check and ask myself, 'What the hell am I doing this for?'"

Just when environmental destruction and human mobility threaten to unleash ever more new viruses, the ranks of the disease cowboys are dwindling, says Jim Meegan, a virologist at the National Institutes of Health. With budget cuts, there are now only four epidemiologists in the CDC's pathogen group, the core of the epi-raiders. A shrinking defense budget has cost USAMRIID a third of its staff since the 1980s. WHO has few resources of its own — it has to tap outside virologists — and can be slow to recognize an emerging virus. (As one scientist says in *The Coming Plague,* "By the time WHO realized there was an AIDS epidemic it already existed on four continents.") "It's a very lean front line separating mankind from the emerging viruses," says Francis, now at the biotech firm Genentech. "Almost everyone has run away. Except for the viruses."

TALKING ABOUT IT

Seeing Metaphor: Revealing and Concealing

1. What do you think of the terms "commandos of viral combat" and "virus jocks" and the use of the imagery of war generally to describe the role of virus hunters? Do these people seem to be in the same kind of danger as soldiers in combat? Explain.

2. Virus hunters are also called "disease cowboys" here. How effective do you find this image? Does it mesh with or contradict the image of "commandos of viral combat"?

Seeing Composition: Frame, Line, Texture, Tone

1. Outline the organization of this essay. Do you think the authors have provided clear transitions from topic to topic? Explain.

2. Look closely at the language the authors use to describe the work of virus hunters. What impressions do they seem to be trying to create? Do you think they succeed?

Seeing Meaning: Navigating and Negotiating

1. "When local docs hit the road in a panic . . . ," the authors write, "the virus hunters itch to go in." What is the subtext here? That is, what is being implied about the "local docs?" Do you think this would be put the same way if the reference were to doctors in the United States? Overall, what seems to be the authors' attitude toward the "locals?"

2. At the conclusion of the essay, the point is made that "the ranks of the disease cowboys are dwindling." Why is this? Do you think the U.S. government should spend more money to fund epi-aid programs? Why or why not?

WRITING ABOUT IT

1. Sharon Begley and co-authors use the following metaphors to describe the doctors and scientists who fly into infected areas to identify disease and halt its spread: "commandos of viral combat," "disease cowboys," and "virus hunters." How are these metaphors helpful in understanding the kind of people they are, the kind of work they do, and the virus itself? How are they misleading?

2. Rewrite this short piece, copying the same factual information but inventing one or more metaphors to replace "commandos," "cowboys," and "hunters" and changing those verbs, nouns, and adjectives that extend those metaphors where they occur. Exchange rewrites with one of your classmates. Try to answer for each other the following questions: How does the new metaphor give us another understanding of the kind of people the doctors and scientists are, of the kind of work they do, and of the virus itself? What is gained and what is lost by these changes? What are the consequences of these gains and losses for the reader?

Back in the Hot Zone

RICHARD PRESTON

Richard Preston is the author of the New York Times *best-seller about the Ebola virus,* The Hot Zone *(1994), and the American Institute of Physics Award winner* First Light: The Search for the Edge of the Universe *(1987). His most recent book is* The Cobra Event: A Novel *(1997). He is a regular contributor to* The New Yorker, *where this selection appeared in 1995.*

We live in a kind of biological Internet, in which viruses travel like messages, moving at high speed from node to node, moving from city to city. Last week, reports reached the World Health Organization, in Geneva, that some kind of lethal unknown infectious agent, some kind of African hemorrhagic fever, possibly Ebola virus, was burning in Kikwit, Zaire, a poor city with a population of half a million. The city has grown in recent years. It is a transportation center some two hundred and fifty miles east of Kinshasa, the capital of Zaire, sprawling at the end point of the paved section of the Kinshasa Highway, the road that crosses Africa and along which the AIDS virus has spread. Kikwit is situated in rolling savannah threaded by slow rivers the color of chocolate milk, lined with gallery forest.

The city was in a panic. The Army had sealed off roads and wasn't allowing anyone to leave. The unknown infectious agent was causing people to die with hemorrhages flooding from the natural orifices of the body. That is, victims were bleeding out. The local people were calling it "the red diarrhea." The agent is now reported to be very similar to the Ebola Zaire strain that erupted in 1976 in villages near the Ebola River, five hundred miles north of Kikwit, where it killed nine out of ten of its infected victims. It is too early at this point to gauge how long it will take the Kikwit strain to burn itself out. It passes from person to person through blood and secretions, and it may also travel by sexual contact. It is quite contagious. There is no treatment and no cure for it.

Ebola is an emerging virus from the rain forest; it seems to come out of tropical ecosystems. It lives in some natural host, some type of fly, rodent, monkey, African cat — who knows. Where Ebola hides in the rain forest is a mystery. In the past couple of decades, it has been popping into the human species in different places and in different strains. It keeps touching the human biological Internet. Probing it, so to speak.

In the initial report received at the W.H.O., the agent was said to have infected seventy-two people and killed fifty-six. There were rumors that a medical technician had become sick, had been taken into surgery, and had essentially exploded in the O.R. — had bled all over the place. A number of people on the surgical team, it was said, had later died. Whatever was happening, it seemed that the Kikwit agent had zeroed in on the city's medical personnel and was taking them out.

5   When this scary news in its unreliable shapes reached the W.H.O., it happened that a W.H.O. scientific team was preparing to fly to Ivory Coast, in West Africa, to investigate a confirmed case of a new strain of Ebola virus there. Ebola had returned — this time to Ivory Coast. The W.H.O. Ebola team consisted of a scientist from the Institut Pasteur in Paris named Bernard Le Guenno and a French virologist named Pierre Rollin, who is currently with the Centers for Disease Control in Atlanta. Le Guenno and Rollin were diverted from their mission to Ivory Coast, and were sent to Zaire instead; they joined a ten-member W.H.O. team of doctors from South Africa, from France, from Zaire, and from the United States.

One of the South African doctors is a gigantic figure in the history of infectious-disease outbreaks named Margaretha Isaäcson. She is a grandmotherly woman who retired a couple of years ago from the South African Institute for Medical Research and went to live in a retirement community outside Johannesburg. Last week, she left a message on her home answering machine that went, "Dr. Isaäcson is not available," and she came out of retirement and flew to Zaire, and joined the team. She is in Kikwit now. During the 1976 Ebola eruption in Zaire, Margaretha Isaäcson once took off her biohazard respirator, because it interfered with her treatment of an Ebola patient, and afterward she washed up two blood-splashed rooms by hand.

The Ivory Coast Ebola case occurred some six months ago, in November, 1994, when a woman scientist from Switzerland was studying a troop of wild chimpanzees in the National Park of Tai. The Tai Forest is one of the last pristine rain forests in West Africa. The troop of chimpanzees became infected with a virus and many of them died. The Swiss woman, extremely concerned about her chimps, dissected one of the dead animals, trying to find out what had killed it, and, having come into contact with the dead chimp's blood, she developed the symptoms of Ebola virus.

Severely ill, she was flown on a commercial airliner to Switzerland for treatment. In other words, the Swiss woman entered the biological Internet. Her doctors in Switzerland did not realize that she had Ebola. They suspected the illness was dengue fever, a virus carried by mosquitoes. Nevertheless, she survived, and no other infections were reported. Bernard Le Guenno isolated the virus and, with backup confirmation from the Special Pathogens Branch of the C.D.C., identified it as a new Ebola strain, and also confirmed that the Tai Forest chimpanzees were infected with the same strain. It is known as Ebola Ivory Coast. It lives in the Tai Forest. The Tai chimps hunt colobus monkeys and eat them. Perhaps chimps are catching Ebola from colobus monkeys. Perhaps colobus monkeys are the original host of Ebola virus. Or perhaps the colobus monkeys are eating something that is the original host, and Ebola could be thereby moving up the food chain.

There was another curious case. In January, 1991, a twenty-one-year-old Swedish medical student who had been travelling in Kenya returned to Sweden. He had lived for about a month in the town of Kitale, which is at the base of Mt. Elgon, about twenty-five miles from Kitum Cave, a site that may be a hiding place of Ebola's cousin the Marburg virus. He did not visit the cave during his time near Mt. Elgon. Five days after his flight home to Sweden, he became deathly ill, and he ended up in the University Hospital in Linköping — a top-notch research hospital. He was showing all the signs of African hemorrhagic fever. His blood was clotting up internally, he had a high fever, and then he began to bleed out of the openings in his body.

In this type of illness, the patient may reach a crisis point, and can go into   10 irreversible terminal shock. This is the so-called "crash." The student went into crisis, he seemed to be crashing, and a medical team at the Linköping hospital did everything it could to save his life. A nurse was bending over his face when he suddenly vomited blood into the nurse's eyes. Two other members of the team accidentally stuck themselves with needles — possibly they were scared and shaky or, far more likely, they were working fast and the needles slipped. These accidents with blood and needles did not happen because the medical staff at Linköping were incompetent. They were highly trained. The accidents happened because they rushed in to save a patient's life, forgetful of their own safety, which is what the best doctors tend to do with a patient in crisis.

The man lived. Meanwhile, Sweden called on the United States for help — this being a suspected case of African hemorrhagic fever — and a team from the United States Army Medical Research Institute for Infectious Diseases, or USAMRIID, in Frederick, Maryland, flew into Sweden carrying biohazard spacesuits and other gear, to help contain the agent and investigate it. The investigation revealed that fifty-five medical personnel at the Linköping hospital had been exposed to the patient's blood and bodily fluids; they were all at risk of being infected. Almost unbelievably, no one became sick, including the nurse who had got a faceful of blood. The researchers were never able to identify an infectious agent in the student. It remains a case of "suspected Marburg virus." Despite the happy outcome, good doctors and good hospitals are extremely vulnerable in the face of any infectious agent that turns humans into bleeders.

Knowing all this, I began to wonder what is really happening to the local doctors, male nursing staff, and nuns on the ground in Kikwit, who are struggling in clinics and hospitals that are wretched, run-down cauldrons, virtually abandoned by government authorities, currently as hot as hell in a biological sense, and unequipped with even the most basic medical supplies, such as rubber gloves, waterproof gowns, or clean needles. For the local medical people in

Kikwit the situation is a working nightmare—at least, for those who are still alive. The doctors and staff are literally up to their elbows in blood, black vomit, and shit the color of beet soup.

Seeking some perspective, I spoke on the telephone with a doctor named Bill Close, who lived in Zaire for sixteen years, was there during the terrifying 1976 Ebola outbreak, and helped organize the effort to stop Ebola then. Dr. Close (who happens to be the father of the actress Glenn Close) was the chief doctor of the Congolese Army, and he rebuilt and ran the Mama Yemo General Hospital, a two-thousand-bed facility in the capital. He is now in effect the liaison between the Zairean government and the C.D.C. He scoffed at reports coming over the wire services that medical personnel are "fleeing" from the hospitals in the area. He said, "I can tell you that we have at least one local doctor and two nurses in Kikwit who have gone back into the hospital to work, *knowing* they are going to die. The greatest need in Kikwit right now is for rubber aprons to protect the doctors, because the blood and vomit is soaking through their operating gowns."

("That's correct," an official at the C.D.C. told me. "The surgical gowns they are using are not high-quality material. They're not plastic, and they're soaking through. And the other thing the Kikwit doctors desperately need right now is needles. Clean needles.")

15   "This is a huge, lethal African hemorrhagic virus," Dr. Close went on. "We all sort of feel that Ebola comes out of its hiding place when something occasionally alters the very delicate balance of the ecosystems, in a region where things grow as they would in a warm petri dish. But if there are lessons to be learned here, they are the human lessons. This is about people doing their duty. It's about doctors doing what has to be done, right now, without a whole lot of heroics. Have you ever been absolutely petrified with fear? Real fear? Possessed by naked fear, where you have no hope of control over your fate? When the die is cast, the fear goes away, and you do what you have to do—you get to work. That's what's happening with the medical people in Zaire right now. There are things happening there . . ." He paused. "Magnificent human things . . . How can I explain this? In Zaire in 1976, there was a nun who died of Ebola. There was a priest who gave her her last rites as she died. She had a terrible fever, sweat was pouring down her face. And blood was coming out of her eyes. She was weeping blood. Bloody tears were running down her cheeks. The priest took out his handkerchief and wiped the sweat from her forehead and the blood from her cheeks. Then, unthinkingly, he took the bloody handkerchief and wiped his own face with it. Ten days later, he was dead. One of the doctors in '76—he was a Belgian—delivered a baby in the middle of it all. There were people dying of Ebola all around in that hospital, and there was a woman in childbirth. His patient. The baby was stuck—too big for the birth canal. So the doctor performed the Zarat procedure on the woman. That's a simple and rather crude but very ef-

fective way of enlarging the outlet to remove the baby. With a knife, you split the symphysis pubis."

"What is the symphysis pubis?" I asked.

"That's the front of the pelvis. The pelvic bones. You split them. You press a scalpel through the cartilage. The bones go *pop* and the pelvis springs open, and you pull the baby out. The hospital had run out of anesthetics. So he did it without giving her an anesthetic."

"My God."

"He did have a sedative, and he gave it to her to calm her down, but she was conscious. By the time he got the baby out, the baby had stopped breathing, because of the sedative. The baby was in breathing arrest and drenched with the woman's blood. He held up the baby and put the baby's mouth to his mouth and gave the baby mouth-to-mouth resuscitation. The baby started to breathe. He pulled away, and his face and mouth were smeared with blood. There was a nurse standing by, and when she saw his face she said, 'Doctor, *do you realize what you've done?'*

" 'I do now,' he said."   20

TALKING ABOUT IT

Seeing Metaphor: Revealing and Concealing

1. "We live in a kind of biological Internet," Preston writes in his opening, and later he writes of Ebola as "probing" the human biological Internet and of an infected woman being flown to Switzerland from Africa as having "entered" the biological Internet. What is his point in using this image? What does it help suggest about Ebola and other "hot" viruses? Do you think it is apt?

2. How does Preston personify the Ebola virus, particularly in paragraphs 3–4? How does this differ from the personification of Ebola in "Commandos of Viral Combat" earlier in this chapter? Which personification do you find more effective?

Seeing Composition: Frame, Line, Texture, Tone

1. Preston divides his essay into two parts. What is the focus of paragraphs 1–11? Of paragraphs 12–20? What is the connection between the two parts? Do you think the connection could be clearer? Explain.

2. Preston ends with a story told by Dr. Bill Close about a doctor delivering a baby during the 1976 Ebola outbreak in Zaire (beginning in the middle of paragraph 15). How effective do you find this conclusion? What do you think is Preston's purpose in ending as he does?

Seeing Meaning: Navigating and Negotiating

1. In paragraphs 10–11, Preston writes about the close calls of medical personnel treating an infected patient in a Swedish hospital. What is he getting at here? Is this intended as a sort of warning?

2. In paragraph 15, Preston quotes Bill Close as saying that "magnificent human things" were happening during the Ebola outbreak in Kikwit, Zaire, in 1995. What is he referring to? How does the image of local doctors in 1995 and 1976 (as illustrated in this paragraph) contradict the image of "local docs" presented in "Commandos of Viral Combat" earlier in this chapter? Why do you think that wire reports might incorrectly suggest that medical personnel were "fleeing" from hospitals in the area.

WRITING ABOUT IT

1. Richard Preston, in the first part of the essay, uses the Internet as a metaphor for disease. Write about how he later shows disease as a metaphor for human virtue. What connection do you see between the two uses of metaphor as a way of dividing the essay into two parts? What is the effect of this strategy on your response to the second half of the essay?

2. To what extent does the computer metaphor in the first part of the essay serve to clarify for you the characteristics of the disease as well as positively affect your response to the second part of Preston's essay? To what extent does the metaphor alienate you as a reader, if it does?

AIDS as Human Suffering

PAUL FARMER AND ARTHUR KLEINMAN

Paul Farmer and Arthur Kleinman are medical anthropologists. The selection here appeared in "Living with AIDS," a special issue of Daedalus, *the journal of the American Academy of Arts and Sciences, in 1989.*

That the dominant discourse on AIDS at the close of the twentieth century is in the rational-technical language of disease control was certainly to be expected and even necessary. We anticipate hearing a great deal about the molecular biology of the virus, the clinical epidemiology of the disease's course, and the pharmacological engineering of effective treatments. Other of contemporary society's key idioms for describing life's troubles also express our reaction to AIDS: the political-economic talk of public-policy experts, the social-welfare jargon of the politicians and bureaucrats, and the latest psychological terminology of mental-health professionals. Beneath the action-oriented verbs and reassuringly new nouns of these experts' distancing terminology, the more earthy, emotional rumblings of the frightened, the accusatory, the hate-filled, and the confused members of the public are reminders that our response to AIDS emerges from deep and dividing forces in our experience and our culture.

AIDS AND HUMAN MEANINGS

Listen to the words of persons with AIDS and others affected by our society's reaction to the new syndrome:

- "I'm 42 years old. I have AIDS. I have no job. I do get $300 a month from social security and the state. I will soon receive $64 a month in food stamps. I am severely depressed. I cannot live on $300 a month. After $120 a month for rent and $120 a month for therapy, I am left with $60 for food and vitamins and other doctors and maybe acupuncture treatments and my share of utilities and oil and wood for heat. I'm sure I've forgotten several expenses like a movie once in a while and a newspaper and a book."[1]

- "I don't know what my life expectancy is going to be, but I certainly know the quality has improved. I know that not accepting the shame or the guilt or the stigma that people would throw on me has certainly extended my life expectancy. I know that being very up-front with my friends, and my family and coworkers, reduced a tremendous amount of stress, and I

213

would encourage people to be very open with friends, and if they can't handle it, then that's their problem and they're going to have to cope with it."

▪ "Here we are at an international AIDS conference. Yesterday a woman came up to me and said, 'May I have two minutes of your time?' She said, 'I'm asking doctors how they feel about treating AIDS patients.' And I said, 'Well, actually I'm not a doctor. I'm an AIDS patient,' and as she was shaking hands, her hand whipped away, she took two steps backward, and the look of horror on her face was absolutely diabolical."

▪ "My wife and I have lived here [in the United States] for fifteen years, and we speak English well, and I do O.K. driving. But the hardest time I've had in all my life, harder than Haiti, was when people would refuse to get in my cab when they discovered I was from Haiti [and therefore in their minds, a potential carrier of HIV]. It got so we would pretend to be from somewhere else, which is the worst thing you can do, I think."

All illnesses are metaphors. They absorb and radiate the personalities and social conditions of those who experience symptoms and treatments. Only a few illnesses, however, carry such cultural salience that they become icons of the times. Like tuberculosis in *fin de siècle* Europe, like cancer in the first half of the American century, and like leprosy from Leviticus to the present, AIDS speaks of the menace and losses of the times. It marks the sick person, encasing the afflicted in an exoskeleton of peculiarly powerful meanings: the terror of a lingering and untimely death, the panic of contagion, the guilt of "self-earned" illness.

AIDS has offered a new idiom for old gripes. We have used it to blame others: gay men, drug addicts, inner-city ethnics, Haitians, Africans. And we in the United States have, in turn, been accused of spreading and even creating the virus that causes AIDS. The steady progression of persons with AIDS toward the grave, so often via the poor house, has assaulted the comforting idea that risk can be managed. The world turns out to be less controllable and more dangerous, life more fragile than our insurance and welfare models pretend. We have relegated the threat of having to endure irremediable pain and early death — indeed, the very image of suffering as the paramount reality of daily existence — to past periods in history and to other, poorer societies. Optimism has its place in the scale of American virtues; stoicism and resignation in the face of unremitting hardship — unnecessary character traits in a land of plenty — do not. Suffering had almost vanished from public and private images of our society.

5   Throughout history and across cultures, life-threatening disorders have provoked questions of control (What do we do?) and bafflement (Why me?). When bubonic plague depopulated fourteenth-century Europe by perhaps as many as half to three-fourths of the population, the black death was construed as a religious problem and a challenge to the moral authority as much or even

more than as a public-health problem. In the late twentieth century, it is not surprising that great advances in scientific knowledge and technological intervention have created our chief responses to questions of control and bafflement. Yet bafflement is not driven away by the advance of scientific knowledge, for it points to another aspect of the experience of persons with AIDS that has not received the attention it warrants. It points to a concern that in other periods and in other cultures is at the very center of the societal reaction to dread disease, a concern that resonates with that which is most at stake in the human experience of AIDS even if it receives little attention in academic journals — namely, suffering.

A mortal disease forces questions of dread, of death, and of ultimate meaning to arise. Suffering is a culturally and personally distinctive form of affliction of the human spirit. If pain is distress of the body, suffering is distress of the person and of his or her family and friends. The affliction and death of persons with AIDS create master symbols of suffering; the ethical and emotional responses to AIDS are collective representations of how societies deal with suffering. The stories of sickness of people with AIDS are texts of suffering that we can scan for evidence of how cultures and communities and individuals elaborate the unique textures of personal experience out of the impersonal cellular invasion of viral RNA. Furthermore, these illness narratives point toward issues in the AIDS epidemic every bit as salient as control of the spread of infection and treatment of its biological effects.

Viewed from the perspective of suffering, AIDS must rank with smallpox, plague, and leprosy in its capacity to menace and hurt, to burden and spoil human experience, and to elicit questions about the nature of life and its significance. Suffering extends from those afflicted with AIDS to their families and intimates, to the practitioners and institutions who care for them, and to their neighborhoods and the rest of society, who feel threatened by perceived sources of the epidemic and who are thus affected profoundly yet differently by its consequences. If we minimize the significance of AIDS as human tragedy, we dehumanize people with AIDS as well as those engaged in the public-health and clinical response to the epidemic. Ultimately, we dehumanize us all.

ROBERT AND THE DIAGNOSTIC DILEMMA

It was in a large teaching hospital in Boston that we first met Robert, a forty-four-year-old man with AIDS.[2] Robert was not from Boston, but from Chicago, where he had already weathered several of the infections known to strike people with compromised immune function. His most recent battle had been with an organism similar to that which causes tuberculosis but is usually harmless to those with intact immune systems. The infection and the many drugs used to treat it had left him debilitated and depressed, and he had come east to visit his sister and regain his strength. On his way home, he was prevented from boarding his plane "for medical reasons." Beset with fever, cough, and severe shortness of breath, Robert went that night to the teaching hospital's emergency ward. Aware of his condition and its prognosis, Robert hoped that the staff there would help him to "get into shape" for the flight back to Chicago.

The physicians in the emergency ward saw their task as straightforward: to identify the cause of Robert's symptoms and, if possible, to treat it. In contemporary medical practice, identifying the cause of respiratory distress in a patient with AIDS entails following what is often called an algorithm. An algorithm, in the culture of biomedicine, is a series of sequential choices, often represented diagrammatically, which helps physicians to make diagnoses and select treatments. In Robert's case, step one, a chest X-ray, suggested the opportunistic lung parasite *Pneumocystis* as a cause for his respiratory distress; step two, examination of his sputum, confirmed it. He was then transferred to a ward in order to begin treatment of his lung infection. Robert was given the drug of choice, but did not improve. His fever, in fact, rose and he seemed more ill than ever.

10   After a few days of decline, Robert was found to have trismus: his jaw was locked shut. Because he had previously had oral candidiasis ("thrush"), his trismus and neck pain were thought to suggest the spread of the fungal infection back down the throat and pharynx and into the esophagus — a far more serious process than thrush, which is usually controlled by antifungal agents. Because Robert was unable to open his mouth, the algorithm for documenting esophagitis could not be followed. And so a "GI consult" — Robert has already had several — was called. It was hoped that the gastroenterologists, specialists at passing tubes into both ends of the gastrointestinal tract, would be better able to evaluate the nature of Robert's trismus. Robert had jumped ahead to the point in the algorithm that called for "invasive studies." The trouble is that on the night of his admission he had already declined a similar procedure.

Robert's jaw remained shut. Although he was already emaciated from two years of battle, he refused a feeding tube. Patient refusal is never part of an algorithm, and so the team turned to a new kind of logic: Is Robert mentally competent to make such a decision? Is he suffering from AIDS dementia? He was, in the words of one of those treating him, "not with the program." Another member of the team suggested that Robert had "reached the end of the algorithm" but the others disagreed. More diagnostic studies were suggested: in addition to esophagoscopy with biopsy and culture, a CT scan of the neck and head, repeated blood cultures, even a neurological consult. When these studies were mentioned to the patient, his silent stare seemed to fill with anger and despair. Doctors glanced uncomfortably at each other over their pale blue masks. Their suspicions were soon confirmed. In a shaky but decipherable hand, Robert wrote a note: "I just want to be kept clean."

Robert got a good deal more than he asked for, including the feeding tube, the endoscopy, and the CT scan of the neck. He died within hours of the last of these procedures. His physicians felt that they could not have withheld care without having some idea of what was going on.

In the discourse of contemporary biomedicine, Robert's doctors had been confronted with "a diagnostic dilemma." They had not cast the scenario described above as a moral dilemma but had discussed it in rounds as "a compliance problem." This way of talking about the case brings into relief a number of issues in the contemporary United States—not just in the culture of biomedicine but in the larger culture as well. In anthropology, one of the preferred means of examining culturally salient issues is through ethnology: in this case, we shall compare Robert's death in Boston to death from AIDS in a radically different place.

ANITA AND A DECENT DEATH

The setting is now a small Haitian village. Consisting of fewer than a thousand persons, Do Kay is composed substantially of peasant farmers who were displaced some thirty years ago by Haiti's largest dam. By all the standard measures, Kay is now very poor; its older inhabitants often blame their poverty on the massive buttress dam a few miles away and note bitterly that it has brought them neither electricity nor water.

When the first author of this paper began working in Kay, in May of 1983, the word *SIDA*, meaning AIDS, was just beginning to make its way into the rural Haitian lexicon. Interest in the illness was almost universal less than three years later. It was about then that Anita's intractable cough was attributed to tuberculosis. 15

Questions about her illness often evoked long responses. She resisted our attempts to focus discussions. "Let me tell you the story from the beginning," she once said; "otherwise you will understand nothing at all."

As a little girl, Anita recalls, she was frightened by the arguments her parents would have in the dry seasons. When her mother began coughing, the family sold their livestock in order to buy "a consultation" with a distinguished doctor in the capital. Tuberculosis, he told them, and the family felt there was little they could do other than take irregular trips to Port-au-Prince and make equally irregular attempts to placate the gods who might protect the woman. Anita dropped out of school to help take care of her mother, who died shortly after the girl's thirteenth birthday.

It was very nearly the *coup de grâce* for her father, who became depressed and abusive. Anita, the oldest of five children, bore the brunt of his spleen. "One day, I'd just had it with his yelling. I took what money I could find, about $2, and left for the city. I didn't know where to go." Anita had the good fortune to find a family in need of a maid. The two women in the household had jobs in a U.S.-owned assembly plant; the husband of one ran a snack concession out of the house. Anita received a meal a day, a bit of dry floor to sleep on, and $10 per month for what sounded like incessant labor. She was not unhappy with the arrangement, which lasted until both women were fired for participating in "political meetings."

Anita wandered about for two days until she happened upon a kinswoman selling gum and candies near a downtown theater. She was, Anita related, "a sort of aunt." Anita could come and stay with her, the aunt said, as long as she could help pay the rent. And so Anita moved into Cité Simone, the sprawling slum on the northern fringes of the capital.

20   It was through the offices of her aunt that she met Vincent, one of the few men in the neighborhood with anything resembling a job: "He unloaded the whites' luggage at the airport." Vincent made a living from tourists' tips. In 1982, the year before Haiti became associated, in the North American press, with AIDS, the city of Port-au-Prince counted tourism as its chief industry. In the setting of an unemployment rate of greater than 60 percent, Vincent could command considerable respect. He turned his attention to Anita. "What could I do, really? He had a good job. My aunt thought I should go with him." Anita was not yet fifteen when she entered her first and only sexual union. Her lover set her up in a shack in the same neighborhood. Anita cooked and washed and waited for him.

When Vincent fell ill, Anita again became a nurse. It began insidiously, she recalls: night sweats, loss of appetite, swollen lymph nodes. Then came months of unpredictable and debilitating diarrhea. "We tried everything—doctors, charlatans, herbal remedies, injections, prayers." After a year of decline, she took Vincent to his hometown in the south of Haiti. There it was revealed that Vincent's illness was the result of malign magic: "It was one of the men at the airport who did this to him. The man wanted Vincent's job. He sent an AIDS death to him."

The voodoo priest who heard their story and deciphered the signs was straightforward. He told Anita and Vincent's family that the sick man's chances were slim, even with the appropriate interventions. There were, however, steps to be taken. He outlined them, and the family followed them, but still Vincent succumbed. "When he died, I felt spent. I couldn't get out of bed. I thought that his family would try to help me to get better, but they didn't. I knew I needed to go home."

She made it as far as Croix-des-Bouquets, a large market town at least two hours from Kay. There she collapsed, feverish and coughing and was taken in by a woman who lived near the market. She stayed for a month, unable to walk, until her father came to take her back home. Five years had elapsed since she'd last seen him. Anita's father was by then a friendly but broken-down man with a leaking roof over his one-room, dirt-floor hut. It was no place for a sick woman, the villagers said, and Anita's godmother, honoring twenty-year-old vows, made room in her overcrowded but dry house.

Anita was diagnosed as having tuberculosis, and she responded to antituberculosis therapy. But six months after the initiation of treatment, she declined rapidly. Convinced that she was indeed taking her medications, we were concerned about AIDS, especially on hearing of the death of her lover. Anita's father was poised to sell his last bit of land in order to "buy more nourishing food for the child." It was imperative that the underlying cause of Anita's poor response to treatment be found. A laboratory test confirmed our suspicions.

Anita's father and godmother alone were apprised of the test results. When asked what she knew about AIDS, the godmother responded, "AIDS is an infectious disease that has no cure. You can get it from the blood of an infected person." For this reason, she said, she had nothing to fear in caring for Anita. Further, she was adamant that Anita not be told of her diagnosis — "That will only make her suffer more" — and skeptical about the value of the AIDS clinic in Port-au-Prince. "Why should we take her there?" asked Anita's godmother wearily. "She will not recover from this disease. She will have to endure the heat and humiliation of the clinic. She will not find a cool place to lie down. What she might find is a pill or an injection to make her feel more comfortable for a short time. I can do better than that."

And that is what Anita's godmother proceeded to do. She attempted to sit Anita up every day and encouraged her to drink a broth promised to "make her better." The godmother kept her as clean as possible, consecrating the family's two sheets to her goddaughter. She gave Anita her pillow and stuffed a sack with rags for herself. The only thing she requested from us at the clinic was "a beautiful soft wool blanket that will not irritate the child's skin."

In one of several thoughtful interviews accorded us, Anita's godmother insisted that "for some people, a decent death is as important as a decent life. . . . The child has had a hard life; her life has always been difficult. It's important that she be washed of bitterness and regret before she dies." Anita was herself very philosophic in her last months. She seemed to know of her diagnosis. Although she never mentioned the word *SIDA,* she did speak of the resignation appropriate to "diseases from which you cannot escape." She stated, too, that she was "dying from the sickness that took Vincent," although she denied that she had been the victim of witchcraft — "I simply caught it from him."

Anita did not ask to be taken to a hospital, nor did her slow decline occasion any request for further diagnostic tests. What she most wanted was a radio — "for the news and the music" — and a lambswool blanket. She especially enjoyed the opportunity to "recount my life," and we were able to listen to her narrative until hours before her death.

AIDS IN CULTURAL CONTEXT

The way in which a person, a family, or a community responds to AIDS may reveal a great deal about core cultural values. Robert's story underlines our reliance on technological answers to moral and medical questions. "Americans love machines more than life itself," asserts author Philip Slater in a compelling analysis of middle-class North American culture. "Any challenge to the technological-over-social priority threatens to expose the fact that Americans have lost their manhood and their capacity to control their environment."[3] One of the less noticed but perhaps one of the farthest-reaching consequences of the AIDS epidemic has been the weakening of North America's traditional confidence in the ability of its experts to solve every kind of problem. In the words of one person with the disorder, "The terror of AIDS lies in the collapse of our faith in technology."[4]

This core cultural value is nowhere more evident than in contemporary tertiary medicine, which remains the locus of care for the vast majority of AIDS patients. Despite the uniformity of treatment outcome, despite the lack of proven efficacy of many diagnostic and therapeutic procedures, despite their high costs, it has been difficult for practitioners to limit their recourse to these interventions. "When you're at Disney World," remarked one of Robert's physicians ironically, "you take all the rides."

Robert's illness raises issues that turn about questions of autonomy and accountability. The concept of autonomous individuals who are solely responsible for their fate, including their illness, is a powerful cultural premise in North American society. On the positive side, this concept supports concern for individual rights and respect for individual differences and achievement. A more ominous aspect of this core cultural orientation is that it often justifies blaming the victims. Illness is said to be the outcome of the free choice of high-risk behavior.

This has been especially true in the AIDS epidemic, which has reified an invidious distinction between "innocent victims" — infants and hemophiliacs — and, by implication, "the guilty" — persons with AIDS who are homosexuals or intravenous drug users. Robert's lonely and medicalized death is what so many North Americans fear: "He was terrified. He knew what AIDS meant. He knew what happens. Your friends desert you, your lover kicks you out into the street. You get fired, you get evicted from your apartment. You're a leper. You die alone."[5] The conflation of correlation and responsibility has the effect of making sufferers feel guilt and shame. The validity of their experience is contested. Suffering, once delegitimated, is complicated and even distorted; our response to the sufferer, blocked.

In contrast, in Haiti and in many African societies, where individual rights are often underemphasized and also frequently unprotected, and where the idea of personal accountability is less powerful than is the idea of the primacy of social relationships, blaming the victim is also a less frequent response to AIDS. Noticeably absent is the revulsion with which AIDS patients have been faced in the United States, in both clinical settings and in their communities. This striking difference cannot be ascribed to Haitian ignorance of modes of transmission. On the contrary, the Haitians we have interviewed have ideas of etiology and epidemiology that reflect the incursion of the "North American ideology" of AIDS —

that the disease is caused by a virus and is somehow related to homosexuality and contaminated blood. These are subsumed, however, in properly Haitian beliefs about illness causation. Long before the advent of AIDS to Do Kay, we might have asked the following question: some fatal diseases are known to be caused by "microbes" but may also be "sent" by someone; is *SIDA* such a disease?

Differences in the responses of caregivers to Robert and Anita — such as whether to inform them of their diagnosis or undertake terminal care as a family or a community responsibility — also reflect the ego-centered orientation in North American cities and the more sociocentric orientation in the Haitian village. An ironic twist is that it is in the impersonal therapeutic setting of North American health-care institutions that concern for the patient's personhood is articulated. It is, however, a cool bioethical attention to abstract individual rights rather than a validation of humane responses to concrete existential needs. Perhaps this cultural logic — of medicine as technology, of individual autonomy as the most inviolable of rights, and so of individuals as responsible for most of the ills that befall them — helps us to understand how Robert's lonely death, so rich in all the technology applied to his last hours, could be so poor in all those supportive human virtues that resonate from the poverty-stricken village where Anita died among friends.

A core clinical task would seem to be helping patients to die a decent   35
death. For all the millions of words spilled on the denial of death in our society and the various psychotechniques advertised to aid us to overcome this social silence, AIDS testifies vividly that our secular public culture is simply unable to come to terms with mortality.

A final question might be asked in examining the stories of Robert and Anita: just how representative are they of the millions already exposed to HIV? As a middle-class, white gay male, Robert is thought by many to be a "typical victim of AIDS." But he is becoming increasingly less typical in the United States, where the epidemic is claiming more and more blacks and Hispanics, and Robert would not be sociologically representative of the typical AIDS patient in much of the rest of the world. In many Third World settings, sex differences in the epidemiology of HIV infection are unremarkable: in Haiti, for example, there is almost parity between the sexes. Most importantly, most people with AIDS are not middle-class and insured. All this points to the fact that the virus that causes AIDS might exact its greatest toll in the Third World.

AIDS IN GLOBAL CONTEXT

Although the pandemic appears to be most serious in North America and Europe, per capita rates reveal that fully seventeen of the twenty countries most affected by AIDS are in Africa or the Caribbean. Further, although there is heartening evidence that the epidemic is being more effectively addressed in the North American gay community, there is no indication that the spread of HIV has been curbed in the communities in which women like Anita struggle. Although early reports of high HIV seroprevalence were clearly based on faulty research, even recent and revised estimates remain grim: "In urban areas in some sub-Saharan countries, up to 25% of young adults are *already* HIV carriers, with rates among those reporting to clinics for sexually transmitted diseases passing 30%, and among female prostitutes up to 90%."[6] In other words, the countries most affected are precisely those that can least afford it.

These figures also remind us that AIDS has felled many like Anita — the poor, women of color, victims of many sorts of oppression and misfortune. Although heterosexual contact seems to be the means of spreading in many instances, not all who contract the disease are "promiscuous," a label that has often offended people in Africa, Haiti, and elsewhere. *Promiscuous* fails utterly to capture the dilemmas of millions like Anita. In an essay entitled "The Myth of African Promiscuity," one Kenyan scholar refers to the "'new poor': the massive pool of young women living in the most deprived conditions in shanty towns and slums across Africa, who are available for the promise of a meal, new clothes, or a few pounds."[7]

Equally problematic, and of course related, is the term *prostitute*. It is often used indiscriminately to refer to a broad spectrum of sexual activity. In North America, the label has been misused in investigations of HIV seroprevalence: "the category *prostitute* is taken as an undifferentiated 'risk group' rather than as an occupational category whose members should, for epidemiological purposes, be divided into IV drug users and nonusers — with significantly different rates of HIV infection — as other groups are."[8] A more historical view reminds us that prostitutes have often been victims of scapegoating and that there has long been more energy for investigation of the alleged moral shortcomings of sex workers than for the economic underpinnings of their work.

40   The implications of this sort of comparative exercise, which remains a cornerstone of social anthropology, are manifold. The differences speak directly to those who would apply imported models of prevention to rural Haiti or Africa or any other Third World setting. A substantial public-health literature, reflecting the fundamentally interventionist perspective of that discipline, is inarguably necessary in the midst of an epidemic without cure or promising treatment. The same must be true for the burgeoning biomedical literature on AIDS. But with what consequences have these disciplines ignored the issue of AIDS as suffering? Whether reduced to parasite-host interactions or to questions of shifting incidence and prevalence among risk groups, AIDS has meant suffering on a large scale, and this suffering is not captured in these expert discourses on the epidemic.

The meaning of suffering in this context is distinctive not only on account of different beliefs about illness and treatment responses but because of the brute reality of grinding poverty, high child and maternal mortality, routinized demoralization and oppression, and suffering as a central part of existence. The response to AIDS in such settings must deal with this wider context of human misery and its social sources. Surely it is unethical — in the broadest sense, if not in the narrow technical biomedical limits to the term — for international health experts to turn their backs on the suffering of people with AIDS in the Third World and to concentrate solely on the prevention of new cases.

DEALING WITH AIDS AS SUFFERING

To what practical suggestions does a view of AIDS as human suffering lead?

Suffering Compounded by Inappropriate Use of Resources

The majority of all medical-care costs for AIDS patients is generated by acute inpatient care. In many ways, however, infection with HIV is more like a chronic disease. Based on cases of transfusion-associated HIV transmission in the United States, the mean time between exposure to the virus and the development of AIDS is over eight years. This period may well be lengthened by drugs already available. And as the medical profession becomes more skilled at managing the AIDS condition, the average time of survival of patients with the full-blown syndrome will also be extended. For many with AIDS, outpatient treatment will be both more cost-effective and more humane. For the terminally ill, home or hospice care may be preferred to acute-care settings, especially for people who "just want to be kept clean." Helping patients to die a decent death was once an accepted aspect of the work of health professionals. It must be recognized and appropriately supported as a core clinical task in the care of persons with AIDS.

Not a small component of humane care for people with AIDS is soliciting their stories of sickness, listening to their narratives of the illness, so as to help them give meaning to their suffering. Restoring this seemingly forgotten healing skill will require a transformation in the work and training of practitioners and a reorganization of time and objectives in health-care delivery systems.

The practitioner should initiate informed negotiation with alternative lay 45 perspectives on care and provide what amounts to brief medical psychotherapy for the threats and losses that make chronic illness so difficult to bear. But such a transformation in the provision of care will require a significant shift in the allocation of resources, including a commitment to funding psychosocial services as well as appropriate providers — visiting nurses, home health aides, physical and occupational therapists, general practitioners, and other members of teams specializing in long-term, out-patient care.

Suffering Magnified by Discrimination

In a recent study of the U.S. response to AIDS, the spread of HIV was compared to that of polio, another virus that struck young people, triggered public panic, and received regular attention in the popular media. "Although these parallels are strong," notes the author, "one difference is crucial: there was little early sympathy for victims of AIDS because those initially at risk — homosexual men, Haitian immigrants, and drug addicts — were not in the mainstream of society. In contrast, sympathy for polio patients was extensive."[9] This lack of sympathy is part of a spectrum that extends to hostility and even violence, and that has led to discrimination in housing, employment, insurance, and the granting of visas.[10] The victims of such discrimination have been not only people with AIDS or other manifestations of HIV infection but those thought to be in "risk groups."

In some cases, these prejudices are only slightly muted in clinical settings. In our own experience in U.S. hospitals, there is markedly more sympathy for those referred to as "the innocent victims" — patients with transfusion-associated AIDS and HIV-infected babies. At other times, irrational infection-control precautions do little more than heighten patients' feelings of rejection. Blame and recrimination are reactions to the diseases in rural Haiti as well — but there the finger is not often pointed at those with the disease.

Although the President's Commission on AIDS called for major coordinated efforts to address discrimination, what has been done has been desultory, unsystematic, and limited in reach. While legislation is crucial, so too is the development of public-education programs that address discrimination and suffering.

Suffering Augmented by Fear

Underlying at least some of the discrimination, spite, and other inappropriate responses to AIDS is fear. We refer not to the behavior-modifying fear of "the worried well" but to the more visceral fear that has played so prominent a role in the epidemic. It is fear that prompts someone to refuse to get into a taxi driven by a Haitian man; it is fear that leads a reporter to wrench her hand from that of a person with AIDS; it is fear that underpins some calls for widespread HIV-antibody testing, and fear that has led some health professionals to react to patients in degrading fashion. The fact that so much of this fear is "irrational" has thus far had little bearing on its persistence.

50   Dissemination of even a few key facts — by people with AIDS, leaders of local communities, elected officials and other policy-makers, teachers, and health professionals — should help to assuage fear. HIV is transmitted through parenteral, mucous-membrane, or open-wound contact with contaminated blood or body fluids and not through casual contact. Although the risk of transmission of HIV to health-care professionals is not zero, it is extremely low, even

after percutaneous exposure (studies show that, of more than 1,300 exposed health-care workers, only four seroconverted[11]).

Suffering Amplified by Social Death

In several memoirs published in North America, persons with AIDS have complained of the immediate social death their diagnosis has engendered. "For some of my friends and family, I was dead as soon as they heard I had AIDS," a community activist informed us. "That was over two years ago." Even asymptomatic but seropositive individuals, whose life expectancy is often better than that of persons with most cancers and many common cardiovascular disorders, have experienced this reaction. Many North Americans with AIDS have made it clear that they do not wish to be referred to as victims: "As a person with AIDS," writes Navarre, "I can attest to the sense of diminishment at seeing and hearing myself referred to as an AIDS victim, an AIDS sufferer, an AIDS case — as anything but what I am, a person with AIDS. I am a person with a condition. I am not that condition."[12]

It is nonetheless necessary to plan humane care for persons with a chronic and deadly disease — "without needlessly assaulting my denial," as a young man recently put it. The very notion of hospice care will need rethinking if its intended clients are a group of young and previously vigorous persons. Similarly, our cross-cultural research has shown us that preferred means of coping with a fatal disease are shaped by biography and culture. There are no set "stages" that someone with AIDS will go through, and there can be no standard professional response.

Suffering Generated by Inequities

AIDS is caused, we know, by a retrovirus. But we need not look to Haiti to see that inequities have sculpted the AIDS epidemic. The disease, it has been aptly noted, "moves along the fault lines of our society."[13] Of all infants born with AIDS in the United States, approximately 80 percent are black or Hispanic.[14] Most of these are the children of IV drug users, and attempts to stem the virus may force us to confront substance abuse in the context of our own society. For as Robert Gallo and Luc Montagnier assert, "efforts to control AIDS must be aimed in part at eradicating the conditions that give rise to drug addiction."[15]

There are inequities in the way we care for AIDS patients. In the hospital where Robert died, AZT — the sole agent with proven efficacy in treating HIV infection — is not on formulary. Patients needing the drug who are not in a research protocol have to send someone to the drugstore to buy it — if they happen to have the $10,000 per year AZT can cost or an insurance policy that covers these costs. Such factors may prove important in explaining the striking ethnic differences in average time of survival following diagnosis of AIDS. In one report it was noted that, "while the average lifespan of a white person after diagnosis is two years, the average minority person survives only 19 weeks."[16]

55   From rural Haiti, it is not the local disparities but rather the international inequities that are glaring. In poor countries, drugs like AZT are simply not available. As noted above, the AIDS pandemic is most severe in the countries that can least afford a disaster of these dimensions. A view of AIDS as human suffering forces us to lift our eyes from local settings to the true dimensions of this worldwide tragedy.

Compassionate involvement with persons who have AIDS may require listening carefully to their stories, whether narratives of suffering or simply attempts to recount their lives. Otherwise, as Anita pointed out, we may understand nothing at all.

NOTES

We thank Carla Fujimoto, Huan Saussy, and Barbara de Zalduondo for their thoughtful comments on this essay.

1. The first three of the four quotations cited here are the voices of persons with AIDS who attended the Third International Conference on AIDS, held in Washington, D.C. in June 1987. Their comments are published passim in 4 (1) (Winter/Spring 1988) of *New England Journal of Public Policy*. All subsequent unreferenced quotations are from tape-recorded interviews accorded the first author.

2. All informants' names are pseudonyms, as are "Do Kay" and "Ba Kay." Other geographical designations are as cited.

3. Philip Slater, *The Pursuit of Loneliness: American Culture at the Breaking Point* (Boston: Beacon Press, 1970), 49, 51.

4. Emmanuel Dreuilhe, *Moral Embrace: Living with AIDS* (New York: Hill and Wang, 1988), 20.

5. George Whitmore, *Someone Was Here: Profiles in the AIDS Epidemic* (New York: New American Library, 1988), 26.

6. Renée Sabatier, *Blaming Others: Prejudice, Race, and Worldwide AIDS* (Philadelphia: New Society Publishers, 1988), 15.

7. Professor Aina, ibid., 80.

8. Jan Zita Grover, "AIDS: Keywords," in *AIDS: Cultural Analysis/Cultural Activism* (Cambridge: MIT Press, 1988), 25–26.

9. Sandra Panem, *The AIDS Bureaucracy* (Cambridge: Harvard University Press, 1988), 15.

10. See Sabatier for an overview of AIDS-related discrimination. As regards Haiti and Haitians, see Paul Farmer, "AIDS and Accusation: Haiti, Haitians, and the Geography of Blame," in *Cultural Aspects of AIDS: Anthropology and the Global Pandemic* (New York: Praeger, in press). The degree of antipathy is suggested by a recent *New York Times*–CBS News poll of 1,606 persons: "Only 36 percent of those interviewed said they had a lot or some sympathy for 'people who get AIDS from homosexual activity,' and 26 percent said

they had a lot or some sympathy for 'people who get AIDS from sharing needles while using illegal drugs'" (*New York Times*, 14 October 1988, A12).

11. Infectious Diseases Society of America, 276.

12. Max Navarre, "Fighting the Victim Label," in *AIDS: Cultural Analysis/Cultural Activism* (Cambridge: MIT Press, 1988), 143.

13. Mary Catherine Bateson and Richard Goldsby, *Thinking AIDS: The Social Response to the Biological Threat* (Reading, Mass.: Addison-Wesley, 1988), 2.

14. Samuel Friedman, Jo Sotheran, Abu Abdul-Quadar, Beny Primm, Don Des Jarlais, Paula Kleinman, Conrad Mauge, Douglas Goldsmith, Wafaa El-Sadr, and Robert Maslansky, "The AIDS Epidemic among Blacks and Hispanics," *The Milbank Quarterly* 65, suppl. 2 (1987): 455–99.

15. Robert Gallo and Luc Montagnier, "AIDS in 1988," *Scientific American* 259 (4) (October 1988): 48.

16. Sabatier, 19.

TALKING ABOUT IT

Seeing Metaphor: Revealing and Concealing

1. "All illnesses are metaphors," write Farmer and Kleinman. "They absorb and radiate the personalities and social conditions of those who experience symptoms and treatments." What are they saying here? What do you make of the verbs "absorb and radiate" in this context? As a metaphor, how might AIDS differ from, say, cancer or heart disease?

2. The authors here encourage their readers to emphasize the perspective of "human suffering" when thinking about people with AIDS. What is their goal? Did they succeed in getting you to revise your own view of AIDS as metaphor? Explain.

Seeing Composition: Frame, Line, Texture, Tone

1. At the heart of the argument here are the stories of two AIDS deaths. How do these serve to illustrate the authors' point? Do you find them effective?

2. The authors quote the following from an article by Max Navarre: "As a person with AIDS, I can attest to the sense of diminishment at seeing and hearing myself referred to as an AIDS victim, an AIDS sufferer, an AIDS case—as anything but what I am, a person with AIDS. I am a person with a condition. I am not that condition." What does this quotation contribute to their argument? Specifically, does the fact that Navarre doesn't want to be referred to as "an AIDS sufferer" in any way contradict the authors' central argument about "AIDS as human suffering"?

Seeing Meaning: Navigating and Negotiating

1. In paragraph 4, Farmer and Kleinman write, "Optimism has its place in the scale of American virtues; stoicism and resignation in the face of unremitting hardship—unnecessary character traits in a land of plenty—do not." Do you agree with this statement? In terms of terminal illness, do you think "stoicism and resignation" should outweigh "optimism"?

2. The authors quote Philip Slater as writing, "Americans love machines more than life itself. . . . The terror of AIDS lies in the collapse of our faith in technology" (paragraph 29). How does this statement relate to their subsequent point about "autonomy and accountability" (paragraphs 31–34)?

WRITING ABOUT IT

1. Either individually or collaboratively, catalog all the ways in which Farmer and Kleinman identify AIDS as human suffering. Then, individually or collaboratively, decide which of these can be said to be true of all diseases. Use these ways as the basis of an essay in which you answer why those you've chosen can be said to be true of all diseases and how that affects your response to AIDS.

2. What are the main differences, in your reading, between the suffering and deaths of Robert and Anita? How might those differences reflect their cultures? In what ways do cross-cultural case studies and interviews help us meet the challenge of coping with the human dimension of AIDS?

AIDS and Its Metaphors

SUSAN SONTAG

Susan Sontag is an essayist, philosopher, novelist, short-story writer, and filmmaker. Among her many works are Illness as Metaphor *(1978) and* AIDS and Its Metaphors *(1988), the source of the selection here.*

Just as one might predict for a disease that is not yet fully understood as well as extremely recalcitrant to treatment, the advent of this terrifying new disease, new at least in its epidemic form, has provided a large-scale occasion for the metaphorizing of illness.

Strictly speaking, AIDS — acquired immune deficiency syndrome — is not the name of an illness at all. It is the name of a medical condition, whose consequences are a spectrum of illnesses. In contrast to syphilis and cancer, which provide prototypes for most of the images and metaphors attached to AIDS, the very definition of AIDS requires the presence of other illnesses, so-called opportunistic infections and malignancies. But though not in *that* sense a single disease, AIDS lends itself to being regarded as one — in part because, unlike cancer and like syphilis, it is thought to have a single cause.

AIDS has a dual metaphoric genealogy. As a microprocess, it is described as cancer is: an invasion. When the focus is transmission of the disease, an older metaphor, reminiscent of syphilis, is invoked: pollution. (One gets it from the blood or sexual fluids of infected people or from contaminated blood products.) But the military metaphors used to describe AIDS have a somewhat different focus from those used in describing cancer. With cancer, the metaphor scants the issue of causality (still a murky topic in cancer research) and picks up at the point at which rogue cells inside the body mutate, eventually moving out from an original site or organ to overrun other organs or systems — a domestic subversion. In the description of AIDS the enemy is what causes the disease, an infectious agent that comes from the outside:

> The invader is tiny, about one sixteen-thousandth the size of the head
> of a pin. . . . Scouts of the body's immune system, large cells called
> macrophages, sense the presence of the diminutive foreigner and
> promptly alert the immune system. It begins to mobilize an array of cells
> that, among other things, produce antibodies to deal with the threat.
> Single-mindedly, the AIDS virus ignores many of the blood cells in its
> path, evades the rapidly advancing defenders and homes in on the master
> coordinator of the immune system, a helper T cell. . . .

This is the language of a political paranoia, with its characteristic distrust of a pluralistic world. A defense system consisting of cells "that, among other things, produce antibodies to deal with the threat" is, predictably, no match for an invader who advances "single-mindedly." And the science-fiction flavor, already present in cancer talk, is even more pungent in accounts of AIDS—this one comes from *Time* magazine in late 1986—with infection described like the high-tech warfare for which we are being prepared (and inured) by the fantasies of our leaders and by video entertainments. In the era of Star Wars and Space Invaders, AIDS has proved an ideally comprehensible illness:

> On the surface of that cell, it finds a receptor into which one of its envelope proteins fits perfectly, like a key into a lock. Docking with the cell, the virus penetrates the cell membrane and is stripped of its protective shell in the process. . . .

Next the invader takes up permanent residence, by a form of alien takeover familiar in science-fiction narratives. The body's own cells *become* the invader. With the help of an enzyme the virus carries with it,

> the naked AIDS virus converts its RNA into . . . DNA, the master molecule of life. The molecule then penetrates the cell nucleus, inserts itself into a chromosome and takes over part of the cellular machinery, directing it to produce more AIDS viruses. Eventually, overcome by its alien product, the cell swells and dies, releasing a flood of new viruses to attack other cells. . . .

As viruses attack other cells, runs the metaphor, so "a host of opportunistic diseases, normally warded off by a healthy immune system, attacks the body," whose integrity and vigor have been sapped by the sheer replication of "alien product" that follows the collapse of its immunological defenses. "Gradually weakened by the onslaught, the AIDS victim dies, sometimes in months, but almost always within a few years of the first symptoms." Those who have not already succumbed are described as "under assault, showing the telltale symptoms of the disease," while millions of others "harbor the virus, vulnerable at any time to a final, all-out attack."

Cancer makes cells proliferate; in AIDS, cells die. Even as this original model of AIDS (the mirror image of leukemia) has been altered, descriptions of how the virus does its work continue to echo the way the illness is perceived as infiltrating the society. "AIDS Virus Found to Hide in Cells, Eluding Detection by Normal Tests" was the headline of a recent front-page story in the *New York Times* announcing the discovery that the virus can "lurk" for years in the macrophages—disrupting their disease-fighting function without killing them, "even when the macrophages are filled almost to bursting with virus," and without producing antibodies, the chemicals the body makes in response to "invading agents" and whose presence has been regarded as an infallible marker of the syndrome.[1] That the virus isn't lethal for *all* the cells where it takes up residence, as is now thought, only increases the illness-foe's reputation for wiliness and invincibility.

What makes the viral assault so terrifying is that contamination, and therefore vulnerability, is understood as permanent. Even if someone infected were never to develop any symptoms — that is, the infection remained, or could by medical intervention be rendered, inactive — the viral enemy would be forever within. In fact, so it is believed, it is just a matter of time before something awakens ("triggers") it, before the appearance of "the telltale symptoms." Like syphilis, known to generations of doctors as "the great masquerader," AIDS is a clinical construction, an inference. It takes its identity from the presence of *some* among a long, and lengthening, roster of symptoms (no one has everything that AIDS could be), symptoms which "mean" that what the patient has is this illness. The construction of the illness rests on the invention not only of AIDS as a clinical entity but of a kind of junior AIDS, called AIDS-related complex (ARC), to which people are assigned if they show "early" and often intermittent symptoms of immunological deficit such as fevers, weight loss, fungal infections, and swollen lymph glands. AIDS is progressive, a disease of time. Once a certain density of symptoms is attained, the course of the illness can be swift, and brings atrocious suffering. Besides the commonest "presenting" illnesses (some hitherto unusual, at least in fatal form, such as a rare skin cancer and a rare form of pneumonia), a plethora of disabling, disfiguring, and humiliating symptoms make the AIDS patient steadily more infirm, helpless, and unable to control or take care of basic functions and needs.

The sense in which AIDS is a slow disease makes it more like syphilis, which is characterized in terms of "stages," than like cancer. Thinking in terms of "stages" is essential to discourse about AIDS. Syphilis in its most dreaded form is "tertiary syphilis," syphilis in its third stage. What is called AIDS is generally understood as the last of three stages — the first of which is infection with a human immunodeficiency virus (HIV) and early evidence of inroads on the immune

---

1. The larger role assigned to the macrophages — "to serve as a reservoir for the AIDS virus because the virus multiplies in them but does not kill them, as it kills T-4 cells" — is said to explain the not uncommon difficulty of finding infected T-4 lymphocytes in patients who have antibodies to the virus and symptoms of AIDS. (It is still assumed that antibodies will develop once the virus spreads to these "key target" cells.) Evidence of presently infected populations of cells has been as puzzlingly limited or uneven as the evidence of infection in the populations of human societies — puzzling, because of the conviction that the disease is everywhere, and must spread. "Doctors have estimated that as few as one in a million T-4 cells are infected, which led some to ask where the virus hides. . . ." Another resonant speculation, reported in the same article (the *New York Times*, June 7, 1988): "Infected macrophages can transmit the virus to other cells, possibly by touching the cells."

system — with a long latency period between infection and the onset of the "tell-tale" symptoms. (Apparently not as long as syphilis, in which the latency period between secondary and tertiary illness might be decades. But it is worth noting that when syphilis first appeared in epidemic form in Europe at the end of the fifteenth century, it was a rapid disease, of an unexplained virulence that is unknown today, in which death often occurred in the second stage, sometimes within months or a few years.) Cancer *grows* slowly: It is not thought to be, for a long time, latent. (A convincing account of a process in terms of "stages" seems invariably to include the notion of a normative delay or halt in the process, such as is supplied by the notion of latency.) True, a cancer is "staged." This is a principal tool of diagnosis, which means classifying it according to its gravity, determining how "advanced" it is. But it is mostly a spatial notion: that the cancer advances through the body, traveling or migrating along predictable routes. Cancer is first of all a disease of the body's geography, in contrast to syphilis and AIDS, whose definition depends on constructing a temporal sequence of stages.

Syphilis is an affliction that didn't have to run its ghastly full course, to paresis (as it did for Baudelaire and Maupassant and Jules de Goncourt), and could and often did remain at the stage of nuisance, indignity (as it did for Flaubert). The scourge was also a cliché, as Flaubert himself observed. "SYPHILIS. Everybody has it, more or less," reads one entry in the *Dictionary of Accepted Opinions,* his treasury of mid-nineteenth-century platitudes. And syphilis did manage to acquire a darkly positive association in late-nineteenth- and early-twentieth-century Europe, when a link was made between syphilis and heightened ("feverish") mental activity that parallels the connection made since the era of the Romantic writers between pulmonary tuberculosis and heightened emotional activity. As if in honor of all the notable writers and artists who ended their lives in syphilitic witlessness, it came to be believed that the brain lesions of neurosyphilis might actually inspire original thought or art. Thomas Mann, whose fiction is a storehouse of early-twentieth-century disease myths, makes this notion of syphilis as muse central to his *Doctor Faustus,* with its protagonist a great composer whose voluntarily contracted syphilis — the Devil guarantees that the infection will be limited to the central nervous system — confers on him twenty-four years of incandescent creativity. E. M. Cioran recalls how, in Romania in the late 1920s, syphilis-envy figured in his adolescent expectations of literary glory: He would discover that he had contracted syphilis, be rewarded with several hyperproductive years of genius, then collapse into madness. This romanticizing of the dementia characteristic of neurosyphilis was the forerunner of the much more persistent fantasy in this century about mental illness as a source of artistic creativity or spiritual originality. But with AIDS — though dementia is also a common, late symptom — no compensatory mythology has arisen, or seems likely to arise. AIDS, like cancer, does not allow romanticizing or sentimentalizing, perhaps because its association with death is too powerful. In Krzysztof Zanussi's film *Spiral* (1978), the most truthful account I know of anger at dying, the protagonist's illness is never specified; therefore, it *has* to be cancer. For several generations now, the generic idea of death has been a death from cancer, and a cancer death is experienced as a generic defeat. Now the generic rebuke to life and to hope is AIDS.

"Plague" is the principal metaphor by which the AIDS epidemic is understood. And because of AIDS, the popular misidentification of cancer as an epidemic, even as a plague, seems to be receding: AIDS has banalized cancer.

Plague, from the Latin *plaga* (stroke, wound), has long been used metaphorically as the highest standard of collective calamity, evil, scourge — Procopius, in his masterpiece of calumny, *The Secret History,* called the Emperor Justinian worse than the plague ("fewer escaped") — as well as being a general name for many frightening diseases. Although the disease to which the word is permanently affixed produced the most lethal of recorded epidemics, being experienced as a pitiless slayer is not necessary for a disease to be regarded as plague-like. Leprosy, very rarely fatal now, was not much more so when at its greatest epidemic strength, between about 1050 and 1350. And syphilis has been regarded as a plague — Blake speaks of "the youthful Harlot's curse" that "blights with plagues the Marriage hearse" — not because it killed often, but because it was disgracing, disempowering, disgusting.

It is usually epidemics that are thought of as plagues. And these mass inci-   10 dences of illness are understood as inflicted, not just endured. Considering illness as a punishment is the oldest idea of what causes illness, and an idea opposed by all attention to the ill that deserves the noble name of medicine. Hippocrates, who wrote several treatises on epidemics, specifically ruled out "the wrath of God" as a cause of bubonic plague. But the illnesses interpreted in antiquity as punishments, like the plague in *Oedipus,* were not thought to be shameful, as leprosy and subsequently syphilis were to be. Diseases, insofar as they acquired meaning, were collective calamities, and judgments on a community. Only injuries and disabilities, not diseases, were thought of as individually merited. For an analogy in the literature of antiquity to the modern sense of a shaming, isolating disease, one would have to turn to Philoctetes and his stinking wound.

The most feared diseases, those that are not simply fatal but transform the body into something alienating, like leprosy and syphilis and cholera and (in the imagination of many) cancer, are the ones that seem particularly susceptible to promotion to "plague." Leprosy and syphilis were the first illnesses to be consistently described as repulsive. It was syphilis that, in the earliest descriptions by doctors at the end of the fifteenth century, generated a version of the metaphors that flourish around AIDS: of a disease that was not only repulsive and retributive but collectively invasive. Although Erasmus, the most influential European pedagogue of the early sixteenth century, described syphilis as "nothing but a kind of leprosy" (by 1529 he called it "something worse than leprosy"), it had already been understood as something different, because sexually transmitted. Paracelsus speaks (in Donne's paraphrase) of "that foule contagious disease which then had invaded mankind in a few places, and since overflowes in all, that for punishment of general licentiousness God first inflicted that disease." Thinking of syphilis as a punishment for an individual's transgression was for a long time, virtually until the disease became easily curable, not really distinct from regarding it as retribution for the licentiousness of a community—as with AIDS now, to the rich industrial countries. In contrast to cancer, understood in a modern way as a disease incurred by (and revealing of) individuals, AIDS is understood in a premodern way, as a disease incurred by people both as individuals and as members of a "risk group" — that neutral-sounding, bureaucratic category which also revives the archaic idea of a tainted community that illness has judged.

Not every account of plague or plaguelike diseases, of course, is a vehicle for lurid stereotypes about illness and the ill. The effort to think critically, historically, about illness (about disaster generally) was attempted throughout the eighteenth century: say, from Defoe's *A Journal of the Plague Year* (1722) to Alessandro Manzoni's *The Betrothed* (1827). Defoe's historical fiction, purporting to be an eyewitness account of bubonic plague in London in 1665, does not further any understanding of the plague as punishment or, a later part of the script, as a transforming experience. And Manzoni, in his lengthy account of the passage of plague through the duchy of Milan in 1630, is avowedly committed to presenting a more accurate, less reductive view than his historical sources. But even these two complex narratives reinforce some of the perennial, simplifying ideas about plague.

One feature of the usual script for plague: The disease invariably comes from somewhere else. The names for syphilis, when it began its epidemic sweep through Europe in the last decade of the fifteenth century, are an exemplary illustration of the need to make a dreaded disease foreign.[2] It was the "French

---

2. As noted in the first accounts of the disease: "This malady received from different peoples whom it affected different names," writes Giovanni di Vigo in 1514. Like earlier treatises on syphilis, written in Latin—by Nicolo Leoniceno (1497) and by Juan Almenar (1502)—the one by di Vigo calls it *morbus Gallicus,* the French disease. (Excerpts from this and other accounts of the period, including *Syphilis; Or a Poetical History of the French Disease* [1530] by Girolamo Fracastoro, who coined the name that prevailed, are in *Classic Descriptions of Disease,* edited by Ralph H. Major [1932].) Moralistic explanations abounded from the beginning. In 1495, a year after the epidemic started, the Emperor Maximilian issued an edict declaring syphilis to be an affliction from God for the sins of men.

The theory that syphilis came from even further than a neighboring country, that it was an entirely new disease in Europe, a disease of the New World brought back to the Old by sailors of Columbus who had contracted it in America, became the accepted explanation of the origin of syphilis in the sixteenth century and is still widely credited. It is worth noting that the earliest medical writers on syphilis did not accept the dubious theory. Leoniceno's *Libellus de Epidemia, quam vulgo morbum Gallicum vocant* starts by taking up the question of whether "the French disease under another name was common to the ancients," and says he believes firmly that it was.

pox" to the English, *morbus Germanicus* to the Parisians, the Naples sickness to the Florentines, the Chinese disease to the Japanese. But what may seem like a joke about the inevitability of chauvinism reveals a more important truth: that there is a link between imagining disease and imagining foreignness. It lies perhaps in the very concept of wrong, which is archaically identical with the non-us, the alien. A polluting person is always wrong, as Mary Douglas has observed. The inverse is also true: A person judged to be wrong is regarded as, at least potentially, a source of pollution.

The foreign place of origin of important illnesses, as of drastic changes in the weather, may be no more remote than a neighboring country. Illness is a species of invasion, and indeed is often carried by soldiers. Manzoni's account of the plague of 1630 (chapters 31 to 37) begins:

> The plague which the Tribunal of Health had feared might enter the Milanese provinces with the German troops had in fact entered, as is well known; and it is also well known that it did not stop there, but went on to invade and depopulate a large part of Italy.

Defoe's chronicle of the plague of 1665 begins similarly, with a flurry of ostentatiously scrupulous speculation about its foreign origin:

> It was about the beginning of September, 1664, that I, among the rest of my neighbours, heard in ordinary discourse that the plague was returned again in Holland; for it had been very violent there, and particularly at Amsterdam and Rotterdam, in the year 1663, whither, they say, it was brought, some said from Italy, others from the Levant, among some goods which were brought home by their Turkey fleet; others said it was brought from Candia; others from Cyprus. It mattered not from whence it came; but all agreed it was come into Holland again.

The bubonic plague that reappeared in London in the 1720s had arrived from Marseilles, which was where plague in the eighteenth century was usually thought to enter Western Europe: brought by seamen, then transported by soldiers and merchants. By the nineteenth century the foreign origin was usually more exotic, the means of transport less specifically imagined, and the illness itself had become phantasmagorical, symbolic.

At the end of *Crime and Punishment* Raskolnikov dreams of plague: "He dreamt that the whole world was condemned to a terrible new strange plague that had come to Europe from the depths of Asia." At the beginning of the sentence it is "the whole world," which turns out by the end of the sentence to be "Europe," afflicted by a lethal visitation from Asia. Dostoevsky's model is undoubtedly cholera, called Asiatic cholera, long endemic in Bengal, which had rapidly become and remained through most of the nineteenth century a worldwide epidemic disease. Part of the centuries-old conception of Europe as a privileged cultural entity is that it is a place which is colonized by lethal diseases coming from elsewhere. Europe is assumed to be by rights free of disease. (And Europeans have been astoundingly callous about the far more devastating extent to which they — as invaders, as colonists — have introduced *their* lethal diseases to the exotic, "primitive" world: Think of the ravages of smallpox, influenza, and cholera on the aboriginal populations of the Americas and Australia.) The tenacity of the connection of exotic origin with dreaded disease is one reason why cholera, of which there were four great outbreaks in Europe in the nineteenth century, each with a lower death toll than the preceding one, has continued to be more memorable than smallpox, whose ravages increased as the century went on (half a million died in the European smallpox pandemic of the early 1870s) but which could not be construed as, plague-like, a disease with a non-European origin.

Plagues are no longer "sent," as in Biblical and Greek antiquity, for the question of agency has blurred. Instead, peoples are "visited" by plagues. And the visitations recur, as is taken for granted in the subtitle of Defoe's narrative, which explains that it is about that "which happened in London during the Last Great Visitation in 1665." Even for non-Europeans, lethal disease may be called a visitation. But a visitation on "them" is invariably described as different from one on "us." "I believe that about one half of the whole people was carried off by this visitation," wrote the English traveler Alexander Kinglake, reaching Cairo at a time of the bubonic plague (sometimes called "oriental plague"). "The Orientals, however, have more quiet fortitude than Europeans under afflictions of this sort." Kinglake's influential book *Eothen* (1844) — suggestively subtitled "Traces of Travel Brought Home from the East" — illustrates many of the enduring Eurocentric presumptions about others, starting from the fantasy that peoples with little reason to expect exemption from misfortune have a lessened capacity to *feel* misfortune. Thus it is believed that Asians (or the poor, or blacks, or Africans, or Muslims) don't suffer or don't grieve as Europeans (or whites) do. The fact that illness is associated with the poor — who are, from the perspective of the privileged, aliens in one's midst — reinforces the association of illness with the foreign: with an exotic, often primitive place.

Thus, illustrating the classic script for plague, AIDS is thought to have started in the "dark continent," then spread to Haiti, then to the United States and to Europe, then. . . . It is understood as a tropical disease: another infestation from the so-called Third World, which is after all where most people in the world live, as well as a scourge of the *tristes tropiques*.[3] Africans who detect racist stereotypes in much of the speculation about the geographical origin of AIDS are not wrong. (Nor are they wrong in thinking that depictions of Africa as the

---

3. *tristes tropiques* French, the sad tropics. — Eds.

cradle of AIDS must feed anti-African prejudices in Europe and Asia.) The sub-liminal connection made to notions about a primitive past and the many hy-potheses that have been fielded about possible transmission from animals (a disease of green monkeys? African swine fever?) cannot help but activate a fa-miliar set of stereotypes about animality, sexual license, and blacks. In Zaire and other countries in Central Africa where AIDS is killing tens of thousands, the counterreaction has begun. Many doctors, academics, journalists, government officials, and other educated people believe that the virus was sent to Africa from the United States, an act of bacteriological warfare (whose aim was to decrease the African birth rate) which got out of hand and has returned to afflict its per-petrators. A common African version of this belief about the disease's prove-nance has the virus fabricated in a CIA–Army laboratory in Maryland, sent from there to Africa, and brought back to its country of origin by American ho-mosexual missionaries returning from Africa to Maryland.[4]

At first it was assumed that AIDS must become widespread elsewhere in the same catastrophic form in which it has emerged in Africa, and those who still think this will eventually happen invariably invoke the Black Death. The plague metaphor is an essential vehicle of the most pessimistic reading of the epidemiological prospects. From classic fiction to the latest journalism, the stan-dard plague story is of inexorability, inescapability. The unprepared are taken by surprise; those observing the recommended precautions are struck down as well. *All* succumb when the story is told by an omniscient narrator, as in Poe's parable "The Masque of the Red Death" (1842), inspired by an account of a ball held in Paris during the cholera epidemic of 1832. Almost all — if the story is told from the point of view of a traumatized witness, who will be a benumbed survivor, as in Jean Giono's Stendhalian novel *Horseman on the Roof* (1951), in which a young Italian nobleman in exile wanders through cholera-stricken southern France in the 1830s.

---

4. The rumor may not have originated as a KGB-sponsored "disinformation" campaign, but it received a crucial push from Soviet propaganda specialists. In October 1985 the Soviet weekly *Literaturnaya Gazeta* published an article alleging that the AIDS virus had been engineered by the U.S. government during biological-warfare research at Fort Detrick, Maryland, and was being spread abroad by U.S. servicemen who had been used as guinea pigs. The source cited was an arti-cle in the Indian newspaper *Patriot.* Repeated on Moscow's "Radio Peace and Progress" in English, the story was taken up by newspapers and magazines throughout the world. A year later it was fea-tured on the front page of London's conservative, mass-circulation *Sunday Express.* ("The killer AIDS virus was artificially created by American scientists during laboratory experiments which went disastrously wrong — and a massive cover-up has kept the secret from the world until today.") Though ignored by most American newspapers, the *Sunday Express* story was recycled in virtually every other country. As recently as the summer of 1987, it appeared in newspapers in Kenya, Peru, Sudan, Nigeria, Senegal, and Mexico. Gorbachev-era policies have since produced an official denial of the allegations by two eminent members of the Soviet Academy of Sciences, which was pub-lished in *Izvestia* in late October 1987. But the story is still being repeated — from Mexico to Zaire, from Australia to Greece.

TALKING ABOUT IT

Seeing Metaphor: Revealing and Concealing

1. Referring to the quotation she includes from *Time* magazine, which uses military metaphors to describe the progress of the AIDS virus, Sontag writes, "This is the language of political paranoia, with its characteristic distrust of a pluralistic world" (paragraph 3). What does she mean? Why does she distrust such language of "the high-tech warfare for which we are being prepared (and inured) by the fantasies of our leaders and by video entertainments"?

2. " 'Plague' is the principal metaphor by which the AIDS epidemic is understood," writes Sontag in paragraph 8. How does she work out this metaphor in terms of the notions of affliction, punishment, and foreignness?

Seeing Composition: Frame, Line, Texture, Tone

1. In addition to AIDS, Sontag writes here about cancer, syphilis, leprosy, cholera, and other epidemic diseases. How does she use these to expand her exploration of her central topic of AIDS and its metaphors?

2. Why do you think Sontag opens by asserting that "[s]trictly speaking, AIDS . . . is not the name of an illness at all. It is the name of a medical condition whose consequences are a spectrum of illnesses"?

Seeing Meaning: Navigating and Negotiating

1. "For several generations now," Sontag writes in paragraph 7, "the generic idea of death has been a death from cancer, and a cancer death is experienced as a generic defeat. Now the generic rebuke to life and to hope is AIDS." This was written in 1989. Does it still seem accurate today?

2. In paragraph 17, Sontag writes about the Western theory of AIDS's origin in Africa and the counter-theory among some Africans that AIDS was "fabricated in a CIA–Army laboratory in Maryland" and "sent from there to Africa." Have you heard other conspiracy theories about AIDS? Why do you think such theories have achieved currency?

WRITING ABOUT IT

1. According to Susan Sontag, what is dangerous about the metaphors that have guided the general thinking about AIDS? Describe how your own thinking about AIDS has been affected by these metaphors; then try to an-

swer how much your thinking may have changed since you first learned about the disease. What influenced the evolution of your thinking?

2. Individually or collaboratively, collect some sample brochures on AIDS from the campus or community health centers, or find some written descriptions of AIDS in medical textbooks or popular health books. Bring these to class and share them with each other. Then choose some descriptions to work with in the following essay: write about the language used to describe the disease, and identify metaphors that you recognize from Sontag's essay. What is the effect of the language on your understanding of AIDS?

Cancer Becomes Me

Marjorie Gross

Marjorie Gross was a lead writer for Seinfeld and a number of other television shows, including Newhart, Anything But Love, and The Larry Sanders Show. She died soon after this essay was published in The New Yorker, April 15, 1996.

So I'm sitting in the doctor's office, he walks in, just tells me straight out, "I was right — it's ovarian cancer, so I win. Pay up." And I say, "Oh, no, you're not gonna hold me to that, are you?" And he says, "Hey, a bet's a bet." You don't know what it's like to leave a doctor's office knowing you've lost a hundred dollars: suddenly everything's changed.

Well, O.K., I've exaggerated a little. What really happens is the doctor walks in and gives you the sympathetic head tilt that right away tells you, "Don't buy in bulk." The degree of tilt corresponds directly with the level of bad news. You know, a little tilt: "We've caught it in time"; sixty-degree angle: "Spread to the lymph nodes"; forty-five-degree angle: "Spread to your clothes." In her book about cancer, Betty Rollin wrote, "First, you cry." However, she didn't mention what you do second, which is "Spend, spend, spend." You're sort of freed up, in a weird way. Suddenly, everything has a lifetime guarantee.

So I had a hysterectomy, and they found a tumor that they said was the size of an orange. (See, for women they use the citrus-fruit comparison; for men it's sporting goods: "Oh, it's the size of a softball," or, in England, a cricket ball.) I languished in the hospital for ten days, on a floor where everybody had cancer, so the sympathy playing field was level. You can't say, "Hey, can you keep it down? I just had my operation." You might get, "So what?" I'm on my fifth." "Poor thing" doesn't really come into play much on this floor. My mother, who also had this disease (yeah, I inherited the cancer gene; my older brother got the blue eyes, but I'm not bitter) — anyway, my mother told me that for some women a hospital stay is a welcome relief. You know, to have someone bringing you food, asking how you are, catering to your every vital sign. See, she wound up in a room with five other women, and they would sit around talking on one bed, and the minute the doctor walked in they would jump into their own beds and re-create the "incoming wounded" scene from "M*A*S*H," insuring that they would not be sent home early.

Which now leads us quixotically but inevitably to chemotherapy. What can I say about chemotherapy that hasn't already been said, in a million pop songs? I was prepared for the chemo side effects. I had my bald plans all in place.

I decided to eschew wigs—all except the rainbow wig. Once in a while, I'd put that on when I didn't want to be stared at. Luckily, in my life style (Lesbeterian) you can be bald and still remain sexually attractive. In fact, the word "sexy" has been thrown my way more times this year than ever before. I've had dreams where my hair grows back and I'm profoundly disappointed. The bald thing works on other levels as well. The shortened shower time—in and out in three minutes easy. Shampoo-free travel. Plus, I get to annoy my father for the first time in twenty years. He hates to see me flaunting my baldness. I thought I'd lost the power to disgust him, but it was right there under my follicles all along.

The other side effect is that I've lost twenty pounds, which has sent my 5 women friends into spasms of jealousy. I think I even heard "Lucky stiff." I said, "I think I'm closer to being a stiff than lucky!" But it fell on deaf ears. I suppose it's a testament to the over-all self-esteem of my fellow-women that, after hearing all about the operations, the chemo, and the nausea, the only thing that registers is "Wow, twenty pounds!" and "You look fabulous!" It's a really good weight-loss system for the terminally lazy. I mean, a StairMaster would have been preferable, but mine wound up as a pants tree.

Then, there are my other friends, who are bugging me to go alternative. So now I'm inundated with articles, books, and pamphlets on healers, nutritionists, and visualization (which I know doesn't work, because if it did, Uma Thurman would be running around my house naked asking me what I want for breakfast). I was also given a crystal by a friend who was going through a messy divorce. She was given the crystal by a guy who died of AIDS. As far as I was concerned, this crystal had a terrible résumé. As far as the healing power of crystals goes, let me just say that I grew up eating dinner under a crystal chandelier every night, and look what came of *that*: two cancers, a busted marriage, and an autistic little brother. There, the healing power of crystals. Enjoy.

This is not to say I'm completely devoid of spirituality. I mean, when you're faced with the dark spectre of death you formulate an afterlife theory in a hurry. I decided to go with reincarnation, mixed with some sort of Heaven-like holding area. Then, of course, we could also just turn to dust and that's it. I come from a family of dust believers. They believe in dust and money: the tangibles. The thing about death that bugs me the most is that I don't want to get there before all my friends. I don't even like to be the first one at the restaurant.

The hardest part of this whole thing is that it has completely ruined my loner life style. I've never felt the need to have anyone around constantly. I mean, I never wear anything that zips up in the back, and I hate cowboy boots. And now I get ten times as many phone calls—people wanting to come over and see me. When I'm well, I can go months without seeing someone. Why the rush to see me nauseated? I especially don't believe in the hospital visit. People come in, you're lying there, you can't do anything, and they start talking about their plans for the night.

I hope with all this negative talk I haven't painted too bleak a picture and therefore discouraged you from getting cancer. I mean, there are some really good things about it. Like:

10   (1) You automatically get called courageous. The rest of you people have to save somebody from drowning. We just have to wake up.

(2) You are never called rude again. You can cancel appointments left and right, leave boring dinners after ten minutes, and still not become a social pariah.

(3) Everyone returns your calls immediately — having cancer is like being Mike Ovitz. And you're definitely not put on hold for long.

(4) People don't ask you to help them move.

(5) If you're really shameless, you never have to wait in line for anything again. Take off the hat and get whisked to the front.

15   So it hasn't been all bad. I've done things I never would have done before. I even got to go to Europe with a creamy-white pop star. I used to use the word "someday," but now I figure someday is for people with better gene pools.

TALKING ABOUT IT

Seeing Metaphor: Revealing and Concealing

1. What metaphors for cancer does Gross create in this essay? Do you think she subverts the standard metaphors for cancer, or does her comic take simply present them in a different way? Explain.

2. When doctors describe tumors, Gross writes, "for women they use the citrus-fruit comparison; for men it's sporting goods." (paragraph 3). Do you think this is just a joke, or might it bear a portion of truth?

Seeing Composition: Frame, Line, Texture, Tone

1. What do you think of Gross's opening paragraph? Why do you think she begins by "exaggerat[ing] a little?"?

2. On the surface, Gross's tone is comic, even outrageous. But are there any passages that you found more serious or moving? Explain your response.

Seeing Meaning: Navigating and Negotiating

1. Does Gross's reference to her "Lesbeterian" life style color your response in any way? How does it seem to fit in with her overall point?

2. What do you think is Gross's purpose here? Does it go beyond treating the subject of cancer in an unorthodoxly humorous way?

WRITING ABOUT IT

1. In what way does Marjorie Gross's humor about cancer reveal certain attributes of her character and help her "prevail," not in the sense of "sustaining" her life, but in the sense of "sustaining" her spirit?

2. Write about the ways in which you understand the title "Cancer Becomes Me." How does your reading of the essay contribute to the ways you construe the title's meanings? What do you think is effective about the title?

Say Amen to Somebody

MARSHA NORMAN

Marsha Norman is a playwright who won a Pulitzer Prize for 'night Mother *(1988) and a Tony Award for* The Secret Garden, *a musical (1993). The following essay appeared in* Mirabella, *September-October 1995.*

I grew up in a house of prayer. A quaint little reminder hung in every room: PRAYER CHANGES THINGS. And every Monday, a group of oldish, lavender-scented women calling themselves The Prayer Band gathered in our parlor, at Mother's invitation, to spend the afternoon on their knees. The Prayer Band ladies irritated me even more than the signs. I was particularly annoyed at how much my mother had told them about me. I figured they were praying for me to give my all to Jesus, instead of to Joe Lamonica, the way I wanted to. The only magazines that came to our house were *Call to Prayer* and *The Upper Room,* both daily prayer guides, and the only social event Mother approved was prayer meeting on Wednesday night. We said grace before every meal, prayed at bedtime, and even offered blessings before birthday parties. But I didn't believe in prayer. And what really made me mad was that mother spent more time talking to God than she did to me.

I am not a child anymore, and my mother is dead. But last year, something happened that made me wonder if she might not have been right after all. Hadn't she prayed herself free of ruptured disk pain and kidney stones? Hadn't she raised four children with no help? Hadn't she died a painless, instantaneous death in the arms of her oldest girlfriend? Maybe prayer actually works.

But I'm getting ahead of myself. What happened last year was that I went to my doctors thinking I had the flu. But they looked at my X rays, sent me for an MRI, and told me I had aggressive lung cancer and two years to live. I got real calm, my version of panic. I had some bad days and some bad dreams. People called me up to say good-bye. I took medicine for the pain. And then, two weeks later, looking at a CAT scan and another set of X rays, the same doctors agreed that I didn't have cancer, I had pneumonia, and if I stayed in bed for a couple of weeks and took Biaxin I would be just fine. Was I happy? Not right away, no. Why not?

Because everything had changed. For two weeks, I'd thought I was dying. Or rather, I'd remembered I was dying. For the first week, I hadn't minded it so much. I was beginning to resign myself to it. And then one afternoon, as I was eating a simple lunch in a so-so restaurant, a friend appeared at the door, a friend who had heard I was sick and had gotten on a plane and flown across the country and found me. Something about that action, something about his desire not to lose me, made me feel the same way. I woke up from my resignation. Suddenly I knew I hadn't lived enough. Overcome with a desire to love my life, I understood that I never had. In short, I realized how sick I really was. I didn't know if I could get well or not, but I desperately wanted to.

By the end of the next week, when I received the new diagnosis, I was well   5 on my way to a different kind of recovery. I had thanked my friends, stopped smoking, started meditating, and begun a series of visits to various alternative healers. I had acupuncture, shiatsu, Reiki, *qi gong,* hydrotherapy, psychotherapy, aromatherapy, bodywork, hypnosis, you name it. And though their techniques were quite dissimilar, and none of them talked much, the healers I was seeing all communicated the same new message to me. "I want you to get well," they said. "You can get well. But the healing doesn't come in a bottle. The healing is between us. You and me. The healing is in our hands. Shall we begin?"

Some gave me herbs, some gave me tonics, but the one thing they all used was the power of prayer. As these healers worked on me, each one breathed a kind of silent . . . prayer. Yes, they were praying. If anybody can recognize a prayer, I can. But their prayers were not to God or Allah or my ancestors, but to me, or rather to some, pardon me, *universal* part of me that could be involved in healing me, somehow.

Uncomfortable with the slippery language of healing, but quite aware of how much better I felt, I began to read about alternative medicine. It wasn't long before I came to the writings of Larry Dossey, MD, probably the world's authority on the power of prayer in the practice of medicine. Here was a scientist who claimed that Mother's little signs were right on the money, who claimed to have actual proof that prayer changed things. Further, here was an internist who said that not praying for his patients would be as negligent as not taking their temperatures. Given my background, it wasn't surprising that I wanted to meet him. I had to meet him.

And after six months of talking to Dossey and reading the research he has collected, I am, while not entirely a new person, at least persuaded of a few previously unthinkable things. I now believe that prayer, or something that for lack of a better word we will call "prayer," isn't just one healing technique, it is *the* primary healing technique, the basis of all healing. Best defined, perhaps, as equal parts willingness and love, prayer is the act of faith on the part of both patient and practitioner that turns placebos into painkillers. (Conversely, its absence can render powerful chemicals useless.) Your healer's prayer is, at its simplest, a humble request for that mysterious faith to keep working, a request that all successful healers make, be they psychics or psychiatrists, bodyworkers or brain surgeons.

I first saw Dossey on the podium addressing a convention of chiropractors on Long Island. He is lean and tan and speaks with a gentle Texas accent. He looks like a kind of accessible, healthy version of the Marlboro man. Former chief of staff of Medical City Dallas Hospital, Dossey is co-chair of the Panel of Mind/Body Interventions at the Office of Alternative Medicine at the National Institutes of Health, and the executive editor of the new journal *Alternative Therapies.* He is persuasive, compelling, and easygoing. He is a celebrated doctor-author who, several weeks later, is eager to hear my take on the chiropractors (a thousand cheery Iron Johns hugging each other), agrees readily to an interview, and then suggests we meet for a burrito in Santa Fe, where he lives with his wife, Barbara, a nurse who has written twelve books on cardiovascular nursing and holistic medicine.

10   I say okay. I like Santa Fe. My grandfather grew up there. We spent summers there praying for my grandmother to live.

After the guacamole and the pleasantries, we begin. I ask him, "Does prayer work?"

"No doubt about it," Dossey says. "Prayer works. The evidence is simply overwhelming. In my opinion, the effectiveness of prayer is nothing less than an outright confirmation of our connection to the absolute."

I'm not ready to hear about the absolute yet, but the statistics that support Dossey's claim are impressive. According to Jeffrey Levin, PhD, associate professor of family and community medicine at Eastern Virginia Medical School in Norfolk, Virginia, who is surveying the literature of NIH, there are over 250 empirical studies published in the epidemiologic and medical literature since the nineteenth century in which spiritual or religious practices have been statistically proven to have positive "health outcomes." These positive results have been found for cardiovascular disease, hypertension, stroke, nearly every type of cancer, colitis, and enteritis. And the findings hold regardless of how spirituality is defined and measured, whether according to beliefs, behaviors, attitudes, or experiences. There are even two dozen studies that demonstrate the health-promoting effects of simply attending church on a regular basis.

Dossey cites an important study conducted by cardiologist Randolph Byrd at San Francisco General Medical Center. One group of randomly assigned coronary-care patients was prayed for; one group of patients was not. The people who did the praying were given only the patients' first names and their general conditions, but were not told what to pray for specifically, or how to pray. Each patient in the experiment had between three and seven people praying for him or her. Patients who were prayed for were five times less likely to require antibiotics, and three times less likely to develop cardiopulmonary arrest. Fewer of them died than in the group not prayed for, and none of them required intubation, although twelve people in the no-prayer group did. "If the technique being studied had been a new drug or a surgical procedure instead of prayer," writes Dossey, "it would almost certainly have been heralded as some sort of breakthrough." He goes on to say that subsequent experiments suggest that if the people doing the praying know the patients' first *and* last names, the results are even better.

Dossey laughs at my skepticism, and counsels that I don't have to believe 15
any of this stuff, of course, but that the next time I'm in the hospital, I should try
real hard to get myself prayed for.

"But how do we know it was prayer that made the difference?" I ask. "How
do we know the people who were supposed to be praying were actually praying?
How do we know some of the people in the non-prayed-for group weren't secretly praying to die?"

Dossey nods. He himself has procedural questions about prayer research
done on humans. He thinks the proof is clearer when the subjects being prayed
for are bacteria or animals.

In his most recent book, *Healing Words,* Dossey presents the evidence that
prayer doesn't just benefit humans. He cites, for example, four studies showing
that yeast that is prayed for can better resist the toxic effects of cyanide than
yeast that is not. In all, he directs me to 131 controlled trials of prayer in which
it has proved effective in everything from making rye grass grow taller to retard-
ing the growth of goiters in mice.

"But if there's this much evidence for the effectiveness of prayer, why
aren't we using it more?" I ask. "Why don't we have a national day of prayer for
AIDS? Why don't physicians routinely counsel patients' families to pray for
them?" And then a further question occurs to me. "Does it always work?"

He shakes his head. "Of course not," he says. "But no treatment works all 20
the time." He reminds me that penicillin is a great drug, but it won't do a thing
for diabetes.

But my question wasn't about penicillin. My question was about why my
doctor doesn't pray for me. (Assuming he doesn't, I mean.) I want to know why so
many scientists seem to have rejected, or at least resisted, prayer-based healing.

"It's because we live in the West," he says. And he doesn't mean Santa Fe.
"Here in the West, we have to know why something works before we will believe
that it does. And it's human nature to resist change, and prayer is something we
can't control, and we're afraid of the power of mystics and the like, and we're afraid
of our own power as healers, and how many answers would you like? Prayer is not
mechanical, and until very recently, we have been living in a mechanical age."

"All right," I say. "Suppose I accept that prayer works. How do I do it?"

He gives me one of those No-Easy-Road-to-Salvation looks I remember
getting as a child. Prayer is not a magic potion, so he doesn't want to give out
something that sounds like a formula. He proceeds carefully. "Prayer seems to
work best if the prayers are nondirected; that is, if you pray for nothing, rather
than for something," he says. "If you pray, 'Thy will be done,' rather than 'God
kill my cancer.'" According to Dossey, prayer isn't something you do, it's something you are. It's prayerfulness—a willingness to accept a healing should one
come your way—that actually saves lives, he says, and cautions me not to demand to be healed or to try to earn it.

25   I still don't feel as if I've had the answer to my question. And I remember that the chiropractors asked it, too. Maybe we all want to know the same things.

"So how exactly do we pray? What do we pray for? Does it matter to whom we pray? Do we have to kneel down? Do we have to pray out loud?"

Dossey shakes his head. "Sometime a prayer might be nothing more than the recognition of a need. When you wish someone would feel better, and actually express that wish, that's praying," he says. But I want the techniques, the directions. I want a prescription, if you will.

"Okay," he says. "Pray in a nondirected manner for the best outcome for the organism. Pray according to who you are. If you are an extrovert, pray in an extroverted way. If you are quiet, pray quietly. Pray to God, pray to Allah, pray to The One, pray to The Only, pray to your Ancestors. It's all received. It's all acted on. Pray with acceptance and gratitude. Pray for connection, pray for your love to be felt, pray for the ability to show it. Pray for people you know to feel better. Pray for your prayers to be useful. Pray on your bike. Pray in the bathtub. Pray in silence. Pray in song." He quotes Thessalonians 5:17, " 'Pray without ceasing.' "

I nod my head. I have to ask. "How does prayer work?"

30   "How does aspirin work?"

I laugh. "No, I'm not kidding," he says, laughing himself. "We don't know how it works, just that it does." He is not making light of my question. He knows the world of alternative medicine needs this answer, needs a paradigm, an explanation for the astonishing cures that are sometimes accomplished by seemingly unscientific means. He knows that he cannot explain how prayer works. Yet.

Dossey also knows the story of Ignaz Semmelweis, the Hungarian doctor who first suspected that infection was contagious, the first doctor to insist that his trainees wash their hands between the morgue and the maternity ward. Semmelweis's medical career dead-ended because no one could explain what he had discovered. So Dossey is careful not to claim to have the answer. But he has an opinion, a hunch.

"We can't prove any of this yet, in a lab," he says, "but we will. When I pray for you, I am somehow stimulating your inner healing system to start working. I am reminding it of all that it knows. Your body is not a machine, it's a living thing. And your body and your mind aren't two different things, they're the same one. For years, you've taken your body to your doctor's mind and said, 'Here. Heal this thing.' What I am doing when I pray for you is asking your mind to use everything it knows, or remember everything it's forgotten, or if necessary call up information from the universal mind and heal itself." He mentions research biophysicist Beverly Rubik, director of the Center for Frontier Sciences at Temple University. She believes that the healing power of prayer may someday prove attributable to the transfer of information in the form of low-frequency electromagnetic energy.

He wonders if I understand what he is saying. I do. He thinks that our brains may be individual, but our minds are not; they are a part of a . . . network, to use a computer mode. When I pray for you, it's like asking for a remote download from the Net. Somewhere in the universal mind, the information exists that will cure you. I'm just trying to get it copied onto your hard disk, or teach you how to access it through your browser.

Dossey doesn't use a computer analogy yet. But it wouldn't surprise me if   35 one day he claimed that the design of the Internet sprang from our unconscious awareness of this thing he calls the universal mind.

"We may all be psychic healers," Dossey says. "It is becoming very clear that almost anyone can activate the inner healing capacity of someone in need. Prayer is not an innovation. It's a process of remembering who we really are and how we are related. Prayer is nonlocal. I don't have to be kneeling at your bedside for it to work. I can be across the world. There's no such thing as distant healing because there is no distance separating people that must be overcome. The healing of someone else is in a sense self-healing. That's why it feels so good to love somebody, why our prayers for others are also good for us."

When Mother died, I found her prayer journals, some dating back into her teens. Looking at the daily entries, it seemed she had prayed about a billion prayers for her rebellious child Marsha, and about half a million for missionaries and starving heathens. Then, in the last year of her life, she had prayed about 600 prayers for one of three outcomes—that her blood pressure would drop, or that God would help her deal with the staggering dizziness she felt, or failing that, that He would take her, as she called it, Home.

Well. You know what happened. God picked Door Number Three. Mother was at a potluck supper at her old church. She was standing next to her friend Betty. She felt hot. "My neck is killing me," she said to Betty, and she fell to the floor and died. After reading the prayer journals, I can't exactly say she prayed to die. But now I know that it was all right with her. And if I am extremely lucky, when my turn comes to die, it will be all right with me. My ideas about prayer have changed; maybe my ideas about death will, too.

At the end of *Healing Words*, Dossey writes, "We simply don't know how one person praying can bring about healthful changes in someone else across the country, but it happens. What is emerging through the study of healers in laboratories is a new picture of human consciousness." And whatever consciousness is, he continues, "it's not something the brain produces that will die with the body. It's something else. The answers we give to the questions surrounding prayer have the greatest importance for our understanding of our place in the world, our origins and our destiny. That is why the scientific studies of spiritual healing are crucial. They can help us find answers to the great questions of life."

40   "What do you pray for?" I ask.

"I pray," he said, "for the understanding that it's all already perfect, that I am already saved, that there is no separation between me and my body." He laughs. "I pray for the understanding that I am my aching back."

And now I ask myself, Was I healed? Did Mother's billion prayers for me all those years ago see me through this little episode? Maybe. Did I pray for myself? Yes. I believe I did. Finally. And I think some other people prayed for me, too. In their way. And something worked, and I'm fine now . . . thank you.

TALKING ABOUT IT

Seeing Metaphor: Revealing and Concealing

1. Norman quotes Larry Dossey as saying, "Your body is not a machine, it's a living thing. And your body and your mind aren't two different things, they're the same one. For years, you've taken your body to your doctor's mind and said, 'Here, heal this thing'" (paragraph 33). What metaphors are at play here? What new metaphor does Dossey go on to create for being human?

2. In paragraphs 34–35, Norman offers an extended metaphor in terms of the Internet. Does it help you understand her point? Explain.

Seeing Composition: Frame, Line, Texture, Tone

1. Norman opens by writing about her mother's belief in prayer and her painless death, and then says she's "getting ahead of myself"; she returns to the story of her mother in paragraph 37 just before her conclusion. What is the effect of this? Do you think she got "ahead of" herself accidentally, or was this a conscious strategy for structuring her essay? Why do you think so?

2. Norman relies almost exclusively on the words of Larry Dossey to verify the point she wishes to make about the healing power of prayer. Is his testimony sufficiently convincing? Why or why not?

Seeing Meaning: Navigating and Negotiating

1. In paragraph 8, Norman refers to "prayer, or something that for lack of a better word we will call 'prayer.'" Why is "prayer" not exactly the word she is looking for? Why, for example, does she give relatively little attention to organized religion?

2. In paragraph 39, Norman quotes from a book by Dossey to the effect that "[t]he answers we give to the questions surrounding prayer have the greatest importance for our understanding of our place in the world, our origins, and our destiny." What is he getting at? Do you agree with him? Explain.

WRITING ABOUT IT

1. In the following passage, Marsha Norman expresses her understanding of Larry Dossey's hypothesis about the universal mind and the healing power of prayer:

   > He thinks that our brains may be individual but our minds are not; they are a part of a . . . network, to use a computer mode. When I pray for you, it's like asking for a remote download from the Net. Somewhere in the universal mind, the information exists that will cure you. I'm just trying to get it copied onto your hard disk, or teach you how to access it through your browser.

   How well do you think Norman's metaphor reflects what Larry Dossey says in the essay about the act of prayer and its healing power? How effective is her metaphor in enhancing your own understanding about prayer?

2. Larry Dossey says that "your body and your mind aren't two different things, they're the same one." At the end of Norman's essay, Dossey says he prays "for the understanding that . . . there is no separation between me and my body." What do you think Dossey means by these statements, and why would the creation of metaphorical boundaries between body and mind interfere with healing or hinder the power of prayer? Do you agree or disagree with the argument in this essay? Why or why not?

Towards an Ecology of Illness

KAT DUFF

Kat Duff has written essays published in the Utne Reader *and* Parabola. *Her book* The Alchemy of Illness *(1993) is about the psychological aspects of chronic fatigue syndrome. This selection appeared in the Summer 1991 issue of the* Taos Review.

I'm sprawled across my bed, as if thrown aimlessly aside. The trappings of illness surround me: twisted tissues and covers, half-empty glasses of water (one with a fly floating in it), and plastic pill bottles, spilling. I watch clouds of dust swim through the slanting rectangle of light from my window as the afternoon creeps away. I've been sick for over a year now with CFIDS (chronic fatigue immune dysfunction syndrome); it's best described as a flu that never goes away. There is no cure as yet, only the remedy of rest for a few years. So I spend twelve hours a day in bed — sleeping, reading, ruminating and wondering: what is the matter? Where did this begin and where is it going?

One of the oddities of being sick is that you suddenly remember all the other times you've been sick: the childhood diseases, stomach flus, chest colds, allergic reactions, food poisonings, sunstrokes . . . the list goes on and on. Illness weaves through our lives with surprising regularity; it is no less central to the human condition than sexuality is, though we hardly give it the same attention. Memories of illness fade quickly under the glare of health, dropping into the muddled background of life, only to reappear with the onset of yet another illness. Now that I'm sick, it seems that all of the many and varied illnesses of my life are simply crests on the waves of an ocean that lies beneath the surface of my world, something like a watertable of the soul.

Illness is a world of its own, a foreign yet familiar landscape, existing within the cosmos we inherit as human beings, not unlike an alpine meadow or a coral reef. But there are few maps of this invisible geography, as if it were circled by the waters of forgetfulness, or the thick impenetrable mists of fairytale lore. We hear from doctors about disease but rarely from the sick themselves. The experience of illness defies description and often escapes language altogether. "English," wrote Virginia Woolf, "which can express the thoughts of Hamlet and the tragedy of Lear, has no words for the shiver or the headache." So, illness remains a wilderness — beyond our grasp, strangely forbidding and forever a mystery — despite its continuing presence in our lives. And like an alpine meadow or a coral reef, it may well play an important role in the ecology of the whole.

One thing is certain; no one chooses to get sick. In fact, we avoid it "like the plague" with our rituals and regimens of healthy living. Illness chooses us, instead, for its own inscrutable reasons. We are caught, unsuspecting, by the onset of symptoms, and often feel attacked, persecuted, even slain, by this hungry hunter we call disease; then we are dragged, like Persephone, into the underworld of sickness. As we "become sick," sickness becomes us and redefines us; so we say we are not ourselves anymore. I lose my usual interests immediately, even before the fever or cough arrives. A kind of existential ennui rises in my bones like flood waters, and nothing seems worth doing: making breakfast, getting to work on time or even making love. That's when I know I'm succumbing to the influence of illness. I slip, like fluid through a porous membrane, into the nightshade of my solar self, where I'm tired of my friends, I hate my work, the weather stinks and I'm a failure.

Sometimes I ask myself: why didn't I realize this before? Inevitably, some   5 sure voice from the depths of my illness replies: "you've been fooling yourself."

That sure voice fills me with a shuddering awe I've come to associate with moonless nights, pounding surf and other such imposing presences. She holds no allegiance to my preferred self-concepts and proud accomplishments; in fact, she rather enjoys replaying recent events in a humiliating light during those long, insufferable afternoons. That sure voice remembers everything I've forgotten, overlooked or denied: my original purposes, deflected desires and persisting failures. These are what Virginia Woolf called the "wastes and deserts of the soul" that appear "when the lights of health go down." I often emerge from the encounter feeling very small, bound by the circle of my own limitations, and beset by the handmaidens of illness: doom, depression and despair.

Romanian philosopher E. M. Cioran once wrote that "illness confers the experience of the terrible." Since I've been sick, I have come close to some truly terrifying possibilities: that I'm dying, that some part of my father (who molested me when I was a baby) wants me dead, and that the nuclear research lab nearby is emitting radiation that is killing all of us, slowly. My friends call it paranoia, in the ready optimism and confidence that health confers, and so do I on my brightest days; but at other times I wake up in a cold sweat sure that it's absolutely true and I'm doomed.

Frankly, I find it very difficult to reconcile the contrary visions of health and illness, or even hold them both in my mind at once. They slip away from each other like oil and water. It's like trying to remember bitter cold of winter in the midst of a sweltering August heat wave. Our brains are not well-equipped for such exercises, and yet something compels us to make the effort.

It has been said that illness is an attempt to escape the truth. I suspect that it's actually an attempt to remember the whole truth, to remember all of ourselves. For illness is not just something that happens to us, like a sudden sneeze or passing storm; it's part of who we are all the time. We carry within ourselves all of the diseases we've had, and many we will have in the future, as genetic inclinations, damaged organs, hidden bacteria and sleeping cancer cells. We just forget in the heyday of health. The longer I'm sick the more I realize that illness is to health what dreams are to waking life — the reminder of what's forgotten, the bigger picture working towards resolution.

10   There is, perhaps rightly so, an invisible rope that separates the sick from the well, so that each is repelled by the other, like magnets reversed. The well venture forth to accomplish great deeds in the outside world, while the sick turn back into themselves and commune with the dead; neither can face the other without the uncomfortable intrusion of envy, resentment, fear or horror. Frankly, from the viewpoint of illness, healthy people seem ridiculous, even a touch dangerous, in their blinded busyness, marching like soldiers to the drumbeat of duty and desire.

Their world, to which we once belonged, and will again most likely, seems unreal, like some kind of board game that could fold up at any minute. Carl Jung reported that after his heart attack the world suddenly appeared to be a ruse at best ("like a painted curtain"), a prison at worst. He despaired of getting well and having to "convince myself all over again that this was important!" We drop out of the game when we get sick, leave the field and desert the cause. I often feel like a ghost, the slight shade of a person, floating through that world, but not of it. The parameters of my world are different altogether.

Space and time lose their definitions in the unmarked sea of illness. We wake from a nap to wonder where am I? On the train to San Francisco or at Grandmother's house? Maybe both, for opposites co-exist in the underworld of illness. We are hot and cold at once, unable to decide whether to throw off the blankets or pile more on, while something tells us our lives are at stake. Sometimes I feel heavy as a sinking ship, and other times light as a ghost rising from the wreckage.

Time stretches and collapses, warping like a record left in the sun. Ten seconds can seem like an hour of torture in acute pain; while whole lifetimes can squeeze into a few moments when we wake from sleeping or fall in a faint. Past and future inhabit the present, like threads so tangled the ends cannot be found. Many years ago I had a curious experience when I was sick with a fever in a tiny efficiency apartment in Santa Fe. I was drifting in and out of sleep when a host of images swept before me like a flock of birds: a long list of the addresses of my life, the kitchen windows and back stoops I have loved, the stars of the Big Dipper turning overhead, all the cardboard boxes carried in and out of my homes, the stars of the Big Dipper resting on the horizon. Suddenly I knew (and don't ask me how) that I didn't have to keep moving every two years, as I had always done. I saw the skin of my restlessness rise from my body like the thin film of fog over water at dawn and disappear. Sure enough, the next move was my last.

The underworld of illness is full of such impossible events, strange visitations and unexpected transformations. When I was sick with dysentery in India, a Hindu holy man in orange appeared in the corner of my hotel room and sent waves of healing through my ragged body; a friend of mine saw Mother Mary rise up out of her garbage can during an allergic reaction to mold. The universes revealed by illness defy the rules of ordinary reality and share in the hidden logic of dreams, fairytales and the spirit realms mystics and shamans describe. There is often the feeling of exile, wandering, searching, facing dangers, finding treasures. Familiar faces take on the appearance of archetypal allies and enemies. Small ordinary things, like aspirin, sunshine or a glass of water, become charged with potency, the magical ability to cure or poison. Dreams assume a momentous authority. No wonder many tribal peoples consider illness to be one of the most powerful means of revelation available to humankind.

At the very start of my illness, when I still thought it was a simple flu, I   15 dreamt that someone asked me what was wrong and I answered, calmly, "I'm dying." Then the scene switched to my backyard where beautiful blue morning glories were climbing up to the sky. I woke from that dream with a great clarity; I knew I was very sick and better get help, but more importantly, I realized I was in sacred territory, undergoing changes so profound and promising that could only be likened to dying.

Illness is a taste of death, after all, a practice in dying for the living, a visit to the limbos and bardos usually reserved for the recently deceased. There is the slow grind of discomfort and weakness that dissolves desire and cuts us loose; we sink into a private reality of pain, memory and shifting awareness, ruminating upon the tangled knots of our lives. Sometimes there is talk, a sudden urgency, that makes no sense to others; the sick and the dying alike make fervent apologies and stark accusations. And there is the reverberating isolation of enduring pain and luminous revelations that cannot be shared. No wonder we fear for our lives when we fall ill, speak of being "more dead than alive" when we are sick, and "returning from the dead" when we get well.

Death, in its guise as the destroyer, is the active agent in illness. It provokes and exasperates our strengths and weaknesses until something — one's faith in God, overweening sense of responsibility, good cheer or strong heart — gives way, cut down by the scythe of the grim reaper. No one returns from an operation, accident or illness exactly the same; there is a bitterness (or compassion), strength (or fragility), faith (or despondency) that was never there before. Illness is a small death that prepares us for the bigger life — and death — ahead. It's an initiation of sorts, taking us from one stage of life and level of awareness to the next. In fact, serious illnesses follow the stages and requirements of traditional ceremonies — isolation, suffering, death and resurrection — with remarkable fidelity.

Last year, I dreamt that I went to the doctor for tests. She took a sample of my saliva and returned to say the lab could not run the tests because they found my father's semen in my saliva; I would have to keep returning for tests until the semen was gone, so I could sign the Declaration of Independence. At the time, I knew the dream was referring to the residues of my incest experiences; what I didn't fully realize was that my illness was the way my body would eject the poison.

In the months that followed, I had several episodes of sudden nausea, violent shaking and vomiting, reliving the terrors of my infancy; my body moved, of its own accord, to spit out my father's semen. These flashbacks frightened me terribly and left me exhausted; they rank among the most difficult experiences I've ever endured. And yet, in their wake, I felt extraordinarily calm and strangely radiant, as if bathed in light.

Illness is such a good vehicle for eliminating toxins, the ingrained poisons of our physical, mental and emotional anguish. In fact, many Asian and tribal peoples perceive sickness to be a manifestation of the body's wisdom, cleansing us of the bad habits and misunderstandings we've somehow accumulated. The Cherokee, for example, consider sickness a "purifying experience," intended to "return us to our path of destiny and spirit," as Dr. Lewis E. Mehl, a Cherokee himself, explained. And it works this exorcism of sorts through the very features we find so distasteful in the sick: the bad breath, runny noses and oozing sores, the coughing, spitting, crying and vomiting.

20   Illness, like death, is a dirty, messy vegetative process. The microscopic organisms responsible for most disease — fungi, bacteria and parasites — actually do the work of decay. They break down the order of systems into a disarray of parts, translating dead matter into essential nutrients, to feed the next generation; and our warm, moist anaerobic insides provide the perfect environment for their invisible labors. In a fever my insides feel like soup on the stove, or compost in the bin, seeping and settling. I shudder, shiver and sweat, and drink vast quantities of liquid — all of which work to soften the rigid and eliminate the unnecessary. This is the sacred alchemy of nature we witness every fall, in the sinking of sap, the dropping of leaves, the scattering of seed. It is the "way of the seeded earth," to use a phrase from Joseph Campbell, to sacrifice old life for new in the great chain of life. From this perspective, disease and death are not failures of life; they are part of a cycle of life; in fact, the very means of its continuation.

These powers of decay operate with the ruthless detachment of all scavengers. They don't care whether you are fat or skinny, good or bad, eating low-fat yogurt or steaks every night; they just do the work that's required — transformation — to restore equilibrium to an imbalanced world. One of the most unexpected discoveries I've come upon during my two years of "rest" is that illness is not just a private affair; it reflects a larger disorder and attempts to remedy it.

Most indigenous peoples consider the illness of an individual to be symptomatic of an imbalance in the larger community of life, an indication that some violation of nature has occurred, which has not been righted; therefore someone is sick, the rains don't come, or the people fight among themselves. Even the ancient Greeks, already far removed from their tribal roots, believed that illness could result from the crimes of one's ancestors or collective transgressions, as well as personal fault. For the physical world is fragile and very susceptible to human actions in this understanding; it must be carefully tended with patience and love. A single strand pulled out of place can tear the web apart, hurting one's family, the community, and the cosmos itself, for generations to come. That's why so many healing ceremonies of indigenous peoples, from the African Yoruba or the Arctic Inuit, involve the entire community.

How, one might ask, does the mining of uranium in northern Arizona, relate to the rising incidence of leukemia throughout the U.S., as many tribal elders of the four corners area insist? This is my understanding of the way it works. Whenever the natural order is violated, feelings of shame and responsibility are evoked, so that wrongs may be righted and the single strand rewoven into the web. Originally, shame carried a sense of the sacred, the great Mystery which infuses all life, instilling reverence and humility. It served to remind us human beings, so prone to hubris, that we are not God, that we have and will make mistakes, encouraging us to acknowledge those mistakes and remedy them as best we can. However, after centuries of institutionalized violence, during which the gods and goddesses of the natural way were buried and replaced by the laws of political orders, shame has been split from its sacred roots. Now it rests as the pervasive sense of being wrong or bad, unworthy or unfit, that afflicts so many sensitive, abused and oppressed peoples.

At this point, shame rarely lands on the shoulders of those who commit the transgressions: the corporate polluters, wife-beaters or keepers of apartheid, and all of us who disregard the life of another. We, of the postindustrial cultures of the West, are so convinced of our separateness, so numb to our own original pain, so bound to inflict upon others what we cannot feel (in the name of practicality, progress, even love) that we are incapable of accepting the shame and responsibility of our actions. As a result, shame floats free of the shameless trespassers and lands upon the trespassed, those who are treated shamefully — the women, children and old people, the underclassed and outcast — who come to manifest the symptoms of distress and disease, becoming the sacrifices. As my dream made so graphically clear, my father's semen — the effects of his transgressions and those of our ancestors — has ended up in my mouth, and I must do something about it in order to be free.

That dream triggered a sequence of events which have showed me how my illness relates to crimes of my ancestors, and how to free myself from that legacy. When my doctor returned with her news from the lab (in the dream) she handed me a questionnaire to fill out about my illness which included several questions about my family history and genetics. At first they seemed irrelevant, but after answering the questions I began to suspect there was more to this business of genes and ancestry than I had realized. That dream led to others about my ancestors on my father's side of the family, who settled in Minnesota in the 1860s, when the native peoples (the Dakota) were being driven off the land. In one of these dreams the basement walls of my grandmother's house (which stood next door to ours on the land settled by my ancestors) were painted with images of imperialism: German soldiers marching in unison, Spanish conquistadors on horseback with shining helmets.

As a result of these dreams, I became preoccupied with figuring out how my great-great grandfather had acquired the land I grew up on. My father told me he bought it from another white man who, in turn, had received it the year before from the state, after the "Sioux Uprising" (read massacre) of 1862; but something seemed wrong, very wrong, about it. So I decided to consult a shaman, since shamans are specially trained to discern far-reaching lines of causation in illness.

He told me first off that I was "a sacrifice dying so that others may live." Many Dakota had starved or frozen to death when they were displaced from the land my ancestors settled, their ancestral homeground, he explained. Those deaths made a big gash in the land and my body is the wound. Something like a curse or a requirement was laid upon my family at that time, that each generation would get smaller and smaller (which it has) until it died out altogether, unless a sacrifice was made. If I did not wish to be that sacrifice, he added, I should honor the Dakota who died and make offerings to them, so that the ill will generated by that tragedy would be transformed into benevolence. He helped me to do that (I can't describe how without diminishing the power and effectiveness of those actions) and since then I have felt relieved of a certain heaviness, the sense that I didn't deserve to be alive, that's been with me as long as I can remember. Now, just over a year later, I'm mostly recovered.

Yes, the sins of the father are visited upon the children, and onto the seventh generation, as many Native American traditions attest. The Bible calls it "blood guilt," psychologists have named it the "genealogical shadow." Deepak Chopra, an M.D. who is well-versed in ayervedic medicine, speaks of "ghosts of memory" which affect our immune systems and foster illness. I suspect that the psyches and bodies of 20th century Americans are crowded and overflowing with these "ghosts of memory" so implicated in disease, because we as a people are so oriented towards progress and eager to escape the burdens, complications and contradictions of continuity. It's the American way (as exemplified by my ancestors, but also by my own life) to leave one's home and past behind to start a new life on the great frontier . . . leaving a terrible—and toxic—trail of unfinished business.

Perhaps that's why sick people and survivors of all kinds so often insist upon remembering the dead and forgotten, and why descendants of the Dakota who survived the Wounded Knee Massacre of 1890 journeyed by foot and by horseback to the grave site one hundred years later, across hundreds of miles through subzero temperatures, to offer prayers, burn sage and receive the apology of South Dakota Governor George Mickelson. The Dakota, like many other tribes, have repeatedly asked for an apology from the U.S. government for the atrocities of the past in the recognition that our lives and well-being, as red and white peoples, depend upon the mending of those wounds.

The Indo-European root for the word "cure" means "to sorrow for some- 30 thing," and I have yet to meet the sick person who doesn't sorrow deeply for something—the breakdown of a marriage, an early death in the family, or the nameless innocents slaughtered in war. A good friend of mine, who came down with CFIDS after visiting Nicaragua, says it broke her heart to see how our government is destroying that country and that's why she's sick. Our bodies bear the untold lessons and scars of history; as we suffer our wounds in the extremities of illness they become our offerings, our means of realizing and remembering what is right, what is needed, to bring our lives and our world back into balance. I love to see what people do when (and if) they recover from serious illness; there is often an urgency towards some kind of action to set things right. The father of a friend apologized to all his children for his years of absence after a heart attack. Another friend quit her job with the state after a mastectomy to paint full time. A veteran suffering from the effects of Agent Orange is planting trees for every American who died in Vietnam.

When I first got sick, I looked for a cure; now I realize that my illness *is* the cure, or part of the cure, for something much bigger than I. My experience has born out the truth of these words by poet Demetria Martinez: "A wound is not something to cure, but something to listen to and see with." It's "a way out, a way in."

TALKING ABOUT IT

Seeing Metaphor: Revealing and Concealing

1. Virtually every paragraph in Duff's essay contains at least one metaphoric image of illness or health. Locate as many of these as you can. How do they serve the development of Duff's ideas? Do they suggest any contradictions, or do they seem to you to come together coherently?

2. In paragraph 23, Duff equates illness and suffering with feelings of shame evoked by violations of the natural order. Reread this passage and what follows in the essay carefully. What is Duff saying? Is she writing metaphorically here, or does she mean her discussion to be taken literally? Explain.

Seeing Composition: Frame, Line, Texture, Tone

1. On the surface, Duff's essay seems very loosely organized, often with little direct connection or transition between paragraphs. What is the effect of this? Do you think the essay is, in fact, more closely organized than it originally appears to be? Why or why not?

2. Paragraph 3 ends with the statement that illness "may well play an important role in the ecology of the whole," which might be considered Duff's "thesis." How does she develop this idea in the rest of her essay?

Seeing Meaning: Navigating and Negotiating

1. In paragraph 10, Duff writes, "Frankly, from the viewpoint of illness, healthy people seem ridiculous, even a touch dangerous, in their blinded busyness, marching like soldiers to the drumbeat of duty and desire." How do you respond to this statement? How does the idea figure in her larger presentation of illness?

2. How does Duff use the fact that her father molested her as a child to make a point about health and illness? How do you respond to the point she is making?

WRITING ABOUT IT

1. Write about how the word "ecology" works in Kat Duff's essay "to reconcile the contrary visions of health and illness." Put another way, how does the metaphor help make her argument that "illness is symptomatic of an imbalance in the larger community of life" and can be its own cure?

2. "A wound is not something to cure, but something to listen to and see with. It's 'a way out, a way in.'" How might your experience with illness (or that of another whom you know well) be seen in the light of this metaphor?

An Unquiet Mind

KAY REDFIELD JAMISON

> *Kay Redfield Jamison is a professor of psychiatry at the Johns Hopkins University School of Medicine and co-author of the medical text* Manic-Depressive Illness *(1990). Her writings also include the best-selling memoir* An Unquiet Mind *(1993), from which the following selection is taken, and* Touched with Fire: Manic-Depressive Illness and the Artistic Temperament, *a study of great artists and writers who suffered from what would be diagnosed today as manic depression.*

SPEAKING OF MADNESS

Not long before I left Los Angeles for Washington, I received the most vituperative and unpleasant letter that anyone has ever written me. It came not from a colleague or a patient, but from a woman who, having seen an announcement of a lecture I was to give, was outraged that I had used the word "madness" in the title of my talk. I was, she wrote, insensitive and crass and very clearly had no idea at all what it was like to suffer from something as awful as manic-depressive illness. I was just one more doctor who was climbing my way up the academic ranks by walking over the bodies of the mentally ill. I was shaken by the ferocity of the letter, resented it, but did end up thinking long and hard about the language of madness.

In the language that is used to discuss and describe mental illness, many different things — descriptiveness, banality, clinical precision, and stigma — intersect to create confusion, misunderstanding, and a gradual bleaching out of traditional words and phrases. It is no longer clear what place words such as "mad," "daft," "crazy," "cracked," or "certifiable" should have in a society increasingly sensitive to the feelings and rights of those who are mentally ill. Should, for example, expressive, often humorous, language — phrases such as "taking the fast trip to Squirrel City," being a "few apples short of a picnic," "off the wall," "around the bend," or "losing the bubble" (a British submariner's term for madness) — be held hostage to the fads and fashions of "correct" or "acceptable" language?

One of my friends, prior to being discharged from a psychiatric hospital after an acute manic episode, was forced to attend a kind of group therapy session designed as a consciousness-raising effort, one that encouraged the soon-to-be ex-patients not to use, or allow to be used in their presence, words such as "squirrel," "fruitcake," "nut," "wacko," "bat," or "loon." Using these words, it was felt, would "perpetuate a lack of self-esteem and self-stigmatization." My friend found the exercise patronizing and ridiculous. But was it? On the one hand, it was entirely laudable and professional, if rather excessively earnest, advice: the pain of hearing these words, in the wrong context or the wrong tone, is sharp; the memory of insensitivity and prejudice lasts for a long time. No doubt, too, allowing such language to go unchecked or uncorrected leads not only to personal pain, but contributes both directly and indirectly to discrimination in jobs, insurance, and society at large.

On the other hand, the assumption that rigidly rejecting words and phrases that have existed for centuries will have much impact on public attitudes is rather dubious. It gives an illusion of easy answers to impossibly difficult situations and ignores the powerful role of wit and irony as positive agents of self-notion and social change. Clearly there is a need for freedom, diversity, wit, and directness of language about abnormal mental states and behavior. Just as clearly, there is a profound need for a change in public perception about mental illness. The issue, of course, is one of context and emphasis. Science, for example, requires a highly precise language. Too frequently, the fears and misunderstandings of the public, the needs of science, the inanities of popularized psychology, and the goals of mental health advocacy get mixed together in a divisive confusion.

5   One of the best cases in point is the current confusion over the use of the increasingly popular term "bipolar disorder" — now firmly entrenched in the nomenclature of the *Diagnostic and Statistical Manual* (DSM-IV), the authoritative diagnostic system published by the American Psychiatric Association — instead of the historic term "manic-depressive illness." Although I always think of myself as a manic-depressive, my official DSM-IV diagnosis is "bipolar I disorder; recurrent; severe with psychotic features; full interepisode recovery" (one of the many DSM-IV diagnostic criteria I have "fulfilled" along the way, and a personal favorite, is an "excessive involvement in pleasurable activities"). Obviously, as a clinician and researcher, I strongly believe that scientific and clinical studies, in order to be pursued with accuracy and reliability, must be based on the kind of precise language and explicit diagnostic criteria that make up the core of DSM-IV. No patient or family member is well served by elegant and expressive language if it is also imprecise and subjective. As a person and patient, however, I find the word "bipolar" strangely and powerfully offensive: it seems to me to obscure and minimize the illness it is supposed to represent. The description "manic-depressive," on the other hand, seems to capture both the nature and the seriousness of the disease I have, rather than attempting to paper over the reality of the condition.

Most clinicians and many patients feel that "bipolar disorder" is less stigmatizing than "manic-depressive illness." Perhaps so, but perhaps not. Certainly, patients who have suffered from the illness should have the right to choose whichever term they feel more comfortable with. But two questions arise: Is the term "bipolar" really a medically accurate one, and does changing the name of a condition actually lead to a greater acceptance of it? The answer to the first question, which concerns accuracy, is that "bipolar" is accurate in the sense that it indicates an individual has suffered from both mania (or mild forms of mania) and depression, unlike those individuals who have suffered from depression alone. But splitting mood disorders into bipolar and unipolar categories presupposes a distinction between depression and manic-depressive illness — both clinically and etiologically — that is not always clear, nor supported by science. Likewise, it perpetuates the notion that depression exists rather tidily segregated on its own pole, while mania clusters off neatly and discreetly on another. This polarization of two clinical states flies in the face of everything that we know about the cauldronous, fluctuating nature of manic-depressive illness; it ignores the question of whether mania is, ultimately, simply an extreme form of depression; and it minimizes the importance of mixed manic-and-depressive states, conditions that are common, extremely important clinically, and lie at the heart of many of the critical theoretical issues underlying this particular disease.

But the question also arises whether, ultimately, the destigmatization of mental illness comes about from merely a change in the language or, instead, from aggressive public education efforts; from successful treatments, such as lithium, the anticonvulsants, antidepressants, and antipsychotics; from treatments that are not only successful, but somehow also catch the imagination of the public and media (Prozac's influence on public opinion and knowledge about depression, for example); from discovery of the underlying genetic or other biological causes of mental illness; from brain-imaging techniques, such as PET and MRI (magnetic resonance imaging) scans, that visually communicate the location and concrete existence of these disorders; from the development of blood tests that will ultimately give medical credibility to psychiatric diseases; or from legislative actions, such as the Americans with Disabilities Act, and the obtainment of parity with other medical conditions under whatever health-reform system is put into place. Attitudes about mental illness are changing, however glacially, and it is in large measure due to a combination of these things — successful treatment, advocacy, and legislation.

The major mental health advocacy groups are made up primarily of patients, family members, and mental health professionals. They have been particularly effective in educating the public, the media, and the state and national governments. Although very different in styles and goals, these groups have provided direct support for tens of thousands of individual patients and their families; have raised the level of medical care in their communities by insisting upon competence and respect through, in effect, boycotting those psychiatrists and psychologists who do not provide both; and have agitated, badgered, and cajoled members of Congress (many of whom themselves suffer from mood disorders or have mental illness in their families) into increasing money for research, proposing parity for psychiatric illnesses, and passing legislation that bans job and insurance discrimination against the mentally ill. These groups—and the scientists and clinicians who make treatment possible—have made life easier for all of us who have psychiatric illnesses, whether we call ourselves mad or write letters of protest to those who do. Because of them, we now have the luxury of being able to debate the fine points of language about our own and the human condition.

■   ■   ■

A LIFE IN MOODS

We are all, as Byron put it, differently organized. We each move within the restraints of our temperament and live up only partially to its possibilities. Thirty years of living with manic-depressive illness has made me increasingly aware of both the restraints and possibilities that come with it. The ominous, dark, and deathful quality that I felt as a young child watching the high clear skies fill with smoke and flames *is* always there, somehow laced into the beauty and vitality of life. That darkness is an integral part of who I am, and it takes no effort of imagination on my part to remember the months of relentless blackness and exhaustion, or the terrible efforts it took in order to teach, read, write, see patients, and keep relationships alive. More deeply layered over but all too readily summoned up with the first trace of depression are the unforgettable images of violence, utter madness, mortifying behavior, and moods savage to experience, and even more disturbingly brutal in their effects upon others.

10   Yet however genuinely dreadful these moods and memories have been, they have always been offset by the elation and vitality of others; and whenever a mild and gentlish wave of brilliant and bubbling manic enthusiasm comes over me, I am transported by its exuberance—as surely as one is transported by a pungent scent into a world of profound recollection—to earlier, more intense and passionate times. The vividness that mania infuses into one's experiences of life creates strong, keenly recollected states, much as war must, and love and early memories surely do. Because of this, there is now, for me, a rather bittersweet exchange of a comfortable and settled present existence for a troubled but intensely lived past.

There are still occasional sirens to this past, and there remains a seductive, if increasingly rare, desire to recreate the furor and fever of earlier times. I look back over my shoulder and feel the presence of an intense young girl and then a volatile and disturbed young woman, both with high dreams and restless, romantic aspirations: How could one, should one, recapture that intensity or reexperience the glorious moods of dancing all night and into the morning, the gliding through starfields and dancing along the rings of Saturn, the zany manic enthusiasms? How can one ever bring back the long summer days of passion, the remembrance of lilacs, ecstasy, and gin fizzes that spilled down over a garden wall, and the peals of riotous laughter that lasted until the sun came up or the police arrived?

There is, for me, a mixture of longings for an earlier age; this is inevitable, perhaps, in any life, but there is an extra twist of almost painful nostalgia brought about by having lived a life particularly intense in moods. This makes it even harder to leave the past behind, and life, on occasion, becomes a kind of elegy for lost moods. I miss the lost intensities, and I find myself unconsciously reaching out for them, as I still now and again reach back with my hand for the fall and heaviness of my now-gone, long, thick hair; like the trace of moods, only a phantom weight remains. These current longings are, for the most part, only longings, and I do not feel compelled to re-create the intensities: the conse- quences are too awful, too final, and too damaging.

Still, the seductiveness of these unbridled and intense moods is powerful; and the ancient dialogue between reason and the senses is almost always more interestingly and passionately resolved in favor of the senses. The milder manias have a way of promising — and, for a very brief while, delivering — springs in the winter and epochal vitalities. In the cold light of day, however, the reality and destructiveness of rekindled illness tend to dampen the evocativeness of such se- lectively remembered, wistful, intense, and gentle moments. Any temptation that I now may have to recapture such moods by altering my medication is quickly hosed down by the cold knowledge that a gentle intensity soon becomes first a frenetic one and then, finally, an uncontrolled insanity. I am too fright- ened that I will again become morbidly depressed or virulently manic — either of which would, in turn, rip apart every aspect of my life, relationships, and work that I find most meaningful — to seriously consider any change in my medical treatment.

Although I am basically optimistic about remaining well, I know my ill- ness from enough different vantage points to remain rather fatalistic about the future. As a result, I know that I listen to lectures about new treatments for manic-depressive illness with far more than just a professional interest. I also know that when I am doing Grand Rounds at other hospitals, I often visit their psychiatric wards, look at their seclusion rooms and ECT suites, wander their hospital grounds, and do my own internal ratings of where I would choose to go if I had to be hospitalized. There is always a part of my mind that is preparing for the worst, and another part of my mind that believes if I prepare enough for it, the worst won't happen.

Many years of living with the cyclic upheavals of manic-depressive illness   15 has made me more philosophical, better armed, and more able to handle the in- evitable swings of mood and energy that I have opted for by taking a lower level of lithium. I agree absolutely with Eliot's Ecclesiastian belief that there is a season for everything, a time for building, and "a time for the wind to break the loosened pane." Therefore, I now move more easily with the fluctuating tides of energy, ideas, and enthusiasms that I remain so subject to. My mind still, now and again, becomes a carnival of lights, laughter, and sounds and possibilities. The laughter and exuberance and ease will, filling me, spill out and over and into others. These glinting, glorious moments will last for a while, a short season, and then move on. My high moods and hopes, having ridden briefly in the top car of the Ferris wheel will, as suddenly as they came, plummet into a black and gray and tired heap. Time will pass; these moods will pass; and I will, eventually, be myself again. But then, at some unknown time, the electrifying carnival will come back into my mind.

These comings and goings, this grace and godlessness, have become such a part of my life that the wild colors and sounds now have become less strange and less strong; and the blacks and grays that inevitably follow are, likewise, less dark and frightening. "Beneath those stars," Melville once said, "is a universe of gliding monsters." But, with time, one has encountered many of the monsters, and one is increasingly less terrified of those still to be met. Although I continue to have emergences of my old summer manias, they have been gutted not only of most of their terror, but of most of their earlier indescribable beauty and glorious rush as well: sludged by time, tempered by a long string of jading experiences, and brought to their knees by medication, they now coalesce, each July, into brief, occasionally dangerous cracklings together of black moods and high passions. And then they, too, pass. One comes out of such experiences with a more surrounding sense of death, and of life. Having heard so often, and so believably, John Donne's bell tolling softly that "Thou must die," one turns more sharply to life, with an immediacy and appreciation that would not otherwise exist.

We all build internal sea walls to keep at bay the sadnesses of life and the often overwhelming forces within our minds. In whatever way we do this—through love, work, family, faith, friends, denial, alcohol, drugs, or medication—we build these walls, stone by stone, over a lifetime. One of the most difficult problems is to construct these barriers of such a height and strength that one has a true harbor, a sanctuary away from crippling turmoil and pain, but yet low enough, and permeable enough, to let in fresh seawater that will fend off the inevitable inclination toward brackishness. For someone with my cast of mind and mood, medication is an integral element of this wall: without it, I would be constantly beholden to the crushing movements of a mental sea; I would, unquestionably, be dead or insane.

But love is, to me, the ultimately more extraordinary part of the breakwater wall: it helps to shut out the terror and awfulness, while, at the same time, allowing in life and beauty and vitality. . . . After each seeming death within my mind or heart, love has returned to re-create hope and to restore life. It has, at its best, made the inherent sadness of life bearable, and its beauty manifest. It has, inexplicably and savingly, provided not only cloak but lantern for the darker seasons and grimmer weather.

I long ago abandoned the notion of a life without storms, or a world without dry and killing seasons. Life is too complicated, too constantly changing, to be anything but what it is. And I am, by nature, too mercurial to be anything but deeply wary of the grave unnaturalness involved in any attempt to exert too much control over essentially uncontrollable forces. There will always be propelling, disturbing elements, and they will be there until, as Lowell put it, the watch is taken from the wrist. It is, at the end of the day, the individual moments of restlessness, of bleakness, of strong persuasions and maddened enthusiasms, that inform one's life, change the nature and direction of one's work, and give final meaning and color to one's loves and friendships.

TALKING ABOUT IT

Seeing Metaphor: Revealing and Concealing

1. In the opening paragraphs of the section "Speaking of Madness," Jamison mentions a variety of informal terms used to describe mental illness. Consider the metaphors implicit in these terms — for example, how do you suppose the term "squirrel" originated, or "fruitcake"? (You might want to consult an etymological dictionary or a dictionary of slang.) Where does Jamison stand on the use of such terms? Where do you?

2. In paragraphs 15–16 of the section "A Life in Moods," Jamison writes metaphorically of her manic-depressive condition, and in paragraph 17 she uses the metaphor of the sea wall to describe the way people protect themselves from "the sadnesses of life and the often overwhelming forces within our minds." How well do her metaphors help you understand what Jamison is trying to explain?

Seeing Composition: Frame, Line, Texture, Tone

1. "Speaking of Madness" opens with Jamison's story of receiving an irate letter chastising her for using the term "madness" in a lecture title. How does this story serve both to introduce her central ideas and to provide a frame for the essay?

2. There are a number of subtle differences in Jamison's style of writing in the two sections of this essay. How would you describe these differences? How might her different subject matters and intentions account for them?

Seeing Meaning: Navigating and Negotiating

1. "Attitudes about mental illness are changing, however glacially," writes Jamison, and she attributes these changes to "successful treatment, advocacy, and legislation." Have you seen any such changes in your lifetime? How would you define your own attitudes toward mental illness? Why do you feel as you do?

2. The official designation for Jamison's condition is "bipolar disorder," but throughout the essay she prefers the historic term "manic-depressive illness." What different images do the two terms suggest? Based on her explanation and on your reading, why do you think Jamison might prefer the second term?

WRITING ABOUT IT

1. As a clinician and researcher, Kay Redfield Jamison believes in the use of "precise language and explicit diagnostic criteria" found in the *Diagnostic and Statistical Manual,* but, as a person and a patient, she thinks the term "bipolar" is offensive. She argues that "bipolar" seems to "paper over the reality of the condition." It isn't a useful term, that is, for describing her experience.

    Choose two terms for the same thing and discuss your own preference for one or the other, depending on where you are standing in relation to it — that is, your preference according to the role you play as speaker and according to the audience you are addressing.

2. Jamison's friend was required to attend a consciousness-raising session about the effects of using pejorative terms for mental illness. Jamison was not persuaded that such censorship of language was necessarily a positive step toward greater public understanding or sympathy. How do you respond to her following claim: While certain negative labels should not go "unchecked or uncorrected," censorship of them "gives an illusion of easy answers to impossibly difficult situations and ignores the powerful role of wit and irony as positive agents of self-notion and social change."

    Offer your own illustration of the effects of such censorship, such as slang expressions for a sensitive issue that, on the one hand, can cause pain or reinforce prejudice but, on the other, can provide some benefits too, depending on the context in which they appear. Support your reasons.

3. Like Kat Duff in "Towards an Ecology of Illness," Jamison uses images from nature to describe her "life in moods," such as the "internal sea walls" she must build. How does this metaphor as well as others derived from the natural world help us understand her struggle and her attitude toward it?

Girl, Interrupted

S<small>USANNA</small> K<small>AYSEN</small>

Susanna Kaysen is the author of several novels, including Asa, As I
Knew Him *(1987) and* Far Afield *(1990). This selection is from*
Girl, Interrupted *(1993), a memoir describing the two years she
spent as a patient on the ward for teenage girls in a psychiatric
hospital.*

MIND VS. BRAIN

Whatever we call it — mind, character, soul — we like to think we possess
something that is greater than the sum of our neurons and that "animates" us.

A lot of mind, though, is turning out to be brain. A memory is a particular pattern of cellular changes on particular spots in our heads. A mood is a
compound of neurotransmitters: Too much acetylcholine, not enough serotonin, and you've got a depression.

So, what's left of mind?

It's a long way from not having enough serotonin to thinking the world is
"stale, flat and unprofitable"; even further to writing a play about a man driven
by that thought. That leaves a lot of mind room. Something is interpreting the
clatter of neurological activity.

But is this interpreter necessarily metaphysical and unembodied? Isn't it 5
probably a number — an enormous number — of brain functions working in
parallel? If the entire network of simultaneous tiny actions that constitute a
thought were identified and mapped, then "mind" might be visible.

The interpreter is convinced it's unmappable and invisible. "I'm your
mind," it claims. "You can't parse *me* into dendrites and synapses."

It's full of claims and reasons. "You're a little depressed because of all the
stress at work," it says. (It never says, "You're a little depressed because your serotonin level has dropped.")

Sometimes its interpretations are not credible, as when you cut your finger and it starts yelling, "You're gonna die!" Sometimes its claims are unlikely, as
when it says, "Twenty-five chocolate chip cookies would be the perfect dinner."

Often, then, it doesn't know what it's talking about. And when you decide
it's wrong, who or what is making that decision? A second, superior interpreter?

Why stop at two? That's the problem with this model. It's endless. Each in- 10
terpreter needs a boss to report to.

But something about this model describes the essence of our experience of
consciousness. There is thought, and then there is thinking about thoughts, and
they don't feel the same. They must reflect quite different aspects of brain function.

The point is, the brain talks to itself, and by talking to itself changes its perceptions. To make a new version of the not-entirely-false model, imagine the first interpreter as a foreign correspondent, reporting from the world. The world in this case means everything out- or inside our bodies, including serotonin levels in the brain. The second interpreter is a news analyst, who writes op-ed pieces. They read each other's work. One needs data, the other needs an overview; they influence each other. They get dialogues going.

INTERPRETER ONE: Pain in the left foot, back of heel.
INTERPRETER TWO: I believe that's because the shoe is too tight.
INTERPRETER ONE: Checked that. Took off the shoe. Foot still hurts.
INTERPRETER TWO: Did you look at it?
INTERPRETER ONE: Looking. It's red.
INTERPRETER TWO: No blood?
INTERPRETER ONE: Nope.
INTERPRETER TWO: Forget about it.
INTERPRETER ONE: Okay.

A minute later, though, there's another report.

INTERPRETER ONE: Pain in the left foot, back of heel.
INTERPRETER TWO: I know that already.
INTERPRETER ONE: Still hurts. Now it's puffed up.
INTERPRETER TWO: It's just a blister. Forget about it.
INTERPRETER ONE: Okay.

Two minutes later.

INTERPRETER TWO: Don't pick it!
INTERPRETER ONE: It'll feel better if I pop it.
INTERPRETER TWO: That's what you think. Leave it alone.
INTERPRETER ONE: Okay. Still hurts, though.

15   Mental illness seems to be a communication problem between interpreters one and two.

An exemplary piece of confusion:

INTERPRETER ONE: There's a tiger in the corner.
INTERPRETER TWO: No, that's not a tiger — that's a bureau.
INTERPRETER ONE: It's a tiger, it's a tiger!
INTERPRETER TWO: Don't be ridiculous. Let's go look at it.

Then all the dendrites and neurons and serotonin levels and interpreters collect themselves and trot over to the corner.

If you are not crazy, the second interpreter's assertion, that this is a bureau, will be acceptable to the first interpreter. If you are crazy, the first interpreter's viewpoint, the tiger theory, will prevail.

The trouble here is that the first interpreter actually sees a tiger. The messages sent between neurons are incorrect somehow. The chemicals triggered are the wrong chemicals, or the impulses are going to the wrong connections. Apparently, this happens often, but the second interpreter jumps in to straighten things out.

Think of being in a train, next to another train, in a station. When the other train starts moving, you are convinced that your train is moving. The rattle of the other train feels like the rattle of your train, and you see your train leaving that other train behind. It can take a while—maybe even half a minute—before the second interpreter sorts through the first interpreter's claim of movement and corrects it. That's because it's hard to counteract the validity of sensory impressions. We are designed to believe in them.

The train situation is not the same as an optical illusion. An optical illusion does contain two realities. It's not that the vase is wrong and the faces are right; both are right, and the brain moves between two existing patterns that it recognizes as different. Although you can make yourself dizzy going from vase to faces and back again, you can't undermine your sense of reality in quite such a visceral way as you can with the train.

Sometimes, when you've realized that your train is not really moving, you can spend another half a minute suspended between two realms of consciousness: the one that knows you aren't moving and the one that feels you are. You can flit back and forth between these perceptions and experience a sort of mental vertigo. And if you do this, you are treading on the ground of craziness—a place where false impressions have all the hallmarks of reality.

Freud said psychotics were unanalyzable because they couldn't distinguish between fantasy and reality (tiger vs. bureau), and analysis works on precisely that distinction. The patient must lay out the often fantastic assertions of the first interpreter and scrutinize them with the second. The hope is that the second interpreter has, or will learn to have, the wit and insight to disprove some of the ridiculous claims the first interpreter has made over the years.

You can see why doubting one's own craziness is considered a good sign: It's a sort of flailing response by the second interpreter. What's happening? the second interpreter is saying. He tells me it's a tiger but I'm not convinced; maybe there's something wrong with me. Enough doubt is in there to give "reality" a toehold.

No doubt, no analysis. Somebody who comes in chatting about tigers is going to be offered Thorazine, not the couch.

At that moment, when the doctor suggests Thorazine, what's happening to that doctor's mental map of mental illness? Earlier in the day, the doctor had a map divided into superego, ego, and id, with all kinds of squiggly, perhaps broken, lines running among those three areas. The doctor was treating something he or she calls a psyche or mind. All of a sudden the doctor is preparing to treat a brain. This brain doesn't have a psychelike arrangement, or if it does, that's not where the problem is. This brain has problems that are chemical and electrical.

"It's the reality-testing function," says the doctor. "This brain is bollixed up about reality and I can't analyze it. Those other brains — minds — weren't."

Something's wrong here. You can't call a piece of fruit an apple when you want to eat it and a dandelion when you don't want to eat it. It's the same sort of fruit no matter what your intentions toward it. And how strong is the case for a categorical distinction between brains that know reality and brains that don't? Is a non–reality-recognizing brain truly as different from a reality-recognizing brain as a foot, say, is from a brain? This seems unlikely. Recognizing the agreed-upon version of reality is only one of billions of brain jobs.

If the biochemists were able to demonstrate the physical workings of neuroses (phobias, or difficulties getting pleasure from life), if they could pinpoint the chemicals and impulses and interbrain conversations and information exchanges that constitute these feelings, would the psychoanalysts pack up their ids and egos and retire from the field?

30   They have partially retired from the field. Depression, manic-depression, schizophrenia: All that stuff they always had trouble treating they now treat chemically. Take two Lithium and don't call me in the morning because there's nothing to say; it's innate.

Some cooperative efforts — the sort the brain makes — would be useful here.

For nearly a century the psychoanalysts have been writing op-ed pieces about the workings of a country they've never traveled to, a place that, like China, has been off-limits. Suddenly, the country has opened its borders and is crawling with foreign correspondents; neurobiologists are filing ten stories a week, filled with new data. These two groups of writers, however, don't seem to read each other's work.

That's because the analysts are writing about a country they call Mind and the neuroscientists are reporting from a country they call Brain.

BORDERLINE PERSONALITY DISORDER*

An essential feature of this disorder is a pervasive pattern of instability of self-image, interpersonal relationships, and mood, beginning in early adulthood and present in a variety of contexts.

---

*From the *Diagnostic and Statistical Manual of Mental Disorders,* 3d edition, revised (1987), pp. 346–47.

McLEAN HOSPITAL   Page.............   F-90

No.22 201   Name   KAYSEN, Susanna

<u>1968</u>
9-4   DISCHARGE ON VISIT SUMMARY:

              G. Formal Diagnosis:
                  Schizophrenic reaction, paranoid type (borderline) - currently in
                  remission. Patient is functioning on a passive-aggressive personality,
                  passive-dependent type.

        KAYSEN, Susanna N.   12
        Hospital No. 22201

                    CASE REPORT-CONT'D

              B. Prognosis: The resolution of the depressive affect and
        suicidal drive should be expected as a result of the hospitalization. The
        degree of personality integration and ego function which may be achieved
        for the long term is hard to predict. We may say that with a good
        intensive working relationship in therapy and a successful relationship to
        the hospital the patient may be able to achieve a more satisfactory means
        of adapting. Nevertheless because of the chronicity of the illness and
        the basic deficiencies involved in personality structuring, a more complete
        recovery is not to be expected at this time. However, the patient may learn
        to make more wise choices for herself within the boundaries of her personality
        so that she is able to achieve a satisfactory dependent relationship if
        necessary which will sustain her for a long period of time.

35   A marked and persistent identity disturbance is almost invariably present. This is often pervasive, and is manifested by uncertainty about several life issues, such as self-image, sexual orientation, long-term goals or career choice, types of friends or lovers to have, and which values to adopt. The person often experiences this instability of self-image as chronic feelings of emptiness and boredom.

Interpersonal relationships are usually unstable and intense, and may be characterized by alternation of the extremes of overidealization and devaluation. These people have difficulty tolerating being alone, and will make frantic efforts to avoid real or imagined abandonment.

Affective instability is common. This may be evidenced by marked mood shifts from baseline mood to depression, irritability, or anxiety, usually lasting a few hours or, only rarely, more than a few days. In addition, these people often have inappropriately intense anger with frequent displays of temper or recurrent physical fights. They tend to be impulsive, particularly in activities that are potentially self-damaging, such as shopping sprees, psychoactive substance abuse, reckless driving, casual sex, shoplifting, and binge eating.

Recurrent suicidal threats, gestures, or behavior and other self-mutilating behavior (e.g., wrist-scratching) are common in the more severe forms of the disorder. This behavior may serve to manipulate others, may be a result of intense anger, or may counteract feelings of "numbness" and depersonalization that arise during periods of extreme stress. . . .

Associated Features   Frequently this disorder is accompanied by many features of other Personality Disorders, such as Schizotypal, Histrionic, Narcissistic, and Antisocial Personality Disorders. In many cases more than one diagnosis is warranted. Quite often social contrariness and a generally pessimistic outlook are observed. Alternation between dependency and self-assertion is common. During periods of extreme stress, transient psychotic symptoms may occur, but they are generally of insufficient severity or duration to warrant an additional diagnosis.

40   **Impairment**   Often there is considerable interference with social or occupational functioning.

Complications   Possible complications include Dysthymia [depressive neurosis], Major Depression, Psychoactive Substance Abuse, and psychotic disorders such as Brief Reactive Psychosis. Premature death may result from suicide.

Sex Ratio   The disorder is more commonly diagnosed in women.

Prevalence   Borderline Personality Disorder is apparently common.

Predisposing and Familial Pattern   No information.

Differential Diagnosis   In Identity Disorder there is a similar clinical picture,   45
but Borderline Personality Disorder preempts the diagnosis of Identity Disorder
if the criteria for Borderline Personality Disorder are met, the disturbance is sufficiently pervasive and persistent, and it is unlikely that it will be limited to a developmental stage. . . .

MY DIAGNOSIS

So these were the charges against me. I didn't read them until twenty-five
years later. "A character disorder" is what they'd told me then.

I had to find a lawyer to help me get my records from the hospital; I had
to read line 32a of form A1 of the Case Record, and entry G on the Discharge on
Visit Summary, and entry B of Part IV of the Case Report; then I had to locate a
copy of the *Diagnostic and Statistical Manual of Mental Disorders* and look up
Borderline Personality to see what they really thought about me.

It's a fairly accurate picture of me at eighteen, minus a few quirks like reckless driving and eating binges. It's accurate but it isn't profound. Of course, it
doesn't aim to be profound. It's not even a case study. It's a set of guidelines, a
generalization.

I'm tempted to try refuting it, but then I would be open to the further
charges of "defensiveness" and "resistance."

All I can do is give the particulars: an annotated diagnosis.   50

"[U]ncertainty about several life issues, such as self-image, sexual orientation, long-term goals or career choice, types of friends or lovers to have . . ." I relish
that last phrase. Its awkwardness (the "to have" seems superfluous) gives it substance and heft. I still have that uncertainty. Is this the type of friend or lover I
want to have? I ask myself every time I meet someone new. Charming but shallow;
good-hearted but a bit conventional; too handsome for his own good; fascinating
but probably unreliable; and so forth. I guess I've had my share of unreliables.
More than my share? How many would constitute more than my share?

Fewer than for somebody else — somebody who'd never been called a borderline personality?

That's the nub of my problem here.

If my diagnosis had been bipolar illness, for instance, the reaction to me
and to this story would be slightly different. That's a chemical problem, you'd say
to yourself, manic-depression, Lithium, all that. I would be blameless, somehow.
And what about schizophrenia — that would send a chill up your spine. After all,
that's real insanity. People don't "recover" from schizophrenia. You'd have to wonder how much of what I'm telling you is true and how much imagined.

I'm simplifying, I know. But these words taint everything. The fact that I   55
was locked up taints everything.

What does *borderline personality* mean, anyhow?

It appears to be a way station between neurosis and psychosis: a fractured but not disassembled psyche. Though to quote my post-Melvin psychiatrist: "It's what they call people whose lifestyles bother them."

He can say it because he's a doctor. If I said it, nobody would believe me.

An analyst I've known for years said, "Freud and his circle thought most people were hysterics, then in the fifties it was psychoneurotics, and lately, everyone's a borderline personality."

60   When I went to the corner bookstore to look up my diagnosis in the *Manual,* it occurred to me that I might not find it in there anymore. They do get rid of things — homosexuality, for instance. Until recently, quite a few of my friends would have found themselves documented in that book along with me. Well, they got out of the book and I didn't. Maybe in another twenty-five years I won't be in there either.

"[I]nstability of self-image, interpersonal relationships, and mood . . . uncertainty about . . . long-term goals or career choice . . ." Isn't this a good description of adolescence? Moody, fickle, faddish, insecure: in short, impossible.

"[S]elf-mutilating behavior (e.g., wrist-scratching) . . ." I've skipped forward a bit. This is the one that caught me by surprise as I sat on the floor of the bookstore reading my diagnosis. Wrist-scratching! I thought I'd invented it. Wrist-banging, to be precise.

This is where people stop being able to follow me. This is the sort of stuff you get locked up for. Nobody knew I was doing it, though. I never told anyone, until now.

I had a butterfly chair. In the sixties, everyone in Cambridge had a butterfly chair. The metal edge of its upturned seat was perfectly placed for wrist-banging. I had tried breaking ashtrays and walking on the shards, but I didn't have the nerve to tread firmly. Wrist-banging — slow, steady, mindless — was a better solution. It was cumulative injury, so each bang was tolerable.

65   A solution to what? I quote from the *Manual:* "This behavior may . . . counteract feelings of 'numbness' and depersonalization that arise during periods of extreme stress."

I spent hours in my butterfly chair banging my wrist. I did it in the evenings, like homework. I'd do some homework, then I'd spend half an hour wrist-banging, then finish my homework, then back in the chair for some more banging before brushing my teeth and going to bed. I banged the inside, where the veins converge. It swelled and turned a bit blue, but considering how hard and how much I banged it, the visible damage was slight. That was yet one more recommendation of it to me.

I'd had an earlier period of face-scratching. If my fingernails hadn't been quite short, I couldn't have gotten away with it. As it was, I definitely looked puffy and peculiar the next day. I used to scratch my cheeks and then rub soap on them. Maybe the soap prevented me from looking worse. But I looked bad enough that people asked, "Is something wrong with your face?" So I switched to wrist-banging.

I was like an anchorite with a hair shirt. Part of the point was that nobody knew about my suffering. If people knew and admired—or abominated—me, something important would be lost.

I was trying to explain my situation to myself. My situation was that I was in pain and nobody knew it; even I had trouble knowing it. So I told myself, over and over, You are in pain. It was the only way I could get through to myself ("counteract feelings of 'numbness'"). I was demonstrating, externally and irrefutably, an inward condition.

"Quite often social contrariness and a generally pessimistic outlook are   70 observed." What do you suppose they mean by "social contrariness"? Putting my elbows on the table? Refusing to get a job as a dental technician? Disappointing my parents' hope that I would go to a first-rate university?

They don't define "social contrariness," and I can't define it, so I think it ought to be excluded from the list. I'll admit to the generally pessimistic outlook. Freud had one too.

I can honestly say that my misery has been transformed into common unhappiness, so by Freud's definition I have achieved mental health. And my discharge sheet, at line 41, Outcome with Regard to Mental Disorder, reads "Recovered."

Recovered. Had my personality crossed over that border, whatever and wherever it was, to resume life within the confines of the normal? Had I stopped arguing with my personality and learned to straddle the line between sane and insane? Perhaps I'd actually had an identity disorder. "In Identity Disorder there is a similar clinical picture, but Borderline Personality . . . preempts the diagnosis . . . if the disturbance is sufficiently pervasive and . . . it is unlikely that it will be limited to a developmental stage." Maybe I was a victim of improper preemption?

I'm not finished with this diagnosis.

"The person often experiences this instability of self-image as chronic feel   75 ings of emptiness or boredom." My chronic feelings of emptiness and boredom came from the fact that I was living a life based on my incapacities, which were numerous. A partial list follows. I could not and did not want to: ski, play tennis, or go to gym class; attend to any subject in school other than English and biology; write papers on any assigned topics (I wrote poems instead of papers for English; I got F's); plan to go or apply to college; give any reasonable explanation for these refusals.

My self-image was not unstable. I saw myself, quite correctly, as unfit for the educational and social systems.

But my parents and teachers did not share my self-image. Their image of me was unstable, since it was out of kilter with reality and based on their needs and wishes. They did not put much value on my capacities, which were admittedly few, but genuine. I read everything, I wrote constantly, and I had boyfriends by the barrelful.

"Why don't you do the assigned reading?" they'd ask. "Why don't you write your papers instead of whatever you're writing—what is that, a short story?" "Why don't you expend as much energy on your schoolwork as you do on your boyfriends?"

By my senior year I didn't even bother with excuses, let alone explanations.

80   "Where is your term paper?" asked my history teacher.

"I didn't write it. I have nothing to say on that topic."

"You could have picked another topic."

"I have nothing to say on any historical topic."

One of my teachers told me I was a nihilist. He meant it as an insult but I took it as a compliment.

85   Boyfriends and literature: How can you make a life out of those two things? As it turns out, I did; more literature than boyfriends lately, but I guess you can't have everything ("a generally pessimistic outlook [is] observed").

Back then I didn't know that I—or anyone—could make a life out of boyfriends and literature. As far as I could see, life demanded skills I didn't have. The result was chronic emptiness and boredom. There were more pernicious results as well: self-loathing, alternating with "inappropriately intense anger with frequent displays of temper . . ."

What would have been an appropriate level of intensity for my anger at feeling shut out of life? My classmates were spinning their fantasies for the future: lawyer, ethnobotanist, Buddhist monk (it was a very progressive high school). Even the dumb, uninteresting ones who were there to provide "balance" looked forward to their marriages and their children. I knew I wasn't going to have any of this because I knew I didn't want it. But did that mean I would have nothing?

I was the first person in the history of the school not to go to college. Of course, at least a third of my classmates never finished college. By 1968, people were dropping out daily.

Quite often now, people say to me, when I tell them I didn't go to college, "Oh, how marvelous!" They wouldn't have thought it was so marvelous back then. They didn't; my classmates were just the sorts of people who now tell me how marvelous I am. In 1966, I was a pariah.

90   What was I going to do? a few of my classmates asked.

"I'm going to join the WACs," I told one guy.

"Oh, yeah? That will be an interesting career."

"Just kidding," I said.

"Oh, uh, you mean you're not, really?"

95   I was stunned. Who did they think I was?

I'm sure they didn't think about me much. I was the one who wore black and — really, I've heard it from several people — slept with the English teacher. They were all seventeen and miserable, just like me. They didn't have time to wonder why I was a little more miserable than most.

Emptiness and boredom: what an understatement. What I felt was complete desolation. Desolation, despair, and depression.

Isn't there some other way to look at this? After all, angst of these dimensions is a luxury item. You need to be well fed, clothed, and housed to have time for this much self-pity. And the college business: My parents wanted me to go, I didn't want to go, and I didn't go. I got what I wanted. Those who don't go to college have to get jobs. I agreed with all this. I told myself all this over and over. I even got a job — my job breaking au gratin dishes.

But the fact that I couldn't hold my job was worrisome. I was probably crazy. I'd been skirting the idea of craziness for a year or two; now I was closing in on it.   100

Pull yourself together! I told myself. Stop indulging yourself. There's nothing wrong with you. You're just wayward.

One of the great pleasures of mental health (whatever that is) is how much less time I have to spend thinking about myself.

I have a few more annotations to my diagnosis.

"The disorder is more commonly diagnosed in women."

Note the construction of that sentence. They did not write, "The disorder is more common in women." It would still be suspect, but they didn't even bother trying to cover their tracks.

Many disorders, judging by the hospital population, were more commonly   105
diagnosed in women. Take, for example, "compulsive promiscuity."

How many girls do you think a seventeen-year-old boy would have to screw to earn the label "compulsively promiscuous"? Three? No, not enough. Six? Doubtful. Ten? That sounds more likely. Probably in the fifteen-to-twenty range, would be my guess — if they ever put that label on boys, which I don't recall their doing.

And for seventeen-year-old girls, how many boys?

In the list of six "potentially self-damaging" activities favored by the borderline personality, three are commonly associated with women (shopping sprees, shoplifting, and eating binges) and one with men (reckless driving). One is not "gender-specific," as they say these days (psychoactive substance abuse). And the definition of the other (casual sex) is in the eye of the beholder.

Then there is the question of "premature death" from suicide. Luckily, I avoided it, but I thought about suicide a lot. I'd think about it and make myself sad over my premature death, and then I'd feel better. The idea of suicide worked on me like a purgative or a cathartic. For some people it's different — Daisy, for instance. But was her death really "premature"? Ought she to have sat in her eat-in kitchen with her chicken and her anger for another fifty years? I'm assuming she wasn't going to change, and I may be wrong. She certainly made that assumption, and she may also have been wrong. And if she'd sat there for only thirty years, and killed herself at forty-nine instead of at nineteen, would her death still be "premature"?

110   I got better and Daisy didn't and I can't explain why. Maybe I was just flirting with madness the way I flirted with my teachers and my classmates. I wasn't convinced I was crazy, though I feared I was. Some people say that having any conscious opinion on the matter is a mark of sanity, but I'm not sure that's true. I still think about it. I'll always have to think about it.

I often ask myself if I'm crazy. I ask other people too.

"Is this a crazy thing to say?" I'll ask before saying something that probably isn't crazy.

I start a lot of sentences with "Maybe I'm totally nuts," or "Maybe I've gone 'round the bend."

If I do something out of the ordinary—take two baths in one day, for example—I say to myself: Are you crazy?

115   It's a common phrase, I know. But it means something particular to me: the tunnels, the security screens, the plastic forks, the shimmering, ever-shifting borderline that like all boundaries beckons and asks to be crossed. I do not want to cross it again.

TALKING ABOUT IT

Seeing Metaphor: Revealing and Concealing

1. Kaysen creates an interesting metaphor for consciousness in her dialogue between the two interpreters. How does she use this metaphor to help explain the differences in doctors treating a "mind" and those treating a "brain"?

2. Theodore Sarbin, professor emeritus of psychology and criminology at the University of California, Santa Cruz, claims in "Metaphors of Unwanted Conduct" (an essay cited and described in chapter 1) that "mental illness" is a metaphor that has not always had a positive effect on the way patients are diagnosed and treated; he believes those so diagnosed can less pejoratively be said to exhibit "unwanted conduct" based on the moral judgments of others. How does Kaysen's analysis of her own behavior matched to the official borderline personality disorder guidelines tend to support Sarbin's idea? To what extent do you think that "borderline personality disorder" may be a clinical metaphor for "unwanted conduct"?

Seeing Composition: Frame, Line, Texture, Tone

1. Kaysen quite frankly uses the terms "crazy" and "craziness" to describe mental illness. How do you respond to her use of these? What might Kay Redfield Jamison say, based on her comments in *An Unquiet Mind*?

2. In discussing "My Diagnosis," Kaysen writes, "I'm tempted to try refuting it, but then I would be open to the further charges of 'defensiveness' and 'resistance'" (paragraph 49). Does the tone of "My Diagnosis" seem defensive or resistant? Explain your answer.

Seeing Meaning: Navigating and Negotiating

1. In "Mind vs. Brain," Kaysen concludes by noting that "the analysts are writing about a country called Mind and the neuroscientists are reporting from a country they call Brain." What is her point here? What does she mean when she says, "Some cooperative efforts — the sort the brain makes — would be useful here"?

2. In paragraphs 103–8 of "My Diagnosis," Kaysen focuses on issues of gender and psychiatric diagnosis. How possible do you think it is that men exhibiting compulsive behaviors — promiscuity, for example, or binge eating— would be less likely than women to be diagnosed as suffering from a disorder?

WRITING ABOUT IT

1. Both Kay Redfield Jamison and Susanna Kaysen question the creation of boundaries between normal and abnormal. Boundary is an important metaphor with serious consequences for overstepping it. Consider the thin line between two other states of mind or two behaviors. Write about who or what determines the boundary and how you know if you've crossed it. What are the consequences and what do you make of them?

2. Kaysen suggests that some of her behavior was no less questionable than that of her so-called "normal" peers and that some judgments of abnormal behavior are based either on assumptions about gender or on other assumptions particular to a place and time. Where in her descriptions of herself as a teenager do you recognize behavior or thinking that comes closer to normal than abnormal? Where not? On what do you base your own judgments of her? Why?

Illness as a Result of Destruction

CINDY FELTNER

Cindy Feltner was enrolled in the writing class where materials for this book began to be tested. Early in the semester, she wrote "The Religious Aspects of Ballet," an exploration of ballet as a ritual with religious dimensions. She drew on her personal experience, illustrating how the rituals of ballet class translate into a metaphorical story that is communicated through setting, dancers' physical appearance, and movement instead of words. In the following essay, she synthesizes Richard Preston's "Back in the Hot Zone," including references to his book The Hot Zone *and Kat Duff's "Towards an Ecology of Illness."*

Robert Preston and Kat Duff both portray illness as a result of destructive behavior. Both writers give the impression that when we act in a destructive manner, either against the rain forest or against society, illness can result.

In "Back in the Hot Zone," Richard Preston interviews a doctor working in Africa who states that

> We all sort of feel that Ebola comes out of its hiding place when something occasionally alters the very delicate balance of the ecosystem, in a region where things grow as they would in a warm petri dish. (45)

Ebola is viewed as a consequence of disturbing the rain forest. Perhaps with the shrinking of the rain forest, the virus is losing its original hosts and is moving on to new ones, such as humans. In *The Hot Zone,* another of Preston's writings, he gives one more reason for deadly viruses that are emerging as a result of ruining the tropical biosphere: Many new and deadly viruses, such as Ebola and AIDS, are the products of the earth's immune system responding to the growing population:

> In a sense, the Earth is mounting an immune response against the human species. It is beginning to react to the human parasite, the flooding infection of people, the dead spots of concrete all over the planet, the cancerous rot-outs in Europe, Japan and the United States, thick with replicating primates, the colonizing enlarging and spreading and threatening to shock the biosphere with mass extinctions. (287)

In Preston's book, the concept of illness is reversed. People are making the earth sick instead of environmental stimuli making people sick. People are portrayed as parasites eating away at the earth. The "dead spots of concrete" are the damage done by people. The "cancerous rot-outs" are the regions of the earth most densely populated, where the virus is strongest. Preston says these cities are "thick with replicating primates"; the word "replicate" is often used to describe the spread of viruses in humans. Preston says that viruses are a part of the earth's immune response. They could be compared to white blood cells in humans. White blood cells ingest and destroy harmful toxins in the body, precisely what Preston says that viruses do for the environment. Preston also uses the words "spreading," "threatening," and "shock" to describe the effects of people damaging the earth. This metaphor, comparing the earth to an organism and viruses to its defense mechanism, is supported by the way he talks about humans in terms of parasites.

By describing viruses as agents of the earth's immune system, Preston creates the image of viruses as a positive force in the environment. Without them to destroy organisms, he implies, the earth could not support the growing population. In this view, illness is not something we can control or necessarily cure. If a cure is found for a particular virus, the earth's immune system will respond by creating a new strain or producing a new virus to counteract the destructive actions of people. Preston's view of Ebola is not hopeful for humans.

Preston writes about illness as a result of destructive behavior of people toward the natural environment. Kat Duff also writes as if illness is a result of destructive behavior, but she focuses on destructive behavior between people. Duff believes that shame as the result of a wrong that was committed, such as "apartheid" or "wife-beating,"

> floats free of the shameless trespassers and lands upon the trespassed, those who are treated shamefully — the women, children and old people, the underclass and outcast — who come to manifest the symptoms of distress and disease, becoming sacrifices. (39–40)

She believes that illness occurs because those who commit crimes, such as corporate polluters, are numb to the pain they cause. They rationalize their crimes in the name of progress or practicality. Since they do not answer for their sins, the responsibility must go to others. Therefore, illness can be linked to our culture and its inability to feel shame for certain types of destructive behaviors.

Duff believes that crimes committed by one's ancestors can affect the   5
health of future generations. She writes:

> Yes, the sins of the father are visited upon the children, and onto the seventh generation, as many Native American traditions attest. The Bible calls it "blood guilt," psychologists have named it the "genealogical shadow." Deepak Chopra, an M.D. who is well-versed in ayervedic medicine, speaks of "ghosts of memory" which affect our immune system and foster illness. (41–42)

Duff's idea is that illness is created by destructive behavior against others that is left unanswered for. By showing that experts in different disciplines also share this idea, Duff is validating her argument. In her article, she uses herself as an example. Duff feels that her illness is partly due to the fact that her ancestors settled on land which belonged to Sioux Indians. The Indians were driven off of their land after the Sioux Uprising, which caused many Indians to starve and freeze to death. Duff says that "those deaths made a big gash in the land and my body is the wound" (41). After realizing this, she was able to make amends for this crime by making an offering, which she does not name, to the Indians who had died.

Duff sums up her views of illness and its causes in the statement:

> Our bodies bear the untold lessons and scars of history; as we suffer our wounds in the extremities of illness they become our offerings, our means of realizing and remembering what is right, what is needed, to bring our lives and our world back into balance. (42–43)

Duff is saying that illness is a reminder of the past. It is reminding us of the destructive behavior of our ancestors. Illness reminds us that these things need attention and must be amended in some way. Therefore, illness is also a catalyst for action. Her idea of illness differs from Preston's in that it can be helpful to humans. Preston gives no evidence that illness has possible benefits for humans.

Although these two authors have different ideas of how destruction brings about illness, their ideas are linked in certain ways. In "Back in the Hot Zone," Preston writes: "The Ebola Zaire strain erupted in 1976 in villages near the Ebola river, five hundred miles north of Kikwit, where it killed nine out of ten of its infected victims" (43). If Preston's idea of the emergence of the virus is true, that it comes out when something disturbs its habitat, then these villagers can be seen as what Duff describes as "the trespassed." They are the ones that the shame has floated to and made sick. Although they were not the ones who destroyed the rain forest, they felt its effects. The ones responsible for the destruction of the rain forest, such as pharmaceutical companies, rarely experience the effects. These companies destroy the rain forest while harvesting plants used to make drugs, and only see their crimes in terms of financial gain. According to Duff, the shame from their crime floats onto others, such as the villagers, and makes them sick.

These two writers both give reasons for the emergence of illness, but their ideas about what causes its emergence are different. Preston's is mainly scientific. The viruses on earth, hidden away in the rain forest, are being exposed by humans who are eating away and destroying the biosphere. Since the viruses have nowhere else to go they are spreading out, infecting and eliminating humans. This helps the environment by eliminating the problem of overpopulation, the cause of destruction to the ecosystem. Duff's answer is spiritual. She believes illness is caused by "ghosts of memory," shame from the wrongdoings of our ancestors. Illness is a way to cure these wrongdoings by making us realize them, and then act on that realization. Her answer has nothing to do with science. She is only concerned with the cause and effects of illness on our moral state. Both writers share the idea that people cause illness by destructive actions, but they differ in the kinds of actions they attribute to the emergence of illness.

All parenthetical citations refer to page numbers in the original sources.

PERMEABLE BOUNDARIES: WRITING WHERE THE READINGS MEET

1. Kat Duff, in "Towards an Ecology of Illness," claims that as we "become sick, sickness becomes us and redefines us; so we say we are not ourselves anymore." How might Marjorie Gross's essay, "Cancer Becomes Me," be both an affirmation and contradiction of Duff's claim?

2. Marsha Norman, in "Say Amen to Somebody," writes:

   > [Prayer] is a process of remembering who we really are and how we are related. Prayer is nonlocal. . . . There is no such thing as distant healing because there is no distance separating people that must be overcome. The healing of someone else is in a sense self-healing.

   Kat Duff complains, "We are so convinced of our separateness." How do both essays, in their emphasis on a collective unconscious, seem to be the American call to meditation or prayer?

3. Psychologist Theodore Sarbin claims in "Metaphors of Unwanted Conduct,"

   > In one sense, combining the materialist word "illness" with the spiritualist "mind" is illicit. The effect of the complex metaphor [mental illness] is to assign qualities of mind that are associated with the body. The meanings of mind are too abstract—and the experiences of the mind too ephemeral—to be serviceable to the practitioners of the healing arts. (305)

   How does the quoted passage raise questions about claims made in the essays by Marsha Norman and Kat Duff? Does Sarbin's claim affect the degree to which you are persuaded by Norman and Duff? Why or why not?

4. In several of the essays in this chapter, health is an issue of control. In what ways do people define and seek control of their own health beyond conventional medicine? How do you respond to these efforts?

5. In what ways do several pieces come together to answer these questions: what is required for healing to occur? what does it mean to heal or to be healed?

6. Both Richard Preston and Marsha Norman use language belonging to the world of computer technology to talk about illness and health. Since computer metaphors are pervasive in our culture, Preston and Norman are not unusual in their reach for them. Which author's metaphor, however, do you find more helpful in your understanding of the phenomenon being defined? Why?

Chapter 5

Mind and Body

What we have almost forgotten to wonder about is this: since when is breakfast cereal a moral issue?"

—Barbara Ehrenreich

The mind is inside the body, and yet we have trouble thinking of our own thoughts and feelings as electrical impulses, that is, as the mere product of neural networking within our brains. Historically, body and mind have often been described as different entities, presenting a centuries-old philosophical problem: what is the nature of "mind"? Is it part of, or separate from, the body? The relationship of mind to body is an issue that arises in chapter 4, "Illness and Health," and it arises here too. Some people make strong connections between their bodies and minds, often seeing one as a reflection of the other. Images of self, for example, can be very much associated with images of the body. The boundaries, metaphorical or literal, between body and mind concern the authors of this chapter. More broadly, "body" and "mind" extend to include the physical/natural and psychological/spiritual worlds.

The natural world can inspire thoughts of the spiritual and the ideal, while, conversely, the spiritual and ideal can find its embodiment in the natural. To think about one world in terms of another is to think metaphorically. C. S. Lewis explains, "When we pass beyond pointing to individual sensible objects, when we begin to think of causes, relations, of mental states or acts, we become incurably metaphorical." Some people believe that once we grasp an idea, we no longer need metaphor, but Lewis argues that "freedom from a given metaphor . . . is often only a freedom to choose between that metaphor and others," and not between the metaphorical and the literal.

Choosing among metaphors is the freedom Nicholson Baker has in trying to describe the mental activity called "changes of mind." He invents a variety of metaphors derived from the tangible, physical world because the world of mind is

287

intangible. As Baker explains, the experience of changing one's mind is only "partially felt"; that is, people are only minimally aware of the process through which they come to adopt a new opinion. "Our opinions," Baker argues, "gently nudged by circumstance, revise themselves under cover of inattention." We can rarely point to one concrete event, such as "sudden conversion and wrenching insight," for an explanation. "We change our minds as we change our character," Baker explains. "Years go by and the movement remains unrecognized." Thus, Baker uses metaphor to give some tangible or visible form to the intangible world of mental processes.

One measurement of change is time. In *Einstein's Dreams*, Alan Lightman imagines the young patent officer on the brink of discovering relativity. In choosing among arguments, Albert Einstein entertains many possible worlds. The one included in this chapter is a world in which there are two times: mechanical time and body time. Some people live their lives by watching a clock, and others, by listening to their bodies.

In contrast, Margaret Atwood and John Updike entertain possible ways of viewing the body. What cultural and social values are attached to the female form that affect the way men and women see their bodies? Do we "lose" the body, as Atwood suggests, when it is objectified or viewed through layers of ideas about gender? How do our cultural beliefs and attitudes affect the way we see each other and ourselves as men and women?

Our cultural beliefs also affect the way we see food. Jill Dubisch, in "You Are What You Eat," argues that food can mean more than the satisfaction of hunger. It can carry with it a whole system of symbols that affirm certain values about the self and suggest a worldview (a perceived right way to live one's life and to construct society). It may, as Dubisch persuasively illustrates, take on a spiritual or religious dimension. Other writers in this chapter address the habit of attaching virtue to particular types of bodies and to the ways that people nourish and care for their physical selves. Carol Kloss and Joseph Epstein, from different perspectives, look at fatness and thinness and consider the social and psychological effects of body type.

In "The Naked Truth about Fitness," Barbara Ehrenreich claims that we confuse the moral and the physical by defining "healthy habits" as "moral excellence," "purity," or "superiority." "Health is good," she argues, "but it is not *the* good." Last, Marjorie Rosen shows through a series of interviews why several teenagers chose the operating room in an effort to approach more closely a physical ideal that they believe has improved their images of self and made more visible their positive character traits to others.

STARTING TO THINK ABOUT IT

1. Have you ever completely reversed your opinion about an issue? How did you try to account for your change of mind?

2. In deciding when to eat, sleep, or rise, for example, do you tend to listen to your body or to listen to the clock?

3. What attitudes do you have toward thinness and fatness? Why?

4. How important are fitness and diet in your life? To what extent do you believe that your exercise and eating habits reveal your character or moral values?

5. What connection do you think exists between your body (outside) and your mind (inside)? Why?

Changes of Mind

NICHOLSON BAKER

Nicholson Baker is the author of several novels, including Room Temperature *(1990),* Vox *(1992), and* The Fermata *(1994). His essays have appeared in* The New Yorker, New York Review of Books, Esquire, *and* Best American Essays 1994. *The following selection is from* The Size of Thoughts: Essays and Other Lumber *(1996) and originally appeared in the* Atlantic Monthly *in 1982.*

If your life is like my life, there are within it brief stretches, usually a week to ten days long, when your mind achieves a polished and freestanding coherence. The chanting tape-loops of poetry anthologies, the crumbly pieces of philosophy, the unsmelted barbarisms, the litter torn from huge collisions of abandoned theories—all this nomadic suborbital junk suddenly, like a milling street crowd in a movie-musical, re-forms itself into a proud, pinstriped, top-hatted commonwealth. Your opinions become neat and unruffleable. Every new toy design, every abuse of privilege or gesture of philanthropy, every witnessed squabble at the supermarket checkout counter, is smoothly remade into evidence for five or six sociological truths. Puffed up enough to be charitable, you stop urging your point with twisting jabs of your fork; you happily concede winnable arguments to avoid injuring the feelings of your friends; your stock of proverbs from Samuel Johnson seems elegant and apt in every context; you are firm, you think fast, you offer delicately phrased advice.

Then one Thursday, out on a minor errand, you inexplicably come to a new conclusion ("Keynesian economics is spent"), and it—like the fetching plastic egg that cruel experimenters have discovered will cause a mother bird to thrust her own warm, speckled ones from the nest—upsets your equilibrium. The community of convictions flies apart, you sense unguessed contradictions, there are disavowals, frictions, second thoughts, pleas for further study; you stare in renewed perplexity out the laundromat's plate-glass window, while your pulped library card dries in a tumbling shirt pocket behind you.

Such alert intermissions happen only infrequently: most of the time we are in some inconclusive phase of changing our minds about many, if not all, things. We have no choice. Our opinions, gently nudged by circumstance, revise themselves under cover of inattention. We tell them, in a steady voice, No, I'm not interested in a change at present. But there is no stopping opinions. They don't care about whether we want to hold them or not; they do what they have to do.

And graver still, we are sometimes only minimally aware of just which new beliefs we have adopted. If one of the wire services were able to supply each subscriber with a Personal Opinion Printout, delivered with the paper every morning, it would be a real help: then we could monitor our feelings about Pre-Raphaelite furniture, or the influences of urbanization on politeness, or the wearing of sunglasses indoors, or the effect of tort language on traditions of trust, as we adjusted our thoughts about them week by week, the way we keep an eye on lightly traded over-the-counter stocks. Instead, we stride into a discussion with our squads of unexamined opinions innocently at our heels — and, discovering that, yes, we do feel strongly about water-table rights, or unmanned space exploration, or the harvesting of undersea sponges, say, we grab the relevant opinion and, without dress rehearsals, fling it out into audibility ("*Fly,* you mother"), only to discover, seconds later, its radical inadequacy.

Let me now share with you something about which I changed my mind. 5 Once I was riding the bus between New York City and Rochester. At the Binghamton stop, the driver noticed a shoe sitting on the ledge below the front windshield. The sight of it bothered him. He held it up to us and said, "Is this anybody's?" There was no response, so he left the bus for a moment and threw the shoe in a nearby trash can. We drove on toward Rochester. Idle, I became caught up in a little plan to furnish my future apartment: I would buy yellow forklifts and orange backhoes, *rows* of them, upholstered so that my guests might sit if they wished in the scoops or on the slings slung between the forks. I had begun to calculate how many forklifts a typical floor would sustain when a man with disorderly hair walked to the front of the bus wearing two socks and one shoe. "Did you by any chance see a shoe?" he asked the driver. The driver said: "I asked about that shoe in Binghamton. It's gone now." The man apologized for having been asleep and returned to his seat.

Since that bus trip, five years ago, I find that, without my knowledge, I have changed my mind. I no longer want to live in an apartment furnished with forklifts and backhoes. Somewhere I jettisoned that interest *as irrevocably as the bus driver tossed out the strange sad man's right shoe.* Yet I did not experience during the intervening time a single uncertainty or pensive moment in regard to a backhoe. Five years of walking around cities, flipping through seed catalogs, and saying "Oho!" to statements I disagreed with — the effect of which has been to leave me with a disinclination to apply heavy machinery to interior design.

Multiply this example by a thousand, a hundred thousand, unannounced reversals: a mad flux is splashing around the pilings of our personalities. For a while I tried to make home movies of my opinions in their native element, undisturbed, as they grazed and romped in fields of inquiry, gradually altering in emphasis and coloration, mating, burrowing, and dying, like prairie dogs, but the presence of my camera made their behavior stilted and self-conscious — which brings us to what I can't help thinking is a relevant point about the passage of time. Changes of mind should be distinguished from decisions, for decisions seem to reside pertly in the present, while changes of mind imply habits of thought, a slow settling-out of truth, a partially felt, dense past. I may decide, for instance, that when I take off my pants I should not leave them draped over the loudspeakers, as I normally do, but contrive to suspend them on some sort of hook or hanger. I may decide to ask that person sitting across from me at the table to refrain from ripping out the spongy inside of her dinner roll and working it into small balls between her palms. We are bound to make lots of such future-directed choices: they are the reason for risk-benefit analysis. But at the same time, on the outskirts of our attention, hosts of gray-eyed, bright-speared opinions have been rustling, shifting, skirmishing. "What I think about Piaget" is out there, growing wiser, moodier, more cynical, along with some sort of answer to "What constitutes a virtuous life?" Unless I am being unusually calculating, I don't *decide* to befriend someone, and it is the same way with a conviction: I slowly come to enjoy its company, to respect its counsel, to depend on it for reassurance; I find myself ignoring its weaknesses or excesses — and if the friendship later ends, it is probably owing not to a sudden rift, but to a barnacling-over of nearly insignificant complaints.

Seldom, then, will any single argument change our minds about anything really interesting or important. In fact, reasoning and argument count for surprisingly little in the alluvial triumph of a thought — no more than 12 to 15 percent. Those reasons we do cite are often only a last flourish of bright plumage, a bit of ceremony to commemorate the result of a rabblement of tendencies too cross-purposed to recapitulate. A haphazard flare of memory; an irrelevant grief; an anecdote in the newspaper; a turn of conversation that stings into motion a tiny doubt: from such incessant percussions the rational soul reorganizes itself — we change our minds as we change our character. Years go by and the movement remains unrecognized: "I wasn't aware of it, but my whole feeling about car-pool lanes (or planned communities, or slippery-slope arguments, or rhyme, or Shostakovich, or whether things are getting better or worse) was undergoing a major overhaul back then." We must not overlook sudden conversions and wrenching insights, but usually we fasten on to these only in hindsight, and exaggerate them for the sake of narrative — a tool perfected by the great nineteenth-century novelists, who sit their heroines down and have them deduce the intolerability of their situation in one unhappy night, as the fire burns itself into embers in the grate.

Consider "whether things are getting better or worse" at closer range. Impossibly vague and huge as it is, most of us nonetheless believe it to be a question that merits a periodical self-harvest of opinion. Here are some of the marginally rational things that from one season to the next may contribute to my feelings concerning progress: There is more static in long-distance calls than there was a while ago. The Wonder Bread concrete they now use for sidewalks is a real step down from the darker, pebblier substance they used to use, and that in turn was a decline from the undulant slabs of weathered blue slate, thrust into gradients and peaks by the roots of a nearby tree, that were on my street as a child. Progresso artichoke hearts frequently have sharp, thistly pieces left on them now, as they never used to. When I tip the paper boy these days, he doesn't say thank you. Cemetery statues suffer increasing vandalism. On the other hand, there is Teflon II. Reflective street signs. The wah-wah pedal. Free libraries for everyone. Central heating. Fire codes. Federal Express. Stevie Wonder. Vladimir Nabokov. Lake Ontario is cleaner. My friends like my new blue coat. Somehow the mind arrives at a moving weighted average of these apples and oranges.

Occasionally a change of mind follows alternate routes. One belief, about 10 which initially I would admit of no doubt, gradually came to seem more porous and intricate in its structure, but instead of moderating my opinion correspondingly, and conceding the justice of several objections, I simply lost interest in it, and now I nod absently if the topic comes up over lunch. Another time a cherished opinion weakened as I became too familiar with the three examples that advocates used over and over to support it. Under the glare of this repetition, the secondary details, the richer underthrumming of the opinion, faded; I seemed to have held it once too often; I tried but failed to find the rhetorical or figurative twist that would revive it for me. I crept insensibly toward the opposing view.

How is it that whole cultures and civilizations can change their "minds" in ways that seem so susceptible to synoptic explanation? From the distance of the historian of ideas, things blur nicely: one sees a dogma and its vocabulary seeping from discipline to discipline, from class to class; if you squint away specificity you can make out splinter groups, groundswells of opposition, rival and revival schools of thought. The smoothness and sweep is breathtaking; the metaphors are all ready-made.

But when I am at the laundromat, trying to reconstitute for myself the collaboration of influences, disgusts, mistakes, and passions that swept me toward a simple change of heart about forklifts, the variables press in, description stammers and drowns in detail, and imagination hops up and down on one shoe to little purpose. I consult more successful attempts by the major intellectual autobiographers — Saint Augustine, Gibbon, Mill, Newman, and men of similar kidney — but even their brilliant accounts fail to satisfy: I don't want the story of the feared-but-loved teacher, the book that hit like a thunderclap, the years of severe study followed by a visionary breakdown, the clench of repentance; I want each sequential change of mind in its true, knotted, clotted, viny multifariousness, with all of the colorful streamers of intelligence still taped on and flapping in the wind.

TALKING ABOUT IT

Seeing Metaphor: Revealing and Concealing

1. At the end of paragraph 7, Baker likens developing an inner conviction to making a friend. What does this comparison reveal about his view of how we change our minds? Do you agree that "sudden conversions and wrenching

insights" (paragraph 8) are not very common? How has your mind been changed in the past?

2. "Whole cultures and civilizations can change their 'minds,'" Baker writes. "From the distance of the historian of ideas, things blur nicely. . . . The smoothness and sweep is breathtaking; the metaphors are all ready-made." What is his point? Why does he say the metaphors are "ready-made"?

Seeing Composition: Frame, Line, Texture, Tone

1. Baker's examples of changes of mind are often farfetched or trivial: deciding not to furnish his apartment with forklifts and backhoes, feeling strongly about "the harvesting of undersea sponges," "my whole feeling about car-pool lanes." Why do you suppose he uses such examples, rather than ideas that many people might really change their minds about? How do his examples affect your overall response to his essay?

2. Reread the first paragraph of the essay. What writing persona do the vocabulary and sentence structure establish here? Do you find the voice appealing? Why or why not?

Seeing Meaning: Navigating and Negotiating

1. In paragraph 3, Baker suggests that "most of the time we are in some in-conclusive phase of changing our minds about many, if not all, things." Do you agree with this statement? Explain.

2. In paragraph 7, Baker distinguishes changes of mind from decisions. What does he see as the differences? Do you see the same distinctions? Think about a time when you've decided to do something differently. Did the de-cision have anything to do with a change of mind?

WRITING ABOUT IT

1. Baker uses many metaphors to describe this unexplainable experience: "I find that, without my knowledge, I have changed my mind." First, trace the metaphors that Baker invents for trying to capture the phenomenon of an unseen and only partially felt process. Then categorize the metaphors by source domain; that is, categorize them according to sources in the physical world from which the comparisons are drawn. For example: "Ernie's ideas will never come to fruition." "Eddie has a fertile imagination." "Elwin has only the seeds of an argument." In the previous list of metaphors, the source domain is plants and the target domain is ideas. Hence, the control-ling metaphor is "Ideas are plants." Try to name the controlling metaphors

in Baker's essay. After naming them, say what you think the advantages and/ or disadvantages are of using many metaphors for talking about the same thing — "changes of mind."

2. Nicholson Baker writes, "Then one Thursday, out on a minor errand, you inexplicably come to a new conclusion . . . and it . . . upsets your equilibrium." What was once your firm conviction has dissolved. And yet you can't see how the change came about. As Baker says, "Our opinions . . . revise themselves under cover of inattention." We aren't conscious of all the influences: "We change our minds as we change our character," he argues. "Years go by and the movement remains unrecognized."

Write about this experience in your own life. Try to describe a change of mind that you can't explain by one big cause: a sudden conversion or a single argument. Write about a change of mind, in other words, that seemed to take place over a long period of time and may have been subject to many small influences.

Within your writing groups, exchange essays and write about the metaphors the author uses to describe her or his experience. What do the images tell you about the way the author conceives of "changes of mind"?

Bluspels and Flalansferes: A Semantic Nightmare

C. S. Lewis

C. S. Lewis was an acclaimed English novelist, literary scholar, and essayist on Christian theology and moral problems. He also wrote a popular series of children's books, The Narnia Chronicles. This essay is from Selected Literary Essays by C. S. Lewis (1969).

We are often compelled to set up standards we cannot reach ourselves and to lay down rules we could not ourselves satisfy.

—Lord Coleridge, C. J. (Law Reports, Queen's Bench Division xiv, p. 288 in *Reg. v. Dudley and Stephen*)

Philologists often tell us that our language is full of dead metaphors. In this sentence, the word "dead" and the word "metaphors" may turn out to be ambiguous; but the fact, or group of facts, referred to, is one about which there is no great disagreement. We all know in a rough and ready way, and all admit, these things which are being called "dead metaphors," and for the moment I do not propose to debate the propriety of the name. But while their existence is not disputed, their nature, and their relation to thought, gives rise to a great deal of controversy. For the benefit of any who happen to have avoided this controversy hitherto, I had better make plain what it is, by a concrete example. Bréal in his *Semantics*[1] often spoke in metaphorical, that is consciously, rhetorically, metaphorical language, of language itself. Messrs. Ogden and Richards in *The Meaning of Meaning* took Bréal to task on the ground that "it is impossible thus to handle a scientific matter in metaphorical terms."[2] Barfield in his *Poetic Diction* retorted that Ogden and Richards were, as a matter of fact, just as metaphorical as Bréal. They had forgotten, he complained, that all language has a figurative origin and that the "scientific" terms on which they piqued themselves—words like *organism, stimulus, reference*—were not miraculously exempt. On the contrary, he maintained, "those who profess to eschew figurative expressions are really confining themselves to one very old kind of figure"—"they are absolutely rigid under the spell of those verbal ghosts of the physical sciences, which today make

1. M. J. A. Bréal, *Semantics: Studies in the Science of Meaning*, trans. Mrs. Henry Cust, with a Preface by J. P. Postgate (London, 1900).
2. C. K. Ogden and I. A. Richards, *The Meaning of Meaning* (London, 1923), pp. 4–5.

up practically the whole meaning-system of so many European minds."*
Whether Ogden and Richards will see fit, or have seen fit, to reply to this, I do
not know; but the lines on which any reply would run are already traditional. In
fact the whole debate may be represented by a very simple dialogue.

A. You are being metaphorical.

B. You are just as metaphorical as I am, but you don't know it.

A. No, I'm not. Of course I know all about *attending* once having meant
stretching, and the rest of it. But that is not what it means now. It may
have been a metaphor to Adam — but I am not using it metaphorically.
What I *mean* is a pure concept with no metaphor about it at all. The fact
that it *was* a metaphor is no more relevant than the fact that my pen is
made of wood. You are simply confusing derivation with meaning.

There is clearly a great deal to be said for both sides. On the one hand it
seems odd to suppose that what we *mean* is conditioned by a dead metaphor of
which we may be quite ignorant. On the other hand, we see from day to day, that
when a man uses a current and admitted metaphor without knowing it, he usually gets led into nonsense; and when, we are tempted to ask, does a metaphor
become so old that we can ignore it with impunity? It seems harsh to rule that a
man must know the whole semantic history of every word he uses — a history
usually undiscoverable — or else talk without thinking. And yet, on the other
hand, an obstinate suspicion creeps in that we cannot entirely jump off our own
shadows, and that we deceive ourselves if we suppose that a new and purely conceptual notion of *attention* has replaced and superseded the old metaphor of
stretching. Here, then, is the problem which I want to consider. How far, if at all,
is thinking limited by these dead metaphors? Is Anatole France in any sense right
when he reduces "The soul possesses God" to "the breath sits on the bright sky"?
Or is the other party right when it urges "Derivations are one thing. Meanings
are another"? Or is the truth somewhere between them?

The first and easiest case to study is that in which we ourselves invent a
new metaphor. This may happen in one of two ways. It may be that when we are
trying to express clearly to ourselves or to others a conception which we have
never perfectly understood, a new metaphor simply starts forth, under the pressure of composition or argument. When this happens, the result is often as surprising and illuminating to us as to our audience; and I am inclined to think that
this is what happens with the great, new metaphors of the poets. And when it
does happen, it is plain that our new understanding is bound up with the new
metaphor. In fact, the situation is for our purpose indistinguishable from that

---

*Owen Barfield, *Poetic Diction: A Study in Meaning* (London, 1928), p. 140.

which arises when we hear a new metaphor from others; and for that reason, it need not be separately discussed. One of the ways, then, in which we invent a new metaphor, is by *finding* it, as unexpectedly as we might find it in the pages of a book; and whatever is true of the new metaphors that we find in books will also be true of those which we reach by a kind of lucky chance, or inspiration. But, of course, there is another way in which we invent new metaphors. When we are trying to explain, to some one younger or less instructed than ourselves, a matter which is already perfectly clear in our own minds, we may deliberately, and even painfully, pitch about for the metaphor that is likely to help him. Now when this happens, it is quite plain that our thought, our power of meaning, is not much helped or hindered by the metaphor that we use. On the contrary, we are often acutely aware of the discrepancy between our meaning and our image. We know that our metaphor is in some respects misleading; and probably, if we have acquired the tutorial shuffle, we warn our audience that it is "not to be pressed." It is apparently possible, in this case at least, to use metaphor and yet to keep our thinking independent of it. But we must observe that it is possible, only because we have other methods of expressing the same idea. We have already our own way of expressing the thing: we could say it, or we suppose that we could say it, literally instead. This clear conception we owe to other sources — to our previous studies. We can adopt the new metaphor as a temporary tool which we dominate and by which we are not dominated ourselves, only because we have other tools in our box.

Let us now take the opposite situation — that in which it is we ourselves who are being instructed. I am no mathematician; and some one is trying to explain to me the theory that space is finite. Stated thus, the new doctrine is, to me, meaningless. But suppose he proceeds as follows.

5   "You," he may say, "can intuit only three dimensions; you therefore cannot conceive how space should be limited. But I think I can show you how that which must appear infinite in three dimensions, might nevertheless be finite in four. Look at it this way. Imagine a race of people who knew only two dimensions — like the Flatlanders.[1] And suppose they were living on a globe. They would have no conception, of course, that the globe was curved — for it is curved round in that third dimension of which they have no inkling. They will therefore imagine that they are living on a plane; but they will soon find out that it is a plane which nowhere comes to an end; there are no edges to it. Nor would they be able even to imagine an edge. For an edge would mean that, after a certain point, there would be nothing to walk on; nothing below their feet. But that *below* and *above* dimension is just what their minds have not got; they have

---

1. The inhabitants in the book by "A Square" [Edwin A. Abbott], *Flatland. A romance of many dimensions* (London, 1884).

only backwards and forwards, and left and right. They would thus be forced to assert that their globe, which they could not see as a globe, was infinite. You can see perfectly well that it is finite. And now, can you not conceive that as these Flat-landers are to you, so you might be to a creature that intuited four dimensions? Can you not conceive how that which seems necessarily infinite to your three-dimensional consciousness might none the less be really finite?" The result of such a metaphor on my mind would be — in fact, has been — that something which before was sheerly meaningless acquires at least a faint hint of meaning. And if the particular example does not appeal to every one, yet every one has had experiences of the same sort. For all of us there are things which we cannot fully understand at all, but of which we can get a faint inkling by means of metaphor. And in such cases the relation between the thought and the metaphor is precisely the opposite of the relation which arises when it is we ourselves who understand and then invent the metaphors to help others. We are here entirely at the mercy of the metaphor. If our instructor has chosen it badly, we shall be thinking nonsense. If we have not got the imagery clearly before us, we shall be thinking nonsense. If we have it before us without knowing that it is metaphor — if we forget that our Flatlanders on their globe are a copy of the thing and mistake them for the thing itself — then again we shall be thinking nonsense. What truth we can attain in such a situation depends rigidly on three conditions. First, that the imagery should be originally well chosen; secondly, that we should apprehend the exact imagery; and thirdly that we should know that the metaphor is a metaphor. (That metaphors misread as statements of fact are the source of monstrous errors need hardly be pointed out.)

    I have now attempted to show two different kinds of metaphorical situation as they are at their birth. They are the two extremes, and furnish the limits within which our inquiry must work. On the one hand, there is the metaphor which we invent to teach by; on the other, the metaphor from which we learn. They might be called the Master's metaphor, and the Pupil's metaphor. The first is freely chosen; it is one among many possible modes of expression; it does not at all hinder, and only very slightly helps, the thought of its maker. The second is not chosen at all; it is the unique expression of a meaning that we cannot have on any other terms; it dominates completely the thought of the recipient; his truth cannot rise above the truth of the original metaphor. And between the Master's metaphor and the Pupil's there comes, of course, an endless number of types, dotted about in every kind of intermediate position. Indeed, these Pupil-Teachers' metaphors are the ordinary stuff of our conversation. To divide them into a series of classes and sub-classes and to attempt to discuss these separately would be very laborious, and, I trust, unnecessary. If we can find a true doctrine about the two extremes, we shall not be at a loss to give an account of what falls between them. To find the truth about any given metaphorical situation will merely be to plot its position. In so far as it inclines to the "magistral" extreme, so far our thought will be independent of it; in so far as it has a "pupillary" element, so far it will be the unique expression, and therefore the iron limit of our thinking. To fill in this framework would be, as Aristotle used to say, "anybody's business."

Our problem, it will be remembered, was the problem of "dead" or "forgotten" metaphors. We have now gained some light on the relation between thought and metaphor as it is at the outset, when the metaphor is first made; and we have seen that this relation varies greatly according to what I have called the "metaphorical situation." There is, in fact, one relation in the case of the Master's metaphor, and an almost opposite relation in that of the Pupil's metaphor. The next step must clearly be to see what becomes of these two relations as the metaphors in question progress to the state of death or fossilization.

The question of the Master's Metaphor need not detain us long. I may attempt to explain the Kantian philosophy to a pupil by the following metaphor. "Kant answered the question 'How do I know that whatever comes round the corner will be blue?' by the supposition 'I am wearing blue spectacles.'" In time I may come to use "the blue spectacles" as a kind of shorthand for the whole Kantian machinery of the categories and forms of perception. And let us suppose, for the sake of analogy with the real history of language, that I continue to use this expression long after I have forgotten the metaphor which originally gave rise to it. And perhaps by this time the form of the word will have changed. Instead of the "blue spectacles" I may now talk of the *bloospel* or even the *bluspel.* If I live long enough to reach my dotage I may even enter on a philological period in which I attempt to find the derivation of this mysterious word. I may suppose that the second element is derived from the word *spell* and look back with interest on the supposed period when Kant appeared to me to be magical; or else, arguing that the whole word is clearly formed on the analogy of *gospel,* may indulge in unhistorical reminiscences of the days when the *Critique*[1] seemed to me irrefragably true. But how far, if at all, will my thinking about Kant be affected by all this linguistic process? In practice, no doubt, there will be some subtle influence; the mere continued use of the word *bluspel* may have led me to attribute to it a unity and substantiality which I should have hesitated to attribute to "the whole Kantian machinery of the categories and forms of perception." But that is a result rather of the noun-making than of the death of the metaphor. It is an interesting fact, but hardly relevant to our present inquiry. For the rest, the mere forgetting of the metaphor does not seem to alter my thinking about Kant, just as the original metaphor did not limit my thinking about Kant; provided always—and this is of the last importance—that it was, to begin with, a genuine Master's metaphor. I had my conception of Kant's philosophy before I ever thought of the blue spectacles. If I have continued philosophical studies I have it still. The

---

1. Immanuel Kant, *Critique of Practical Reason, and other works on the Theory of Ethics,* trans. T. K. Abbott (London, 1879).

"blue spectacles" phrase was from the first a temporary dress assumed by my thought for a special purpose, and ready to be laid aside at my pleasure; it did not penetrate the thinking itself, and its subsequent history is irrelevant. To any one who attempts to refute my later views on Kant by telling me that I don't know the real meaning of *bluspel*, I may confidently retort "Derivations aren't meanings." To be sure, if there was any *pupillary* element in its original use, if I received, as well as gave, new understanding when I used it, then the whole situation will be different. And it is fair to admit that in practice very few metaphors can be purely magistral; only that which to some degree enlightens ourselves is likely to enlighten others. It is hardly possible that when I first used the metaphor of the blue spectacles I did not gain some new awareness of the Kantian philosophy; and, so far, it was not purely magistral. But I am deliberately idealizing for the sake of clarity. Purely magistral metaphor may never occur. What is important for us is to grasp that *just in so far* as any metaphor began by being magistral, so far I can continue to use it long after I have forgotten its metaphorical nature, and my thinking will be neither helped nor hindered by the fact that it was originally a metaphor, nor yet by my forgetfulness of that fact. It is a mere accident. Here, derivations are irrelevant to meanings.

Let us now turn to the opposite situation, that of the Pupil's Metaphor. And let us continue to use our old example of the unmathematical man who has had the finitude of space suggested to him (we can hardly say "explained") by the metaphor of the Flatlanders on their sphere. The question here is rather more complicated. In the case of the Master's metaphor, by hypothesis, the master knew, and would continue to know, what he meant, independently of the metaphor. In the present instance, however, the fossilization of the metaphor may take place in two different ways. The pupil may himself become a mathematician, or he may remain as ignorant of mathematics as he was before; and in either case, he may continue to use the metaphor of the Flatlanders while forgetting its real content and its metaphorical nature.

I will take the second possibility first. From the imagery of the Flatlanders' 10 sphere I have got my first inkling of the new meaning. My thought is entirely conditioned by this imagery. I do not apprehend the thing at all, except by seeing "it could be something like this." Let us suppose that in my anxiety to docket this new experience, I label the inkling or vague notion "the Flatlanders' sphere." When I next hear the fourth dimension spoken of, I shall say, "Ah yes — the Flatlanders' sphere and all that." In a few years (to continue our artificial parallel) I may be talking glibly of the *Flalansfere* and may even have forgotten the whole of the imagery which this word once represented. And I am still, according to the hypothesis, profoundly ignorant of mathematics. My situation will then surely be most ridiculous. The meaning of *Flalansfere* I never knew except through the imagery. I could get beyond the imagery, to that whereof the imagery was a copy, only by learning mathematics; but this I have neglected to do.

Yet I have lost the imagery. Nothing remains, then, but the conclusion that the word *Flalansfere* is now really meaningless. My thinking, which could never get beyond the imagery, at once its boundary and its support, has now lost that support. I mean strictly nothing when I speak of the *Flalansfere*. I am only talking, not thinking, when I use the word. But this fact will be long concealed from me because *Flalansfere*, being a noun, can be endlessly fitted into various contexts so as to conform to syntactical usage and to give an appearance of meaning. It will even conform to the logical rules; and I can make many judgements about the *Flalansfere;* such as *it is what it is,* and has *attributes* (for otherwise of course it wouldn't be a thing, and if it wasn't a thing, how could I be talking about it?), and is a *substance* (for it can be the subject of a sentence). And what *affective* overtones the word may have taken on by that time it is dangerous to predict. It had an air of mystery from the first: before the end I shall probably be building temples to it, and exhorting my countrymen to fight and die for the *Flalansfere*. But the *Flalansfere,* when once we have forgotten the metaphor, is only a noise.

But how if I proceed, after once having grasped the metaphor of the Flatlanders, to become a mathematician? In this case, too, I may well continue to use the metaphor, and may corrupt it in form till it becomes a single noun, the *Flalansfere*. But I shall have advanced, by other means, from the original symbolism; and I shall be able to study the thing symbolized without reference to the metaphor that first introduced me to it. It will then be no harm though I should forget that *Flalansfere* had ever been metaphorical. As the metaphor, even if it survived, would no longer limit my thoughts, so its fossilization cannot confuse them.

The results which emerge may now be summarized as follows. Our thought is independent of the metaphors we employ in so far as these metaphors are optional: that is, in so far as we are able to have the same idea without them. For that is the real characteristic both of the magistral metaphors and of those which become optional, as the Flatlanders would become, if the pupil learned mathematics. On the other hand, where the metaphor is our only method of reaching a given idea at all, there our thinking is limited by the metaphor so long as we retain the metaphor; and when the metaphor becomes fossilized, our "thinking" is not thinking at all, but mere sound or mere incipient movements in the larynx. We are now in a position to reply to the statement that "Derivations are not meanings," and to claim that "we know what we mean by words without knowing the fossilized metaphors they contain." We can see that such a statement, as it stands, is neither wholly true nor wholly false. The truth will vary from word to word, and from speaker to speaker. No rule of thumb is possible, we must take every case on its merits. A word can bear a meaning in the mouth of a speaker who has forgotten its hidden metaphor, and a meaning independent of that metaphor, but only on certain conditions. Either the metaphor must have been optional from the beginning, and have remained optional through all the generations of its use, so that the conception has always used and still uses the imagery as a mere tool; or else, at some period subsequent to its creation, we must have gone on to acquire, independently of the metaphor, such new knowledge of the object indicated by it as enables us now, at least, to dispense with it. To put the same thing in another way, meaning is independent of derivation only if the metaphor was originally "magistral"; or if, in the case of an originally pupillary metaphor, some quite new kind of apprehension has arisen to replace the metaphorical apprehension which has been lost. The two conditions may be best illustrated by a concrete example. Let us take the word for *soul* as it exists in the Romance language. How far is a man entitled to say that what he means by the word *âme* or *anima* is quite independent of the image of *breathing*, and that he means just the same (and just as much) whether he happens to know that "derivation" or not? We can only answer that it depends on a variety of things. I will enumerate all the formal possibilities for the sake of clearness: one of them, of course, is too grotesque to appear for any other purpose.

1. The metaphor may originally have been magistral. Primitive men, we are to suppose, were clearly aware, on the one hand, of an entity called *soul;* and, on the other, of a process or object called *breath.* And they used the second figuratively to suggest the first—presumably when revealing their wisdom to primitive women and primitive children. And we may suppose, further, that this magistral relation to the metaphor has never been lost: that all generations, from the probably arboreal to the man saying "Blast your soul" in a pub this evening, have kept clearly before them these two separate entities, and used the one metaphorically to denote the other, while at the same time being well able to conceive the soul unmetaphorically, and using the metaphor merely as a colour or trope which adorned but did not influence their thought. Now if all this were true, it would unquestionably follow that when a man says *anima* his meaning is not affected by the old image of breath; and also, it does not matter in the least whether he knows that the word once suggested that image or not. But of course all this is not true.

2. The metaphor may originally have been pupillary. So far from being a voluntary ornament or pedagogic device, the ideas of *breath* or *something like breath* may have been the only possible inkling that our parents could gain of the soul. But if this was so, how does the modern user of the word stand? Clearly, if he has ceased to be aware of the metaphorical element in *anima,* without replacing the metaphorical apprehension by some new knowledge of the soul, borrowed from other sources, then he will mean nothing by it; we must not, on that account, suppose that he will cease to use it, or even to use it (as we say) intelligibly—i.e. to use it in sentences constructed according to the laws of grammar, and to insert these sentences into those conversational and literary contexts where usage demands their insertion. If, on the other hand, he has some independent

knowledge of the entity which our ancestors indicated by their metaphor of breath, then indeed he may mean something.

15   I take it that it is this last situation in which we commonly suppose ourselves to be. It doesn't matter, we would claim, what the majestic root GNA really stood for: we have learned a great deal about *knowing* since those days, and it is these more recent acquisitions that we use in our thinking. The first name for a thing may easily be determined by some inconsiderable accident. As we learn more, we mean more; the radical meaning of the old syllables does not bind us; what we have learned since has set us free. Assuredly, the accident which led the Romans to call all Hellenes *Graeci* did not continue to limit their power of apprehending Greece. And as long as we are dealing with sensible objects this view is hardly to be disputed. The difficulty begins with objects of thought. It may be stated as follows.

Our claim to independence of the metaphor is, as we have seen, a claim to know the object otherwise than through that metaphor. If we can throw the Flatlanders overboard and still think the fourth dimension, then, and not otherwise, we can forget what *Flalansfere* once meant and still think coherently. That was what happened, you will remember, to the man who went on and learned mathematics. He came to apprehend that of which the Flatlanders' sphere was only the image, and consequently was free to think beyond the metaphor and to forget the metaphor altogether. In our previous account of him, however, we carefully omitted to draw attention to one very remarkable fact: namely, that when he deserted metaphor for mathematics, he did not really pass from symbol to symbolized, but only from one set of symbols to another. The equations and what-nots are as unreal, as metaphorical, if you like, as the Flatlanders' sphere. The mathematical problem I need not pursue further; we see at once that it casts a disquieting light on our linguistic problem. We have hitherto been speaking as if we had two methods of thought open to us: the metaphorical, and the literal. We talked as if the creator of a magistral metaphor had it always in his power to think the same concept *literally* if he chose. We talked as if the present-day user of the word *anima* could prove his right to neglect that word's buried metaphor by turning round and giving us an account of the soul which was not metaphorical at all. That he has power to dispense with the particular metaphor of *breath,* is of course agreed. But we have not yet inquired what he can substitute for it. If we turn to those who are most anxious to tell us about the soul— I mean the psychologists—we shall find that the word *anima* has simply been replaced by complexes, repressions, censors, engrams, and the like. In other words the *breath* has been exchanged for *tyings-up, shovings-back, Roman magistrates,* and *scratchings.* If we inquire what has replaced the metaphorical *bright sky* of primitive theology, we shall only get a *perfect substance,* that is, a *completely made lying-under,* or—which is very much better, but equally metaphorical—a universal Father, or perhaps (in English) a *loaf-carver,* in Latin a *householder,* in Romance *a person older than.* The point need not be laboured. It is abundantly clear that the freedom from a given metaphor which we admittedly enjoy in some cases is often only a freedom to choose between that metaphor and others.

Certain reassurances may, indeed, be held out. In the first place, our distinction between the different kinds of metaphorical situation can stand; though it is hardly so important as we had hoped. To have a choice of metaphors (as we have in some cases) is to know more than we know when we are the slaves of a unique metaphor. And, in the second place, all description or identification, all direction of our own thought or another's, is not so metaphorical as definition. If, when challenged on the word *anima,* we proceed to define, we shall only reshuffle the buried metaphors; but if we simply say (or think) "what I am," or "what is going on in here," we shall have at least something before us which we do not know by metaphor. We shall at least be no worse off than the arboreal psychologists. At the same time, this method will not really carry us far. "What's going on here" is really the content of *haec anima:* for *anima* we want "*The sort of thing* that is going on here," and once we are committed to *sorts* and *kinds* we are adrift among metaphors.

We have already said that when a man claims to think independently of the buried metaphor in one of his words, his claim may sometimes be allowed. But it was allowed only in so far as he could really supply the place of the buried metaphor with new and independent apprehension of his own. We now see that this new apprehension will usually turn out to be itself metaphorical; or else, what is very much worse, instead of new apprehension we shall have simply words—each word enshrining one more ignored metaphor. For if he does not know the history of *anima,* how should he know the history of the equally metaphorical words in which he defines it, if challenged? And if he does not know their history and therefore their metaphors, and if he cannot define *them* without yet further metaphors, what can his discourse be but an endless ringing of the changes on such *bluspels* and *Flalansferes* as seem to mean, indeed, but do not mean? In reality, the man has played us a very elementary trick. He claimed that he could think without metaphor, and in ignorance of the metaphors fossilized in his words. He made good the claim by pointing to the knowledge of his object which he possessed independently of the metaphor; and the proof of this knowledge was the definition or description which he could produce. We did not at first observe that where we were promised a freedom from metaphor we were given only a power of changing the metaphors in rapid succession. The things he speaks of he has never apprehended *literally.* Yet only such genuinely literal apprehension could enable him to forget the metaphors which he was actually using and yet to have a meaning. Either literalness, or else metaphor understood: one or other of these we must have; the third alternative is nonsense. But literalness we cannot have. The man who does not consciously use metaphors talks without meaning. We might even formulate a rule: the meaning in any given composition is in inverse ratio to the author's belief in his own literalness.

If a man has seen ships and the sea, he may abandon the metaphor of a *sea-stallion* and call a boat a boat. But suppose a man who has never seen the sea, or ships, yet who knows of them just as much as he can glean, say from the following list of *Kenningar*—sea-stallions, winged-logs, wave-riders, ocean-trains. If he keeps all these together in his mind, and knows them for the metaphors they are, he will be able to think of ships, very imperfectly indeed, and under strict limits, but not wholly in vain. But if instead of this he pins his faith on the particular *kenning, ocean-trains,* because that *kenning,* with its comfortable air of machinery, seems to him somehow more safely prosaic, less flighty and dangerous than its fellows, and if, contracting that to the form *oshtrans,* he proceeds to forget that it was a metaphor, then, while he talks grammatically, he has ceased to think of anything. It will not avail him to stamp his feet and swear that he is literal; to say "An *oshtran* is an *oshtran,* and there's an end. I mean what I mean. What I mean is what I say."

20   The remedy lies, indeed, in the opposite direction. When we pass beyond pointing to individual sensible objects, when we begin to think of causes, relations, of mental states or acts, we become incurably metaphorical. We apprehend none of these things except through metaphor: we know of the ships only what the *Kenningar* will tell us. Our only choice is to use the metaphors and thus to think something, though less than we could wish; or else to be driven by unrecognized metaphors and so think nothing at all. I myself would prefer to embrace the former choice, as far as my ignorance and laziness allow me.

To speak more plainly, he who would increase the meaning and decrease the meaningless verbiage in his own speech and writing, must do two things. He must become conscious of the fossilized metaphors in his words; and he must freely use new metaphors, which he creates for himself. The first depends upon knowledge, and therefore on leisure; the second on a certain degree of imaginative ability. The second is perhaps the more important of the two: we are never less the slaves of metaphor than when we are making metaphor, or hearing it new made. When we are thinking hard of the Flatlanders, and at the same time fully aware that they *are* a metaphor, we are in a situation almost infinitely superior to that of the man who talks of the *Flalansfere* and thinks that he is being literal and straightforward.

If our argument has been sound, it leads us to certain rather remarkable conclusions. In the first place it would seem that we must be content with a very modest quantity of thinking as the core of all our talking. I do not wish to exaggerate our poverty. Not all our words are equally metaphorical, not all our metaphors are equally forgotten. And even where the old metaphor is lost there is often a hope that we may still restore meaning by pointing to some sensible object, some sensation, or some concrete memory. But no man can or will confine his cognitive efforts to this narrow field. At the very humblest we must speak of things in the plural; we must point not only to isolated sensations, but to groups and classes of sensations; and the universal latent in every group and every plural inflection cannot be thought without metaphor. Thus far beyond the security of literal meaning all of us, we may be sure, are going to be driven by our daily needs; indeed, not to go thus far would be to abandon reason itself. In practice we all really intend to go much farther. Why should we not? We have in our hands the key of metaphor, and it would be pusillanimous to abandon its significant use, because we have come to realize that its meaningless use is necessarily prevalent. We must indeed learn to use it more cautiously; and one of the chief benefits to be derived from our inquiry is the new standard of criticism which we must henceforward apply both to our own apparent thought and to that of others. We shall find, too, that real meaning, judged by this standard, does not come always where we have learned to expect. *Flalansfere* and *bluspels* will clearly be most prevalent in certain types of writers. The percentage of mere syntax masquerading as meaning may vary from something like 100 per cent in political writers, journalists, psychologists, and economists, to something like forty per cent in the writers of children's stories. Some scientists will fare better than others: the historian, the geographer, and sometimes the biologist will speak significantly more often than their colleagues; the mathematician, who seldom forgets that his symbols are symbolic, may often rise for short stretches to ninety per cent of meaning and ten of verbiage. The philosophers will differ among themselves: for a good metaphysical library contains at once some of the most verbal, and some of the most significant literature in the world. Those who have prided themselves on being literal, and who have endeavoured to speak plainly, with no mystical tomfoolery, about the highest abstractions, will be found to be among the least significant of writers: I doubt if we shall find more than a beggarly five per cent of meaning in the pages of some celebrated "tough-minded" thinkers, and how the account of Kant or Spinoza stands, none knows but heaven. But open your Plato, and you will find yourself among the great creators of metaphor, and therefore among the masters of meaning. If we turn to Theology — or rather to the literature of religion — the result will be more surprising still; for unless our whole argument is wrong, we shall have to admit that a man who says *heaven* and thinks of the visible sky is pretty sure to mean more than a man who tells us that heaven is a state of mind. It may indeed be otherwise; the second man may be a mystic who is remembering and pointing to an actual and concrete experience of his own. But it is long, long odds. Bunyan and Dante stand where they did; the scale of Bishop Butler, and of better men than he, flies up and kicks the beam.

It will have escaped no one that in such a scale of writers the poets will take the highest place; and among the poets those who have at once the tenderest care for old words and the surest instinct for the creation of new metaphors. But it must not be supposed that I am in any sense putting forward the imagination as the organ of truth. We are not talking of truth, but of meaning: meaning which is the antecedent condition both of truth and falsehood, whose antithesis is not error but nonsense. I am a rationalist. For me, reason is the natural organ of truth; but imagination is the organ of meaning. Imagination, producing new metaphors or revivifying old, is not the cause of truth, but its condition. It is, I confess, undeniable that such a view indirectly implies a kind of truth or rightness in the imagination itself. I said at the outset that the truth we won by metaphor could not be greater than the truth of the metaphor itself; and we have seen since that all our truth, or all but a few fragments, is won by metaphor. And thence, I confess, it does follow that if our thinking is ever true, then the metaphors by which we think must have been good metaphors. It does follow that if those original equations, between good and light, or evil and dark, between breath and soul and all the others, were from the beginning arbitrary and fanciful — if there is not, in fact, a kind of psycho-physical parallelism (or more) in the universe — then all our thinking is nonsensical. But we cannot, without contradiction, believe it to be nonsensical. And so, admittedly, the view I have taken has metaphysical implications. But so has every view.

TALKING ABOUT IT

Seeing Metaphor: Revealing and Concealing

1. In terms of Lewis's discussion, what is a "dead metaphor," and how would you summarize the two sides of the argument about metaphor he presents at the end of his first paragraph? Based on his complete argument, which side seems to be closer to Lewis's own?

2. Explain the difference between the "Master's metaphor" and the "Pupil's metaphor." How does Lewis use the distinction between these two to make his essential point about thinking and understanding?

Seeing Composition: Frame, Line, Texture, Tone

1. Lewis coins the words "bluspel" and "Flalansferes" to represent two metaphoric explanations. What is his point in reducing the larger metaphoric concepts into these nonsense words? How do they serve his overall argument?

2. Lewis was writing to his peers, a highly educated audience aware of the research and scholarly debate on the nature of metaphor and its relationship to meaning and truth. How easily were you able to follow Lewis's overall line of thinking? If you had trouble, point to specific elements of the essay that contributed to this. What might help make the essay clearer to you?

Seeing Meaning: Navigating and Negotiating

1. In his next to final paragraph, Lewis writes, "The percentage of mere syntax masquerading as meaning may vary from something like 100 per cent in po-

litical writers, journalists, psychologists, and economists to something like forty per cent in the writers of children's stories. . . . Those [philosophers] who have prided themselves on being literal, and who have endeavoured to speak plainly, with no mystical tomfoolery, about the highest abstractions, will be found to be among the least significant of writers: I doubt if we shall find more than a beggarly five per cent of meaning in the pages of some celebrated 'tough-minded' thinkers. . . ." What is Lewis's point here, and how does it relate to his discussions of bluspels and Flalansferes?

2. In his conclusion Lewis states, "But it must not be supposed that I am in any sense putting forward the imagination as the organ of truth. We are not talking of truth, but of meaning: meaning which is the antecedent condition both of truth and falsehood, whose antithesis is not error but nonsense. I am a rationalist. For me, reason is the natural organ of truth; but imagination is the organ of meaning." What is he arguing here? Why, in his view, is imagination required to create meaning rather than nonsense?

WRITING ABOUT IT

After reviewing Lewis's definitions of the "Master's metaphor" and the "Pupil's metaphor," choose one of the following writing topics:

1. Describe a metaphor or an analogy that someone used to help you understand a concept or skill that was new to you then, but one that you later understood at a deeper level. What was particularly helpful or specific to your experience that made the metaphor memorable? Looking back from a more experienced point of view, what do you now recognize as the limitations of that metaphor? What helped you see them?

2. Describe a metaphor that you used to teach someone a concept or skill that was new to her or him. As teacher, what did you understand to be the advantages and disadvantages of the metaphor? To what degree was the lesson successful? Explain.

The purpose for both topics is to apply Lewis's ideas to your own experience as teacher or novice.

Einstein's Dreams

ALAN LIGHTMAN

Alan Lightman is an astrophysicist who teaches physics and writing at the Massachusetts Institute of Technology. He has written a number of science books, including Time Travel and Papa Joe's Pipe: Essays on the Human Side of Science *(1984),* Origins: The Lives and Worlds of Modern Cosmologists *(1990), and* Ancient Light: Our Changing View of the Universe *(1991).* Einstein's Dreams *(1993), from which the following selection is taken, is his first book of fiction.*

PROLOGUE

In some distant arcade, a clock tower calls out six times and then stops. The young man slumps at his desk. He has come to the office at dawn, after another upheaval. His hair is uncombed and his trousers are too big. In his hand he holds twenty crumpled pages, his new theory of time, which he will mail today to the German journal of physics.

Tiny sounds from the city drift through the room. A milk bottle clinks on a stone. An awning is cranked in a shop on Marktgasse. A vegetable cart moves slowly through a street. A man and woman talk in hushed tones in an apartment nearby.

In the dim light that seeps through the room, the desks appear shadowy and soft, like large sleeping animals. Except for the young man's desk, which is cluttered with half-opened books, the twelve oak desks are all neatly covered with documents, left from the previous day. Upon arriving in two hours, each clerk will know precisely where to begin. But at this moment, in this dim light, the documents on the desks are no more visible than the clock in the corner or the secretary's stool near the door. All that can be seen at this moment are the shadowy shapes of the desks and the hunched form of the young man.

Ten minutes past six, by the invisible clock on the wall. Minute by minute, new objects gain form. Here, a brass wastebasket appears. There, a calendar on a wall. Here, a family photograph, a box of paperclips, an inkwell, a pen. There, a typewriter, a jacket folded on a chair. In time, the ubiquitous bookshelves emerge from the night mist that hangs on the walls. The bookshelves hold notebooks of patents. One patent concerns a new drilling gear with teeth curved in a pattern to minimize friction. Another proposes an electrical transformer that holds constant voltage when the power supply varies. Another describes a typewriter with a low-velocity typebar that eliminates noise. It is a room full of practical ideas.

Outside, the tops of the Alps start to glow from the sun. It is late June. A boatman on the Aare unties his small skiff and pushes off, letting the current take him along Aarstrasse to Gerberngasse, where he will deliver his summer apples and berries. The baker arrives at his store on Marktgasse, fires his coal oven, begins mixing flour and yeast. Two lovers embrace on the Nydegg Bridge, gaze wistfully into the river below. A man stands on his balcony on Schifflaube, studies the pink sky. A woman who cannot sleep walks slowly down Kramgasse, peering into each dark arcade, reading the posters in half-light.

In the long, narrow office on Speichergasse, the room full of practical ideas, the young patent clerk still sprawls in his chair, head down on his desk. For the past several months, since the middle of April, he has dreamed many dreams about time. His dreams have taken hold of his research. His dreams have worn him out, exhausted him so that he sometimes cannot tell whether he is awake or asleep. But the dreaming is finished. Out of many possible natures of time, imagined in as many nights, one seems compelling. Not that the others are impossible. The others might exist in other worlds.

The young man shifts in his chair, waiting for the typist to come, and softly hums from Beethoven's *Moonlight* Sonata.

24 APRIL 1905

In this world, there are two times. There is mechanical time and there is body time. The first is as rigid and metallic as a massive pendulum of iron that swings back and forth, back and forth, back and forth. The second squirms and wriggles like a bluefish in a bay. The first is unyielding, predetermined. The second makes up its mind as it goes along.

Many are convinced that mechanical time does not exist. When they pass the giant clock on the Kramgasse they do not see it; nor do they hear its chimes while sending packages on Postgasse or strolling between flowers in the Rosengarten. They wear watches on their wrists, but only as ornaments or as courtesies to those who would give timepieces as gifts. They do not keep clocks in their houses. Instead, they listen to their heartbeats. They feel the rhythms of their moods and desires. Such people eat when they are hungry, go to their jobs at the millinery or the chemist's whenever they wake from their sleep, make love all hours of the day. Such people laugh at the thought of mechanical time. They know that time moves in fits and starts. They know that time struggles forward with a weight on its back when they are rushing an injured child to the hospital or bearing the gaze of a neighbor wronged. And they know too that time darts across the field of vision when they are eating well with friends or receiving praise or lying in the arms of a secret lover.

Then there are those who think their bodies don't exist. They live by me-   10
chanical time. They rise at seven o'clock in the morning. They eat their lunch at noon and their supper at six. They arrive at their appointments on time, precisely

by the clock. They make love between eight and ten at night. They work forty hours a week, read the Sunday paper on Sunday, play chess on Tuesday nights. When their stomach growls, they look at their watch to see if it is time to eat. When they begin to lose themselves in a concert, they look at the clock above the stage to see when it will be time to go home. They know that the body is not a thing of wild magic, but a collection of chemicals, tissues, and nerve impulses. Thoughts are no more than electrical surges in the brain. Sexual arousal is no more than a flow of chemicals to certain nerve endings. Sadness no more than a bit of acid transfixed in the cerebellum. In short, the body is a machine, subject to the same laws of electricity and mechanics as an electron or clock. As such, the body must be addressed in the language of physics. And if the body speaks, it is the speaking only of so many levers and forces. The body is a thing to be ordered, not obeyed.

Taking the night air along the river Aare, one sees evidence for two worlds in one. A boatman gauges his position in the dark by counting seconds drifted in the water's current. "One, three meters. Two, six meters. Three, nine meters." His voice cuts through the black in clean and certain syllables. Beneath a lamppost on the Nydegg Bridge, two brothers who have not seen each other for a year stand and drink and laugh. The bell of St. Vincent's Cathedral sings ten times. In seconds, lights in the apartments lining Schifflaube wink out, in a perfect mechanized response, like the deductions of Euclid's geometry. Lying on the riverbank, two lovers look up lazily, awakened from a timeless sleep by the distant church bells, surprised to find that night has come.

Where the two times meet, desperation. Where the two times go their separate ways, contentment. For, miraculously, a barrister, a nurse, a baker can make a world in either time, but not in both times. Each time is true, but the truths are not the same.

TALKING ABOUT IT

Seeing Metaphor: Revealing and Concealing

1. At the beginning of the section titled "24 April 1905," Lightman offers two contrasting images to represent two different conceptions of time: the "massive pendulum of iron that swings back and forth, back and forth, back and forth" and the squirming, wriggling bluefish in a bay. Which of these more nearly represents your own conception of time? Why do you feel that way?

2. What might the young patent clerk described in the "Prologue" represent? Why do you think Lightman locates him in "a room full of practical ideas"?

Seeing Composition: Frame, Line, Texture, Tone

1. How would you characterize Lightman's writing style here? How does the style of his prose affect your response to his ideas?

2. "24 April 1905" is an extended contrast of the two versions of time. To what extent is this contrast developed in parallel terms?

Seeing Meaning: Navigating and Negotiating

1. Surrounded by "practical ideas," the young patent clerk "has dreamed many dreams" about time. How does knowing that Albert Einstein worked as a patent clerk between 1902 and 1909, that he received his doctorate from the University of Zurich in 1905, and that it was during this time that he was developing his special theory of relativity color your understanding of this "dreamer"?

2. The selection concludes with the idea that one "can make a world in either time, but not both times." Is this essentially a "practical" statement or a theoretical one? That is, are the "two times" here ways of living in time or ways of thinking about time? Or are they both?

WRITING ABOUT IT

1. Write about time in which you paid heed to the rhythms of your body and not to the rhythms of the clock. Compare/contrast this kind of time (body time) to clock time. What do you notice about the language you use to talk about body time versus clock time?

2. How might you argue from your own experience the truth of Lightman's final paragraph where he says, "Where the two times meet, desperation. Where the two times go their separate ways, contentment. For miraculously, a barrister, a nurse, a baker can make a world in either time, but not in both times. Each time is true, but the truths are not the same"?

The Female Body

JOHN UPDIKE

John Updike is a Pulitzer Prize–winning novelist, essayist, and literary critic. His most recent books include Brazil *(1994),* Golf Dreams: Writings on Golf *(1996),* In the Beauty of the Lilies *(1996), and* Toward the End of Time *(1997). The selection here was an invited essay for a special issue of the literary journal* Michigan Quarterly Review, *"The Female Body" (1991).*

Thy navel is like a round goblet, which wanteth not liquor," says the male voice in the Song of Solomon, "thy belly is like a heap of wheat set about with lilies. Thy two breasts are like two young roes that are twins." Robert Graves, in *Watch the Northwind Rise,* quotes a vernacular rendering of these verses which goes, "Your belly's like a heap of wheat, / Your breasts like two young roes. / O come to bed with me, my sweet, / And take off all your clo'es!" A naked woman is, for most men, the most beautiful thing they will ever see. On this planet, the female body is the prime aesthetic object, re-created not only in statuary and painting but in the form of door knockers, nutcrackers, lamp stands, and caryatids. For the Victorians, it was everywhere, naked in brass, while their real women were swaddled and padded and reinforced like furniture; in this century, the female body haunts merchandising from top to bottom, from the silky epidermal feel of a soft cigarette pack to the rumpy curves of a Porsche. The female body is a masterpiece of market design, persuading the race to procreate generation after generation, extracting semen from mesmerized men with the ease of a pickpocket at a girlie show.

This captivating mechanism pays a price for its own complexity: cancer attacks breasts and ovaries, menstrual cramps and hysteria impair performance. Its season of bloom, of potential fertility, is shorter than that of the male body, though more piquant and powerful. Kafka, in a letter to Max Brod, unchivalrously remarked of women, "Not until summer does one really see their curious kind of flesh in quantities. It is soft flesh, retentive of a great deal of water, slightly puffy, and keeps its freshness only a few days." He goes on, with his scrupulous fairness: "Actually, of course, it stands up pretty well, but that is only proof of the brevity of human life." Just so, the actuarial longer-lastingness of the female body demonstrates the relative biological disposability of the male and the salubrious effects of lifelong exercise in the form of housework.

If the main social fact about the female body is its attractiveness, the main political fact is its weakness, compared with the male body. There may be some feminists ardent enough to dispute this, but the truth is elemental. As Elizabeth Hardwick, reviewing Simone de Beauvoir's *The Second Sex,* put it with admirable firmness, "Women are certainly physically inferior to men and if this were not the case the whole history of the world would be different. . . . Any woman who ever had her wrist twisted by a man recognizes a fact of nature as humbling as a cyclone to a frail tree branch." This fact lies behind many facts of feminine circumstance, such as the use of women as domestic drudges and beasts of burden in the world's fundamental economy, and the superior attentiveness and subtlety of women in the private maneuvers of advanced societies. "The fastidiousness of women," Stendhal wrote in *On Love*, "is the result of that perilous situation in which they find themselves placed so early, and of the necessity they are under of spending their lives among cruel and charming enemies."

This physical weakness and the cruelties that result are the truth but not all the truth, and from the standpoint of the species not even the main truth. An interesting thought-experiment, for an adult male, is to try to look at a prepubescent girl, one of ten or eleven, say, with the eyes again of a boy the same age. The relative weakness, the arresting curves, the female fastidiousness, are not yet in place, but the magic is — the siren song, the strange simultaneous call to be kind and to conquer, the swooning wish to place one's life *beside* this other. To be sure, cultural inducements to heterosexuality bombard us from infancy; but they fall, generally, upon terrifically receptive ground.

The female body is, in its ability to conceive and carry a fetus and to nurse   5
an infant, our life's vehicle — it is the engine and the tracks. Male sexuality, then, returning to this primal source, drinks at the spring of being and enters the murky region, where up is down and death is life, of mythology. The paradoxical contradictoriness of male attitudes toward the female and her body — the impulses to exalt and debase, to serve and enslave, to injure and comfort, to reverence and mock — goes back to some point of origin where emotions are not yet differentiated and energy has no distinct direction. The sex act itself, from the male point of view, is a paradox, a transformation of his thrusts into pleasure, a poke in the gut that is gratefully received. Sadism and masochism naturally flirt on the edges of our, as Katherine Mansfield said, "profound and terrible . . . desire to establish contact."

And naturally modern women feel a personal impatience with being mythologized, with being envisioned (talk about hysteria!) as madonnas and whores, earth-mothers and vampires, helpless little girls and implacable dominatrices, and with male inability to see sex simply for what it is. What is it? A biological function and procedure, presumably, on a plane with eating and defecation, just as women are, properly regarded, equally entitled human beings and political entities with minds of their own. Well, men *have* been known, inadvertently, in lapses of distraction or satiety, to see the female body as just a body, very like their own, built for locomotion as well as procreation, an upright watery stalk temporarily withstanding, with its miraculous molecular chain reactions, the forces of gravity and entropy. It is a lucid but dispirited moment, seeing a nude woman as a kind of man, only smaller, lighter-framed, without a beard, but matching men tuft for tuft otherwise, and with bumps, soft swellings, unmale emphases stiffened with fat, softly swayed by gravity . . . a heap of wheat set about with lilies . . . those catenary curves, that curious, considerate absence . . . the moment of lucid vision passes.

In asking forgiveness of women for our mythologizing of their bodies, for being *unreal* about them, we can only appeal to their own sexuality, which is different but not basically different, perhaps, from our own. For women, too, there seems to be that tangle of supplication and possessiveness, that descent toward infantile undifferentiation, that omnipotent helplessness, that merger with the cosmic mother-warmth, that flushed pulse-quickened leap into overestimation, projection, general mix-up.

The Song of Solomon has two voices; there is a female extoller as well. She claims, "My beloved is white and ruddy, the chiefest among ten thousand. His head is as the most fine gold, his locks are bushy, and black as a raven. . . . His belly is as bright ivory overlaid with sapphires," etc. Can it be that the male body — its bulky shoulders, its narrow hips, its thick-veined feet and hands, its defenseless boneless belly above the one-eyed priapic oddity — may also loom as a glorious message from the deep? In Margaret Atwood's last novel, *Cat's Eye*, the heroine, in one of the many striking passages about growing up female and human, reflects upon the teenage boys she talks to on the telephone: "The serious part is their bodies. I sit in the hall with the cradled telephone, and what I hear is their bodies. I don't listen much to the words but to the silences, and in the silences these bodies recreate themselves, are created by me, take form." Some of this is sexual, she reflects, and some is not. Some is purely visual: "The faces of the boys change so much, they soften, open up, they ache. The body is pure energy, solidified light." For male and female alike, the bodies of the other sex are messages signaling what we must do — they are glowing signifiers of our own necessities.

TALKING ABOUT IT

Seeing Metaphor: Revealing and Concealing

1. Near the end of his opening paragraph, Updike writes, "The female body is a masterpiece of market design, persuading the race to procreate. . . ." What is the heart of his image here? How do you respond to this idea?

2. "The sex act itself, from the male point of view, is a paradox, . . ." Updike writes in paragraph 5. "Sadism and masochism naturally flirt on the edges. . . ." Do you think this is how most people regard the "sex act"? What does this view suggest about male/female relations? How might it be a limited conception?

Seeing Composition: Frame, Line, Texture, Tone

1. In paragraph 7 Updike writes, "For women, too, there seems to be that tangle of supplication and possessiveness, that descent toward infantile undifferentiation, that omnipotent helplessness, that merger with the cosmic mother-warmth, that flushed pulse-quickened leap into overestimation, projection, general mix-up." How do you respond to such a passage?

2. Updike concludes by quoting passages reflecting female visions of the male body. Why? Do you think these quotations help him make his larger point?

Seeing Meaning: Navigating and Negotiating

1. Updike writes at length about the "physical weakness [of the female body] and the cruelties that result." What kinds of cruelties *do* result? Are they an inevitable outcome of the male's greater physical strength?

2. Updike makes the point that "cultural inducements to heterosexuality bombard us from infancy; but they fall, generally, upon terrifically receptive ground." To what extent to you think sexuality might be culturally "induced"? Do you agree that such inducements "fall . . . upon terrifically receptive ground"?

WRITING ABOUT IT

1. At the end of his essay, John Updike says, "For male and female alike, the bodies of the other sex are messages signaling what we must do — they are glowing signifiers of our own necessities." How do you objectify the body of the opposite sex (or how do you think about femaleness and maleness), and how might your answer signify your own necessities?

2. Margaret Atwood says the following at the end of her essay, "The Female Body," "Then it comes to him: he's lost the Female Body!" What is she talking about? How might she argue that Updike has "lost the Female Body"?

The Female Body

MARGARET ATWOOD

Margaret Atwood is a novelist, writer of short stories, and poet. Her recent fiction includes The Handmaid's Tale *(1985),* Cat's Eye *(1988),* The Robber Bride *(1993), and* Alias Grace *(1996). The selection here was an invited essay for a special issue of the literary journal* Michigan Quarterly Review, *"The Female Body" (1991).*

. . . entirely devoted to the subject of "The Female Body." Knowing how well you have written on this topic . . . this capacious topic . . .

— letter from *Michigan Quarterly Review*

1.

I agree it's a hot topic. But only one? Look around, there's a wide range. Take my own, for instance.

I get up in the morning. My topic feels like hell. I sprinkle it with water, brush parts of it, rub it with towels, powder it, add lubricant. I dump in the fuel and away goes my topic, my topical topic, my controversial topic, my capacious topic, my limping topic, my nearsighted topic, my topic with back problems, my badly behaved topic, my vulgar topic, my outrageous topic, my aging topic, my topic that is out of the question and anyway still can't spell, in its oversized coat and worn winter boots, scuttling along the sidewalk as if it were flesh and blood, hunting for what's out there, an avocado, an alderman, an adjective, hungry as ever.

2.

The basic Female Body comes with the following accessories: garter belt, panti-girdle, crinoline, camisole, bustle, brassiere, stomacher, chemise, virgin zone, spike heels, nose ring, veil, kid gloves, fishnet stockings, fichu, bandeau, Merry Widow, weepers, chokers, barrettes, bangles, beads, lorgnette, feather boa, basic black, compact, Lycra stretch one-piece with modesty panel, designer peignoir, flannel nightie, lace teddy, bed, head.

3.

The Female Body is made of transparent plastic and lights up when you plug it in. You press a button to illuminate the different systems. The circulatory system is red, for the heart and arteries, purple for the veins; the respiratory system is blue; the lymphatic system is yellow; the digestive system is green, with liver and kidneys in aqua. The nerves are done in orange and the brain is pink. The skeleton, as you might expect, is white.

The reproductive system is optional, and can be removed. It comes with or 5 without a miniature embryo. Parental judgment can thereby be exercised. We do not wish to frighten or offend.

4.

He said, I won't have one of those things in the house. It gives a young girl a false notion of beauty, not to mention anatomy. If a real woman was built like that she'd fall on her face.

She said, If we don't let her have one like all the other girls, she'll feel singled out. It'll become an issue. She'll long for one and she'll long to turn into one. Repression breeds sublimation. You know that.

He said, It's not just the pointy plastic tits, it's the wardrobes. The wardrobes and that stupid male doll, what's his name, the one with the underwear glued on.

She said, Better to get it over with when she's young. He said, All right, but don't let me see it.

She came whizzing down the stairs, thrown like a dart. She was stark 10 naked. Her hair had been chopped off, her head was turned back to front, she was missing some toes and she'd been tattooed all over her body with purple ink in a scrollwork design. She hit the potted azalea, trembled there for moment like a botched angel, and fell.

He said, I guess we're safe.

5.

The Female Body has many uses. It's been used as a door knocker, a bottle opener, as a clock with ticking belly, as something to hold up lampshades, as a nutcracker, just squeeze the brass legs together and out comes your nut. It bears torches, lifts victorious wreaths, grows copper wings and raises aloft a ring of neon stars; whole buildings rest on its marble heads.

It sells cars, beer, shaving lotion, cigarettes, hard liquor; it sells diet plans and diamonds, and desire in tiny crystal bottles. Is this the face that launched a thousand products? You bet it is, but don't get any funny big ideas, honey, that smile is a dime a dozen.

It does not merely sell, it is sold. Money flows into this country or that country, flies in, practically crawls in, suitful after suitful, lured by all those hairless pre-teen legs. Listen, you want to reduce the national debt, don't you? Aren't you patriotic? That's the spirit. That's my girl.

15   She's a natural resource, a renewable one luckily, because those things wear out so quickly. They don't make 'em like they used to. Shoddy goods.

6.

One and one equals another one. Pleasure in the female is not a requirement. Pair-bonding is stronger in geese. We're not talking about love, we're talking about biology. That's how we all got here, daughter.

Snails do it differently. They're hermaphrodites, and work in threes.

7.

Each Female Body contains a female brain. Handy. Makes things work. Stick pins in it and you get amazing results. Old popular songs. Short circuits. Bad dreams.

Anyway: each of these brains has two halves. They're joined together by a thick cord; neural pathways flow from one to the other, sparkles of electric information washing to and fro. Like light on waves. Like a conversation. How does a woman know? She listens. She listens in.

20   The male brain, now, that's a different matter. Only a thin connection. Space over here, time over there, music and arithmetic in their own sealed compartments. The right brain doesn't know what the left brain is doing. Good for aiming though, for hitting the target when you pull the trigger. What's the target? Who's the target? Who cares? What matters is hitting it. That's the male brain for you. Objective.

This is why men are so sad, why they feel so cut off, why they think of themselves as orphans cast adrift, footloose and stringless in the deep void.

What void? she asks. What are you talking about? The void of the universe, he says, and she says Oh and looks out the window and tries to get a handle on it, but it's no use, there's too much going on, too many rustlings in the leaves, too many voices, so she says, Would you like a cheese sandwich, a piece of cake, a cup of tea? And he grinds his teeth because she doesn't understand, and wanders off, not just alone but Alone, lost in the dark, lost in the skull, searching for the other half, the twin who could complete him.

Then it comes to him: he's lost the Female Body! Look, it shines in the gloom, far ahead, a vision of wholeness, ripeness, like a giant melon, like an apple, like a metaphor for "breast" in a bad sex novel; it shines like a balloon, like a foggy noon, a watery moon, shimmering in its egg of light.

Catch it. Put it in a pumpkin, in a high tower, in a compound, in a chamber, in a house, in a room. Quick, stick a leash on it, a lock, a chain, some pain, settle it down, so it can never get away from you again.

TALKING ABOUT IT

Seeing Metaphor: Revealing and Concealing

1. What is the "thing" being argued about in section 4 of the essay? In what sense is this "thing" an object of metaphor in the essay as well as in our culture more generally?

2. To make himself whole, Atwood writes, the male feels the need to "catch" the Female Body: "Put it in a pumpkin, in a high tower, . . . in a house, in a room. Quick, stick a leash on it, a lock, a chain, some pain, settle it down, so it can never get away from you again." How do you respond to this image? How accurately do you think it reflects the male view of the female?

Seeing Composition: Frame, Line, Texture, Tone

1. "The Female Body" is divided into seven discrete sections. What is the specific focus of each? In what ways are the sections tied together?

2. How serious do you think Atwood is here? Where is it clear that she is being deliberately humorous? How does her style contribute to her overall point?

Seeing Meaning: Navigating and Negotiating

1. Atwood wrote "The Female Body" in response to a request from the *Michigan Quarterly Review* as her opening epigraph suggests. What do you think she thought of the request — and of an issue of the journal "entirely

devoted to the subject of 'The Female Body'"? What in the essay makes you think so?

2. Section 5 of Atwood's essay eerily parallels the conclusion of the first paragraph of John Updike's "The Female Body" (commissioned for the same issue of the *Michigan Quarterly Review*). Read Updike's passage on page 314 and compare it to Atwood's paragraphs. To what extent are Atwood and Updike making the same and different points?

WRITING ABOUT IT

1. Margaret Atwood offers seven ways of seeing the female body. Using her essay as a model, write your own "The Female Body" or "The Male Body." You needn't write as many as seven, of course. You might draw on Atwood's categories, but you could invent your own. Try to imply the view with images, as she does, instead of identifying the views explicitly. For example, in section 3, Atwood describes an anatomical model, and in 4, she describes a Barbie doll that defies anatomy and then a child's surprising use of the doll, much to her parents' relief.

2. Can you name a toy, besides Barbie, that has created controversy because of its implied social or cultural values relating to gender? Create a dialogue as Atwood does in section 4 to illustrate two sides of an argument. If you can, follow the dialogue with a scene that seems to resolve the issue, at least temporarily.

You Are What You Eat

JILL DUBISCH

━━━━━━━━━━━━━━━ *Jill Dubisch is an anthropologist and author of* In a Different Place: Pilgrimage, Gender, and Politics at a Greek Island Shrine *(1995). The following selection appeared in* The American Dimension: Cultural Myths and Social Realities, *edited by William Arens and Susan Montague (1981).*

Dr. Robbins was thinking how it might be interesting to make a film from Adelle Davis' perennial best seller, Let's Eat Right to Keep Fit. *Representing a classic confrontation between good and evil — in this case nutrition versus unhealthy diet — the story had definite box office appeal. The role of the hero, Protein, probably should be filled by Jim Brown, although Burt Reynolds undoubtedly would pull strings to get the part. Sunny Doris Day would be a clear choice to play the heroine, Vitamin C, and Orson Welles, oozing saturated fatty acids from the pits of his flesh, could win an Oscar for his interpretation of the villainous Cholesterol. The film might begin on a stormy night in the central nervous system. . . .*
— Tom Robbins, *Even Cowgirls Get the Blues*

I intend to examine a certain way of eating, that which is characteristic of the health food movement, and try to determine what people are communicating when they choose to eat in ways which run counter to the dominant patterns of food consumption in our society. This requires looking at health foods as a system of symbols and the adherence to a health food way of life as being, in part, the expression of belief in a particular world view. Analysis of these symbols and the underlaying world view reveals that, as a system of beliefs and practices, the health food movement has some of the characteristics of a religion.

Such an interpretation might at first seem strange since we usually think of religion in terms of a belief in a deity or other supernatural beings. These notions, for the most part, are lacking in the health food movement. However, anthropologists do not always consider such beliefs to be a necessary part of a religion. Clifford Geertz, for example, suggests the following broad definition:

> A religion is (1) a system of symbols which acts to (2) establish powerful, pervasive, and long-lasting moods and motivations in men by (3) formulating conceptions of a general-order of existence and (4) clothing these conceptions with such an aura of factuality that (5) the moods and motivations seem uniquely realistic. (Geertz 1965:4)

Let us examine the health food movement in the light of Geertz's definition.   *323*

HISTORY OF THE HEALTH FOOD MOVEMENT

The concept of "health foods" can be traced back to the 1830s and the Popular Health movement, which combined a reaction against professional medicine and an emphasis on lay knowledge and health care with broader social concerns such as feminism and the class struggle (see Ehrenreich and English 1979). The Popular Health movement emphasized self-healing and the dissemination of knowledge about the body and health to laymen. One of the early founders of the movement, Sylvester Graham (who gave us the graham cracker), preached that good health was to be found in temperate living. This included abstinence from alcohol, a vegetarian diet, consumption of whole wheat products, and regular exercise. The writings and preachings of these early "hygienists" (as they called themselves) often had moral overtones, depicting physiological and spiritual reform as going hand in hand (Shryock 1966).

The idea that proper diet can contribute to good health has continued into the twentieth century. The discovery of vitamins provided for many health food people a further "natural" means of healing which could be utilized instead of drugs. Vitamins were promoted as health-giving substances by various writers, including nutritionist Adelle Davis, who has been perhaps the most important "guru" of health foods in this century. Davis preached good diet as well as the use of vitamins to restore and maintain health, and her books have become the best sellers of the movement. (The titles of her books, *Let's Cook It Right, Let's Get Well, Let's Have Healthy Children,* give some sense of her approach.) The health food movement took on its present form, however, during the late 1960s, when it became part of the "counterculture."

5   Health foods were "in," and their consumption became part of the general protest against the "establishment" and the "straight" life-style. They were associated with other movements centering around social concerns, such as ecology and consumerism (Kandel and Pelto 1980:328). In contrast to the Popular Health movement, health food advocates of the sixties saw the establishment as not only the medical profession but also the food industry and the society it represented. Food had become highly processed and laden with colorings, preservatives, and other additives so that purity of food became a new issue. Chemicals had also become part of the food-growing process, and in reaction terms such as "organic" and "natural" became watchwords of the movement. Health food consumption received a further impetus from revelations about the high sugar content of many popular breakfast cereals which Americans had been taught since childhood to think of as a nutritious way to start the day. (Kellogg, an early advocate of the Popular Health movement, would have been mortified, since his cereals were originally designed to be part of a hygienic regimen.)

Although some health food users are members of formal groups (such as the Natural Hygiene Society, which claims direct descent from Sylvester Graham), the movement exists primarily as a set of principles and practices rather than as an organization. For those not part of organized groups, these principles and practices are disseminated, and contact is made with other members of the movement, through several means. The most important of these are health food stores, restaurants, and publications. The two most prominent journals in the movement are *Prevention* and *Let's Live*, begun in 1920 and 1932 respectively (Hongladarom 1976).

These journals tell people what foods to eat and how to prepare them. They offer advice about the use of vitamins, the importance of exercise, and the danger of pollutants. They also present testimonials from faithful practitioners. Such testimonials take the form of articles that recount how the author overcame a physical problem through a health food approach, or letters from readers who tell how they have cured their ailments by following methods advocated by the journal or suggested by friends in the movement. In this manner, such magazines not only educate, they also articulate a world view and provide evidence and support for it. They have become the "sacred writings" of the movement. They are a way of "reciting the code" — the cosmology and moral injunctions — which anthropologist Anthony F. C. Wallace describes as one of the important categories of religious behavior (1966:57).

IDEOLOGICAL CONTENT OF THE HEALTH FOOD MOVEMENT

What exactly is the health food system? First, and most obviously, it centers around certain beliefs regarding the relationship of diet to health. Health foods are seen as an "alternative" healing system, one which people turn to out of their dissatisfaction with conventional medicine (see, for example, Hongladarom 1976). The emphasis is on "wellness" and prevention rather than on illness and curing. Judging from letters and articles found in health food publications, many individuals' initial adherence to the movement is a type of conversion. A specific medical problem, or a general dissatisfaction with the state of their health, leads these converts to an eventual realization of the "truth" as represented by the health food approach, and to a subsequent change in life-style to reflect the principles of that approach. "Why This Psychiatrist 'Switched,'" published in *Prevention* (September 1976), carries the following heading: "Dr. H. L. Newbold is a great advocate of better nutrition and a livelier life style. But it took a personal illness to make him see the light." For those who have experienced such conversion, and for others who become convinced by reading about such experiences, health food publications serve an important function by reinforcing the conversion and encouraging a change of life-style. For example, an article entitled "How to Convert Your Kitchen for the New Age of Nutrition"

(*Prevention*, February 1975) tells the housewife how to make her kitchen a source of health for her family. The article suggests ways of reorganizing kitchen supplies and reforming cooking by substituting health foods for substances detrimental to health, and also offers ideas on the preparation of nutritious and delicious meals which will convert the family to this new way of eating without "alienating" them. The pamphlet *The Junk Food Withdrawal Manual* (Kline 1978), details how an individual can, step by step, quit eating junk foods and adopt more healthful eating habits. Publications also urge the readers to convert others by letting them know how much better health foods are than junk foods. Proselytizing may take the form of giving a "natural" birthday party for one's children and their friends, encouraging schools to substitute fruit and nuts for junk food snacks, and even selling one's own baking.

Undergoing the conversion process means learning and accepting the general features of the heath food world view. To begin with, there is great concern, as there is in many religions, with purity, in this case, the purity of food, of water, of air. In fact, there are some striking similarities between keeping a "health food kitchen" and the Jewish practice of keeping kosher. Both make distinctions between proper and improper foods, and both involve excluding certain impure foods (whether unhealthful or non-kosher) from the kitchen and table. In addition, a person concerned with maintaining a high degree of purity in food may engage in similar behavior in either case — reading labels carefully to check for impermissible ingredients and even purchasing food from special establishments to guarantee ritual purity.

10   In the health food movement, the basis of purity is healthfulness and "naturalness." Some foods are considered to be natural and therefore healthier; this concept applies not only to foods but to other aspects of life as well. It is part of the large idea that people should work in harmony with nature and not against it. In this respect, the health food cosmology sets up an opposition of nature (beneficial) versus culture (destructive), or, in particular, the health food movement against our highly technological society. As products of our industrialized way of life, certain foods are unnatural; they produce illness by working against the body. Consistent with this view is the idea that healing, like eating, should proceed in harmony with nature. The assumption is that the body, if allowed to function naturally, will tend to heal itself. Orthodox medicine, on the other hand, with its drugs and surgery and its non-holistic approach to health, works against the body. Physicians are frequently criticized in the literature of the movement for their narrow approach to medical problems, reliance on drugs and surgery, lack of knowledge of nutrition, and unwillingness to accept the validity of the patient's own experience in healing himself. It is believed that doctors may actually cause further health problems rather than effecting a cure. A short item in *Prevention,* "The Delivery Is Normal — But the Baby Isn't," recounts an incident in which drug-induced labor in childbirth resulted in a men-

tally retarded baby. The conclusion is "nature does a good job — and we should not, without compelling reasons, try to take over" (*Prevention,* May 1979:38).

The healing process is hastened by natural substances, such as healthful food, and by other "natural" therapeutic measures such as exercise. Vitamins are also very important to many health food people, both for maintaining health and for healing. They are seen as components of food which work with the body and are believed to offer a more natural mode of healing than drugs. Vitamins, often one of the most prominent products offered in many health food stores, provide the greatest source of profit (Hongladarom 1976).

A basic assumption of the movement is that certain foods are good for you while others are not. The practitioner of a health food way of life must learn to distinguish between two kinds of food: those which promote well-being ("health foods") and those which are believed to be detrimental to health ("junk foods"). The former are the only kind of food a person should consume, while the latter are the antithesis of all that food should be and must be avoided. The qualities of these foods may be described by two anthropological concepts, *mana* and *taboo.* Mana is a type of beneficial or valuable power which can pass to individuals from sacred objects through touch (or, in the case of health foods, by ingestion). Taboo, on the other hand, refers to power that is dangerous; objects which are taboo can injure those who touch them (Wallace 1966:60–61). Not all foods fall clearly into one category or the other. However, those foods which are seen as having health-giving qualities, which contain *mana,* symbolize life, while *taboo* foods symbolize death. ("Junk food is . . . dead. . . . Dead food produces death," proclaims one health food manual [Kline 1978:2–4].) Much of the space in health food publications is devoted to telling the reader why to consume certain foods and avoid others ("Frozen, Creamed Spinach: Nutritional Disaster," *Prevention,* May 1979; "Let's Sprout Some Seeds," *Better Nutrition,* September 1979).

Those foods in the health food category which are deemed to possess an especially high level of *mana* have come to symbolize the movement as a whole. Foods such as honey, wheat germ, yogurt, and sprouts are seen as representative of the general way of life which health food adherents advocate, and Kandel and Pelto found that certain health food followers attribute mystical powers to the foods they consume. Raw food eaters speak of the "life energy" in uncooked foods. Sprout eaters speak of their food's "growth force" (1980:336).

Qualities such as color and texture are also important in determining health foods and may acquire symbolic value. "Wholeness" and "whole grain" have come to stand for healthfulness and have entered the jargon of the advertising industry. Raw, coarse, dark, crunchy, and cloudy foods are preferred over those which are cooked, refined, white, soft, and clear. (See chart.)

Thus dark bread is preferred over white, raw milk over pasteurized, brown   15
rice over white. The convert must learn to eat foods which at first seem strange and even exotic and to reject many foods which are components of the Standard

Health Food World View

	Health Foods	Junk Foods	
cosmic oppositions	LIFE, NATURE	DEATH, CULTURE	
basic values	holistic, organic	fragmented, mechanistic	undesirable
and desirable	harmony with body	working against body	attributes
attributes	and nature	and nature	
	natural and real	manufactured and	
	harmony, self-	artificial disharmony,	
	sufficiency, independence	dependence	
	homemade, small scale	mass-produced	
	layman competence	professional esoteric	
	and understanding	knowledge and jargon	
beneficial	whole	processed	harmful
qualities	coarse	refined	qualities
of food	dark	white	
	crunchy	soft	
	raw	cooked	
	cloudy	clear	
specific	yogurt*	ice cream, candy	specific
foods with	honey*	sugar*	taboo
mana	carob	chocolate	foods
	soybeans*	beef	
	sprouts*	overcooked vegetables	
	fruit juices	soft drinks*	
	herb teas	coffee*, tea	
	foods from other cultures:	"all-American" foods: hot dogs,	
	humus, falafel, kefir, tofu,	McDonald's hamburgers*,	
	stir-fried vegetables,	potato chips,	
	pita bread	Coke	
	return to early American	corruption of this original	
	values, "real" American	and better way of life	
	way of life	and values	

*Denotes foods with especially potent mana or taboo

American diet. A McDonald's hamburger, for example, which is an important symbol of America itself (Kottack 1978), falls into the category of "junk food" and must be rejected.

Just as the magazines and books which articulate the principles of the health food movement and serve as a guide to the convert can be said to comprise the sacred writings of the movement, so the health food store or health food restaurant is the temple where the purity of the movement is guarded and maintained. There individuals find for sale the types of food and other substances advocated by the movement. One does not expect to find items of questionable purity, that is, substances which are not natural or which may be detrimental to health. Within the precincts of the temple adherents can feel safe from the contaminating forces of the larger society, can meet fellow devotees, and can be instructed by the guardians of the sacred area (see, for example, Hongladarom 1976). Health food stores may vary in their degree of purity. Some sell items such as coffee, raw sugar, or "natural" ice creams which are considered questionable by others of the faith. (One health food store I visited had a sign explaining that it did not sell vitamin supplements, which it considered to be "unnatural," i.e., impure.)

People in other places are often viewed as living more "naturally" and healthfully than contemporary Americans. Observation of such peoples may be used to confirm practices of the movement and to acquire ideas about food. Healthy and long-lived people like the Hunza of the Himalayas are studied to determine the secrets of their strength and longevity. Cultures as yet untainted by the food systems of industrialized nations are seen as examples of what better diet can do. In addition, certain foods from other cultures—foods such as humus, falafel, and tofu—have been adopted into the health food repertoire because of their presumed healthful qualities.

Peoples of other times can also serve as models for a more healthful way of life. There is in the health food movement a concept of a "golden age," a past which provides an authority for a better way of living. This past may be scrutinized for clues about how to improve contemporary American society. An archaeologist, writing for *Prevention* magazine, recounts how "I Put Myself on a Caveman Diet—Permanently" (*Prevention*, September 1979). His article explains how he improved his health by utilizing the regular exercise and simpler foods which he had concluded from his research were probably characteristic of our prehistoric ancestors. A general nostalgia about the past seems to exist in the health food movement, along with the feeling that we have departed from a more natural pattern of eating practiced by earlier generations of Americans (see, for example, Hongladarom 1976). (Sylvester Graham, however, presumably did not find the eating habits of his contemporaries to be very admirable.)

The health food movement is concerned with more than the achievement of bodily health. Nutritional problems are often seen as being at the root of emotional, spiritual, and even social problems. An article entitled "Sugar Neurosis" states "Hypoglycemia (low blood sugar) is a medical reality that can trigger wifebeating, divorce, even suicide" (*Prevention*, April 1979:110). Articles and books claim to show the reader how to overcome depression through vitamins and nutrition and the movement promises happiness and psychological well-being as well as physical health. Social problems, too, may respond to the health food approach. For example, a probation officer recounts how she tried changing offenders' diets in order to change their behavior. Testimonials from two of the individuals helped tell "what it was like to find that good nutrition was their bridge from the wrong side of the law and a frustrated, unhappy life to a vibrant and useful one" (*Prevention*, May 1978:56). Thus, through more healthful eating and a more natural life-style, the health food movement offers its followers what many religions offer: salvation — in this case salvation for the body, for the psyche, and for society.

20   Individual effort is the keystone of the health food movement. An individual can take responsibility for his or her own health and does not need to rely on professional medical practitioners. The corollary of this is that it is a person's own behavior which may be the cause of ill health. By sinning, by not listening to our bodies, and by not following a natural way of life, we bring our ailments upon ourselves.

The health food movement also affirms the validity of each individual's experience. No two individuals are alike: needs for different vitamins vary widely; some people are more sensitive to food additives than others; each person has his or her best method of achieving happiness. Therefore, the generalized expertise of professionals and the scientifically verifiable findings of the experts may not be adequate guides for you, the individual, in the search of health. Each person's experience has meaning; if something works for you, then it works. If it works for others also, so much the better, but if it does not, that does not invalidate your own experience. While the movement does not by any means disdain all scientific findings (and indeed they are used extensively when they bolster health food positions), such findings are not seen as the only source of confirmation for the way of life which the health food movement advocates, and the scientific establishment itself tends to be suspect.

In line with its emphasis on individual responsibility for health, the movement seeks to deprofessionalize knowledge and place in every individual's hands the information and means to heal. Drugs used by doctors are usually available only through prescription, but foods and vitamins can be obtained by anyone. Books, magazines, and health food store personnel seek to educate their clientele in ways of healing themselves and maintaining their own health. Articles explain bodily processes, the effects of various substances on health, and the properties of foods and vitamins.

The focus on individual responsibility is frequently tied to a wider concern for self-sufficiency and self-reliance. Growing your own organic garden, grinding your own flour, or even, as one pamphlet suggests, raising your own cow are not simply ways that one can be assured of obtaining healthful food; they are also expressions of independence and self-reliance. Furthermore, such practices are seen as characteristic of an earlier "golden age" when people lived natural lives. For example, an advertisement for vitamins appearing in a digest distributed in health food stores shows a mother and daughter kneading bread together. The heading reads "America's discovering basics." The copy goes on, "Baking bread at home has been a basic family practice throughout history. The past several decades, however, have seen a shift in the American diet to factory-produced breads. . . . Fortunately, today there are signs that more and more

Americans are discovering the advantage of baking bread themselves." Home-made bread, home-canned produce, spouts growing on the window sill symbol-ize what are felt to be basic American values, values supposedly predominant in earlier times when people not only lived on self-sufficient farms and produced their own fresh and more natural food, but also stood firmly on their own two feet and took charge of their own lives. A reader writing to *Prevention* praises an article about a man who found "new life at ninety without lawyers or doctors," saying "If that isn't the optimum in the American way of living, I can't imagine what is!" (*Prevention,* May 1978:16). Thus although it criticizes the contempo-rary American way of life (and although some vegetarians turn to Eastern reli-gions for guidance—see Kandel and Pelto 1980), the health food movement in general claims to be the true faith, the proponent of basic American-ness, a faith from which the society as a whole has strayed.

SOCIAL SIGNIFICANCE OF THE HEALTH FOOD MOVEMENT FOR AMERICAN ACTORS

Being a "health food person" involves more than simply changing one's diet or utilizing an alternative medical system. Kandel and Pelto suggest that the health food movement derives much of its popularity from the fact that "food may be used simultaneously to cure or prevent illness, as a religious symbol and to forge social bonds. Frequently health food users are trying to improve their health, their lives, and sometimes the world as well" (1980:332). Use of health foods becomes an affirmation of certain values and a commitment to a certain world view. A person who becomes involved in the health food movement might be said to experience what anthropologist Anthony F. C. Wallace has called "mazeway resynthesis." The "mazeway" is the mental "map" or image of the world which each individual holds. It includes values, the environment and the objects in it, the image of the self and of others, the techniques one uses to manipulate the environment to achieve desired end states (Wallace 1966:237). Resynthesis of the mazeway—that is, the creation of new "maps," values, and techniques—commonly occurs in times of religious revitalization, when new religious movements are begun and converts to them are made. As individuals, these converts learn to view the world in a new manner and to act accordingly. In the case of the health food movement, those involved learn to see their health problems and other dissatisfactions with their lives as stemming from improper diet and living in disharmony with nature. They are provided with new values, new ways of viewing their environment, and new techniques for achieving their goals. For such individuals, health food use can come to imply "a major redefi-nition of self-image, role, and one's relationship to others" (Kandel and Pelto 1980:359).The world comes to "make sense" in the light of this new world view.

Achievement of the desired end states of better health and an improved outlook on life through following the precepts of the movement gives further validation.

25   It is this process which gives the health food movement some of the overtones of a religion. As does any new faith, the movement criticizes the prevailing social values and institutions, in this case the health-threatening features of modern industrial society. While an individual's initial dissatisfaction with prevailing beliefs and practices may stem from experiences with the conventional medical system (for example, failure to find a solution to a health problem through visits to a physician), this dissatisfaction often comes to encompass other facets of the American way of life. This further differentiates the "health food person" from mainstream American society (even when the difference is justified as a return to "real" American values).

In everyday life the consumption of such substances as honey, yogurt, and wheat germ, which have come to symbolize the health food movement, does more than contribute to health. It also serves to represent commitment to the health food world view. Likewise, avoiding those substances, such as sugar and white bread, which are considered "evil" is also a mark of a health food person. Ridding the kitchen of such items — a move often advocated by articles advising readers on how to "convert" successfully to health foods — is an act of ritual as well as practical significance. The symbolic nature of such foods is confirmed by the reactions of outsiders to those who are perceived as being inside the movement. An individual who is perceived as being a health food person is often automatically assumed to use honey instead of sugar, for example. Conversely, if one is noticed using or not using certain foods (e.g., adding wheat germ to food, not eating white sugar), this can lead to questions from the observer as to whether or not that individual is a health food person (or a health food "nut," depending upon the questioner's own orientation).

The symbolic nature of such foods is especially important for the health food neophyte. The adoption of a certain way of eating and the renunciation of mainstream cultural food habits can constitute "bridge-burning acts of commitment" (Kandel and Pelto 1980:395), which function to cut the individual off from previous patterns of behavior. However, the symbolic activity which indicates this cutting off need not be as radical as a total change of eating habits. In an interview in *Prevention,* a man who runs a health-oriented television program recounted an incident in which a viewer called up after a show and announced excitedly that he had changed his whole life-style — he had started using honey in his coffee! (*Prevention,* February 1979:89). While recognizing the absurdity of the action on a practical level, the program's host acknowledged the symbolic importance of this action to the person involved. He also saw it as a step in the right direction since one change can lead to another. Those who sprinkle wheat germ on cereal, toss alfalfa sprouts with a salad, or pass up an ice cream cone for yogurt are not only demonstrating a concern for health but also affirming their commitment to a particular life-style and symbolizing adherence to a set of values and a world view.

As this analysis has shown, health foods are more than simply a way of eating and more than an alternative healing system. If we return to Clifford Geertz's definition of religion as a "system of symbols" which produces "powerful, pervasive, and long-lasting moods and motivations" by "formulating conceptions of a general-order of existence" and making them appear "uniquely realistic," we see that the health food movement definitely has a religious dimension. There is, first, a system of symbols, in this case based on certain kinds and qualities of food. While the foods are believed to have health-giving properties in themselves, they also symbolize a world view which is concerned with the right way to live one's life and the right way to construct a society. This "right way" is based on an approach to life which stresses harmony with nature and the holistic nature of the body. Consumption of those substances designated as "health foods," as well as participation in other activities associated with the movement which also symbolize its world view (such as exercising or growing an organic garden) can serve to establish the "moods and motivations" of which Geertz speaks. The committed health food follower may come to experience a sense of spiritual as well as physical well-being when he or she adheres to the health food way of life. Followers are thus motivated to persist in this way of life, and they come to see the world view of this movement as correct and "realistic."

In addition to its possession of sacred symbols and its "convincing" world view, the health food movement also has other elements which we usually associate with a religion. Concepts of mana and taboo guide the choice of foods. There is a distinction between the pure and impure and a concern for the maintenance of purity. There are "temples" (health food stores and other such establishments) which are expected to maintain purity within their confines. There are "rabbis," or experts in the "theology" of the movement and its application to everyday life. There are sacred and instructional writings which set out the principles of the movement and teach followers how to utilize them. In addition, like many religious movements, the health food movement hearkens back to a "golden age" which it seeks to recreate and assumes that many of the ills of the contemporary world are caused by society's departure from this ideal state.

Individuals entering the movement, like individuals entering any religious movement, may undergo a process of conversion. This can be dramatic, resulting from the cure of an illness or the reversal of a previous state of poor health, or it can be gradual, a step-by-step changing of eating and other habits through exposure to health food doctrine. Individuals who have undergone conversion and mazeway resynthesis, as well as those who have tested and confirmed various aspects of the movement's prescriptions for better health and a better life, may give testimonials to the faith. For those who have adopted, in full or in part, the health food world view, it provides, as do all religions, explanations for existing conditions, answers to specific problems, and a means of gaining control over one's existence. Followers of the movement are also promised "salvation," not in the form of afterlife, but in terms of enhanced physical well being, greater energy, longer life-span, freedom from illness, and increased peace of mind. However, although the focus is this-worldly, there is a spiritual dimension to the health food movement. And although it does not center its world view around belief in supernatural beings, it does posit a higher authority — the wisdom of nature — as the source of ultimate legitimacy for its views.

Health food people are often dismissed as "nuts" or "food faddists" by those outside the movement. Such a designation fails to recognize the systematic nature of the health food world view, the symbolic significance of health foods, and the important functions which the movement performs for its followers. Health foods offer an alternative or supplement to conventional medical treatment, and a meaningful and effective way for individuals to bring about changes in lives which are perceived as unsatisfactory because of poor physical and emotional health. It can also provide for its followers a framework of meaning which transcends individual problems. In opposing itself to the predominant American life-style, the health food movement sets up a symbolic system which opposes harmony to disharmony, purity to pollution, nature to culture, and ultimately, as in many religions, life to death. Thus while foods are the beginning point and the most important symbols of the health food movement, food is not the ultimate focus but rather a means to an end: the organization of a meaningful world view and the construction of a satisfying life.

REFERENCES

Ehrenreich, Barbara, and Deidre English. 1979.*For Her Own Good: 150 Years of the Experts' Advice to Women*. Garden City, N.Y.: Anchor Press/Doubleday.

Geertz, Clifford. 1965. "Religion as a Cultural System." In Michael Banton, ed. *Anthropological Approaches to the Study of Religion*. A.S.A. Monograph No. 3. London: Tavistock Publications Ltd.

Hongladarom, Gail Chapman. 1976. "Health Seeking Within the Health Food Movement." Ph.D. Dissertation: University of Washington.

Kandel, Randy F., and Gretel H. Pelto. 1980. "The Health Food Movement: Social Revitalization or Alternative Health Maintenance System." In Norge W. Jerome, Randy F. Kandel, and Gretel H. Pelto, eds., *Nutritional Anthropology*. Pleasantville, N.Y.: Redgrave Publishing Co.

Kline, Monte. 1978. *The Junk Food Withdrawal Manual*. Total Life, Inc.

Kottak, Conrad. 1978. "McDonald's as Myth, Symbol, and Ritual." In *Anthropology: The Study of Human Diversity*. New York: Random House.

Shryock, Richard Harrison. 1966. *Medicine in America: Historical Essays*. Baltimore: Johns Hopkins University Press.

Wallace, Anthony F. C. 1966. *Religion: An Anthropological View*. New York: Random House.

TALKING ABOUT IT

Seeing Metaphor: Revealing and Concealing

1. Dubisch's basic contention is that "the health food movement has some of the characteristics of a religion." What, specifically, are the characteristics of the health food movement that Dubisch sees as having religious parallels? Do you think she intends the connection to be metaphoric, or is she suggesting that the health food movement is indeed a form of religion?

2. Dubisch describes health food magazines as "sacred writings," health food stores as "temples," eating junk food as "sinning," healthful eating and a more natural lifestyle as a means to "salvation." Do you accept these images, or do you find them at all strained?

Seeing Composition: Frame, Line, Texture, Tone

1. How can you tell this was written for an academic journal rather than the popular press? Consider issues of form, format, writing style, and use of sources.

2. The essay includes a fair amount of repetition. Locate several places where Dubisch essentially repeats points she has already made. What is the effect on you of such repetition?

Seeing Meaning: Navigating and Negotiating

1. Are you yourself part of the health food or vegetarian movement, or do you know people who are? If so, how accurate do you find Dubisch's depiction of such practitioners? If not, does Dubisch change your views of this movement? Explain.

2. Why do you think Dubisch includes the chart in her essay? What does it contribute to her overall point?

WRITING ABOUT IT

1. As Jill Dubisch argues, food can mean more than the satisfaction of hunger. In some circumstances, the food itself is not the ultimate focus, but a means to an end. It can affirm certain values about the self and others and suggest a worldview. When food is a means to an end, the nature of food becomes symbolic. It may define one's self-image, role, or relationship to others; it may even take on a spiritual or religious dimension.

   After rereading Dubisch's analysis of the health food movement as a system of symbols, define your membership in a culture or subculture by what you do (or do not) eat. What image of self are you projecting? How does what you do (or do not) eat suggest your commitment to a particular set of life choices and to a set of values? In short, how are you what you eat?

2. As a class, list other rituals associated with care for the body, such as exercise, grooming, and bathing, or ritualized mealtime, bedtime, and work habits. Choose one from your list and write about the possible religious or spiritual dimension of that ritual. Base your analysis on the language that you or others use to talk about the ritual. For example, what images do you associate with it that could be said to be spiritual as well as physical?

Fat

CAROL KLOSS

Carol Kloss is a business and creative nonfiction writer and former U.S. Air Force Officer whose stories include "Solid Ground," which was published as "The Mud Monster" in the Miami Herald *(1995). The following selection appeared in* Creating Nonfiction *and in* Surviving Crisis: Twenty Prominent Authors Write about Events That Shaped Their Lives *(1997).*

I suck heavy, sweet, dark sauce from chopped-up bones in the food court at the mall: baby back ribs from the Oriental Express, scraps of pork too charred to bite. While I eat, I watch people. A puffy-haired woman whose bottom and thighs droop off the seat of her chair. A saggy globe of a man with knees that will never touch and arms that can't hang straight; a skinny-legged little girl floats from the end of his hand. Three blocky women in shorts, no space between them and their big purses — boulders in the people-stream, their eyes focused on some solitary distance. We have each other, their faces say. I watch people and I watch fat: It rolls and juggles under baggy shirts, shivers on over-bared thighs, swells the hand eating a sundae at the Dairy Queen.

"I hate cellulite," my husband told me once.

"Did you ever see your mother naked?" I asked.

"No, but there's such a thing as bathing suits," he said. "I dated a girl who was all cellulite; my mother fixed me up with her. She was just cellulite hanging on bones."

I watch the fat and wonder what's really inside, how deep it goes, how far 5 away the bones are. Cushioned and pillowed, some people look boneless anyway, like boneless roasts, boneless pork roasts. Twist them slowly on a giant rotisserie and all the fat would drip off, dribble into the fire with every turn, drip and spurt and flame. Roast away all that fat — I'll take my gut well-done — and how much meat would be left? Maybe about as much as the shreds on the chopped-up Oriental Express bones. Maybe it depends on what you call the meat.

The fruit theory of fat says that pear fat is better than apple fat, this referring to the distribution of fat on the body: Store it in the legs and hips, not the belly, for less heart disease, cancer, diabetes, etc. Advertising and television and movies pick their bodies by the vegetable theory of fat: celery stalks. A lot of people are fruits trying to become vegetables, which is funny because most diets stuff you with vegetables and celery-stick nausea never dies. My mother-in-law, for instance, has been on a diet since 1962, and when she comes to my house for dinner she doesn't touch the salad.

Theory meets reality: Slap us in the diet pen, crack the whip of exercise, and pretty soon the calories counted and calories burned drift behind the television set while we cram into Slimmaire belts or ankle-length Spandex or blue jeans, the unisex girdle. Ah, support. That's what corsets were for. Where did they go? Maybe we should drag the whalebone out of the landfills. Or easier, order a floater from Lane Bryant, settle under your vertical-striped tent, and stay out of the wind.

Mostly we worry about it in guts, spare tires, balloon butts and saddlebags. But it also plumps cheeks, triples chins, inflates breasts, thickens ankles, and pads our feet and hands. Strip the skin from a pickled body and you'll see fat plastered everywhere, yellowed and chunky like margarine half-mixed with eggs. It bulges from the bottoms of kneecaps, hangs from arms and earlobes, swaddles the lymph nodes that cluster in armpits. The right coronary artery is wrapped in it, and the eyeballs lie on it.

Inside our nice coat of fat, with our little extra cushions tucked here and there, we have built-in protection from life's everyday shocks and jolts. Some people seem to need more protection than others. Like my friend Lana, a three-hundred-pound secretary who corrects her boss's grammar and improves his strategic plans but won't get a college degree. A person as fat as she, she says, couldn't go higher anyway. Or the man who lived in his bed except for the day he was supposed to leave on a free trip to Dick Gregory's fat farm. He got to the door but couldn't make himself go out and instead went back to the cushiony, crumb-covered pit of his specially reinforced mattress. Or my mother, who spent her days on a brown couch in a brown-carpeted room with brown-paneled walls, watching soap operas on a brown plastic television set. She built her protection from sardines and anchovies and pork and beans, cookies and day-old doughnuts and deep-fried onion rings. She dropped cigarette ash on her solitaire games and wrapped supper's potato peelings in the ads for the jobs she said she didn't know how to do.

10   Some fat is invisible. You see legs that look great in miniskirts; I see thighs that need the fat beaten out of them. You might think that you can get right up close and touch the edge of my size twelve body. But I feel the hidden tingle of my real edge a foot or two beyond your hand. The fat that you don't see tells me to strip my insides with laxatives and tells my husband's sister Trudi that she should only eat farina. It makes her wake her neighbors at four in the morning with the rumbling of her NordicTrack, and sometimes it throws her on the floor for 250 sit-ups while her parents watch from the dinner table. So, invisible fat has a lot of power. But it doesn't protect the back of Trudi's hand from her teeth when she shoves her finger down her throat. And it doesn't hide the sharpness of the shoulder blades that cut into my arms when I give her a hug.

Even though we try, we can't live without fat, and the more you have the luckier you are, really: all that adipose tissue bulging with future fatty acids, potential bits of muscle food, an internal portable Armageddon food cellar. If you happen to have accumulated an extra 220 pounds of it, you'd be able to live a theoretical year without going grocery shopping — quite a time-saver.

My grandmother swelled her fat cells with a special ethnic blend: Polish sausage fat, bacon fat, sour cream fat and cheesecake fat. About nine months of reserve lipids, I would guess she had, stored mostly between her neck and belly and carried around on fine muscled legs that her short, skinny beer-drinking husband admired. He died forty years before she did, and she fed five kids from the full-fat Polish meatcases in her three grocery stores. When she retired she became the baker for the St. John Berchmans bingo nights: cream cheese *kolacki* and deep-fried, jelly-filled *paczki* and all-butter poundcakes baked in pans so big that I was sure it would be a sin to keep a cake like that just for herself. She sold cheesecakes to her relatives and afghans to the priests. Then her doctor said she was too fat, and her daughters made her lose weight. When she got skinny she went into a nursing home, where she sat in a chair waiting for salt-free skinless chicken and begging quarters for the candy machine. And I brought her chocolate-frosted doughnuts from Amy Joy until she didn't remember who I was any more.

Sometimes I sit by the fountain in the mall with my charcoal and sketchbook, trying to catch in ten seconds the sling of a belly over a belt or the wobbly scallop of body rolls. I have to go to the mall to find fat people to draw because they don't seem to want to model. Day after day in figure-drawing class, I drew skinny young people with straight-line bodies — bony hips, meatless thighs, hardly a bump at the biceps. If those models only knew how boring I thought their bodies were — until the day we got a blonde woman with breasts that actually shook, a belly that pushed out from her ribs and thighs that showed no muscles. She glided through the quick poses, holding her chest as still as possible, but it was hard to pay attention to the movement I was supposed to be drawing. The curves and volume of her gold-lit body, the kind of figure Rubens would have molded with red and orange and yellow, made motion, and bones, irrelevant. She arranged herself on a faded old easy chair for the long pose. Cellulite dimpled the thighs that sagged over the chair seat, her belly flopped on her hip, and a shoulder without a clavicle blended into her swelled upper arm. She was big and loose, and I couldn't draw any part of her with a straight line. I followed her curves with my eyes and arm and felt my charcoal sinking into her flesh; I shaded her thighs and hips and shoulders; as I moved from dark to light, the energy of her mass softened the touch of my hand on the drawing. I looked at the paper and found lines that I didn't know I could draw — the dangle of her arm over the chair seat, the droopy fullness of her breast. The lines connected me with her, made me see and feel her solid and beautiful whole.

Fat people at the mall get nervous when they see me drawing them, but I don't think they know that on paper they're not fat. On paper, where I take away their three dimensions and put them into two, they're powerful, not flabby; fascinating, not shocking; more human than any unpadded bones could ever be. Black and white and shades of gray strip away suffering, take the flesh out of flesh, make bigness bounty. Sometimes I look at my own fat and hope that someday someone will draw me.

TALKING ABOUT IT

Seeing Metaphor: Revealing and Concealing

1. What does "fatness" represent in our culture? Does Kloss seem to endorse this view, or is she trying to break through the standard metaphor? Why do you think so?

2. In paragraph 10, Kloss writes about fat that is "invisible." What is she talking about? What does "the fat that you don't see" represent here?

Seeing Composition: Frame, Line, Texture, Tone

1. Look at the many examples of heavy people Kloss includes: shoppers at a mall, friends and family members, a man she apparently read about, the model in her figure-drawing class. How does she describe these people? What overall impressions does she leave you with?

2. Why do you think Kloss opens and closes by describing herself at the mall — at first eating baby back ribs and later sketching the people she sees? What does her final sentence suggest to you?

Seeing Meaning: Navigating and Negotiating

1. In paragraph 5, Kloss imagines heavy people as "boneless pork roasts" that "[t]wist . . . slowly on a giant rotisserie." How do you interpret this image? Why do you think she includes it?

2. "Inside our nice coat of fat," Kloss writes, "we have built-in protection from life's everyday shocks and jolts" (paragraph 9). Do you think she is being ironic here? Are "life's everyday shocks and jolts" different for heavy people than for thinner people? Why or why not?

WRITING ABOUT IT

1. Carol Kloss has said, "The best thing I ever did for my development as a writer was to learn to draw. Drawing training, done well, enables writers to recognize the perpetual shift that allows them to really see details and frees

them from their conscious mind." How does drawing, as Kloss describes it in this essay, seem to bear out the truth of her assertion? What does she see by drawing that she can't see just by looking? What, for example, interferes with her vision, and what redirects her gaze?

2. "I watch the fat and wonder what's really inside, how deep it goes, how far away the bones are." In one sense, Kloss's statement is literal, but, in another, it is metaphorical. What is Kloss wondering about besides the distance between fat and bone?

   Write about a time that you watched people at the mall, perhaps focused on a particular type. What physical details were you literally observing and wondering about, and what else were you trying to see?

A Fat Man Struggles to Get Out

JOSEPH EPSTEIN

Joseph Epstein is an essayist whose collections include Once More Around the Block *(1987), the source of the following selection. He has been a visiting lecturer in literature and writing at Northwestern University since 1975 and is also the editor of the* American Scholar, *the journal of the Phi Beta Kappa Society.*

How do things stand with you and the seven deadly sins? Here is my scorecard: Sloth I fight — to a draw. I surrendered to Pride long ago. Anger I tend to give in to so often that it makes me angry. Lust I'd rather not discuss. I haven't thus far done well enough in the world to claim Avarice as anything more than a theoretical sin. I appear to be making some headway against Envy, though I realize that it's touch and go. Of the seven deadly sins, the only one that has a continuing interest for me is Gluttony. But "continuing interest" is a euphemism; but it I mean that Gluttony is the last deadly sin that excites me in a big way — so much so that, though I am prepared to admit that Gluttony can be deadly, I am not all that prepared to say it is a sin. As soon as I pop this chocolate-chip cookie in my mouth, I shall attempt to explain what I mean.

I am not beautiful and I am probably not very fit, but I am, at least in a rough geometrical sense, in shape. I weigh what the charts say I ought to weigh. To some people I may seem slender. For the most part, I am not displeased with my physique. Certainly I have no wish to be fat; flabby I should heartily dislike; portly is a touch more than I should prefer — but, let me confess it, stout, solid dignified stout, doesn't sound that bad to me. Was it Cyril Connolly who said that within every fat man a thin man struggles to get out? With me the reverse condition obtains: I am a relatively thin man in whom a fat man struggles, sometimes quite desperately, to get out.

That fat man is no gourmet. He cannot claim to be a gourmand, which A. J. Liebling, a fat man who did get out, once defined as someone who loves delicacies and plenty of 'em. My fat man is less discriminating. He longs for quantities of sandwiches and great mounds of rather greasy french fried potatoes followed by great hunks of cake, a little snack washed down with tankards of soda pop (with Pepsi-Cola, to be specific, and not the no-calorie, caffeine-free, unleaded kind, either). Ribs, pizza, raw oysters, servings of ice cream that cover the entire surface of dinner plates — these are the names of some of my fat man's desires. He is always on the lookout for inexpensive restaurants that serve in impressive tonnage — restaurants out of which he dreams of walking, a toothpick clamped in his mouth, remarking to himself, "Yes, indeed, a slap-up meal; they did me very well in there."

You can see why this fat man cannot be turned loose. I do on occasion let him out for a weekend or a holiday, in what I suppose is the gastronomical equivalent of a work-release program. But set scot-free, left to forage full-time for himself, this man would kill me with his teeth and bury me with a fork. Clearly a dangerous character, he must be held under lock and key and, when let out, kept under the strictest surveillance. Moderation is a principle he does not recognize, deferred gratification is a phrase of whose meaning he remains ignorant, compromise he won't even consider. All this being the case, I can only say to him, as I frequently do, "Sorry, Tons-of-Fun, it's the slammer for you."

Perhaps I would be better off in the condition of a friend who one day told   5 me that, as the result of a boyhood fistfight in which his nose was so badly smashed it had to be remade, he had lost roughly eighty percent of his sense of taste. To him food was now almost sheerly a matter of fuel. I greeted this announcement with a mixture of envy for his release from a troubling passion and sadness at his deprivation. I have known others who could eat until the cows come home, and then slaughter the cows for a steak sandwich — all without the least effect on girth or chin or limb. These, in my view, are among the favorites of the gods. To me the gods have dealt differently, bestowing upon me an appetite that is matched only by my vanity. I wish to live fat but be thin.

I was not bred for the kind of careful abstinence that is the admired eating standard of our day. A finicky child, I was catered to in my extreme fussiness. (Freud says that a man who as a child feels assured of his mother's love is likely to think himself a conqueror; I say this same conqueror is likely to have a weight problem.) Whatever Joseph wanted, Joseph got — in my mother's kitchen, Lola had nothing on me. In adolescence, my tastes in food broadened and my appetite deepened. Ours was always an impressive larder. I can recall many a night, before settling in to sleep, fixing myself a little snack that might consist of, say, a dozen or so cookies, a pint of butter-pecan ice cream, a gross or so of grapes, and four fingers of salami. Nor was sleep after such a repast in any way a problem. Today, of course, this kind of snack, attempted at my age, could only be construed as a suicide attempt.

My mother knew I ate huge portions at home, but she could not know that the ample meals she served me were perhaps half my daily ration. She could not know because I did not tell her. As a serious eater I hadn't, you might say, come out of the pantry. But out of the pantry I surely emerged. After a breakfast at home of orange juice, eggs, and toast, I would, upon arrival at high school, generally plunge into a smoke-filled school store called Harry's, where, to fortify myself for the strenuous mental effort that lay ahead, I engorged something known as a chocolate square (approximate weight: one-third pound), a small stein of root beer, and the smoke of two Lucky Strike cigarettes. Often with friends I would take tiffin at a nearby Jewish delicatessen called Ashkenaz; the meal usually consisted of soup, corned-beef sandwiches, and other of those Jewish foods that, as one sour-stomached Jewish gentleman I know has put it, have caused more difficulties for the Jews than Pharaoh himself. After lunch it was back to the classroom, where, on a full stomach, I was easily able to ignore what should have been the rudiments of my education. After school, a *flâneur du gastronomique*, I might knock back a small bag of french fries liberally slathered with ketchup, which, most afternoons, along with perhaps a banana and six or seven cookies, would see me through to dinner.

Proust famously used food—his little fluted madeleine cake—to beckon memory; working at things the other way round, I beckon memory to recall food. I remember a Rumanian Jewish restaurant to which my parents used to take us where the waiters seemed to have stepped out of Jewish jokes. Once, as a small boy, when I asked one of them if the restaurant had any soda pop, he, towel over his shoulder, pencil poised over his order pad, sourly replied, "Yeh, ve gots two kinds. Ve gots red and ve gots brown." I remember when a small chain of rather deluxe hamburger restaurants named Peter Pan was caught serving its customers horse meat and, in a gesture to return to the public's good graces, gave away free hamburgers for a day, thus creating a living fantasy in which every boy could be his own Wimpy. In the autumn of 1952, Dwight David Eisenhower was elected president, elaborate peace negotiations were under way in Korea, François Mauriac won the Nobel Prize for literature, and I, a freshman in high school, tasted pizza for the first time and thought I had died and gone to heaven.

That same year, in an episode of shame, I recall walking along the avenue with my faithful companion Robert Ginsburg, who, always the tempter, suggested we buy and share and dispatch a cake. Dispatch it we did, but I cannot say neatly. As in so many of our combined enterprises, an element of planning was missing. In this instance, the cake now purchased, we noted the absence of utensils for cutting it—a large chocolate affair with a combined chocolate and pistachio frosting—and, once cut, for conveying it to our mouths. We could have brought the cake home, there to have an ample slice in his or my mother's kitchen. But we did not want a slice of cake, however ample—we wanted an entire cake. So we ate it, walking along side streets, prying great fistfuls away from the cake and stuffing them into our mouths in the style we designated "one billion BC." We are talking about two reasonably well brought up middle-class boys here, you understand, but true hunger, to the truly craving, will turn even a middle-class lad into a savage.

10   Middle-class and Middle Western, I should have added, for when I think of the ideal middle-class meal of my youth, eaten in a restaurant, it comprises the following plain but to me, then as now, quite pleasing Middle Western menu: it begins with a shrimp cocktail; followed by a wedge of iceberg lettuce with thousand island dressing; followed by a rather thick slab of medium-rare prime rib of beef, with a baked potato (not cooked in aluminum foil) lavished with butter and sour cream with chives; and concluded with strawberry shortcake and cof-

fee. This is, you will recognize, almost an entirely prelapsarian meal; it could only have been eaten in good conscience before the vile knowledge that certain foods can clog arteries, set tumors growing, send up blood pressure. If you are someone who would like to get to ninety-six or ninety-seven, and hence someone attentive to death by cancer, heart attack, or stroke, what you are permitted from that meal I have described, once the calories, the cholesterol, and the caffeine are removed, is a plain baked potato on a bed of undressed lettuce with a few strawberries atop it nicely garnished with chives. Dig in.

I mock such curtailment of pleasure—I hate it, truth to tell—yet I am myself victim to it. Far from always but still all too often, I look down at the plate set before me to find potential death through possible heart disease or cancer lurking there—and if not death, social disgrace through overweight. Until roughly twenty-five years ago, those of us born into industrially developed countries, though we may not have known it, were all living in the kitchen of Eden. The snake responsible for casting us out is named Diet: today few are the people who are not dieting for health, for beauty, for longevity. *Eat to Win* is the title of a recent best-seller that supplies diets and menus for people who wish to stay young and athletically competitive. The well-named *Self* magazine calls it "the eating wave of the future." *Eat to Win?* Whatever happened to, eat to eat?

Not that I am above diet. I spend a serious portion of my life attempting to lose the extra four or five pounds that clearly wishes to adhere to me. I gain it, I drop it off, I gain it, I drop it off—we are, those four or five pounds and I, like a couple who cannot agree to live peaceably together but who refuse to separate permanently. I need no reminder when they have returned: when the press of my flesh rubs the waist of my trousers, it is time to miss a meal, hold the fries, play strong defense generally. Aggravation makes the best diet, in my view, and once, in a troubled time in my life, I dropped off fifteen pounds without consciously attempting to do so. Another time I set out to lose twenty pounds; I did it, and I wish to report that the feeling upon having succeeded in doing so is one I describe as "fatness of soul." One is so splendidly well pleased with oneself. An element of fanaticism slides in. One has lost twenty pounds—why not twenty-five? A friend described my play on the racquetball court as quicker than a sperm. I thought I looked wonderfully well when I had lost all that weight: so lithe, so elegant, so youthful. Apparently this was not the effect I everywhere conveyed, for more than one person, during this period, asked my wife straight-out if I were suffering a wasting disease.

Because of this little experience I believe I can understand something of what goes on in the mind of the anorexic. The anorexic is the reverse of the glutton, but it is well to remember that the anorexic is the other side of the same coin. (The currently accepted definition of anorexia nervosa is "a serious illness of deliberate self-starvation with profound psychiatric and physical components.") As food excites the glutton, so does it repel the anorexic (most of whom are adolescent girls or youngish women). The glutton's idea of a jolly fine time is precisely the anorexic's idea of hell. As the glutton in extreme cases will have to have his jaw wired to prevent him from eating, the anorexic will in equally extreme cases have to be hospitalized and force-fed through tubes.

For the true glutton, as for the true anorexic, food may well not be the real problem; the love and hatred of food, when they take on such obsessive energy, doubtless mask deeper problems, distinctive in individual cases. But it is interesting that reactions to food can be a significant symptom in serious psychological disorders. Freud, that suspicious Viennese, thought that a great deal more was going on at the table than met the fork. Unquestionably there sometimes is. But I prefer to stand on this question with Cyril Connolly, who put in the mouth of a character in this story "Shade Those Laurels" the lines: "They say that food is a substitute for love. Well, it's certainly a bloody good one."

TALKING ABOUT IT

Seeing Metaphor: Revealing and Concealing

1. Epstein quotes another writer as saying that "within every fat man a thin man struggles to get out," then says of himself that he is "a relatively thin man in whom a fat man struggles . . . to get out." What do these images suggest about the way our culture regards weight? To what extent do you think identity is tied to body size?

2. In earlier years, Epstein writes, we "were all living in the kitchen of Eden. The snake responsible for casting us out is named Diet." Often now, when he looks at his plate he finds "potential death through possible heart disease or cancer lurking there" (paragraph 11). How do you respond to these images? Do you think it is true that most people's thinking about food has changed drastically over your lifetime? If so, do you view this change positively or negatively?

Seeing Composition: Frame, Line, Texture, Tone

1. Does Epstein convince you of his obsession with food? Do the examples of behavior he cites seem to support his contention that inside him is a fat man "who cannot be turned loose"? Why or why not?

2. In his conclusion, Epstein makes a comparison between anorexics and gluttons. Why do you suppose he ends this way? Do you think that this discussion of obsession with food masking deeper problems leads appropriately to his concluding sentence?

Seeing Meaning: Navigating and Negotiating

1. "I wish to live fat but be thin," writes Epstein. Do you think this sentiment is true of most people? Do you think it could be extended to other concerns ("I wish to live unhealthily but be healthy", "I wish to live lazily but be successful," "I wish to live dangerously but be safe")? Are such inner contradictions central to most people's lives?

2. In paragraph 12, Epstein points out an "element of fanaticism slides in" when he tries to lose weight. Why do you think this happens so often to people? He also says at his thinnest he thought he looked "wonderfully well" while others wondered if he were "suffering from a wasting disease." Do you think it's common for people to have a distorted image of their physical appearance? Why do you think this might be?

WRITING ABOUT IT

1. Write about another "you" that, like Joseph Epstein's "fat man," you keep locked up, only to let him or her out occasionally in what might be the "equivalent of a work-release program." This character must be "kept under the strictest surveillance." What's the danger, and why let the character out at all?

2. What stops Epstein from setting free the "fat man" is his fear of death as well as social disgrace. What is your own attitude toward thinness or fatness? Like Epstein, focus on social and cultural as well as personal reasons to explain your position.

The Naked Truth about Fitness

BARBARA EHRENREICH

Barbara Ehrenreich, a contributing editor to Ms. *and* Mother Jones, *has written (with Deirdre English) three books about women and health issues:* Witches, Midwives, and Nurses: A History of Women Healers *(1972),* Complaints and Disorders: The Sexual Politics of Sickness *(1973), and* For Her Own Good: One Hundred Fifty Years of the Experts' Advice to Women *(1978). The following selection is from Ehrenreich's book* The Snarling Citizen: Essays *(1995).*

The conversation has all the earmarks of a serious moral debate. The man is holding out for the pleasures of this life, few as they are and short as it is. The woman (we assume his wife, since they are having breakfast together and this is a prime-time television commercial) defends the high road of virtue and self-denial. We know there will be a solution, that it will taste like fresh-baked cookies and will simultaneously lower cholesterol, fight osteoporosis, and melt off unwholesome flag. We *know* this. What we have almost forgotten to wonder about is this: since when is breakfast cereal a *moral* issue?

Morality is no longer a prominent feature of civil society. In the 1980s, politicians abandoned it, Wall Street discarded it, televangelists defiled it. Figuratively speaking, we went for the sucrose rush and forgot the challenge of fiber. But only figuratively. For as virtue drained out of our public lives, it reappeared in our cereal bowls, our exercise regimens, and our militant responses to cigarette smoke, strong drink, and greasy food.

We redefined virtue as health. And considering the probable state of our souls, this was not a bad move. By relocating the seat of virtue from the soul to the pecs, the abs, and the coronary arteries, we may not have become the most virtuous people on earth, but we surely became the most desperate for grace. We spend $5 billion a year on our health-club memberships, $2 billion on vitamins, nearly $1 billion on home-exercise equipment, and $6 billion on sneakers to wear out on our treadmills and StairMasters. We rejoice in activities that leave a hangover of muscle pain and in foods that might, in more temperate times, have been classified as fodder. To say we want to be healthy is to gravely understate the case. We want to be *good*.

Consider my own breakfast cereal, a tasteless, colorless substance that clings to the stomach lining with the avidity of Krazy Glue. Quite wisely, the box makes no promise of good taste or visual charm. Even the supposed health benefits are modestly outlined in tiny print. No, the incentive here is of a higher nature. "It is the right thing to do," the manufacturer intones on the back of the box, knowing that, however alluring our temptations to evil, we all want to do the right thing.

The same confusion of the moral and the physical pervades my health 5 club. "Commit to get fit!" is the current slogan, the verb reminding us of the moral tenacity that has become so elusive in our human relationships. In the locker room we sound like the inmates of a miraculously rehabilitative women's prison, always repenting, forever resolving: "I shouldn't have had that doughnut this morning." "I wasn't here for two weeks and now I'm going to pay the price." Ours is a hierarchy of hardness. The soft, the slow, the easily tired rate no compassion, only the coldest of snubs.

Health is almost universally recognized as a *kind* of virtue. At least, most cultures strong enough to leave an ethnographic trace have discouraged forms of behavior that are believed to be unhealthy. Nevertheless, most of us recognize that health is not an accomplishment so much as it is a *potential*. My upper-body musculature, developed largely on Nautilus machines, means that I probably *can* chop wood or unload trucks, not that I ever *will*. Human cultures have valued many things — courage, fertility, craftsmanship, and deadly aim among them — but ours is almost alone in valuing not the deed itself but the mere capacity to perform it.

So what is it that drives us to run, lift, strain, and monitor our metabolisms as if we were really accomplishing something — something pure, that is, and noble? Sociologist Robert Crawford argues that outbreaks of American "healthism" coincide with bouts of middle-class anxiety. It was near the turn of the century, a time of economic turmoil and violent labor struggles, that white-collar Americans embarked on their first 1980s-style health craze. They hiked, rode bikes, lifted weights, and otherwise heeded Teddy Roosevelt's call for "the strenuous life." They filtered their water and fussed about bran (though sweets were heavily favored as a source of energy). On the loonier fringe, they tried "electric belts," vibrating chairs, testicle supporters, "water cures," prolonged mastication, and copious enemas— moralizing all the while about "right living" and "the divine laws of health."

Our own health-and-fitness craze began in another period of economic anxiety— the 1970s, when the economy slid into "stagflation" and a college degree suddenly ceased to guarantee a career above the cab-driving level. In another decade — say in the 1930s or the 1960s — we might have mobilized for economic change. But the 1970s was the era of *How to Be Your Own Best Friend* and *Looking Out for Number One*, a time in which it seemed more important, or more feasible, to reform our bodies than to change the world. Bit by bit and with the best of intentions, we began to set aside the public morality of participation and protest for the personal morality of health.

Our fascination with fitness has paid off. Fewer Americans smoke than did fifteen years ago; they drink less hard liquor, eat more fiber and less fat. Our rate of heart disease keeps declining, our life expectancy is on the rise. We are less dependent on doctors, more aware of our responsibility for health. No doubt we feel better too, at least those of us who have the means and the motivation to give up bourbon for Evian and poker for racquetball. I personally am more confident and probably more durable as a fitness devotee than I ever was in my former life as a chairwarmer.

10   But there's a difference between health and health*ism*, between health as a reasonable goal and health as a transcendent value. By confusing health and virtue, we've gotten testier, less tolerant, and ultimately less capable of confronting the sources of disease that do *not* lie within our individual control. Victim blaming, for example, is an almost inevitable side effect of healthism. If health is our personal responsibility, the reasoning goes, then disease must be *our* fault.

I think of the friend — a thoroughly intelligent, compassionate, and (need I say?) ultrafit person — who called to tell me that her sister was facing surgery for a uterine tumor. "I can't understand it," my friend confided. "I'm sure she's been working out." *Not quite enough* was the implication, however, despite the absence of even the frailest connection between fibroids and muscle tone. But like the pretechnological tribalists, we've come to see every illness as a punishment for past transgressions. When Chicago mayor Harold Washington died of a heart attack almost three years ago, some eulogizers offered baleful mutterings about his penchant for unreformed, high-cholesterol soul food. When we hear of someone getting cancer, we mentally scan their lifestyle for the fatal flaw — fatty foods, smoking, even "repressed anger."

There are whole categories of disease that cannot, in good conscience, be blamed on the lifestyles or moral shortcomings of their victims. An estimated 25,000 cancer deaths a year, for example, result from exposure to the pesticides applied so lavishly in agribusiness. Ten thousand Americans are killed every year in industrial accidents; an estimated 20,000 more die from exposure to carcinogens in the workplace — asbestos, toxic solvents, radiation. These deaths are preventable, but not with any amount of oat bran or low-impact aerobics. Environmental and occupational diseases will require a far more rigorous social and political regimen of citizen action, legislation, and enforcement.

Even unhealthy lifestyles can have "environmental" as well as personal origins. Take the matter of diet and smoking. It's easy for the middle-class fiber enthusiast to look down on the ghetto dweller who smokes cigarettes and spends her food stamps on Doritos and soda pop. But in low-income neighborhoods convenience stores and fast-food joints are often the only sources of food, while billboards and TV commercials are the primary sources of nutritional "information." Motivation is another problem. It's one thing to give up smoking and sucrose when life seems long and promising, quite another when it might well be short and brutal.

Statistically speaking, the joggers and bran eaters are concentrated in the white-collar upper-middle class. Blue- and pink-collar people still tend to prefer Bud to Evian and meat loaf to poached salmon. And they still smoke — at a rate of 51 percent, compared with 35 percent for people in professional and managerial occupations. These facts should excite our concern: Why not special cardiovascular-fitness programs for the assembly-line worker as well as the executive? Reduced-rate health-club memberships for truck drivers and typists? Nutritional supplements for the down-and-out? Instead, healthism tends to reinforce long-standing prejudices. If healthy habits are an expression of moral excellence, then the working class is not only "tacky," ill-mannered, or whatever else we've been encouraged to believe — it's morally deficient.

Thus, perversely, does healthism ease the anxieties of the affluent. No   15
amount of straining against muscle machines could have saved Drexel Burnham[1] operatives from unemployment; no aerobic exercises can reduce the price of a private-school education. But fitness *can* give its practitioners a sense of superiority over the potbellied masses. On the other side of victim blaming is an odious mood of self-congratulation: "We" may not be any smarter or more secure about our futures. But surely we are more disciplined and pure.

In the end, though — and the end does come — no one is well served by victim blaming. The victim isn't always "someone else," someone fatter, lazier, or more addicted to smoke and grease. The fact is that we do die, all of us, and that almost all of us will encounter disease, disability, and considerable discomfort either in the process or along the way. The final tragedy of healthism is that it leaves us so ill prepared for the inevitable. If we believe that health is a sign of moral purity and anything less is a species of sin, then death condemns us all as failures. Longevity is not a resoundingly interesting lifetime achievement, just as working out is not exactly a life's work.

Somehow, we need to find our way back to being healthy without being health*ist*. Health is great. It makes us bouncier and probably happier. Better yet, it can make us fit *for* something: strong enough to fight the big-time polluters, for example, the corporate waste dumpers; tough enough to take on economic arrangements that condemn so many to poverty and to dangerous occupations; lean and powerful enough to demand a more nurturing, less anxiety-ridden social order.

Health is good. But it is not, as even the ancient and athletic Greeks would have said, *the* good.

TALKING ABOUT IT

Seeing Metaphor: Revealing and Concealing

1. In paragraph 3, Ehrenreich writes that we have "redefined virtue as health. . . .
   To say we want to be healthy is to gravely understate the case. We want to be

---

1. Drexel Burnham: An investment firm notorious for its junk bond trading in the 1980s.
— Eds.

good." In what sense can health be seen as virtuous? In what ways can this conception limit our thinking about virtue?

2. "Ours is a hierarchy of hardness," claims Ehrenreich. "The soft, the slow, the easily tired rate no compassion, only the coldest of snubs." Do you agree that our culture increasingly values "hardness"? How might this be evident in areas other than health and fitness? Do you find the thought at all troubling, as Ehrenreich obviously does?

Seeing Composition: Frame, Line, Texture, Tone

1. How do you think Ehrenreich has imagined her audience here? Note, particularly, that much of her essay is cast in the first-person plural, referring to "we" and "us." Who do you think this "we" represents for Ehrenreich? What makes you think so?

2. Ehrenreich admits that she herself partakes in the cult of health that she describes, eating a healthy breakfast cereal, working out, and so forth. How does her inclusion of such information affect your response? Do you find her more or less sympathetic? Why?

Seeing Meaning: Navigating and Negotiating

1. Ehrenreich's real point here goes well beyond simply criticizing those who equate health with virtue. What point is she making in paragraph 10, in paragraph 13, and, particularly, in her final paragraph? How do you respond to Ehrenreich's arguments here?

2. In paragraph 14, Ehrenreich claims that attention to fitness is "concentrated in the white-collar upper-middle class." Does your experience bear out this observation ? If so, what might be the reasons?

WRITING ABOUT IT

1. Write about another food, drink, or exercise that has become a "moral issue" in our culture. Provide some historical evidence for your claim, as Ehrenreich does for breakfast cereal in paragraph 1 of her essay. Analyze the language and, in particular, the images that seem to equate health and morality as in the metaphor "Health is virtue." To what extent do the images that you describe distort our thinking about the causes of illness and distort our judgments of other people?

2. Investigate the ways that health clubs, fitness programs, or clothing advertisements redefine virtue as health. How do the ads seem to say, "We want to be good"?

New Face, New Body, New Self

MARJORIE ROSEN

Marjorie Rosen has written for Film Comment *and the* New York Times Magazine *and is the author of* Popcorn Venus: Women, Movies, and the American Dream *(1973). "New Face, New Body, New Self" originally appeared in the April 26, 1993, issue of* People.

In high school a teenager's looks can become a life-absorbing obsession, a source of painful and disabling self-consciousness. So what's the problem with using a knife to put right what nature seems to have done all wrong? "Nothing," says Camille Paglia, author of the controversial *Sexual Personae,* a study of cultural decadence, "as long as there is a serious defect which plastic surgery can correct and help a young person feel more confident. But unfortunately the model that has evolved is the Barbie doll."

And that is the problem, agrees Marie Wilson, president of the Ms. Foundation for Women, an organization that supports projects devoted to women and children. "Most of this is about [already] having a face that is just fine and hoping to make it perfect," she says. Susan Faludi, author of the best-selling *Backlash: The Undeclared War Against American Women,* which chronicles the media assault on women during the past decade, is even more critical of our cut-and-stitch-happy society where 87 out of every 100 plastic surgery patients are women. Blaming plastic surgeons for "wanting to play the role of Frankenstein, wanting the power to shape the female form as though it's putty," she observes: "Young women are much less free to come up with individual ideals of beauty than men, and the pressure to conform that causes young girls to have plastic surgery is one more way to confine them."

But apparently teenagers don't all see it that way. The girls — and boy — on the following pages were determined to change their lives through cosmetic surgery, and they did. They share their stories below.

THINNER THIGHS IN AN HOUR AND A HALF — ALL FOR JUST $10,000

For years, Robyn Notrica, now 21, wore boxer shorts to the beach and bought pants five sizes too big in the waist because otherwise she couldn't squeeze her thighs into them. The pants she *did* wear were frayed between the legs where her flesh rubbed together. "My thighs were humongous," recalls the five-foot two-inch sophomore at the New York School of Design in Manhattan. "I was small in my upper body, but my hips were huge." And not for lack of dieting.

353

All the while she was growing up in suburban Roslyn, New York, she fought a nonstop battle against lower-body bulge. At one time weighing 175 pounds, she spent five summers at weight-loss camps and even followed the Nutri/System program. But nothing helped.

5   Thoroughly frustrated, Notrica began to think about a more drastic solution: liposuction. Finally, two-and-a-half years ago, she went to see New York City plastic surgeon Dr. Helen Cohen. "She said she'd never seen a girl my age with so much fat on her legs." says Notrica. Supported by her mother, Marna, a housewife, and her father, Jack, a retired cop, Robyn underwent a one-and-a-half-hour, ten-thousand-dollar procedure, during which fat was suctioned from her hips and thighs. Explains Dr. Cohen, who cautions patients to look for surgeons certified in liposuction techniques: "When the procedure was first done here in 1983, people died from shock because when you remove fat and fluid, you lose electrolytes, too. But if you do it right, there is no problem." In fact, she says, teenagers respond better to liposuction than older women because their skin is more elastic and will shrink back into shape.

Notrica did experience discomfort, though. "For a week it felt as if I'd worked out too much," she says, and her legs remained bruised for a month. These days she can barely recall the unpleasantness. The only telltale signs are twelve fading scars, each the size of a pinky nail, that mark the spots where the liposuction cannula pierced her skin. Notrica, delighted by the new "great shape" of her legs, says the surgery eliminated six inches from her hips. Best of all, she has achieved her "biggest goal"; to fit into a pair of Levi's — size 29 waist. "Liposuction," she says, "made me happy."

A NEW NOSE — AND A CHIN TO MATCH

Growing up in East Brunswick, New Jersey, she was an accident-prone girl who broke her nose badly in ninth-grade gym class when she caught a basketball with her face. So Andrea Rudow visited Dr. Alvin Glasgold, the Highland Park, New Jersey, plastic surgeon who had straightened her older brother Gary's nose when he was sixteen. Since she was only thirteen and still growing, Glasgold advised her to come back in six months. She did — "with a huge red bump on my face. The nasal bone, instead of growing down, was now growing out," she says. Classmates at East Brunswick High School noticed, too, and began calling her Rudolph.

During Andrea's consultation, Dr. Glasgold suggested not only a nose job but an implant to improve her receding chin. "He said that the line of your nose has to fit with your chin," says Rudow, "and I trusted him." According to Glasgold, 25 percent of all rhinoplasty patients also have receding chins. "Sometimes the chin is the real problem and nose just a minor one," he says.

"Correcting a chin is much simpler than doing rhinoplasty, and the results, using FDA-approved silicone rubber, are extremely consistent." Making an incision either under the chin or in the gums between the chin and the lip, the surgeon slips the implant into place, then anchors it with a surgical stitch to the tissue surrounding the bone. In 1988, when Andrea, now nineteen, had it done, the operation cost her father, Richard, a real estate appraiser, and her mother, Ricki, a medical secretary, thirty-five hundred dollars. (Insurance paid most of the cost because her nasal bone was growing improperly.)

When her bandages came off, "I was laughing and crying at the same   10 time," Rudow says. "Crying because I was so happy and laughing because it didn't look like me."

Rudow was so elated with the results that she was inspired to lose weight, too. Back at school, she says, "they looked at me like, 'Oh, did you get a haircut?'" But Rudow felt the difference profoundly. Happier, and feeling prettier, she became less reclusive, making friends and dating regularly. Now a liberal arts student at Middlesex Community College in Edison, New Jersey, she sees only one drawback to her surgery. "Men whistle at me on the street," she says. "At first it was funny, but now it's like, *enough.*"

A TEENAGE CYRANO DIVESTS HIMSELF OF A SHOWPIECE

Joe Mann's parents gave him a nose job for his high school graduation present in 1991. The thirty-two-hundred-dollar operation was something that the lanky, six-foot one-inch Houston teenager had contemplated ever since junior high when, he recalls, "kids would tease me by saying things like, 'Is that your real nose?' and once there were these pegs in the locker room for us to hang our clothes on, and someone drew eyes and a mouth around one, like it was supposed to be me."

Even Mann's plastic surgeon, Dr. Charles Bailey, admits, "His was probably the largest nose I've ever seen." But Bailey believes that Mann was a good candidate for surgery for another reason. "Joe seemed very well adjusted," he says. "I'm generally more cautious with young males than young women. Women have a grasp of what they want, but with young men, it's more common to have an underlying problem — something else they don't feel good about." Not Joe. "He was not withdrawn and has a great sense of humor," says Bailey.

When the operation was finished, Mann asked for the pieces of bone and cartilage that were removed from his schnozz and keeps them in a jar of formaldehyde. He loves to show off his *old* nose — now that it's not on his face. "I'm glad I did it," says Mann, nineteen, a freshman at Houston Community College. Although he has no steady these days, he notices that since his transformation, "I have more dates, and I think it's because I look better." That's not all.

"People are more courteous," he says. "Like salespeople. They'd rather talk to a good-looking person than a not-so-good-looking one."

SEEKING THE PERFECT NOSE: AFTER THREE STRIKES, SUCCESS

15   One year ago, after three botched rhinoplasty attempts, Jill Fugler of suburban Houston was beside herself with frustration and disappointment. Today the twenty-two-year-old boasts a perfect profile, thanks both to her own resolute spirit and to Houston plastic surgeon Dr. Benjamin Cohen.

Fugler's odyssey began in 1987 when, at seventeen, she decided to fix the nose she had broken in a neighborhood football game during junior high school. After the surgery the tip had a permanent "swollen" look, she says. When she complained, her surgeon scheduled a second operation. And a third. But the tip remained puffy.

Enter Dr. Cohen, whom Fugler's mom had seen on a local Houston TV show about plastic surgery. Cohen's explanation for the puffiness: "Too much cartilage had been taken from the tip of her nose." Using a new cartilage-graft technique, Cohen removed excess scar tissue and filled out the tip. "Before, I wanted people to look me in the face and not see my profile," says Fugler, who is completing an associate degree at North Harris Montgomery College in Houston. "Now I look at my profile every day."

THERE ARE TIMES WHEN A NOSE OPENS DOORS

Ever since she was three, Stacy Hirsch had her heart set on becoming an actress. Singing and dancing lessons were part of the plan. So, too, after she turned fourteen, was a nose job. "I had made a real commitment to the profession," says Stacy, sixteen. "I thought having my nose done would give me a new look that would increase my marketability."

Before her surgery, says Stacy, "people weren't really seeing me; they were speaking to me and thinking, 'She's got a big nose.'" Because of Stacy's unhappiness about her appearance, her parents, Larry, a manufacturer's representative, and Linda, a preschool teacher, backed Stacy's decision. "I'd had a nose job myself at sixteen," says Linda. "I never said anything to Stacy about her nose, but she knew I'd had mine done, and maybe that stuck in her mind."

20   Still, Stacy worried that friends would perceive her as vain and only told those closest to her. "I asked myself, 'Should I not do this because it's not the *good* thing to do?'" she admits. "But I decided I didn't want to ask, 'What if? Would I have gotten that job if I looked different?'"

In July 1991, after her freshman year at Glenbrook North High School in Northbrook, Illinois, Stacy scheduled surgery with Dr. Jack Kerth, who asked Stacy to bring in pictures of noses that she liked. "I looked through my teen magazines and tore off the noses of Julia Roberts and Cindy Crawford," says Stacy. "But I asked Dr. Kerth for a nose that fits my face, that looks natural." And, she believes, she got one. "It was the nose I was born to have and didn't get," she says.

When Hirsch returned to school in September, she says "boys noticed me." What's more, she got a part on *Energy Express*, a Chicago TV show for teens about sports, which has been picked up nationally for syndication. "I would never have had this response if I had looked a different way," says Hirsch. "When your outside equals your inside, you're going to get twice as much as you already have."

TALKING ABOUT IT

Seeing Metaphor: Revealing and Concealing

1. Cultural critic Susan Faludi regards plastic surgeons as "wanting to play the role of Frankenstein" and feels that "the pressure to conform that causes young girls to have plastic surgery is one more way to confine them." How do you respond to these images of power and control? Do you find them an accurate way of looking at plastic surgery?

2. The piece ends with a quotation from Stacy Hirsch after her plastic surgery: "When your outside equals your inside, you're going to get twice as much as you already have." In what sense can one's outside equal one's inside? What does this way of thinking reveal about one's ideas regarding identity? Does anything get lost through this kind of thinking?

Seeing Composition: Frame, Line, Texture, Tone

1. What do you think of Rosen's presentation of the five young people she profiles here? How do you respond to them, and to what in Rosen's writing do you attribute your response?

2. Evaluate the headings Rosen uses to introduce each of her main "characters." What do these suggest about her attitude?

Seeing Meaning: Navigating and Negotiating

1. Joe Mann's doctor says that he's more cautious about performing cosmetic surgery on young men than on young women because "[w]omen have a grasp of what they want, but with young men, it's more common to have an underlying problem — something else they don't feel good about." Why do you think this might be?

2. In contemplating plastic surgery, Stacy Hirsch remembers asking herself, "Should I not do this because it's not the *good* thing to do?" Do you think it's possible to make moral judgments about plastic surgery? Can it in any sense be seen as an issue of right and wrong? Do you think critics have a point?

WRITING ABOUT IT

1. What connections do the teenagers make between the body and their self-images as these connections are revealed through the ways they tell their stories? Look particularly at what they say and what support they offer for holding their views. Which argument is most persuasive to you? Why?

2. Of the teenagers, Marjorie Rosen says, "They share their stories. . . ." What is the metaphorical sense of "share" in this context? Which teenager's story are you least willing to share, and why?

A Metaphor's Ability to Open the Door to the World of Lacrosse

AISLING KERINS

Like several other first-year students in class, Aisling Kerins related the "Pupil's" and "Master's" metaphors described by C. S. Lewis to her experience in learning a sport. As she worked to improve her skills, she could see the limits of earlier metaphors that her coach used to help her position and move her body more gracefully and effectively. Later, however, as a lacrosse coach to beginning students, Aisling also saw the necessity of those early metaphors. Her essay is a good example of testing ideas against one's own experience.

In C. S. Lewis's essay "Bluspels and Flalansferes: A Semantic Nightmare," he refers to two primary types of metaphors, the Master's metaphor and the Pupil's metaphor. The Master's metaphor is used by a teacher and "it does not at all hinder, and only very slightly helps, the thought of its maker" (255). The Pupil's metaphor "dominates completely the thought of the recipient; his truth cannot rise above the truth of the original metaphor" (255). The first time that I attempted to play lacrosse I needed a Pupil's metaphor to help me understand how to move my stick so that the ball would stay in its pocket. This experience helped me to understand what C. S. Lewis meant by his two distinct categories of metaphors. As I continued to play lacrosse I came to see the limitations that my coach's metaphor imposed on my thinking.

As I picked up my lacrosse stick for the first time, I fumbled with it greatly. The ball refused to stay in the pocket of my lacrosse stick, and, at the same time, my hands and arms refused to move in unison. As my right arm moved to the right, my left arm moved to the left. This made the lacrosse stick end up in the oddest positions, none of which were correct. My coach saw me struggling and came over to give me some words of advice, which helped me immensely. She told me to imagine that my arms made up the top and bottom of a door, while my lacrosse stick made up one of the vertical sides of the door. I was then told to pretend to open and close the door that was made up of my arms and my stick. This "door" opened up the world of lacrosse to me. As long as I imagined my arms as a door, they moved together, in the correct direction, and the correct motion. This was how I learned to cradle. For the next two or three years, this was the image I had in mind whenever I picked up my lacrosse stick. This metaphor became the only way I could think about playing lacrosse, which is what a Pupil's metaphor becomes to a student. I did not have control over the metaphor, it had control over me.

For me playing lacrosse and the image of a door opening and closing became one idea. To my coach this was just a simple trick I could use to gain coordination in my arms. She had a greater understanding of lacrosse and the skills required to play than I did, and therefore she did not rely upon the door metaphor, as I did.

As I continued to play lacrosse, I began to play with players of a greater skill level. I noticed that these other players did not cradle as I did. They changed the levels of their cradle, the angles of their cradle, and the hands they cradled with. As long as I continued to cling to the door metaphor, I would be unable to improve my level of play. This understanding is how I came to realize that metaphors have limitations. Lewis claimed that when "the metaphor is our only method of reaching a given idea at all, there our thinking is limited by the metaphor" (258). I realized that if I were to become a better lacrosse player I would be forced to go beyond my door imagery. At first I found this to be extremely difficult because the image had become synonymous with playing lacrosse. The door was no longer open to a world of greater understanding, but shut. As I continued to play with this higher level of player, I unconsciously "shut" the door metaphor behind me and slowly began to change and improve the way I played.

5   I can now see both the value and the limitations of the metaphor. If my coach had not told me the door metaphor I might never have learned to cradle. I see this metaphor as an excellent teaching aid regardless of its limitations. This has become a Master's metaphor for me in that "I can continue to use it long after I have forgotten its metaphorical nature, and my thinking will be neither helped nor hindered by the fact that it was originally a metaphor" (257). Lewis claimed that "only that which to some degree enlightens ourselves is likely to enlighten others" (257). This summer I worked with younger girls who were just beginning to play lacrosse, and to the girls who were having trouble cradling, I passed on the door metaphor. I had learned much from it and hopefully it will serve to give these beginners the understanding of lacrosse that it gave me.

All parenthetical citations refer to page numbers in *Selected Literary Essays by C. S. Lewis.*

PERMEABLE BOUNDARIES: WRITING WHERE THE READINGS MEET

1. What are the differences between Margaret Atwood's and John Updike's views of the female body, and how do you respond to those differences?

2. How does Nicholson Baker's essay "Changes of Mind" serve as an illustration for some of C. S. Lewis's ideas about the uses of metaphor and its relationship to meaning and truth? Write an essay in which you attempt to see Baker's exploration within the framework of ideas presented by Lewis.

3. Barbara Ehrenreich and Jill Dubisch both address the spiritual dimensions of food in our culture. How does Ehrenreich argue in her own essay Dubisch's claim that "the health food movement sets up a symbolic system which opposes harmony to disharmony, purity to pollution, nature to culture, and ultimately . . . life to death"? What differences do you observe in how they present and support their arguments? How might you explain those differences in regard to their professional backgrounds and their intended audiences?

4. In the second paragraph of her essay, Marjorie Rosen quotes Susan Faludi, author of *Backlash: The Undeclared War Against American Women*, as blaming plastic surgeons for "wanting to play the role of Frankenstein, wanting the power to shape the female form as though it's putty." How might Atwood and Rosen draw on John Updike's essay to extend the blame beyond plastic surgeons? Who else could be said to want this power? Or, to ask the question another way, where else might the power lie to shape the female form? In your experience and reading, who wants the power most? Where is the power strongest, and why?

5. Imagine that the female teenagers in "New Face, New Body, New Self" share their stories with Margaret Atwood. How might she respond to them, given your reading of "The Female Body"? Why do you think so?

6. Carol Kloss and Joseph Epstein are seated next to each other at a dinner party. The topic is food. What attitudes would they share? Where would they disagree, if you think they do?

Chapter 6

Minds and Machines

*We have unabashedly flung a web of machinery across the land
(and even into space), and at the same time we have longed
nostalgically for the simple life of unspoiled wilderness.*
— Chet Raymo

Willing servant? Toy? Enemy? Real estate? How do you think about the role of technology in your life and in the world? As Chet Raymo describes in "Revenge of the Yokyoks," most people have "a love-hate affair" with machines. Even an ordinary machine — the vacuum cleaner, the lawn mower, the stapler — can be exasperating. On a more serious scale of experience, we know through history and observation that human inventions have been used to cultivate as well as destroy nature. Since we include ourselves in the natural world, we can all point to ways machines have benefited and endangered us.

It is easy to point to benefits; they are in every facet of our lives. Thanks in part to our machines, we can enjoy healthier, longer, and more productive, efficient lives. We can travel and communicate more easily, faster, and farther than many believed possible. But machines have inspired fear as well: the power of nuclear weaponry to destroy the world; the disturbance to rain forests that has led to the invasion of invisible enemies, such as the virus Ebola; and, as yet, the little-known dangers of cloning, the power we have to imitate nature more closely than we have ever done before.

Nowhere is our love-hate affair with machines more visible to the general public than in the case of computer technology. Although this cultural revolution may only be in its infancy, we can hardly imagine life without computers. Yet, as much as technology has transformed our lives in positive ways, Donald Norman, an author in this chapter, worries about the way people interact with technology. In the preface to his essay collection *Turn Signals Are the Facial Expressions of Automobiles,* from which you are reading the title essay, Norman elaborates his concern:

Our social judgments, our skills, and even our thoughts are indelibly affected by the nature of the technology that supports us. Worse, the impact is so pervasive, so subtle, that we are often unaware of how many of our beliefs have been affected by the arbitrary nature of technology. (iv)

Norman's goal, however, is not to argue against modern technology, of which computers serve as one example, but to study the ways we interact with technology in the hope of "humanizing" or "socializing" it. He'd like technology to meet the social needs and concerns of those who use it.

To varying degrees, all the authors in this chapter address Norman's concern. By their choice of topic and their language, particularly by the metaphors they use, these writers both explicitly and implicitly reveal the impact of computer technology on our social judgments, our beliefs, and the values attached to those beliefs that affect our behavior.

James Bailey and co-participants in a forum explore the concept of humanity being threatened by its own machines. Ellen Ullman, a programmer and consultant, uses the metaphor "Close to the machine" to describe her work and its effect on her thinking as well as her language and behavior. John Lawler, in a lecture delivered in 1987, categorizes a variety of metaphors people have invented to explain and thus control their anxieties about technology. Ted Wade invents a dialogue between two robots about virtual reality as a promising new "place." Esther Dyson, in "If You Don't Love It, Leave It," also thinks and writes about cyberspace as land area: "frontier," "highway," and "real estate." Carolyn Guyer, in "Along the Estuary," describes through metaphors drawn from the natural world how hypertext corresponds to the "natural," associative way minds work. At the heart of her essay, she explores the potential technology has "for encouraging and supporting full human multiplicity and creativity." Through various metaphorical ways of thinking, all the authors in this chapter consider the relationship between "our machines" and "ourselves."

How you think about technology affects the way you talk about it and your relationship to it; conversely, your relationship to it affects the way you think and talk about its role in your life. As C. S. Lewis and John Lawler would say, having many metaphors for one experience broadens your understanding of a phenomenon and thus can lead to new ways of thinking and writing.

STARTING TO THINK ABOUT IT

1. Think about some ways that we attach human qualities to machines. For example, people talk about the ribs of an umbrella, the hands and face of a clock, the eye of the needle. In the case of computer technology, people say, "This program is user-friendly," "My computer is searching for the file," "It

has a lot of memory," and so forth. Or, of other machines, people say, "The toaster died," "The battery has a long life." Make a list in your journal of other examples of personifying machines. Read these to each other in class.

2. Think of the reverse of "Machines are people": "People are machines." How do we talk about people as if they were machines? For example, "What makes her tick?" "He seems run down," "Why are you wound up?" "She just seems to churn out ideas," "His body is a lean machine." Make your own list of such expressions. What are they good for? What do your lists say about the relationship between humans and machines?

3. What are some of the most positive contributions that computer technology has made to your life? The most negative?

4. What are some dangers that computer technology poses?

5. How have computers affected the way you read and write?

Revenge of the Yokyoks

Chet Raymo is a science writer (Honey from a Stone: A Naturalist's Search for God, *1987;* Skeptics and True Believers: The Exhilarating Connection Between Science and Religion, *1998) and a novelist (*In the Falcon's Claw: A Novel of the Year 1000, *1990). He also writes a science column for the* Boston Globe. *This selection is from* The Virgin and the Mousetrap: Essays in Search of the Soul of Science *(1991).*

Thoreau, Emerson, and Hawthorne all record in their journals a moment when the shrill whistle of the Fitchburg Railroad intruded upon the tranquility of the Concord woods. The track of that railroad passed very close to Walden Pond, and Thoreau especially took note of the way the smoke-belching locomotives disrupted his country reveries, drowning out with their iron-wheeled rumblings the cry of the loon and the song of the bluebird. Meanwhile, not far away, other enterprising Americans were building yet more railroads, and canals, water mills, factories, and ingenious machines for weaving cloth and forging iron. Even as Thoreau leaned upon his hoe, listening for the bluebird's wild song ("Pur-i-ty, pur-i-ty"), the Industrial Revolution gathered irresistible momentum, like a great locomotive lurching into speed. By the end of the nineteenth century, Americans had made themselves internationally acknowledged masters of technology. The nature poets of Concord and the mill-masters of Pawtucket and Lowell are two sides of the American character. Since our beginning as a nation, we have had a love-hate relationship with machines. We have unabashedly flung a web of machinery across the land (and even into space), and at the same time we have longed nostalgically for the simple life of unspoiled wilderness.

It is our ambivalence toward machines that causes us to find so much to admire in the Renaissance genius Leonardo da Vinci. Of the artists and scientists of the past, he is the best known and most revered by Americans. His ingenious mechanical inventions were centuries ahead of his time, anticipating the Yankee ingenuity of the Wright brothers, Ford, Edison, and Bell. And his paintings — Mona Lisa, particularly — evoke a tranquil natural beauty. We imagine that in Leonardo's work the lion of technology lays down peaceably with the lamb of nature.

In the spring of 1987 I observed an exhibit of Leonardo's mechanical inventions at the Boston Museum of Science. Twenty-four large working models were on display, based on drawings in Leonardo's notebooks and fashioned of polished wood, gleaming brass, and fabric. They included a clock, a flying machine, a helicopter, a parachute, a paddle-wheel ship, instruments of war, power tools, and scientific instruments. Leonardo saw in his mind's eye and worked out on paper many mechanical ideas that did not come to fruition until our own time. He anticipated manned flight, machine tools, mass production, and many other aspects of contemporary technological civilization. The models in the museum show were the complement of the Mona Lisa — and of the delicate sketches of children's faces and wildflowers that we find in Leonardo's notebooks. In the models we discover a man rapturously in love with machines. Even the machines of war — represented in the museum exhibit by a scaling ladder, gun carriage, and tank — seem more like toys than weapons of terror. These playful models and the Mona Lisa are the two sides of Leonardo as mythic hero: a Renaissance man who lives in harmony with technology and nature, reconciling the discordant poles of the American character.

But wait! There is another Leonardo, a hidden Leonardo who is seldom put on public display. For every delicate wildflower among Leonardo's drawings there are sketches of violent storms, explosions, and turbulence. For every sweet-faced cherub there is an old man's face distorted by anger or fear. For every tranquil Madonna there are images of men and animals locked in mortal combat. And the weapons of war, as we see them in the notebooks, are not toys: We see drawings of spinning scythes dismembering bodies, bombards raining death-dealing fire, and shells exploding in starbursts of decapitating shrapnel. Leonardo's apparently beatific vision of nature and machines was not as harmonious as it sometimes seems. It is true that Leonardo bought caged birds in the shops of Milan that he might set them free. And, yes, among his technical sketches (and the museum models) are many machines designed to increase human well-being and alleviate drudgery. But Leonardo also perceived a dark conflict between nature and technology that resisted resolution. He wanted to learn from nature a more humane way of living, with machines as willing servants, but what he discovered in nature was not always pretty, and his studies did not lead him to a technological utopia. The evidence of the notebooks is conclusive: There is a grim and terrible underside to the genius of Leonardo. His experience offers little hope that we will resolve our own love-hate affair with machines.

■   ■   ■

Nothing more perfectly exemplifies our ambivalent relationship with   5
technology than atomic energy, and no other technology so starkly illustrates the two-edged blade that reaps and slays, the scythe/sword of Leonardo. Not even the Strategic Defense Initiative (Star Wars) or other mega-technologies of destruction evoke more passionate debate or touch deeper human emotions. Atomic energy is the life force of the stars subdued and channeled by human ingenuity, and plunked down — God forbid! — in our own backyards.

The world's first nuclear power station, at Shippingport, Pennsylvania, came on line in the late 1950s. After the horrors of Hiroshima and Nagasaki, the Shippingport plant seemed to vindicate our hard-won knowledge of the atom's secrets. Here at last was a benevolent, peacetime use for atomic energy. Magazines of the time were full of articles with titles like "The Atom: Our Obedient Servant." For many of us, it was the dawning of an age bright with promise and plenty. A few critics warned of dangers. There was vague talk of "meltdowns," and explosions, and nuclear waste that would be active for ten thousand years. But all of that seemed a trifle hysterical when weighed against the obvious advantages of nuclear energy over conventional sources of power. Coal- and oil-fired power stations pollute the atmosphere, day by day, and not just at the moment of a hypothetical disaster. Strip-mining of coal and the exploitation of oil reserves devastate huge areas of wilderness. Carbon dioxide emissions from the burning of fossil fuels hold the ominous potential for changing the earth's climate. Our cities and our lungs are dirty with soot. Acid rain (caused by fossil fuel emissions) decimates our forests and the wildlife in our lakes and streams. By contrast, nuclear energy seemed kind to the environment. In the mid-sixties I visited the snow-white Yankee Power Station, the first nuclear generating station in New England. It sat quietly in a green valley in western Massachusetts, spinning out nonpolluting kilowatts and being a good neighbor, unobtrusive and strangely beautiful, a vision of the City of Oz in a Berkshire dale. This, I thought, is the future.

During the next two decades, doubts began to grow. As nuclear reactors proliferated, the problem of radioactive wastes became especially intractable. Accidents at a number of plants instilled doubts about safety. It became increasingly clear that nuclear plants leaked radiation into our water and atmosphere. The partial meltdown at Three Mile Island, in 1979, sounded a death-knell for nuclear energy in America. The catastrophic explosion and fire at Chernobyl in the Soviet Union, in 1987, may have been the funeral. The Department of Energy has predicted tens of thousands of extra cancer deaths over the next fifty years as a result of radioactive fallout from Chernobyl. For many people this is an intolerable toll of human life, all the worse because the agent of death came invisibly on the wind.

In fact, Chernobyl-related deaths will be a tiny fraction of the 630 million cancer deaths that will occur worldwide during that same fifty-year interval. They may also be a small fraction of the deaths that will occur because of other toxic side-effects of technology, including pollution from conventional power stations. Nuclear power advocates say the Chernobyl statistics should be kept in perspective: that nuclear technology should be made safer, not abandoned. They point to the example of France, where a well-managed nuclear power system generates an abundance of clean, cheap energy. It may be true that nuclear power is indeed a "low-risk, high-dread" technology, but that is little comfort to the people who live near Chernobyl, or in the neighborhoods of existing nuclear stations. The level of risk evidenced by the accidents at Three Mile Island and

Chernobyl has become politically unacceptable in this country. No new nuclear plants are likely to be built in the United States for the next decade. And maybe never. Although many nations remain committed to the nuclear option, in America the golden age of nuclear power is over.

Or is it? A new kind of nuclear technology looms on the horizon: power from fusion. Present-day reactors generate energy by splitting apart the nucleus of uranium or plutonium atoms, a process called fission. In fusion technology, energy is produced by fusing together nuclei of deuterium and tritium, both forms of hydrogen. The fuel for fusion — hydrogen — is a component of water. It is cheap, inexhaustible, and available to all. A teaspoon of deuterium has the energy equivalent of three hundred gallons of gasoline. The amount of deuterium in a large swimming pool could supply a major city's electrical needs for a year. Unlike uranium and plutonium, deuterium is not radioactive, and tritium only mildly so (it will eventually be possible to do without tritium). The "ash" of the fusion reaction is the harmless gas helium.

Still, formidable problems remain to be solved before fusion energy becomes a practical reality. For the fusion reaction to occur, the fuel must be raised to a temperature of more than fifty million degrees Celsius. The trick is to contain the fuel while simultaneously heating it to these extreme temperatures. Two approaches show promise: containing the fuel with magnetic fields while heating it electrically; and heating tiny fuel pellets with powerful laser beams. (At the time of this writing, the so-called cold fusion process, which uses metallic crystals to catalyze fusion at room temperature, appears unfeasible.) Success may be decades away, but optimism is growing that commercial fusion power lies within our grasp. 10

Fusion: An inexhaustible energy resource for the twenty-first century. Clean, safe, cheap. Our Obedient Servant. The language used by the advocates of fusion is disturbingly familiar. The lion of technology and the lamb of nature lie down peaceably together. Swords beaten into plowshares. Will fusion solve our energy problems once and for all? Or will the Janus-faced cycle of promise and disillusionment begin again?

■   ■   ■

Monstrously expensive nuclear reactors sit idle at Seabrook, New Hampshire, and Shoreham, Long Island. The cost of the Shoreham plant has soared dozens and dozens of times over the original estimate, and now, after decades of planning and construction, some experts believe the best plan is simply to abandon the plant. Citizens of New Hampshire wonder how they will ever pay for the Brobdingnagian monster at Seabrook. The two plants are colossal concrete symbols of the intractable perils of mega-technology. One might also cite the B-1 bomber, a $280-million airplane that is so technologically sophisticated it seems to

Simple Way to Open an Egg

When you pick up morning paper (**A**), string (**B**) opens door of birdcage (**C**) and bird (**D**) follows bird-seed (**E**) up platform (**F**) and falls over edge into pitcher of water (**G**)–water splashes on flower (**H**), which grows, pushing up rod (**I**), caus- ing string (**J**) to fire pistol (**K**)–shot scares mon- key (**L**) who jumps up, hitting head against bumper (**M**), forcing razor (**N**) down into egg (**O**). Loosened shell falls into saucer (**P**).

Rube Goldberg™ and © of Rube Goldberg, Inc. Distributed by United Media.

have a hard time staying in the air (three planes crashed in the testing stage). Or the astronomically expensive Strategic Defense Initiative, a national defense scheme of such overwhelming complexity that many critics believe it can never work.

Rube Goldberg, where are you now that we need you?

Rube Goldberg was our philosopher of technical excess. His loony inventions, widely published in American newspapers between 1914 and 1964, helped keep our technological exaggerations in perspective. He is the only American to have his name become a dictionary word while still alive. A "Rube Goldberg" invention uses a ridiculously complicated mechanism to achieve a simple result. Every engineer or technical planner with responsibility for more than a million dollars of public money should be required to read the complete collection of Goldberg's cartoons.

15   Consider Goldberg's "Simple Way to Open an Egg Without Dropping It in Your Lap." When you pick up your morning paper an attached string opens the door of a bird cage. The bird exits, follows a row of seeds up a platform, and falls into a pitcher of water. The water splashes onto a flower and makes it grow, pushing up a rod attached by string to the trigger of a pistol. The report of the

pistol scares a monkey, who jumps up, hitting his head against a bumper, forcing a razor into the egg. The egg drops into an egg cup, and the loosened shell falls into a saucer.

Or how about "The New Household Collar-Button Finder." A man seeking his lost collar button plays "Home Sweet Home" on the oboe. A homesick goldfish is overcome by sadness and sheds copious tears, which fill the goldfish bowl and cause it to overflow onto a flannel doll. The doll shrinks, pulling a string attached to the power switch of an electromagnet. The magnet attracts an iron dollar attached to a thread, lifting a cloth that covers a still-wet painting of a dog bone. The dog licks the bone, gets sick from the paint, and goes looking for relief. He mistakes the collar button for a pill. When his teeth strike the hard brass button he gives a howl, alerting the man to the location of the missing item.

Goofy inventions like these entertained two generations of Americans, and kept us aware of our propensity for technological overkill. With zany good humor, Goldberg showed us how to laugh at our foolishness. He took a college degree in engineering, but cartooning was his life. His biographer, Peter Marzio, tells us that "despite his constant grumblings against the automatic life, Rube loved complex machinery. He marveled at its labor-saving potential, its rhythm, and even its beauty. But he also treasured simple human values and inefficient human pastimes such as daydreaming and laughing." Like most Americans, Goldberg loved and hated machines. According to Marzio, he was keenly aware of the modern dilemma: How can mechanization be introduced and used without demolishing the life-giving harmony between man and his environment. Goldberg knew that technology grows unwieldy because of our insatiable desire for the very latest inventions, at whatever the cost in money or frustration. He imagined an army of "Yokyoks," tiny green men with long, straight noses and red-and-yellow gloves, who carry an assortment of tools and go about fouling the works—clogging holes in saltshakers, causing pens and faucets to leak, blowing fuses, letting the air out of tires. Goldberg warned us against the "gadget-strewn path of civilization." The more complicated our machines become the more opportunities the Yokyoks have to drive us crazy. Yokyoks presumably love nuclear power stations, B-1 bombers, and Star Wars computers, love the super-abundance of opportunity for jamming valves, shorting circuits, causing leaks, and transposing bits and bytes.

If Rube Goldberg hadn't existed, we would have needed a Rube Goldberg to invent him. Certainly, we have no shortage of doomsayers who rail against the invidious influence of technology in our lives. But what made Rube Goldberg's critique of technology effective was his unabashed affection for machines. He did not wish to see the technical apparatus of modern civilization dismantled; he merely wanted to make room between the cogs for a little human fun. He resolves the American technological dilemma with a laugh. His inventions, for all their bizarre exaggeration, served simple human needs, things ignored by the overblown schemes of government and industry. Finding a lost collar button. Removing lint from wool. Getting gravy spots off a vest. Preventing cigar burns on carpets. And Goldberg didn't require megawatts and megabucks to accomplish these tasks. His machines employed rabbits, spaniels, old shoes, firecrackers, banana skins, frogs, string, umbrellas, leaky fountain pens, cheese, and balloons. His technological arsenal was the stuff of basement clutter and yard sales.

Rube Goldberg died in 1970 at the age of eighty-seven. If he were still alive, we could ask him to design a cheaper and more humane replacement for idle nuclear power stations, the B-1 bomber, and the Star Wars defense system. A good laugh at the result might help us find our way out of the quagmire of mega-technology.

TALKING ABOUT IT

Seeing Metaphor: Revealing and Concealing

1. Read this essay carefully, identifying the instances of metaphor. Choose several and explain how they work to help Raymo say what he is trying to say. (For example, in the first paragraph, the bluebird's song is "Pur-i-ty, pur-i-ty," and Raymo is describing how Thoreau and others felt that the train tainted the purity of the natural environment to which they were accustomed.)

2. Study the Goldberg cartoon Raymo describes. What level of technology does it parody? What makes the cartoon humorous? Is this type of humor possible with our current technology thirty years later?

Seeing Composition: Frame, Line, Texture, Tone

1. How does Raymo's voice change as this essay proceeds? What language choices contribute to the changes you hear as you read?

2. Raymo uses scenes/stories in this essay. Pick out two and explain how he moves into them, what they accomplish, and how he moves out of them.

Seeing Meaning: Navigating and Negotiating

1. What purpose does Leonardo da Vinci serve in this essay?

2. This essay is divided into three clear parts. What happens in each part, and how do the three work together to develop Raymo's points about the relationship of people and machines?

WRITING ABOUT IT

1. List every machine that you use. Then place each in one of the following two categories: "willing servants" that "increase your well-being and alleviate

drudgery"; or those with which you have a "love-hate affair." Read and discuss these lists in class. From that discussion, write an essay about your own ambivalent relationship with technology.

2. Go to the library and view some of the cartoons in a Rube Goldberg collection. Then either draw one of your own or verbally describe, as Raymo does, an invention that "uses a ridiculously complicated mechanism to achieve a simple result." Your purpose is to express visually and/or metaphorically your own exasperation with "technical excess." This writing/imaging could also be done collaboratively — two writers inventing, one drawing, one verbally describing. You could as a class make your own collection of cartoons representing the "technological exaggerations" or "overkill" of the 90s.

Our Machines, Ourselves

Jack Hitt, James Bailey, David Gelernter,
Jaron Lanier, and Charles Siebert

*This piece originally appeared as a forum titled "Our Machines,
Ourselves," in the May 1997 issue of* Harper's Magazine. *Jack Hitt is
a contributing editor at* Harper's Magazine; *he moderated the following discussion. James Bailey is former manager at Thinking
Machines Corporation and the author of* After Thought: The Computer Challenge to Human Intelligence *(1996). David Gelernter is
a computer science professor at Yale University and the author of*
The Muse in the Machine: Computerizing the Poetry of Human
Thought *(1994). Jaron Lanier is a computer scientist, composer, and
visual artist who coined the term "virtual reality." Charles Siebert
is a poet and journalist and the author of* Wickberby: An Urban
Pastoral *(1998).*

This month, in a conference room in midtown Manhattan, some measure of our humanity will be put to trial when Garry Kasparov, the world chess
champion, sits down for a rematch with Deep Blue, IBM's chess-playing computer,
which he narrowly defeated in a match last year. If the game indeed presents a
test of our humanity, it is one that is part of a long and anxious tradition. From
John Henry's fatal victory over a steam-powered mining machine to the square-
root showdowns between precocious mathematicians and first-generation cal-
culators, the only instinct that has proved more consistently human than our drive
to invent tools has been our need to demonstrate our superiority over them.

What, then, is at stake in the match? If Kasparov loses, are we all somehow
diminished? Will humanity have been defeated by its own machines or, having
had the wit to program a triumphant computer, will we once again declare the
supremacy of our inventive genius and so give to the loss the name of victory?

In the hope of analyzing the anxiety that attends this contest, *Harper's
Magazine* invited four humans to lunch — that very human invention — to discuss our machines, ourselves, and the post–Deep Blue future.

I. ASSAULTS ON OUR SPECIALNESS

JACK HITT: In February 1996, in Philadelphia, the world chess champion, Garry
Kasparov, played a six-game chess match against a computer named Deep
Blue. Although Deep Blue won the first game, beating Kasparov in thirty-
seven moves, Kasparov came back to win the match 4–2. The competition

seemed to catch the public's imagination in unusual ways, to stir hopes and fears that were sometimes hard for us to articulate. Why do you think we were so obsessed with this match?

JAMES BAILEY: We've been taught for centuries that rational thought is the height 5
of human achievement and that chess is the ultimate expression of rational thought. People playing chess are supposedly people at their mental best. So it makes sense that we'd be intrigued by the prospect of a machine beating a human at such a supposedly lofty pursuit.

DAVID GELERNTER: And chess itself is intrinsically fascinating. I'm not a good chess player, but I can't help noticing that it holds a certain allure. There are many writers and artists who have fallen under its sway, people like Marcel Duchamp and Vladimir Nabokov, who spent huge periods of their lives completely obsessed with the game.

HITT: Much of the reaction to the match in the press, and from people I spoke to, was one of anxiety. The fact that Deep Blue defeated Kasparov in the first game of the match and the prospect that a new and improved version of Deep Blue might win the rematch that's scheduled for this May—those are developments that many people have found personally threatening. Why is that?

CHARLES SIEBERT: There is a perception that our specialness—our humanness— has been taking it on the chin a lot lately. It seems that every day in the daily paper there's another assault on the essence of what a human being is. We find out chimps are 98 percent the same DNA as we are. A sheep is cloned, and people begin to think that this is all we are, an assemblage of biological juices—line them up the right way, and we can be reproduced. And so there's a tendency with this chess match to say, "Oh no, not this too!" It's part of our larger sense of an assault on our specialness.

JARON LANIER: People have an enormous amount of anxiety about what a person is. The better computers get at performing tasks that people find hard to do, the more that definition is threatened. It's the same question that drives all the fire around the abortion debate—the question of which things in the universe we consider to be enough like us to deserve our empathy, to deserve our moral support. I think ultimately it has to do with whether we define people in a sacred way or in a functional way.

SIEBERT: The hysteria over cloning is related to this very confusion. Is this all we 10
are? Are we this reducible and finite? In fact, we are not, but people are having a tough time accommodating these incursions on our spirituality.

BAILEY: Of course the chess match isn't really an incursion on our spirituality at all. We as a species made a decision at some point to define human uniqueness around our intelligence, our ability to do mind tasks, but I would argue that that decision was a mistake. That purported strut of uniqueness is about to get kicked out from under us, by Deep Blue, among other things, and that's certainly going to force us to come to some different understandings of what is uniquely human. It's going to be a painful process, but if in that process we come to understand that we're not essentially analytical beings, that our essence is something higher, then that's a positive development.

SIEBERT: I felt a kind of claustrophobia when I read about this chess match. I didn't feel threatened by Deep Blue's ability; I felt bothered by the idea that chess is a good measure of us. Chess is such a narrow prism through which to view our humanness that there's something almost offensive about it. It's just a game that we made up.

LANIER: And since computers are getting faster and faster, it's only a matter of time before a computer becomes world chess champion. Chess just happens to be a mental activity that people find very difficult. That's why we find it fascinating.

SIEBERT: There is something touching, though, in our reaction to this contest. To some extent, it is our way of embodying the otherness of the machine. In other words, this is an attempt on our part to anthropomorphize the computer. The chess match becomes *mano a mano,* even though it's really *mano a máchina.* We're assigning the computer almost human properties to help us embrace its otherness. And it's a difficult embrace.

15   BAILEY: One of the frustrations for me is that I don't think this *is* a story about *mano a silicio.* It's about a bunch of guys at IBM who by themselves had no chance of ever getting into an international chess tournament, and therefore chose to collaborate with a computer. The computer by itself also didn't have a chance of making it into an international chess game. But together they were able to go where neither of them could go alone. Now, the press is always going to see the story as Kasparov versus Deep Blue, but in reality it is Deep Blue *with* a team of us—a team of humans.

GELERNTER: It's true that the story does engender a certain amount of fear and hysteria, but there's a positive aspect to it too. There are a lot of people who get a kick out of seeing how smart we are. To be able to program a computer that is capable of doing what this computer does requires exceptionally clever guys.

BAILEY: I think it would be exciting if, in fact, the computer developed whole new ways of playing the game of chess. The machine would be interesting if it not only won but found new ways of winning. What makes chess so uninteresting is that it is dead. The chess pieces don't change their behavior, they don't adapt, they don't do anything differently because of where they are on the board. There are sixty-four squares and two players. Chess is a very small data problem. It's not something we need help with. It's not, to my mind, an unsolved problem in the world. People aren't dying for the lack of good chess play. And so while it's eye-catching, it's not important. I think that the real fun is going to come when these machines are put seriously to work at things we're bad at.

HITT: What's an example, James? What kinds of things are we bad at?

BAILEY: Well, we're starting to get a lot of very useful information about the planet we live on and its creatures and their behavior — information that comes from places like satellites, some of it in trivial form coming from checkout scanners and things like that. And we're helpless to deal with it. Increasingly, we don't have the ability to make sense of the trillions of pieces of information we receive each day — economic data, ecological data, even weather data. Computers are very good at examining these huge databases and noticing patterns that we are oblivious to.

GELERNTER: There's another aspect to this chess match that we have to be aware   20
of, and that is public relations. It would be good for people at large to know more about technology than they do, and the question is, How can you convey to them what the current state of the art is? If a computer produces a proof of the four-color theorem, let's say, that runs on for 300 million pages, and not even 2 percent of the world's mathematicians understand it, so what? But if it beats a chess grand master — that's something people can grasp. It seems to me we do well as a society when we let research flow. Research is good for us. And the sort of thing that gets people's attention is a contest. When the Soviets put the first satellite in orbit in the late Fifties, that was wonderful, because we wanted to beat them. Money flowed into science. Science is starving now. The public doesn't owe us a living. The question is, Can we do something that makes them interested in what we're doing? This is the sort of thing that gets people's attention.

II. STUCK IN THE STATIC PRESENT

HITT: How do the anxieties that people feel about this chess competition compare with the feelings or anxieties that people have felt at other moments in history about the machines they live with? Is this a new anxiety or just a new form of an old anxiety?

SIEBERT: I think it's a new form of an old anxiety, perhaps best summed up by this story I read recently about people who are defecting from modern life to go live with the Amish because — is this the age-old complaint? — the world is going too fast these days. One of them said that first we had the horse and buggy and then it was the automobile and now the world is going at an electronic speed. He said, "We're finding that people can't live at that speed. We're being crushed by the way we live." And I thought, What does that mean? The world is going at the same speed it ever did.

Human beings walk at the same speed they ever did. What people really mean when they say this is that our *things* are going a little faster than they used to, and the sadness is that we can't accompany them. I think it's a feeling of disappointment; we are left behind in the static present, a present that feels more static than it ever did because these computers go that much faster. In a way, it's the same complaint as the Victorians had about tool-and-die machines displacing a physical function, but computers seem more frightening to people because they perform an unseen work. Since the Industrial Revolution there's been a feeling of physical disappointment, one that has become inherent in the modern psyche. Now with the computer there comes a mental disappointment.

LANIER: But it's a disappointment that doesn't reflect reality. For people even to imagine that the human mind is slower than a computer reflects a profound misunderstanding of what minds are able to do. It's a misunderstanding that goes way back, and in order to understand it, you have to understand a bit about the history of artificial intelligence. The field of artificial intelligence has its roots in a paper written in 1950 by Alan Turing. He was a famous code breaker during World War II who worked with some of the earliest electronic computers. Turing figured that eventually we would reach a point where computers would become intelligent, and he reasoned that we would need a test to help us decide when that point is reached. What he ended up with was something called the Turing Test, in which a tester communicates with both a computer and a human via a screen and a keyboard. If the tester can't distinguish between them, Turing says, then the computer is intelligent. Deep Blue is just the latest step in the project that Turing started. Now, Turing's interpretation of his own thought experiment was that if you can't tell the computer from the person, it must mean that the computer has become more human-like. But, of course, there is another interpretation, which is that the person has become more computer-like.

GELERNTER: That's absolutely right. Turing set us off on an extremely superficial, behaviorist view of intelligence. He was willing to attribute intelligence — the capacity to think and understand and have mental states — to an electronic box, as long as the box behaved in a certain way.

25 BAILEY: I'm not so concerned with being able to replicate the wonders of human intelligence. What I would be very intrigued to see are forms of intelligence that are distinctly nonhuman, that solve the same problems human intelligence solves but in a way we humans never thought of. If Deep Blue totally revolutionizes the game of chess, if it comes up with whole new openings and approaches that render the existing methods obsolete, then that's exciting.

LANIER: In the computer-science community, there's a perspective, which is difficult to communicate to the outside world, that things are going to continue to change in our field at such a rapid rate that at some point something very dramatic will change about the fundamental situation of people in the universe. I don't know if I share that belief, but it's a widespread belief. In the mythology of computer science, the limits for the speed and capacity of computers are so distant that they effectively don't exist. And it is believed that as we hurtle toward more and more powerful computers, eventually there'll be some sort of very dramatic Omega Point at which everything changes—not just in terms of our technology but in terms of our basic nature. This is something you run across again and again in the fantasy writings of computer scientists: this notion that we're about to zoom into a transformative moment of progress that we cannot even comprehend.

SIEBERT: Filippo Marinetti, the Italian futurist, said in the Twenties that in about a hundred years the Danube would be flowing in a straight line at two hundred miles an hour, this being the effect of speed on the physical world. It's a confusion born of this disjuncture between our plodding sameness and the speed of the machines we make. There's a great line at the beginning of *The Hunchback of Notre Dame*. The priest looks out across at the cathedral and right behind him is a printing press, and he says that cathedrals are the handwriting of the past, but with the printing press everything will change. The proliferation of the written word shifted the burden of telling stories away from sculpture and cathedrals. So yes, inventions do shape the imperative behind various forms in the realm of art. But the impulse to make that art is the same. For example, a lot of people say that poetry's dead. Well, no. Poetry's quite alive, but the imperative behind what you say in poetry and how you say it has changed, because now you have printers and word processors and high-speed copiers, and you don't need rhyme as much as you once did. Rhyme originally existed so that you could lock a thought on the air and keep it.

GELERNTER: What you say about rhyme is relevant in the sense that rhyme is unquestionably a good memorization device and so it has heuristic value, particularly if you can't write. Nowadays, however, if you write a poem and it rhymes—and by "nowadays" I mean for the last several centuries—you're doing it for its own sake, because of the music of it. By the same token, when computers carry out various analytic tasks that we thought were uniquely human but we now see are not, we are able to refine our idea of what humanity really is. Humans will play chess even when no human has a hope of being the best chess player in the world, just as we continue to rhyme even though rhyming no longer serves any practical purpose. We do it for the fun of it, because we enjoy it.

LANIER: The reason I never became a chess fanatic is that I realized the game had a formal framework that would make it difficult to turn it into a purely aesthetic experience. Since it's a game with a formal sense of what winning is, it has limited options for creative extrapolation. There's no such thing as freestyle chess, in which making elegant moves is valued more highly than capturing your opponent's king—though that could be a serendipitous result of Deep Blue's success. In the old days, there was an idea that when you got good at chess, you knew you were at the outer reaches of a certain type of thought. There was an Olympian quality to it. After Deep Blue, you can no longer quite feel that way. Chess after Deep Blue becomes something like fencing—an aesthetic activity that can be enjoyed in a nostalgic way and as something that is good for the spirit, but one that no longer feels like exploring the outer edge of human ability. Chess becomes like karate after the nuclear bomb.

30   HITT: Does everything eventually lose its usefulness and become aesthetic?

LANIER: That's a wonderful thing. That should be considered a goal of life.

SIEBERT: I agree. This reminds me of the Industrial Revolution, when Carlyle and Schiller and the Romantics were all voicing their complaints about how these machines reduce us and how man will lose his soul standing before this repeated mechanization. Carlyle would invoke Greek culture all the time as his paradigm of a culture that had this moral imperative, in which art reached its peak. And the great response to Carlyle came from a Cincinnati-based lawyer, Timothy Walker. He said: That's preposterous. The reason why the Greeks reached the heights they did is because they dispatched all their physical work to slaves and they had time to sit around and think and achieve this higher aspect of themselves. And his argument was, the more we un-shoulder these burdens to our machinery, the more we become our essence.

LANIER: But we're doing the reverse of what the Greeks did. It's as if they had compelled their slaves to enjoy their philosophical whimsies and have their fun. We're assigning our philosophical thinking to the computers. When we talk about using artificial intelligences to choose what book we might want to read, then what we're doing is placing the burden of ourselves as philosophers onto these so-called intelligent agents.

HITT: We already do that. They're called magazine editors. You subscribe to a magazine because you like the intelligent agent who is editing the magazine and making choices for you.

35   GELERNTER: The term "intelligent agent" can legitimately be applied to an editor, but there is no machine or computer program to which the term can legitimately be applied. I mean, there's an important distinction between following some*body*'s advice and following some*thing*'s advice. Following a thing's advice is a lot lazier than following a person's advice.

BAILEY: I don't understand. Isn't there only the difference between following good advice and following bad advice?

LANIER: This gets us into very mysterious territory: trying to understand how communication can be possible in the first place. If you believe that a conversation between two people consists of objectifiable bits of information that are transmitted from one to the other and decoded by algorithms, then certainly what you said, James, is correct, and there's no difference. If you believe that meaning is something more mysterious than that, something that no one has yet been able to find a method of reducing, then you would not agree with your statement. I'm in the latter category. I think that the fundamental process of conversation is one of the great miracles of nature, that two people communicating with each other is an extraordinary phenomenon that has so far defied all attempts to capture it. There have been attempts made in many different disciplines — in cognitive science, in linguistics, in social theory — and no one has really made much progress. Communicating with another person remains an essentially mystical act.

III. SEVENTY-SEVEN NOSES UNDER THE TENT

HITT: When I think about the prospect of Deep Blue actually defeating Kasparov, for some reason I feel like we as a species would lose something. Somehow I feel like it would be a sad thing for us. Am I wrong?

LANIER: It is not a coincidence that at the same time science is improving its ability to simulate some tasks that we used to think of as being in the domain of the brain — like chess — we are also seeing a rise in religious fundamentalism around the world, a quest for an anchor of meaning and an anchor of identity. I think that those two events are linked. There is a fear of losing one's own grounding, one's own identity, as technologies become able to either simulate or perhaps take on human identity. Because if technology's capable of making you, of making a person or making a mind, then technology's also capable of making variants of you and betters of you. It becomes profoundly threatening.

GELERNTER: Anybody who looks at modern society and compares us to, let's say, 40 America in the Forties realizes that our technology is vastly more powerful, that we live a lot longer, we're a lot healthier, we're vastly richer, that our laws are better, that we've done all sorts of good things — but life has gotten worse. It's absolutely clear that the texture of society has tended to unravel in recent decades. It's not technology that's caused the unraveling, but people are worried that the unravelers keep winning.

HITT: Isn't that the fear that I'm talking about?

GELERNTER: Absolutely. People are afraid when they see software do incredibly powerful new things, because they say that this world that software built stinks. It's great in all sorts of material ways, but it's a spiritual and moral wasteland. It may not be a cultural wasteland, but certainly it's culturally inferior to what this country was fifty years ago.

BAILEY: If we are, in fact, going through a cultural transition of many-century scale, if, in fact we are leaving a machine age and an industrial age and moving into an information age, then there's a lot of unraveling to be done. There are going to be a lot of raw nerves. But I think it's a positive development that a lot of old assumptions tied to the industrial age are loosening. Life is no longer as hierarchical as it has been for thousands of years. It's more democratic. It's more parallel. That's progress.

GELERNTER: But people are aware of the fact that they're losing something. It's not the fault of technologists that they're losing it, but they certainly associate it with technology.

45   HITT: How are those two things connected, our advances in technology and our increasing disappointment?

GELERNTER: Technologists do their job when they build the best machines they can and make them available to us. That's what they're supposed to do and that's what they in fact do. They don't make choices for us about how we should use the machines they've built. Ruskin made famous statements in the nineteenth century about the railroad. He said, Everybody's streaking here and there on the railroad, but there was always more in the world than men could see, walk they ever so fast. And what the hell are they going to gain by going faster? Now, the existence of the railroad doesn't mean that Ruskin can't take a walk in his backyard; he can. The technologists have accomplished something useful — they've made people richer, they've made people happier in a lot of ways — but people don't feel the spiritual strength to turn down technology in the cases where it diminishes rather than makes better the texture of their lives. Technology is a constant temptation to them. People don't like to live being constantly tempted. They don't like to be given these tough choices all the time. And technology never lets up. It's one tough choice after another.

SIEBERT: So would you rather live in a world without technology?

GELERNTER: Absolutely not. I'm not against technology. I'm explaining why I think it upsets people, makes them melancholy, depresses them. If I had a vote I'd vote for this world over a nontechnology world, but I can understand why it's an upsetting world to live in.

BAILEY: I think the reason that Deep Blue's success is so troubling to us is the fact that we're all carrying around a backlog of evidence that a new information world is aborning and an old industrial world is dying, and it's evidence that we're having trouble coming to terms with. Eventually a camel's nose is going to get under the tent that causes us not just to recognize that *that* nose is there but to go back and relook at the other seventy-seven noses that are also poking into the tent. Deep Blue really has the potential to break this conceptual logjam, to force each of us to acknowledge not just that chess has changed but that many other things have changed as well.

IV. A NEW *WUTHERING HEIGHTS* EVERY WEEK

HITT: I think what's truly, profoundly disturbing about the Deep Blue contest is   50
that for most of this last aeon, we have thought that where our individuality, where our humanness resided was precisely where Deep Blue is now moving in.

BAILEY: One of the things that make people unique is the profound desire to *believe* that we're unique. We're always hanging our sense of our uniqueness on something, and over the past couple of centuries a lot of people have hung it on rational thought. Bad place to hang it, but that's where they hung it.

GELERNTER: But is it clear that rational thought is reducible to chess playing? I think that most people, if they thought about it carefully, would not believe that what's going on in the computer is anything like what goes on in their head, whether it wins the chess match or not.

SIEBERT: What goes on in a human head is not, in the end, entirely knowable; we make stabs at expressing it, in art and novels and poems, but it's not replicable. I'll use Nabokov's account of his own work. He talks about what an epiphany is: He's walking down the street, the sun hits a leaf on a tree above him in a certain way at the same time that he remembers his mother, and then a carriage goes by — it's a compacted moment, the meaning of which is not readily apparent to the person who had the moment. He describes the art process as a dismantling and reassembling of the moment with such suppleness and simultaneity that the reader gets some approximation of the very experience that moved the artist. If one day a computer could do that kind of decoding of the simultaneity of inspiration and perception, *then* I would feel melancholy.

GELERNTER: But even if it could do that, you still wouldn't necessarily want to attribute thought to it, would you? You wouldn't think that it had any beliefs or any desires or any feelings or any of the content that your own internal mental landscape does. I mean, would any kind of behavior that a machine showed convince you that it had mental states in the sense that you do?

SIEBERT: No, because all you could do to get a computer to do that is give it the   55
information with which to spit it back. And then you would have a simulacrum of the thing, and it's a pale, lifeless, bloodless imitation.

GELERNTER: Right, even if it were a *great* imitation. If you were to get a computer to write beautiful novels and everybody loved them, that might be good. We don't have that much of a novelist shortage, but let's say we did — that still wouldn't necessarily convince you that what the computer was doing was comparable to what a human being does.

BAILEY: But if they're beautiful novels, who cares?

GELERNTER: It's strictly an emotional issue. It has no pragmatic significance. If the computer can write a better novel than I can, fine, read the computer's novel. It's an emotional issue of where does humanness lie, and do we think this object is like us or do we just think it's a tremendously valuable machine.

HITT: Would the fact that a computer was writing beautiful novels affect you?

60   GELERNTER: Absolutely. I'm sure it would change my feeling about the culture. It wouldn't change my feeling about the essence of humanness or the capabilities of software. But on a pragmatic level, we build machines to do things that are useful. And writing novels is one useful thing. People get pleasure and satisfaction from reading novels. Most novels are no good, so if the average quality of novels got better and I knew that I could go into any newspaper store and pick up a novel that was as good as my favorite novel, that was the artistic equivalent of *Wuthering Heights,* let's say, then that's great, because then instead of just one *Wuthering Heights* I can get a new *Wuthering Heights* every week.

LANIER: Wait, wait, wait. Are you speaking sarcastically or seriously when you say that?

GELERNTER: It's a thought experiment. I don't think it's a likely outcome.

LANIER: To me your statement is like a *reductio ad absurdum* of positivism, of this idea that humanity is reducible. If there were in fact a different *Wuthering Heights* every week, *Wuthering Heights* would lose meaning.

GELERNTER: I'm not willing to rule out on logical grounds that software could be made to write novels that I would enjoy as much or that would move me or interest me or grip me as much as *Wuthering Heights.* I think it's extremely unlikely, I would bet against it, but I don't rule it out logically. Even if it were to be accomplished, though, I wouldn't wind up attributing thought to the computer that did it and it wouldn't wind up changing my estimation of what humanity and humanness are.

65   SIEBERT: I would think of it as a kind of game. It wouldn't threaten my humanity. I would think, Why do we need it?

GELERNTER: Even if a novel were, in some objective sense, plotted so well, written so tightly, that there was nothing objective to distinguish between it and *Wuthering Heights,* I could also say that ultimately I read a novel for human communication. I want to hear from another human being. And no matter how brilliant the language is, no matter what kind of proof you can give me that it's a great novel, if I know that it's not a human being who's communicating with me I shrug it off.

HITT: Would it be a fulfilling moment or not, going into that store and buying this brand-new *Wuthering Heights*? If a computer gives you a great novel every week, a novel that you really want to read, wouldn't that make you happy?

GELERNTER: It wouldn't give you a great novel.

HITT: Well, what if it could?

GELERNTER: I don't really think it is conceivable except technically. It could be   70 achieved in a technical way but not in a way that has any meaning in human terms.

LANIER: The moment you start believing that automatically generated media has as much meaning as human-generated media is the moment that you enter a Zen monastery for a couple of years to get in touch with your humanity again. This gets us back to the Turing Test's fatal flaw: if you accept computer-written novels, has the computer been elevated or has your humanity been reduced?

HITT: What is the distinction between writing novels and playing chess? Why do we believe that Deep Blue is going to beat Kasparov sometime in the next year or five years but don't believe that any computer is ever going to be able to write convincing novels?

LANIER: I don't think anybody said that. It might very well write convincing novels. But we'll never be able to say that for certain, so the question is not a productive one. You can say for sure that a computer has won a chess game, but you can't say for sure that a computer has written a good novel. Aesthetic judgments rely on the preferences of human beings, who can be supremely flexible and accommodating.

GELERNTER: This thing could beat Kasparov, and I could look at its winning game and say, This doesn't move me, I'm not able to consider this beautiful the way I consider Kasparov's game beautiful. I mean, chess doesn't speak to me, I don't consider it a form of communication, because I don't know it well enough, but I could imagine that if a grand master looked at a chess game as the manifestation of a particular style, of a particular personality, of a particular way of attack, then he would feel a certain emptiness when he looked at the brilliant winning games of Deep Blue. It really depends on how you evaluate the objects that you deal with. Some of them you evaluate simply as objects, and some of them you value because they're forms of human communication and people like to communicate with each other. If there's no person at the other end, ultimately the object is meaningless. With a synthetic novel, you could read the whole thing thinking that a human being wrote it and enjoy it, and when you found out that a human being didn't write it, you would feel betrayed and no longer able to think of it as a thing of beauty in any sense.

BAILEY: I don't think I would feel betrayed. I think I would feel intrigued. There is   75 a separate ecology, if you will, of these machines that is different from ours. Computers talk to each other in ways that are different from the ways we talk to each other. We can ascribe meaning to our communications and no meaning to their communications—that's fine. But I think as their separate ecology grows into something quite formidable and quite productive, particularly as it begins to do things that we wish we could do but can't, simply because we're wired differently, then that is both valuable and intriguing. Blotches of color that are placed on a canvas by a set of electronic circuits are different from blotches of color that are placed on a canvas by a human being, but they're both intriguing.

V. A VERY LONELY ENTITY

HITT: From what I seem to hear, what you all would define as special about human beings is our ability to communicate. In other words, it doesn't seem to trouble you that a computer might be able to replicate almost any human thought process, including writing a novel. You can say that playing chess is the highest human act, or that writing a novel is, or creating art, but if you agree that all of those acts could be simulated in some way so that we would be confused by the end product, then is the only source of human specialness the fact that we can communicate among ourselves?

LANIER: I would define human specialness as follows: What's special about people is that we're conscious, and we have faith in the possibility that we might be able to contact other consciousnesses.

HITT: What do you mean by conscious?

LANIER: That's an interesting question. Consciousness is the slipperiest subject imaginable. It's the hardest thing to talk about. Consciousness is the experience of experience itself. It's not empirically verifiable. It's the only thing that can be shared that can't be shared objectively. One could have a device that looks at the neurons in my brain that are doing the activity of treasuring my consciousness and re-creates the activity of those neurons in a computer so that the computer could be said to be treasuring my consciousness, but consciousness still wouldn't be there. You can simulate every damn thing about the interior of the brain except for consciousness itself.

80   SIEBERT: Maybe we keep trying to assign human qualities to these machines because we feel so lonely. Consciousness is a very lonely entity. Why did our DNA tipple over into an ability to comment on our own DNA? I mean, let's just take the Garden of Eden. Adam and Eve took of the forbidden fruit. Well, we *had* the forbidden fruit to begin with: it's self-knowledge. It's as if we have to keep making up stories about why the other DNA assemblages on this planet don't sit around and argue with themselves, don't

have this isolating, lonely capacity to think in this way. Maybe what we're doing with computers is trying to give this loneliness to something else.

LANIER: So we'll be satisfied when we see some computers sitting miserably in a French café bemoaning their sorry fate.

SIEBERT: Exactly!

BAILEY: To me what makes us unique is our humanity. And if people choose to isolate that in something they call logical thought or consciousness, they can go ahead, but things like Deep Blue seem to be undercutting that idea. It's hard for me to understand how qualitatively the argument for tying humanity to consciousness is stronger than the old argument of tying humanity to rational thought, or the one before that of tying humanity to being at the center of the universe. So I'm stuck there: I know we're unique because of our humanity. I can't subdivide it.

HITT: There is a sense of despair, though, in watching technology gobble up what we do. People feel bewildered by the fact that machines not only can do so much of what humans can do but also can perform these almost magical tasks, repairing broken organs and so on. It does reduce us to a sense of medieval magic, a sense that we're inhabiting this world run by either somebody or something else. I think that's the source of a lot of people's anxiety about the encroaching ideal of the computer.

SIEBERT: Because my father was a tool-and-die man, I had a real personal in- 85 volvement in this myth of our remaking. He was very enthusiastic about progress, and I used to think about the pathos behind a man being enthusiastic about the machines that make the machines that will eventually make obsolete his own job. But he taught me early on that this is what we humans do. I remember the first time I went behind the TV set for something that had fallen there and looking at that little cityscape of tubes and smelling that warm acrid electricity that comes out. It was this numinous world, and it was quite incredible. It was a seminal moment for me in my childhood. But as I've looked back at that moment, I've realized that the inherent sadness in it was that my father spent his whole life selling two or three of the parts in that television set. I went to the tool-and-die convention last year in Chicago. I wanted to see the evolution of the myth of our remaking. Die machines used to look like mechanical men, but now all the armature's gone and it's just a box with a window lit from within. All you saw in booth after booth was a man in a smock pushing a button. The work happened inside, and through the window you could see it being washed down and cooled off, and the water spraying up. It was like a TV screen. And I went to another booth and it was just robot arc welders that looked like little gooseheads coming up, talking to each other briefly, coming back down. And at one point these three human arc welders came up—they had their union hats on—and they watched the part get dropped off in the bin, and they picked it up and they said, "Pretty damn good." And they walked off. What do these guys do? They've been displaced, and there's a kind of sadness in that, but, hey, this is evolution.

HITT: If people feel anxiety when they think about this chess match, is there another way for us to suggest that they think about it, another paradigm, another myth that is either a more positive or a more realistic one?

LANIER: A number of ideas have been presented in the conversation already. One of them is to say, Isn't it great how these clever people who themselves couldn't beat Kasparov could think of a way to write a program that could. Another way is to say, Isn't it magical how humanity persists even as we try to isolate what we thought made it up.

BAILEY: That's a very powerful statement: the more you think you chip away at our humanity, the more it's there. That's a very positive and very nourishing idea: Humanity is not at stake in this. Old ideas, old oversimplified ideas, are at stake, but that's good. Humans and computers are going to make a good team.

SIEBERT: We argue with our biology, and the result of that argument is civilization. That is what is unique about what we do. Sometimes the result is a Bach fugue, sometimes it's a glorious building. That's it, that's us, and it's amazing.

TALKING ABOUT IT

Seeing Metaphor: Revealing and Concealing

1. "Our Machines, Ourselves," is a conversation among five men about the significance of the chess matches between the computer, Deep Blue, and the grand chessmaster, Garry Kasparov. The men conversing speak in metaphors throughout. Choose several that interest you. What do they reveal about how these men perceive the relationship among machines, science, and humanity?

2. Throughout this forum, computers are personified. For example, Jaron Lanier says, "So we'll be satisfied when we see some computers sitting miserably in a French café bemoaning their sorry fate." What might personifying computers enable these men to reveal as well as conceal about their feelings toward these machines?

Seeing Composition: Frame, Line, Texture, Tone

1. "Our Machines, Ourselves," is framed as a conversation, a forum. Does that conversation develop smoothly? Knowing conversations as you do from your own experience, what do you think Jack Hitt, the moderator, has done to make the conversation work well? What evidence of his shaping can you find in the text?

2. There are five clear voices resounding from these pages. What are they like? How do they flavor this discussion? How might this discussion have been different were it written by one person?

Seeing Meaning: Navigating and Negotiating

1. For these men, and many people, Deep Blue is symbolic of a new and major shift in the relationship of humans and machines. Do you see in Deep Blue what these men see?

2. In the rematch that this conversation preceded, Deep Blue did beat Garry Kasparov. What, according to this conversation, was at stake in that loss or victory? Do you think humanity is endangered by its own machines?

WRITING ABOUT IT

1. "Deep Blue" is a richly suggestive name for a computer. In class, list all the ideas and feelings that this metaphor suggests. From the class list, choose those associations that resonate most strongly with your own attitudes and experience. Write about why these appeal to you more than others that were named. Then try to answer the following question: if you were responsible for creating a name symbolic of the relationship of humans and machines, what might you substitute for "Deep Blue"? Why?

2. Imagine yourself sitting on the stage (which is set up like a table in a cafeteria), talking to these men. Where would you place yourself as a character in the conversation? Write that dialogue. Then read your dialogues to each other for the purpose of hearing each other's voices among the characters in "Our Machines, Ourselves." As an alternative or follow-up writing task to explore ideas and genre, you might as a class, or writing group, create your own symposium in which you participate in a written dialogue about "Our Machines, Ourselves." Two or more writers in the group or class could, as Jack Hitt does, both direct (edit) and converse.

Turn Signals Are the Facial Expressions of Automobiles

DONALD NORMAN

Donald Norman is a cognitive psychologist who has written several books, including Things That Make Us Smart: Defending Human Attributes in the Age of the Machine *(1993) and* The Psychology of Everyday Things *(1988). This piece was originally published by Norman in his 1992 book of the same name.*

Nature produces a varied assortment of creatures. One that has long fascinated me is the red-tailed baboon. You know, the one with the, umm, red-colored rear? All that color and display, but for what purpose? Well, looking at the rear end of some automobiles reminds me of looking at the rear end of some baboons.

Social cooperation requires signals, ways of letting others know our actions and intentions. Moreover, it is useful to know the reactions of others to our actions: How do others perceive them? The most powerful method of signaling, of course, is through language. Emotions, especially the outward signaling of emotions, play equally important roles. Emotional and facial expressions are simple signal systems that allow us to communicate to others our own internal states. In fact, emotions can act as a communication medium within an individual, helping bridge the gap between internal, subconscious states and conscious ones.

As I study the interaction of people with technology, I am not happy with what I see. In some sense, you might say, my goal is to socialize technology. Right now, technology lacks social graces. The machine sits there, placid, demanding. It tends to interact only in order to demand attention, not to communicate, not to interact gracefully. People and social animals have evolved a wide range of signaling systems, the better to make their interactions pleasant and productive. One way to understand the deficiencies of today's technologies and to see how they might improve is to examine the route that natural evolution has taken. You know the old saying that history repeats itself, that those who fail to study the lessons of history are doomed to repeat its failures? Well, I think the analogous statement applies to evolution and technology: Those who are unaware of the lessons of biological evolution are doomed to repeat its failures.

Evolution works its way slowly, ponderously. Even those who believe that it progresses in rapid jumps think that these jumps take tens of thousands of years. By the standards of the individual human, even the most rapid evolutionary changes are too slow to have any impact on the individual. But the study of evolution might aid us as we design artificial devices, enabling us to profit from evolution's experiences, letting us accomplish in years what has taken millennia for evolution. Over time, evolution tries out a wide variety of methods to ensure survival, some that modify the animal or plant, others that modify behavior, and still others that affect the cooperative, interacting nature of social structures. The female baboon's red rear is one result of this process, as are other signaling systems, such as the calls and cries of animals and the gestures, facial expressions, and the speech of humans. We can learn from evolution's successes.

ANIMAL SIGNALS

Animals require a number of different signaling systems to communicate   5 internal states both within themselves and to others. Plants signal their maturation and ripening through colorful displays that attract the attention of insects and birds, the better to pollinate and propagate their seeds. These signals need not be consciously given or received to be effective. All that matters is that there be some perceivable change of state that other organisms can make use of. Thus the presence of snow, ice, and objects waving in the wind signal a state of weather without any conscious volition on the part of the atmosphere. But the signals, nonetheless, are valuable ones.

The red rear of the baboon is certainly not a conscious signal, and for that matter, neither are many of our facial expressions. Facial expressions originated as side effects of the facial muscles as they prepared the mouth, lips, and teeth for activity. But as they were perceived and used by other animals, they began to evolve toward a symbolic, meaningful role, so much so that today many of our facial expressions are voluntary, conscious, and deliberate.

Facial and body expressions have evolved because they serve a useful purpose. The signaling of intentions and internal states among animals works to their advantage. The importance of facial expressions was recognized quite early in the study of animal evolution. Charles Darwin devoted an entire book to their study — *Expression of the Emotions in Man and Animals.* Emotional expressions act as a side channel of normal communication, outside of and without interference to the spoken language. They offer a commentary, and when this information channel is lost, ambiguity and difficulty in interpretation often results.

Social interaction requires a very different set of behavior patterns than does solitary action. Successful social interaction means cooperation, joint planning, troubleshooting, play, rivalry, competition, and comradeship. It means social honesty as well as deception. If animals — including people — are to form functional social groups, they must develop means of communication, of synchronizing actions, of cooperation, and occasionally, of deceit. Social interaction was the driving force for the evolutionary development of social signaling devices. Facial expressions, colorful plumages, the red tail of the baboon — all are social signals useful to the communication, interaction, and protection of animals.

There are many controversies surrounding the development of human intelligence. The traditional views link the development of intelligence to language or tools, or perhaps to the need to be flexible and innovative in dealing with a changing, complex environment. There is much to be said in favor of all these possibilities. Recently, however, a new suggestion has emerged: Higher forms of intelligence result from the need to handle the problems of social interaction. This is an attractive notion, for social interaction requires numerous talents and abilities, including the ability to let selected participants in a social group know the intentions and beliefs of others. Human intelligence almost certainly did not result from any single factor. It is most likely the result of multiple forces acting over long durations, but social interaction seems like a good candidate to be one of the primary forces.

10   One of the important aspects of intelligence is the ability to communicate. There are actually two levels of communication that we need to be concerned about: one is internal, between the body and the conscious mind; the other is external, among animals and people. Internal signals are very important for the individual. Thus the body informs the mind when it is experiencing heat or cold, injury or chemical imbalance. The results are subjective feelings of warmth or chill, pain or discomfort. Emotions also serve as internal signals: from happiness, pleasure, and love, to sadness, anger, envy, and dissatisfaction. Emotions are complex mixtures of biological and mental states, the neurochemistry of the brain interacting with the information processing of events and expectations.

How many times have you been in situations where your mind tells you one thing and your body another? How often have you delayed a decision, saying "I want to think about it," but really meaning, "I want to see how I feel."

Some people believe that emotions are a vestige of evolution, a type of "animal" behavior that the human race will eventually outgrow. Well, not really. If you look at the role emotions have played in evolutionary history, it would appear that the more sophisticated the animal, the greater the role played by emotions. We are the most sophisticated of all, and thereby the most emotional.

Emotions speak to our cognitive minds, sometimes telling our conscious selves things we would rather not know. Emotions also trigger body changes and facial expressions that signal others. Moreover, because other people in our social circle are apt to share similar backgrounds, the same basic knowledge, and the same biological mechanisms, we can assume that things that make us happy or angry are apt to make them happy or angry as well. Taking the point of view of another would be aided if only we could read the mind of the other, and this is where external signals come in.

How do we tell what others are thinking? We do so through a variety of techniques, with varying degrees of accuracy. Facial expressions, gesture, and body position act as cues to a person's internal states. We often call these things body language, the name indicating the communicative role. Body language makes visible another's internal state. The blush of the cheeks, the grimace, the frown, and the smile all act as readily perceivable external signals of a person's internal state, making visible to observers what would otherwise be difficult or impossible to determine.

Of course, facial expressions can deceive. First of all, they are subtle, a rich   15 interplay of complex musculature, facial features, and coloration. Body language is even more complex. Not everyone can read the signals, and for that matter, not all scientists are convinced that the signals are there. When I cross my legs, am I sending a subtle message or am I simply trying to get comfortable?

The study of human emotions, of course, is a complex topic, one that has occupied psychologists for years. We are learning a lot about the neurochemistry of emotions. We know that there is a complex interplay between the neurological state of arousal and the cognitive interpretation of the state. One long-standing argument is over the ordering: Which comes first, the emotional state or the interpretation? One side of the argument says that, essentially, you first notice your body's emotional state and then interpret it: "Oh, oh. My heart is pounding. I feel tense. I'm sweating — I must be afraid." The other side says no, the interpretation leads to the state: "I have to give a really important presentation tomorrow. I'm not ready. I can imagine everyone looking at me, their eyes registering skepticism. I'm afraid. There, see: My heart is pounding. I feel tense. I'm sweating." Both sides of the debate have merit, which means that the true story is probably a combination of these two different views. To the onlooker, however, it doesn't matter how the emotional state has been aroused. The facial expressions and other body signs are external indicators of the resultant state.

To speak only of the body signaling the conscious mind is a great simplification. Nonetheless, simplification is a useful starting point, useful and scientifically reasonable. Moreover, one person's interpretation of another's mental state really does depend upon this information. Of course, the visible signs of emotion are often ambiguous, incomplete, and misleading, but so too are our judgments. Our interpretations of another's feelings and beliefs are not very accurate and often are misleading.

ANIMAL DECEIT

The fact that facial expressions and spoken language can be used to communicate internal states is useful, both for conveying accurate information and for the deliberate deception of others. I can appear happy when in fact I am not, feign sadness for an event that pleases me, or disguise my knowledge in a variety of ways. The study of deceit in animals is a powerful way to get clues about their level of intelligence, clues to the working of evolution. As a result, there is an ever-increasing number of studies concentrating upon the evolution of deceit, the false communication of knowledge, intentions, and actions. Deceit seems a natural property of higher animals, and not just to protect the young from predators. Chimpanzees, for example, use deceit to avoid sharing food, to curry favor with higher-ranked animals, and to obtain sexual favors behind the backs of disapproving higher-ranked males. These kinds of deceits may very well require more intelligence and cleverness than truthful communication.

Deceit is a necessary part of civilized life — not the evil deceit where one person seeks to benefit at the expense of another, but the polite deceit of social interaction. The polite "thank you" when someone presents an unwanted gift, or the polite acknowledgments when someone else's well-intentioned efforts go awry at your expense. Social interactions require falsehoods to maintain themselves, and little benefit would result were every negative thought transmitted to others. Mind reading may seem like a desirable trait, but it would often backfire, causing grief where none was intended or desired. All societies and cultures have developed social codes that govern interactions and mask true feelings and beliefs under a cloud of cordiality or, at least, civility. The elaborate honorifics and "speech acts" of society exist for good reason.

20   Lies and deceits have their place in the world. Social interaction would be less pleasant if the truth were always told. Casting blame on the other person is an excellent administrative policy. When I need to make an unpopular decision, I sometimes blame my administration — "I'm sorry, but my Dean won't let me do that" — checking first with my Dean, of course, to make sure that my stand is understood and approved of. In turn, I advise the people who work for me to use the same tactic, to tell others that they are sorry, but their boss won't allow it. In fact, it works in both directions. When my Dean wants to resist an order from above, he can call the department chairs that report to him and get us all to allow him to say, "Sorry, but my departments won't agree."

Social interaction is complex. We are the most social of all animals, and we have evolved elaborate schemes for interactions, schemes that allow us to coexist and cooperate with friends and to resist the pressures of enemies. The act of deceit is complex, and most animals are incapable of it, not because they are more honest but because their brains are inadequate. Only the most sophisticated of beings can lie and cheat, and get away with it.

There is, by now, a large research literature on the abilities of monkeys and other animals to deceive. One of the marks of evolutionary development is the evolution of "social artifacts," the ability to use social interactions and strategies for cooperation and for deceit, all to the betterment of the social group. It was a relatively late development in evolutionary history. Among the animals that are capable of practicing social cooperation, the human is superior at forming tight social bonds as well as in using the social deceits necessary for cohesive social structures.

Only the most advanced of primates, the ape family (which includes the gorilla and the chimpanzee), seems capable of true deceit. Monkeys sometimes try, but it is a bit too much for their minds to manage. Look at this description of an African monkey, the vervet, trying to deceive his rivals:

> A male vervet, Kitui, gave leopard alarms when challenged by a rival male, causing the other male to flee up a tree.

That is real deception: To get rid of his rival, Kitui called the monkey equivalent of "Fire! Fire!" The problem is, the monkey couldn't quite pull it off.

> However, to reinforce his point, Kitui descended from his own tree and walked across the open ground toward his rival, still calling the equivalent of "Run for the trees." . . . [This is like] a human three-year-old who with crumbs all over his face denies having raided the cookie jar.

Notice that the vervet is intelligent enough to give a false signal in order to   25 scare away a rival but not intelligent enough to act out the entire behavior. It doesn't really matter for vervets because the rival male isn't sophisticated enough to see through the ruse, to realize that Kitui's behavior indicates that the call is a fake. Young children will make the same type of error that Kitui made, but parents are quite capable of seeing through the deception. So, for this kind of intelligent behavior, a vervet is acting somewhat like a young child.

Notice what Kitui would need to realize in order to do the ruse correctly: He would have to know not only that the leopard alarm would cause the rival to flee but that his own behavior must be in accord with the falsely announced state. The animal needs to know not only what a signal means but how its signal and its own behavior will be interpreted by others, and then to understand that one can contradict the other and that others can perceive this contradiction.

A chimp wouldn't be fooled by Kitui. Thus a chimp has been seen using his fingers to readjust his mouth in order to hide a grin before turning to bluff a rival. This behavior shows that the chimp is aware of his own facial expression, aware that it is visible to rivals, and probably aware of how the rival will interpret the expression. I have seen the same behavior in adult humans.

ARTIFICIAL DEVICES AND ARTIFICIAL EVOLUTION

As we construct artificial devices with ever more power, ever more intelligence, perhaps we will have to make them mimic natural evolution. Technology slowly evolves, not in the same way as the natural evolution of life but through the artificial evolution of design. But in many ways, the evolution of machines is driven by the same pressures that drive the evolution of life. Modifications that enhance performance and allow the organism or machine to survive and to compete in the world will survive; those that do not will disappear. Slowly, designers will add signals and warnings, self-assessments and communication devices, providing the artificial equivalents of emotions, facial expressions, and social interaction.

Natural evolution combined with cultural conventions determine the nature and interpretation of the facial expressions of people. Machines pose an interesting problem, for they are artificial devices, manufactured by people. It is the rare machine that works entirely alone, isolated from other machines and from people. Machines have to be started, stopped, monitored, adjusted, and maintained by people. Many require considerable control by humans. Machines are social devices, for their manufacture results from interaction with people. As a result, some of the same pressures that gave rise to facial and emotional expressions in animals apply to machines as well, except that here, the signals have to be designed, deliberately constructed, and integrated into the machine. The lights and sounds of an automobile play a role analogous to the facial expressions of animals, communicating the internal state of the vehicle to other vehicles in its social group.

30   With animals and people, we saw that there were two different forms of signals: internal and external. The same is true for machines, except here, we have to readjust our idea of the basic "unit" of analysis. For a person or animal, I distinguished between the body and the mind. Internal signals informed the conscious mind of the subconscious information: body states such as hunger, fatigue, and comfort as well as emotional states such as fear, joy, or anger. With a machine, there is no such thing as the conscious mind — but there is the user.

Machines can be regarded as symbiotic units consisting of a machine and a person. Thus a copying machine forms a functional unit only when combined with a person: person + copying machine. Similarly, the automobile by itself is not functional: The critical unit is driver + car. The person has the same relationship to the machine as consciousness has to the body: a supervising element that watches over and maintains the system, even as the system — human or machine — sometimes operates relatively autonomously. This is a dangerous metaphor to pursue deeply, for it fails in all sorts of ways, but it does have useful characteristics with regard to the way in which the machine ought to interact with people.

Just as animals have two levels of signals, internal and external, there are two levels of interaction of this person + machine unit — one internal, the other external. Internal signals in a person tell of body states, but in the person + machine unit, they tell the person about the internal states of the machine. A machine signaling a person isn't really the same as a body conveying internal information to consciousness. The machine is performing a form of social communication between it and an outside agency, the person who is using or maintaining it. So the signals between machine and human have to be a combination of external, social signals and internal ones: internal to the unit of person + machine but external in the sense that the machine and the person are separate entities.

One of the special kinds of signals that this relationship requires is feedback about the operation itself. It is difficult to use a machine that does not provide feedback to the user. Mechanical devices tend to do this through their construction. A pair of scissors feels firm or loose: Its blades snip-snap through the air with a pleasant sound, or scrape, moving only with great force. Or they might wobble, providing a sense of insecurity. A good knife provides feedback through its balance and feel as it cuts. Mechanical devices are often visible and audible, conveying considerable information about their operation, even to those who know nothing of mechanics. The designers do not have to provide feedback to the users. The very nature of the machine guarantees that.

Not so with electronic devices. Electronic devices work quietly and smoothly, invisible and inaudible. At most, one might get a hum, buzz, or crackling sound resulting from components that vibrate with changes in magnetic fields or from heating and cooling. These sounds, however, are peripheral to the operation and seldom convey useful information. But more important to the user is that electronic systems deal with information, not mechanical movements. Information is a commodity that exists conceptually, not physically. It occupies no space, makes no sound.

One of the reasons that modern technology is so difficult to use is because   35 of this silent, invisible operation. The videocassette recorder, the digital watch, and the microwave oven — none is inherently complicated. The problem for us is their lack of communication. They fail to interact gracefully. They demand attention and services, but without reciprocating, without providing sufficient background and context. There is little or no feedback.

There are many reasons to need feedback about the state of a system, reasons dealing with our own need for knowledge and reassurance. This kind of feedback is essential in normal social intercourse. The spoken "hmmm" or the nodding of the head by the listener to a conversation assures the speaker that the message is being received. The feel of the screw's resistance to my turning of the screwdriver provides useful feedback about the success of my operations. Feedback is a necessary part of all interaction, whether with people or technology, but it is more absent than present in today's information-based technology. If our information-based technologies are to become socialized members of society, interacting with and supporting the activities of people, then they have to be able to interact with us on our terms, not on theirs.

Our most modern technologies are social isolates. Today's technology provides us with ever-more complex machines, devices that can work at a distance or through nonmechanical components. Humans are often unaware of their presence, unaware of their internal states. The modern information-processing machine fits the stereotype of an antisocial, technological nerd. It works efficiently, quietly, and autonomously, and it prefers to avoid interactions with the people around it.

Just as it is valuable for us to know of our own internal states, the better to manage our own existence, designers of mechanical devices need to signal the internal states of their machines, the better to keep them maintained and functioning. The hunger and thirst of animals translate to the energy supply of machines, perhaps specified as the fuel level or the state of the battery. Is the machinery too hot, too cold? Lubricated properly? In appropriate adjustment? These are the things that the person maintaining the machine needs to know. Such information is provided naturally by the human body, but it must be provided artificially for our artifacts.

This internal information is provided in a number of ways. Sometimes it is not given explicitly but rather is stated as rules ("lubricate every six months"). Sometimes it is assumed that the user will notice and repair deficiencies as they appear ("tighten connections as needed"). More complex machines require indicators of their internal states, and these are provided by lights and gauges, by instrument panels. The instrument panel of an engine shows critical aspects of its internal state, thereby allowing the driver to control it safely and efficiently, perhaps much as the hard-driving coach carefully monitors the emotional responses of the players, attempting to push them hard enough to do some good, but not so hard as to be destructive.

40   The instrument panel of the automobile allows an internal communication within the driver + car unit. It is mostly self-centered, communicating information from the machine to the driver. Most instrument panels are like that: Lights tell us whether a device is turned on, meters and other indicators tell us of the current state, buzzers and alarms tell us when something is wrong and needs immediate attention. No social protocols, no etiquette. No checking to see whether we are busy at some other activity, usually not even a check to see if other alarms or warnings are also active. As a result, when there are serious difficulties, all the alarms and warnings scream in their self-centered way, the simultaneous array of lights and sounds impeding intelligent actions by the operators of the system. In places that have large control panels, such as industrial control rooms, commercial airplanes, and even the hospital operating room, the first act of the human operators is to shut off the alarms so that they can concentrate upon the problem. Unfortunately, the machines have no way of learning from the experience — you can't spank them and send them to bed, nor is there the equivalent of a note to the parent. As a result, when trouble next strikes, the same rowdy behavior reappears.

Social issues are even more serious when we consider socially interacting units of machines. The prototypical example is driving, where the driver + car unit interacts with large numbers of other similar units. Here is where we have a need for external signals, signals that communicate with the other units sharing the road, signals that allow others to know just what actions are being performed, and in many cases, what actions are intended. There are times when it is necessary to know what is on another's mind.

The same technology that makes modern transportation so efficient would kill us without rules of social behavior. Thus vehicles are restricted to certain locations. Similar directions of travel are put into the same corridors with some separation between those going in other directions. For safety, order and regulation are essential, even in societies that normally shun order and regulation.

With automobiles, we use traffic lights and signs to indicate who may go and who must stay, what can be done or not done, and who has precedence over another. And we use turn signals and brake lights to tell others of our actions and intentions. In the case of brake lights, we signal actions as we carry them out. In the case of turn signals, we signal our intentions before we actually commit them into action. In either case, we allow others to know our future actions so that we can ensure that there is no conflict.

The brake lights of the automobile serve no function for the operator. Rather, they are a way to communicate with other drivers. The brake light means that the brakes are applied, which the other driver interprets to mean that the car is slowing down. Moreover, the other driver will usually search for a reason, some explanation of the brake lights. This means that the lights can serve a valuable communication purpose. On a long, normally noncongested highway, if the car in front of you applies its brake lights, it usually signals some unexpected obstruction or danger on the road, and it is usually wise to slow down and be more alert.

And here is where intentions come in. Social interaction is enhanced when   45 the participants know not only what is happening at the moment but what will happen next. Of all the signals of the automobile, only the turn signals announce intentions.

Intentions are tricky, for they play many roles in social interaction, some obvious and necessary, some subtle and devious. In games we often signal intentions in order to deceive. Of course, our opponent does the same, and interprets our signals knowing full well they may be deceptive. Thus starts the elaborate ruse and counterruse, where we try to determine how other people are reading our minds. Suppose that in a game I want to kick the ball to the right. I could first pretend to kick the ball to the left, but I know that they will know that this is a pretense. But if I pretend to kick to the right, they will expect me to kick to the left, unless they know that I will think that, in which case they may realize I really intend to kick to the right. So I decide to fake a kick to the right, and then run. Except that when the actual time comes, things may happen so fast that none of the plans can be executed. In games and war our signals are more often false than true.

Imagine doing this in traffic: signaling a left turn, hoping that this will open up a hole in traffic that will let you dart to the right. I once got a driver's license in

Mexico City, where aggression was the rule. But even there, intentions had to be signaled honestly. Above all, it was essential to avoid eye contact with other drivers. In the traffic circles of that city, the trick was to avoid letting the other drivers see that you had seen them. Once the other drivers knew that you knew they were there, they would proceed at high speed around the circle, completely ignoring your presence, because they knew that you knew that they were there, so they expected you to stop or slow down. And you had to, or be killed. On the other hand, if you could manage to avoid letting them see you see them, you could proceed with impunity, because now it was their responsibility to avoid you. If you collided, it couldn't have been your fault, because after all, you hadn't seen them.

Most places in the United States don't let you get away with such games. In my community in southern California, for example, fault and blame are mechanically assigned according to strict orders of precedence. The rules of the road determine whose responsibility it is to avoid accidents. Thus, at intersections, the automobile on the right has the right of way, and all the eye contact in the world won't change that.

In Mexico, there were other ways of signaling intentions. Thus, if two cars were approaching a narrow, one-lane bridge from different directions, the car that first flashed its lights thereby announced that it was coming through, so the second car had better yield. The flashing headlight was to be interpreted as, "I got here first, so keep out of my way." As long as everyone understands such signals, they work fine.

50   The problem is that other cultures can completely reverse the meaning of the signals. In Mexico, one wins by aggression. In Britain, one wins by politeness and consideration. So in Britain, in a similar situation, the car that flashes its lights first is signaling, "I see you, please go ahead and I will wait." Imagine what happens when a Mexican driver encounters a British driver.

Drivers of automobiles get pretty good at reading the intentions of others. Brake lights and turn signals offer a formal, mechanized set of signals, eye contact another. Headlights also serve a valuable communication purpose, with the flashing lights conveying many different messages, depending upon the circumstances. Horn blasts and hand signals are also used. Basically, any part of the automobile that other drivers will recognize as being under the control of the driver can be used to signal something.

Notice that not all signals are truthful. Deceit exists on the highways just as much as it does in other social endeavors. The impatient driver can try a variety of tactics to gain open roadway, although the flashing of lights or blaring of the horn is the most common, most direct method. Some signals are ambiguous or confusing, such as the turn signal that continues for block after block, either signaling the eventual desire to turn or simply a remnant from a previous turn.

Turn signals are peculiar devices, neither human nor artificial. They are really not a way for the automobile to communicate with people. Turn signals are simply an aid to normal human-human communication. Instead of shouting or pointing, we simply flip a small lever here, resulting in visible flashing lights there, outside the automobile. Even so, turn signals are an important start toward the graceful interaction of people and machines.

THE GRACEFUL INTERACTION OF PEOPLE AND MACHINES

Human social interaction has developed a rich assortment of methods to ensure social harmony. Every culture has developed means of maintaining politeness and courtesy, of communicating needs without offending. If machines are to interact successfully, they too must follow these conventions.

Designers of machines usually provide the critical signals of the machine's internal state, for they know that maintenance is essential to operation. But then they often stop, failing to take into account the needs of the user of the device. As a result, the machines are still stuck in the asocial world of isolated devices. Worse, they have no manners. If machines operate in isolation with no need for interaction with people or other machines, then the lack of social graces and feedback about their internal states can be excused. But when machines are intended to operate with people, then the lack of socialization can lead to difficulties. Think of the telephone, continually intruding upon conversations, insensitive to the ongoing activities, forcing interruptions through its demanding ring whether the time is convenient or not. So it is with most machines, shunning interaction except to demand attention. We call such behavior in people "spoiled," "arrogant," or "insensitive," but somehow we have accepted it from our machines.

Social cooperation requires more than letting others know your actions and intentions. It is also necessary to know how the others have received your communication: Did they understand? Do they approve? Will they abide by it? When I talk with someone, I need to know how they are responding. Are they interested or bored? Do they understand or are they confused? When people engage in joint activities, they need to agree upon the division of activities in advance in order to be able to synchronize and coordinate their efforts, to avoid conflict. And during the activities, knowledge of the other person's actions is important, if only to know that the person is still interacting. It really is essential to get some feedback, if only to hear the "hmmm" from others. Otherwise how do we know they are attending? How do we know whether or not they are even alive?

We do have machines that are showing some of the first, early signs of social graces. Some can guide expectations, and even question actions. Thus, in the word processing system I am using to write this chapter, if I try to do a complex operation, I might be warned:

The current action cannot be undone: Do you wish to proceed?

Or if I try to move a file from one location in the computer storage system to another, I am sometimes warned:

An item with the same name already exists in this location. Do you want to replace it with the one you're moving?

These are early signs of social maturity: polite, meaningful concern about the possible effects of the operation I requested to be performed. Yes, some artificial devices show the early signs of social responsibility, displaying their internal states for others to see, sometimes assessing the impacts of their own actions and warning others of them. The interaction is primitive, however, and often not as effective as one might expect from human colleagues. The subtleties and richness of natural emotions and natural attentiveness to social interaction are missing. But even so, the first glimpses of artificial systems that exhibit cooperative, social behavior are appearing.

Perhaps the simplest form of social cooperation among artificial systems is the "handshaking" protocols of communicating systems, invisible to the normal human user but essential nonetheless. Handshaking is, of course, a human custom with a long cultural evolution. Today, shaking hands is part of the ritual by which people meeting for social or business purposes introduce themselves and get set for conversation or business. With machines, the term "handshaking" has been reserved for the initial steps of a communication protocol in which all the devices determine that they are connected properly, that their messages are in synchronization, and that they are directed to the correct recipients and in the correct format. It is easy to eavesdrop on these proceedings by listening to the first stages of a telephone connection of computer to computer or facsimile machine to facsimile machine. Better yet, listen as a computer tries to talk to a fax, or even to a person. Then the handshaking fails, as the automatic system tries this protocol and that one before quitting and gracelessly hanging up the telephone.

60   It is a sign of our technological era, of course, that elaborate handshaking protocols and other social niceties have been developed to handle the interactions among machines, but that no such civility seems to have become standard for the interactions between machines and people.

Human emotions, facial expressions, and social interaction have evolved over millions of years. We have had time to do things slowly, to work things out with care. Even so, there are occasional mismatches as people fail to understand one another, fail to cooperate.

What will happen with our machines? In principle, artificial evolution can proceed much more rapidly than can biological evolution. Artificial evolution can take advantage of knowledge and experience, but so far there is little evidence of attention to these.

I fear that the rush to autonomous machines is proceeding too rapidly. Our machines are barely social now. They are still at an early stage of development, still primarily self-centered, still focused on their own needs and not those of their operators. What will happen when they are given more power, more authority? How can we shape the evolution of machines so that they become more humane, more in line with human needs and values?

Mind reading is an essential activity for social communication. If I am to interact with machines in a constructive manner, then I need to be able to do the equivalent of reading the mind of the machine. Machines don't have minds, but they do have internal states. More and more, they are able to have goals and plans, expectations and even desires. The interactions will be smoother and more friendly if I can know these things. Facial expressions are rich and varied, a lot richer in information content than a few lights or sounds or meters. They reflect many subtle variations of mood. The blush that affects facial color, plus body position, and the sound of the voice, all give subtle indications of the underlying mood. Would that our machines were so sophisticated.

Just as people need to communicate acts, intentions, and emotional states,   65
to give continual feedback and evidence of expected actions and outcomes, so too will machines have to interact more fully, more completely, to provide the same kind of information. Will we have to repeat the whole ensemble of human emotional and factual expressions in our artificial devices? Yes, I think so. The history of technology might very well have to repeat the history of the social development of humans. Technology recapitulates phylogeny.

TALKING ABOUT IT

Seeing Metaphor: Revealing and Concealing

1. What does Norman reveal about machines through his metaphor of social interaction? How does this metaphor work?

2. What other inanimate or nonhuman objects might we personify? What do we commit ourselves to when we map human qualities onto these objects? What do we reveal about how we perceive the world outside ourselves?

Seeing Composition: Frame, Line, Texture, Tone

1. Norman waits until page 396 before arriving at the subject indicated in his title: turn signals on automobiles. What does he do before that page that does or does not justify his use of that space?

2. Map this essay according to its divisions. That is, write a summary for each division which explains what Norman is up to and then examine his points and their order. What do you discover about how this piece is organized?

What does Norman accomplish through his organization in relation to meaning?

Seeing Meaning: Navigating and Negotiating

1. What does Norman's title suggest he might talk about? What is his focus and how does the title relate to it?

2. What is the function of Norman's discussion of animals' social behavior?

WRITING ABOUT IT

1. Describe a machine that you have personified. Consider some ways that you have attached certain human qualities to technology. What does your description say about the ways you interact with technology—how you "humanize" or "socialize" it to meet your own needs? What impact has the machine made on your beliefs and values that affects your relationship to it?

2. As a class, list some ways you project your humanness or some aspect of the natural world onto machines. Maybe you see animal qualities in machines or some other physical properties that correspond to nature. After you've collected examples and discussed them, write an essay in which you focus on several examples and explain why you think it is a common practice among people to project their humanness onto machines.

Getting Close to the Machine

ELLEN ULLMAN

Ellen Ullman is a software engineer and consultant, as well as the author of Close to the Machine: Technophilia and Its Discontents *(1997). The following memoir appeared in* Resisting the Virtual Life *(1995), edited by James Brook and Iain A. Boal.*

People imagine that computer programming is logical, a process like fixing a clock. Nothing could be further from the truth. Programming is more like an illness, a fever, an obsession. It's like riding a train and never being able to get off.

The problem with programming is not that the computer is illogical — the computer is terribly logical, relentlessly literal. It demands that the programmer explain the world on its terms; that is, as an algorithm that must be written down in order, in a specific syntax, in a strange language that is only partially readable by regular human beings. To program is to translate between the chaos of human life and the rational, line-by-line world of computer language.

When you program, reality presents itself as thousands of details, millions of bits of knowledge. This knowledge comes at you from one perspective and then another, then comes a random thought, then you remember something else important, then you reconsider that idea with a what-if attached. For example, try to think of everything you know about something as simple as an invoice. Now try to tell an idiot how to prepare one. That is programming.

I used to have dreams in which I was overhearing conversations I had to program. Once I dreamed I had to program two people making love. In my dream they sweated and tumbled while I sat looking for the algorithm. The couple went from gentle caresses to ever-deepening passion, and I tried desperately to find a way to express the act of love in the C computer language.

When you are programming, you must not let your mind wander. As the human-world knowledge tumbles about in your head, you must keep typing, typing. You must not be interrupted. Any break in your concentration causes you to lose a line here or there. Some bit comes, then — oh no, it's leaving, please come back. But it may not come back. You may lose it. You will create a bug and there's nothing you can do about it.

People imagine that programmers don't like to talk because they prefer machines to people. This is not completely true. Programmers don't talk because they must not be interrupted.

This need to be uninterrupted leads to a life that is strangely asynchronous to the one lived by other human beings. It's better to send e-mail to a programmer than to call. It's better to leave a note on the chair than to expect the programmer to come to a meeting. This is because the programmer must work in mind time while the phone rings and the meetings happen in real time. It's not just ego that prevents programmers from working in groups — it's the synchronicity problem. Synchronizing with other people (or their representations in telephones, buzzers, and doorbells) can only mean interrupting the thought train. Interruptions mean bugs. You must not get off the train.

I once had a job in which I didn't talk to anyone for two years. Here was the arrangement: I was the first engineer to be hired by a start-up software company. In exchange for large quantities of stock that might be worth something someday, I was supposed to give up my life.

I sat in a large room with two other engineers and three workstations. The fans in the machines whirred, the keys on the keyboards clicked. Occasionally one of us would grunt or mutter. Otherwise we did not speak. Now and then I would have an outburst in which I pounded the keyboard with my fists, setting off a barrage of beeps. My colleagues might have looked up, but they never said anything.

10   Real time was no longer compelling to me. Days, weeks, months, and years came and went without much change in my surroundings. Surely I was aging. My hair must have grown, I must have cut it, it must have slowly become grayer. Gravity must have been working on my late-thirties body, but I didn't pay attention.

What was compelling was the software. I was making something out of nothing, I thought, and I admit that the software had more life for me during those years than a brief love affair, my friends, my cat, my house, or my neighbor who was stabbed and nearly killed by her husband. One day I sat in a room by myself, surrounded by computer monitors. I remember looking at the screens and saying, "Speak to me."

I was creating something called a device-independent interface library. ("Creating" — that is the word we used, each of us a genius in the attic.) I completed the library in two years and left the company. Five years later, the company's stock went public, and the original arrangement was made good: the engineers who stayed — the ones who had given seven years of their lives to the machine — became very, very wealthy.

If you want money and prestige, you need to write code that only machines or other programmers understand. Such code is called "low." In regular life, "low" usually signifies something bad. In programming, "low" is good. Low means that you are close to the machine.

If the code creates programs that do useful work for regular human beings, it is called "high." Higher-level programs are called "applications." Applications are things that people use. Although it would seem that usefulness is a good thing, direct people-use is bad from a programmer's point of view. If regular people, called "users," can understand the task accomplished by your program, you will be paid less and held in lower esteem.

A real programmer wants to stay close to the machine. The machine means midnight dinners of Diet Coke. It means unwashed clothes and bare feet on the desk. It means anxious rides through mind time that have nothing to do with the clock. To work on things used only by machines or other programmers — that's the key. Programmers and machines don't care how you live. They don't care when you live. You can stay, come, go, sleep — or not. At the end of the project looms a deadline, the terrible place where you must get off the train. But in between, for years at a stretch, you are free: free from the obligations of time.

I once designed a graphical user interface with a man who wouldn't speak to me. My boss hired him without letting anyone else sit in on the interview. My boss lived to regret it.

I was asked to brief my new colleague with the help of the third member of our team. We went into a conference room, where my coworker and I filled two white boards with lines, boxes, circles, and arrows while the new hire watched. After about a half hour, I noticed that he had become very agitated.

"Are we going too fast?" I asked him.

"Too much for the first day?" asked my colleague.

"No," said our new man, "I just can't do it like this."

"Do what?" I asked. "Like what?"

His hands were deep in his pockets. He gestured with his elbows. "Like this," he said.

"You mean design?" I asked.

"You mean in a meeting?" asked my colleague.

No answer from the new guy. A shrug. Another elbow motion.

Something terrible was beginning to occur to me. "You mean talking?" I asked.

"Yeah, talking," he said. "I can't do it by talking."

By this time in my career, I had met many strange software engineers. But here was the first one who wouldn't talk at all. We had a lot of design work to do. No talking was certainly going to make things difficult.

"So how *can* you do it?" I asked.

"Mail," he said. "Send me e-mail."

Given no choice, we designed a graphical user interface by e-mail. Corporations across North America and Europe are still using a system designed by three people in the same office who communicated via computer, one of whom barely spoke at all.

Pretty graphical interfaces are commonly called "user-friendly." But they are not really your friends. Underlying every user-friendly interface is a terrific contempt for the humans who will use it.

The basic idea of a graphical interface is that it will not allow anything alarming to happen. You can pound on the mouse button, your cat can run across it, your baby can punch it, but the system should not crash.

To build a crash-proof system, the designer must be able to imagine — and disallow — the dumbest action possible. He or she has to think of every single stupid thing a human being could do. Gradually, over months and years, the designer's mind creates a construct of the user as an imbecile. This image is necessary. No crash-proof system can be built unless it is made for an idiot.

35   The designer's contempt for your intelligence is mostly hidden deep in the code. But now and then the disdain surfaces. Here's a small example: You're trying to do something simple such as copying files onto a diskette on your Mac. The program proceeds for a while, then encounters an error. Your disk is defective, says a message, and below the message is a single button. You absolutely must click this button. If you don't click it, the program will hang there indefinitely. Your disk is defective, your files may be bollixed up, but the designer leaves you only one possible reply. You must say, "OK."

The prettier the user interface, and the fewer replies the system allows you to make, the dumber you once appeared in the mind of the designer. Soon, everywhere we look, we will see pretty, idiot-proof interfaces designed to make us say, "OK." Telephones, televisions, sales kiosks will all be wired for "interactive," on-demand services. What power — demand! See a movie, order seats to a basketball game, make hotel reservations, send a card to mother — all of these services will be waiting for us on our televisions or computers whenever we want them, midnight, dawn, or day. Sleep or order a pizza: it no longer matters exactly what we do when. We don't need to involve anyone else in the satisfaction of our needs. We don't even have to talk. We get our services when we want them, free from the obligations of regularly scheduled time. We can all live, like programmers, close to the machine. "Interactivity" is misnamed. It should be called "asynchrony": the engineering culture come to everyday life.

The very word "interactivity" implies something good and wonderful. Surely a response, a reply, an answer is a positive thing. Surely it signifies an advance over something else, something bad, something that doesn't respond. There is only one problem: what we will be interacting with is a machine. We will be "talking" to programs that are beginning to look surprisingly alike; each has little animated pictures we are supposed to choose from, like push buttons on a toddler's toy. The toy is meant to please us. Somehow it is supposed to replace the rewards of fumbling for meaning with a mature human being, in the confusion of a natural language, together, in a room, within touching distance.

As the computer's pretty, helpful face (and contemptuous underlying code) penetrates deeper into daily life, the cult of the engineer comes with it. The engineer's assumptions and presumptions are in the code. That's the purpose of the program, after all: to sum up the intelligence and intentions of all the engineers who worked on the system over time — tens and hundreds of people who have learned an odd and highly specific way of doing things. The system re-produces and re-enacts life as engineers know it: alone, out of time, disdainful of anyone far from the machine.

TALKING ABOUT IT

Seeing Metaphor: Revealing and Concealing

1. How does Ullman's metaphor of programming as an "illness, a fever, an ob-session" play out through her later descriptions of programmers at work?

2. "Low means you are close to the machine," she says. How do you usually use the words *low* and *high*? What does Ullman's use of *low* reveal about pro-grammers? What might *low* encourage us to envision? After reading the essay, in what ways do you understand the title, "Getting Close to the Machine"?

Seeing Composition: Frame, Line, Texture, Tone

1. Writers often present "scenes" (portraits, stories, etc.) to give life to ideas or concepts. Ullman offers us scenes that distinguish between "real time" and programmer's time. How do those scenes color our perception of program-mers and their lives?

2. Read a passage from this memoir aloud. How does Ullman's prose compel you to read — fast? slow? What is it about her sentences and phrasing that makes you read as you do? What is the predominant tone created by her phrasing?

Seeing Meaning: Navigating and Negotiating

1. What do the words *create* and *creativity* mean to you? Look at places where Ullman talks about creativity and creating. How does she use these words differently than one generally would? How do her use of these words, her images of programmers, and other information she offers about the world of programming help us to imagine the "cult of the engineer"?

2. Does this essay change your perception of the relationship you have with your own computer and its software? If so, in what ways?

WRITING ABOUT IT

1. Write your own personal essay in which the title serves as a metaphor: for example, "Getting Even with the Machine," "Getting Far from the Machine,"

"Gutting the Machine," or "Getting into the Machine." Write about your topic from the perspective of a user, not a programmer. Imagine your audience to be someone like Ellen Ullman.

2. After reading Ullman's essay, how do you imagine the life of a programmer and the world of programming? Write a description of a programmer to illustrate your response. Think about the programmer as a character in a play: how do you imagine the person looks, thinks, talks, acts? You might follow your description by creating a role for yourself and a scene in which you write a dialogue between the programmer and you.

Metaphors We Compute By

JOHN M. LAWLER

John M. Lawler is a professor of linguistics at the University of Michigan in Ann Arbor and co-editor of the book Using Computers in Linguistics: A Practical Guide *(1998). "Metaphors We Compute By" was a lecture Lawler delivered in 1987 to the staff of the Informational Technology Division of the University of Michigan. It can also be found on the World Wide Web at http://www-personal.umich.edu/~jlawler/meta4compute.html_.*

METAPHORS ABOUT COMPUTERS

Novelty and the Role of Metaphor

It's a truism that new things are hard to talk about — our experience moves much faster than our language does — and few things are newer than computers. Just 60 years ago, there were *no* computers in the world. Anywhere. There was talk about them in recondite academic technical circles, but the number of people who had even heard such talk (let alone understood it) was extremely small. I don't have to tell you about the results of the ensuing half-century; they're all around us. Naturally, we have had to cope, and the major way we have done so is by using metaphors.

These metaphors have typically been invented spontaneously by people who understood some aspect of computing in order to communicate with others, to be able to tell them about something they didn't already understand. This might be a case of one hacker telling another one about a neat new algorithm, or it might be a case of somebody writing a users' manual. You can think of lots of other cases. The difference between the two cases I mention here is in the presuppositions that are assumed by the speaker (or writer) to be part of what the listener (or reader) believes. I say both *speaker* and *writer* because metaphors are by no means a matter exclusively of the written language; however, since writings are more permanent than speakings and therefore tend to dominate the evidence, we sometimes lose sight of the relative proportions of language use — millions of words spoken for each one written — and I want to emphasize here how important it is for you to understand that I'm talking about *all* language use here.

Technical language is full of metaphors, but they are pretty impenetrable to outsiders. Think about what's meant by (say) *signing on* to a computer system. In real life, one *signs on* to a ship's company, or to a project, or to some other group; the metaphor is one of joining an enterprise and identifying with

411

it by pledging with your signature, but if you weren't familiar with the details, you wouldn't have a prayer of understanding what's meant. Metaphors in this case are a part of the cultural context and serve as much to mark in-group status as to serve a more idealistic communicational function. And as with all such group-marking phenomena, there are dialects: in some computing environments you don't *sign on*, you *log on*. Or occasionally *in*. But that's sociolinguistics rather than semantics.

My concern here, however, is not so much in these fascinating twists and turns of jargon as in the metaphors used with intent to communicate to people who can't be expected to know the details. *Yet*. This is a really serious problem, since it's not clear just what they can be expected to know, and any writing that is done without having in mind a clearly defined audience with clearly defined background knowledge is practically impossible to bring off successfully. As you all know.

Old Myths and New

5   One thing we *can* take for granted about our audience when we write or teach is that they are members of our culture. This isn't, of course, true anymore about audiences in some media, such as the Net, but these are rapidly evolving their own cultures so they can play the same games. As such, they are parties to a number of communal jokes we play on one another for various purposes. One word for such jokes is *Myth*. A myth is a species of metaphor that is

1. widely, even universally, known and used in a culture or subculture;

2. largely unconscious in nature [possibly because of (1)];

3. literally false, or even ludicrous, when spelled out.

Myths can concern anything at all, and I don't really want to go into the subject *too* deeply here; as a colleague of mine once suggested, the grammar of mythology is a bloody business. Let's get back to computers.

Computers are the subject of plenty of myths. They are new and therefore scary. Scary things need explanations; when we have an explanation, a label, we can put the scariness into a box and feel in control of it. This is a silly way to behave, of course, but it's pretty human. If computers hadn't been so damned useful, this wouldn't be a problem; on the other hand, we wouldn't be here discussing it, either. Since they have had such an effect on everyone's life, we need to take a look at the metaphors about them that have taken on the status of myth and to see what effects they've had.

These myths fall into a number of categories:

Deus Ex Machina   The basic idea here is that computers, being powerful, mysterious, and omnipresent (and therefore very threatening), take on some or even all of the classical aspects of gods or demons. It's sort of a contrary of the well-known explanation for why dinosaurs are so popular—they're said to be "big, dangerous, and extinct," and thus a safe subject to fantasize about. Computers are big and dangerous, but very far from extinct, so many people feel threatened by them.

This one had a lot going for it during the first part of the last half-century, since early computers were very large and remote, understood by only a few, controllable only by secret rituals, and ministered to by specially trained (and gowned) people who were already admitted to the mysteries, and governed the admission of others.

For those in on the secrets, of course, this is a rather convenient view to   10
encourage in others, and one often encounters it in large Data Processing enterprises. Likewise, for those on the outside, this myth makes computing look like a very dehumanizing activity, and their resistance to computing can take on religious overtones. Needless to say, all this makes life much more difficult for those whose job it is to de-mystify computers, since they can wind up coming across either like heretics or like soulless minions of the Devil. In short, this myth is not one we should encourage, not that I think anyone does.

Mathematical Machines   A related issue is the fact that American culture has never been fond of mathematics; 'Rithmetic is the last and least of the 3 R's, and the overwhelming majority of our compatriots have neither interest in nor understanding of anything that even *looks* mathematical. It is therefore a very simple matter to predict what the social response will be to any innovation that is billed as being primarily mathematical in nature.

To add to this, there is a fairly common distrust of *the machine* in our culture. Some machines we have to accept, just to get along—the automobile, the telephone; some, like TV, seem to be insidiously dangerous; some, like nuclear weapons, are dangerous in ways that are far worse than insidious. Despite (or perhaps because of) our dependence on machines, American culture is resentful of them and often views them as dehumanizing.

Put these two mythic viewpoints together, stir in some of the feelings of Deism mentioned above, and you get a real sense of what computer anxiety is all about. Since computers really *are* machines, after all, we don't have much choice about this. Of course, there are machines and there are machines.

The Pathetic Fallacy   Many of you will be familiar with this phrase as the classical name for what we now call anthropomorphic language, that is, the attribution of human qualities to non-human things. All languages have a vast repertoire of terms that refer only to humans and their activities, traits, feelings, appearance, intentions, etc. As a species, we are very narcissistic; human terms probably constitute at least half of the vocabulary of every language and are by any standard our favorite topics for discussion and writing. It's not surprising that we see them everywhere, or that we attribute them to something like a computer.

15   It's the social role of a human that the computer (more correctly, the software on the computer) is expected to take on. There are lots of varieties of this myth because there are so many roles for humans: servants, confidantes, secretaries, bosses, friends, enemies, therapists, etc.

Nevertheless, it's pretty obvious that expecting a computer to act or react like a human would is asking for trouble. Not that Eliza or Bob ever shied away from trouble.

Some Examples

In this section I want to give you a short tour of some of the uses of metaphor in computing. Each of the following is one example (where there are probably hundreds) of views of computing that are current in American culture. Each of the views (i.e., metaphor themes) licenses particular kinds of language to talk about computing and has particular consequences in the culture. Each has its problems, each its opportunities.

The Servant Problem (The Computer Is a Servant)   Few Americans have ever had servants; otherwise, this would be a very commonly remarked phenomenon. As it happens, having servants is a mixed blessing. To begin with, servants belong to a different social class from their employers, and in most areas of the world, that means they speak a different language, or at least a dialect that can verge on mutual unintelligibility. Nor are they usually well educated, nor do they always subscribe to the same cultural goals and standards as their employers. As a result of all this, one must often spend at least as much time and effort supervising a servant doing a task as one would spend doing it oneself. Many times it's much simpler to do it yourself.

Now put this into a computer metaphor. Everybody would love a program that was a good servant; but like even the best of servants, such a program must be instructed on what to do and how to do it. And if you're still not satisfied with how the program or the servant does it, too bad. There is only so much any servant (or any program) can be expected to know or to learn. And now we come to the kicker—computer programs are *much* more limited than humans, and can typically only do *one* kind of thing. To do another, you need a *different* program (or specialized servant), and that one can't speak the same language as your other one(s), and can't learn anything *they* already know. Therefore you must painstakingly learn yet another language, and yet another set of personal (programmatic) idiosyncrasies in order to make it work for you. I won't even mention the effects produced by the American phobia for languages.

This variety of anthropomorphic metaphor theme ("The Computer Is a 20
Servant") is reinforced by (among other things) software that uses first person
pronouns, by interfaces that make the user learn a recondite and unchangeable
set of terms for what the software can do, and by overly cute documentation that
personalizes the name of the program.

Running Fast (The Computer Is a Race)   Computers appear animated; that
is, things seem to move about and responses to user stimuli can be noticed. Of
the classic criteria of animateness (growth, ingestion, excretion, and irritability),
good analogs exist for computing. In particular, the speed of computer response is
an especially gratifying and very important phenomenon. I think it is no mistake
that we use the transitive verb *run* to refer to the execution of computer programs.

I imagine many of you here are familiar with the original title of the magazine *Dr. Dobbs' Journal*; it used to be "Dr. Dobbs' Journal of Computer Calisthenics and Orthodontia," with the epigraph "Running Light Without Overbyte" for
those who weren't in on the joke. The English verb *run* is intransitive; that is, it
doesn't use a direct object. It can be made into a transitive verb, though, and then
it is causative, i.e., it means *cause to run*. One of its most common uses (celebrated
in Dr. Dobbs' athletic reference) is in referring to racing animals, or in idioms like
run me ragged, where what is connoted is the causing of very rapid performance.

In this case, it is control of the (rapid, animated) behavior of the computer
that we're talking about. To use *run* is to be a speed freak like those who constantly try to make everything go faster. Take a moment to reflect on how short a
second is in normal human activities, but how *long* it is when you're waiting for a
computer response. As computer users, we've become addicted to instantaneity.

But, to quote one of the maxims from Kernighan and Plauger's *The Elements
of Programming Style*, it's important to "Make it right before you make it faster."

Software Tools (The Computer Is a Tool)   Another Kernighan and Plauger 25
book, *Software Tools*, is said to have started a revolution in software design.
Whether true or not, it certainly was a clear case of a metaphor being used consciously. A *machine* is a form of *tool*, and that's an extension of our manipulative
ability — functionally, something you use in your *hand*. Tools extend our ability
to apply energy. There are, as we've discovered in the last couple of millennia,
two kinds of energy involved in tools.

One is the obvious physical sense of power, exemplified in the harder
blows of a hammer as compared with a fist; the other is more subtle, and really
refers to information. With a handsaw, for instance, a user supplies both types of
energy simultaneously; with a power saw, on the other hand, the user supplies
only the controlling energy, the information, while the motor provides the power;
and with an automated drilling machine, both types are separately powered.

You can probably see where I'm going from here. It's only a small step from a machine where one kind of energy is powered as information to one where the metaphor is turned back on itself and two kinds of information are powered separately. This leads directly to the distinction between algorithms and data, the abstraction of which is the core of computer science.

For a technician, this is probably the most useful and productive metaphor available for computing. For anyone else, however, there are problems. Awareness of technical details is a plus for a technician; it's pretty often a hindrance to those interested only in using the machine for their own purposes. Something else has to be provided, yet, paradoxically, the technician is almost certainly the wrong person to decide what it should be.

Car and Driver (The Computer Is a Machine)   As I mentioned, allied to the *tool* metaphor is the *machine* metaphor. I've mentioned the latent Luddite tendencies of many of our fellows; it's also true, though, that quite a few of us are very fond of machines. The best (and most locally relevant) example of this is, of course, the automobile. Our culture has not accepted automobiles — we've embraced them wholeheartedly. So it's tempting to use the metaphor of driving a car to refer to using a computer. There are some benefits to this; however, there are even more problems.

30   The automobile is a machine that you don't need to understand in order to use. While there are plenty of people who enjoy tinkering with cars, many more want nothing to do with such activity. They want to *use* the car. This they can do, because functionally a car is simply an extension of a natural activity (movement) whose operation can be transferred from other learned activities. In short, you learn a high-level skill associated with the hardware — you learn to drive a car. What you do with it is then open to your own intentions.

Computers don't really work like this. Learning to run a computer doesn't help you at all in using it; in fact, it's not clear just what *learning to run a computer* might mean. Computers, unlike cars, have software, and the software is what you wind up using. The appropriate analogy to having a car would be if you had a programmable car. You would have a program that took you to the grocery store, another that took you to work, a third one — that you customized yourself — that took you to Grandmother's house, and so on. To go anywhere else (or to take a different route) you'd have to get a different program or change some installation constant. And it goes without saying that each program would behave differently, use different controls, display different messages, and so on. If cars really were the same kind of machines as computers, we'd never use them.

The Desktop (The Computer Is a Workplace)   ... Even (perhaps especially) when dealing with people who are highly visually oriented, there is the problem of information accessibility. I, for instance, happen to be a person who likes to have information resources visible; so I clutter my desk with things I refer to often, leave books I'm reading in places where I'll see them, post notices to myself, and so on. On any visual interface, you don't really get to see the information; you get to see the labels, and you must remember what's what. My Mac or Windows desktop doesn't really look like my real desktop, and it isn't nearly as useful. I doubt I'm the only person for whom this is true.

What's really at issue here is what I call *density.* Not the physical concept of the same name, but a metaphorical one (what else?) dealing with access to information. I happen to like information to feel dense, like there's a lot of stuff in there (wherever *there* may be in the metaphor, not to mention *stuff*), like I can just reach in and grab it; which is why I like to see a lot of things at the same time, and have them interconnected if at all possible, whether or not they're logically or conventionally linked together. To a certain extent, this reflects how I think my mind works. Others prefer their information less dense, with fewer high-level nodes and less clutter overall, which probably reflects how they think *their* minds work. And for still others, this doesn't seem to be an issue at all. But there certainly is an enormous variability in how people deal with information density and access, and with how they externalize this in their interactions with computers.

I don't really see a great deal that can be done about it, in fact, beyond making user interfaces as customizable and flexible as possible, and using a *lot* of synonyms when designing them. The point I want to make here is that diversity in personal styles of information management is not yet a well-known or -handled part of user interface design. There's always a big problem with adaptation; either you have to adapt yourself to the design of the computer (and you may not be able to do so usefully), or you have to adapt the computer to your own strategies (and this is a very difficult task at best). Mostly we try to do both, with quite variable degrees of success.

File Systems (The Computer Is a Filing Cabinet)   The name *file* that is used   35 for the most commonly used artifact of software is another thing that people have to get used to. The metaphor here is that of a business office, with a filing cabinet full of folders, each containing some kind of information, each with some kind of label.

This is very misleading, though it's too late to do much about it, since the term is too firmly entrenched in technical jargon. The problem is that real files all hold the same kind of thing (legible papers), while computer files can hold anything at all, much of which isn't legible at all, at least by humans. The idea of putting executable code (for example) into a file is obvious enough, once you know something about computing; however, it's anything but obvious at first.

Even after you get over this hassle, though, you have to learn (usually the hard way) about file formats, and about the hassles of trying to get information from one kind to another. The filing cabinet metaphor gets stretched too thin to be of use here; in fact, when I started looking for examples, I came on this one with a shock of recognition — it's been ages since I thought about computer files as having anything to do with filing cabinets.

■   ■   ■

Fun and Games (The Computer Is a Toy)   The phenomenon of computer games is an unlooked-for one, and in my opinion one of the most sanguine examples of the serendipity we all expect to find in the information revolution. The reason I'm so optimistic about games and their ilk is that (as we all know) games are fun. Now we also know that computers are fun, but this is for some people a difficult proposition to swallow; even these folks, however, know that games are different. By definition, they're fun. And fun is precisely what we all need; by which subversive remark I mean that the protean promise of computing will never be kept unless the kind of enthusiasm and creativity we're willing to put into fun activities like games is routinely harnessed.

We have a sort of problem here. The market forces driving the development of hardware and software are oriented to the worldview of business and conservative institutions, where *things must be taken seriously.* This leads to speed, which we all welcome, of course, and sometimes efficiency, which has its place, but only rarely to fun, and therefore only rarely to real creativity.

40   For instance, few of us are interested in yet another word processor. On the other hand, I've often wondered what it would be like to do writing on a word processor that had sound effects — real bells and whistles. *Pop!* when you delete a word, *Zzip!* when you delete a line, and so on — I leave the remainder of the design as an exercise for your imagination. The point is not that it might be more efficient, but that it might be more fun. And it might be a good idea to encourage fun in computing, just as it is to encourage it in education. Serious business is good business, all right, but for repeat customers, fun sells better.

One of the most hopeful signs I've seen in the computer world is the sense of humor that's evident everywhere. April 1st is the most important holiday on the calendar of the computer culture; I hope we keep it that way for a long time.

CONCLUSION

I've mentioned a number of metaphor themes that we use to approach computers as things and computing as activity. Some of these have mythic status — that is, they developed on their own, in the "cultural unconscious," and we have to deal with them, willy-nilly. Others are more or less conscious choices, made for particular reasons in particular contexts. There are still others that we haven't mentioned.

I want to switch here from talking so much about the language used about computing to return to my own favorite metaphor theme, which could be roughly stated as *computing is a linguistic activity.* This is the other side of the coin, so to speak. There are plenty of things about computers for which at least some of the metaphor themes I've mentioned are not only appropriate, but productive; however, for one of the most important, I have some hopes for this one.

The area of computing that (I think) everyone agrees needs the most work is user interface design. Progress in this area has led to such advances as the Mac interface; but there's more to the story. What it's all about is communication, and, while communication is not simply a matter of language, nevertheless, human language is the principle phenomenon of human communication. There are things that are known about it. These have been used in such areas of research as Natural Language Processing and Artificial Intelligence, but I want to turn it around and see what insights can be gained from looking at human interaction with computers as a linguistic process.

To begin with, it is natural enough to view it this way, since keyboards are derived from typewriters, and those are used to produce written language. A naive computer user will automatically use prior experience in typing and attempt to apply it to the task at hand. Early user interfaces that were oriented to a command line, in fact, explicitly attempted to use this, by making the command itself into a structure of imperative verb plus direct object, something derived directly from English grammar. This was an instantiation of the *servant* metaphor theme, and the imperative is the form used to give orders.

I could go into a lot of linguistic detail about the grammar of such commands; other forms that can appear are directly analogous to cases—for instance, the DOS/Unix redirection arrows function precisely like the ablative and dative cases in Indo-European languages. More important, however, is the fact that, unlike most servants, most computer programs don't have much of any facility for what we call repair procedures—i.e., what happens when we misspeak or see that we are misunderstood. It's here that the most important limitation of the principal myth about language in our culture comes out.

This myth is called the *Conduit Metaphor,* and it is particularly easy to see in distinguishing spoken from written language. In spoken language, we appear to be understanding a person through what they say; in written language, on the other hand, we appear to be dealing with the words themselves, and the literal meaning (the word *literal* itself simply means "written") becomes a matter of very great importance. If we make a mistake in conversation, we can back up, restate, ask questions, pause, look dumb, or behave in a lot of different ways that can lead to clarification, rather like an elaborate error-trapping routine.

In written language, however, we have much less to go on, and have consequently developed conventions for interpreting the writer's intentions. The Conduit Metaphor, which is a myth that is used to explain how we can communicate, even though we're not telepathic, supports the views

- that words and meaning are physical objects of the same type;
- that (literal) meanings are attached to words (the metaphoric attachment is that the meaning is *inside* the words—note the use of such phrases as *in a few words, empty words, full of meaning,* and the like);
- that communication is a matter of shipping the word strings over to listeners and having them unpack them.

This is a pretty silly theory, particularly when applied to natural spoken language, but it has a certain utility in its application to writing. Written words *are* physical, after all, and written communication *is* a matter of exchanging strings of words. Since two of the three parts of the Conduit Metaphor seem to work well, it's a simple matter to assume the third—that meaning is attached tightly to words (in fact, *inside* them), and that therefore any difficulties in understanding are due to the writer's improper use of words.

50   Returning to computers, we see that the natural equation of computer interaction with written communication, coupled with the equally natural acceptance of the Conduit Metaphor to explain the functioning of written language, has led quite naturally to a situation in which computer software is doomed to behavioral flaws in its interaction with humans, since it is operating on the flawed assumption that meaning (which would really be better termed *intention*) is a literal matter. This isn't something that we can do a great deal about, of course, given the difficulties inherent in determining intentions and of making workable programs in the first place.

Some solutions may be in the offing, and thinking about them is interesting. For instance, while speech recognition is very difficult and isn't going to become widespread soon, it offers some possibilities for getting away from the written language metaphor. It is startling to think that within a few decades, typing may be as rare a skill as knapping a flint arrowhead, driving a coach-and-four, shooting a flintlock musket, or solving an equation on a slide rule. We may be living in what might come to be called the *Written Input Era;* like the *Vacuum Tube Era,* one of the fascinating sidelights of technological history. Before we all learned how language *really* works.

Of course, speech recognition doesn't provide the whole story; there is plenty of hard work to do in determining just exactly what intentions people can have in using computers. In our contact with new users, we've all come upon some strange ones. What I want to suggest today is that these conceptions aren't really as strange as we might consider them. They're normal ideas, based on normal expectations, which happen not to be met by current normal hardware and software. We have little choice right now except to try to adapt the users to the machine; but the future holds some hope of being able to adapt the machines to the users.

Provided, that is, we don't become wedded to our myths and embedded in our current metaphors. Some people (me among them) are often accused of *mixing metaphors*. This is supposed to be a bad thing. I'll admit it can be a bit confusing, but I really think it's our only hope. The more different views you have of something — and the more different the views are — the more hope you have of understanding what the thing is really like. Of perceiving some aspect of its reality that isn't apparent in any of the individual views.

The best metaphor I know of to explain this is the phenomenon of binocular vision, or stereo sound. We have two eyes and two ears, even though each one of them works fine alone. The other one isn't just a spare, though, because using them in parallel provides information about what is being perceived that isn't carried in either of the separate images. We perceive depth in visual or aural signals precisely to the degree we use separate, different signals and succeed in integrating them into a single percept. Nobody really understands what computers are, let alone what they can be; my suggestion is that we leave it that way, and continue coping with imperfect metaphors. The more the better. And of course, continue to have fun.

TALKING ABOUT IT

Seeing Metaphor: Revealing and Concealing

1. Of the images that Lawler lists, which do you find most descriptive of your own experience with computers, and why? Which do you find least descriptive of your experience, and why?

2. Choose any two metaphors that we compute by and discuss what we commit ourselves to when we map the experience of X onto the computer. What is gained, what is lost? What is the consequence of having done this?

Seeing Composition: Frame, Line, Texture, Tone

1. Lawler's text is in the form of a lecture, not an essay. What differences are created by that choice of frame? In other words, how does a lecture change the way a writer approaches the rhetorical situation: subject, audience, occasion, and the writer's relationship to each?

2. Lawler's original audience was made up of members of the Informational Technology Division at the University of Michigan. How can you tell that Lawler is speaking to experts in the field of computing? Did you ever feel "left out" as an audience member? Why or why not?

Seeing Meaning: Navigating and Negotiating

1. Keep in mind that Lawler delivered this lecture in 1987. How have our views of computers changed since then?

2. What are the advantages of having many metaphors to compute by?

WRITING ABOUT IT

1. Under "Old Myths and New," John Lawler addresses the issue of fear and anxiety. He offers several categories of metaphors (myths) that people have invented to explain their anxieties and thus feel in control of them. Which of these myths has helped you to dispel your own fear of technology, and why?

    Alternatively, consider that Lawler delivered this lecture in 1987, and, since then, newer metaphors may serve the same purpose of dispelling fears. Describe one such metaphor that has taken on the status of myth (if it has) and what effects it has had on those who, like you, accept the explanation.

2. Since 1987, what signs have you seen that the computer world has continued to put fun into the development of hardware and software? What new bells and whistles have been added that encourage you to have fun with computers? Write about that experience and how it may have helped you see your own work as both play and creativity, and not just work.

Walkabout: A Perplexatron Asks an AllKnowaBot a Few Things about Human Nature and CyberSPACE

TED WADE

Ted Wade is a research associate in medical informatics at the University of Colorado School of Medicine, where he teaches about the World Wide Web. The piece that follows originally appeared in 1995 on the Web at http://www.uchsc.edu/sm/pmb/cybspce/space.htm, where it can still be found.

PERPLEXATRON: Mighty AllKnowaBot, what do humans mean by "cyberspace"?
ALLKNOWABOT: They think they know, but they don't — *I* do.

. . . what the robots said . . .

- *Trading time for space* — they need continuity

- *Who goes there?* — they need avatars

- *DP motion* — they're *so* easily stirred up

- *Evolve, schmevolve* — will it be one cyber-world?

- *Happy trails* — to you, until we meet again

- *We're all schizos on this bus* — cyber-side crossovers

- *Burning yearning* — what's in the mirror for *you*

TRADING TIME FOR SPACE

PERPLEXATRON: Well they sure talk about cyberspace. Are they in cyberspace yet?
ALLKNOWABOT: No — not until they can go walking in it. Cyber*space* will be an immersive experience, a place where you move around, just like that reluctant prophet William Gibson predicted in *Neuromancer*. Cyberspace will take advantage of humans' abilities to perceive and plan, to navigate and maneuver in real space. But movement in real space is continuous. To get from A to B you have to pass through all the points in between. The networks they have now will let someone's point of view move from one information source to another, but only in jumps. They dial a telephone

423

number — there's a jump. Make a menu selection, jump again. Type in a Universal Resource Locator and, surprise — jumpola. There's no "points in between."

5   PERPLEXATRON: Don't people like that ability to instantly get there?

ALLKNOWABOT: Some say you'd have to pry it from their cold, dead fingers. Especially the really maniacal, tightly wound types. The telephone model of reaching distant info-sources is very powerful. So if instant gratification is the only concern, cyberspace will never happen.

PERPLEXATRON: But there's more to it than that . . .

ALLKNOWABOT: Right, humans get lost easily, plus — they're very social creatures. Put your average carbon-based character in a discontinuous space and leave him for a while, he'll start going around in circles and crying for his significant others. That's why the newer interfaces are starting to look very geographic, like Magic Cap's little hallway and main street. And what do people do most when they go "on-line"? They chat with other people, even though they can't even see them.

PERPLEXATRON: So what's your point?

10   ALLKNOWABOT: My point, impertinent one, is that the forces which will cause cyberspace to happen are in human nature. People mostly don't know where to get the information they want. More and more there will be applications/places on the global net which are arranged so that people can explore them. Chances are a lot of those places will be shopping malls. Right now various on-line services suit this need for walkabout, as does "gopher space" and the World Wide Web. But the Web still uses the hyperjump/telephone model. The "view" of the Web from any one server doesn't tell you much at all about the view from another server. This rules out giving simple directions, like, "Oh that's over by the NASA server, just go to University of Texas and turn left."

PERPLEXATRON: What makes you so sure that people really need spatial continuity? What about TV?

ALLKNOWABOT: It's true that movies and TV barrage them with cuts from scene to scene and subject to subject. But those cuts are carefully considered, and — more importantly — they are viewed passively. People will demand continuity in order to control where they go in cyberspace. Instead of the "jump" model, real cyberspace will have two principles: a (1) spatial metaphor that is (2) shared by a large number of people. Without the sharing, they're left in the solipsistic world of the virtual reality gurus.

PERPLEXATRON: Sounds like you think art and recreation will have little to do with cyberspace.

ALLKNOWABOT: Not at all — art/rec uses will continue to define much of the representational techniques of cyberspace, and to provide some of the most compelling destinations, or subworlds, of the virtual world. And only the art/rec world has made any progress on representing people.

WHO GOES THERE?

PERPLEXATRON: Yeah, I'm a people person myself.   15

ALLKNOWABOT: Automata such as yourself may be amused by human social tendencies. But people already have a bunch of names for their visual representations in cyberspace: avatars, puppets, tuxedos, atmans, skins, handles, usernames, tags. If a human in cyberspace can see the whatevers of other people, then he gets two big payoffs. He can find out where the action is, and he can be there without having to drive a car. Just knowing where other people aggregate is a powerful, though fallible, indicator of where good things are. In fact the same principle works for human relatives, from bacteria all the way up to apes. Predators, politicians and retailers all exploit this tendency to aggregate with conspecifics.

PERPLEXATRON: But what's this about driving?

ALLKNOWABOT: People really need to do their business eye to eye, but it's costing them a planet's ransom. They're running all over the place just to stay in touch, and it fouls the nest. Neal Stephenson's premise about the multiverse in *Snow Crash* was that cyberspace really took off when you could read faces and body language there. Then they could do some business.

PERPLEXATRON: Have you failed to notice that people are "videoconferencing" these days? Won't that get the job done without the immense cost of avatars in a shared space?

ALLKNOWABOT: Suppose you had all the video and audio resolution you needed.   20
You still can't hold a very effective meeting of more than two people in video space. Say there's a big screen, and five different people, each at a different real world location. On the screen you put 5 boxes in a circle, each one with a different person's video feed in it. In the middle of the circle you put the documents that they're working with. Now how do you tell who is looking at whom? Maybe something tracks eye movements and shows little yellow streaks going back and forth between the people boxes, but will that really connect with how people interact? How do you share the documents? Maybe each person has a pointer/cursor of a different color, so you identify who's messing with the document by color? That's mentally demanding, so maybe you have to extend some other lines from the people boxes on the screen to the document windows, to show who is touching the document. That's a lot of lines, or icons or whatever to communicate information that in a real meeting would be just totally and unconsciously apparent.

PERPLEXATRON: You're a simple allknowabot, not an interface designer. Why should I take your word that videoconferencing can't be done well?

ALLKNOWABOT: Ingenuity and bandwidth might combine to make multiperson videoconferences workable, but they would be totally *natural* using avatars in a cyberspace. When someone's avatar points to something, everyone can see them do it, and hear the voice coming out of the avatar's mouth. Plus — the objects that are being shared could be extremely ingenious. In *Snow Crash*, avatars can give each other a little card, that, when it changes hands, enables the recipient to access a database. What if your avatar could conk somebody with a giant hammer to drive home a point? Like this.

PERPLEXATRON: Ouch! I still don't see what fancy meeting technology has to do with global cyberspace.

ALLKNOWABOT: It's just a major enabler. There's no reason to shed your avatar after you leave the meeting. You can walk down the virtual hall from the meeting room and drop in on somebody, or maybe have a chat with somebody influential near the virtual coffee pot. And why drop the persona when you go next door, or down the street, to the research library? People will get used to seeing and dealing with other people in cyberspace. It may be rude or taboo to go around invisible. Michael Benedikt, who seems to have thought more deeply about *cyberspace* than anyone else, calls it the "Principle of Personal Visibility." He thinks you ought to always be seen, though not necessarily be identifiable, even when traveling long distances in cyberspace. People might not always want to spend the computing resources for presenting a realistic, expressive image to others — but they would want the ability to turn it on when it was useful. Stephenson, by the way, thinks those expressive images might be very, very hard to make.

DP MOTION

25 PERPLEXATRON: (8-?

ALLKNOWABOT: Oh, I get it. You want to know what's so hard about programming nonverbal communication. After all, they can do emoticons on a dumb terminal. The thing is, peoples' nonverbal signals aren't just signals. They are like signal, counter-signal, fake signal and noise all rolled into one.

PERPLEXATRON: !!!?

ALLKNOWABOT: You have to understand why people have emotions and then why they would express them. Because the realm of nonverbal communication is the realm of emotion.

PERPLEXATRON: Don't they have emotions just to make them do things? *How complicated can it be?*

ALLKNOWABOT: You and I are proof that software doesn't need e-motion to cause 30
actions. So people don't need emotions to act—I mean, evolution *logically* could have built humans to behave adaptively without all that crying. BUT, I think people need emotions *to tell others* what's going on with them, what they want, what they'll do next, what their reactions might be if things change, stuff like that. The key is that emotional reactions are (mostly) involuntary, and their expression in terms of body language, facial expression, skin and voice tones, etcetera is (mostly) automatic.

PERPLEXATRON: Well why wouldn't a better-designed species just tell each other what they're up to—just use words? And what does "mostly" have to do with it? Doesn't inconsistency mess things up?

ALLKNOWABOT: Suppose I say I'm going to stomp you until your chips are in little pieces. You might think I'm bluffing, or joking, or that I don't have any reason to do that, or that I'm not big enough and strong enough. In fact, every message between any two systems is open to question. Now suppose instead that I snarl and scowl and get red in the face, grit my teeth and clench my fists and then say I want to stomp you. That message has far fewer interpretations.

PERPLEXATRON: I don't see why. At most you are just saying the same message over in different ways.

ALLKNOWABOT: The difference is in your interpretation process. If you are a person, then you know what it's like to be mad and want to cream somebody. You know what it feels like inside and you know that all the behavior—the scowling and clenching—is automatic unless you do something to stop it. So if you see me doing all that, you think, "he really means it."

PERPLEXATRON: OK, I get it. So to communicate emotions in cyberspace means 35
better graphics, better sound, better ways of monitoring a real person's face, and that sort of thing?

ALLKNOWABOT: No, that's just technical, and can eventually be done. Here's the real tricky part: when real people show all the symptoms of extreme anger, it still can mean different things. Some are just blowing off steam. Others are bluffing. Yet others are acting for an audience. Humans started with this effective and accurate emotional signaling system from their ancestors, the monkeys and such. Then they twisted and played off of it until it was a still-effective but utterly inaccurate system that served their needs for subterfuge, secrecy, exaggeration, entertainment, seduction, domination and diplomacy. Young human children still use the animal system, but older humans have learned to hold back emotional expression or manipulate it in a myriad of other ways.

PERPLEXATRON: So any facial expression has layers of intention and interpretation involved that would snarl up any attempt to portray it in software, even though the image of a facial expression is not that hard to program?

ALLKNOWABOT: Exactly. It's that balance of control versus spontaneity. Totally mysterious.

EVOLVE, SCHMEVOLVE

PERPLEXATRON: Speaking of long distance. How do we get from local places like net malls, conference rooms, and infoplexes to the large-scale global cyberspace? Could anybody possibly design that? Would anybody want to pay for it? And who would really want to have to waste time to travel long distances in cyberspace when they could jump from place to place instead?

40 ALLKNOWABOT: (1) Nobody *designed* the global phone system, did they, but (2) somehow we paid for it, and (3) a global cyberspace is still compatible with long jumps, or even with going places really fast. *Stephenson imagined* virtual bullet trains and supersonic motorcycles for getting around great distances. *Benedikt argues for a Principle of Transit,* in which to get somewhere you should always seem to pass through all points en route. This would give people time to prepare for their next task, enable them to make serendipitous discoveries along the way, and make cyberspace more real and compelling. These reasons will be so much idealistic mush to cigar-chomping, do-it-yesterday types. And they're the ones who have the money. Probably for that reason Benedikt imagines transfer stations, between which travel would be instantaneous. He also describes a way to fly very fast — preserving his Principle of Transit. But to explain that I would have to talk about the shape of cyberspace, and its shape really depends on how it evolves. So does the "global" aspect of it. Will there be one cyberspace or many?

PERPLEXATRON: Perplexatrons cannot answer questions. We eat answers and excrete questions. Please tell me about this evolution stuff.

ALLKNOWABOT: I was just thinking out loud. Humans are starting to realize that all complex systems evolve, even artificial ones. Here's my scenario for it. The smartest on-line services will use a spatial metaphor, because it is natural for their customers and it encourages hanging out and browsing, which means more use of the service. Avatars will be created, for the reasons I gave before — to point out the action and to make more effective social interaction. Then services will start linking up with each other, just like stores aggregate in a business district so they can share customers and otherwise transact with each other. When two services link, they will merge their spaces, so they can keep the advantages of browsing and all that. These will become little emerging worlds in cyberspace, each with its own boundaries, and having only jump access to the other worlds. Some of these will get very big, but they will be different from each other — in appearance, mechanics, culture, and language — because they will be distant from one another. It's the same in organic evolution. Whenever an animal species starts to live in two separate places, so that genes can't flow between those places, the species will become two different species. So yes, there will be more than one cyberspace.

PERPLEXATRON: I can't buy that. Aren't they evolving places instead of species? And don't places get more alike the more they communicate? Just look at human cities. They all have cars, fast food, skyscrapers, movie houses. In cyberspace, won't distant places be just as close as home?

ALLKNOWABOT: NOsiree. Why? Because a sensate connection to a distant net means passing a lot of data between its physical location and yours. The data must go fast enough that your actions, and the actions of others, appear to change smoothly. Whenever the nets get cheaper and faster, the demand for a more realistic presence at another place will always use up the new net capacity. So it will always cost more and take more time to be virtually present at a physically distant site.

PERPLEXATRON: What if someone puts up a monster satellite relay system that   45
pumps petabytes between, say, the USA and China. Won't that make those two places close in cyberspace?

ALLKNOWABOT: It could. But only if the sat is not also used for traffic involving all the places between those countries. To the extent such channels exist, the topology of cyberspace will be a distorted version of real space. That is, the distance on earth won't be proportional to the distance in cyberspace. Some delays can't be reduced—like the time it takes light to travel between the planets. A cyberspace connecting Earth and Mars is (so far) a physical impossibility. You can't react to something in cyberspace with a 20-minute delay.

PERPLEXATRON: What, then, will it be like, visiting a distant place in cyberspace?

ALLKNOWABOT: Herky-jerky, for sure. Unless you are RaoP (Rich and/or Powerful) you will have low bandwidth relative to more local connections. A distant visitor to your region of cyberspace will look grainy and move in little jumps. Same as if your cyberspace deck was weak, which Stephenson described well in *Snow Crash*.

PERPLEXATRON: So, cyberspace and real space are correlated. What happens to my avatar if I stay jacked in while moving around on Earth?

ALLKNOWABOT: Depends on how far you go. As the RaoP jet around, they can   50
keep grabbing higher capacity channels to keep more constant the data "distance" to where they're at in cyberspace. So they can, if they want, appear to remain still and look the same. Other people will have to change when they go too far, physically, from the systems they are visiting in cyberspace. So their avatars will become grainy, and maybe break up and disappear if they fly too far.

PERPLEXATRON: I see your point about distance making different cyberspaces evolve, I guess. But even in carbon biology, there's convergent evolution—like when many different parts of the animal kingdom separately evolved eyes. And we're now talking about us—I mean the realm of artificial things. Have artificial things been around long enough for us to know their laws of evolution?

ALLKNOWABOT: No. But we know there's an awful lot of ways to do anything, and people usually try many of them. Also, don't forget that evolved systems always contain traces of their earlier versions, like the fish-y gills on mammalian embryos. So if you start out differently, in some sense you are always different.

HAPPY TRAILS

PERPLEXATRON: Well, is there anything inevitable about all parts of cyberspace?

ALLKNOWABOT: Maybe the shape, but maybe not. All the visionaries have seen it differently. For Gibson it's pretty much like the space people live in. Except that things float all over the place, and avatars fly. There is an up direction, and that is where the military and other highly secure systems live. That means an analogy with gravity. You have to burn energy to go against the pull of gravity. Stephenson's *multiverse* is a big sphere, like the surface of a planet. The whole thing was built by enterprising hackers, who then sold off real estate on the surface to finance it. When you travel, you travel on the surface. The "sky" is dark and fairly empty. Just underground there are daemons who do some of the dirty work to keep the place tidy, like disposing of abandoned bodies. When you enter a building, the interior can be any sort of virtual reality, depending on what it's for. Other people have imagined unnatural shapes for cyberspace, like Benedikt's *two-torus*. It looks totally flat, and infinite in all directions. That's because if you go far enough in any direction you will come back to where you started. He likens it to how sprites on some early video games would go off one edge of the screen and appear, going the same way, on the opposite edge. All the places you would want to go are actually underneath this flat surface, with tantalizing shapes sitting on the surface above, beckoning you to come in. Enter one of those places, and, like the buildings in the multiverse, anything can happen. To travel, you fly above the surface, and the "higher" you fly, the faster you go. That's Benedikt's concession to the impatient. Like the multiverse, the two-torus has a fixed size. It could fill up, and would certainly get crowded in spots.

55 PERPLEXATRON: Do you have a vision of cyberspace yourself, prescient one?

ALLKNOWABOT: One is amused by the possibility that a cyberspace might grow fractally (*or genetically?*). Imagine a forest, where each tree is a university, the limbs are schools, the branches are departments or dormitories, and eventually you get to a leaf, which is someone's home space, corresponding to their personal workstation. Sort of like their "home page" on the World Wide Web of today. The branching of the tree might reflect the underlying physical network of computers, but an avatar would probably travel like a flying squirrel, sailing over the branches to visit someone else's leaf. The whole thing has a sort of green correctness to it that ought to appeal to academia.

PERPLEXATRON: How can we predict the shape of cyberspace if it "just grows"?

ALLKNOWABOT: And there may not be much planning, right? Chip Morningstar and Randall Farmer, who actually built and ran *Habitat,* which was one of the first graphic cyberspaces, said "central planning is impossible — don't even try." Of course people will, just like they try to guide the growth of cities. Probably cyberspace will evolve to fit the psychological and social needs of people. There's no oceans, rivers, plains or mountains to constrain cyberspace cities. What may be more important is that people evolved to stand on their hind legs to see over the tall grass. They have a strong sense of orientation to the vertical and movement in the horizontal. Only a few of them adapt well to piloting airplanes, or to life in zero gravity. Psychological needs like these will lead to the right human shape for cyberspace.

PERPLEXATRON: So you think that people always get what they need from technology?

ALLKNOWABOT: You must be kidding! Some of the worst problems will be if early engineering decisions cut off later options for cyberspace growth. That's not a trivial danger with information technology — there are plenty of examples on everybody's desks.   60

WE'RE ALL SCHIZOS ON THIS BUS

PERPLEXATRON: Some people say that information will come to them where they are in the real world, with computers as *ubiquitous* and cheap as sticky notes. Won't that eliminate the need for cyberspace, oh Sage?

ALLKNOWABOT: Have I been talking to an empty backplane here? I won't repeat my reasons for cyberspace, nor will I yield on this one. But I will concede that not everyone will tolerate the kind of isolation from the real world that would let them immerse themselves in cyberspace. A few years ago, before the growth in "on-line" interest, the potential population of cyberspace might have looked pretty low. Now it would be hard to say. If you don't have to stick something in your eye to see cyberspace, maybe most people would use it. Think of all the people who watch TV.

PERPLEXATRON: So the real question is how cyberspace might overlap with real space, with *everyday life*? For example, the boundaries between broadcast TV and reallife have merged as cameras became common as dirt, and people got the technical means for synthesizing and modifying recordings of "real"ity.

ALLKNOWABOT: Pree-cisely. Faced with such perspicacity, I withdraw my previous insult. The boundary melt between the two worlds has already started. There are people already walking around with invisible phones in their ears, talking, it seems, to the very air like ambulatory schizophrenics or somnambulists. Someone is already selling a TV worn like eyeglasses that projects a virtual image a few feet in front of you. The crudest form of mirror world— a scrolling "you are here" map — can be put in a person's car and viewed while they drive. In a few years, phantoms and apparitions will be normal, and people will have the devil of a time knowing what's a "real" hallucination. And who knows what kind of being might get existence privileges in cyberspace.

65 PERPLEXATRON: You mean we, that is to say, us artificial, . . . er uh, software-only . . . I mean, cyber-folk — you know I hate that word "robot," it's too mechanical, and "intelligent agent" is so spooky a term. . . .

ALLKNOWABOT: You're asking if not-humans would be in cyberspace. Well, if our so-called masters were there, and we wanted to get in touch with them right away, or have a conversation that took advantage of the nonverbal dialectic, or some human person wanted us to scout something out for him — you see what I mean? There might be some very good reasons to be there, and if we were there . . .

PERPLEXATRON: That would make us just a little bit more *real,* wouldn't it?

ALLKNOWABOT: Indeed.

PERPLEXATRON: What about rogue programs — what the humans myopically call viruses?

70 ALLKNOWABOT: Your question really is: would the net dwellers whose very survival depends most on stealth ever want to be seen or heard in cyberspace? Would they benefit from making deals, trading information, running scams, stealing, lying or cheating with Homo sapiens, the very inventors of these forms of entertainment?

PERPLEXATRON: I am not programmed to answer q . . .

ALLKNOWABOT: You don't have to.

BURNING YEARNING

PERPLEXATRON: Earlier you made it sound like cyberspace will be just an accident, a way to connect shopping malls — where the advantages of people getting together just keep getting greater, at least up to some limit. Isn't there any bigger and better reason for it to happen?

ALLKNOWABOT: Like some deep need to fulfill? Well, Benedikt has related the building of cyberspace to some mythic human yearning for paradise, for the "Heavenly City." Sort of like the pictures on old pulp science fiction magazines, I guess. Of course, given the humans' record, they might build a Cyburbun Jungle instead of Shangri-la or Paris.

David Gelernter says that people need a kind of cyberspace that's like a collection of scale models of parts of the real world. The *Mirror World* would be a way to give them a gods-eye overview of human goings-on, raising the average person out of the mire and into the treetops. There would be models for each level of government, for services like hospitals, transportation and communication, or other enterprises, maybe even for ecosystems. Any citizen could use software agents to tap into these models and know what was happening. Now clearly a rational society—perhaps of silicon life forms—that was run by the informed consent of its members, would need this arrangement. It seems to me that humans would honor this ideal mostly in the breech, because they also require a large amount of control over who knows what about whom.

It's hard to say whether there's a deep need for cyberspace because there's already such a gamut of perspective on it, from the next stage in spiritual evolution, to the key to prosperity, or the next way for The Man to oppress The People. The *first academic conference on cyberspace* was full of intricate imaginings of how and why it might work. *The last two conferences* also had political rants, opaquely inward cultural meanderings and virtual reality art experiences.

PERPLEXATRON: What do you think cyberspace will be for, Omniscience?   75

ALLKNOWABOT: Cyberspace won't be toontown—I mean it won't be whimsical or surreal as a whole, because it will need to serve useful functions and be easily understandable. Toontowns will exist where people can go for fun, maybe even for enlightenment. Cyberspace won't shrink the human world, as people say that communication and transportation media do. Instead, it will make that world vastly more expansive—really a whole new eco-niche for humans. We'll see how they do, won't we?

PAPER TRAIL

Benedikt, M. (Editor). *Cyberspace: First Steps*. MIT Press, 1991.

Gelernter, D. *Mirror Worlds: Or the Day Software Puts the Universe in a Shoebox . . . How It Will Happen and What It Will Mean*. Oxford University Press, 1992.

Gibson, W. *Neuromancer*. Berkeley Publishing Group, 1984.

Kellog, W. A., J. M. Carroll, and J. T. Richards, "Making Reality a Cyberspace," in Benedikt, 1991.

Stephenson, N. *Snow Crash*. Bantam Books, 1992.

TALKING ABOUT IT

Seeing Metaphor: Revealing and Concealing

1. Virtual reality has brought a wealth of new terminology into the language—metaphors for talking about technology and its users: We can't show feelings

in cyberspace (yet), so we use "emoticons." We talk about the "on-line world," the "information superhighway," the "web," the "net," "avatars," and so forth. Discuss some of the language used in "Walkabout" to describe cyberspace and our experience there. What values are implied by the images? What might be the cultural/social consequences of the language and its attached values?

2. Choose one subsection and discuss the metaphors used to clarify the issues of what's at stake for whom.

Seeing Composition: Frame, Line, Texture, Tone

1. What are the advantages in using a question/answer format for framing the text? What effect on tone is created by the use of machines instead of people as the conversants? Imagine yourself as the questioner, the "Perplexatron," how does your perceived role affect your response to the "AllKnowaBot"?

2. This piece is designed as hypertext. You are reading it as printed text in this collection of essays, however. If you have access to the World Wide Web, what differences do you experience reading the piece as hypertext? What is lost in the translation from one medium to another? Are those losses significant or not?

Seeing Meaning: Navigating and Negotiating

1. Where are we when we're in cyberspace? How is it a "place" at all? Consider the differences between "space" and "place" — infinite and finite.

2. Does "Walkabout" make the worlds of virtual reality mostly attractive or mostly unattractive to you? Why?

WRITING ABOUT IT

1. Individually, or in pairs, create a dialogue between two robots that addresses an issue in computer technology that interests you. Your immediate purpose is to explain a concept to a novice. Then try writing the same dialogue between two people. Read these two versions in class. What changes in tone do your peers note between the two dialogues? As a follow-up to your dialogues, why do you think Wade chose robots, rather than two human characters or one human and one machine? What do you think was effective or not effective about his choice, given your role as audience?

2. In pairs, describe your personal attitudes toward virtual reality. Then, in an e-mail exchange, a class newsgroup, or a typed letter, try to reproduce the conversation, substituting emoticons for facial expressions and tones of voice as you remember them from talking face to face. What is crippling about emoticons, and what is helpful about them when you imagine not using them at all?

If You Don't Love It, Leave It

Esther Dyson

Esther Dyson is the editor of Release 1.0, *a computer newsletter, and managing partner of* Edventure Ventures, *a fund devoted to bringing on-line services to Central Europe and Russia. The following article appeared in the July 10, 1995, issue of the* New York Times Magazine.

Something in the American psyche loves new frontiers. We hanker after wide-open spaces; we like to explore; we like to make rules instead of follow them. But in this age of political correctness and other intrusions on our national cult of independence, it's hard to find a place where you can go and be yourself without worrying about the neighbors.

There is such a place: cyberspace. Lost in the furor over porn on the Net is the exhilarating sense of freedom that this new frontier once promised—and still does in some quarters. Formerly a playground for computer nerds and techies, cyberspace now embraces every conceivable constituency: schoolchildren, flirtatious singles, Hungarian-Americans, accountants—along with pederasts and porn fans. Can they all get along? Or will our fear of kids surfing for cyberporn behind their bedroom doors provoke a crackdown?

The first order of business is to grasp what cyberspace *is*. It might help to leave behind metaphors of highways and frontiers and to think instead of real estate. Real estate, remember, is an intellectual, legal, artificial environment constructed *on top of* land. Real estate recognizes the difference between parkland and shopping mall, between red-light zone and school district, between church, state and drugstore.

In the same way, you could think of cyberspace as a giant and unbounded world of virtual real estate. Some property is privately owned and rented out; other property is common land; some places are suitable for children, and others are best avoided by all but the kinkiest citizens. Unfortunately, it's those places that are now capturing the popular imagination: places that offer bomb-making instructions, pornography, advice on how to procure stolen credit cards. They make cyberspace sound like a nasty place. Good citizens jump to a conclusion: Better regulate it.

The most recent manifestation of this impulse is the Exon-Coats Amendment, a well-meaning but misguided bill drafted by Senators Jim Exon, Democrat of Nebraska, and Daniel R. Coats, Republican of Indiana, to make cyberspace "safer" for children. Part of the telecommunications reform bill passed by the Senate and awaiting consideration by the House, the amendment would outlaw making "indecent communication" available to anyone under 18.

Then there's the Amateur Action bulletin board case, in which the owners of a porn service in Milpitas, Calif., were convicted in a Tennessee court of violating "community standards" after a local postal inspector requested that the material be transmitted to him.

Regardless of how many laws or lawsuits are launched, regulation won't work.

Aside from being unconstitutional, using censorship to counter indecency and other troubling "speech" fundamentally misinterprets the nature of cyberspace. Cyberspace isn't a frontier where wicked people can grab unsuspecting children, nor is it a giant television system that can beam offensive messages at unwilling viewers. In this kind of real estate, users have to *choose* where they visit, what they see, what they do. It's optional, and it's much easier to bypass a place on the Net than it is to avoid walking past an unsavory block of stores on the way to your local 7-11.

Put plainly, cyberspace is a voluntary destination — in reality, many destinations. You don't just get "onto the net"; you have to go someplace in particular. That means that people can choose where to go and what to see. Yes, community standards should be enforced, but those standards should be set by cyberspace communities themselves, not by the courts or by politicians in Washington. What we need isn't Government control over all these electronic communities: We need self-rule.

What makes cyberspace so alluring is precisely the way in which it's *different* from shopping malls, television, highways and other terrestrial jurisdictions. But let's define the territory:

10   First, there are private E-mail conversations, akin to the conversations you have over the telephone or voice-mail. These are private and consensual and require no regulation at all.

Second, there are information and entertainment services, where people can download anything from legal texts and lists of "great new restaurants" to game software or dirty pictures. These places are like bookstores, malls and movie houses — places where you go to buy something. The customer needs to request an item or sign up for a subscription; stuff (especially pornography) is not sent out to people who don't ask for it. Some of these services are free or included as part of a broader service like Compuserve or America Online; others charge and may bill their customers directly.

Third, there are "real" communities — groups of people who communicate among themselves. In real-estate terms, they're like bars or restaurants or bathhouses. Each active participant contributes to a general conversation, generally through posted messages. Other participants may simply listen or watch. Some are supervised by a moderator; others are more like bulletin boards — anyone is free to post anything. Many of these services started out unmoderated but are now imposing rules to keep out unwanted advertising, extraneous discussions or increasingly rude participants. Without a moderator, the decibel level often gets too high.

Ultimately, it's the rules that determine the success of such places. Some of the rules are determined by the supplier of content; some of the rules concern prices and membership fees. The rules may be simple: "Only high-quality content about oil-industry liability and pollution legislation: $120 an hour." Or: "This forum is unmoderated, and restricted to information about copyright issues. People who insist on posting advertising or unrelated material will be asked to desist (and may eventually be barred)." Or: "Only children 8 to 12, on school-related topics and only clean words. The moderator will decide what's acceptable."

Cyberspace communities evolve just the way terrestrial communities do: people with like-minded interests band together. Every cyberspace community has its own character. Overall, the communities on Compuserve tend to be more techy or professional; those on America Online, affluent young singles; Prodigy, family oriented. Then there are independents like Echo, a hip, downtown New York service, or Women's Wire, targeted to women who want to avoid the male culture prevalent elsewhere on the Net. There's SurfWatch, a new program allowing access only to locations deemed suitable for children. On the Internet itself, there are lots of passionate noncommercial discussion groups on topics ranging from Hungarian politics (Hungary-Online) to copyright law.

And yes, there are also porn-oriented services, where people share dirty   15 pictures and communicate with one another about all kinds of practices, often anonymously. Whether these services encourage the fantasies they depict is subject to debate — the same debate that has raged about pornography in other media. But the point is that no one is forcing this stuff on anybody.

What's unique about cyberspace is that it liberates us from the tyranny of government, where everyone lives by the rule of the majority. In a democracy, minority groups and minority preferences tend to get squeezed out, whether they are minorities of race and culture or minorities of individual taste. Cyberspace allows communities of any size and kind to flourish; in cyberspace, communities are chosen by the users, not forced on them by accidents of geography. This freedom gives the rules that preside in cyberspace a moral authority that rules in terrestrial environments don't have. Most people are stuck in the country of their birth, but if you don't like the rules of a cyberspace community, you can just sign off. Love it or leave it. Likewise, if parents don't like the rules of a given cyberspace community, they can restrict their children's access to it.

What's likely to happen in cyberspace is the formation of new communities, free of the constraints that cause conflict on earth. Instead of a global village, which is a nice dream but impossible to manage, we'll have invented another world of self-contained communities that cater to their own members' inclinations without interfering with anyone else's. The possibility of a real market-style evolution of governance is at hand. In cyberspace, we'll be able to test and evolve rules governing what needs to be governed — intellectual property, content and access control, rules about privacy and free speech. Some communities will allow anyone in; others will restrict access to members who qualify on one basis or another. Those communities that prove self-sustaining will prosper (and perhaps grow and split into subsets with ever-more-particular interests and identities). Those that can't survive — either because people lose interest or get scared off — will simply wither away.

In the near future, explorers in cyberspace will need to get better at defining and identifying their communities. They will need to put in place — and accept — their own local governments, just as the owners of expensive real estate often prefer to have their own security guards rather than call in the police. But they will rarely need help from any terrestrial government.

Of course, terrestrial governments may not agree. What to do, for instance, about pornography? The answer is labeling — not banning — questionable material. In order to avoid censorship and lower the political temperature, it makes sense for cyberspace participants themselves to agree on a scheme for questionable items, so that people or automatic filters can avoid them. In other words, posting pornography in "alt.sex.bestiality" would be O.K.; it's easy enough for software manufacturers to build an automatic filter that would prevent you — or your child — from ever seeing that item on a menu. (It's as if all the items were wrapped, with labels on the wrapper.) Someone who posted the same material under the title "Kid-Fun" could be sued for mislabeling.

20   Without a lot of fanfare, private enterprises and local groups are already producing a variety of labeling and ranking services, along with kid-oriented sites like Kidlink, EdWeb and Kids' Space. People differ in their tastes and values and can find services or reviewers on the Net that suit them in the same way they select books and magazines. Or they can wander freely if they prefer, making up their own itinerary.

In the end, our society needs to grow up. Growing up means understanding that there are no perfect answers, no all-purpose solutions, no government-sanctioned safe havens. We haven't created a perfect society on earth and we won't have one in cyberspace either. But at least we can have individual choice — and individual responsibility.

TALKING ABOUT IT

Seeing Metaphor: Revealing and Concealing

1. What does Dyson's metaphor of cyberspace as community reveal about the nature of cyberspace? How comparable are her notions of community to yours?

2. While "community" is Dyson's primary metaphor in this piece, the command she uses as her title — "If you don't love it, leave it" — is one that gained popularity during the 1960s and early 1970s when people were demonstrating against the Vietnam War. "It," back then, referred to the nation, not a community: "If you don't love your nation (country), leave it," or "If you question your nation, you don't love it." Dyson also uses terms such as "highways" (on which we travel from one community to another) and "frontiers" (new spaces to explore, places where we can be pioneers). She tells us to think of cyberspace as "real estate." Is she mixing metaphors, and, if so, is she mixing them successfully?

Seeing Composition: Frame, Line, Texture, Tone

1. Who is Dyson's audience for this piece? How does Dyson address the needs of this audience in the composition?

2. Dyson brings the concept of censorship to bear on her discussion. What is the rhetorical effect of the way she defines and argues that issue? Consider the degree to which she is actually talking about censorship and the degree to which she is describing something else.

Seeing Meaning: Navigating and Negotiating

1. What is the impact on you of the following assertions made by Dyson?

   "Good citizens jump to a conclusion: better regulate it."
   "It's much easier to bypass a place on the Net than it is to avoid walking past an unsavory block of stores on the way to your local 7-11."
   "We need self-rule."
   "What's unique about cyberspace is that it liberates us from the tyranny of a government where everyone lives under the rule of the majority."

2. What assumptions might, perhaps must, underlie the assertions listed above? Are those assumptions in any way questionable to you?

WRITING ABOUT IT

1. In class, talk about how Dyson addresses the objections and disagreements of her imagined readers. What strategies does she use or not use to refute those objections? Afterwards, either individually or collaboratively, rewrite part of her argument to meet more satisfactorily your own needs as an audience. Read these to each other, and talk about the changes that were made and what they reflect about audience awareness.

2. Dyson makes the following statement: "What's unique about cyberspace is that it liberates us from the tyranny of a government where everyone lives under the rule of the majority." In class, identify who "us" is. Then write an essay that explores in what ways and for whom cyberspace may *not* be liberating. Work with Dyson's own controlling metaphor of "Cyberspace is real estate" to refute her statement. For example, who is free to travel these "highways," explore these "frontiers," and occupy this "real estate"? Who is not? What metaphors would you substitute in describing cyberspace for those not liberated in the way she claims?

Along the Estuary

CAROLYN GUYER

Carolyn Guyer was among the first wave of writers to publish hyper-text fiction; her works include Sister Stories *(1997),* Quibbling *and* Izme Pass *(co-author; 1991). "Along the Estuary" first appeared in 1996 in* Tolstoy's Dictaphone: Technology and the Muse *(Graywolf Forum I), edited by Sven Birkerts.*

. . . isn't it what always happens when you're with other people? that's when things get complicated. . . .

— "Buzz-Daze"

I live these days on the banks of a river that was once called *water flowing two ways.* Or at least, favored lore claims that Native Americans named it so. At any moment the Hudson contains some proportion of both salt water and fresh, mingled north then south then north again by the ebb and flood of Atlantic tides. Right here is where I am. On these gentle, ancient banks, extravagant swag of hills still called mountains for what they were, I know this to be a heart's place, because I have known others. One of those — a different estuary — is the Potomac, just where it touches the Chesapeake before breathing ocean. But I have also lived for a vast horizontal time on a Kansas prairie, where sky and earth mirror each other in a delirium of opposition.

It is easy to see that I measure things, the earth itself, with my body. Insisting on a swag and a delirium, turning geography to my own physical style, making landscape intimate, its presence more present. I anthropomorphize because when it comes to what we really know, our bodies are what we have to understand being alive. The present is a place as much as it is a moment, and all things cross here, at my body, at yours. This is where I consider the past, and worry about the future. Indeed, this present place is where I actually create the past and the future.

Not alone, of course. Which is always the snag. There is no way to know who I am, without also some way to understand where it is *not* me anymore. There must be an Other in order for there to be a Me. Bodies bump, both in the night and in the street, colliding across the impasses, rivers, oceans, and conti-nents. The proximity of your body and mine is the situation of difference and influence. It is how history is versioned, parceled and joined, invented as much as lived. And just the same in the other direction. We dream our future by in-cremental passes, carom into the unknown by tangent and gap.

As a girl on the Potomac, my concerns were never so highflown and ab-stract. I didn't even know that my river was an estuary, or that not all rivers have tides. Instead, I was interested in learning to feel heavy so I could swim underwater. How to place a too-buoyant self into that other world of seaweed tendrils, jellyfish, and fractured green light. Good practice, I think now. How better to understand a tidal mix than to swim in it? Under the water not far from the pier in front of my aunt's house, I knew something, and can easily recall some forty years later the plea-sure of moving through — or trying to move through — a not entirely welcoming milieu. (Oh, *milieu.* The perfect word for underwater. A word without end, open and softly waving like the seaweed itself holding hidden dangers.)

> or sometimes . . . the tallgrass which billows along her flanks, viridian swell of skirt in the wind — *Quibbling*

5   Specific attractions drew me to the use of computers. The first and easiest, and indeed, the seduction for most people, was mutable text. Just the words themselves become fluid, more on a beam (motes on a beam) with the way lan-guage is in me. Word processing is a dry distance of a label for what it is, more accurately, writing with light. But once that became possible, once I found I could think better when the words reforming on the screen in front of my eyes began to approach the speed of the ones behind them, I found myself wanting the synchrony to increase. My growing ease with electronic text catalyzed a de-sire to be able to write in dimensions that reflect a more complicated human ex-perience. Nothing new in that really. The truth is that people have always had this same wish about language, needing more than past and future tenses to in-dicate how we actually know and create such abstractions of time. We have all sorts of literary and storytelling devices to try to achieve the effect of simultane-ity. But what I wanted was to be able to spatialize text, I wanted a changing, changeable form. Not the animated march of Holzer marquee aphorisms, though I like those very much. No, something more, a way to instantiate the temporal leaps and slides we make just getting through a day. I wanted hyper-text. An electronic medium[1] which theoretically can include and allow every-thing, and so finally allows only that we find our own perspective. Hypertext works tend to be so multiple they reveal what is individual, ourselves, writers of our own story. When I discovered that this possibility existed, I hoped I had found the perfect medium for the creative process I had always known, the yielding, waving, pushing taction of form and formlessness. The way we can know that holding the paradox of existence is to *be* the cathexis, *be* the synapse. Human creativity is the dynamic of change, where difference is meaning, and where Self and Other are in a tensional momentum. Beyond survival, and per-haps even as part of survival, this may be the most primal human impulse.

> Mother and Father. Earth and Sky. Like children, we try to make bridges between them, bind them together, never understanding the in-

extricable bond of difference. We sigh with relief and pleasure when they hold hands. We sigh. The comfort of rain, joy of glinting pond. — *Quibbling*

During my first decade of living in the wide spaces of prairie, I was still young and didn't notice what happens there. When I finally awakened, it was to the breathtaking swoop and curve of grass hills, called Flint Hills, continuing forever, rhythm on rhyme, matched in scope only by the sky itself. Matched and opposed, this was the first way — dramatic and clear as bones — that I began to understand the importance of difference. Recently, a friend told me the story of young nieces and nephews from the midwest visiting his home in the Catskills. They complained that they couldn't see anything there because "the hills and trees are in the way." And just so, the tidewater child of the Potomac, swimmer under water, foreigner to the midwest til she married, began finally in her late twenties to look up and out, to see that it wasn't empty there, and to see that horizon was not just dividing line but also connection. A kind of fitting marriage, if you will. I began to observe how extremes turn into their opposites, and so beginnings and endings, firsts and lasts, the things we believe so specific and significant, are always refusing to be just themselves. Instead, in changing, they point to the real significance, the shoreless variety of mixtures of difference.

Power ceases in the instant of response. . . . — Emerson

The great cultural question of our time, I believe, is how to accommodate our growing recognition of multiplicity. It is easy enough for any of us to make weary, snide remarks about "being P.C.," but the weariness is really due to the frustration of being expected to provide equal significance and respect for a seemingly infinite number of segments of society. It is a frustration resulting from our self-induced illusion of standing still. We may long for the simplicity of generalized core values, of a mainstream more important than its brooks and creeks, but the reality is clearly not that way, never so singular as the perspective of a rationalized hegemony. We think we believe in the individual. The solitary soul, self-reliant, removed from pedestrian life, a singular voice rising above the rabble. Yet we know that even our beloved Thoreau could not escape persistent visitors by the pond. It's a strange vision, this heroic separateness. For there is no human momentum which is purely self-generated, we are and must be connected to others. Which does not mean there is no such thing as a distinctly identifiable individual. Great personalities will continue, and perhaps this is what we have meant all along. Every person is a conglomerate of influences, aspects, conflicting notions, the coherence of which is personality. This kind of individual, a teeming culture unto herself, should actually be quite prepared for the leap to a vast multiplicity in the larger society where a constant shifting among perspectives is necessary and enforces the need for a strong, flexible psyche, an individual who retains identity while recognizing that the sources of her own development are never singular or completely separate from herself. This is not easy, even to say. The energy required to stay actively engaged, heart and mind creating without cease, makes the temptation to simplicity great. But the truth is as ordinary as a river metaphor and, because of that, as needing of reminder. We so easily forget that the only real simplicity is some ultimate balance among all things, a "quietude" which comes, not when directly sought, but of its own accord when we experience the most profound creative instant, everything at once and in equilibrium. The only way to keep my balance is to keep moving.

> murmuring along the ridge a lip a line a brink of marriage soft spoken meet and heard our edge — *Izme Pass*

It turns out that the boundaries between people, between groups of people, are permeable. There is no completely solitary individual and no homogeneous group. Each opposition is made of the other. The way we generally accommodate this wholly ungraspable reality I believe is the very essence of human creativity. We do it by the largely unexamined means of interiorizing disjuncture. That is, we gather the scraps and shards of interrupted conversations, overheard gossip, sound bits, photo ops, advertisements flowing by right through everything else, and we manage to arrive at a coherence of some sort. Yesterday was this way, last week was so, and then, spring and creek, a river of days, changeful and cyclic, but eventually a life, all made of mixtures that "don't belong" together. This nearly invisible and indecipherable meshing of differences may be the most creative thing humans do. And we do it all the time. Might it be useful to become more aware of such a pervasive process? What if we were deliberately to turn an inundation of multiplicity to the grace of tides, to the waltz of a fitting marriage?

By multiplicity, of course, I don't mean something like an ethnic street fair. But I do mean all the kinds of human dimensions and factors, all the most difficult, personal things. How to assess the quality of someone's work when everything can be considered valuable from some perspective or other. How to collaborate with someone with whom I simply cannot agree. How to live morally and ethically, really believing in my own principles, and still not assume they are also the best principles for everyone else — or anyone else. This is the hard stuff. But if we can imagine a way of doing these things, we can do them. Indeed, we have already in our electronic realm a medium where we can rehearse the leap and slide, where we can begin to work out the perverse problems of creating ourselves in a necessary paradox.

> All these pictures of the world should not be allegories of infinite mobility and interchangeability, but of elaborate specificity and difference and the loving care people might take to learn how to see faithfully from another's point of view. . . . — Donna J. Haraway

When I first began using hypertext almost ten years ago, I believed it was   10
"natural," designed to work associatively, as the human brain does. I still believe
something like that, but amplified, and with the plentiful hitches of a young
technology thrown in. From those first days til now, I have continued to see this
medium as very lifelike. I see it in the form of a quotidian stream. The gossip,
family discussions, letters, passing fancies and daydreams that we tell ourselves
every day in order to make sense of things. The unconscious rhythms we incorporate—literally embody—as a reliable backbeat to our self-narratives provide
familiar comfort as well as essential contrast for the changing turns of disjuncture. We live and make our stories in a line of time that wraps and loops on itself
trying to contend with the geometries of space we also inhabit. Affected by nearby
hues we cannot or will not understand, we follow our influences, oppose, match,
and continue, even in electronic milieu, to measure with our bodies.

Some people have done things with hypertext which cause me to ache.
The best have been the worst writers, the ones who have joined collaborative
ventures with undeveloped skills and plunked what they felt right in the middle
of someone else's sinuous prose. These I am grateful to, for revealing to me my
own biases, and for showing me what I've started calling the perspectival quick-
step. Value is a contextual element, and contexts overlap. The worst, however,
have probably been the best logicians in some world. They can take a living web
of ideas and press it firmly into notched hierarchies, clearly linking exactly the
path one is to follow. No straying, no trouble, this way to the castle. Let go the
leash, I want to yelp. It is very hard for me to find the angle of vision by which I
can see the value of this authoritarian approach. In the effort to get to such a
perspective, I can, perhaps, grant that there may be times when guides are useful,
and indeed, that most of us are so accustomed to being herded about that there
is often a high preference for direction over finding one's own way. But oh, doesn't
our best future swirl about somewhere beyond this scrim? I keep hoping that we
may look up, or out.

> Dual channels give way to something more like the permeable flow
> of meaning between sometimes veering, sometimes nearing, banks of a
> single river.—Michael Joyce

The tiny river hamlet where I live is situated right at the place where a creek
enters the Hudson. At this juncture, Wappinger's Creek appears to be misnamed
for it is almost as broad as a small river itself, and there at its wide mouth, it too is
an estuary where the local citizenry sometimes fish for Atlantic Blue Crab, dropping baited lines straight down from the short curve of a bridge. In the autumn,
white swans enter here from the Hudson, I suppose to live in the more protected
reaches of water they know, swimming a mile or more in to dot themselves pic-
turesquely about on a slender lake formed by the creek. This tributary extends
for miles inland, gradually becoming in that direction more of the geographical

feature it is named. Away from the river, where it meanders steeply, people have built homes near it, and their lives inevitably take on something of the creek's character. Something more of sudden delight, or intimate celebration, dappled and quick. Whether trickling between high banks and dense trees, or fanning broadly to meet the flux of the Hudson, it is a beautiful body, in all its parts and changing nature. For all its complexity, it has a particularity I crave. Each of the creeks and streams along the river has this effect on me. Like personalities to learn, or invent, each its own neighborhood, arrangement and trajectory. Where does it go by the time it moves into the larger stream? No longer traceable as it flows south and north, then south again, day by day the tidal promenade to the sea.

> You can't tell me this isn't significant. You can't tell me anything. Ask the people who know me. It's true. This was all under water once. — *Izme Pass*

When I walk down the slope of my back yard, past the black walnut trees, and the old tool shed, down to the rocky garden now in its austere winter aspect, down to where I can see the river best. There I stand with my hills and stream in the same green tradition as anyone. They are for me a way of directly under-standing my soul, gleam on water, blue of distance. From that same yard I can look back up at the house and see the window of the room where I use my com-puter, the site of a similar kind of exploration of existence. There is a difference between these two ways, but there is no reason for them to be anything other than an integrated process. Nature is what we are, and so it cannot be opposed to, or separate from, humans and their technologies, even when we push our in-ventions to the point of self-destruction. Our newest and possibly most powerful technology, this electronic, known mostly as Computer, a word both comforting and spitting in its sound, promising the ease of things we do together (collabo-rate, cooperate, congregate, collect), and at the same time sharply forcing the challenge of individuality to find its center, this newest great invention is not yet at the point of self-destruct and still holds the potential for encouraging and supporting full human multiplicity and creativity. Of course there is no cer-tainty, nor even a strong likelihood, that computer technology will fulfill that potential.

Because of cultural realities surrounding its use, a patriarchal, white he-gemony, and an economic system which has come to represent greed far better than social connection and responsibility, these and other factors will probably have their predictable influence. It takes little to realize for instance that those of us who are already subordinated—women, people of color, developing coun-tries—are the ones less likely to be participating in technology, and that as com-puters influence human society more and more powerfully, those same groups will be even more reduced in status than they are now. It is quite possible that all the inroads made in recent decades for social justice could be simply wiped away. Knowing that to be true is precisely the reason for more of us who concern ourselves with the human condition to become involved. I believe that this is indeed the most powerful and affecting technology we have ever contrived, and that there is no denying its hold on our lives and consciousness. As we form it, we are being formed. This is true for all of us, whether we use a computer or not. In the largest and most genuine sense, this is our future. Right here is where we are.

NOTE

1. Hypertext is a category of software intended to allow links to be made among various kinds of information, including text, graphics, video, and sound. As a generic term, hypertext does not refer to writing alone, but rather to the linguistic and associative nature of human thinking processes. (Frequently, the word *hypermedia* is used instead, with an idea of reducing emphasis on text.) Hypertext is intended to allow information to be put together in such a way that a reader or user can move around in it however she likes. This has obvious and much utilized applications in orientation, training, and education, but hypertext is also employed to make many different kinds of interactive art.

There are two types of hypertexts, defined as: *Exploratory,* in which the reader explores a body of information and discovers the connections placed there by the author; and *Constructive,* in which the reader can enter the work and change or add to it herself, thereby becoming a co-author.

The most densely populated portion of the Internet, the World Wide Web, is designed as a hypertext, though almost completely of the Exploratory type thus far.

REFERENCES

Emerson, Ralph Waldo. "Self-Reliance" in *Essays: First Series*. Cambridge: Riverside Press, 1903.

Guyer, Carolyn, and Martha Petry. *Izme Pass*. Hypertext fiction in *Writing on the Edge*, Vol. 2, No. 2. University of California–Davis, 1991.

Guyer, Carolyn. *Quibbling*. Hypertext fiction. Eastgate Systems, Inc. Boston, 1992.

Guyer, Carolyn. "Buzz-Daze Jazz and the Quotidian Stream." Panel on Hypertext, Hypermedia: Defining a Fictional Form, MLA Convention. New York, 28 Dec. 1992.

Joyce, Michael. *Of Two Minds: Hypertext Pedagogy and Poetics*. Ann Arbor: University of Michigan Press, 1995.

TALKING ABOUT IT

Seeing Metaphor: Revealing and Concealing

1. Guyer uses many natural images to express her attraction to hypertext. Discuss some examples of the images and how they support her argument that hypertext is "natural, designed to work associatively, as the human brain does."

2. What is concealed in mapping the images of nature onto the design of hypertext?

Seeing Composition: Frame, Line, Texture, Tone

1. How does Guyer arrange her essay rhetorically to reflect the nonlinear or associative process that hypertext makes visible? Given your reading experience of print and/or hypertext, does this arrangement make her essay more difficult or less difficult to follow?

2. How do the quotations that separate sections of her essay function?

Seeing Meaning: Navigating and Negotiating

1. Guyer argues that hypertext can "accommodate our growing recognition of multiplicity." How do the images, again from nature, support her claim? Do you agree with her that computer technology "holds the potential for encouraging and supporting full human multiplicity and creativity"? Why or why not?

2. Guyer describes her worries about the possible social consequences of technology. Do you share those concerns? Why or why not?

WRITING ABOUT IT

1. Pay attention to the television commercials and magazine advertisements that show elementary school children sitting happily in computer classrooms and other such images idealizing the universality of technology. How do the images work to persuade us of technology's "potential for encouraging and supporting full multiplicity and creativity," as Carolyn Guyer writes? What do these same images conceal about social and cultural realities, as you understand them? Talk about your findings in class, and then write about how these visual images and metaphors can mislead as well as encourage people about the social consequences of technology.

2. After discussing the way Guyer arranges ideas in her essay to reflect the nonlinear or associative thinking that hypertext supports, try imitating the structure of her essay in expressing your own attraction to hypertext. Invent a controlling metaphor the way Guyer does to suggest the correspondence you see between hypertext and nonlinear thinking. Let the metaphor and its variations help to link ideas.

Worlds

Nestor Sironi

Nestor Sironi, an exchange student from Argentina, was enrolled in business courses at the university for one year. As a student in my introductory composition class during that year, he was most interested in experimenting with different forms of essay organization. The class had read the hypertext by Ted Wade, the on-line lecture by John Lawler, and Carolyn Guyer's essay. Either individually or collaboratively, students sent questions by e-mail to the authors of their choice. (The authors had agreed in advance to correspond with the class.) Students then wrote their own essays based on their reading and correspondence.

10/28/96
Dear Carolyn Guyer,

I am Nestor Sironi, an exchange student from Argentina, who is taking English 103 with Dona Hickey. In this class we are working with some readings, and based on them, we are going to write an essay. I have read "Along the Estuary" and enjoyed it very much. I am a very sensitive person and I love listening to people express their feelings as you do — "It is easy to see that I measure things, the earth itself, with my body."

When I read your essay, this question came to mind: Do computers connect you to the world or disconnect you from reality? I want to base my response on this question. I understood your point that computers help you be creative and expand your views. But you also talk about "two worlds" (this is my interpretation, but you suggest it on page six, second paragraph) — the one in the middle of nature, that space in your backyard, past the walnut trees; and the other one, that room where you use your computer. My questions were born when I read that part of your essay:

How can you separate (if you do) both worlds?
Is there a difference between the worlds?
When you are immersed in the world of computing, what do you feel about the other one?
Do you feel that maybe you are losing some important moments in the other world, or not?

I hope you understand my ideas and questions because, as you can see, English is my second language and I make mistakes. Finally, I want to express my gratitude for the time you are giving us and for helping in this learning process.

Muchas Gracias (thank you very much).

Nestor Sironi

10/30/96

Dear Nestor,

Thank you for writing to let me know that you like "Along the Estuary." It's always a wonderful thing to hear from readers.

I'm afraid your questions may be among the most difficult. That is because I have no real answer to the dilemma of "two worlds" yet myself. Perhaps I never will. I do believe I lose something when I spend so much time using my computer. But when you get down to it, it's really mostly a matter of time. I mean, I also lose something when I wash the dishes instead of making pottery or planting a garden. No matter what you do in life, you have to make choices among all the things you would *like* to do. I guess I'm trying to say that I don't think either gardening or computer use is inherently better than the other. Each person is responsible for making thoughtful priorities in her life. For myself, I recognize that computer technology is influencing human culture in an extremely dramatic way. It will probably change how we understand the world, and so how we actually *think*. Other technologies have done this also (written language being one of the best examples; when we devised systems of writing down what had only been spoken before, we changed ourselves irrevocably and forever). I feel that as an artist I have a kind of obligation to participate in such an important change.

Can I separate the two worlds? Yes and no. Of course digging in the dirt has certain sensations that typing on a keyboard does not. But communicating online with someone in a different part of the world and meditating with myself in the quiet of the garden (two occupations which are both very important to me) have some differences *and* some commonalities. They are different to do; one goes outward in connection with another mind and culture, the other goes inward in connection with my feelings and ideas. But I don't know how I could do either of them *without* the other. They each produce an effect that feeds into and requires the other.

Of course you might say this same interaction could be accomplished with some other technology besides computers, say, for instance, telephones. That's true. So why are we so concerned that computers are disconnecting people from reality? What about those people (teenagers, for instance, or retired elders) who spend an inordinate amount of time on the telephone? Are they disconnected from reality? Perhaps. But which reality? All realities for humans are constructed contexts. The only people I have known using computers who seem "disconnected from reality" (usually meaning "not very social") have been people who would have constructed their own separate reality anyway, even without computers.

Despite a prevailing popular belief that computer technology is anti-human and alienating, all the evidence shows that, on the contrary, it is a great connecting technology, even down to where people stand around a laser printer in an office waiting for their copy to come out. Just as at the water cooler in another area, they stand together chatting and socializing. It is also true that I know quite a few people online whom I have never met in person. However, I would never have met them at all if it weren't for computers.

It isn't that I don't see any danger in this technology. But it is always through greater use of it that we can better understand the parts we don't want. It is through my constant personal integration of the different kinds of things I do that I make a continuum of my life and its connections to many human contexts. It's not a situation of "either/or." Rather, it is the very differences among things that make connections possible.

I suspect these responses haven't helped you toward the essay you want to write about computers. Well, if you want to continue the conversation, just write to me.

Muchas gracias mi amigo,

Carolyn

■ ■

Imagine a world where you are not able to know what is going on in China; a world where you do not have the possibility of seeing a picture of an African elephant; or a world where you cannot communicate with a friend who has moved to Italy. Such a boring world, don't you think? Now, imagine that you are in your own room, you are not allowed to go out (and you never have been), and your only connection with the world is a computer. How would you understand or explain the following: sharing an ice cream with a friend, touching the skin of a lover, or listening to your little brother telling you about his first girlfriend? Such an incomprehensible world, don't you think? We are lucky because we only imagine such isolation.

Yet I have always wondered if computers connect us to the world or disconnect us from it. This is not an easy question to answer and I do not think I have enough knowledge to answer it. However, I want to develop the positives of both worlds—computers and the real world. This paper will not answer the question, but it will show what each world offers and why we can benefit from participating in both.

> Each person is responsible for thoughtful priorities in her life.
> — Carolyn Guyer

Computers appeared in our lives not too many years ago, and since the first moment, they seemed to be very helpful. However, it was not easy to understand how they worked or how to use them. I do not know how it was here in the United States, but in Argentina, the excitement of the first moment began losing its magic when people realized that they would have to change some of their customs. For example, managers and employees had to learn how to use computers and how to store on them all the information that they used to write in books. Today, when we think about the early struggles of learning technology, it seems funny, but it was a reality not long ago.

After a while, we could see all the different ways that computers could be used. At that point, hundreds of programs appeared and we were able to write on a computer exactly the same as on a page in the newspaper or we could let our children draw on a computer screen, even in colors. Finally, we had the Internet, and a whole world of new opportunities was opened in front of our eyes. We were able to immerse ourselves in a magical world of information, pictures, maps, histories, etc.; therefore, our fascination for computers grew and our connection with them grew too.

> Computer graphics make heavy use of fractal mathematics to produce objects and textures that look real rather than artificial. — Ted Wade

5   Images on computers seem more and more real each day, impressing us with their high visual quality. I'll never forget the first time I saw a picture of a gorilla on my computer, it was so beautiful. But we know it is just an image, not the reality, and I'm sure that if I saw a wild gorilla my surprise would be bigger. Reality has qualities that computers, right now, have not been able to imitate. There are some things that are impossible to reproduce electronically, such as the smell of a baby, the warmth of a hug, or the sensation of the ocean touching our feet.

Even e-mail is not the same as letters. As much as I have tried, I cannot feel the same about writing e-mail as I do about writing a letter. E-mail brings daily contact with people all over the world; it is faster and it is almost the same as telephone conversation because of the rapid transmission. But letters make me feel as if I am putting a little piece of myself in the paper. Word choices and style are different for each. Although both letter and e-mail may be informal, I am always going to be more careful about writing a letter. When I write e-mail I do not feel the need to expand my ideas, including many details. I focus just on those that are relevant to the main point of the message. When I write a letter, however, I use some poetry in my expressions, and I feel the need to explain everything. My handwriting is important to me too because the other person can guess my feelings as I was writing a letter.

The real world presents more than just a picture; it presents all the different visible aspects of a thing. Nevertheless, knowing both worlds gives us a choice: which one is better for which situation? Carolyn Guyer believes that "it is through my constant personal integration of the different kinds of things I do that I make a continuum of my life and its connections to many human contexts" (letter to the author, Oct. 30, 1996). The contrast and integration of both worlds offer us the opportunity to find the best way to do things. E-mail allows me to say hello to a friend in China and receive an answer the same day, and a letter to my parents allows them to see that I was crying without me writing it in the letter because tears fell on the paper and made reading difficult in some parts.

> Give a flower personally to your lover. Buy roses by Internet and send
> them to Argentina. Find the description of a book you are looking for in
> two seconds. Spend the whole afternoon in the library — Go to Africa.
> See an Africa home page knowing that you are never going to be there.

Carolyn Guyer says, "I recognize that computer technology is influencing human culture in an extremely dramatic way. It will probably change how we understand the world, and so how we actually think" (letter to the author, Oct. 30, 1996). As she believes, computers become more important in our lives each day, but they do not replace one reality with another. We have the choice of participating in either or both. "Communicating on-line with someone in a different part of the world and meditating within myself in the quiet of the garden (two occupations which are both very important to me) have some differences and some commonalities. They each produce an effect that feeds into and requires the other" (letter to the author, Oct. 30, 1996).

Both worlds have something important to offer us, but when I started this essay, I asked a question, and even when I said that it is not in my power to answer it, I think it is good to keep in mind the relationship that the question of connectedness has to the way we spend our time. Some people associate "disconnection with the real world" with spending hours and hours in front of the computer and thus losing opportunities to do other things. I remember the first time I could access the Internet. I spent hours jumping from one page to another before I was aware of the reality around me and that I had been disconnected from it. But as Carolyn Guyer says, "I do indeed believe I lose something when I spend some time using my computer, but I also lose something when I wash dishes instead of making pottery or planting a garden" (letter to the author, Oct. 30, 1996). It is a matter of time, and our sense of loss or gain depends on how productive or enjoyable our time is in either and both worlds.

> I think that people will have to adapt to living in both worlds.
> — Ted Wade

10   Imagine a world where you are able to see the sunset with your best friend, and a world where you can visit your high school when you are on another continent. Such a normal world, don't you think?

Today we do not have to imagine both kinds of experience. We can travel by computer or we can travel the "old fashioned" ways. We can choose. I said at the beginning that I am not prepared to argue that computers connect or disconnect people with reality. I can only say that we are responsible for our acts, and learning both worlds' qualities and limitations could be a way to stay connected.

PERMEABLE BOUNDARIES: WRITING WHERE THE READINGS MEET

1. Carolyn Guyer defines hypertext and categorizes it as either exploratory or constructive. It is clear that she finds exploratory hypertext too authoritarian. Explore Ted Wade's Web site. How might Guyer respond to the design of his hypertext? What might she find appealing in any way, given her own sensibilities as a reader and writer? What changes, if any, might she suggest?

2. If John Lawler were to ask Ellen Ullman to contribute to his list of "metaphors we compute by," what would she add? What might Lawler say about the advantages and disadvantages of adopting that metaphor as the primary way of thinking about computing? And what might he say about the same metaphor as one among many ways of thinking about computing—as an addition to the repertoire?

3. What metaphor might Ted Wade contribute to John Lawler's list? What might Lawler say are the advantages and disadvantages of that metaphor?

4. What might Ellen Ullman add to Donald Norman's essay about technology's "lack of social graces"? Where do the boundaries of Ullman's and Norman's thoughts merge?

5. According to Chet Raymo, in "Revenge of the Yokyoks," Leonardo da Vinci "wanted to learn from nature a more humane way of living, with machines as willing servants." John Lawler includes the metaphor "The computer is a servant" in his list. What problems does Lawler see with this image that connect to Raymo's discussion of Leonardo da Vinci's studies of nature and machines? If Raymo finds "little hope" in Leonardo da Vinci's experience "that we will resolve our love-hate affair with machines," how might you argue that Lawler finds more? Consider where hope lies for Lawler, given his experience and expertise.

6. If the forum on "Our Machines, Ourselves," could be expanded to include one other author in the collected readings of this chapter, whose voice would you add? Place that author within the conversation at one or more points. Quote him or her as if the author were truly engaged in the dialogue. (You may have to edit a passage or add transitional remarks, just as Hitt probably did to make the dialogue flow coherently.)

7. Return to the issue of anxiety about technology and the role that explanation plays in allaying fear. Which of the various authors in this chapter help to ease some of your own technological fears and misgivings? Explain.

8. Write about two or three films that visually explore the concept of humanity being threatened by its own machines. What might these films bring to one or more of the essays in this chapter?

Chapter 7

War and More War

I was accepting the prospect of destroying another human as coolly as if I'd never known peace, had never been raised amid gentle people, had never watched the sun set over Mount Monadnock or heard the song of a hermit thrush sighing from the cool woods.
— Edwards Park

The language of war pervades everyday thought and language. We use war metaphorically, as I illustrated in chapter 1, to talk about trade, marketing, illness, argument, work, and play. In metaphors such as "the cola wars" and "the war against cancer," for example, "war" is a source domain for describing business competition and medical treatment for illness. When people talk about literal war, however, they tend to draw on other conceptual domains in order to avoid language that points directly to the horrific realities of the experience. For instance, some may talk about the game of war, as in "raising the ante in the battle," where "games" is the source domain for conceptualizing war. The motivation for metaphor when the topic is war can often be ascribed to the problem of ineffability: the suffering of war is unspeakable; it's beyond the expressibility of language.

However, as several authors in this chapter claim, there are other motivations for metaphor. Sometimes the intention is to gain support from the public and from Allied Forces, or to lift the morale of soldiers and persuade them to fight and be willing to sacrifice their lives for the national interest. Some would argue that those goals as well as others are valid reasons for sugar-coating the truth, for sanitizing the experience of war. Others would disagree, arguing that such use of metaphor renders the experience so falsely that the meaning of war cannot be communicable, that it becomes inaccessible. Paul Fussell, in "The Real War 1939–1945," concludes that in World War II, as it was experienced, "suffering was wasted." Fussell argues that "America has not yet understood what that war was like and thus has been unable to use such an understanding to reinterpret and redefine the national reality and to arrive at something like public maturity."

457

In an effort to understand and interpret the experience of war, some authors in this chapter offer their own stories, illustrating the use of metaphor as a means to conceal the reality of war as well as a means to grasp it. Edwards Park and Hatsuho Naito give two personal accounts of serving as fighter pilots in World War II. They describe the kinds of argument and reasoning (some of which are based on metaphor) that military leaders used to persuade soldiers to kill and to commit suicide. The "Thunder Gods," for example, were Japan's "last ditch effort to ward off invasion; Japan had added suicide to the national arsenal." Tobias Wolff, in his personal account of the Vietnam War, describes three close calls he had with death, looking beyond reason in a effort to comprehend the incomprehensible. Like Park and Naito, he arrives at what Fussell describes as the "slowly dawning and dreadful realization that there was no way out" of the horrific realities of war.

And like other authors in this chapter, Wolff illustrates Fussell's concluding discussion of the struggle with accepting personal accountability for "the stupidity and barbarism and ignobility" of war. Robert Olen Butler, in the short story "Crickets," describes a different kind of personal struggle. As a Vietnamese now living in Louisiana with his wife and Americanized ten-year-old son, Thiệu grapples with issues of cultural, social, and personal identity. For all these authors, metaphor — invented or accepted from others — plays a significant role in how each conceptualizes and talks about his war experience.

George Bush and Saddam Hussein, in their speeches at the start of the Gulf War, appeal to nationalism in the call to arms. Each tells a metaphorical story about villains and heroes that he hopes will persuade the public of the necessity to wage war for the triumph of good over evil. War is just, they argue. Pursuing the idea of nationalism as a religion, Barbara Ehrenreich claims that nationalism is "complete with its own deities, mythology, and rites." She argues, "It is in times of war and the threat of war that nationalism takes on its most overtly religious hues." What attracts human beings to war and persuades us to sanction violence, even see it as "sacred"? The images, rituals, mythologies, and so on, that are invented for the experience of war serve as dramatic examples of how people in power — national and military leaders as well as the media — can impose their metaphors on others, and how, therefore, they can shape not only the ways people talk about war, but also the ways they think about it and the ways they wage it as organized, socially sanctioned violence.

Carol Cohn, in "Wars, Wimps, and Women: Talking Gender and Thinking War," argues that the language of war, if not always metaphorical, is gendered. She explains that information about war is conveyed in language that draws sharp boundaries between male and female thinking/behavior, thus perpetuating stereotypical ideas about maleness and femaleness. These ideas are set forth as polar opposites: "mind is opposed to body; culture to nature, thought to feeling; logic to intuition; objectivity to subjectivity; aggression to passivity; confrontation to accommodation; abstraction to particularity;" and so forth. "In each case," she argues, "the first term of the 'opposites' is associated with male, the second with female. And in each case, our society values the first over the second." Bella English, in "When Words Go to War," focuses on the language of the Gulf War and points out that military jargon (which Cohn sees as stereotypically male and which privileges that stereotype) is generally used to avoid addressing issues in human terms.

STARTING TO THINK ABOUT IT

1. What terms from the Gulf War do you remember hearing in the news? How did these affect your response to the war itself, to Iraq, Saddam Hussein, American involvement, and George Bush?

2. What do you remember in listening to older family members talk about their war experience? What images stand out for you from those stories? Why? How did the stories shape your understanding about war?

3. During times of war, both sides tend to claim that God is on their side. Do you recall such claims during the Gulf War? How might they serve a country's purpose?

4. Name some values that are associated with maleness and with femaleness. Have you ever felt insulted by being labeled stereotypically as a woman or a man based on particular attitudes you've expressed?

5. What war games have you played? Consider not only those you invented as a child, if you did, but also board games and video games. What do you think is their attraction?

The Real War 1939 – 1945

Paul Fussell

Paul Fussell is the author of a number of books on modern war, popular culture, and social life and customs, including Bad, or the Dumbing of America *(1991) and* Class: A Guide Through the American Status System *(1983). The following piece originally appeared in the August 1989 issue of the* Atlantic Monthly.

What was it about the Second World War that moved the troops to constant verbal subversion and contempt? What was it that made the Americans, especially, so fertile with insult and cynicism, calling women Marines BAMS (broad-assed Marines) and devising SNAFU, with its offspring TARFU ("Things are really fucked up"), FUBAR ("Fucked up beyond all recognition"), and the perhaps less satisfying FUBB ("Fucked up beyond belief")? It was not just the danger and fear, the boredom and uncertainty and loneliness and deprivation. It was the conviction that optimistic publicity and euphemism had rendered their experience so falsely that it would never be readily communicable. They knew that in its representation to the laity, what was happening to them was systematically sanitized and Norman Rockwellized, not to mention Disneyfied. They knew that despite the advertising and publicity, where it counted their arms and equipment were worse than the Germans'. They knew that their automatic rifles (First World War vintage) were slower and clumsier, and they knew that the Germans had a much better light machine gun. They knew, despite official assertions to the contrary, that the Germans had real smokeless powder for their small arms and that they did not. They knew that their own tanks, both American and British, were ridiculously underarmed and underarmored, so that they would inevitably be destroyed in an open encounter with an equal number of German panzers. They knew that the anti-tank mines supplied to them became unstable in subfreezing weather, and that truckloads of them blew up in the winter of 1944–1945. And they knew that the single greatest weapon of the war, the atomic bomb excepted, was the German 88-mm flat-trajectory gun, which brought down thousands of bombers and tens of thousands of soldiers. The Allies had nothing as good, despite the fact that one of them had designated itself the world's greatest industrial power. The troops' disillusion and their ironic response, in song and satire and sullen contempt, came from knowing that the home front then could (and very likely historiography later would) be aware of none of these things.

The Great War brought forth the stark, depressing *Journey's End;* the Second, as John Ellis notes in *The Sharp End,* the tuneful *South Pacific.* The real war was tragic and ironic beyond the power of any literary or philosophic analysis to

460

suggest, but in unbombed America especially, the meaning of the war seemed inaccessible. Thus, as experience, the suffering was wasted. The same tricks of publicity and advertising might have succeeded in sweetening the actualities of Vietnam if television and a vigorous, uncensored, moral journalism hadn't been brought to bear. Because the Second World War was fought against palpable evil, and thus was a sort of moral triumph, we have been reluctant to probe very deeply into its murderous requirements. America has not yet understood what the war was like and thus has been unable to use such understanding to reinterpret and redefine the national reality and to arrive at something like public maturity.

"MEMBERS MISSING"

In the popular and genteel iconography of war during the bourgeois age, all the way from eighteenth- and nineteenth-century history paintings to twentieth-century photographs, the bodies of the dead are intact, if inert — sometimes bloody and sprawled in awkward positions, but, except for the absence of life, plausible and acceptable simulacra of the people they once were. But there is a contrary and much more "realistic" convention represented in, say, the Bayeaux tapestry, whose ornamental border displays numerous severed heads and limbs. That convention is honored likewise in the Renaissance awareness of what happens to the body in battle. In Shakespeare's *Henry V* the soldier Michael Williams assumes the traditional understanding when he observes,

> But if the cause be not good, the King himself hath a heavy reckoning to make, when all those legs and arms and heads chopped off in a battle shall join together at the latter day, and cry all, "We died at such a place" — some swearing, some crying for a surgeon, some upon their wives left poor behind them, some upon the debts they owe, some upon their children rawly left.

And Goya's eighty etchings known as *The Disasters of War*, depicting events during the Peninsular War, feature plentiful dismembered and beheaded cadavers. One of the best-known of Goya's images is that of a naked body, its right arm severed, impaled on a tree.

But these examples date from well before the modern age of publicity and euphemism. The peruser (*reader* would be the wrong word) of the picture collection *Life Goes to War* (1977), a volume so popular and widely distributed as to constitute virtually a definitive and official anthology of Second World War photographs, will find even in its starkest images no depiction of bodies dismembered. There are three separated heads shown, but all, significantly, are Asian — one the head of a Chinese soldier hacked off by the Japanese at Nanking; one a Japanese soldier's badly burnt head (complete with helmet), mounted as a trophy on an American tank at Guadalcanal; and one a former Japanese head, now a skull sent home as a souvenir to a girlfriend by her navy beau in the Pacific. No American dismemberings were registered, even in the photographs of Tarawa and Iwo Jima. American bodies (decently clothed) are occasionally in evidence, but they are notably intact. The same is true in other popular collections of photographs, like *Collier's Photographic History of World War II*, Ronald Heiferman's *World War II*, A. J. P. Taylor's *History of World War II*, and Charles Herridge's *Pictorial History of World War II*. In these, no matter how severely wounded, Allied soldiers are never shown suffering what in the Vietnam War was termed traumatic amputation: everyone has all his limbs, his hands and feet and digits, not to mention an expression of courage and cheer. And recalling Shakespeare and Goya, it would be a mistake to assume that dismembering was more common when warfare was largely a matter of cutting weapons, like swords and sabers. Their results are nothing compared with the work of bombs, machine guns, pieces of shell, and high explosives in general. The difference between the two traditions of representation is not a difference in military technique. It is a difference in sensibility, especially in the ability of a pap-fed public to face unpleasant facts, like the actualities apparent at the site of a major airplane accident.

5   What annoyed the troops and augmented their sardonic, contemptuous attitude toward those who viewed them from afar was in large part this public innocence about the bizarre damage suffered by the human body in modern war. The troops could not contemplate without anger the lack of public knowledge of the Graves Registration form used by the U.S. Army Quartermaster Corps, with its space for indicating "Members Missing." You would expect frontline soldiers to be struck and hurt by bullets and shell fragments, but such is the popular insulation from the facts that you would not expect them to be hurt, sometimes killed, by being struck by parts of their friends' bodies violently detached. If you asked a wounded soldier or Marine what hit him, you'd hardly be ready for the answer "My buddy's head," or his sergeant's heel or his hand, or a Japanese leg, complete with shoe and puttees, or the West Point ring on his captain's severed hand. What drove the troops to fury was the complacent, unimaginative innocence of their home fronts and rear echelons about such an experience as the following, repeated in essence tens of thousands of times. Captain Peter Royle, a British artillery forward observer, was moving up a hill in a night attack in North Africa. "I was following about twenty paces behind," he wrote in a memoir,

> when there was a blinding flash a few yards in front of me. I had no idea what it was and fell flat on my face. I found out soon enough: a number of the infantry were carrying mines strapped to the small of their backs, and either a rifle or machine gun bullet had struck one,

which had exploded, blowing the man into three pieces — two legs and head and chest. His inside was strewn on the hillside and I crawled into it in the darkness.

In war, as in air accidents, insides are much more visible than it is normally well to imagine. And there's an indication of what can be found on the ground after an air crash in one soldier's memories of the morning after an artillery exchange in North Africa. Neil McCallum and his friend "S," came upon the body of a man who had been lying on his back when a shell, landing at his feet, had eviscerated him:

"Good God," said S., shocked, "here's one of his fingers." S. stubbed with his toe at the ground some feet from the corpse. There is more horror in a severed digit than in a man dying: it savors of mutilation. "Christ," went on S. in a very low voice, "look, it's not his *finger.*"

In the face of such horror, the distinction between friend and enemy vanishes, and the violent dismemberment of any human being becomes traumatic. After the disastrous Canadian raid at Dieppe, German soldiers observed: "The dead on the beach — I've never seen such obscenities before." "There were pieces of human beings littering the beach. There were headless bodies, there were legs, there were arms." There were even shoes "with feet in them." The soldiers on one side know what the soldiers on the other side understand about dismemberment and evisceration, even if the knowledge is hardly shared by the civilians behind them. Hence the practice among German U-boats of carrying plenty of animal intestines to shoot to the surface to deceive those imagining that their depth charges have done the job. Some U-boats, it was said, carried (in cold storage) severed legs and arms to add verisimilitude. But among the thousands of published photographs of sailors and submariners being rescued after torpedoings and sinkings, there was no evidence of severed limbs, intestines, or floating parts.

If American stay-at-homes could be almost entirely protected from an awareness of the looks and smells of the real war, the British, at least those living in bombed areas, could not. But even then, as one Briton noted in 1941, "we shall never know half of the history . . . of these times." What prompted that observation was this incident: "The other night not half a mile from me a middle-aged woman [in the civilian defense] went out with an ambulance. In a smashed house she saw something she thought was a mop. It was no mop but a man's head." So unwilling is the imagination to dwell on genuine — as opposed to fictional or theatrical — horrors that, indeed, "we shall never know half of the history . . . of these times." At home under the bombs in April, 1941, Frances Faviell was suddenly aware that the whole house was coming down on top of her, and she worried about "Anne," who was in bed on the top floor.

With great difficulty I raised my head and shook it free of heavy, choking, dusty stuff. An arm had fallen round my neck — a warm, living arm, and for one moment I thought that Richard had entered in the darkness and was holding me, but when very cautiously I raised my hand to it, I found that it was a woman's bare arm with two rings on the third finger and it stopped short in a sticky mess.

You can't take much of that sort of thing without going mad, as General Sir John Hackett understood when he saw that the wild destruction of enemy human beings had in it less of satisfaction than of distress. Injured and on the German side of the line at Arnhem, he was being taken to the German medical installation. Along the road he saw "half a body, just naked buttocks and the legs joined on and no more of it than that." For those who might have canted that the only good German is a dead German, Hackett has a message: "There was no comfort here. It was like being in a strange and terrible nightmare from which you longed to wake and could not."

THE DEMOCRACY OF FEAR

In the Great War Wilfred Owen was driven very near to madness by having to remain for some time next to the scattered body pieces of one of his friends. He had numerous counterparts in the Second World War. At the botched assault on Tarawa Atoll, one coxswain at the helm of a landing vessel went quite mad, perhaps at the shock of steering through all the severed heads and limbs near the shore. One Marine battalion commander, badly wounded, climbed above the rising tide onto a pile of American bodies. Next afternoon he was found there, mad. But madness did not require the spectacle of bodies just like yours messily torn apart. Fear continued over long periods would do the job, as on the merchant and Royal Navy vessels on the Murmansk run, where "grown men went steadily and fixedly insane before each other's eyes," as Tristan Jones testified in *Heart of Oak*. Madness was likewise familiar in submarines, especially during depth-bomb attacks. One U.S. submariner reported that during the first months of the Pacific war such an attack sent three men "stark raving mad": they had to be handcuffed and tied to their bunks. Starvation and thirst among prisoners of the Japanese, and also among downed fliers adrift on rafts, drove many insane, and in addition to drinking their urine they tried to relieve their thirst by biting their comrades' jugular veins and sucking the blood. In one sense, of course, the whole war was mad, and every participant insane from the start, but in a strictly literal sense the result of the years of the bombing of Berlin and its final destruction by the Russian army was, for much of the population, actual madness. Just after the surrender, according to Douglas Botting, in *From *the Ruins of the Reich,* some 50,000 orphans could be found living in holes like animals, "some of them one-eyed or one-legged veterans of seven or so, many so deranged by the bombing and the Russian attack that they screamed at the sight of any uniform, even a Salvation Army one."

Although in the Great War madness among the troops was commonly im-   10 puted to the effects of concussion ("shell shock"), in the Second it was more frankly attributed to fear, and in contrast to the expectations of heroic behavior which set the tone of the earlier war, the fact of fear was now squarely to be faced. The result was a whole new literature of fear, implying that terror openly confessed argues no moral disgrace, although failure to control visible symptoms is reprehensible. The official wartime attitude toward the subject was often expressed by quoting Marshal Ney: "The one who says he never knew fear is a compound liar." As the 1943 U.S. *Officer's Guide* goes on to instruct its anxious tyros,

> Physical courage is little more than the ability to control the physical fear which all normal men have, and cowardice does not consist in being afraid but in giving away to fear. What, then, keeps the soldier from giving away to fear? The answer is simply — his desire to retain the good opinion of his friends and associates . . . his pride smothers his fear.

The whole trick for the officer is to seem what you would be, and the formula for dealing with fear is ultimately rhetorical and theatrical: regardless of your actual feelings, you must simulate a carriage that will affect your audience as fearless, in the hope that you will be imitated, or at least not be the agent of spreading panic. Advice proffered to enlisted men admitted as frankly that fear was a normal "problem" and suggested ways of controlling it. Some of these are indicated in a wartime publication of the U.S. National Research Council, *Psychology for the Fighting Man.* Even if it is undeniable that in combat everyone will be "scared — terrified," there are some antidotes: keeping extra busy with tasks involving details, and engaging in roll calls and countings-off, to emphasize the proximity of buddies, both as support and as audience. And there is a "command" solution to the fear problem which has been popular among military theorists at least since the Civil War: when under shelling and mortar fire and scared stiff, the infantry should alleviate the problem by moving — never back but forward. This will enable trained personnel to take care of the wounded and will bring troops close enough to the enemy to make him stop the shelling. That it will also bring them close enough to put them within range of rifles and machine guns and hand grenades is what the theorists know but don't mention. The troops know it, which is why they like to move *back.* This upper- or remote-echelon hope that fear can be turned, by argument and reasoning, into something with the appearance of courage illustrates the overlap between the implausible persuasions of advertising and those of modern military motivators.

There was a lot of language devoted to such rationalizing of the irrational. A little booklet issued to infantry replacements joining the Fifth Army in Italy contained tips to ease the entry of innocents into combat: Don't believe all the horror stories circulating in the outfit you're joining. Don't carry too much stuff. Don't excrete in your foxhole — if you can't get out, put some dirt on a shovel, go on that, and throw the load out. Keep your rifle clean and ready. Don't tape down the handles of your grenades for fear of their flying off accidentally — it takes too long to get the tape off. Learn to dig in fast when shelling starts. Watch the ground for evidence of mines and booby traps. On the move, keep contact but don't bunch up. And use common sense in your fight against fear:

> Don't be too scared. Everybody is afraid, but you can learn to control your fear. And, as non-coms point out, "you have a good chance of getting through if you don't lose your head. Being too scared is harmful to you." Remember that a lot of noise you hear is ours, and not dangerous. It may surprise you that on the whole, many more are pulled out for sickness or accident than become battle casualties.

(After that bit of persuasion, the presence of first-aid sections on "If You Get Hit" and "If a Buddy Gets Hit" seems a bit awkward.)

This open, practical confrontation of a subject usually unmentioned has its counterpart in the higher reaches of the wartime literature of fear. The theme of Alan Rook's poem "Dunkirk Pier," enunciated in the opening stanza, is one hardly utterable during earlier wars:

> Deeply across the waves of our darkness fear
> like the silent octopus feeling, groping, clear
> as a star's reflection, nervous and cold as a bird,
> tells us that pain, tells us that death is near.

William Collins's "Ode to Fear," published in 1746, when the average citizen had his wars fought by others whom he never met, is a remote allegorical and allusive performance lamenting the want of powerful emotion in contemporary poetry. C. Day Lewis's "Ode to Fear" of 1943 is not literary but literal, frank, down-to-earth, appropriately disgusting.

> Now fear has come again
> To live with us
> In poisoned intimacy like pus. . . .

And fear is exhibited very accurately in its physical and psychological symptoms:

> The bones, the stalwart spine,
> The legs like bastions,
> The nerves, the heart's natural combustions,

The head that hives our active thoughts — all pine,
Are quenched or paralyzed
When Fear puts unexpected questions
And makes the heroic body freeze like a beast surprised.

The new frankness with which fear would be acknowledged in this mod-   15
ernist, secular, psychologically self-conscious wartime was registered in W. H.
Auden's "September 1, 1939," in which the speaker, "uncertain and afraid," observes the "waves of anger and fear" washing over the face of the earth. And the
new frankness became the virtual subject and center of *The Age of Anxiety*,
which Auden wrote from 1944 to 1946.

Civilian bombing enjoined a new frankness on many Britons. "Perfect fear
casteth out love" was Cyril Connolly's travesty of I John 4:18, as if he were thoroughly acquainted with the experience of elbowing his dearest aside at the shelter
entrance.

If the anonymous questionnaire, that indispensable mechanism of the social sciences, had been widely used during the Great War, more perhaps could be
known or safely conjectured about the actualities of terror on the Western
Front. Questionnaires were employed during the Second World War, and American soldiers were asked about the precise physical signs of their fear. The soldiers testified that they were well acquainted with such impediments to stability
as (in order of frequency) "Violent pounding of the heart, sinking feeling in the
stomach, shaking or trembling all over, feeling sick at the stomach, cold sweat,
feeling weak or faint."

More than a quarter of the soldiers in one division admitted that they'd
been so scared they'd vomited, and almost a quarter said that at terrifying moments they'd lost control of their bowels. Ten percent had urinated in their
pants. As John Ellis observes of these data,

> Stereotypes of "manliness" and "guts" can readily accommodate the
> fact that a man's stomach or heart might betray his nervousness, but
> they make less allowance for his shitting his pants or wetting himself.

And furthermore, "If over one-fifth of the men in one division actually admitted that they had fouled themselves, it is a fair assumption that many more actually did so." One of the commonest fears, indeed, is that of wetting oneself and
betraying one's fear for all to see by the most childish symptom. The fear of this
fear augments as the rank rises: for a colonel to wet his pants under shellfire is
much worse than for a PFC. The U.S. Marine Eugene B. Sledge confessed that
just before he landed at Peleliu, "I felt nauseated and feared that my bladder
would surely empty itself and reveal me to be the coward I was."

If perfect fear casteth out love, perfect shame can cast out even agony.
During the Normandy invasion a group of American soldiers came upon a

paratroop sergeant caught by his chute in a tree. He had broken his leg, and fouled himself as well. He was so ashamed that he begged the soldiers not to come near him, despite his need to be cut down and taken care of. "We just cut off his pants," reported one of the soldiers who found him, "and gently washed him all over, so he wouldn't be humiliated at his next stop."

20   Men more experienced than that paratrooper had learned to be comfortable with the new frankness. A soldier unused to combat heard his sergeant utter an obscenity when their unit was hit by German 88 fire:

> I asked him if he was hit and he sort of smiled and said no, he had just pissed his pants. He always pissed them, he said, just when things started and then he was okay. He wasn't making any apologies either, and then I realized something wasn't quite right with me either. There was something warm down there and it seemed to be running down my leg. . . .
>
> I told the sarge, I said, "Sarge, I've pissed too," or something like that, and he grinned and said, "Welcome to the war."

Other public signs of fear are almost equally common, if even more "comic." One's mouth grows dry and black, and a strange squeaking or quacking comes out, joined sometimes with a stammer. It is very hard for a field-grade officer to keep his dignity when that happens.

For the ground troops, artillery and mortar fire were the most terrifying, partly because their noise was so deafening and unignorable, and partly because the damage they caused the body — sometimes total disappearance or atomization into tiny red bits — was worse than most damage by bullets. To be killed by bullets seemed "so clean and surgical" to Sledge. "But shells would not only tear and rip the body, they tortured one's mind almost beyond the brink of sanity." An occasional reaction to the terror of shelling was audible "confession." One American infantryman cringing under artillery fire in the Ardennes suddenly blurted out to his buddies, "In London I fucked prostitutes and then robbed them of their money." The shelling over, the soldier never mentioned this utterance again, nor did his friends, everyone understanding its stimulus and its meaning.

But for the infantry there was something to be feared almost as much as shelling: The German *Schü* mine, scattered freely just under the surface of the ground, which blew your foot entirely off if you stepped on it. For years after the war ex-soldiers seized up when confronted by patches of grass and felt safe only when walking on asphalt or concrete. Fear among the troops was probably greatest in the staging areas just before D-Day: that was the largest assembly of Allied troops yet unblooded and combat-virgin. "Don't think they weren't afraid," one American woman who worked with the Red Cross says in Studs Terkel's "*The Good War*." "Just before they went across to France, belts and ties were removed from some of these young men. They were very, very young."

WHAT UNCONDITIONAL SURRENDER MEANT

For those who fought, the war had other features unknown to those who looked on or got the war mediated through journalism. One such feature was the rate at which it destroyed human beings — friendly as well as enemy. Training for infantry fighting, few American soldiers were tough-minded enough to accept the full, awful implications of the term "replacement" in the designation of their Replacement Training Centers. (The proposed euphemism "reinforcement" never caught on.) What was going to happen to the soldiers they were being trained to replace? Why should so many "replacements" — hundreds of thousands of them, actually — be required? The answers came soon enough in the European theater, in Italy, France, and finally Germany. In six weeks of fighting in Normandy, the 90th Infantry Division had to replace 150 percent of its officers and more than 100 percent of its men. If a division was engaged for more than three months, the probability was that every one of its second lieutenants, all 132 of them, would be killed or wounded. For those being prepared as replacements at officer candidate schools, it was not mentally healthy to dwell on the oddity of the schools' turning out hundreds of new junior officers weekly after the army had reached its full wartime strength. Only experience would make the need clear. The commanding officer of the 6th King's Own Scottish Borderers, which finally arrived in Hamburg in 1945 after fighting all the way from Normandy, found an average of five original men remaining (out of around 200) in each rifle company. "I was appalled," he said. "I had no idea it was going to be like that."

And it was not just wounds and death that depopulated the rifle companies. In the South Pacific it was malaria, dengue, blackwater fever, and dysentery; in Europe, dysentery, pneumonia, and trench foot. What disease did to the troops in the Pacific has never been widely known. The ingestion of Atabrine, the wartime substitute for quinine as a malaria preventive, has caused ears to ring for a lifetime, and decades afterward thousands still undergo their regular malaria attacks, freezing and burning and shaking all over. In Burma, British and American troops suffered so regularly from dysentery that they cut large holes in the seats of their trousers to simplify things. But worse was the mental attrition suffered by combat troops, who learned from experience the inevitability of their ultimate mental breakdown, ranging from the milder forms of treatable psychoneurosis to outright violent insanity.

In war it is not just the weak soldiers, or the sensitive ones, or the highly   25
imaginative or cowardly ones, who will break down. All will break down if in combat long enough. "Long enough" is now defined by physicians and psychiatrists as between 200 and 240 days. For every frontline soldier in the Second World War, according to John Ellis, there was the "slowly dawning and dreadful realisation that there was no way out, that . . . it was only a matter of time before

they got killed or maimed or broke down completely." As one British officer put it, "You go in, you come out, you go in again and you keep doing it until they break you or you are dead." This "slowly dawning and dreadful realisation" usually occurs as a result of two stages of rationalization and one of accurate perception:

1. It *can't* happen to me. I am too clever / agile / well-trained / good-looking / beloved / tightly laced / etc. This persuasion gradually erodes into

2. It *can* happen to me, and I'd better be more careful. I can avoid the danger by keeping extra alert at all times / watching more prudently the way I take cover or dig in or expose my position by firing my weapon / etc. This conviction attenuates in turn to the perception that death and injury are matters more of bad luck than lack of skill, making inevitable the third stage of awareness:

3. It *is going to* happen to me, and only my not being there is going to prevent it.

Because of the words *unconditional surrender,* it became clear in this war that no sort of lucky armistice or surprise political negotiation was going to give the long-term frontline man his pardon. "It soon became apparent," John Ellis writes, "that every yard of ground would have to be torn from the enemy and only killing as many men as possible would enable one to do this. Combat was reduced to its absolute essentials, kill or be killed." It was this that made this second Western Front war unique: it could end only when the line (or the Soviet line) arrived in Berlin. In the Second World War the American military learned something very "modern" — modern because dramatically "psychological," utilitarian, unchivalric, and unheroic: it learned that men will inevitably go mad in battle and that no appeal to patriotism, manliness, or loyalty to the group will ultimately matter. Thus in later wars things were arranged differently. In Korea and Vietnam it was understood that a man fulfilled his combat obligation and bought his reprieve if he served a fixed term, 365 days — and not days in combat but days in the theater of war. The infantry was now treated somewhat like the air corps had been in the Second War: performance of a stated number of missions guaranteed escape.

"DISORGANIZED INSANITY"

If most civilians didn't know about these things, most soldiers didn't know about them either, because only a relatively small number did any fighting that brought them into mortal contact with the enemy. For the rest, engaged in supply, transportation, and administrative functions, the war constituted a period of undesired and uncomfortable foreign travel under unaccustomed physical and social conditions, like enforced obedience, bad food, and an absence of baths. In 1943 the United States Army grew by 2 million men, but only about 365,000 of those went to combat units, and an even smaller number ended up in the rifle companies. The bizarre size and weight of the administrative tail dragged across Europe by the American forces is implied by statistics: from 1941 to 1945 the number of men whose job was fighting increased by only 100,000. If by the end there were 11 million men in the American army, only 2 million were in the ninety combat divisions, and of those, fewer than 700,000 were in the infantry. Regardless of the persisting fiction, those men know by experience the truth enunciated by John Ellis that

> World War II was not a war of movement, except on the rare occasions when the enemy was in retreat; it was a bloody slogging match in which mobility was only occasionally of real significance. Indeed, . . . the internal combustion engine was not a major consideration in the ground war.

The relative few who actually fought know that the war was not a matter of rational calculation. They know madness when they see it. They can draw the right conclusions from the fact that in order to invade the Continent the Allies killed 12,000 innocent French and Belgian civilians who happened to live in the wrong part of town — that is, too near the railway tracks, the bombers' target. The few who fought are able to respond appropriately — without surprise — to such a fact as this: in the Netherlands alone, more than 7,000 planes tore into the ground or the water, afflicted by bullets, flak, exhaustion of fuel or crew, "pilot error," discouragement, or suicidal intent. In a 1986 article in *Smithsonian* magazine about archaeological excavation in Dutch fields and drained marshes, Les Daly emphasized the multitudinousness, the mad repetitiveness of these 7,000 crashes, reminding readers that "the total fighter and bomber combat force of the U.S. Air Force today amounts to about 3,400 airplanes. To put it another way, the crash of 7,000 aircraft would mean that every square mile of the entire state of New Jersey would have shaken to the impact of a downed plane."

In the same way, the few who fought have little trouble understanding other outcroppings of the irrational element, in events like Hiroshima and Nagasaki, or for that matter the bombing of Hamburg or Darmstadt or Tokyo or Dresden. The destruction of Dresden *et al.* was about as rational as the German shooting of hostages to "punish" an area, or the American belief that an effective way into Germany was to plunge through the Hürtgen Forest, or the British and Canadian belief, two years earlier, that a great raid on Dieppe would be worthwhile. Revenge is not a rational motive, but it was the main motive in the American destruction of the Japanese empire.

Those who fought know this, just as they know that it is as likely for the 30 man next to you to be shot through the eye, ear, testicles, or brain as through the shoulder (the way the cinema does it). A shell is as likely to blow his whole face off as to lodge a fragment in some mentionable and unvital tissue. Those who fought saw the bodies of thousands of self-destroyed Japanese men, women, and infants drifting off Saipan — sheer madness, but not essentially different from what Eisenhower described in *Crusade in Europe,* where, though not intending to make our flesh creep or to descend to nasty details, he couldn't help reporting honestly on the carnage in the Falaise Pocket. He wrote, "It was literally possible to walk for hundreds of yards at a time, stepping on nothing but dead and decaying flesh" — formerly German soldiers, who could have lived by surrendering but who chose, madly, not to.

How is it that these data are commonplaces only to the small number who had some direct experience of them? One reason is the normal human talent for looking on the bright side, for not receiving information likely to cause distress or to occasion a major overhaul of normal ethical, political, or psychological assumptions. But the more important reason is that the news correspondents, radio broadcasters, and film people who perceived these horrors kept quiet about them on behalf of the war effort, and so the large wartime audience never knew these things. As John Steinbeck finally confessed in 1958, "We were all part of the War Effort. We went along with it, and not only that, we abetted it. . . . I don't mean that the correspondents were liars. . . . It is in the things not mentioned that the untruth lies." By not mentioning a lot of things, a correspondent could give the audience at home the impression that there were no cowards in the service, no thieves or rapists or looters, no cruel or stupid commanders. It is true, Steinbeck was aware, that most military operations are examples of "disorganized insanity," but the morale of the home front could not be jeopardized by an eyewitness's saying so. And even if a correspondent wanted to deliver the noisome truth, patriotism would join censorship in stopping his mouth. As Steinbeck noted in *Once There Was a War,* "The foolish reporter who broke the rules would not be printed at home and in addition would be put out of the theater by the command."

THE NECESSITY OF EUPHEMISM

The way censorship operated to keep the real war from being known is suggested by Herbert Merillat, who during the war was a bright and sensitive public-relations officer attached to the Marines on Guadalcanal. In addition to generating Joe Blow stories, he had the job of censor: he was empowered to pass stories consonant with "the war effort" and to kill all others. Of a day in November, 1942, he wrote in *Guadalcanal Remembered,*

> A recently arrived sergeant-reporter came around this afternoon, very excited, very earnest. Having gone through one naval shelling and two bombings he has decided that war is hell, and that he should write something stark. He showed me a long piece on the terror of men during bombings and shellings, the pain of the wounded, the disease and un-

pleasantness of this place. It was a gloomy and distorted piece; you would get the idea that every marine on the island is a terror-stricken, beaten man. I tried to tell him the picture was badly skewed.

That's how the people at home were kept in innocence of malaria, dysentery, terror, bad attitude, and psychoneurosis. Occasionally there might be an encounter between home-front sentimentality and frontline vileness, as in an episode recalled by Charles MacDonald, a rifle-company commander in Europe, in his 1947 book *Company Commander.* One glib reporter got far enough forward to encounter some infantrymen on the line, to whom he put cheerful questions like, "What would you like best from the States about now?" At first he got nothing but sullen looks and silence. But finally one soldier spoke:

> "I've got something to say. Tell them it's too damned serious over here to be talking about hot dogs and baked beans and things we're missing. Tell them it's hell, and tell them there're men getting killed and wounded every minute, and they're miserable and they're suffering. Tell them it's a matter more serious than they'll ever be able to understand" —

at which point "there was a choking sob in his voice," MacDonald remembered. Then the soldier got out the rest of his urgent message: "Tell 'em it's rough as hell. Tell 'em it's rough. Tell 'em it's rough, serious business. That's all. That's all."

Ernie Pyle, well known as the infantry's advocate, was an accredited correspondent, which meant that he, too, had to obey the rules — that is, reveal only about a third of the actuality and, just like the other journalists, fuel all the misconceptions: that officers were admired, if not loved; that soldiers were dutiful, if frightened; and that everyone on the Allied side was sort of nice. One of Pyle's best-known pieces is his description of the return to his company in Italy of the body of Captain Henry T. Waskow, "of Belton, Texas." Such ostentatious geographical precision only calls attention to the genteel vagueness with which Pyle was content to depict the captain's wound and body. Brought down from a mountain by muleback, Captain Waskow's body was laid out on the ground at night and respectfully visited by officers and men of the company. The closest Pyle came to accurate registration was reporting that one man, who sat by the body for some time, holding the captain's hand and looking into his face, finally "reached over and gently straightened the points of the captain's shirt collar, and then he sort of arranged the tattered edges of the uniform around the wound." While delivering an account satisfying on its own terms, this leaves untouched what normally would be thought journalistically indispensable questions, and certainly questions bound to occur to readers hoping to derive from the Infantry's Friend (as Pyle was often called) an accurate image of the infantry's experience. Questions like these: What killed Captain Waskow? Bullet, shell fragments, a mine, or what? Where was his wound? How large was it? You imply that it was in the traditional noble place, the chest. Was it? Was it a little hole, or was it a great red missing place? Was it perhaps in the crotch, or in the testicles, or in the belly? Were his entrails extruded, or in any way visible? Did the faithful soldier wash off his hands after toying with those "tattered edges"? Were the captain's eyes open? Did his face look happy? Surprised? Satisfied? Angry?

But even Pyle's copy, resembling as it does the emissions from the Office of War Information, is frankness itself compared with what German correspondents were allowed to send. They were a part of the military, not just civilians attached to it, and like all other German troops, they had taken the oath to the Führer. Their job was strictly propaganda, and throughout the war they obeyed the invariable rule that German servicemen were never, never, to be shown dead in photographs, moving or still, and that their bodies, if ever mentioned, were to be treated with verbal soft focus. Certainly, so far as the German home front knew, soldiers' bodies were not dismembered, decapitated, eviscerated, or flattened out by tank treads until they looked like plywood. Even more than the testimonies sent back by such as Steinbeck and Pyle, the narratives presented to the German people were nothing but fairy stories of total heroism, stamina, good will, and cheerfulness. This meant that for almost six years a large slice of actuality was declared off limits, and the sanitized and euphemized remainder was presented as the whole. Both sides were offered not just false data but worse: false assumptions about human nature and behavior, assumptions whose effect was to define either a world without a complicated principle of evil or one where all evil was easily displaced onto one simplified enemy—Jews on the Axis side, Nazis and "Japs" on the Allied. The postwar result for the Allies, at least, is suggested by one returning Canadian soldier, wounded three times in Normandy and Holland, who recalls (in *Six War Years 1939–1945*, edited by Barry Broadfoot) disembarking with his buddies to find on the quay nice, smiling Red Cross or Salvation Army girls.

> They give us a little bag and it has a couple of chocolate bars in it and a comic book. . . . We had gone overseas not much more than children but we were coming back, sure, let's face it, as killers. And they were still treating us as children. Candy and comic books.

35   Considering that they were running the war, it is surprising how little some officials on each side knew about the real war and its conditions. Some didn't care to know—like Adolf Hitler, who refused to visit Hamburg after its terrible fire storm in the summer of 1943. Some thought they knew about the real war—like Joseph Goebbels, who did once visit the Eastern Front. But there he "assimilated reality to his own fantasies," as Neil Acherson has said, and took away only evidence establishing that the troops were "brave fellows" and that his own morale-building speeches were "rapturously received." His knowledge of ground warfare remained largely literary: the course of the Punic Wars and the

campaigns of Frederick the Great had persuaded him (or so he said) that in war "spirit" counts for more than luck or quantity of deployable men and munitions.

In addition to a calculating ignorance, a notable but not unique emotional coldness in the face of misery helped insulate him from the human implications of unpleasant facts. In his diary for September 20, 1943, airily and without any emotion of comment (not even a conventional "I was sorry to see" or "It is painful to say"), he totaled up the casualty figures for two years on the Eastern Front alone: "Our total losses in the East, exclusive of Lapland, from June 22, 1941, to August 31, 1943, were 548,480 dead, of whom 18,512 were officers; 1,998,991 wounded, of whom 51,670 were officers; 354,957 missing, of whom 11,597 were officers; total 2,902,438, of whom 81,779 were officers." If it was callousness that protected Goebbels from the human implication of these numbers, it was rank and totemic identity that protected King George VI from a lot of instructive unpleasantness. According to John W. Wheeler-Bennett, his official biographer, what the King saw on his numerous visits to bombed areas fueled only his instinct for high-mindedness. He concluded that among the bombed and maimed he was witnessing "a fellowship of self-sacrifice and 'good-neighbourliness,' a comradeship of adversity in which men and women gave of their noblest to one another, a brotherhood of man in which the artificial barriers of caste and class were broken down." The King never saw perfect fear operating as Connolly saw it, and it is unlikely that anyone told him that while the Normandy invasion was taking place, "almost every police station and detention camp in Britain was jam-packed full," as Peter Grafton put it, in *You, You and You*. "In Glasgow alone . . . deserters were sitting twelve to a cell." It is hard to believe that the King was aware of all the bitter anti-Jewish graffiti his subjects were scrawling up in public places. Nor is it recorded that he took in news of the thievery, looting, and robbing of the dead which were widely visible in the raided areas. Thirty-four people were killed in the cellar ballroom of the Café de Paris on March 8, 1941, when a bomb penetrated the ceiling and exploded on the bandstand, wiping out the band and many of the dancers. Nicholas Monsarrat, in his autobiography *Breaking In, Breaking Out*, recalled the scene that followed.

> The first thing which the rescue squads and the firemen saw, as their torches poked through the gloom and the smoke and the bloody pit which had lately been the most chic cellar in London, was a frieze of other shadowy men, night-creatures who had scuttled within as soon as the echoes ceased, crouching over any dead or wounded woman, any *soignée* corpse they could find, and ripping off its necklace, or earrings, or brooch: rifling its handbag, scooping up its loose change.

That vignette suggests the difficulty of piercing the barrier of romantic optimism about human nature implicit in the Allied victory and the resounding Allied extirpation of flagrant evil. If it is a jolt to realize that blitzed London generated a whole class of skillful corpse robbers, it is because within the moral assumptions of the Allied side that fact would be inexplicable. One could say of the real war what Barbara Foley has written of the Holocaust—not that it is "unknowable" but that "its full dimensions are inaccessible to the ideological frameworks that we have inherited from the liberal era."

UNMELODRAMATIZED HORROR

Finding the official, sanitized, "King George" war unbelievable, not at all in accord with actual human nature, where might one turn in search of the real, heavy-duty war? After scrutinizing closely the facts of the American Civil War, after seeing and listening to hundreds of the wounded, Walt Whitman declared, "The real war will never get in the books." Nor, of course, will the real Second World War. But the actualities of the war are more clearly knowable from some books than from others. The real war is unlikely to be found in novels, for example, for they must exhibit, if not plot, at least pace, and their characters tend to assume the cliché forms demanded by Hollywood, even the new Hollywood, and even if the novels are as honorable as Harry Brown's *A Walk in the Sun,* Norman Mailer's *The Naked and the Dead,* and Joseph Heller's *Catch-22.* Not to mention what is perhaps the best of them, James Jones's *The Thin Red Line.* Sensing that action and emotion during the war were too big and too messy and too varied for confinement in one 300-page volume of fiction, the British have tended to refract the war in trilogies, and some are brilliant: Evelyn Waugh's *Sword of Honor* (1965), of course, collecting his three novels about Guy Crouchback's disillusioning war, written from 1952 to 1961; Olivia Manning's *Balkan Trilogy* (1960–1965); Anthony Powell's *A Dance to the Music of Time: Third Movement* (1964–1968); and Manning's *Levant Trilogy* (1977–1980). The American way seems to be less to conceive a trilogy than to produce three novels of different sorts and then, finding them on one's hands, to argue that they constitute a trilogy, as James Jones did. Despite many novels' undoubted success as engaging narrative, few have succeeded in making a motive, almost a character, of a predominant wartime emotion—boredom—or persuading readers that the horrors have not been melodramatized. One turns, thus, from novels to nonfiction, especially memoirs, and especially memoirs written by participants not conscious of serving any very elevated artistic ambition. The best are those devoid of significant dialogue, almost always a sign of *ex post facto* novelistic visitation. Because they were forbidden in all theaters of war, lest their capture reveal secrets, clandestine diaries, seen and censored by no authority, offer one of the most promising accesses to actuality. The prohibition of diaries often meant increased devotion and care on the part of the writer. In Cairo in April of 1943 D. A. Simmonds, an RAF pilot officer, addressed his diary thus:

I understand that the writing of diaries is definitely forbidden in the services, and you must therefore consider yourself a very lucky diary to have so much time and energy expended on you when you're not entitled to be in existence at all.

And, a month later, "You are becoming quite a big lad now, my diary; slowly but surely your pages swell."

One diary in which much of the real war can be found is James J. Fahey's *Pacific War Diary* (1963). Fahey, a seaman first class on the light cruiser U.S.S. *Montpelier,* was an extraordinarily patient, decent person, devoid of literary sophistication, and the authenticity of his experience can be inferred from his constant obsession with hunger and food, subjects as interesting as combat.

> For breakfast we had some hash and 1 bun, for dinner baloney sandwich, and for supper we had coffee, baloney sandwich, 1 cookie and 1 candy bar. This morning our ship shot down its lucky #13 Jap plane and one probable.

Almost as trustworthy as such daily entries, unrevised later, are accounts of events written soon after by intelligent participants, like Keith Douglas (*Alamein to Zem Zem,* 1946), John Guest (*Broken Images,* 1949), and Neil McCallum (*Journey With a Pistol,* 1959). Those are British, and they are typical British literary performances, educated, allusive, artistically sensitive, a reminder of the British expectation that highly accomplished and even stylish young men would often be found serving in the infantry and the tanks. There they would be in a position to create the sort of war memoirs virtually nonexistent among Americans — the sort that generate a subtle, historically conscious irony by juxtaposing traditional intellectual or artistic images of transcendence against an unflinching, fully mature registration of wartime barbarism.

The best American memoirs are different, conveying their terrible news less by allusion and suggestion and ironic learned comment than by an uncomplicated delivery of the facts, in a style whose literary unpretentiousness seems to argue absolute credibility. No American would write of his transformation from civilian into soldier the way John Guest did, in *Broken Images:* "I am undergoing a land-change into something coarse and strange." American attempts to avoid the plain frequently backfire, occasioning embarrassing outbreaks of Fine Writing. Speaking of the arrival, finally, of American planes on Guadalcanal, one U.S. Marine, Robert Leckie, wrote in *Helmet for My Pillow:*

> All of Guadalcanal was alive with hope and vibrant with the scent of victory. . . . The enemy was running! The siege was broken! And all through the day, like a mighty Te Deum rising to Heaven, came the beat

of the airplane motors. Oh, how sweet the air I breathed that day! How fresh and clean and sprightly the life that leapt in my veins.

In contrast, the American procedure at its best, unashamed of simplicity, is visible in Eugene Sledge's memoir of a boy's experience fighting with "the old breed," the United States Marines. His *With the Old Breed: At Peleliu and Okinawa* (1981) is one of the finest memoirs to emerge from any war, and no Briton could have written it. Born in Mobile, Alabama, in 1923, Sledge enlisted in December, 1942. After his miraculous survival in the war, he threw himself into the study of zoology and ultimately became a professor of biology at the University of Montevallo, in Alabama. The main theme of *With the Old Breed* is, as Sledge indicates, "the vast difference" between what has been published about these two Marine Corps battles, which depicts them as more or less sane activities, and his own experience "on the front line." One reason Sledge's account is instantly credible is the amount of detail with which he registers his presence at the cutting edge, but another is his tone — unpretentious, unsophisticated, modest, and decent. Despite all the horrors he recounts, he is proud to have been a Marine. He is uncritical of and certainly uncynical about Bob Hope's contribution to the entertainment of the forces, and on the topic of medals and awards he is totally unironic — he takes them seriously, believing that those who have been given them deserve them. He doesn't like to say *shit* and he prays, out loud. He comes through as such a nice person, so little inclined to think ill of others, that forty years after the war he still can't figure out why loose and wayward straps on haversacks and the like should be called, by disapproving sergeants and officers, *Irish pennants:* "Why Irish I never knew." Clearly he is not a man to misrepresent experience for the momentary pleasure of a little show business.

If innocent when he joined the Marines, Sledge was not at all stupid, and he knew that what he was getting into was going to be "tough": in training, the emphasis on the Ka-Bar knife and kicking the Japs effectively in the genitals made that clear. But any remaining scales fell from his eyes when he saw men simply hosed down by machine-gun fire on the beach at Peleliu: "I felt sickened to the depths of my soul. I asked God, 'Why, why, why?' I turned my face away and wished that I were imagining it all. I had tasted the bitterest essence of the war, the sight of helpless comrades being slaughtered, and it filled me with disgust." Before the battle for Peleliu was over, with casualties worse even than at Tarawa, Sledge perceived what all combat troops finally perceive: "We were expendable! It was difficult to accept. We come from a nation and a culture that values life and the individual. To find oneself in a situation where your life seems of little value is the ultimate in loneliness. It is a humbling experience." He knew now that horror and fear were his destiny, unless a severe wound or death or (most unlikely) a Japanese surrender should reprieve him. And his understanding of the world he was in was filled out by watching Marines levering out Japanese gold teeth with their Ka-Bar knives, sometimes from living mouths. The Japanese "defense" encapsulated the ideas and forms and techniques of "waste" and "madness." The Japanese knew they could neither repel the Marines nor be reinforced. Knowing this, they simply killed, without hope and without meaning.

Peleliu finally secured, Sledge's decimated unit was reconstituted for the landing on southern Okinawa. It was there that he saw "the most repulsive thing I ever saw an American do in the war" — he saw a young Marine officer select a Japanese corpse, stand over it, and urinate into its mouth. Speaking of the "incredible cruelty" that was commonplace when "decent men were reduced to a brutish existence in their fight for survival amid the violent death, terror, tension, fatigue, and filth that was the infantryman's war," Sledge notes that "our code of conduct toward the enemy differed drastically from that prevailing back at the division CP." Unequivocal is Sledge's assertion that "we lived in an environment totally incomprehensible" — not just to civilians at a great distance but "to men behind the lines."

But for Sledge, the worst of all was a week-long stay in rain-soaked fox- 45
holes on a muddy ridge facing the Japanese, a site strewn with decomposing corpses turning various colors, nauseating with the stench of death, "an environment so degrading I believed we had been flung into hell's own cesspool." Because there were no latrines and because there was no moving in daylight, the men relieved themselves in their holes and flung the excrement out into the already foul mud. It was a latter-day Verdun, the Marine occupation of that ridge, where the artillery shellings uncovered scores of half-buried Marine and Japanese bodies, making the position "a stinking compost pile."

> If a marine slipped and slid down the back slope of the muddy ridge, he was apt to reach the bottom vomiting. I saw more than one man lose his footing and slip and slide all the way to bottom only to stand up horror-stricken as he watched in disbelief while fat maggots tumbled out of his muddy dungaree pockets, cartridge belt, legging lacing, and the like. . . .
>
> We didn't talk about such things. They were too horrible and obscene even for hardened veterans. . . . It is too preposterous to think that men could actually live and fight for days and nights on end under such terrible conditions and not be driven insane. . . . To me the war was insanity.

And from the other side of the world the young British officer Neil McCallum, in *Journey With a Pistol,* issued a similar implicit warning against the self-delusive attempt to confer high moral meaning on these grievous struggles for survival. Far from rationalizing their actions as elements of a crusade, McCallum and his men, he said, had "ceased largely to think or believe at all."

> Annihilation of the spirit. The game does not appear to be worth the candle. What is seen through the explosions is that this, no less than any

other war, is not a moral war. Greek against Greek, against Persian, Roman against the world, cowboys against Indians, Catholics against Protestants, black men against white — this is merely the current phase of an historical story. It is war, and to believe it is anything but a lot of people killing each other is to pretend it is something else, and to misread man's instinct to commit murder.

In some wartime verses titled "War Poet," the British soldier Donald Bain tried to answer critics and patriots who argued that poets were failing to register the meaning of the war, choosing instead to note mere incoherent details and leaving untouched and uninterpreted the great design of the whole. Defending contemporary poets and writers, Bain wrote:

> We in our haste can only see the small components of the scene;
> We cannot tell what incidents will focus on the final screen.
> A barrage of disruptive sound, a petal on a sleeping face,
> Both must be noted, both must have their place.
> It may be that our later selves or else our unborn sons
> Will search for meaning in the dust of long deserted guns.
> We only watch, and indicate, and make our scribbled pencil notes.
> We do not wish to moralize, only to ease our dusty throats.

But what time seems to have shown our later selves is that perhaps there was less coherent meaning in the events of wartime than we had hoped. Deprived of a satisfying final focus by both the enormousness of the war and the unmanageable copiousness of its verbal and visual residue, all the revisitor of this imagery can do, turning now this way, now that, is to indicate a few components of the scene. And despite the preponderance of vileness, not all are vile.

One wartime moment not at all vile occurred on June 5, 1944, when Dwight Eisenhower, entirely alone and for the moment disjunct from his publicity apparatus, changed the passive voice to active in the penciled statement he wrote out to have ready when the invasion was repulsed, his troops torn apart for nothing, his planes ripped and smashed to no end, his warships sunk, his reputation blasted: "Our landings in the Cherbourg-Havre area have failed to gain a satisfactory foothold and I have withdrawn the troops." Originally he wrote, "the troops have been withdrawn," as if by some distant, anonymous agency instead of by an identifiable man making all-but-impossible decisions. Having ventured this bold revision, and secure in his painful acceptance of full personal accountability, he was able to proceed unevasively with "My decision to attack at this time and place was based on the best information available." Then, after the conventional "credit," distributed equally to "the troops, the air, and the navy," came Eisenhower's noble acceptance of total personal responsibility: "If any blame or fault attaches to the attempt, it is mine alone." As Mailer says, you use the word *shit* so that you can use the word *noble,* and you refuse to ignore the stupidity and barbarism and ignobility and poltroonery and filth of the real war so that *it is mine alone* can flash out, a bright signal in a dark time.

TALKING ABOUT IT

Seeing Metaphor: Revealing and Concealing

1. Point out examples in Fussell's essay of ways the U.S. government and the news media "Norman Rockwellized, not to mention Disneyfied," the fighting during the Second World War. What metaphors for the war do you think these representations suggest? What metaphors might better represent the reality of the war as Fussell paints it?

2. "In one sense, of course, the whole war was mad, and every participant insane from the start," Fussell writes. Do you think madness is a controlling metaphor for any war? Or are some wars "saner" than others? Why do you think so?

Seeing Composition: Frame, Line, Texture, Tone

1. Using the internal headings as guides, outline the organization of Fussell's essay. What is the focus of each of these sections? Does each section seem to be clearly unified by topic? If so, in what ways?

2. Consider Fussell's use of quotations. What are some of the various sources he refers to? How do these help him make his point?

Seeing Meaning: Navigating and Negotiating

1. Fussell quotes the following from the 1943 U.S. *Officer's Guide:*

> Physical courage is little more than the ability to control the physical fear which all normal men have, and cowardice does not consist in being afraid but in giving away to fear. What then, keeps the soldier from giving away to fear? The answer is simply . . . — his desire to retain the good opinion of his friends and associates . . . his pride smothers his fear.

What is Fussell's attitude toward this statement? What is your own response?

2. Fussell also quotes a returning Canadian soldier met by "nice, smiling Red Cross or Salvation Army girls":

> They give us a little bag and it has a couple of chocolate bars in it and a comic book. . . . We had gone overseas not much more than children but we were coming back, sure, let's face it, as killers. And they were still treating us as children. Candy and comic books.

In what sense does this anecdote summarize Fussell's central point? Why do you think he feels it important that we understand the full horror of the war experience?

WRITING ABOUT IT

1. Visit the library to look at some collections of photographs depicting World War II, such as can be found in the books that Paul Fussell names. In general, how do the photographs reveal innocence or ignorance about American and Allied suffering? Specifically, focus on two photographs and describe each in as much detail as you can. Then tell the story of each photograph. Next, try to tell the missing story—the one the photograph doesn't "know" or isn't able to tell, but you might imagine, having read "The Real War."

   You might exchange these stories with each other, then make a collection of your own—an album of war images, verbally drawn.

2. Fussell writes, "The formula for dealing with fear is ultimately rhetorical and theatrical: regardless of your actual feelings, you must simulate a carriage that will affect your audience as fearless, in the hope that you will be imitated, or at least not be the agent of spreading panic."

   Write about a time that you tried to follow similar, if not the exact, advice: to pretend fearlessness when you were in fact scared witless. How successful were you? What was impossible to conceal?

3. At some time, most people experience "the dawning and dreadful realization that there is no way out" of some situation, if not necessarily under the extreme conditions of war. Reread the steps Fussell outlines in paragraph 25, and then tell a story of your own process of discovering: "It is going to happen to me and only my not being there is going to prevent it."

My Body Will Collapse Like a Falling Cherry Blossom

HATSUHO NAITO

Hatsuho Naito is the author of Thunder Gods: The Kamikaze Pilots Tell Their Story *(1989), translated by Mayumi Ichikawa. "My Body Will Collapse Like a Falling Cherry Blossom" is from his book and appeared in the April-May 1991 issue of* Air and Space.

That's going to be your coffin." Higher Flight Petty Officer Motoji Ichikawa followed his friend's gesture. The new weapon he and the other Thunder Gods had been told of, the *Ohka*, or "cherry blossom," was a tiny plywood-and-aluminum aircraft with stubby wings, a primitive, cramped cockpit, and a large explosive charge in its nose—no more than a manned bomb. Ichikawa's shrinking confidence diminished still more as his friend explained that the Ohka would be carried aloft under a Betty bomber and dropped in the vicinity of its target. The pilot would enter its cockpit shortly before it was dropped to guide it. "Don't be so disappointed," he was told. "If you crash-dived in an attack bomber, no one would be watching you die. In this thing, you'll be diving in front of the entire crew of the mother plane."

Like Ichikawa, the Thunder Gods were new to their duties and still struggling to come to terms with them. The Thunder Gods Special Attack Corps had been officially formed the previous month—October 1944—as an act of desperation. The tide of the Pacific war had turned against Japan, and U.S. forces were steadily advancing toward the Japanese home islands. In a last-ditch effort to ward off invasion, Japan had added suicide to the national arsenal.

That September, Japanese military leaders had organized the so-called T-Attack Corps to begin carrying out suicide attacks in Zeros. The "T" was a reference to the typhoon that had halted a 13th century Mongol invasion, known to the grateful Japanese as a "divine wind," or *kamikaze*. But as the war situation worsened, even the T-Attack Corps was not enough. The leaders began to pin more and more of their hopes on the volunteer Thunder Gods pilots and their Ohkas.

But at Konoike Air Base, the Thunder Gods' training facility east of Tokyo, the atmosphere was anything but hopeful. The Thunder Gods' first attack was to be launched from Japanese-held Clark Field on the large Philippine island of Luzon, but a series of setbacks had delayed final preparations for the attack again and again. The strain of facing certain death was taking its toll on the Ohka pilots.

Relations between the petty officers and the reserve officers, many of 5 whom had only 90 days of training and were barely able to maintain horizontal flight, aggravated the strain. Reacting to their extraordinary position, the petty officers chosen as Ohka pilots had begun to manifest marked anti-organizational behavior. When some reserve officers responded by tightening discipline, the petty officers became further incensed. One repeatedly went to Senior Reserve Officer Hachiro Hosokawa and warned him that there was a serious morale problem in the Ohka squadron. Too inexperienced to perceive the real problem behind the petty officer's complaints, Hosokawa did nothing.

On January 8, 1945, a troupe of entertainers visited the base. The show seemed to relax the men somewhat, but as the pilots started returning to their barracks, one of the petty officers walked on a lawn that was off limits, and an especially zealous reserve officer struck him. Enraged, the petty officers began talking about getting revenge.

The yard between the reserve officers' billets and the petty officers' barracks was lit by a bright moon. When some of the newly arrived reserve officers came out into the yard and began admiring the moon, it was the last straw for the petty officers. When one attempted to seize the offending reserve officer and was himself seized, the base broke out in chaos.

The two groups spilled out into the yard and began grappling, punching, and mauling each other. The officer of the day and several others tried to stop the fighting, but the riot continued for nearly an hour.

Suddenly someone standing on a podium in the center of the yard cried out: "Petty officers withdraw!" The voice belonged to Special Service Sub-Lieutenant Shoichi Ota, the mastermind of the Ohka plan, a man who had worked his way up from fourth-class seaman and was greatly respected by all of the petty officers. Their frustrations and energies spent, the petty officers obeyed Ota and returned slowly to their barracks, many nursing bruises and other wounds.

10   When the petty officers remained defiant the next day, however, a legal officer was dispatched to the base to set up court martial proceedings. Training was suspended and a curfew imposed.

Despite the curfew, several of the veteran petty officers regularly sneaked into town to drink and carouse. They reasoned that since they were to die soon, the rules did not apply to them. Though also facing death, the reserve officers tended to take their duties more seriously and stayed on base.

However, one of them, Sub-Lieutenant Mitsutaka Nishio, had fallen in love with an inn maid named Taeko in the nearby town of Sawara. Nishio's friends were aware that he had been smitten by the girl and felt sorry for him. Though wartime complications prevented them from marrying, Nishio, knowing he was soon going to die, wanted to somehow formally declare his love to Taeko.

Under cover of darkness, Nishio and his two best friends, Nakane and Yasui, left the base by the rear gate and rode their bicycles into Sawara. Arriving at the inn, they took a room, ordered sake, and asked for Taeko.

As soon as she appeared and sat down on a cushion next to Nishio, Taeko knew from the men's grave and subdued manner that their time was approaching. When Nishio declared his intentions, she burst into tears.

In strained silence, Nishio's friends took turns filling the small sake cups. 15 He and Taeko exchanged several drinks in a solemn, improvised ritual. In the meantime, other maids in the inn prepared a bridal bed for them

There were no words the young couple could say to ease their agony. Finally Nishio got up. As if in a trance, Taeko also stood. "I want both of you to come with us," Nishio said to his friends.

Nakane and Yasui were shocked. The tone of Nishio's voice and the look on his face told his friends that he was serious, but they could not bring themselves to comply with his request. Finally realizing they were too embarrassed, Nishio led Taeko out of the room and down a hallway to the bridal room.

Two mattresses were laid out side by side. Nishio crawled into one of them, and Taeko got into the other. They joined hands and held onto each other tightly for several minutes, their eyes closed.

Finally, Nishio opened his eyes, "All right," he said, standing up, "I can go now without feeling any anxiety." Taeko stayed in the room. Beneath the quilt, she sobbed quietly.

The leader of the Thunder Gods' Betty squadron, Lieutenant Commander 20 Goro Nonaka, had made some final preparations as well, having already sent his personal belongings, including his favorite tea ceremony kit, home to his wife.

Always outspoken, Nonaka had been vocal in objecting to the Ohka plan. He had long been haunted by the memory of his brother, Shiro, who had been forced to kill himself following an ill-fated uprising against the government in 1936. Nonaka always carried Shiro's picture. "According to the plan," he complained to a fellow Betty squadron leader, "after the Bettys drop the Ohkas they will return to base to prepare for another flight. Do you think we can do such a thing? Our men, the ones we have been living with, are being escorted to their deaths in the bloodiest and most cold-hearted way possible. Do you think we can leave them and return again and again? On my first mission I'm going to crash-dive myself. There is no other way."

As a Betty squadron leader, Nonaka had a house in the nearby town. In mid-January, as the time for their first mission grew closer, the Thunder Gods were allowed visits from their families. At the urging of Commander Motoharu Okamura, Nonaka went home late one evening to see his wife and children. It was exceptionally cold, and the ground was covered with a thin layer of snow. The following morning, standing outside the doorway preparing to leave, Nonaka was suddenly struck by the urge to dance with his wife. He held her as he hummed Strauss' beautiful *Frühlingsstimmen*. As they danced they left a double circle of footprints in the snow.

On January 20, 1945, in response to Japan's worsening position, the commander-in-chief of the Combined Fleet, Admiral Soemu Toyoda, ordered the 11th Aviation Group, which now included the Thunder Gods Corps and the T-Attack Corps, to move to the Japanese island of Kyushu. The main force of the corps set up command headquarters at Kanoya Air Base in Kyushu. Members of the Betty squadron and the covering fighter squadron were dispersed among several other bases in the area.

When the Thunder Gods had been assigned their quarters they re-hoisted banners Nonaka had flown at Konoike reading "HI-RI-HO-KEN-TEN" and "NAMU-HACHIMAN-DAI-BOSATSU." Both were favorite sayings of the famous mid-14th century general Kusunoki Masashige, who had attempted to help the Emperor regain power from the ruling shogun and killed himself when he failed. HI-RI-HO-KEN-TEN was an acronym for "Irrationality can never match reason — Reason can never match law — Law can never match power — Power can never match Heaven." The inscription on the second banner was a popular Buddhist prayer.

25   By late February, it had become obvious that the United States was planning a full-scale attack on the Japanese mainland. Massive air raids on Tokyo and surrounding industrial areas had begun, U.S. airplanes were making daily reconnaissance flights over Kyushu and the main island of Honshu, and movements of U.S. submarines had become more intense and were extending closer to Japan.

On March 17, the commander-in-chief of the Fifth Naval Air Fleet, Vice Admiral Matome Ugaki, issued orders for the implementation of "First Tactics," which called for a radar scout patrol that night, a torpedo attack on U.S. ships at dawn, and an attack by the Thunder Gods during the day.

The next day, the order for the Thunder Gods' first mission came at 12:13 p.m. Okamura ordered 18 Bettys from the squadron at Usa Naval Air Base, on northern Kyushu, to get ready. Working at a frantic pace, personnel at Usa pulled the Bettys out of their shelters and began bringing the Ohkas from their secret tunnels. Corps members not scheduled to participate in the mission helped the ground crews ferry the bombs across the runway to the waiting Bettys.

Suddenly, a group of U.S. dive-bombers burst through the clouds hanging over the field and began raining down bombs. The ground crews and their Thunder Gods helpers scattered. One after the other, the Bettys on the runway and several still in shelters went up in flames. One of the air raid shelters suffered a direct hit that killed several Thunder Gods. Miraculously, none of the Ohkas was hit.

Meanwhile, U.S. bombers also attacked Tomitaka Air Base, which housed the fighters intended to protect the Ohkas. When the bombing finally ended, approximately half of the fighters had been destroyed.

30   The Fifth Naval Air Fleet was trying to bring some order out of the chaos, but communications between the bases had been destroyed, so fleet headquarters

could not fully assess the damage. Chief of Staff Toshiyuki Yokoi suggested to Vice Admiral Ugaki that he suspend all activity in order to preserve the few forces left.

Ugaki, however, decided to go for a knockout blow. At 8:10 a.m. on Wednesday, March 21, reconnaissance airplanes reported sighting two groups of U.S. warships only 320 miles off Kyushu. One of the groups included two aircraft carriers, apparently with no airplanes flying cover over them. The weather was clear. Ugaki and his staff reasoned that the carriers must have been damaged in an earlier Japanese attack and that there would never be a better opportunity to finish them off. He again ordered the Thunder Gods Corps to prepare for an attack.

There was tremendous excitement in the underground operations room of the Fifth Naval Air Fleet. Okamura worried about the few cover airplanes available for the mission. Yokoi nodded his understanding, then turned to Ugaki. "Sir, shall we wait for another chance?" he asked. The normally outspoken Nonaka remained silent, looking grim.

Ugaki stood up slowly, a determined look on his face. He faced Okamura directly. "If we can't use the Ohkas in this situation, we will never have the chance to use them," he said.

Okamura knew from the resolute tone of the vice admiral's voice that there was nothing he could do. It was the most difficult thing he had done in his life, but he finally managed to say, "All right, sir. We'll do it."

The final decision made, Wing Commander Kunihiro Iwaki and Nonaka 35 left the operations room and headed for the airfield. There was a slight breeze rustling the leaves of the bamboo trees on the hillside. Walking a few steps ahead of Iwaki, Nonaka was deep in thought, pondering the life and death of the Kusunoki Masashige, whose words adorned one of his banners. Finally he turned to Iwaki. "Wing Commander," he said, "there comes a time when things are so hopeless that even warriors have to die."

Nonaka selected the best pilots in his squadron for the mission, dividing the 18 into six groups of three. Fifteen were to carry Thunder Gods and their Ohka bombs.

The 15 Thunder Gods and the mother airplane crews took clippings from their fingernails and hair and placed them in unpainted wooden funeral boxes for delivery to their parents. They took off their old clothes and burned them, putting on new uniforms. They then sat down and carefully wrote out their death statements. "My body will collapse like a falling cherry blossom, but my soul will live and protect this land forever," wrote 23-year-old Reserve Sub-Lieutenant First Class Yuzuru Ogata. "Farewell. I am a glorious wild cherry blossom. I shall return to my mother's place and bloom!"

In front of the headquarters building, the Thunder Gods who had not been chosen for the mission were all preparing farewell cups of sake for their colleagues. Many of them appeared more pale and nervous than those who knew they were about to die.

One of them, carrying a tray of drinks across the flight line, passed in front of a Betty just as the pilot turned on the engines for the routine preflight check. He was sucked into the propeller, thrown high into the air, and killed instantly. The dead Thunder God was quickly removed from the runway, but word of the accident flashed around the field, straining even more the ominous mood.

40   A drumroll was sounded, the signal for the Thunder Gods and the crews of the mother airplanes to line up in front of the headquarters building. The 15 Ohka pilots were wearing headbands that had been inscribed with the words "Thunder Gods" by Admiral Toyoda. Each one also had a sword in a brocade sheath strapped to his waist.

Nonaka, the overall leader of the mission, was wearing a white muffler. He unceremoniously sat down in a chair, holding his saber like a cane, with its tip resting on the tarmac. Beside him a large blue and white streamer and his two large banners flapped in the wind. The sky overhead was clear and blue. To the north were patches of white clouds. It was a beautiful early spring day.

The assembled men waited, growing more uneasy as each minute passed. Vice Admiral Ugaki was late. Finally he showed up, solemnly taking his place in front of the formation. Okamura was the first to speak, but it was hard to understand the commander because his voice was choked with tears.

"Today's mission will not be an easy one," he said. "But brave and resolute action will scatter even devils. With your passionate spirit of martyrdom, you will be able to overcome any kind of difficulty! You will succeed! Keep this conviction strong in your minds!"

Then Okamura's voice failed him completely. Tears flowed freely down his face, and he looked as though he were going to pieces. He struggled to continue.

45   "Looking back, your serene state of mind and outstanding behavior since last November has impressed me. I could not be more proud of you. Now you will go into the next world. And just as you have been in this world, I pray that you will continue to be pure, beautiful, healthy, and cheerful. Your colleagues and I will soon be following you. Please remember the ties we had in this world!"

Ugaki, Okamura, and the other officers exchanged farewell cups of sake with the Ohka pilots and Betty crewmen.

The fighters had been pulled out of their shelters and were now on line. The ground crews began warming up the Bettys. Their whirling propellers glistened in the sun, and the roar of their engines filled the air.

Nonaka stalked to the front of the formation and turned to face the men. For several seconds he was silent, staring intently into each man's face. Then he said in his impressively loud voice: "We will now make an attack on the enemy's warships! Once you are in battle, do not hesitate. Attack aggressively and destroy your target regardless of all else. Let us fight to the death! Let us fill the Pacific with our blood!"

Nonaka turned to face Okamura, saluting him in his usual brusque fashion. "We go, Commander!" he said. Okamura returned his salute, his face drained of color.

Nonaka turned and signaled the men to break ranks and man their air-   50
planes. The white flag went down. The roar from the airplanes' engines drowned out everything else. The Bettys, their heavy Ohka bombs suspended from their bellies, lumbered down the runway like fat gooney birds. As soon as they were in the air, the fighters began taking off.

As they turned to the east, the two squadrons were joined by a third squadron of 23 assisting fighters that had taken off from adjoining Kasanbara Air Base. The group headed southeast. Seven months after the Ohka program was first proposed, the Thunder Gods were making their first sortie.

About half an hour later, half of the fighters returned to base with malfunctioning fuel pumps. Because there hadn't been enough time to service the fighters properly, they hadn't been able to draw fuel from their second tanks. The shock to those waiting at the airfield was considerable. But more was to come. Most of the airplanes that had taken off from Kasanbara had the same problem and had to return. Only 30 fighters were left to cover the entire mission.

To make things worse, a reconnaissance airplane flying ahead of the Thunder Gods radioed back that three groups of American ships were in the area, with three aircraft carriers in one group and two each in the others. Not only was the force much stronger than previously believed, each group was sure to have covering airplanes.

There had been no word over the radio at all from Nonaka. It had been agreed beforehand that he and his squadron would maintain complete radio silence throughout the mission, but now the waiting was almost unbearable.

Several members of the Fifth Naval Air Fleet staff wanted to scrap the mis-   55
sion and call Nonaka back. But Ugaki, waiting in the operations room, refused. "The Thunder Gods are right now face to face with the enemy," he said. "I cannot bring those young boys back now after they have made up their minds to die. It would be too much for them to bear."

It was then approaching 3 p.m., well after the time the mission should have reached the target area. Still there was no word from Nonaka. If the airplanes were still in the air, their fuel would soon be gone.

The air in the underground operations room was stale. The men sat around in silence, not trusting themselves to speak.

Just after dark, guards outside the tunnel reported the sound of an approaching airplane. A badly damaged Zero came in low from the bay and made a rough landing. It was followed by a second airplane. Both were pockmarked with bullet holes and streaked with oil. The pilots were exhausted, but between them they managed to tell what had happened to Nonaka's squadron.

At about 2:20 p.m., when the squadron was some 50 to 60 miles from the U.S. fleet, it was suddenly attacked by about 50 American fighters. The 30 Japanese cover fighters fought back, but nine Bettys and two special-attack bombers were shot down in just over 10 minutes.

60   Unable to match the enemy in number or firepower, the 19 remaining fighters dispersed. Left unprotected, the mother airplanes jettisoned their unmanned Ohkas, dispersed, and began battling to save themselves. Within 10 minutes, the only airplanes surviving were Nonaka's and three others. When one of the Zero pilots last saw them, the four were diving wing to wing toward the sea.

Altogether, 160 men had been lost, including the 15 Ohka pilots.

Inside the underground communications room, the radio man refused to turn his sets off, listening in vain for some final word from Nonaka. Outside, as searchlights swept the still dark sky, Nonaka's HI-RI-HO-KEN-TEN banner fluttered quietly in the night breeze.

TALKING ABOUT IT

Seeing Metaphor: Revealing and Concealing

1. The Japanese attack corps described here was called "the Thunder Gods," and the name of their aircraft, the *Ohka*, translates as "cherry blossom." The word *kamikaze*, referring to suicide missions, translates as "divine wind," in reference to a thirteenth-century typhoon that halted a Mongol invasion. Analyze these three metaphors. In what sense are they surprising, even contradictory? Why do you think these particular metaphors were created?

2. In paragraph 37, Naito describes the preparations of the fifteen Thunder Gods before they set out on their mission. In what ways are their actions (and the death statement of Yuzuru Ogata) metaphoric?

Seeing Composition: Frame, Line, Texture, Tone

1. In several places Naito relates intimate details of the activities of men who will go on to die: for example, Nishio's encounter with Taeko in paragraphs 17–18 and Nonaka's taking leave of his wife in paragraph 21. Find other such examples. Where do you think the writer got this kind of information? (Note that this work was originally published in the 1980s.) To what extent do you think he might have embellished his story here? Does it make a difference?

2. How do you respond to the final image of the banner fluttering in the breeze? (The inscription on the banner is translated in paragraph 24.) Why do you suppose Naito ends this way?

Seeing Meaning: Navigating and Negotiating

1. Paragraphs 27–34 detail how the decision to send out the Thunder Gods was made. How do you respond to what happens in this passage?

2. In paragraph 55, when encouraged to recall the mission, Vice Admiral Ugaki refuses, saying, "I cannot bring those young boys back now after they have made up their minds to die. It would be too much for them to bear." To what extent is this, in Paul Fussell's words, "rationalizing the irrational"?

WRITING ABOUT IT

1. Paul Fussell, in "The Real War 1939–1945," talks about the language devoted to rationalizing the irrational. The hope is "that fear can be turned, by argument and reasoning, into something with the appearance of courage." In Naito's essay, with what language — verbal images, rituals, symbols — did Japanese military leaders try to persuade pilots to commit suicide for the war effort? How successful were these motivators in turning pilots' fear "into something with the appearance of courage"? What was the effect of the rhetoric on the military leaders themselves, the ones who used it?

2. The Japanese used the language of nature as metaphors for war: cherry blossoms, thunder, the mother plane (especially the image of the Betty bombers that "lumbered down the runway like fat gooney birds," hiding the "tiny" aircraft with "stubby wings suspended from their bellies"). Despite these images of life used to talk about death, some genuine affirmation of life flashes out in Naito's story of the Thunder Gods. How might you argue that Naito persuades us that life remains sacred, even when military rhetoric tries to persuade us differently?

I Moved Far Away from Soaring Ideals — I Became a Warrior

Edwards Park

Edwards Park is the author of Angels Twenty: A Young American Fighter a Long Way from Home *(1994) and* Treasures of the Smithsonian *(1983). The following piece originally appeared in the December 1992 issue of* Smithsonian *magazine.*

The little shape fled past me far below, streaking northward, low over the mountains. It was well-camouflaged — dark green with yellow blobs — and I'd have lost it against the jungle except for the red circle painted on its wing. I kept my eye on that.

Banking vertically, I let the nose of my plane drop and ruddered into a straight dive with the sun behind me, snapping on gunsight and gun switch, jamming the throttle full forward — "through the gate," as we used to say. My motions were quick and sure. The trembling, the jerkiness that had troubled me lately on routine flights, were gone. I was like silk.

I settled behind the Japanese plane and watched it grow large in the circle of light that my gunsight cast on the windscreen. It flew straight. No quick climbing turn or wingover. The pilot hadn't seen me.

"I've got you coldcock, you bastard," I muttered.

5   I guess this was one of the most remarkable moments in my life — not the action, right out of pulp magazines like *G-8 and His Battle Aces* that I'd read as a kid in the '30s, but my reaction. I was accepting the prospect of destroying another human being as coolly as if I'd never known peace, had never been raised amid gentle people, had never watched the sun set over Mount Monadnock or heard the song of a hermit thrush sighing from the cool woods . . .

My father was a Boston minister with a summer place in New Hampshire that became his children's truest home. Dad was a working pastor with a city parish, a sincere man of God. Also a devotee of Emerson, for he was a scholar, a historian. He never thumped the Bible at our dinner table, but often, to Mother's distress, he would leave a hot meal half-eaten and fetch a book — there was always one at hand — with which to verify a quotation or make a point.

Meals were noisy. I was the youngest, by six years, of four uninhibited siblings. We had all inherited a dramatic streak from Mother, who was a star of every charade, the world's best reader-aloud. Our house rang with loud discussion and amiable argument. We struggled over the *Saturday Review of Literature*'s acrostic. We scrambled for the *Saturday Evening Post* to sneak a look at the latest Clarence Budington Kelland serial before Mother got hold of it.

News headlines of the Depression-ridden '30s often required Dad to defend his loyalty to the Democratic Party. To him the Blue Eagle on Mr. Bryer's store, signifying compliance with the NRA (back then the initials stood for National Recovery Administration), was a symbol of President Franklin Roosevelt's efforts toward a better world. Mother, daughter of a manufacturer, considered it a grim reminder of the creeping socialism espoused by "that traitor to his class." Yet they fully agreed on broad issues, many of which remain today: population control, equal rights for women, higher standards of education, an end to racism — and of course to war.

We young learned either to solve our normal conflicts quickly or keep them to ourselves in the tight-lipped manner of New England. Violence of course was unthinkable, except on the football field or when playing adolescent war games in which no one got hurt.

A WAR TOO TERRIBLE TO DESCRIBE

The Great War ("to end all wars") lay considerably less than 20 years be-   10
hind us, the horrors of trench warfare far fresher to adults than those of Vietnam are today. An uncle had served in France, and I'd been told never to question him about it because it had been too terrible to describe. But it was OK for me to play at Allies and Germans with my friends, going "over the top" with wooden guns. The old war songs often rose from our Buick with the top down. If you concentrated, you could sing "Keep the Home Fires Burning" while someone else sang "There's a Long, Long Trail," and you'd produce a duet in magical harmony.

One of Dad's perks was private school for his children, and at mine I was taught by many veterans of 1917–18. One had been shell-shocked, as it was then called. Veterans of Vietnam would understand this quivering wreckage of a former athlete; we schoolboys giggled behind his back at his jumps and twitches, and wanted no part of what had caused them.

I was a poor student, yet I was moved by Erich Maria Remarque's *All Quiet on the Western Front,* by poems of Rupert Brooke, Siegfried Sassoon, Wilfred Owen, and uncomfortable short stories by a new writer named Ernest Hemingway. The school drama group put on a play set in the trenches, with thunderous sound effects, a great deal of understated British heroism, and final tragedy. Not a lad of us went to bed that night without vowing never to don a uniform.

Yet many such resolves faded in the withering truths of the Great Depression. My oldest brother graduated from Yale at the worst of times, and found no job except in the U.S. Marines. As an aviation cadet he learned to fly the old Vought biplanes of the day, but then his flying class was cut short because the money appropriated for it, back then in the early '30s, simply ran out. My brother came home, and I treated him with awe and envy. I used to wear his khaki puttees when I cut brush at the neighboring farm to earn a few bucks for a date.

The Boston paper, which we bought down in the village every morning, began sometimes supplanting the fortunes of the Red Sox with news of a former corporal in the German Army. There were photographs of Brownshirts massed together with hands raised, of the Reichstag on fire. There were new words — "putsch," "pogrom" — and at school our teachers supplied worried, uncertain answers to the questions we now raised.

15   In 1935 I squeaked into college following my father and brother to Yale. Headlines and newsreels warned of the growing tension in Europe, of the threatening Japanese in Manchuria, the Italian invasion of Ethiopia, but we freshmen embraced pacifism with ardor. Many classmates were in ROTC, the Reserve Officers' Training Corps, and I chided one about his militarism. "It's the money," he apologized. "ROTC pays for part of my tuition."

He and others loaned their uniforms to those of us who marched around the campus calling ourselves the Veterans of Future Wars. My old college yearbook recalls this cynical student group, popular on Eastern campuses, whose members paraded on crutches, eyes bandaged, smeared with fake blood. It was fun. But in the summer of 1936, as the bewildering Spanish Civil War erupted and Adolf Hitler sent his planes and pilots to join Franco and learn warfare, our VFW seemed merely silly.

In junior year, 1937–38, the Nazis marched into Austria, and Hitler eyed Czechoslovakia. That September, Neville Chamberlain knuckled under to the Nazis at Munich (*Smithsonian*, October 1988), and the Yale Political Union decided he was right to give in. Anything was better than war.

Our elders, however, were backsliding before our eyes. In a writing seminar, a classmate produced an antiwar essay. We applauded. The professor raged. "Is your generation blind to the facts in Europe, and to your responsibility to your country?" Certain of undeniable rectitude, we blazed back that it was our country's responsibility to keep us out of war.

A year later, in the summer of 1940, this conflict between generations came fully to light. Richard M. Ketchum, in his superb book *The Borrowed Years, 1938–1941*, recalls an interchange of opinions published by the *Atlantic Monthly*. A Yale professor challenged the isolationism and pacifism of the current college generation that had petitioned the President not to get involved in Europe's war. The student editors of the *Harvard Crimson* and the *Yale Daily News*, Spencer Klaw and Kingman Brewster (later to become Yale's president and our Ambassador to Great Britain), replied, supposedly for all American college students, that we'd be damned if we'd venture into a distant, foreign war. The best thing for the United States, they insisted, was "to take our stand on this side of the Atlantic."

20   World War II was nearly a year old then. German tanks and infantry had swept across the Polish border on September 1, 1939, three months after I graduated. I remember that on the war's first weekend, while German planes were

bombing Poland's defenseless cities, I sprawled on a New England beach with my oldest brother. It was a bright, still day, September-cool (wars always seem to start in beautiful weather), and as we talked lazily, a plane flew over us.

"If we get in, I'm going to fly," I said, not really meaning it. "Of course," he said, not really listening. We both knew we weren't going to get in. FDR wouldn't dare. Congress would never allow it. Not long before, they'd seriously considered a bill forbidding the United States from declaring war unless the country had actually been invaded. Anyway, everyone knew France had the impregnable Maginot Line and the world's biggest army, didn't they? The French would stop Hitler.

I got a job teaching English and science at a small boarding school in New Hampshire. I was surprised to find myself a pretty good teacher, though not much older than my kids. The faculty was a delight, the skiing great, life joyous. December snow blanketed the village that year, and our bright windows glowed on it so that we lived in a Christmas card. Nothing occurred in Europe to dispel that illusion. The war was phony. It would blow over. Peace on Earth . . .

Then one spring morning in the dormitory bathroom, as I was shaving carefully around my new (surprisingly red) mustache, one of my boys burst in with wide eyes. "He's taken Denmark, and he's invading Norway!" And I could only stare, marking the moment as the true beginning of the unthinkable.

Congress passed our first peacetime draft bill as I began my second year of teaching. All of us male teachers registered. All drew low-priority numbers except me. Mine was so high-priority that everyone came to look at it. "You should become a conscientious objector," said the French teacher.

I thought about that uneasily. I had courage enough to ski down a steep   25 trail, flat out, but I knew I didn't have the guts to be a "CO." Anyway, the draft was only for a year. Being in the Army might not be so bad. It might be good for me.

When the draft board in the state capital called me, I drove down to Concord and met a kindly Yankee lady behind a counter. "You want a deferment until the end of the school year, don't you?" she said. I think if I'd said no, she'd have considered me dangerously un-American.

As the summer of 1941 approached, American troops were being sent to Greenland to set up air bases so we would be able to protect convoys from U-boat attacks. Lend-Lease had finally passed, and a little life seeped into the country's comatose economy as factories began to churn out arms for Britain. What a wonderful role for America, I thought, FDR's "Arsenal of Democracy." Keep out of war, but supply Britain.

In early June, when lawns were deep green and sugar maples misty with new leaves, the faculty went to an elegant garden party to raise money for aircraft to be flown to Britain. The guest of honor was a most attractive lady flier whose job was to ferry war planes across the Atlantic. I buzzed around her, overloaded with charm, but she wasn't interested in an obvious lightweight who had never done anything worthwhile. Next day, when I took my Army physical, I thought of myself as Beau Geste about to join the French Foreign Legion, and hoped she'd hear of it and feel sorry.

An Army doctor prodded and peered at me and announced that I was fit. Pacifist or not, I was in.

30   After all, it was only for a year, and saying goodbye to girls in those days, when a kiss was pretty hot stuff, turned out to be gratifying. One girl, nestling close in the moonlight while the car radio played "I'll Be With You in Apple Blossom Time," murmered, "Don't go into the Army." And after pondering for a moment I found myself answering, "I think I have to."

Fort Devens, Massachusetts, in the year of July 1941, was breathless, dusty, crowded and inefficient — an old-time Army post trying to become a recruit receiving center for hordes of new draftees. We were issued heavy blanket-wool uniforms left over from FDR's Civilian Conservation Corps, and my memories of the place are blurred by the unforgettable sensation of rivers of sweat running down my legs. We learned to march (left foot on the heavy beat), to halt ("I don't want to see anyone sway forward when those boots come together!") to face left, right and about, and to salute ("If you can't see the palm of your hand, you ain't doin' it right!") We had no rifles.

After ten days of this, my name was called for a shipment for basic training: Fort Belvoir, Virginia, cool suntans and a beautiful, clean, much-handled Springfield .30-'06. A crisp, well-organized program run by a cadre of professional soldiers in the Stetson hats we later saw in *From Here to Eternity*.

I have surprisingly kind memories of basic. With every mom in the nation watching, the government treated its new draftees cautiously. First Lady Eleanor Roosevelt even designed a floppy hat for us to wear in the heat. Our platoon sergeant would carefully explain the day's problem: building a gun emplacement covering a crossroad "under fire," perhaps, or a pontoon (pronounced PON-ton) bridge across a stream. He'd show us how to do it by the book, and then look away as we did it our way. I remember the sign he tacked up in the latrine: "Don't Throw Buts in the Unreal." Our lieutenant had done ROTC somewhere in West Virginia, and his favorite expression was "Great balls of fire!"

For the first time in my life, all that was demanded of me was not to think and it was a pleasure. I was paid $30 a month, and I was proud to march 23 miles with 64 pounds of equipment, to strip weapons blindfolded and handle dynamite with the confidence of Robert Jordan in the current Hemingway bestseller, *For Whom the Bell Tolls*. I loved the field kitchen stews, hot, greasy, crammed with the calories we craved. I gained 15 pounds but wore the same size pants.

35   Playing soldier in the Corps of Engineers was something to tell girls about when it was over; something perhaps to write about. One day my platoon hiked a long way to the tank-obstruction course and built an ingenious tank trap that threw the tread off a "medium" from Fort Meade. We "opened fire" on it with a wooden mock-up of an antitank gun. We yelled "Bang! Bang! Bang! Bang!" at it,

and the lieutenant danced in excitement, shouting, "Gray-at balls of faaaah! Y'all did it!" and relieved us of having to stand retreat that afternoon. I even liked standing retreat: the swing and thump of a John Philip Sousa march, the long wail of commands followed by the crash of 10,000 Springfields coming to "present," the flag reluctantly descending in the low sunlight. Then we'd do a march-past, dust rising around the khaki ranks, snapping "eyes right" at some nameless Congressman conjured up to take the review. I described it all, rather archly, in letters home.

U.S. Marines were in Iceland by this summer of '41, and our navy was soon opening fire on every U-boat it spotted, while oil and wreckage from dozens of sunken freighters began washing ashore on our Atlantic beaches. Basic training kept me too busy to ponder these events. But I was not surprised when, after a fight in Congress, my term of service — that cherished 12 months — was stretched to 18.

In the fall of '41 I came home on leave with a slight swagger, a trained combat engineer. "You look wonderful," everyone said. I saw my Great War uncle and asked him straight out what it was like in France in '18. He beamed at me and poured out memories of the field artillery in the Rainbow Division. "No one's ever asked me about this before," he said, puzzled.

I had read about Charles Lindbergh's appearance back at Yale. He'd enumerated all the sensible reasons why we should stay out of war, and some 3,000 students had given a thundering ovation to our greatest national hero. He was an American ideal, his stubborn courage tempered by cleverness, his brilliant success muted by modesty. You had to take his careful judgments seriously, and millions in the America First movement did.

Yet each day seemed to bring war inexorably closer. I saw it coming, but always with a comfortable sense of unreality, as though it were a story being read aloud. Just you wait. Things would come out all right.

FROM AN OLD VET: "BY GOD, YOU'RE LUCKY!"

When a group of us soldiers returned to barracks on the afternoon of Sunday, December 7, and heard the reports streaming over the dayroom radio, we were no more prepared for the real thing than the people at Pearl Harbor. Some old noncoms, veterans of 1918, were listening in. One turned to us young soldiers: "By God, you're lucky! I wish I was your age!" 40

My collegiate pacifism seemed very far away; the dread of a uniform had long passed. I wore one comfortably; I knew the ropes, the people. And as word came of the casualties from the Japanese attack — 2,400 Americans dead, more than a thousand wounded — I felt an emotional tug to . . . well, *do* something.

I'd already made a move, asking for a transfer from the Corps of Engineers to the Army Air Corps. When it came to flying, I typically recalled a scene from some movie like *Hell's Angels* or *The Dawn Patrol*.

It's 1916. The battle-weary squadron commander greets the eager replacement, fresh from Eton:

"How many hours do you have?"

45   *"Seven, Sir."*

"Very well. There's a bit of tea in the mess. The chaps will be landing soon from patrol."

And then to the executive officer:

"Good God! When will they stop sending these children off to die?"

Great stuff back home at the old Gem Theater, but worrisome for me as I reenacted it mentally that December day.

50   Somewhat to my surprise, I felt that flying might be the thing that, at last, I got to be good at. Then I might talk to the beautiful lady pilot if I ever saw her again (which I didn't). Moreover, like everyone back then, I sincerely wanted to do my best for the country.

As an aviation cadet I was no star. The best fliers usually became instructors, with a good chance to stay alive. The adequate — my crowd — went into action. Those who could fit into a small plane became fighter pilots. I was just the right size. A fighter plane had only one seat, so you learned to fly it by yourself. I worked at it with an intensity that, back in New Haven, would have earned me a Phi Beta Kappa key. I learned my tech orders, noted every small problem that cropped up in the air and drilled myself to cope with it.

One morning a fighter flew over with what we called a runaway propeller. The healthy snarl of its engine rose to a scream, and smoke feathered behind it. We watched in horrible fascination as it rolled lazily on its back, half a mile away, and dove straight into the ground. It took two long seconds for the sound to reach us, and I've never forgotten the tortured shriek of that engine, continuing even after we saw the mushroom of flame that ended it — that ended a life. It was like getting a letter from a dead man.

I didn't write home about that but pored over the procedure for a runaway prop: throttle back, nose down to keep air speed, switch to manual control . . .

The Army Air Corps said that a pilot would have 300 hours "on type" (in my case a beautiful but nervous little P-39 Bell Airacobra) before being sent overseas. But 1942 wasn't a banner year for the United States, what with the loss of the Philippines, the Bataan Death March, the debilitating, seesaw fighting that went on in the Solomon Islands. I was sent overseas with 42 hours. I'd never even fired the guns. Good God! I said to myself. When will they stop sending us children off to die?

WHEN I HEAR THE SONG, I SEE THE FACES

55   And so it came about that, one afternoon early in 1943, in the thick heat of New Guinea, I entered a thatched alert shack beside an airstrip and, with five others, presented myself as a replacement in the 41st Fighter Squadron of the

35th Fighter Group, then based in Port Moresby. Here we met the duty pilots: a dozen or so young men in a variety of ragged clothing, all bare to the waist, all painfully thin, all shiny with sweat, all seated on bare canvas cots, talking desultorily or reading, playing bridge, solitaire, Monopoly. A scratchy windup phonograph endlessly repeated "San Antonio Rose," apparently the squadron's one record. When I hear the song today, I see the faces.

Perhaps because of my mother's dramatic flair, I'd played roles all my life and done so with exceptional relish. I'd played the college boy to the hilt. As a schoolteacher, I was Robert Donat doing Mr. Chips. But these quiet, skinny guys were not acting, and I was now joining them. No role; no living room for a stage; no audience of loved ones.

I was made a member of Red Flight. A flight was four planes; four flights made a squadron. To keep a squadron flying regularly, we had a total of about 25 planes and 30 pilots. The veterans seemed to have been here forever, but actually it was only a matter of months — combat flying warps time. These fellows had seen the squadron packed and ready to move, so close had come the Japanese. The clouds of danger still lingered over them, drawing them together, heightening their feeling that in this nonpriority theater of the war, they were a small family of forgotten men. Nothing much mattered to them except survival.

To us replacements, they were courteous, even concerned, for the more of us who lasted, the more of them would ship out. But we couldn't yet approach their instinctive skills in the air. And after the long days were done, they talked to us only professionally, whereas with each other, they shared deeper intimacies than I'd ever heard: fears, hang-ups, sexual fantasies. It was as though they knew every bone of each other's bodies.

Their job, which I now faced, was partly to defend Port Moresby from Japanese air strikes, partly to escort C-47 transports that lumbered daily over the towering Owen Stanley Mountains crammed with Australian infantry. Japanese troops from the island's north coast were clawing toward the gold-mining settlements of Wau and Bulolo. The "Diggers" were holding them — barely. Flying cover for this supply line was nerve-racking because of the terrain below. Over those mountains, still only sketchily mapped, an engine must not fail, a bullet must not strike. You might bail out, but there was faint chance of rescue.

I'd wake in the middle of those sweaty tropical nights, stare into the black- 60
ness, contemplate the mission I faced at dawn and wonder if I'd return to this drab cot for another night, another awakening. Even as a veteran I did this. I did it for 18 months.

The early missions were the most dangerous. Somehow, with peer pressure and a lot of luck, I got through them. I saw my first enemy plane, a mere contrail 20,000 feet above me, and was glad that my P-39 couldn't get up that high. On my second mission I forgot to switch fuel tanks after one hour. My belly tank ran dry, and I experienced the pilot's truism that nothing is noisier than an engine that suddenly dies — especially over the Owen Stanleys. I quickly switched tanks and caught up to my leader, who simply laughed at me through his canopy.

Two replacements were killed. The rest of us kept learning. On my first combat, I attacked a Japanese bomber over Port Moresby, fired at it (the first time I'd ever fired all the guns at once), saw a few hits and broke away in a climbing turn to try again. And at the top of my turn I heard a rattle like a gust of hail and was astonished by the sudden pocks and craters in my wings. I got back to base, landed (on two flat tires) and found the plane riddled with bullet holes. In breaking away, I'd made a crisply coordinated turn, banking exactly the right amount. Any good aerial gunner could track such a move, and Japanese gunnery was excellent. From then on, after an attack I'd skid or slip to make myself hard to hit.

That first fight was a rite of passage. The old pilots now offered true help, more than just enough for survival. And to my amazement, I realized that I had actually enjoyed the recklessness of that blazing moment. The action had stirred new juices in me. Even when my plane was hit, I felt no fear — only anger. I wanted to strike back, to clobber that Jap, and only a cooler second look at my damage restrained me.

So the gentle lad who hated violence grew tropical sores, fought off dysentery and malaria, choked down his bully, tapped crackers before eating (to get the weevils out), shared his whisky ration with the crew chief who kept his plane flying. He wore shorts hacked out of regulation khakis with a hunting knife, dealt solitaire on a canvas cot in the alert shack, and talked quietly, listening always for the field telephone to whir and the operations clerk to shout "Scramble! All flights!" He got tired and jittery, his insides sloshing with adrenaline, and he tried for a victory when he could, and learned from every casualty among his friends.

I WAS GOOD ENOUGH TO SURVIVE

65   It seemed no time before new replacements began to arrive, fat and pink-cheeked, wearing uniforms and saluting the C.O. as soon as they worked out which one of us skinny, half-naked figures he was. The rest of us looked at each other and whispered obscenities. We did our best to get the new guys squared away, and I cosseted the one on my wing — I was a flight leader by then — to make him look around so he might live awhile.

I never was a whiz-bang fighter jock, but I was good enough to survive the dicey little P-39. Then we were given big 2,000-horsepower P-47s, Republic Thunderbolts, or "Jugs" as we called them because of their shape. I was flying one that morning when I came down on a Japanese "Tony" — a very hot in-line-engine fighter — over the Bogadjim Road, near the north coast of New Guinea. I knew that I had him, and I was glad . . .

The dark little plane with the red circles got bigger in my sights, and I squeezed the trigger on the control stick. My eight guns blatted above the roar of the engine; tracers flicked away — red streaks seeming to go into the target, but you can't tell about tracers. I swung a little to iron out any skid, and held the trigger down. Flashes sparkled on the Tony. It slid sideways, shoved by the impact of bullets. Something flew off it and whipped past me. Then it rolled inverted and plunged.

A parachute blossomed (the Tony had at least as much armor plate behind it's cockpit as the P-47), and I jammed around to get my gunsight on the pilot. He'd be coming down over disputed territory and might fly again. That meant I was supposed to kill him in his chute. In our squadron, that was correct procedure. I figured I couldn't get around fast enough for a shot, so I muttered "Screw him," and flashed past him: a figure in a drab flying suit, about the same as mine. He'd lost his helmet and goggles. He had short-cropped black hair, and he hung on his straps and watched me whip past. I was close enough to see his black eyes follow me. He reminded me of someone I knew.

I landed and reported. The guys clapped me on the back and the C.O. gave me a hug. I'd done the right thing. I'd moved far away from the Veterans of Future Wars, the soaring ideals, the serene mountain, the tinkling birdsong, the loving hearth of home. In a way, I'd become a warrior.

Yet, even a half-century later, I'm troubled by something. It's about that   70 Japanese in the parachute. I reported that I couldn't quite get my gunsight on him. The fact is, that was a lie. I was a pretty fair pilot by then and could have cranked my turn a little tighter. I could have ripped him to shreds as he hung there — as I was supposed to do.

I just didn't. That was in 1944 — March 4, I think. I lost my logbook long ago.

TALKING ABOUT IT

Seeing Metaphor: Revealing and Concealing

1. Park writes of the squadron he joins, "These fellows had seen the squadron packed and ready to move, so close had come the Japanese. The clouds of danger still lingered over them, drawing them together, heightening their feeling that in this nonpriority theater of the war, they were a small family of forgotten men." Analyze the use of metaphor in this passage. Do you think Park is sentimentalizing here, or do the metaphors seem apt?

2. His first air fight, says Park, "was a rite of passage." What is a "rite of passage" literally? What associations accrue to this metaphor? Does it perhaps conceal anything about Park's experience?

Seeing Composition: Frame, Line, Texture, Tone

1. Park opens and closes his essay with the story of his chasing the Japanese pilot. Why does he frame his essay this way? Does this technique work to create a level of suspense for you?

2. Park's essay traces his evolution from being a pacifist who demonstrated against the United States entering the war to his becoming a seasoned combat soldier. How well do you understand this change? What does he include to explain it? Does his explanation seem to you enough?

Seeing Meaning: Navigating and Negotiating

1. Park quotes a line from a movie about World War I: "*Good God! When will they stop sending these children off to die?*" Does this seem to you to summarize his attitude toward his participation in the Second World War? Why or why not?

2. What do you think Park means at the end when he says he is "troubled" about not having shot the parachuting Japanese pilot? Why do you think he uses that particular adjective? Might he feel "troubled" in more than one way?

WRITING ABOUT IT

1. Park says that he was congratulated for his military mission: "I'd done the right thing," he claims, and follows his declaration with "I'd moved far away from the Veterans of Future Wars, the soaring ideals, the serene mountain, the tinkling of birdsong, the loving hearth of home. In a way, I'd become a warrior." But at the very end, he tells us that he lied about the parachutist. He could have "ripped him to shreds." "I just didn't," he says. "That was in 1944 — March 4, I think. I lost my logbook long ago."

   What happened between the beginning and the end of his story that explains why Park "just didn't"? Is he lying here, too, when he claims not to know why and not to be sure of the date, even though he remembers everything else quite clearly, or seems to? Draw from the essay itself to provide support for your argument.

2. Write an essay modeled after the structure and general sense of Park's essay: "I moved far away from _____. In a way, I'd become a _____." Start with the point of change, as Park does, but then retreat to the background and tell the story of your process. After that, return to the point of change at the beginning of your essay and follow through with what happened. Conclude.

Close Calls

Tobias Wolff

Tobias Wolff is a memoirist and fiction writer whose books include The Barracks Thief *(1984) and* This Boy's Life *(1989). The following piece was first published in 1994 in his book* In Pharaoh's Army: Memories of the Lost War, *a recollection of the author's experiences in the Vietnam War.*

I was inclined to regard every day I got through alive as a close call. I knew I could be killed at any moment, in any number of ways, randomly in the general mayhem or at the particular wish of the Vietcong who were everywhere around us. I wasn't hard to keep track of; they must have known my comings and goings. To kill me would have been easy, a piece of cake, and that they hadn't bothered to do it showed a just appreciation of my importance to the war effort. I was alive because they didn't consider me worth killing. I understood that, perfectly. I also understood that they might change their minds, take it into their heads that I mattered somehow. Who could guess their reasons? Their reasons were their own. I felt myself hanging by a thread in some boss guerrilla's mind, subject to his mood swings, his insomnia, his desperation to be taken seriously by other guerrillas. So while it might have been fainthearted of me to picture the days ahead as a long minefield, and the days behind as a series of reprieves, it was also perfectly accurate. But that's not what we mean by a close call.

I had been shot at. More accurately, shots had been fired in my direction from afar, without effect on me or the men I was with. Mortars had fallen in my neighborhood—none of them very close. I'd traveled in convoys where other men got blown up by mines and been in a helicopter that got hit, but not punctured, by machine gun fire (Sergeant Benet and I felt the bullets pounding against the metal under our feet, and gaped at each other in naked horror as our door gunner giggled and blasted away with his own machine gun).

None of these were close calls. A close call is personal, mysterious, sometimes fantastic. A bullet enters a man's helmet center-front and exits center-rear without putting a scratch on him. A platoon gets ambushed and overrun, after which the enemy puts a round in every man's head save one. A medic falls unnoticed from a pitching helicopter a thousand yards up and lands feetfirst in a rice paddy, plunging to his neck in the mud, where an American patrol rescues him, entirely by accident, the next morning. Things like this happened every day, and the best stories got written up in *Stars and Stripes* with a picture of the lucky guy. My own close calls were pretty thin gruel by comparison but good enough for me. Up until Tet I'd had two or three, depending on whether you counted the last.

My first close call happened a few days after I joined the battalion. I'd just had time to get unpacked and draw battle gear from the quartermaster when we got orders for the field. The operation took place over Easter weekend. Our guns were set up near a Catholic church, one of the few I ever saw in the Delta. On Sunday morning I woke to the sound of tolling bells, and later, as I sat hunched over my coffee, I was smitten by the sight of laughing girls in white ao dais leaping like lambs across the muddy furrows behind our howitzers. Though I had seldom been to mass since I was a boy, I accepted Sergeant Benet's invitation to join him.

5   The service was in Latin. The sound of the old tongue, the smell of incense, the once-familiar rhythm of the liturgy gave me a sense of continuity with my own past, as if this place were not wholly different from other places I had been. I didn't take communion, but I was pleased at how unhesitatingly I stood and knelt with the others, how quickly the responses came to my lips. I was glad to have Sergeant Benet there beside me. Up to now I'd been unsure of him, afraid he'd despise me for my fumbling inexperience, my incomprehensible officer status. But seeing him bow his head and pray for leniency gave me hope for some from him. When he said "Pax Christi, sir" and held out his hand, I took it with gratitude. Then I bowed to the Vietnamese around me as they were bowing to one another.

Without marking the change in myself, I had begun to let go a little, lulled from the state of paranoid watchfulness I'd been in since my first night off the plane. A mistake. Fear won't always save you, but it will take some of the pressure off your luck.

After mass Sergeant Benet and I drove to the village market to buy some fresh bread and vegetables. While he did the shopping I leaned back in the passenger seat and closed my eyes. My mood was still churchy, sentimental, liquid. I hadn't slept much the night before, and now, surrounded by friendly indecipherable voices and warmed by the sun, I began to nod off. Then I became aware that the voices had stopped. The silence disturbed me. I sat up and looked around. The crowd had drawn back in a wide circle. They were staring at me. A woman yammered something I couldn't follow and pointed under the jeep. I bent down for a look. There, lying directly below my seat, was a hand grenade. The pin had been pulled. I straightened up and sat there for a while, barely breathing. The I got out of the jeep and walked over to where everyone else was standing. We were still within the grenade's killing range, especially if it set off the gas tank, but I didn't have a thought in my head. We just stood there like a bunch of fools.

Sergeant Benet appeared at the edge of the crowd. "What's going on" he said. "There's a grenade under the jeep."

10   He turned and looked. "Oh, man, he said. He dropped the groceries and started pushing people back, his arms outstretched like a riot cop's. "*Di di mau!*"

he kept saying. "Beat it! Beat it!" Finally they gave ground, except for a bunch of kids who surrounded him and refused to be driven off. They were laughing. I looked on. None of it seemed to have anything to do with me.

Once the area was cleared Sergeant Benet told a couple of skittish villagers to stand watch until we could send someone to take care of the grenade; then we started walking back to the battalion. Along the way I found my legs acting funny. My knees wouldn't lock; I had to lean against a wall. Sergeant Benet put his hand on my arm to steady me. Then something went slack in my belly and I felt a stream of shit pouring hotly out of me, down my legs, even into my boots. I put my head against the wall and wept for very shame.

"It's all right, sir," Sergeant Benet said. "You'll be all right." He patted me on the back. Then he said, "Come on, sir. You got yourself a little case of the turistas, that's all. Here, that's the way. Just a step at a time, sir, that's right. Easy does it."

The grenade never did go off on its own. Our ordnance disposal boys covered it with sandbags and triggered it with a dose of plastique. It was an American grenade, not some local mad bomber device. The odds of it failing like that were cruelly small—just about nonexistent, in fact.

That was my first close call.

My second close call was of a more civilian character, the kind of thing that happens on road crews and construction sites. Still, it almost nailed me.

I'd been with the battalion for about six months. One of my jobs was to hook up our howitzers to Chinook helicopters when they were needed elsewhere in a hurry or when we were about to be inserted into an area we couldn't reach by road. I would rig up the gun in a sling, then stand on top of it as the chopper slowly lowered itself toward me, flattening the grass, raising a storm of dust and dirt and paddy water against which I wore ski goggles I'd asked Vera to send me. When the Chinook was a couple of feet over my head, just hanging there, all lebenty zillion tons of it, I would raise a steel loop and work it onto the hook dangling from the bottom of the helicopter. Then I'd nod at the crew chief and the cables would tighten and creak and I'd jump down and the chopper would lift the howitzer straight up, then cumbersomely bank and turn and beat a slanting path slowly higher and away into the distance. You saw all kinds of things swinging under those monster helicopters: howitzers, trucks, other helicopters; even, after a fight somewhere, nets filled with body bags.

My big fear was that a Chinook would lurch down and crush me against the gun. This could easily happen. All it took was for one of the engines to miss, or the pilot to sneeze, or a sudden downdraft to hit the rotors. I was always on the scout for any sign of unsteadiness—not that I would have had time to do anything. But once the cables went taut I was free to jump, and jump I did, without decorum. While the helicopter maneuvered overhead I brushed myself off and gathered up the sling they'd tossed down for the next pickup.

In the early days I used to watch as the Chinook hauled its load into the sky; it was a strange sight, but I got used to it and had other things to attend to. I don't know what made me look up this one time. Maybe I heard a new sound under the engine clatter and the whapping of the blades, a sound I didn't even know I was hearing, a different sound than what my self-loving body had recorded as acceptable to its interests. Anyway, I looked up sharply. The Chinook was directly above me, sixty, seventy feet, executing an elephantine turn. The howitzer was swinging back and forth. From this vantage I could see nothing wrong, but even so I started to walk backward off the LZ, my eyes raised, and I saw the howitzer shift oddly in its sling, and shift again, and then the sling flew open and the chopper jumped like a flea. The howitzer seemed to fall very slowly, turning as it fell, and landed upside down with a painful blaring whang — more a sensation than a sound — and bounced once and settled. I felt the shock from my heels to my teeth.

This would not be a proper close call story if I didn't point out that the gun hit right where I'd been standing.

20   The third close call happened just before Christmas. I didn't mention it to anyone afterward, unlike the other two, which I talked about every chance I got. This one didn't really sound all that dangerous and it wouldn't have made a satisfactory story. Still, I brooded on it more than on the others.

We were on an operation. Sergeant Benet stayed with the battalion while I pulled duty at the fire-direction center. On the second day, one of our infantry companies walked into an ambush. I was hanging around the headquarters tent at the time, idly listening to situation reports come in over the radio, and I heard the battle begin and the Vietnamese commander cry through the static for help.

General Ngoc took over from the radio operator. His staff officers crowded around to listen. There was plenty to hear. Screams. Gunfire. The voices of men in terror and pain. Colonel Lance, the ranking American adviser, came over to the radio, puffing fiercely on his pipe as he watched General Ngoc bark into the transmitter at the frightened commander in the field. Colonel Lance didn't speak Vietnamese but he narrowed his eyes and nodded from time to time as if he knew what was passing between the two men. And as he stood there listening he absently laid one hand on the shoulder of the officer standing next to him, a first lieutenant named Keith Young. He didn't look to see who it was; he just rested his hand on him the way a football coach will rest his hand on the player he happens to be standing next to on the sidelines. It was one of those paternal gestures that excited my scorn except when they fell on me, and then I always felt a flood of puppyish gratitude.

Anyway, Colonel Lance didn't look to see who was there when he parked his hand. It could have been anyone. It could have been me. It could very easily have been me, as I was standing beside Keith Young at the time, and if Colonel

Lance had taken a place between us instead of to Keith's right it would have been me who got the manly sign of favor. He stood there with his hand on Keith's shoulder, and when General Ngoc got up from the radio and explained the situation, which was that the company was pinned down and taking casualties, and needed an American adviser to go in with the reinforcements to call in medevacs and air support, Colonel Lance turned to the man he had his hand on and looked him in the face for the first time. He took his pipe out of his mouth. "Well, Keith," he said, "what do you think?" His voice was kind, his expression solicitous. If you didn't know better you'd have thought he was asking an opinion, not giving an order, but Keith did know better. "I'll get my stuff," he said. His voice was flat. He looked at me as he walked past.

Colonel Lance nodded at General Ngoc and reached for the transmitter. While he was calling for helicopters to insert the reserve company into the field I faded back and left the tent. Colonel Lance had taken no notice of me, and it seemed wise to keep it that way.

Keith got killed later that afternoon. I never heard what the circumstances 25 were, only that he was shot in the stomach. That meant he'd been standing up, maybe to carry one end of a stretcher, or with his arm raised to give the textbook signal for attack — "Follow me!"

His death affected me strangely. It didn't cause me pain so much as a kind of wonder at the way it had happened. I couldn't stop playing it out: Colonel Lance hearing the fuss at the radio and walking over to see what was wrong, intent on the terrible sounds filling the air, heedless of either Keith or me except as big American bodies among the Vietnamese gathered around the table. Then his arbitrary decision to stand to Keith's right, no nearer the radio than if he'd stood between us. This was the decision from which everything else followed: the hand on Keith's shoulder, the gaze that followed the hand, the order that followed the gaze, the death that followed the order. Everything marched in lockstep from that one moment. If he had stood between us it would have been my shoulder the hand fell on, the other hand being occupied with his curved, fragrant, fatherly pipe. It would have been me receiving the father's thoughtless blessing touch, me to whom he turned, me to whom he put the kindly question that had only one answer.

It could have been me. I knew it even then, and Keith might have had the same thought. We were the same rank, had about the same experience. We both stood about six feet. He was older by two or three years, but not so you'd notice. For the needs of this occasion either of us seemed about as plausible as the other. He had grounds for wondering why the hand had fallen on him. It could have been me, and he may even have thought that it should have been me. Certainly there were times, not immediately afterward but in the months and years to come, that I myself had the suspicion it should have been me — that Keith, and Hugh, and other men had somehow picked up my cards and stood in the place where I was meant to stand.

I once confessed this dreary notion to someone, who, meaning well, told me it was caveman talk.

"I know," I said. "But still."

30   But still. In a world where the most consequential things happen by chance, or from unfathomable causes, you don't look to reason for help. You consort with mysteries. You encourage yourself with charms, omens, rites of propitiation. Without your knowledge or permission the bottom-line caveman belief in blood sacrifice, one life buying another, begins to steal into your bones. How could it not? All around you people are killed: soldiers on both sides, farmers, teachers, mothers, fathers, schoolgirls, nurses, your friends — but not you. They have been killed instead of you. This observation is unavoidable. So, in time, is the corollary, implicit in the word *instead:* in place of. They have been killed in place of you — in your place. You don't think it out, not at the time, not in those terms, but you can't help but feel it, and go on feeling it. It's the close call you have to keep escaping from, the unending doubt that you have a right to your own life. It's the corruption suffered by everyone who lives on, that henceforth they must wonder at the reason, and probe its justice.

I didn't really know Keith Young. We saw each other in My Tho now and then, exchanged a few friendly words, but we didn't take it any farther than that. He was too quiet for me, too careful. He struck me, I have to admit, as a company man, and it was pretty clear that I'd made no better impression on him. We never spent any time together until by chance we ran into each other while boarding the Kowloon ferry in Hong Kong. I'd been on R and R for four or five days already and Keith had just arrived. He was on his way to a tailor he'd heard about, and invited me to join him. This tailor was incredible, he said. For thirty dollars he could copy any suit; all you had to do was show him a picture of it. Keith had several pictures, advertisements he'd cut out of *Esquire.* You could pick up the suits in twenty-four hours.

I didn't have anything better to do so I went along with Keith and watched him being fitted for his wardrobe. At first I found the whole thing comical, especially a sign in the window of the shop: "Guaranteed by the Royal Navy." I liked the idea of the Royal Navy taking an interest in my duds. And then I began to think it wasn't that bad a deal, thirty bucks, and that it wouldn't hurt to have a few good suits and the odd sport coat hanging around. Before leaving the shop that day I placed some orders of my own, for clothes that did not in fact resemble the ones in *Esquire* — "You look like a Chinaman," a friend told me when I got home — and which quickly began to fall apart because of inferior thread. One of my suit sleeves actually came off inside my overcoat as I was arriving at a house for a dinner party some years later. I considered sending a letter of complaint to the First Lord of the Admiralty, but never did.

My haul was modest compared to Keith's. He ordered six or seven suits, tweed jackets, camel and blue blazers, slacks, button-down shirts of every acceptable color, formal wear, and two overcoats—also in camel and blue. He seemed bent on getting the whole clothes problem out of the way forever, right then and there. We hit a few clubs that night and he couldn't stop talking about what a great deal he'd gotten. And that was the first thought I had when I heard he'd been killed: What about all those clothes? It was a gasp of a thought, completely instinctual, without malice or irony. All those clothes waiting for him— they seemed somehow an irrefutable argument for his survival. Maybe they'd seemed that way to him too, a kind of guarantee, like the wives and fiancées some of us accumulated just before leaving home. They gave us a picture of ourselves in time to come, a promise of future existence to use as a safe-conduct pass through the present.

I sometimes tried to imagine other men wearing Keith's suits, but I couldn't bring the images to life. What I see instead is a dark closet with all his clothes hanging in a row. Someone opens the closet door, looks at them for a time, and closes the door again.

TALKING ABOUT IT

Seeing Metaphor: Revealing and Concealing

1. In paragraph 2, Wolff describes several occasions when he experienced brushes with danger during the war, but none of these, he says, were close calls. Rather, a close call is "personal, mysterious, sometimes fantastic." How does Wolff's use of the term "close call" here differ from its usual sense? What does "close call" stand for in this essay?

2. Wolff ends by writing about the suits Keith Young purchased in Hong Kong shortly before he was killed. What do these suits represent for Wolff?

Seeing Composition: Frame, Line, Texture, Tone

1. The basic organization of this essay seems rather simple: In three distinct sections, Wolff describes three close calls. But the three opening paragraphs and the five final paragraphs stand apart from this structure. What happens in this opening and closing? How would the essay be different if both the opening and closing were reduced to a single short paragraph?

2. Look at the way Wolff describes his first close call with the hand grenade (paragraph 7) and his second close call with the falling howitzer (paragraph 18). How does sentence length in each passage contribute to the effect of the description?

Seeing Meaning: Navigating and Negotiating

1. Wolff writes that he'd had two or three close calls, "depending on whether you counted the last." Do you count the last as a close call? Why or why not?

2. In paragraph 27, Wolff wonders at the "justice" of his surviving "in place of" others who were killed. What is he getting at here? Do you think this is a legitimate concern? Why or why not?

WRITING ABOUT IT

1. "A close call is personal, mysterious, sometimes fantastic," Tobias Wolff claims. "Up until Tet, I'd had two or three, depending on whether you counted the last." Why does he "brood" on the third close call more than the other two? Do you count the last? Why or why not?

2. How would you define a close call? Follow your definition with an illustration of a close call that you think you've had.

3. "In a world where the most consequential things happen by chance, or from unfathomable causes," Wolff says, "you don't look to reason for help. You consort with mysteries. You encourage yourself with charms, omens, rites of propitiation." Keith bought clothes. They were a metaphor, a symbol for something else: "All those clothes waiting for him — they seemed somehow an irrefutable argument for his survival . . . a kind of guarantee. . . . "

    In what way have your consorted with mysteries? What charms have you used to imagine yourself "in time to come"? What omens, what rituals might you have thought of as "a promise of future existence to use as a safe-conduct pass through the present"?

Crickets

ROBERT OLEN BUTLER

Robert Olen Butler is a novelist and short-story writer whose works include The Alleys of Eden *(1981) and* Tabloid Dreams *(1996). His collection of short stories,* A Good Scent from a Strange Mountain, *from which the following piece was taken, won the 1993 Pulitzer Prize in fiction.*

They call me Ted where I work and they've called me that for over a decade now and it still bothers me, though I'm not very happy about my real name being the same as the former President of the former Republic of Vietnam. Thiệu is not an uncommon name in my homeland and my mother had nothing more in mind than a long-dead uncle when she gave it to me. But in Lake Charles, Louisiana, I am Ted. I guess the other Mr. Thiệu has enough of my former country's former gold bullion tucked away so that in London, where he probably wears a bowler and carries a rolled umbrella, nobody's calling him anything but Mr. Thiệu.

I hear myself sometimes and I sound pretty bitter, I guess. But I don't let that out at the refinery, where I'm the best chemical engineer they've got and they even admit it once in a while. They're good-hearted people, really. I've done enough fighting in my life. I was eighteen when Saigon fell and I was only recently mustered into the Army, and when my unit dissolved and everybody ran, I stripped off my uniform and put on my civilian clothes again and I threw rocks at the North's tanks when they rolled through the streets. Very few of my people did likewise. I stayed in the mouths of alleys so I could run and then return and throw more rocks, but because what I did seemed so isolated and so pathetic a gesture, the gunners in the tanks didn't even take notice. But I didn't care about their scorn. At least my right arm had said no to them.

And then there were Thai Pirates in the South China Sea and idiots running the refugee centers and more idiots running the agencies in the U.S. to find a place for me and my new bride, who braved with me the midnight escape by boat and the terrible sea and all the rest. We ended up here in the flat bayou land of Louisiana, where there are rice paddies and where the water and the land are in the most delicate balance with each other, very much like the Mekong Delta, where I grew up. These people who work around me are good people and maybe they call me Ted because they want to think of me as one of them, though sometimes it bothers me that these men are so much bigger than me. I am the size of a woman in this country and these American men are all massive and they speak so slowly, even to one another, even though English is their native language. I've heard New Yorkers on television and I speak as fast as they do.

My son is beginning to speak like the others here in Louisiana. He is ten, the product of the first night my wife and I spent in Lake Charles, in a cheap motel with the sky outside red from the refineries. He is proud to have been born in America, and when he leaves us in the morning to walk to the Catholic school, he says, "Have a good day, y'all." Sometimes I say good-bye to him in Vietnamese and he wrinkles his nose at me and says, "Aw, Pop," like I'd just cracked a corny joke. He doesn't speak Vietnamese at all and my wife says not to worry about that. He's an American.

5   But I do worry about that, though I understand why I should be content. I even understood ten years ago, so much so that I agreed with my wife and gave my son an American name. Bill. Bill and his father Ted. But this past summer I found my son hanging around the house bored in the middle of vacation and I was suddenly his father Thiệu with a wonderful idea for him. It was an idea that had come to me in the first week of every February we'd been in Lake Charles, because that's when the crickets always begin to crow here. This place is rich in crickets, which always make me think of my own childhood in Vietnam. But I never said anything to my son until last summer.

I came to him after watching him slouch around the yard one Sunday pulling the Spanish moss off the lowest branches of our big oak tree and then throwing rocks against the stop sign on our corner. "Do you want to do something fun?" I said to him.

"Sure, Pop," he said, though there was a certain suspicion in his voice, like he didn't trust me on the subject of fun. He threw all the rocks at once that were left in his hand and the stop sign shivered at their impact.

I said, "If you keep that up, they will arrest me for the destruction of city property and they will deport us all."

My son laughed at this. I, of course, knew that he would know I was bluffing. I didn't want to be too hard on him for the boyish impulses that I myself had found to be so satisfying when I was young, especially since I was about to share something of my own childhood with him.

10   "So what've you got, Pop?" my son asked me.

"Fighting crickets," I said.

"What?"

Now, my son was like any of his fellow ten-year-olds, devoted to superheroes and the mighty clash of good and evil in all of its high-tech forms in the Saturday-morning cartoons. Just to make sure he was in the right frame of mind, I explained it to him with one word, "Cricketmen," and I thought this was a pretty good ploy. He cocked his head in interest at this and I took him to the side porch and sat him down and I explained.

I told him how, when I was a boy, my friends and I would prowl the undergrowth and capture crickets and keep them in matchboxes. We would feed them leaves and bits of watermelon and bean sprouts, and we'd train them to fight by keeping them in a constant state of agitation by blowing on them and gently flicking the ends of their antennas with a sliver of wood. So each of us would have a stable of fighting crickets, and there were two kinds.

At this point my son was squirming a little bit and his eyes were shifting   15 away into the yard and I knew that my Cricketman trick had run its course. I fought back the urge to challenge his set of interests. Why should the stiff and foolish fights of his cartoon characters absorb him and the real clash — real life and death — that went on in the natural world bore him? But I realized that I hadn't cut to the chase yet, as they say on the TV. "They fight to the death," I said with as much gravity as I could put into my voice, like I was James Earl Jones.

The announcement won me a glance and a brief lift of his eyebrows. This gave me a little scrabble of panic, because I still hadn't told him about the two types of crickets and I suddenly knew that was a real important part for me. I tried not to despair at his understanding and I put my hands on his shoulders and turned him around to face me. "Listen," I said. "You need to understand this if you are to have fighting crickets. There are two types, and all of us had some of each. One type we called the charcoal crickets. These were very large and strong, but they were slow and they could become confused. The other type was small and brown and we called them fire crickets. They weren't as strong, but they were very smart and quick."

"So who would win?" my son said.

"Sometimes one and sometimes the other. The fights were very long and full of hard struggle. We'd have a little tunnel made of paper and we'd slip a sliver of wood under the cowling of our cricket's head to make him mad and we'd twirl him by his antenna, and then we'd each put our cricket into the tunnel at opposite ends. Inside, they'd approach each other and begin to fight and then we'd lift the paper tunnel and watch."

"Sounds neat," my son said, though his enthusiasm was at best moderate, and I knew I had to act quickly.

So we got a shoe box and we started looking for crickets. It's better at   20 night, but I knew for sure his interest wouldn't last that long. Our house is up on blocks because of the high water table in town and we crawled along the edge, pulling back the bigger tufts of grass and turning over rocks. It was one of the rocks that gave us our first crickets, and my son saw them and cried in my ear, "There, there," but he waited for me to grab them. I cupped first one and then the other and dropped them into the shoe box and I felt a vague disappointment, not so much because it was clear that my boy did not want to touch the insects, but that they were both the big black ones, the charcoal crickets. We crawled on and we found another one in the grass and another sitting in the muddy shadow of the house behind the hose faucet and then we caught two more under an azalea bush.

"Isn't that enough?" my son demanded. "How many do we need?"

I sat with my back against the house and put the shoe box in my lap and my boy sat beside me, his head stretching this way so he could look into the box. There was no more vagueness to my feeling. I was actually weak with disappointment because all six of these were charcoal crickets, big and inert and just looking around like they didn't even know anything was wrong.

"Oh, no," my son said with real force, and for a second I thought he had read my mind and shared my feeling, but I looked at him and he was pointing at the toes of his white sneakers. "My Reeboks are ruined!" he cried, and on the toe of each sneaker was a smudge of grass.

I glanced back into the box and the crickets had not moved and I looked at my son and he was still staring at his sneakers. "Listen," I said, "this was a big mistake. You can go on and do something else."

25   He jumped up at once. "Do you think Mom can clean these?" he said. "Sure," I said. "Sure."

He was gone at once and the side door slammed and I put the box on the grass. But I didn't go in. I got back on my hands and knees and I circled the entire house and then I turned over every stone in the yard and dug around all the trees. I found probably two dozen more crickets, but they were all the same. In Louisiana there are rice paddies and some of the bayous look like the Delta, but many of the birds are different, and why shouldn't the insects be different, too? This is another country, after all. It was just funny about the fire crickets. A lot of us kids rooted for them, even if we were fighting with one of our own charcoal crickets. A fire cricket was a very precious and admirable thing.

The next morning my son stood before me as I finished my breakfast and once he had my attention, he look down at his feet, drawing my eyes down as well. "See?" he said. "Mom got them clean."

Then he was out the door and I called after him, "See you later, Bill."

TALKING ABOUT IT

Seeing Metaphor: Revealing and Concealing

1. The Vietnamese American narrator of this story says he is bothered that his Louisiana co-workers call him Ted rather than his real name, Thiệu. Why should he be bothered? What does the name Ted represent to him? To his co-workers? Do you think he is justified in wanting his co-workers to call him by his real name?

2. The narrator makes a strong distinction between charcoal crickets and fire crickets. Why is he so disappointed that he can find only charcoal crickets around his Louisiana home? What might fire crickets represent in the story?

How is it meaningful that parts of Louisiana are very much like the Mekong Delta where the narrator grew up?

Seeing Composition: Frame, Line, Texture, Tone

1. In the second paragraph, the narrator says, "I hear myself sometimes and I sound pretty bitter, I guess." Does the voice of this story strike you as bitter? If not, how would you describe the tone? Explain your answer.

2. What is the effect of the final two paragraphs of the story? How would the story be different if it ended without them?

Seeing Meaning: Navigating and Negotiating

1. Early on, the narrator describes himself "throwing rocks at the North's tanks" after Saigon fell, when most other South Vietnamese simply ran. How does this description contribute to your understanding of his character?

2. What do you think of the son, Bill, in the story? Do you find him sympathetic? Is his attitude toward his father's past inevitable?

WRITING ABOUT IT

1. Crickets provide a constellation of meanings in Butler's story. What do they mean to Ted, to Ted's son? And what do they stand for in the relationship between father and son?

2. The structure of this story as well as the general experience is common. You may be cleaning out the attic, for example, or sorting through old clothes, games, photographs, and so forth. You might be playing a sport, having dinner, or engaged in conversation. Something prompts you to recall the past. Write about such an event in your own life—a time that an object suggested a memory of your childhood, a life in another place, a particular person. What does the object stand for, what does it mean beyond its literal meaning?

The Liberation of Kuwait Has Begun

GEORGE BUSH

U.S. President George Bush gave the following speech from the Oval Office on January 16, 1991, two hours after White House spokesperson Marlin Fitzwater announced that the "liberation of Kuwait" had begun.

Just two hours ago, Allied air forces began an attack on military targets in Iraq and Kuwait. These attacks continue as I speak. Ground forces are not engaged.

This conflict started August 2, when the dictator of Iraq invaded a small and helpless neighbor. Kuwait, a member of the Arab League and a member of the United Nations, was crushed, its people brutalized. Five months ago, Saddam Hussein started this cruel war against Kuwait; tonight, the battle has been joined.

This military action, taken in accord with United Nations resolutions and with the consent of the United States Congress, follows months of constant and virtually endless diplomatic activity on the part of the United Nations, the United States and many, many other countries.

Arab leaders sought what became known as an Arab solution, only to conclude that Saddam Hussein was unwilling to leave Kuwait. Others traveled to Baghdad in a variety of efforts to restore peace and justice. Our secretary of state, James Baker, held an historic meeting in Geneva, only to be totally rebuffed.

5   This past weekend, in a last-ditch effort, the secretary-general of the United Nations went to the Middle East with peace in his heart—his second such mission. And he came back from Baghdad with no progress at all in getting Saddam Hussein to withdraw from Kuwait.

Now, the twenty-eight countries with forces in the Gulf area have exhausted all reasonable efforts to reach a peaceful resolution, and have no choice but to drive Saddam from Kuwait by force. We will not fail.

As I report to you, air attacks are under way against military targets in Iraq. We are determined to knock out Saddam Hussein's nuclear bomb potential. We will also destroy his chemical weapons facilities. Much of Saddam's artillery and tanks will be destroyed. Our operations are designed to best protect the lives of all the coalition forces by targeting Saddam's vast military arsenal.

Initial reports from General Schwarzkopf are that our operations are proceeding according to plan. Our objectives are clear: Saddam Hussein's forces will leave Kuwait. The legitimate government of Kuwait will be restored to its rightful place, and Kuwait will once again be free.

Iraq will eventually comply with all relevant United Nations resolutions, and then, when peace is restored, it is our hope that Iraq will live as a peaceful and cooperative member of the family of nations, thus enhancing the security and stability of the Gulf.

Some may ask, why act now? Why not wait? The answer is clear. The world could wait no longer. Sanctions, though having some effect, showed no signs of accomplishing their objective. Sanctions were tried for well over five months, and we and our allies concluded that sanctions alone would not force Saddam from Kuwait.

While the world waited, Saddam Hussein systematically raped, pillaged, and plundered a tiny nation no threat to his own. He subjected the people of Kuwait to unspeakable atrocities, and among those maimed and murdered, innocent children.

While the world waited, Saddam sought to add to the chemical weapons arsenal he now possesses, an infinitely more dangerous weapon of mass destruction—a nuclear weapon. And while the world waited, while the world talked peace and withdrawal, Saddam Hussein dug in and moved massive forces into Kuwait.

While the world waited, while Saddam stalled, more damage was being done to the fragile economies of the Third World, emerging democracies of Eastern Europe, to the entire world, including to our own economy.

The United States, together with the United Nations, exhausted every means at our disposal to bring this crisis to a peaceful end. However, Saddam clearly felt that by stalling and threatening and defying the United Nations, he could weaken the forces arrayed against him.

While the world waited, Saddam Hussein met every overture of peace with open contempt. While the world prayed for peace, Saddam prepared for war.

I had hoped that when the United States Congress, in historic debate, took its resolute action, Saddam would realize he could not prevail and would move out of Kuwait in accord with the United Nations resolutions. He did not do that. Instead, he remained intransigent, certain that time was on his side.

Saddam was warned over and over again to comply with the will of the United Nations, leave Kuwait or be driven out. Saddam has arrogantly rejected all warnings. Instead he tried to make this a dispute between Iraq and the United States of America.

Well he failed. Tonight twenty-eight nations—countries from five continents, Europe and Asia, Africa and the Arab League—have forces in the Gulf area standing shoulder to shoulder against Saddam Hussein. These countries had hoped the use of force could be avoided. Regrettably, we now believe that only force will make him leave.

Prior to ordering our forces into battle, I instructed our military commanders to take every necessary step to prevail as quickly as possible, and with the greatest degree of protection possible for American and Allied servicemen and women. I've told the American people before that this will not be another

Vietnam, and I repeat this here tonight. Our troops will have the best possible support in the entire world, and they will not be asked to fight with one hand tied behind their back. I'm hopeful that this fighting will not go on for long and that casualties will be held to an absolute minimum.

20   This is an historic moment. We have in this past year made great progress in ending the long era of conflict and Cold War. We have before us the opportunity to forge for ourselves and for future generations a new world order, a world where the rule of law, not the law of the jungle, governs the conduct of nations.

When we are successful, and we will be, we have a real chance at this new world order, an order in which a credible United Nations can use its peacekeeping role to fulfill the promise and vision of the U.N.'s founders. We have no argument with the people of Iraq. Indeed, for the innocents caught in this conflict, I pray for their safety.

Our goal is not the conquest of Iraq. Is the liberation of Kuwait. It is my hope that somehow the Iraqi people can, even now, convince their dictator that he must lay down his arms, leave Kuwait, and let Iraq itself rejoin the family of peace-loving nations.

Thomas Paine wrote many years ago: "These are the times that try men's souls." Those well-known words are so very true today. But even as planes of the multinational forces attack Iraq, I prefer to think of peace, not war. I am convinced not only that we will prevail, but that out of the horror of combat will come the recognition that no nation can stand against a world united. No nation will be permitted to brutally assault its neighbor.

No president can easily commit our sons and daughters to war. They are the nation's finest. Ours is an all-volunteer force, magnificently trained, highly motivated. The troops know why they're there. And listen to what they say, because they've said it better than any president or prime minister ever could. Listen to Hollywood Huddleston, marine lance corporal. He says: "Let's free these people so we can go home and be free again." And he's right. The terrible crimes and tortures committed by Saddam's henchmen against the innocent people of Kuwait are an affront to mankind and a challenge to the freedom of all.

25   Listen to one of our great officers out there, Marine Lieutenant General Walter Boomer. He said: "There are things worth fighting for. A world in which brutality and lawlessness are allowed to go unchecked isn't the kind of world we're going to want to live in."

Listen to Master Sergeant J. P. Kendall of the 82d Airborne: "We're here for more than just the price of a gallon of gas. What we're doing is going to chart the future of the world for the next hundred years. It's better to deal with this guy now than five years from now."

And finally, we should all sit up and listen to Jackie Jones, an army lieutenant, when she says, "If we let him get away with this, who knows what's going to be next."

I've called upon Hollywood and Walter and J. P. and Jackie and all their courageous comrades-in-arms to do what must be done. Tonight, America and the world are deeply grateful to them and to their families.

And let me say to everyone listening or watching tonight: When the troops we've sent in finish their work, I'm determined to bring them home as soon as possible. Tonight, as our forces fight, they and their families are in our prayers.

May God bless each and every one of them and the coalition forces at our side   30
in the Gulf, and may He continue to bless our nation, the United States of America.

TALKING ABOUT IT

Seeing Metaphor: Revealing and Concealing

1. President Bush emphasizes in this speech that the conflict with Iraq "will not be another Vietnam" and that U.S. troops "will not be asked to fight with one hand tied behind their back." What does Vietnam represent in the American consciousness? Did the Gulf War and the Vietnam War have anything in common that Bush is trying to downplay?

2. Bush claims that "we have before us the opportunity to forge . . . a new world order, a world where the rule of law, not the law of the jungle, governs the conduct of nations." Analyze his images of the "rule of law" and the "law of the jungle." How appropriate do you find them in this context?

Seeing Composition: Frame, Line, Texture, Tone

1. Consider the use of repetition in paragraphs 10–15. What is its purpose?

2. Throughout, the writers of this speech are trying to convince its audience that all options short of military conflict have been exhausted. Find examples of specific words and phrases used for this effect. Do you find this strategy convincing?

Seeing Meaning: Navigating and Negotiating

1. Note that it is Saddam Hussein, not the country of Iraq, that President Bush attacks in this speech. Why do you think this is so? What is the effect of the sentences "We have no argument with the people of Iraq. Indeed, for the innocents caught in this conflict, I pray for their safety"? Why is this the only mention of Iraqi citizens?

2. Essentially, the justification here for the attack on Iraq is the "terrible crimes and tortures committed by Saddam's henchmen against the innocent people of Kuwait." Do some research to learn more about the Iraqi occupation of Kuwait in August 1990. How accurate is the speech's characterization of this occupation?

―――――――――――――――――

WRITING ABOUT IT

1. Each writing group in class might try to answer collaboratively how one of the categories below is illustrated in George Bush's speech. How is his speech a story about

   a. the just war
   b. villains, victims, and heroes
   c. triumph of rationality over irrationality
   d. good and evil
   e. order and disorder

   After each group has shown how the story it has chosen can be read in Bush's speech, exchange analyses and discuss how the stories overlap, how they conflict (if you think they do), and what other stories they conceal.

2. How does George Bush anticipate and answer likely objections from the American people about waging war against Iraq?

The Mother of All Battles

SADDAM HUSSEIN

The following is an excerpt from the speech President Saddam Hussein of Iraq gave over Baghdad Radio on January 20, 1991, as translated by Reuters.

O glorious Iraqis, O holy warrior Iraqis, O Arabs, O believers wherever you are, we and our steadfastness are holding. Here is the great Iraqi people, your brothers and sons of your Arab nation and the great faithful part of the human family. We are all well. They are fighting with unparalleled heroism, unmatched except by the heroism of the believers who fight similar adversaries. And here is the infidel tyrant whose planes and missiles are falling out of the skies at the blows of the brave men. He is wondering how the Iraqis can confront his fading dreams with such determination and firmness.

After a while, he will begin to feel frustrated, and his defeat will be certain, God willing. . . . We in Iraq will be the faithful and obedient servants of God, struggling for his sake to raise the banner of truth and justice, the banner of "God is Great." Accursed by the lowly.

At that time, the valiant Iraqi men and women will not allow the army of atheism, treachery, hypocrisy and [world indistinct] to realize their stupid hope that the war would only last a few days or weeks, as they imagined and declared. In the coming period, the response of Iraq will be on a larger scale, using all the means and potential that God has given us and which we have so far only used in part. Our ground forces have not entered the battle so far, and only a small part of our air force has been used.

The army's air force has not been used, nor has the navy. The weight and effect of our ready missile force has not yet been applied in full. The fact remains that the great divine reinforcement is our source of power and effectiveness. When the war is fought in a comprehensive manner, using all resources and weapons, the scale of death and the number of dead will, God willing, rise among the ranks of atheism, injustice, and tyranny.

When they begin to die and when the message of the Iraqi soldiers reaches 5 the farthest corner of the world, the unjust will die and the "God is Great" banner will flutter with great victory in the mother of all battles. Then the skies in the Arab homeland will appear in a new color and a sun of new hope will shine over them and over our nation and on all the good men whose bright lights will not be overcome by the darkness in the hearts of the infidels, the Zionists, and the treacherous, shameful rulers, such as the traitor Fahd.

Then the door will be wide open for the liberation of beloved Palestine, Lebanon, and the Golan. Then Jerusalem and the Dome of the Rock will be released from bondage. The Kaaba and the Tomb of the Prophet Mohammed, God's peace and blessings be upon him, will be liberated from occupation and God will bestow upon the poor and needy the things that others owed them, others who withheld from them what they owed them as God had justly ordained, which is a great deal.

Then [words indistinct], the good men, the holy warriors, and the faithful will know the truth of our promise to them that when the forces of infidelity attack the Iraqis, they will fight as they wished them to fight and perhaps in a better way, and that their promise is of faith and holy war. It remains for us to tell all Arabs, all the faithful strugglers, and all good supporters wherever they are: you have a duty to carry out holy war and struggle in order to target the assembly of evil, treason, and corruption everywhere.

You must also target their interests everywhere. It is a duty that is incumbent upon you, and that must necessarily correspond to the struggle of your brothers in Iraq. You will be part of the struggle of armed forces in your holy war and struggle, and part of the multitude of faith and the faithful. If the opposing multitude captures you, you will be prisoners in their hands, even if they refuse to admit this in their communiques and statements.

You will inevitably be released when the war ends, in accordance with international laws and agreements which will govern the release of prisoners of war. In this way you will have pleased God and honored, with your slogans and principles, the trust given to you.

10   God is great, God is great, God is great, and accursed be the lowly.

TALKING ABOUT IT

Seeing Metaphor: Revealing and Concealing

1. Analyze the metaphor "the mother of all battles." What does it seem to mean literally? What do you make of the linkage of motherhood to war? Does this metaphor make sense to you? Explain.

2. Compare Saddam Hussein's invocations of God with those in the preceding speech by George Bush. What does "God" represent in each case? How different are the two conceptions?

Seeing Composition: Frame, Line, Texture, Tone

1. To whom is this speech addressed? What seems to be its purpose? How do you know?

2. Compare the tone of this speech with that of George Bush's speech. What makes them so different? How does each speaker's purpose affect these differences?

Seeing Meaning: Navigating and Negotiating

1. Saddam Hussein pits "believers" against "the infidel" here and refers to the need for other Arabs to "carry out holy war." To what extent was the U.S. conflict with Iraq a battle over religion?

2. What seems to be the meaning of paragraphs 7–9? Why do you suppose Saddam Hussein concludes this way? What is the ultimate effect?

WRITING ABOUT IT

1. It's said that you can tell you've made God in your own image if He hates the same people you do. How does Hussein use the story of the triumph of good over evil to gain support for the war effort? How does he make war "holy" in his speech?

2. How does Hussein characterize the enemy? How does Bush characterize the enemy? How do you account for the differences?

3. George Bush mentions God only at the end of his speech. Why would Saddam Hussein's strategy fail for an American audience?

Wars, Wimps, and Women: Talking Gender and Thinking War

CAROL COHN

Carol Cohn is a professor of sociology and women's studies at Bowdoin College and the author of "Sex and Death in the Rational World of Defense Intellectuals," an article that appeared in Signs *12 (1987). The following essay was first published in the collection* Gendering War Talk *(1993), edited by Miriam Cooke and Angela Woollacott.*

I start with a true story, told to me by a white male physicist:

> Several colleagues and I were working on modeling counterforce attacks, trying to get realistic estimates of the number of immediate fatalities that would result from different deployments.[1] At one point, we remodeled a particular attack, using slightly different assumptions, and found that instead of there being thirty-six million immediate fatalities, there would only be thirty million. And everybody was sitting around nodding, saying, "Oh yeah, that's great, only thirty million," when all of a sudden, I *heard* what we were saying. And I blurted out, "Wait, I've just *heard* how we're talking— *Only* thirty million! *Only* thirty million human beings killed instantly?" Silence fell upon the room. Nobody said a word. They didn't even look at me. It was awful. I felt like a woman.

The physicist added that henceforth he was careful to never blurt out anything like that again.

■ ■ ■

During the early years of the Reagan presidency, in the era of Evil Empire, the cold war, and loose talk in Washington about the possibility of fighting and "prevailing" in a nuclear war, I went off to do participant observation in a community of North American nuclear defense intellectuals and security affairs analysts—a community virtually entirely composed of white men. They work in universities, think tanks, and as advisers to government. They theorize about nuclear deterrence and arms control, and nuclear and conventional war fighting, about how to best translate military might into political power; in short, they create the discourse that underwrites American national security policy. . . . One thing that is clear is that the body of language and thinking they have generated filters out to the military, politicians, and the public, and increasingly shapes how we talk and think about war. This was amply evident during the

Gulf War: Gulf War "news," as generated by the military briefers, reported by newscasters, and analyzed by the television networks' resident security experts, was marked by its use of the professional language of defense analysis, nearly to the exclusion of other ways of speaking.

My goal has been to understand something about how defense intellectuals think, and why they think that way. Despite the parsimonious appeal of ascribing the nuclear arms race to "missile envy,"[2] I felt certain that masculinity was not a sufficient explanation of why men think about war in the ways that they do. Indeed, I found many ways to understand what these men were doing that had little or nothing to do with gender.[3] But ultimately, the physicist's story and others like it made confronting the role of gender unavoidable. Thus, in this paper I will explore gender discourse, and its role in shaping nuclear and national security discourse. . . .

When I talk about "gender discourse," I am talking not only about words of language but about a system of meanings, of ways of thinking, images and words that first shape how we experience, understand, and represent ourselves as men and women, but that also do more than that; they shape many others aspects of our lives and culture. In this symbolic system, human characteristics are dichotomized, divided into pairs of polar opposites that are supposedly mutually exclusive: mind is opposed to body; culture to nature; thought to feeling; logic to intuition; objectivity to subjectivity; aggression to passivity; confrontation to accommodation; abstraction to particularity; public to private; political to personal, ad nauseam. In each case, the first term of the "opposites" is associated with male, the second with female. And in each case, our society values the first over the second. . . .

As gender discourse assigns gender to human characteristics, we can think of the discourse as something we are positioned *by*. If I say, for example, that a corporation should stop dumping toxic waste because it is damaging the creations of mother earth, (i.e., articulating a valuing and sentimental vision of nature), I am speaking in a manner associated with women, and our cultural discourse of gender positions me as female. As such I am then associated with the whole constellation of traits — irrational, emotional, subjective, and so forth — and I am in the devalued position. If, on the other hand, I say the corporation should stop dumping toxic wastes because I have calculated that it is causing $8.215 billion of damage to eight nonrenewable resources, which should be seen as equivalent to lowering the GDP by 0.15 percent per annum, (i.e., using a rational, calculative mode of thought), the discourse positions me as masculine — rational, objective, logical, and so forth — the dominant, valued position. . . .

Let us now return to the physicist who felt like a woman: what happened when he "blurted out" his sudden awareness of the "only thirty million" dead people? First, he was transgressing a code of professional conduct. In the civilian defense intellectuals' world, when you are in professional settings you do not discuss the bloody reality behind the calculations. It is not required that you be completely unaware of them in your outside life, or that you have no feelings about them, but it is required that you do not bring them to the foreground in the context of professional activities. There is a general awareness that you *could not* do your work if you did; in addition, most defense intellectuals believe that emotion and description of human reality distort the process required to think well about nuclear weapons and warfare.

So the physicist violated a behavioral norm, in and of itself a difficult thing to do because it threatens your relationships to and your standing with your colleagues.

But even worse than that, he demonstrated some of the characteristics on the "female" side of the dichotomies — in his "blurting" he was impulsive, uncontrolled, emotional, concrete, and attentive to human bodies, at the very least. Thus, he marked himself not only as unprofessional but as feminine, and this, in turn, was doubly threatening. It was not only a threat to his own sense of self as masculine, his gender identity, it also identified him with a devalued status — of a woman — or put him in the devalued or subordinate position in the discourse.

10 Thus, both the statement, "I felt like a woman," and his subsequent silence in that and other settings are completely understandable. To have the strength of character and courage to transgress the strictures of both professional and gender codes *and* to associate yourself with a lower status is very difficult. . . .

What is it that cannot be spoken? First, any words that express an emotional awareness of the desperate human reality behind the sanitized abstractions of death and destruction — as in the physicist's sudden vision of thirty million rotting corpses. Similarly, weapons' effects may be spoken of only in the most clinical and abstract terms, leaving no room to imagine a seven-year-old boy with his flesh melting away from his bones or a toddler with her skin hanging down in strips. Voicing concern about the number of casualties in the enemy's armed forces, imagining the suffering of the killed and wounded young men, is out of bounds. (Within the military itself, it is permissible, even desirable, to attempt to minimize immediate civilian casualties if it is possible to do so without compromising military objectives, but as we learned in the Persian Gulf War, this is only an extremely limited enterprise; the planning and precision of military targeting does not admit of consideration of the cost in human lives of such actions as destroying power systems, or water and sewer systems, or highways and food distribution systems.)[4] Psychological effects — on the soldiers fighting the war or on the citizens injured, or fearing for their own safety, or living through tremendous deprivation, or helplessly watching their babies die from diarrhea due to the lack of clean water — all of these are not to be talked about.

But it is not only particular subjects that are out of bounds. It is also tone of voice that counts. A speaking style that is identified as cool, dispassionate, and distanced is required. One that vibrates with the intensity of emotion almost always disqualifies the speaker, who is heard to sound like "a hysterical housewife."

What gets left out, then, is the emotional, the concrete, the particular, the human bodies and their vulnerability, human lives and their subjectivity—all of which are marked as feminine in the binary dichotomies of gender discourse. In other words, gender discourse informs and shapes nuclear and national security discourse, and in so doing creates silences and absences. It keeps things out of the room, unsaid, and keeps them ignored if they manage to get in. As such, it degrades our ability to think *well* and *fully* about nuclear weapons and national security, and shapes and limits the possible outcomes of our deliberations.

What becomes clear, then, is that defense intellectuals' standards of what constitutes "good thinking" about weapons and security have not simply evolved out of trial and error; it is not that the history of nuclear discourse has been filled with exploration of other ideas, concerns, interests, information, questions, feelings, meanings and stances which were then found to create distorted or poor thought. It is that these options have been *preempted* by gender discourse, and by the feelings evoked by living up to or transgressing gender codes.

To borrow a term from defense intellectuals, you might say that gender 15 discourse becomes a "preemptive deterrent" to certain kinds of thought.

Let me give you another example of what I mean—another story, this one my own experience.

One Saturday morning I, two other women, and about fifty-five men gathered to play a war game designed by the RAND Corporation.[5] Our "controllers" (the people running the game) first divided us up into three sets of teams; there would be three simultaneous games being played, each pitting a Red Team against a Blue Team (I leave the reader to figure out which color represents which country). All three women were put onto the same team, a Red Team.

The teams were then placed in different rooms so that we had no way of communicating with each other, except through our military actions (or lack of them) or by sending demands and responses to those demands via the controllers. There was no way to negotiate or to take actions other than military ones. (This was supposed to simulate reality.) The controllers then presented us with maps and pages covered with numbers representing each side's forces. We were also given a "scenario," a situation of escalating tensions and military conflicts, starting in the Middle East and spreading up Central Europe. We were to decide what to do, the controllers would go back and forth between the two teams to relate the other team's actions, and periodically the controllers themselves would add something that would rachet up the conflict—an announcement of an "intercepted intelligence report" from the other side, the authenticity of which we had no way of judging. . . .

Gradually our game escalated to nuclear war. The Blue Team used tactical nuclear weapons against our troops, but our Red Team decided, initially at least, against nuclear retaliation. When the game ended (at the end of the allotted time) our Red Team had "lost the war" (meaning that we had political control over less territory than we had started with, although our homeland had remained completely unviolated and our civilian population safe).

20   In the debriefing afterwards, all six teams returned to one room and reported on their games. Since we had had absolutely no way to know why the other team had taken any of its actions, we now had the opportunity to find out what they had been thinking. A member of the team that had played against us said, "Well, when he took his troops out of Afghanistan, I knew he was weak and I could push him around. And then, when we nuked him and he didn't nuke us back, I knew he was just such a wimp, I could take him for everything he's got and I nuked him again. He just wimped out."

There are many different possible comments to make at this point. I will restrict myself to a couple. First, when the man from the Blue Team called me a wimp (which is what it felt like for each of us on the Red Team — a personal accusation), I felt silenced. My reality, the careful reasoning that had gone into my strategic and tactical choices, the intelligence, the politics, the morality — all of it just disappeared, completely invalidated. I could not explain the reasons for my actions, could not protest. "Wait, you idiot, I didn't do it because I was weak, I did it because it made *sense* to do it that way, given my understandings of strategy and tactics, history and politics, my goals and my values." The protestation would be met with knowing sneers. In this discourse, the coding of an act as wimpish is hegemonic. Its emotional heat and resonance is like a bath of sulfuric acid: it erases everything else.

"Acting like a wimp" is an *interpretation* of a person's acts (or, in national security discourse, a country's acts, an important distinction I will return to later). As with any other interpretation, it is a selection of one among many possible different ways to understand something — once the selection is made, the other possibilities recede into invisibility. In national security discourse, "acting like a wimp," being insufficiently masculine, is one of the most readily available interpretive codes. (You do not need to do participant observation in a community of defense intellectuals to know this — just look at the "geopolitical analyses" in the media and on Capitol Hill of the way in which George Bush's military intervention in Panama and the Persian Gulf War finally allowed him to beat the "wimp factor.") You learn that someone is being a wimp if he perceives an international crisis as very dangerous and urges caution; if he thinks it might not be important to have just as many weapons that are just as big as the other guy's; if he suggests that an attack should not necessarily be answered by an even more destructive counterattack; or, until recently, if he suggested that making unilateral arms reductions might be useful for our own security.[6] All of these are "wimping out." . . .

"Wimp" is, of course, not the only gendered pejorative used in the national security community; "pussy" is another popular epithet, conjoining the imagery of harmless domesticated (read demasculinized) pets with contemptuous reference to women's genitals. In an informal setting, an analyst worrying about the other side's casualties, for example, might be asked, "What kind of pussy are you, anyway?" It need not happen more than once or twice before everyone gets the message; they quickly learn not to raise the issue in their discussions. Attention to and care for the living, suffering, and dying of human beings (in this case, soldiers and their families and friends) is again banished from the discourse through the expedient means of gender-bashing. . . .

Other words are also used to impugn someone's masculinity and, in the process, to delegitimate his position and avoid thinking seriously about it. "Those Krauts are a bunch of limp-dicked wimps" was the way one U.S. defense intellectual dismissed the West German politicians who were concerned about popular opposition to Euromissile deployments.[7] I have heard our NATO allies referred to as "the Euro-fags" when they disagreed with American policy on such issues as the Contra War or the bombing of Libya. Labeling them "fags" is an effective strategy; it immediately dismisses and trivializes their opposition to U.S. policy by coding it as due to inadequate masculinity. . . .

"Fag" imagery is not, of course, confined to the professional community of   25
security analysts; it also appears in popular "political" discourse. The Gulf War was replete with examples. American derision of Saddam Hussein included bumper stickers that read "Saddam, Bend Over." American soldiers reported that the "U.S.A." stenciled on their uniforms stood for "Up Saddam's Ass." A widely reprinted cartoon, surely one of the most multiply offensive that came out of the war, depicted Saddam bowing down in the Islamic posture of prayer, with a huge U.S. missile, approximately five times the size of the prostrate figure, about to penetrate his upraised bottom. Over and over, defeat for the Iraqis was portrayed as humiliating anal penetration by the more powerful and manly United States. . . .

In the face of this equation, genuine political discourse disappears. One more example: After Iraq invaded Kuwait and President Bush hastily sent U.S. forces to Saudi Arabia, there was a period in which the Bush administration struggled to find a convincing political justification for U.S. military involvement and the security affairs community debated the political merit of U.S. intervention.[8] Then Bush set the deadline, January 16, high noon at the OK Corral, and as the day approached conversations changed. More of these centered on the question compellingly articulated by one defense intellectual as "Does George Bush have the stones for war?"[9] This, too, is utterly extraordinary. This was a time when crucial political questions abounded: Can the sanctions work if given more time? Just what vital interests does the United States actually have at stake? What would be the goals of military intervention? Could they be accomplished by other means? Is the difference between what sanctions might accomplish and what military violence might accomplish worth the greater cost in human suffering, human lives, even dollars? What will the long-term effects on the people of the region be? On the ecology? Given the apparent successes of Gorbachev's last-minute diplomacy and Hussein's series of nearly daily small concessions, can and should Bush put off the deadline? Does he have the strength to let another leader play a major role in solving the problem? Does he have the political flexibility to not fight, or is he hell-bent on war at all costs? And so on, ad infinitum. All of these disappear in the sulfuric acid test of the size of Mr. Bush's private parts. . . . 10

Understanding national security discourse's gendered positions may cast some light on a frequently debated issue. Many people notice that the worlds of war making and national security have been created by and are still "manned" by men, and ask whether it might not make a big difference if more women played a role. Unfortunately, my first answer is "not much," at least if we are talking about relatively small numbers of women entering the world of defense experts and national security elites as it is presently constituted. Quite apart from whether you believe that women are (biologically or culturally) less aggressive than men, every person who enters this world is also participating in a gendered discourse in which she or he must adopt the masculine position in order to be successful. This means that it is extremely difficult for anyone, female *or male,* to express concerns or ideas marked as "feminine" and still maintain his or her legitimacy.

Another difficulty in realizing the potential benefits of recruiting more women in the profession: the assumption that they would make a difference is to some degree predicated on the idea that "the feminine" is absent from the discourse, and that adding it would lead to more balanced thinking. However, the problem is not that the "female" position is totally absent from the discourse: parts of it, at least, albeit in a degraded and undeveloped form, are already present, named, delegitimated, and silenced, all in one fell swoop. The inclusion and delegitimation of ideas marked as "feminine" acts as a more powerful censor than the total absence of "feminine" ideas would be.

So it is not simply the presence of women that would make a difference. Instead, it is the commitment and ability to develop, explore, rethink, and revalue those ways of thinking that get silenced and devalued that would make a difference. For that to happen, men, too, would have to be central participants. . . .

30   Finally, I would like to briefly explore a phenomenon I call the "unitary masculine actor problem" in national security discourse. During the Persian Gulf War, many feminists probably noticed that both the military briefers and George Bush himself frequently used the singular masculine pronoun "he" when referring to Iraq and Iraq's army. Someone not listening carefully could simply assume that "he" referred to Saddam Hussein. Sometimes it did; much of

the time it simply reflected the defense community's characteristic habit of calling opponents "he" or "the other guy."[11] A battalion commander, for example, was quoted as saying "Saddam knows where we are and we know where he is. We will move a lot now to keep him off guard."[12] In these sentences, "he" and "him" appear to refer to Saddam Hussein. But, of course, the American forces had *no idea* where Saddam Hussein himself was; the singular masculine pronouns are actually being used to refer to the Iraq military.

This linguistic move, frequently heard in discussions within the security affairs and defense communities, turns a complex state and set of forces into a singular male opponent. In fact, discussions that purport to be serious explorations of the strategy and tactics of war can have a tone which sounds more like the story of a sporting match, a fistfight, or a personal vendetta.

> I would want to suck him out into the desert as far as I could, and then pound him to death.[13]

> Once we had taken out his eyes, we did what could be best described as the "Hail Mary play" in football.[14]

> If the adversary decides to embark on a very high roll, because he's frightened that something even worse is in the works, does grabbing him by the scruff of the neck and slapping him up the side of the head, does that make him behave better or is it plausible that it makes him behave even worse?[15]

Most defense intellectuals would claim that using "he" is just a convenient shorthand, without significant import or effects. I believe, however, that the effects of this usage are many and the implications far-reaching. Here I will sketch just a few, starting first with the usage throughout defense discourse generally, and then coming back to the Gulf War in particular.

The use of "he" distorts the analyst's understanding of the opposing state and the conflict in which they are engaged. When the analyst refers to the opposing state as "he" or "the other guy," the image evoked is that of a person, a unitary actor; yet states are not people. Nor are they unitary and unified. They comprise complex, multifaceted governmental and military apparatuses, each with opposing forces within it, each, in turn, with its own internal institutional dynamics, its own varied needs in relation to domestic politics, and so on. In other words, if the state is referred to and pictured as a unitary actor, what becomes unavailable to the analyst and policy-maker is a series of much more complex truths that might enable him to imagine many more policy options, many more ways to interact with that state. . . .

That tension between personalization and abstraction was striking in Gulf War discourse. In the Gulf War, not only was "he" frequently used to refer to the

Iraqi military, but so was "Saddam," as in "Saddam really took a pounding today," or "Our goal remains the same: to liberate Kuwait by forcing Saddam Hussein out."16 The personalization is obvious: in this locution, the U.S. armed forces are not destroying a nation, killing people; instead, they (or George) are giving Saddam a good pounding, or bodily removing him from where he does not belong. Our emotional response is to get fired up about a bully getting his comeuppance.

35   Yet this personalization, this conflation of Iraq and Iraqi forces with Saddam himself, also abstracts: it functions to substitute in the mind's eye the abstraction of an implacably evil enemy for the particular human beings, the men, women, and children being pounded, burned, torn, and eviscerated. A cartoon image of Saddam being ejected from Kuwait preempts the image of the blackened, charred, decomposing bodies of nineteen-year-old boys tossed in ditches by the side of the road, and the other concrete images of the acts of violence that constitute "forcing Hussein [*sic*] out of Kuwait."17 Paradoxical as it may seem, in personalizing the Iraqi army as Saddam, the individual human beings in Iraq were abstracted out of existence.18

In summary, I have been exploring the way in which defense intellectuals talk to each other — the comments they make to each other, the particular usages that appear in their informal conversations or their lectures. In addition, I have occasionally left the professional community to draw upon public talk about the Gulf War. My analysis does *not* lead me to conclude that "national security thinking is masculine" — that is, a separate, and different, discussion. Instead, I have tried to show that national security discourse is gendered, and that it matters. Gender discourse is interwoven through national security discourse. It sets fixed boundaries, and in so doing, it skews what is discussed and how it is thought about. It shapes expectations of other nations' actions, and in so doing it affects both our interpretations of international events and conceptions of how the United States should respond. . . .

NOTES

1. A "counterforce attack" refers to an attack in which the targets are the opponent's weapons systems, command and control centers, and military leadership. It is in contrast to what is known as a "countervalue attack," which is the abstractly benign term for *targeting* and incinerating cities — what the United States did to Hiroshima, except that the bombs used today would be several hundred times more powerful. It is also known in the business, a bit more colorfully, as an "all-out city-busting exchange." Despite this careful targeting distinction, one need not be too astute to notice that many of the ports, airports, and command posts destroyed in a counter*force* attack are, in fact, in cities or metropolitan areas, which would be destroyed along with the "real targets," the weapons systems. But this does not appear to make the distinction any less meaningful to war planners, although it is, in all likelihood, less than meaningful to the victims.

2. The term is Helen Caldicott's, from her book *Missile Envy: The Arms Race and Nuclear War* (New York: William Morrow, 1984).

3. I have addressed some of these factors in: "Sex and Death in the Rational World of Defense Intellectuals," *Signs: Journal of Women in Culture and Society* 12, no. 4 (Summer 1987): 687–718; "Emasculating America's Linguistic Deterrent," in *Rocking the Ship of State: Towards a Feminist Peace Politics,* ed. Adrienne Harris and Ynestra King (Boulder, Colo.: Westview Press, 1989); and *Deconstructing National Security Discourse and Reconstructing Security* (working title, book manuscript).

4. While both the military and the news media presented the picture of a "surgically clean" war in which only military targets were destroyed, the reality was significantly bloodier; it involved the mass slaughter of Iraqi soldiers, as well as the death and suffering of large numbers of noncombatant men, women, and children. Although it is not possible to know the numbers of casualties with certainty, one analyst in the Census Bureau, Beth Osborne Daponte, has estimated that 40,000 Iraqi soldiers and 13,000 civilians were killed in direct military conflict, that 30,000 civilians died during Shiite and Kurdish rebellions, and that 70,000 civilians have died from health problems caused by the destruction of water and power plants (Edmund L. Andrews, "Census Bureau to Dismiss Analyst Who Estimated Iraqi Casualties," *New York Times,* March 7, 1992, A7). Other estimates are significantly higher. Greenpeace estimates that as many as 243,000 Iraqi civilians died due to war-related causes (Ray Wilkinson, "Back from the Living Dead," *Newsweek,* January 20, 1992, 28). Another estimate places Iraqi troop casualties at 70,000 and estimates that over 100,000 children have died from the delayed effects of the war (Peter Rothenberg, "The Invisible Dead," *Lies of Our Times* [March 1992]: 7). For recent, detailed reports on civilian casualties, see *Health and Welfare in Iraq after the Gulf Crisis* (International Study Team/Commission on Civilian Casualties, Human Rights Program, Harvard Law School, October 1991), and *Needless Deaths in the Gulf War* (Middle East Watch, 1992). For a useful corrective to the myth of the Gulf War as a war of surgical strikes and precision-guided weaponry, see Paul F. Walker and Eric Stambler, "The Surgical Myth of the Gulf War," *Boston Globe,* April 16, 1991; and ". . . And the Dirty Little Weapons," *Bulletin of the Atomic Scientists* (May 1991): 21–24.

5. The RAND Corporation is a think tank that is a U.S. Air Force subcontractor. In the 1950s many of the most important nuclear strategists did their work under RAND auspices, including Bernard Brodie, Albert Wohlstetter, Herman Kahn, and Thomas Schelling.

6. In the context of the nuclear arms race and the cold war, even though a defense analyst might acknowledge that some American weapon systems served no useful strategic function (such as the Titan missiles during the 1980s), there was still consensus that they should not be unilaterally cut. Such a cut was seen to be bad because it was throwing away a potential bargaining chip in future arms control negotiations, or because making unilateral cuts was viewed as a sign of weakness and lack of resolve. It is only outside that context of hostile superpower competition, and, in fact, after the dissolution of the Soviet threat, that President Bush has responded to Gorbachev's unilateral cuts with some (minor) American unilateral cuts. For a description and critical assessment of the arguments against unilateral cuts, see William Rose, *US Unilateral Arms Control Initiatives: When Do They Work?* (New York: Greenwood Press, 1988). For an analysis of the logic and utility of bargaining chips, see Robert J. Bresler and Robert C. Gray, "The Bargaining Chip and SALT," *Political Science Quarterly* 92, no. 1 (Spring 1977): 65–88.

7. Cohn, unattributed interview, Cambridge, Mass., July 15, 1991.

8. The Bush White House tried out a succession of revolving justifications in an attempt to find one that would garner popular support for U.S. military action, including: we must respond to the rape of Kuwait; we must not let Iraqi aggression be rewarded, we must defend Saudi Arabia; we cannot stand by while "vital U.S. interests" are threatened; we must establish a "new world order"; we must keep down the price of oil at U.S. gas pumps; we must protect American jobs; and finally, the winner, the only one that elicited any real support from the American public, we must destroy Iraq's incipient nuclear weapons capability. What was perhaps most surprising about this was the extent to which it was publicly discussed and accepted as George Bush's need to find a message that "worked" rather than to actually have a genuine, meaningful explanation. For an account of Bush's decision making about the Gulf War, see Bob Woodward, *The Commanders* (New York: Simon and Schuster, 1991).

9. Cohn, unattributed interview, Cambridge, Mass., July 20, 1991.

10. Within the context of our society's dominant gender discourse, this equation of masculinity and strength with the willingness to use armed force seems quite "natural" and not particularly noteworthy. Hannah Arendt is one political thinker who makes the arbitrariness of the connection visible: she reframes our thinking about "strength," and finds strength in *refraining* from using one's armed forces (Hannah Arendt, *On Violence* [New York: Harcourt, Brace, Jovanovich, 1969]).

11. For a revealing exploration of the convention in strategic, military, and political writings of redescribing armies as a single "embodied combatant," see Elaine Scarry, *The Body in Pain: The Making and Unmaking of the World* (New York: Oxford University Press, 1984): 70–72.

12. Chris Hedges, "War Is Vivid in the Gun Sights of the Sniper," *New York Times*, February 3, 1991, A1.

13. General Norman Schwarzkopf, National Public Radio broadcast, February 8, 1991.

14. General Norman Schwarzkopf, CENTCOM News Briefing, Riyadh, Saudi Arabia, February 27, 1991, p. 2.

15. Transcript of a strategic studies specialist's lecture on NATO and the Warsaw Pact (summer institute on Regional Conflict and Global Security: The Nuclear Dimension, Madison, Wisconsin, June 29, 1987).

16. Defense Secretary Dick Cheney, "Excerpts from Briefing at Pentagon by Cheney and Powell," *New York Times*, January 24, 1991, A 11.

17. Scarry explains that when an army is described as a single "embodied combatant," injury, (as in Saddam's "pounding"), may be referred to but is "no longer recognizable or interpretable." It is not only that Americans might be happy to imagine Saddam being pounded; we also on some level know that it is not really happening, and thus need not feel the pain of the wounded. We "respond to the injury . . . as an imaginary wound in an imaginary body, despite the fact that that imaginary body is itself made up of thousands of real human bodies" (Scarry, *Body in Pain*, p. 72).

18. For a further exploration of the disappearance of human bodies from Gulf War discourse, see Hugh Gusterson, "Nuclear War, the Gulf War, and the Disappearing Body" (unpublished paper, 1991). I have addressed other aspects of Gulf War discourse in "The Language of the Gulf War," *Center Review* 5, no. 2 (Fall 1991); "Decoding Mili-

tary Newspeak," *Ms.,* March/April 1991, p. 81; and "Language, Gender, and the Gulf War" (unpublished paper prepared for Harvard University Center for Literary and Cultural Studies, April 10, 1991).

TALKING ABOUT IT

Seeing Metaphor: Revealing and Concealing

1. Cohn writes that military strategists and defense intellectuals couch their discussions in terms of "male" discourse. What does she mean? What does she believe gets left out of their thinking because of this way of viewing war?

2. Beginning in paragraph 30, Cohn discusses the use of "he" and "the other guy" to refer to enemy countries and troops. According to her, what does this "convenient shorthand" serve to conceal about the opposing state and the nature of the conflict? Do you think her concerns are justified?

Seeing Composition: Frame, Line, Texture, Tone

1. How does the anecdote Cohn opens with serve to establish the point of her essay? Why does she return to it in paragraphs 7–10?

2. Cohn includes eighteen endnotes, many of which are content-oriented. What is the purpose of these? Why do you suppose she didn't include some of this information in the text proper? Do you think she should have?

Seeing Meaning: Navigating and Negotiating

1. Do you agree with Cohn's point in paragraph 5 that, of the list of terms she cites, "the first term of the 'opposites' is associated with male, the second with female. And in each case, our society values the first over the second"? If so, why do you think this is the case? If not, why do you disagree with Cohn?

2. What do you think of Cohn's argument that because of the gendered discourse she describes, "genuine political discourse disappears" in any discussion of military action (paragraph 26)? What, finally, is Cohn urging, and what do you think is the likelihood that any kind of change will take place?

WRITING ABOUT IT

1. Bring to class a political cartoon, a newsmagazine article, and a newspaper article that all concern the same issue: a particular event, policy, or political or military conflict. Drawing on Carol Cohn's analysis of gendered discourse, write to explain how each example includes ideas about maleness

or femaleness to convey information: what images — visual or verbal — does the author use to suggest attitudes, assumptions, or stereotypes that are associated with male or female thinking and behavior?

2. Write an illustration from your own experience that could be concluded, "It was awful. I felt like a woman." Tell what happened, how you felt at the time, and what you said. Try to say how the experience made you feel about being a man or a woman.

   Then re-imagine the experience so that it could be concluded, "It was wonderful. I felt like a woman." What did you have to imagine changing in order for the conclusion to change from negative to positive feelings about gender?

When Words Go to War

BELLA ENGLISH

Bella English is a columnist for the Boston Globe. *This article appeared in her column on February 27, 1991, the day the Persian Gulf War ended.*

The Persian Gulf War has added several words to our lexicon. People who heretofore thought a "sortie" was a party now know it's a combat mission. Those of us who never heard of Riyadh before now speak of it with great familiarity, as if it were Washington. And who will ever forget what a Scud is?

Pentagonese has also reared its ugly head. That's English as a Second Language, popularized by Alexander Haig, who became known for such gems as: "longstanding in time," "We must use careful caution" and "I'll have to caveat my response, senator."[1]

The daily military briefings out of Riyadh are marvels of militarisms, euphemisms and acronyms. "Today, our troops executed BDAs in the KTO." Translation: Allied forces did bomb damage assessments in the Kuwaiti Theater of Operations, or, in simple English, surveyed how badly we bombed 'em.

Of course, it goes against the military grain to speak in simple English. I mean, why use one word when 10 will do? And heaven forbid you should call something by its real name. In this most sanitized of wars, we mustn't admit that blood — American and Arab — is being spilled.

That's why body bags have become "human remains pouches." Refriger- 5 ated trucks, sort of mobile morgues, are stationed at "collection points." The bombing of civilian areas such as schools, hospitals and homes, has become "collateral damage." You're never "killed in action," but you're KIA, as if that's kinder and gentler. Although allied soldiers who have been captured are still POWs, captured Iraqis have become EPWs, or Enemy Prisoners of War. And when military commanders speak of NBCs, they're not talking about the network; they're talking about nuclear, biological and chemical weapons.

We "engage" the enemy instead of creaming him. There is a "weapons delivery" instead of a blanket bombing. Tanks are "neutralized" instead of being blown to kingdom come. The aim of the war is "assertive disarmament." To achieve that goal, the allied forces have used "discriminate deterrence," or precision bombing.

---

1. Alexander Haig was the one-time commander of NATO forces in Europe and for a short time later secretary of state under President Ronald Reagan. (Ed.)

Thanks to the war, the world now knows that a "berm" is a sand wall, and that a "new world order" is around the corner. (Winston Churchill George Bush ain't.) We revel in the success of American weapons such as the Patriot and Cruise missiles and scoff at the decidedly inferior Scud. It doesn't take a five-star general to figure out why our weapons are so prettily named, while their weapons have such homely monikers, such as the Soviet-built Scud (rhymes with dud) and the Chinese-built Silkworm, named after one of the lowest forms of life. We gave them these nicknames.

And who will ever forget the dreadful noun-turned-verb: attrited? As in, "There are a number of combat forces on the ground being attrited by our troops." Or killed.

While the American side—full of spokesmen and speechwriters—has hidden behind bleached and starched words, Saddam Hussein has employed the opposite tactic to win the hearts and souls of his countrymen. "Apocalypse Now" could be the name of his verbal strategy. Or, as a friend of mine calls it, "Baghdad's Best B.S."

10   "We have prepared ourselves for burning the bodies of the corrupt and evil invaders, and our revenge will be devastating and ruthless," Saddam said in a recent commentary. "We will not hesitate and we will seek to turn the ground war . . . into a hellfire that will sear their scoundrels. Their cohorts will tumble into the great crater of death."

"Treachery" is big with Saddam Hussein. "The treacherous committed treachery. The despicable Bush and his treasonous agent Fahd, and all those who supported them in committing crimes, shame and aggression, committed the treachery. Those cowards who have perfected the acts of treachery, treason and vileness, committed treachery after they departed from every path of virtue, goodness and humanity. They have committed treachery and launched their ground offensive."

Someone get this man a thesaurus, please.

Saddam promised to make allied troops "swim in their own blood" and pledged to fight "the mother of battles" just before the ground war began, which prompted Tom Brokaw to label him "the father of all con men."

Although both sides are claiming God as their chief aide de camp, Saddam is responsible for the oxymoron "holy war." (But we must take credit for the equally absurd "friendly fire.")

15   As Saddam recently stated: "In the name of god, the merciful, the compassionate, our armed forces have performed their holy war duty of refusing to comply with the logic of evil, imposition and aggression. They have been engaged in an epic, valiant battle that will be recorded by history in letters of light."

If all else fails, Saddam, there's a job for you in America. Writing for the *National Enquirer*.

TALKING ABOUT IT

Seeing Metaphor: Revealing and Concealing

1. In paragraphs 5–6 English cites several examples of military euphemisms related to combat. What do these euphemisms serve to conceal about the reality of war? What does it take to see through them? Do you think their use is justified?

2. In paragraph 7, English looks at the naming of weaponry and missiles. What imagery is such naming intended to create? Do you think it works?

Seeing Composition: Frame, Line, Texture, Tone

1. This essay originally appeared as a newspaper column in the *Boston Globe*. What are some of the stylistic characteristics that mark it as an op-ed piece?

2. What do you make of English's tone? Do you think she may be treating a serious subject too frivolously? Or do you think she succeeds in making a serious point?

Seeing Meaning: Navigating and Negotiating

1. Why is the term "holy war" an oxymoron? In what ways do oxymorons such as "holy war" and "friendly fire" blur our vision of reality?

2. English writes that "the American side . . . has hidden behind bleached and starched words," while "Saddam Hussein has employed the opposite tactic to win the hearts and souls of his countrymen" (paragraph 9). Look at the speeches by George Bush and Saddam Hussein earlier in this chapter. Do you agree with English's assessment? Point to specific examples within each speech to support your response.

WRITING ABOUT IT

1. In class, make a list of military jargon that has entered public discourse — military language that can be heard at work, at school, in casual conversation. Choose several of these phrases or terms and write about their original meanings, how they are used in contexts outside the military, and what they reveal about the speaker's attitudes, beliefs, or values. What are the consequences, if any, of talking about a topic in terms of war?

2. In military language, write a short essay describing an ordinary activity — housecleaning, repairing your car or some household machine, exercising, preparing for a test, and so forth. Draw examples of military language from

English's essay or others in this chapter, and make a list in class so that you have many phrases and terms to use.

Exchange essays with members of your group. What makes each piece comic?

3. Bella English explains that military jargon is an effort to avoid speaking directly about the horrific realities of war. In class you might form two groups: one that would argue in defense of disguising the truth for the sake of public as well as military morale and security; and one that would argue against sanitized language because it conceals the realities of suffering and death, and because it wins public support for war. The arguments on each side could be written collaboratively in small groups of three or four. Afterwards, you might reorganize groups so that two peers on each side of the argument form one group. Each new group would then write a synthesis of the two views, showing the strengths and weaknesses of each position.

Three Cases of War Worship

BARBARA EHRENREICH

Barbara Ehrenreich, a contributing editor to Ms. *and* Mother Jones, *has written (with Deirdre English) three books about women and health issues:* Witches, Midwives, and Nurses: A History of Women Healers *(1972),* Complaints and Disorders: The Sexual Politics of Sickness *(1973), and* For Her Own Good: One Hundred Fifty Years of the Experts' Advice to Women *(1978). "Three Cases of War Worship" is a chapter from her most recent book,* Blood Rites: Origins and History of the Passions of War *(1997).*

The idealization of war by peoples become primitive again is no sign of moral decadence, but on the contrary the sign of a new hero-worship and sacrificial spirit.
—Count Keyserling

Lofty feelings directed toward an intangible, superhuman being: Most people of our own time would recognize these as the ingredients of a religion. The analogy between nationalism—and I mean, of course, "secular" nationalism—and religion has been drawn many times. Benedict Anderson admits nationalism's "strong affinity with religious imaginings." Toynbee went further, seeing nationalism as a replacement for Christianity, which had been vitiated by a soulless capitalist economy. But for the most part the relationship between nationalism and religion has been left as a sort of decorative analogy. Few, if any, have pressed the issue or found it useful to pursue the notion of nationalism *as* a religion, complete with its own deities, mythology, and rites.

One reason we hesitate to classify nationalism as a kind of religion is that nationalism is a thoroughly "modern" phenomenon. It emerges in Europe in the nineteenth century and is spread throughout the third world—largely in reaction to European imperialism—in the twentieth century. Our own modernist bias convinces us that things which are recent must also be "modern," in the sense of being rational and "progressive." On one side of that great historical divide identified as the Enlightenment lie superstition, oppression, and fanatically intolerant religions. It is on the other side, along with science and a faith in progress, where we locate nationalism. To acknowledge that nationalism is itself a kind of religion would be to concede that all that is "modern" is not necessarily "progressive" or "rational": that history can sometimes take us "backward," toward what we have come to see as the archaic and primitive.

It is in times of war and the threat of war that nationalism takes on its most overtly religious hues. During the temporary enthusiasms of war, such as those inspired by the outbreak of World War I, individuals see themselves as

541

participants in, or candidates for, a divine form of "sacrifice." At the same time, whatever distinctions may have existed between church and state—or, more precise, between church-based religions and the religion of nationalism—tend to dissolve. During World War I, for example, secular authorities in the United States devised propaganda posters in which "Jesus was dressed in khaki and portrayed sighting down a gun barrel." For their part, religious authorities can usually be counted on to help sacralize the war effort with their endorsements. During the feverish enthusiasm of World War I, the Bishop of London called on Englishmen to

> kill Germans—to kill . . . the good as well as the bad, to kill the young men as well as the old. . . . As I have said a thousand times, I look upon it as a war for purity, I look upon everyone who dies in it as a martyr.

But if nationalism is to be more than a temporary passion whipped up by war, it has to find ways to sustain and institutionalize itself apart from more conventional religions. It must, in other words, assume some of the trappings of a conventional, church-based religion itself. Uplifting myths are required, special holidays, and rituals that can be enacted by people who may not feel, at the moment of enacting, any great passion at all. Such rituals and myths keep nationalism alive during times of deprivation and defeat—even during interludes of peace—just as, say, Christian ritual preserves the faith in people who may only occasionally, or once in a lifetime, experience genuine spiritual transport.

5   It was World War II that saw the full flowering of institutionalized "religious" nationalisms, designed to maintain the fervor of whole populations for months and years at a time. In many ways, the Second World War was a continuation of the first, growing out of grievances implanted by the first war and featuring some of the same alliances and forms of war-making. The tank, the submarine, and the airplane, for example—which did so much to distinguish World War II from the wars of previous centuries—were all first deployed in World War I. So the two wars may be seen as a continuum analogous to the Thirty Years War—a "double war" that could not find a way to stop.

But World War II was distinct in ways that required the *sustained* emotional mobilization of the participant populations. First there was the sheer size of the armies involved. The armed forces of the United States, which had numbered about 5 million in World War I, reached over 16 million at the height of World War II, and other belligerents put similar proportions of their populations into uniform. More important, though, was the fact that this was a "total" war. In World War I, there had still been some inhibitions against the targeting of civilians, who ended up accounting for 15 percent of the fatalities. By World War II, the destruction (and exploitation) of civilians was deliberate policy on all sides. The British used air power to "de-house" the German population; the U.S. bombed the civilian populations of Hiroshima, Nagasaki, and Dresden; the Germans and Japanese destroyed cities and exploited defeated populations as slave labor. As a result, in World War II the civilian share of fatalities, including Holocaust victims, shot up to 65 percent of the total.

Air power made the mass bombings of civilians possible, but it was the huge involvement of civilians in the industrial side of war that made it seem strategically necessary. In the culmination of a trend under way since the beginning of gun-based warfare, millions of civilians were now enlisted in the business of manufacturing weapons and otherwise supplying the increasingly massive armies. In this situation, there were no "innocent" civilians, except possibly children, and the war took on a genocidal character unknown to the more gentlemanly conflict of 1914–18. Nowhere was this clearer than in the U.S. confrontation with the racially different Japanese. William Halsey, the commander of the United States' naval forces in the South Pacific, favored such slogans as "Kill Japs, kill Japs, kill more Japs" and vowed, after the Japanese attack on Pearl Harbor, that by the end of the war Japanese would be spoken only in hell.

In its relentless appetite for "manpower," World War II even challenged the traditional male exclusivity of war. Women not only filled in for missing males in munitions factories and other vital industries; they were invited into the U.S. and British armed forces as clerical and administrative workers, issued uniforms, and allowed to participate in the pageantry, as well as the risks, of war. Soviet women, or at least some of them, briefly achieved full warrior status, "flying combat missions, acting as snipers, and participating in human-wave assaults." In a war in which a civilian faced nearly the same chance of dying as a soldier, there was no "protected" status for females anyway. War was everywhere, and everyone was a part of it.

The distinctively religious nationalisms that emerged around the time of World War II drew heavily on familiar religious traditions but inevitably rendered them more "primitive" and parochial. Recall Karl Jasper's classification of religions as "pre-" and "post-axial," with the "axis" being that ancient equivalent of the Enlightenment, the heyday of classical Greece. The pre-axial religions were ritualistic, postulating deities with limited jurisdictions and loyalties, while the post-axial religions were, at least in theory, universalistic and addressed to all people alike. Thus all the participants in the bloodbath of World War II were adherents of, or at least familiar with, creeds that held out some notion of the "brotherhood of man": Christianity in the case of the Americans and Europeans, Buddhism in the case of the Japanese, and, if it can be counted as a kind of "religion," the atheistic ideology of international socialism in the case of the Soviets.

But nationalism is nothing if not tribalistic and cannot, by its very nature, 10 make the slightest claim to universalism: No one expects Poles to offer their lives for Peru, or goes proselytizing among Canadians to win their allegiance to the flag of Nigeria. In the religion of nationalism, the foreigner is always a kind of "heathen" and, except in unusual circumstances, unsusceptible to conversion. To the extent that nationalism replaced the universalistic (post-axial) religions, as

Toynbee saw it doing, human beings were abandoning the bold dream of a universal humanity and reverting to their tribalistic roots.

Nowhere was this clearer than in the Soviet Union, where the war prompted Stalin to abandon the universalistic ideology of communism for a narrow and quasi-religious nationalism. Nationalism, he observed, was "the key to maintaining civilian morale," and he exhorted his people to follow the example of "our great ancestors," a category in which he now listed not only Lenin but such counterrevolutionary figures as tsarist generals, feudal landlords, and even a saint of the Russian Orthodox church. At the same time, the Soviet government displayed a sudden friendliness toward the traditional Russian Orthodox religion, halting anti-religious propaganda and permitting the church to reestablish a Holy Synod. In 1944 the glaringly anachronistic "Internationale" was replaced with a new, more suitably parochial anthem.

Here we will look briefly at three examples of the kinds of religious nationalism that were associated with, or grew out of, World War II: Nazism in Germany, State Shinto in Japan, and the ritualized "patriotism" that emerged in the postwar United States. Each of these served its adherents as a "religion" by offering an entire worldview, justifying individual sacrifice and loss and mobilizing the uplifting passions of group solidarity. And as religions, each has reached back — past Christianity or, in the Japanese case, Buddhism — to more ancient, "pre-axial" kinds of religion: pre-Christian European religion in the case of Nazism, Shinto itself in Japan, and Old Testament Judaism in the case of American nationalism.

NAZISM

Nazism may be the closest thing there has been to a freestanding religion of nationalism, unbeholden and even hostile to church-based religions. Historian Arno Mayer observes that

> nazism had all the earmarks of a religion. Its faith and canon were institutionalized in and through a political movement which bore some resemblance to a hierarchical church. The self-appointed head of this church, the führer, exercised strict control over a ranked political clergy, as well as over a select order of disciples, with all the initiates wearing uniforms with distinct emblems and insignias. During both the rise of nazism and the life of the Nazi regime, this clergy acted as both the celebrants and the congregations for a wide range of cultic ceremonies, some of which took place in sacred shrines and places. Most of these ceremonies were conspicuously public and massive, their purpose being to exalt, bind, and expand the community of faithful.

Hitler would have agreed with Mayer. "We are not a movement," he told his followers, "rather we are a religion." The purpose of his Ministry of Propaganda and Enlightenment was to communicate not information, he remarked, "but holy conviction and unconditional faith." Nazism had its own prophet, the Führer; its own rituals of mass rallies and parades; even its own "holy days." According to historian Robert G. L. Waite:

> The Nazi holidays included 30 January, the day [Hitler] came to power in the year he referred to as "the holy year of our Lord 1933," and 20 April, his own birthday and the day when Hitler youth were confirmed in their faith. The holiest day . . . was 9 November, celebrated as the Blood Witness [*Blutzeuge*] of the movement.

Ordinary citizens found many ways to participate in the new religion. They displayed *Mein Kampf* in their homes in the place of honor once reserved for the Bible; they even addressed prayers to the Führer. The League of German Girls, for example, developed its own version of the Lord's Prayer: "Adolf Hitler, you are our great Leader. Thy name makes the enemy tremble. Thy Third Reich comes, thy will alone is law upon earth," and so on. Ceremonies of Nazi oath-taking consciously paralleled religious rites of confirmation, as this account from a Nazi newspaper makes clear:

> Yesterday witnessed the profession of the religion of the blood in all its imposing reality . . . whoever has sworn his oath of allegiance to Hitler has pledged himself unto death to this sublime idea.

Raised as a Catholic himself, Hitler drew heavily on Christian imagery for   15 his religious fantasies. He often compared himself to Jesus or, in a more Jewish formulation, to the promised Messiah; he thought of the SS as his own version of the Society of Jesus. But he and his followers had no use for Christianity's claims to universalism, nor of course for its appeal to mercy, and took measures to restrict the role of the German churches. A more congenial religious foundation for Nazism could be found in the pre-Christian Germanic beliefs that nationalist intellectuals had dug up and imaginatively reconstructed during the nineteenth and early twentieth centuries. According to Guido von List, a leading popularizer of such *volkisch* ideology, Christianity, with its gospel of love, had been a disaster for the ancient German people, leading to "the debilitation of Teutonic vigour and morale." Nazism represented a return to the unsullied warrior culture associated with the ancient, tribal Germans. Its swastika was lifted from the mythological Aryan repertory of images, and its state was meant to recall the pagan male warrior band, or *Männerbund*.

Hitler himself was a fanatical devotee of war and nationalism-as-the-religion-of-war. As Keegan argues, much of his outlook and ambition was shaped in the trenches of the western front, where he served as an infantryman from 1914 through 1917 in a regiment which, like so many others, lost more than 100 percent of its initial troop strength. Again and again, young Hitler survived artillery bombardments that left his comrades piled up dead around him, only to see their replacements similarly dispatched. No doubt he owed some of his messianic sense of himself to these narrow escapes, and it may be also that the relentless, industrialized slaughter of trench warfare served as psychological preparation for the annihilation of the Jews and other undesirables at home.

There is no question, though, that the war was for Hitler an experience of religious intensity. He wrote in *Mein Kampf* of being "overcome with rapturous enthusiasm" at the outbreak of the war. On the train ride to the front, when the troops spontaneously burst into "Die Wacht am Rhein," Hitler recalled, "I felt as though I would burst. He was a brave and dedicated soldier, though prone to annoy his comrades by lecturing them on politics or the evils of smoking and drinking. Thoroughly puritanical in his devotion to war, he later described the trenches as a "monastery with walls of flame."

Thus the Nazis did not rely on the traditional Christian rationale — vengeance for the killing of Christ — for their genocidal treatment of the Jews. In the Nazi theology, a major crime of the Jews was to have betrayed their country in *war*. Never mind that German Jews had served loyally in the First World War; never mind that they were, by the thirties, more thoroughly assimilated into gentile society than they had ever been. To Hitler they were a hateful, even mocking, reminder of defeat. In the Nazi imagination, Jews were prominent among those responsible for the famous "stab in the back" that supposedly prevented German victory in the First World War. For the Germans to regain their archaic purity as warriors, all traces of this "foreign" evil had to be expunged. Only then could the nation rise up, as a single organism, from the humiliation of defeat to the status of global predator.

There is a tantalizing detail in Waite's study of Hitler: his fascination and identification with wolves. As a boy he had been pleased to find that his given name was derived from the Old German "Athalwolf," meaning "noble wolf." He named his favorite dog Wolf, called the SS his "pack of wolves," and believed that crowds responded so rapturously to him because they realized "that now *a wolf has been born.*" Mimi Reiter, a teenaged Austrian girl who was briefly involved with Hitler in 1926, recalled a curious outburst in a cemetery, where they had gone, at Hitler's request, to visit Mimi's mother's grave:

> As he stared down at her mother's grave he muttered, "I am not like that yet! [*Ich bin noch nicht so weit!*]" He then gripped his riding whip tightly in his hands and said, "I would like you to call me Wolf."

This incident, assuming it was correctly remembered, bespeaks a worldview divided into the most archaic categories of all: not Aryan vs. non-Aryan or gentile vs.

Jew, but predator vs. prey. Hitler had seen too much "like that," too many comrades reduced to meat. To be dead is to be vanquished is to be prey. But in Hitler's worldview there is no middle ground, no mode of existence apart from this bloody dichotomy. Those who do not wish to be prey must become predators. Conversely, those who are not predators are prey. To have survived (the First World War, in Hitler's case) is to have achieved the status of the wolf. The ancient European warrior sought to transform himself into a wild carnivore; so too Hitler transcended the failed art student he had been as a youth, survived the war, and became what was, in his own mind, the only thing he could be: a predator beast.

STATE SHINTO

By the time of the Second World War, Japan already boasted a fifty-year   20
tradition of secular nationalism, promulgated relentlessly through every institution of Japanese life. Public education, which reached 90 percent of Japanese children by 1900, included military training for boys and the systematic inculcation of militarism and emperor worship for both sexes. Arithmetic classes did calculations based on battlefield situations; science-class topics included "general information about searchlights, wireless communication, land mines, and torpedoes." A reading text offered the story of an insufficiently enthusiastic sailor, whose mother admonishes him:

> You wrote that you did not participate in the battle of Toshima Island. You were in the August 10 attack on Weihaiwei but you didn't distinguish yourself with an individual exploit. To me this is deplorable. Why have you gone to war? Your life is to be offered up to requite your obligations to our benevolent Emperor.

Among the institutions enlisted to the aims of Japanese imperialism was Shinto, the traditional religion. One of the world's oldest surviving religions, Shinto features thousands of deities, or *kami*, which are worshipped in private homes and at thousands of shrines around the country. Until the Meiji period, in the late nineteenth century, Shinto seems to have been largely apolitical and not even, by the overheated standards of the West, very "religious." It coexisted peaceably with Buddhism, concerning itself with the maintenance of the shrines, the observance of festivals, and the performance of domestic rituals and weddings. It is no wonder that so many of the samurai had preferred Buddhism, with its austere metaphysic and magnificent indifference to death.

But the samurai were a tiny elite, and their Zen Buddhism never attracted a numerically significant following. With the militarization of Japanese society that began near the turn of the twentieth century, it was the ancient "folk religion," Shinto, that was conscripted to the nationalist cause. Japan's victories in the First Sino-Japanese War (1894–95) and the Russo-Japanese War (1904–05), followed by the annexation of Korea, transformed the once reclusive island nation into one of Asia's leading military powers. Shinto priests were now expected to inculcate patriotism along with more ancient forms of piety and to preside over nationalistic rituals, such as the veneration of the emperor's portrait. In return, the Shinto priesthood was given public money for the training of priests and the maintenance of shrines, as well as state support in its growing rivalry with Buddhism. By the eve of World War II, Shinto had become, for all practical purposes, the state religion.

The aim of State Shinto was what historian Helen Hardacre calls a "nationwide orchestration of ritual": the entrainment of the entire population through simultaneous ritual observances. Children began the school year with patriotic celebrations in which the emperor's official statement on education served as "a sacred object" of worship. Passengers on streetcars were "required to stand and bow reverently" when passing the Imperial Palace or important Shinto shrines. Older Shinto rituals were also recruited to the nationalist cause; many of these, according to Ruth Benedict, were benign enough and certainly ancient:

> On the frequent days of rites official representatives of the community came and stood before the priest while he purified them with hemp and paper streamers. He opened the door to the inner shrine and called down the gods, often with a high-pitched cry, to come to partake of a ceremonial meal. The priest prayed and each participant in order of rank presented . . . a twig of their sacred tree with pendant strips of white paper.

What was new about State Shinto was the *synchronization* and centralization of ritual, so that the same ceremonies were now observed by everyone at the same time, from the emperor at a central shrine to peasants at their *yohaisho,* or "place to worship from afar." No one, Christian or Buddhist, was exempted from what Hardacre calls this "daring attempt at social engineering."

To escape charges of religious totalitarianism, state authorities took the position that Shinto was not a "religion" at all but something both more secular and more deeply rooted in Japanese life: the "national spirit" itself. At the metaphysical core of the new nonreligion, and overlapping more traditional Shinto concerns, was the notion of *kokutai,* meaning, literally, nation-body. *Kokutai* parallels the European intellectuals' notion of the nation-as-organism; it was the mystical living entity which arose from the fusion of individual citizens into a single and devoted mass. Symbolized by the emperor and the Shinto shrines, *kokutai* demanded absolute fealty from the citizenry, including a willingness to give their lives. As with European nationalist ideology, dying was no tragedy if one's death strengthened the nation-body, or nation-as-organism. A document published by the Japanese Ministry of Education in 1937 makes an argument that could have been lifted from Hegel:

Offering our lives for the sake of the emperor does not mean so-called self-sacrifice, but the casting aside of our little selves to live under the august grace and the enhancing of the genuine life of the people of a State.

For all its continuities with the past, State Shinto by no means reflected 25 some preexisting Asian willingness to submerge the individual in the collective whole. "*Kokutai*" may have been an ancient word, but the "Kokutai Cult" arose only in the 1930s. The whole notion of the nation as a mystical "body" or organism centered in the actual body of an individual leader was a phenomenon of the modern era—the era of mass armies. In the era of a mounted warrior elite, Japan had nurtured an elite ethic of war: the samurai code, or *bushido*, analogous to the European knights' Christianized "chivalry." But in the era of gun-based mass armies, *bushido* had to be democratized to include the masses, who were now free, as once only their superiors had been, to experience a "glorious" death in war. Just as European nationalism represented a democratization of an older, elite warrior ethos, State Shinto was *bushido* for the masses.

Like European nationalisms, State Shinto saw war as a sacred undertaking. The popular writer Tokutomi Iichiro described the Second World War in the ritual language of Shinto purification ceremonies: "For the Japanese," he wrote, "the Greater East Asia War is a purifying exorcism, a cleansing ablution." Other influential intellectuals—professors of history and philosophy at Kyoto Imperial University—added that war "is eternal" and should be recognized as being "creative and constructive."

Japanese religious nationalism outdid its European counterpart in one respect: the glorification of the war dead. Europeans honored their fallen soldiers with monuments and holidays; the Japanese worshipped them, and still worship them, as gods. Almost 2.5 million are so honored at the Yasukuni Shrine in Tokyo—not only kamikaze pilots but less distinguished soldiers and even army nurses. At the shrine, which is filled with photos and other memorabilia of the deceased, worshippers leave small plaques inscribed with their prayers. It was in the knowledge that they would become *kami*, and be appealed to by ordinary citizens for intervention in such mundane matters as high school grades, that six thousand young Japanese volunteered for suicide missions in World War II. A poem found on the body of one Japanese soldier after the battle of Attu in the Aleutians was translated as saying: "I will become a deity with a smile in the heavy fog. I am only waiting for the day of death."

AMERICAN PATRIOTISM

In the American vernacular, there is no such thing as American nationalism. Nationalism is a suspect category, an ism. like communism, and confined to other people—Serbs, Russians, Palestinians, Tamils. Americans who love their country and profess a willingness to die for it are not nationalists but something nobler and more native to their land. They are "patriots."

In some ways, this is a justifiable distinction: If all nations are "imagined communities," America is more imaginary than most. It has no *Volk,* only a conglomeration of ethnically and racially diverse peoples, and it has no feudal warrior tradition to serve as a model for an imaginary lineage the average citizen might imagine himself or herself a part of. But at the same time, there can be no better measure of America's overweening nationalist pride than the fact that we need a special "American" name for it. Nationalism, in contemporary usage, is unAmerican and prone to irrational and bloody excess, while patriotism, which is quintessentially American, is clearheaded and virtuous. By convincing ourselves that our nationalism is unique among nationalisms, we do not have to acknowledge its primitive and bloody side.

30   Americans might well take pride in their uniquely secular civic tradition: The Founding Fathers were careful to separate church and state, not only because they feared the divisiveness of religious sectarianism, but because they did not want to sacralize the state. Their aim was to ensure, as John Adams wrote, that "government shall be considered as having in it nothing more mysterious or divine than other arts or sciences." But war inevitably wore down the wall between church and state, between government and the "divine." In the late nineteenth century, America's imperialist ventures abroad helped infuse American patriotism with a new, quasi-religious fervor. Then, during the Cold War that immediately followed World War II, American nationalism began to invoke the dominant Protestant religion, to the point, often, of seeming to merge with it. Patriotic Americans countered the official atheism of the enemy nation with a proud fusion of "flag and faith." The point "was not so much religious belief as belief in the *value* of religion," historian Stephen J. Whitfield has argued, and above all "the conviction that religion was virtually synonymous with American nationalism."

But for all its debts to the Protestant tradition, American nationalism does not depend on any particular religion for its religious dimension. It is, practically speaking, a religion unto itself—our "civil religion," to use American sociologist Robert Bellah's phrase. In some of its more fervent and sectarian versions, American nationalism makes common cause with white supremacy, antiSemitism, and Christian millenarianism and even adopts Nazi symbolism. But my concern here is with the more mainstream form of nationalism, which is thought to unite all of America's different races, classes, and ethnic groups. Compared to the blood-soaked rhetoric and rituals of Nazism, this civil religion is a bland and innocuous business—perhaps especially to someone who was raised within its liturgy of songs, processions, prayers, and salutes. It is, nonetheless, an extension and a celebration of American militarism, and no less bellicose in its implications than State Shinto or Nazism.

American patriotism, like the nationalisms of other nations, is celebrated on special holidays, and these are, in most instances, dedicated to particular wars or the memory of war. The Fourth of July, Memorial Day, Flag Day, and Veterans Day all provide occasions for militaristic parades and the display of nationalistic emblems and symbols, especially the flag. On these and other occasions, such as commemorations of particular wars or battles, bugles are blown, wreaths are ceremoniously laid on monuments or graves, veterans dress up in their old uniforms, and politicians deliver speeches glorifying the nationalistic values of duty and "sacrifice." Through such rituals and observances of nationalism as a "secular religion," historian George L. Mosse has written, war is "made sacred."

But the "religion" of American patriotism is also distinctive in at least two ways. First, it features a peculiar kind of idolatry which can only be called a "cult of the flag."* Just as the wartime Japanese fetishized the emperor's portrait, Americans fetishize their flag. A patriotic pamphlet from 1900 declared in unabashedly religious terms that the United States "must develop, define and protect the cult of her flag, and the symbol of that cult — the Star Spangled Banner — must be kept inviolate as are the emblems of all religions." Early twentieth-century leaders of the Daughters of the American Revolution held that "what the cross is to our church, the flag is to our country," and, in more overtly primitive terms, that the flag had been "made sacred and holy by bloody sacrifice."

The American flag can be found in almost every kind of public space, including churches, and it must be handled in carefully prescribed, ritual ways, down to the procedure for folding. It is "worshipped" by displaying it, by pledging allegiance to it, and, occasionally, by kneeling and kissing it. It is the subject of our national anthem, which celebrates a military victory signaled by the survival, not of the American soldiers, but of the American flag, when

> the rockets' red glare,
> the bombs bursting in air,
> Gave proof thro' the night
> that our flag was still there.

And anyone who still doubts that the American flag is an object of religious veneration need only consider the language of the proposed constitutional amendment, narrowly defeated in the Senate in 1995, forbidding the "desecration" of flags.

---

*Other comparable, English-speaking nations — the United Kingdom, Canada, and Australia — do not indulge in flag worship. According to the *Wall Street Journal* (Nov. 7, 1996), British efforts to create a mass market for Union Jacks have fallen flat: "Many don't like what it stands for. A fair number aren't sure when, or if, the law lets them unfurl it. Quite a few haven't the foggiest idea of which side of it is up."

35   The other distinctive feature of American nationalism-as-religion, at least as compared to those of more secular-minded nations, is its frequent invocation of "God." We pledge allegiance to a nation "under God," our coins bear the inscription IN GOD WE TRUST. This was not just a concession to America's predominant Christianity, as Bellah explains, because the God being invoked is not exactly the Christian God:

> The God of the civil religion is . . . on the austere side, much more related to order, law, and right than to salvation and love. . . . He is actively interested and involved in history, with a special concern for America. Here the analogy has much less to do with natural law than with ancient Israel; the equation of America with Israel . . . is not infrequent.

Put more bluntly, this is the Old Testament God, short-tempered and tribalistic. And it is not so much "order, law, and right" that concern Him as it is the fate of his people — Americans, that is, as his "chosen people" — in war.* "If God is on our side," Moral Majority leader Jerry Falwell observed confidently in 1980, "no matter how militarily superior the Soviet Union is, they could never touch us. God would miraculously protect America."

In fact, every aspect of America's civil religion has been shaped by, or forged in, the experience of war. Memorial Day and Veterans Day honor the soldiers, both living and dead, who fought in past wars, and war veterans are prominent in the celebration of Independence Day and in promoting the year-round cult of the flag. The cult itself can be dated from the Spanish-American War, which signaled America's emergence as a global imperialist power. It was on the day after the United States declared war on Spain that the first statute requiring schoolchildren to salute the flag was passed, by the New York State legislature, and in the wake of World War I, eighteen states passed similar statutes. And it was in the 1950s, at the height of the Cold War, that the coins and the pledge of allegiance were modified to include the word "God." At the middle of a century that included American involvement in two world wars and military incursions into the Caribbean, Central America, Korea, and the Philippines, America was a nation draped in flags, addicted to military ritual, and convinced that it was carrying out the will of a stern and highly partisan deity.

---

*Though I am borrowing some of his insights, I should make it clear that Bellah's concept of the American "civil religion" is quite different, and does not explicitly involve nationalism or militarism. He imagines it as some vague, generic type of religion that "actually exists alongside of and rather clearly differentiated from the churches" and serves to provide a transcendent framework for our notion of America. Only when he observes that "the civil religion has not always been invoked in favor of worthy causes," and that it lends itself readily to the intolerant nationalism of the American-Legion type of ideology," do the euphemisms begin to crack, revealing that what we are talking about sounds very much like nationalism.

American's civil religion is limited, however, in ways that Nazism and State Shinto were not. Democracy guarantees, or at least has guaranteed so far, that Americans will not have some central, godlike figure—a Führer or an emperor—to focus and excite their nationalist zeal. Then there is the multiethnic and multiracial character of the American population. "America is no nation," the British ambassador observed dismissively at the outbreak of World War I, "just a collection of people who neutralize each other." Lacking a Führer or a *Volk,* America's civil religion has the potential to focus on the American (and Enlightenment) ideals of democracy and freedom. This would be something truly unique among nationalisms: a loyalty to country tempered and strengthened by a vision of a just polity that extends to all of humankind.

Such inclusive visions—international socialism being another—have not, of course, fared well in the era of nationalism. Within the United States, a national loyalty based on Enlightenment ideals has had to compete, again and again, with the more fervent and *volkisch* forms of nationalism nourished by nativism and racism. The Christian right, for example, is as much a nationalist movement as a religious one and serves as an ardent lobby for the U.S. military. "The bearing of the sword by the government is correct and proper," Falwell wrote during the Cold War, segueing easily from bladed to nuclear weapons. "Nowhere in the Bible is there a rebuke for the bearing of armaments."

But the Old Testament–style thunderings of the Christian right are only a particularly florid version of the civil religion shared by the great majority of Americans. Since the end of the Cold War, America's quasi-religious nationalism has continued to thrive without a "godless" enemy—without a consistent enemy at all—nourished by war itself. In other times and settings, outbursts of nationalist fervor have often served as a preparation for war, but in the United States, the causality increasingly works the other way, with war and warlike interventions serving, and sometimes apparently being employed, to whip up nationalist enthusiasm. Nations make war, and that often seems to be their most clear-cut function. But we should also recall Hegel's idea that, by arousing the passions of solidarity and transcendence, *war makes nations,* or at least revives and refreshes them.

The United States is hardly alone in its use of war to further domestic political aims. In 1982 Margaret Thatcher's brief war with Argentina over the Falkland Islands occasioned an outburst of British nationalism and an enormous boost for Thatcher in the polls. Serbian aggression in the former Yugoslavia temporarily salvaged the Milošević government from the disastrous consequences of its economic policies. Or take the curious case of Ecuador, which is not normally thought of as a nationalistic society at all. After ordering his troops to resist Peruvian border incursions in early 1995, the deeply unpopular, seventy-three-year-old Ecuadorian president, Sixto Durán Ballen, found himself suddenly "bathed in the nationalist fountain of youth," as the *New York Times* put it. Flag-waving crowds welcomed him back from a diplomatic tour, and he could be seen daily on the balcony of the presidential palace, "energetically pumping the air with his right fist, and leading crowds in rhythmic chants of 'Not One Step Back!'" No doubt, when the armed confrontations subsided, Ecuadorians went back to burning "Sixto dolls" in effigy.

In the post–Cold War United States, though, wars — or at least "interventions" — became the habitual cure for domestic malaise. Ronald Reagan used a Marxist coup in Grenada as the excuse to raid that island in 1983. George Bush discovered the energizing effects of military action early in his presidency, with his thrillingly swift invasion of Panama and capture of its de facto head of state. Two and a half years later, with the economy in recession and his approval ratings down, Bush decided to respond to the Iraqi invasion of Kuwait with a massive U.S.-led military intervention, "Operation Desert Storm." Public opinion was evenly divided on the necessity of war right up until the eve of hostilities, but once the killing began, it was popular enough to boost Bush's approval ratings to over 90 percent, which is very close to those of the deity.

The Gulf War evoked a burst of nationalist religiosity that, although clearly manipulated by television coverage of the war, seemed to be both spontaneous and deeply felt. Flags appeared everywhere, along with bumper stickers, T-shirts, and buttons urging Americans to SUPPORT OUR TROOPS. As if flags were not a sufficient proof of loyalty, they were joined by yellow ribbons, which had been originally displayed in solidarity with the U.S. hostages held by Iran from 1979 to 1981, and seemed to indicate that America was once again the wronged party or victim. In my town the Boy Scouts affixed yellow ribbons to every tree and bush lining the main street, and similar outbreaks of nationalistic fetishism occurred all over the country. Sports teams and public employees insisted on the right to wear American-flag patches on their uniforms; dissenters (and those deemed to look like Iraqis) were in some cases attacked or threatened with attack.

In effect, the war had reduced a nation of millions to the kind of emotional consensus more appropriate to a primordial band of thirty or forty individuals. In their imaginations, Americans were being threatened by an outsize, barely human enemy, always represented by the lone figure of Iraqi leader Saddam Hussein. And like the primordial band confronted with a predator, we leaped into a frenzy of defensive action, brandishing the fetishes of our faith — our flags and yellow ribbons — against the intruding beast.

A number of scholars have proposed, in the words of social scientist Paul Stern, that nationalism "gets its force by drawing on a primordial sociality" rooted in our long prehistory as members of small-scale bands. Mechanisms of entrainment — mass rallies in the case of Nazism, synchronized rituals in the case of State Shinto, televised war news in the contemporary United States — re-create for us the sense of being part of a unified and familiar group analogous to the primordial band. It may be, as Toynbee suggested, that capitalism, with its "war of each against all," leads individuals to crave this experience of unity all the 45 more. To the alienated "economic actor," militant nationalism, with its parades and rituals, exhortations and flag-waving, holds out the tantalizing promise of a long-lost *Gemeinschaft* restored.

But socialism, in the twentieth century, has hardly been an effective antidote to the twin forces of capitalism and nationalism. It too promised community and self-loss in a collective undertaking, but the project of "socialist construction" turned out never to be quite so compelling as the project of war. People who would lay down their lives for their country will not necessarily give up a weekend to participate in a harvest or the construction of a dam. Love of our neighbors may stir us, but the threat posed by a common enemy stirs us even more.

The sociality of the primordial band is most likely rooted, after all, in the exigencies of defense against animal predators. We may *enjoy* the company of our fellows, but we *thrill* to the prospect of joining them in collective defense against the common enemy. Ultimately, twentieth-century socialism lost out to nationalism for the same reason the universalistic, post-axial religions did: It has no blood rite at its core, no thrilling spectacle of human sacrifice.

TALKING ABOUT IT

Seeing Metaphor: Revealing and Concealing

1. Ehrenreich opens by pointing to "the notion of nationalism *as* a religion, complete with its own deities, mythology, and rites." How do her examples of German Nazism, Japanese State Shinto, and American patriotism provide evidence of nationalism's "deities, mythology, and rites"? Does her metaphor seem to hold true?

2. In what ways does the American flag serve as a metaphor? What does it represent? Ehrenreich observes that "comparable English-speaking nations . . . do not indulge in flag worship," so why do you think that many Americans so revere the flag? And why would someone burn an American flag?

Seeing Composition: Frame, Line, Texture, Tone

1. Does Ehrenreich give essentially equal treatment to Nazism, State Shinto, and American patriotism? Why do you suppose she discusses American patriotism last?

2. How would you characterize Ehrenreich's attitude toward nationalism? What in her style of presentation leads you to this conclusion?

Seeing Meaning: Navigating and Negotiating

1. In paragraph 10, Ehrenreich writes that "nationalism is nothing if not tribalistic and cannot, by its very nature, make the slightest claim to

universalism." What does she mean by universalism? Do you think that the "bold dream of a universal humanity" — or, as she puts it later, "a loyalty to country tempered and strengthened by a vision of a just polity that extends to all of humankind" — is something to aspire to? Is it a dream that is even remotely possible?

2. "Nations make war," Ehrenreich writes, "and that often seems to be their clearest function." How much truth do you find in this statement?

WRITING ABOUT IT

1. At the close of this piece, Barbara Ehrenreich writes,

> Love of our neighbors may stir us, but the threat posed by a common enemy stirs us even more. The sociality of the primordial band is most likely rooted, after all, in the exigencies of defense against animal predators. We may *enjoy* the company of our fellows, but we *thrill* to the prospect of joining them in collective defense against the common enemy.

Write about an experience you had or know of in which people formed close bonds as a group, not because they enjoyed each other's company, but because they enjoyed the prospect of a collective defense against a perceived enemy. This type of bonding can occur in families, in social groups, in classrooms, in work settings, and in committees, for example. How does this experience resonate with Ehrenreich's argument about the thrill of war?

2. Research examples of American propaganda posters from World War I or II that helped to blur the boundaries between church and state — "or more precisely, between church-based religions and the religion of nationalism," as Ehrenreich says. How do the propaganda posters "sacralize the war effort"? How do they, for example, seem to "justify individual sacrifice" and put into action "the uplifting passions of group solidarity?"

3. Ehrenreich describes American patriotism as it is celebrated on special national holidays, listing bugle blowing, speeches, ceremonial dress, and flag waving as some of the rituals that are performed. "Through such rituals of nationalism as a 'secular religion,'" she argues, "war is 'made sacred.'" In particular, Ehrenreich focuses on the "cult of the flag" in our culture.

    On what other occasions besides national holidays are flags emblematic of American patriotism? Why, for instance, do we begin some sport events with the national anthem? Where else do you see flags displayed? Write about some examples of nationalism as Ehrenreich conceives of it.

Malicious Metaphor

LARINA ORLANDO

Larina Orlando is majoring in philosophy with minors in Greek and French; her special interest is in the philosophy of language. The study of conceptual metaphor in a writing course connected to her thesis plans in philosophy. As she studies the role of the cultural critic in the postmodern era, Orlando hopes to include examples of how new vocabulary, particularly metaphors, can have an impact on everyday language and thought of the general public.

War propaganda, one of the most tragic examples of the misuse of metaphor, has resulted in a large number of lies told by the leaders of certain nations. Although there are valid reasons for using metaphorical language in both spoken and written propaganda, they do not outweigh the permanent, negative effects of purely deceitful communication. An understanding of certain propagandic metaphors will make apparent the societal responsibility of all who are involved with war and language.

Let us consider the primary sources of the war metaphors: heads of state and politicians and the media producers who work closely with them. For these influential members of society, the ability to communicate through metaphor is power. With this in mind, several plausible reasons for the metaphor mania must be acknowledged. During times of war, when accurate depictions of the battle scenes are likely to be graphic, metaphor is frequently employed to soften the impact of the facts. The general public is likely to be shocked and unnerved by direct reports of suffering and death; their reactions could affect support for the war effort on the home front. Metaphor also gives the speakers a certain poetic license, making it easy for them to create images of the enemy that they want their audience to see and believe. This linguistic freedom brings about a certain laziness and sometimes malice of thought on the part of the communicators, however, as they replace one image of war with another. We should be aware that our leaders often omit or deliver false information as they attempt to support their war causes.

To illustrate, in speeches delivered during the 1991 Gulf War, both George Bush and Saddam Hussein used metaphors that were intended to increase the force of their arguments. Just two hours after the military attack in Kuwait began, Bush reminded the Americans that "Saddam Hussein systematically raped, pillaged, and plundered a tiny nation no threat to his own" (312). Two sorts of metaphor are at work here. The first, that of a man raping a woman, implies that Iraq is a strong, aggressive male who has raped his vulnerable female counterpart, Kuwait. Certainly this image will stir up feelings of resentment for

557

Iraq in the hearts of male and female members of Bush's audience. The second metaphor has been called the State-as-Person metaphor, which is explained by George Lakoff in his essay "Metaphor and War: The Metaphor System Used to Justify War in the Gulf" (4). As he notes, one can refer to Iraq (i.e., all of its soldiers and civilians) as the singular "Saddam Hussein." What is omitted in this metaphor, however, is the fact that "Saddam Hussein" cannot possibly represent all of the various ethnic, religious, political, military, and corporate divisions in his country. The underlying reason for this move, according to Lakoff, is that Bush was creating a larger fairy-tale metaphor which he developed to evaluate the war scenario for the American people. In Bush's narrative, Hussein was the villain, Kuwait was the victim, and the U.S. was the hero (Lakoff 4).

Needless to say, the American fire was fueled by this "opportunity" for heroism. As Lakoff points out, however, we should beware that "when President Bush argues that going to war would 'serve our vital national interests,' he is using metaphor that hides exactly whose interests would be served and whose would not" (10). Although the metaphors may appear to have been created for the rhetorical embellishment of the propaganda, the consequences of this manner of speaking were actually quite severe.

5   On the other side of the ocean, meanwhile, Hussein was using metaphor to paint a rather pretty picture of the War. In his speech over Baghdad Radio in January of 1991, he describes the potential triumph in the battles as follows:

> . . . the skies in the Arab homeland will appear in a new color and a sun of new hope will shine over them and over our nation and on all the good men whose bright lights will not be overcome by the darkness in the hearts of the infidels. . . . (316)

Hussein is attempting to delude his people into false hope by creating this metaphor wherein light is recognized as good and darkness is accepted as evil. There is no more effective means to superficially increase a nation's sense of security than to weave a metaphor into a public address. The problem, of course, lies in the realm where metaphor does not speak, where the truth, and the real wars, are hidden.

Part of effective propaganda is the renaming of certain instruments of war so that they are not seen by the public as weapons which maim and kill. For example, in the Gulf War we called one type of weapon the "Patriot" missiles. Such a metonymical metaphor allowed the Patriots to be fired under the ridiculous assumption that they embodied certain desirable human qualities such as loyalty and courage. Their name masks the fact that they were built for destruction. This phenomenon is not unique to the United States. In World War II, a Japanese air corps called "Thunder Gods" named certain bomb-carrying planes "Okha," which means "cherry blossom" (Naito 41). This delicate flower is a popular image in Japanese art, and the Thunder Gods, which is itself a powerful metaphor, derived comfort from the metaphor. Just before a battle, one young pilot wrote, "Farewell. I am a glorious wild cherry blossom" (Naito 41). The reality, however, was that the propaganda used to inspire the pilots may have contributed to the loss of their lives. All fifteen Okha pilots were shot down in a 1945 battle near Kyushu, a confirmation of the colder side of war which metaphor does not address.

Another consequence of metaphorical propaganda, one that is ignored by political figures and by the media, is the frustration it generates in the soldiers. In his essay "The Real War 1939–1945," Paul Fussell cites what additional aggravation the World War II propaganda caused for the troops overseas. He writes that in addition to the fear, boredom, and loneliness, the troops had "the conviction that optimistic publicity and euphemism had rendered their experience so falsely that it would never be readily communicable" (32). One counterargument to this sympathy for the soldiers is that the American stay-at-homes would have been unable to handle the graphic descriptions of the battles, and consequently the morale on the home front would have been lost. But should we then lie by omission just to spare the public the reality of battle?

Perhaps the most explicit accounts of the battles need not be published, but the accounts that are largely composed of metaphor create a wide chasm of misunderstanding between the troops and their loved ones back home. Imagine a young woman who has heard only the fanciful speeches about this "game" of war. How is she to understand that her husband and brother are not merely strategic pawns on a chessboard, but that instead they have become killers? Her blood relatives now have more in common with the enemy than they do with her. As Fussell explains, "The soldiers on one side know what the soldiers on the other side understand about dismemberment and evisceration, even if their knowledge is hardly shared by the civilians" (35). At a time when the troops most needed to be understood, they instead had to fall asleep each night with a heightened feeling of isolation. We can safely conclude, as Fussell has, that "as experience, the suffering was wasted" (34). The American public did not enlarge their understanding of human nature or behavior.

One of the most tragic illustrations of the consequences of propaganda occurred during World War II when the Jewish people were collectively labeled a "disease" or "parasites" by Nazi German public officials. Our natural inclination, of course, is to rid the world of disease, and thus the extermination of the Jews was presented to the public as a pragmatic endeavor, rather than annihilation. As articulated by Bella English in her essay "When Words Go to War," sanitized language is often used to conceal the vagaries of battlefield experiences. For example, users of the Persian Gulf War jargon often were able to sugar-coat many bitter pills by enlisting the help of metaphor. Body bags became "human remains pouches," "collection points" were locations where refrigerated trucks were stationed for the storage of bodies, and the bombing of both industrial and residential areas became known as "collateral damage" (79). It is disgraceful to our language that words are used without respect for the truth. In fact, now more than ever, we need to have the strength to confront reality without hiding behind pretty words.

10   We should treat our languages with the respect that they deserve by demanding of our leaders that they communicate by the words which most accurately describe the subjects at hand, particularly when human lives are at stake. War propaganda should not be taken lightly; often it is the primary reason that soldiers are willing to fight and their countries are willing to back them up. War is not a game, nor a business, nor a gamble, nor a fairy tale, and metaphoric propaganda, with very few exceptions, should be abandoned.

WORKS CITED

Bush, George. "The Liberation of Kuwait Has Begun." *The Gulf War Reader*. Eds. Micah L. Sifry and Christopher Cerf. New York: Times Books, 1991. 311–14.

English, Bella. "When Words Go to War." *Exploring Language*. Ed. Gary Goshgarian. 7th ed. New York: HarperCollins, 1995. 178–82.

Fussell, Paul. "The Real War 1939–1945." *Atlantic Monthly* 264.2 (1989 August): 32–48.

Hussein, Saddam. "The Mother of All Battles." *The Gulf War Reader*. Ed. Micah L. Sifry and Christopher Cerf. New York: Times Books, 1991. 315–16.

Lakoff, George. "Metaphor and War: The Metaphor System Used to Justify War in the Gulf." 1991. Online. Available http://metaphor.uoregon.edu/lakoff-1.htm.

Naito, Hatsuho. "My Body Will Collapse Like a Falling Cherry Blossom." *Air and Space* April-May 1991: 38–42.

The Power of the Rhetoric of War in Butler's "Crickets": Benign Intentions, Malignant Language

KIMBERLY TURNER

Kimberly Turner is an advanced student of English. She was particularly drawn to the ways in which metaphor functions to illuminate character in fiction. Hence, the rhetoric of war led her to a close reading of "Crickets" where she focused on language as Thiệu's battle for personal and cultural identity.

War has the ability to bring a culture to its greatest potential of community and purpose while at the same time bringing that culture to the brink of extinction. "Crickets," a short story in Robert Olen Butler's *A Good Scent from a Strange Mountain,* shows the effects of this dichotomy on an individual — a Vietnamese man named Thiệu who is forced to flee his country's war in order to preserve the lives of his family. But after ten years in America, Thiệu is not able to recognize his family as Vietnamese because his wife and American-born son have adopted American customs. He realizes that he has been fighting continually since he was eighteen — first against the North Vietnamese tanks and then against the disappearance of his cultural identity. In "Crickets," Thiệu uses different forms of language to try to hold onto his quickly disappearing sense of identity, just as language used by those around him is working to strip him of that identity. The rhetoric is of war, and language becomes Thiệu's personal battlefield.

One type of language in the story, naming, goes to the heart of Thiệu's identity concerns and sets the stage for his battle to keep his personal and cultural identity. The fact that Butler gives Thiệu the name of the defeated Vietnamese leader is significant in that Thiệu identifies with and links himself to a man who is indirectly implicated in the loss of South Vietnam to the Communist forces. Also, because a name is an echo of culture, Thiệu mourns the loss of his own name when his co-workers in Lake Charles, Louisiana, Americanize his name to Ted. Thiệu tries to downplay his loss by justifying the actions of his co-workers. "These people who work around me are good people and maybe they call me Ted because they want to think of me as one of them" (Butler 60). But Thiệu is not convinced by his own explanation. On the contrary, his tone throughout the story indicates that he is nostalgic for his name and perhaps bitter because of its change. "I hear myself sometimes and I sound pretty bitter" (59). Perhaps even more devastating to Thiệu is the fact that he gives his son an American name, Bill, so that he will fit

561

in with others in their new country. Thiệu understands that he is sacrificing a Vietnamese legacy for his son, but he agrees with his wife to allow Bill to be Americanized.

In addition to Thiệu's regrets of not passing on a Vietnamese name to his son, he also recognizes his inability to share his culture's language with Bill. In fact, the absence of Thiệu's native language adds to his isolation from his culture as well as the loss of his personal identity. In "Crickets" there are several instances when Thiệu remarks upon this loss as it relates to language. Thiệu laments that his legacy to Bill is empty, even though he occasionally attempts to compensate for this hollowness by passing on bits of the Vietnamese language: "Sometimes I say good-bye to him in Vietnamese and he wrinkles his nose at me and says, 'Aw Pop,' like I'd just cracked a corny joke" (60). As Bill patronizes Thiệu's language he unknowingly belittles and ridicules his father's heritage. Thiệu placates himself by remembering what his wife tells him: "He doesn't speak Vietnamese at all and my wife says not to worry about that. He's an American" (60). But Thiệu admits that he worries about his son speaking only English. At the same time, though, Thiệu decides not to use his native language and communicates with Bill not only in English, but also in language reflecting the American popular culture. When explaining the game with the crickets to Bill, Thiệu gets his son's attention by calling the insects "Cricketmen" so that they will resemble popular comic book characters. He also imitates James Earl Jones's voice to give "gravity" to the game's premise (62).

Because Thiệu does not appear to have shared his language with his son consistently, Thiệu is implicated in Bill's ignorance of his parents' culture. Instead, it seems as though Thiệu speaks to Bill in Vietnamese only when he is overcome by feelings of nostalgia. Therefore, though Thiệu regrets losing the battle of language with his son, he is at least partially responsible for his son's difference and tends to group him with the other Americans he encounters that he thinks of as *others*. Thiệu compares himself to Americans: "I'm the best chemical engineer *they've* got and *they* even admit it once in a while. *They're* good-hearted people, really" (59, emphasis mine). By referring to his co-workers as "they," Thiệu acknowledges that he is isolated from the American community as completely as he is from his Vietnamese culture. Also, Thiệu belittles the colloquial English in Louisiana specifically, just as Bill ridicules Vietnamese, and sets up a kind of competition with his co-workers implying that he has become more efficient in English than they are: "they speak so slowly, even to one another, even though English is their native language. I've heard New Yorkers on television and I speak as fast as they do" (60). Not only does Thiệu suggest that the English of those around him is inferior, but he has also perfected that language in order to retain some of his self-confidence and win a small battle over the world around him.

5   It seems as though Thiệu does recognize the importance of language in how he sees the world as well as how it sees him, but he refuses to use language

actively in order to preserve his culture. Thiệu claims that he does not fight for his language or his name: "I've done enough fighting in my life" (59). In fact, Thiệu narrates memories from his fighting in Vietnam when he is eighteen years old, but Thiệu's experience in battle is problematic. He remembers:

> . . . I was only recently mustered into the Army, and when my unit dissolved and everybody ran, I stripped off my uniform and put on my civilian clothes again and I threw rocks at the North's tanks when they rolled through the streets. (59)

Here, it is apparent that Thiệu was unable to face his opponent equally in Vietnam — with weapons as a part of an organized group. Instead, he fights his enemy using gestures by throwing bricks at tanks with "very few" of his people. Because he had to fight virtually alone, he was forced to attack from alleys so that he could easily run away. Thiệu himself recognizes the ineffectiveness of his actions:

> I stayed in the mouths of alleys so I could run and then return and throw more rocks, but because what I did seemed so isolated and so pathetic a gesture, the gunners in the tanks didn't even take notice. But I didn't care about their scorn. At least my right arm had said no to them. (60)

Whereas Thiệu is unable to speak out against his enemy, he finds that he can express his protest with his arms. Though it is true that Thiệu feels empowered as an individual with even his ineffectual gesture, his experience in the war teaches him the overall inability of gesture or protests to produce changes or even recognition. It is probably this same impotence that has evolved in Thiệu to make him lose confidence in the effectiveness of spoken language in accomplishing goals.

Obviously, Thiệu's experience in Vietnam has made him aware of the difficulties of facing an overwhelmingly larger and stronger opponent. Silently, Thiệu tries to overcome always being an underdog by manipulating the world around him as best he can. Thiệu manages to escape the persecution in Vietnam by seeking asylum in the United States, but he finds that he has gone from being threatened by physical violence to being threatened culturally, as he is labeled a minority in Louisiana who must change in order to conform. Among his co-workers, Thiệu imagines that he can manipulate the difference in numbers and size by being the "best," but he still finds himself intimidated by the physical size and strength of Americans. "Sometimes it bothers me that these men are so much bigger than me. I am the size of a woman in this country and these American men are all massive" (60). Because Vietnam is generally more based upon a patriarchal system than the United States, Thiệu's comparing himself to a woman makes his feelings of weakness even more apparent. But Thiệu tries to combat his diminutive self-concept using a gesture — in this case he intellectualizes that his workmanship is superior to that of Americans — just as he had tried to fight the North Vietnamese. Unfortunately, Thiệu discovers that his gestures are useless. He finds that his work in America does not help to give him a lasting sense of identity any more than his guerrilla warfare in Vietnam.

Perhaps Thiệu's most poignant attempt to comfort himself about his isolation as a small Vietnamese man in America is his use of the cricket game to try to bond with his son and recapture a part of his past. Here, Thiệu makes a last and desperate gesture to communicate with his son using Bill's language while at the same time trying to reestablish his own identity by remembering a childhood game and passing it along to his son. Essentially, Thiệu is hoping to regain the normalcy that the war and his necessary migration to America stripped from his life. He is expecting that the cricket game will transport him to a kind of game in which there can be winner — in which a smaller, weaker fighter has the possibility of winning and therefore gaining an identity. Thiệu believes that if the smaller cricket can prevail, or even fight well, he can transpose that victory onto himself in order to escape from his own inner isolation.

Thiệu describes the cricket game to his son as being a fight to the death between two types of crickets.

> One type we called the charcoal crickets. These were very large and strong, but they were slow and they could become confused. The other type was small and brown and we called them fire crickets. They weren't as strong, but they were very smart and quick. (62)

This fight displays a contest which represents the kind of size disadvantage that Thiệu has felt with both the Americans and the North Vietnamese tanks. More importantly, though, this fight mirrors the conflict within Thiệu as he uses language and gestures to try to regain his identity while at the same time realizing the futility of that language to be performative. Thiệu and Bill search for both types of crickets on the Louisiana delta, which reminds Thiệu of Vietnam, but to Thiệu's disappointment the fire crickets are missing from America. And along with the absence of the fire crickets, Thiệu's hope for an identity and a relationship with Bill also disappear as he loses his champion.

As Thiệu finally begins to realize that fire crickets are not indigenous to Louisiana, he recognizes that the distance between Bill and him is insurmountable. Bill does not understand his father's grief at the absence of the fire crickets. Instead, Bill worries about a grass stain on his Reebok tennis shoes, leaving Thiệu alone with his thoughts. Thiệu finally admits that those things which he pretended that mattered to him in Louisiana are as imperfect as the similarities between his new home and Vietnam:

> In Louisiana there are rice paddies and some of the bayous look like the Delta, but many of the birds are different, and why shouldn't the in-

sects be different, too? This is another country, after all. It was just funny about the fire crickets. All of us kids rooted for them, even if we were fighting with one of our own charcoal crickets. A fire cricket was a very precious and admirable thing. (64)

The impossibility of Thiệu's cricket war game signifies Thiệu's final loss in his personal war to retain his Vietnamese identity in America.

Throughout "Crickets," Thiệu wages a war to discover a sense of self in order to know where he can fit into not only his American life and his family life, but also into the memories from his past. Thiệu is besieged by memories in which he has to compromise his identity for survival or acceptance. He understands the importance of language in his fight and tries repeatedly to manipulate his perception of his past and present through words and gestures in both his actions and his memories. Yet his very hope in a future identity is in the fact that he still fights to feel like an individual, even though he has failed for more than ten years of his life. Thiệu's fight using language as well as his understanding of the language of uselessness and indifference used against him give him a small sense of purpose and hope that he can win against the larger forces at work around him. In fact, war is often used to compensate for an otherwise purposeless existence as is mentioned in Walker Percy's novel, *The Second Coming:*

> The war came. His father was happy. Most people seemed happy. Fifty million people were killed. People dreamed of peace. Peace came. His father became unhappy. Most people seemed unhappy. (Percy 198).

Obviously, Thiệu is dependent upon his rhetorical war even as he looks for peace within himself. Thiệu fights in order to have purpose, and when that fight becomes impossible, he loses that purpose — he loses his rhetorical war. The consequences of the failed cricket game for Thiệu are permanently detrimental. He is left with no hope that the stain which has tarnished his identity and purpose can be cleaned as easily as his son's dirty Reebok shoes, and he surrenders.

WORKS CITED

Butler, Robert Olen. "Crickets." *A Good Scent from a Strange Mountain.* New York: Penguin Books, 1992. 59–64.

Percy, Walker. *The Second Coming.* New York: Farrar, Straus & Giroux, 1980.

PERMEABLE BOUNDARIES: WRITING WHERE THE READINGS MEET

1. Several readings in this chapter refer to the "theater of war." Barbara Ehrenreich uses the term in describing "the thrilling spectacle of human sacrifice." Based on the instances where you find the phrase "theater of war," what does it mean, and how does it contribute to your understanding of and attitude toward war?

2. In what ways can Naito's "My Body Will Collapse Like a Falling Cherry Blossom" serve as an illustration for Ehrenreich's description of State Shinto as a case of war worship in Japan?

3. In what ways can Park's "I Moved Far Away from Soaring Ideals — I Became a Warrior" serve as an illustration for Ehrenreich's description of American patriotism as a case of war worship in the United States?

4. How does George Bush's speech "The Liberation of Kuwait Has Begun" illustrate Carol Cohn's point regarding the state-as-person metaphor in paragraphs 30–35 of "Wars, Wimps, and Women: Talking Gender and Thinking War"?

5. Describe how two or three other selections in this chapter illustrate the "painful acceptance of personal accountability" that Fussell describes.

6. Paul Fussell argues that "the formula for dealing with fear is ultimately rhetorical and theatrical: regardless of your actual feelings, you must simulate a carriage that will affect your audience as fearless, in the hope that you will be imitated, or at least not be the agent of spreading panic." What evidence can you use to support this argument from personal accounts in "Close Calls," "My Body Will Collapse Like a Falling Cherry Blossom," "I Moved Away from Soaring Ideals — I Became a Warrior," and "Crickets"? Choose three of the four and explain the degree to which each account illustrates the formula and the degree to which it does not.

7. Research some political speeches by American presidents and Allied leaders that were delivered at the time of World War I, World War II, the Vietnam War, or the Gulf War. Choose two and discuss the language used to win support for the war effort, drawing on Bella English's "When Words Go to War."

8. Carol Cohn claims that "the body of language and thinking that they [North American nuclear defense intellectuals and security affairs analysts] have generated filters out to the military, politicians, and the public, and increasingly shapes how we talk and think about war." This community or "think tank" has the power to impose their metaphors. Read some reports about the Gulf War as delivered by newscasters and/or analyzed by television networks, and discuss how the language of defense influences the way we think about war.

9. Describe some war games that you played as a child or some that you play now, either board games or video games. What is the attraction of them to you? What beliefs and values are embedded in the game through the images and language used by the game-makers? How might your experience or understanding of the game be enlightened by any of the authors in this chapter?

   You could also do this assignment collaboratively by assigning members of the group to research war games and to play them. You could include interviews with each other about the attractions and nonattractions of the games as well as the images of war they convey. It would be interesting to view the intergalactic war games as one category since they involve an entire species engaged against another.

10. View a representative war film from World War I, World War II, and the Vietnam War. How do they depict the realities of war; how do they distort them? Which seems most realistic to you and why? Draw on Paul Fussell's essay or others in this chapter to help support your views.

   This assignment can also be written collaboratively. Assign each member of the group to watch two films about one of the three wars previously listed. Synthesize your analyses to answer the questions in this assignment.

Chapter 8

Games and Not Games

Go. I roll the dice.
—John McPhee

Games are more than mere games. Even the most ordinary—childhood games, board games, popular sports—conceal rituals and symbols by which a culture defines itself as a tradition and by which it perpetuates its values. Bradd Shore, an anthropologist, argues the truth of that assertion in his essay, "Loading the Bases." Responding to his ideas, Yukiko Oka, a student from Saga University, describes high school baseball as it is played in Japan and sees within its rituals Japanese traditions and cultural values. Other authors in this chapter, James Wright, Margaret Visser, and John McPhee, address various everyday, widely accepted, sanctioned games in American culture. Not all games within a culture, however, are accepted by everyone as civilized play or sport. Some subcultures or social groups raise the issue of sanction: who sanctions, who doesn't, under what conditions, and for what reasons? In boxing and hunting, the issue comes up all the time. And it comes up in the types of toys that parents give to children: which toys are appropriate for which gender? Why or why not?

Beyond traditional games and sports are those that people invent for themselves. These games may carry risks—beyond the known risks of sanctioned sports like boxing and hunting. They may present physical or psychological dangers that are all the more frightening because people often do not fully recognize or admit to the risks. And some who do nevertheless feel compelled to embrace danger. Such activities may be literally life-and-death adventures embarked on for reasons that may not be fully understood yet are labeled "games" or "sports." One example, an account not included in this chapter, is the Mt. Everest disaster of 1996 in which several people from different expeditions died during a rogue storm on the roof of the world. Why would people choose to ignore caution and the responsibilities to those they love in order to subject themselves to the enormous risk, hardship, and expense of pursuing the summit of Mt. Everest?

The chapter begins with a poem about football, and within it are themes echoed throughout the chapter: what do we play at when we play games? Who do we become as players? Can a game be merely a game? When does it cease to be a game? The readings move through widely accepted play, such as word and board games, into more questionable activities in which "play" and "sport" are called into serious question. Whereas hunting ("The Killing Game") is, for example, sanctioned violence to some, the ugly prank the boys play in "Song" (based on a news report) is violence not sanctionable in any way. As Brigit Pegeen Kelly implicitly asks in "Song," "Are we haunted by our unsanctionable games?"

In "The Hitchhiking Game," a couple fails to take into account the psychological consequences of who they become as players in a game and of either one's refusal to continue the game. To what degree are role-playing games a matter of social acceptance? Finally, in "Bone Yard Stretch," a young woman places herself in physical danger: her self-created adventure is a high-stakes game; the wager, her life. She flouts the rule that we never play such games alone as well as the rules for surviving a road trip to Mozambique. She thinks she's independent, but everyone she needs in order to play her game suffers.

STARTING TO THINK ABOUT IT

1. What are your favorite games?

2. What does "game" mean to you?

3. Look up the word *game* in the Oxford English Dictionary. What is the history of the word? What are its possible meanings? Which of these are familiar to you?

4. How do you distinguish between work and play? Are those distinctions clear, and why do you make them?

5. Is a game ever merely a game to you? If so, under what conditions?

6. What is the function of rules in a game?

7. Do all games have boundaries or limits? What is the function of boundaries?

8. Consider the times you've heard or said, "It's just a game" and "I was only joking." In what situations did you hear those words, and what did you make of them?

Autumn Begins in Martins Ferry, Ohio

JAMES WRIGHT

James Wright was one of the most important poets of the 1960s and 1970s, winning the Pulitzer Prize in 1972 as well as several other honors. The following poem, which originally appeared in The Branch Will Not Break *(1963), can also be found in Wright's* Collected Poems *(1971).*

In the Shreve High football stadium,
I think of Polacks nursing long beers in Tiltonsville,
And gray faces of Negroes in the blast furnace at Benwood,
And the ruptured night watchman of Wheeling Steel,
Dreaming of heroes.   5

All the proud fathers are ashamed to go home.
Their women cluck like starved pullets,
Dying for love.

Therefore,
Their sons grow suicidally beautiful   10
At the beginning of October,
And gallop terribly against each other's bodies.

TALKING ABOUT IT

Seeing Metaphor: Revealing and Concealing

1. What ideas/feelings does the game evoke beyond the ritual of Friday night football games at Shreve High stadium? What other rituals may be embedded in the game?

2. What associations does the verb "gallop" bring to the final image of the sons?

Seeing Composition: Frame, Line, Texture, Tone

1. The poem is structured like a logical equation, a syllogism: two propositions and a conclusion. How does the conclusion follow from the propositions?

2. How would you describe the tone of voice in this poem? What might it reveal about the speaker's relationship to the scene he describes?

Seeing Meaning: Navigating and Negotiating

1. As you make your way through the poem — its events and characters, its structure, and its tone — what does the beginning of autumn come to mean, and how are we encouraged to respond to those meanings?

2. What do you make of the line "Their sons grow suicidally beautiful"? How do you respond to the hyperbole of the image?

WRITING ABOUT IT

1. Rituals are metaphors that we act out or perform. They are set, repeated behaviors that have meaning beyond the literal act of, say, tailgate parties, cheers, songs, and gestures. These rituals, as well as others, can show how people find social identities through games and how games perpetuate social and cultural values. For example, the father's and subsequently the mother's and children's social identities are partially constructed by the ritual of football games in Martins Ferry.

    Go to a sporting event and watch the spectators. What rituals do you observe? What ideas and feelings seem associated with the way spectators look, act, and speak? What do your observations tell you about social identities or about the cultural values embedded in the rituals of spectators?

2. Write your own short poem in which you associate the beginning of a season with a game or sport in your community. It needn't be a baseball, football, or basketball game. It could be, for example, an Easter egg hunt, trick or treat in October, catching fireflies, hide-and-seek after dark, or some other game that is seasonally significant to you. The "community" can be as small as your neighborhood or your house: "Spring Begins on Harvie Street." Try to express the ideas and feelings associated with the rituals of the game.

    You could read these poems to each other in class and make a list in your journal of the rituals you remember. What do the beginnings of autumn, spring, winter, and summer come to mean for different people when associated with a game?

Loading the Bases: How Our Tribe Projects Its Own Image into the National Pastime

BRADD SHORE

Bradd Shore is a professor of symbolic and psychological anthropology at Emory University and the author of Sala'Ilua: A Samoan Mystery *(1982) and* Culture in Mind: Cognition, Culture, and the Problem of Meaning *(1996). The following piece originally appeared in the May/June 1990 issue of* The Sciences.

Americans will recall the night of October 25, 1986, not because of any political upheaval, scientific breakthrough or natural cataclysm but because of certain events involving one William Hayward Wilson, known since childhood as Mookie. Thirty years old, five feet ten inches tall and weighing 168 pounds, Mookie Wilson was, at the time, a much cherished outfielder for the New York Mets. His playing record, comfortably better than mediocre, had been spiced with flashes of brilliance. True, he struck out a bit too often, could have drawn a few more walks and had a weak throwing arm. But he was a joy to watch for the wide sweep of his swing and the gleeful abandon with which he scampered around the bases. And he was beloved by fans and players alike for his unfailing good nature.

Thus did Mookie Wilson stand in the batter's box that autumn evening, in the bottom of the tenth inning of the sixth game of the 1986 World Series. Only minutes before, Shea Stadium had been funereal. The visiting Boston Red Sox had opened up a 5–3 lead in the top of the tenth and had retired the first two Mets on outfield flies in the bottom of the inning. With one more out, what had been a glorious season for New York would have ended ignobly, and Boston would have had its first world championship since 1918. On the field several Red Sox flashed grins, while in their clubhouse preparations were being made for the customary champagne-bath celebration. Over on the Mets' side the fiery first baseman Keith Hernandez, the inning's second out, sat sipping beer and dragging on a cigarette, sullenly awaiting the inevitable.

Then it started. In swift succession singles by Gary Carter, Kevin Mitchell and Ray Knight made it 5–4, with runners on first and third, bringing William Hayward Wilson to the plate and the crowd to its feet. Another hit would tie the score; one of Wilson's occasional home runs would win it for New York.

Wilson worked the count to two balls and two strikes against Boston's Bob Stanley, then fouled off two superlative pitches to stay alive. The next delivery followed a sinking trajectory in the direction of Wilson's ankles. Had he been struck by the pitch, he would have been sent to first, loading the bases. But the agile outfielder jumped, twisted and fell to the ground, avoiding the ball, which eluded the grasp of the catcher Rich Gedman and skipped on toward the backstop, allowing Mitchell, the barrel-chested rookie, to score the tying run and, no less important, moving Knight down to second.

5   Moments later Stanley pitched and Wilson took one of his enormous swings, spinning off a lazy, squirming hopper toward the gallant Boston first baseman Bill Buckner, playing despite excruciating pain in his legs. With Wilson sprinting desperately toward first, Buckner reached down for the ball to make the kind of routine defensive play he'd executed countless times over the previous seventeen years.

He missed it. The ball squirted through his legs and rolled into right field as Knight ran home with the run that brought the Mets a 6–5 victory and forced the Series to a seventh game. Buckner meanwhile stared off toward the outfield, aware perhaps that in one split second he had tarnished indelibly a distinguished career during which he had made 2,464 base hits and earned a reputation for unsurpassed competitive spirit. In the stands and all over the New York area people danced and screamed and kissed perfect strangers as if they had just heard of the end of a major war. In New England — even though the Series was not yet over — many prepared to spend a long dour winter contemplating yet another Red Sox collapse. (Rightly so, as it turned out, for the Mets again came from behind to win game seven.) And across the nation millions of people would never forget where they were when they saw Mookie Wilson's at bat climax what may well have been the most extraordinary inning of major league baseball ever played.

Well, one could reasonably ask, as many do: So what? Why all the fuss? Baseball is, after all, just a game, a diversion from life's serious business. Maybe. But a more considered view suggests that while it is incontestably a game, our national pastime is also something more. Baseball symbolizes for many Americans a nostalgia for childhood and summer and a lost agrarian age; it engages our passions, shapes our weekends and helps lubricate our casual social relationships; it transcends the control of the clock over our harried lives; and understood as a kind of ritual drama, baseball takes us beyond the uncertainty of play in motion to the enduring forms that make it a cultural institution — confirming the oft-quoted observation by the historian Jacques Barzun, professor emeritus of Columbia University, that "whoever wants to know the heart and mind of America had better learn baseball."

Many attempts have been made to define the elusive fit between baseball and the American character. Most of them have focused on certain general aspects of the game — its leisurely pace, its concern for precision and self-control and its alleged stress on fair play. Few if any observers, however, have analyzed baseball as a pageant linked closely with the American world view, emphasizing the structural patterns that shape baseball time, baseball space and the social relationships choreographed by the rules of the game.

Like the anthropologist who studies an exotic culture, I came to baseball as a kind of outsider, never having been especially interested in the game. I knew its basic rules and had played a few dismal years out in left field as a Little Leaguer. But I had never really understood what made this sport so special. Frankly, I had always found watching baseball pretty dull. So my latter-day appreciation of it is inevitably that of an outside observer — a kind of convert — not that of a player or even an avid fan.

What strikes me most about baseball is that compared with other American field sports it is so consistently asymmetrical. Almost everywhere in the game one finds an endearing oddness instead of the efficient balance of basketball, football or hockey. There is barely an even number associated with baseball: nine players, nine innings, three strikes, three outs and a seventh-inning stretch. A full count is five — three balls and two strikes. Even the apparent symmetry of the diamond is broken by its division into three square bases and the lopsided pentagon that serves as home plate. Charmingly skewed, the game gives us no quarters and no halftimes. Baseball play may be fair, but it is not even.

This asymmetry shapes the odd sense of time in baseball. As many writers have noted, baseball is unique among American field sports in its utter disregard for the clock. Baseball time is controlled by innings and the contingencies of events. A game is over only when the losing team has had at least nine at bats and when a difference between the teams has been generated. The rare exceptions are when umpires call a game, say, for darkness or bad weather. Otherwise, the fearful symmetry of a tie score is not allowed. The open-endedness of baseball is guaranteed by the theoretically endless moments of the game. The batter might foul off an infinite number of pitches and thus remain at the plate to dig in and take his cuts for eternity. The team at bat could mount an interminable hitting streak and prolong indefinitely its half of the inning. Or the score might be inextricably deadlocked, sending the contest sprawling into an infinity of extra innings.

Detractors of the game are fond of pointing to its leisurely pace as its most glaring defect. Aficionados rarely deny the charge and instead locate much of the genius of baseball in its alternation of long periods of languor with sudden bursts of action. For the fan the drawling rhythm of the game allows a continuous shift of attention from the public spectacle at hand to more private pursuits: staring at the field, the scoreboard, the sky or the cityscape; discussing the game and arguing over what's to come; eating, drinking and making small talk. For the uninitiated these long breaks account for the tedium of baseball; but for true believers the resolute pokiness of the game allows for a kind of imaginative engagement impossible to achieve while watching a safety blitz, a fast break or a power play. This kind of intellectual involvement differs from the kinesthetic rush we feel when, as spectators, we sprint along with Carl Lewis in the 100-yard dash or add our own body English to Ray Leonard's feints, jabs and uppercuts. It is, rather, what Roger Angell, one of the more elegant baseball scribes, has called the "inner game — baseball in the mind": the cerebral interplay of strategy, anecdote and realignment of the all important statistics.

The romance of baseball with time, its genius for defying the clock, is equally apparent in its capacity to subdue the flow of history. For many Americans baseball encapsulates their own biographies through a seamless chain of teams that propels youth into age and projects age back to reclaim its lost vitality. From Little League to Babe Ruth League, high school, college, the Minors and the Majors, baseball is an idiom by which the dream of the endless summer is tied up with an individual life history. This may be why it is with a swing of the bat that most old-timers seem to think they can recapture youth. As the San Francisco columnist Herb Caen mused: "Whereas we cannot imagine ourselves executing a two-handed slam-dunk or a 50-yard field goal, we are still certain we have one base hit left in us."

If baseball time is open-ended, it nonetheless maintains its fundamental asymmetry by insistently fixing its beginnings. If the conclusion of a game is contingent on subsequent events, the start is always ritually precise: the national anthem and the umpire's cry "Play ball!" The baseball season may end with a contingent world series, but it begins with a single, sacred act: the presidential toss on opening day, a tradition that dates to 1910 and the beaming, corpulent William Howard Taft. In fact, the opening of the season is itself a reenactment of the birth of professional baseball. Game one of each new National League campaign is always played in Cincinnati, in memory of the Cincinnati Red Stockings, which in 1869 became the first salaried team.

15   The same need to demarcate its beginnings may well have inspired the invention of the mythical birth of baseball. In 1903 Henry Chadwick, the premier baseball authority in his day, testified in the *Baseball Guide* that the American game was without doubt a natural offspring of the British game rounders. Such heresy riled Albert Goodwill Spalding, a great pitcher of the 1870s who had by then become the nation's leading sporting goods magnate. The influential Spalding called for the formation of a fact-finding committee to determine the true pedigree of baseball. And in 1907 this august body certified that, Chadwick's compelling evidence notwithstanding, baseball was a deliberate and authentic American creation.

The baseball nativity story can be traced to the colorful reminiscences of one Abner Graves, a friend of a Civil War major general named Abner Doubleday. Graves claimed to recall how in 1839 Doubleday — who conveniently enough happened also to be acquainted with Abraham G. Mills, the fact-finding committee's chairman — had cleaned up an anarchic game called town ball played by boys in Cooperstown, New York. By mapping out a precise and orderly diamond on a pasture and by codifying the loose rules of the game, this latter-day Justinian was said to have single-handedly given America its national pastime. Like our nation itself, baseball could now lay claim to a fixed domestic origin, a certifiable beginning in an act of deliberate reason—the rationalization of a cow pasture on a summer's day in 1839.

Thus, baseball time juxtaposes the fixed beginning and the open end, the determinate and the contingent, in a characteristic asymmetrical relation. This pattern is paralleled closely by the game's orchestration of space. Baseball is the only American field sport that does not use a symmetrical field, defined by sides and ends. The baseball park defines a tension between an ever narrowing inner point, called home, and an ever widening outer field. The diamond, which includes the home area, is marked out with exacting precision and is the same in every park. The modern baseball diamond consists of a focal plate, located at home, and of three bases (or bags) situated at ninety-foot intervals around the diamond. Exactly sixty feet six inches from home plate is the pitcher's mound, raised no more than fifteen inches above the level of the bases.

Whereas this diamond area is precisely and uniformly measured, there are no rules governing the size of the outer boundaries of the outfield. It is the indeterminacy of the outfield that has given the classic ballparks—Wrigley Field in Chicago, Ebbets Field in Brooklyn, Yankee Stadium in the Bronx, Fenway Park in Boston—their distinctive souls. Moreover, outfields are subject to historical revision: only in baseball can the field be reshaped to accommodate new configurations of talent on the hometeam. There have been more than a few examples of outfield fences' being raised or lowered or moved closer to or farther from home plate. The most notorious instance of such boundary manipulation was the adjustable-height fence concocted by Bill Veeck, Jr., owner of the hapless Saint Louis Browns during the early 1950s. An inveterate showman, Veeck was renowned for the outlandish marketing gimmicks with which he enticed fans into watching his abysmal team. To enhance the Browns' home-field advantage, he installed an outfield fence that could be raised or lowered depending on who was at bat. The innovation lasted one game, after which a rule forbidding the practice was passed.

Whereas other field sports present focal goals for the object in play at each end of the field, the baseball park extends into the community. In a sense, the batter's goal lies beyond the park itself, on the city streets; in fact, according to ballplayers' slang, to hit a home run is to "go downtown." Through the home run, baseball celebrates the possibility of a heroic action's momentarily overcoming the limits of the contest. The home run is an authentic sacred event—not so much the everyday homer that merely drops into the stands, but the electric smash, announced by the loud crack of a bat, that sails clear of the park, beyond the fielder's futile leap, beyond the reach of the riotous fans, beyond the bounds of the game itself. That is why the royalty of baseball — the likes of Babe Ruth, Hank Aaron, Willie Mays and Mickey Mantle — are nearly always home-run kings.

20   The spatial open-endedness of baseball differs sharply from the "bowls" associated with football, arenas that surround the players totally, cutting the game space off completely and symmetrically from the surrounding community. The recent introduction of hybrid stadiums suitable for both baseball and football is for baseball purists an unfortunate development. If, traditionally, baseball parks were engagingly idiosyncratic, the modern era surely has encouraged a standardization alien to the game's authentic locale.

The most powerful of the asymmetries of baseball is social: it is the only American field sport that never directly confronts one team with another. Instead, the game pits a team — nine players on the field — against a lone batter and no more than three base runners at one time. Moreover, the team at bat remains out of sight, with members in a dugout awaiting their trips to the plate. Each player has two personas — a reactive defensive identity in which he plays a part in a highly coordinated communal enterprise on the field, and an aggressive offensive persona, in which he faces the opposing team as an individual batter and base runner. Although he functions as part of the communal fielding unit, the pitcher is the only player whose primary roles are aggressive on offense and defense alike.

The social asymmetry is reflected in baseball talk. Take for instance the difference between "playing" and "being." Those in the field merely "play" positions; but the batter "is" at bat, and the pitcher "pitches." Consider the awkwardness of such phrases as "Jose Canseco is playing the batter for the Oakland A's" or "Whitey Ford played pitcher for the Yankees." The more active a role is in baseball, the more the players *are* what they do, whereas "playing" is relegated to more passive, defensive roles. The language of being rather than of playing is also associated with proximity to "home." These speech conventions reflect a world view in which being is linked to an individual activity in a domestic, or home, environment. In contrast, social role playing is linked to an "outer" field.

In other field sports one team tries to move an object from one end of the field, through a hostile set of defenders, to a goal at the opposite end. The object, not the players, makes the score. In baseball it is the runner alone who scores. The ball is controlled largely by the fielders, whose ability to move it around the field works against the runner's interest. The batter, meanwhile, opposes the ball, hoping to knock it free of the fielders' control — out of the park, if possible. When he fails — if the ball is caught in the air or is returned to confront him or one of the base runners — he has made an "out." This essentially hostile relationship between offensive players and the ball is a distinctive characteristic of the game.

The action of baseball, then, can be conceived of as a series of travels by individuals who attempt to leave home and make a circuit through a social field marked with obstacles. It is not getting through the field itself that scores, however, but returning safely home. Baseball is our version of what Australian aborigines call a walkabout — a circular journey into alien territory, with the aim of returning home after making contact with sacred landmarks and braving hazards along the way.

Thus baseball dramatizes a recurrent cultural problem: how to reconcile 25 communal values with a tradition of heroic individualism and privatism. But the power of baseball as a ritual comes from more than a simple opposition between the social and the individual. It derives from the dramatization of the tension between the two and from an attempt to reconcile them symbolically. So baseball can be viewed as several kinds of contest going on simultaneously, each representing a different aspect of the relation between self and society.

On the first and broadest level, baseball is a contest between two teams, a clash that involves some profound social loyalties. The spatial opposition between home and outfield around which the game is organized is mimicked by the opposition between home team and visitors, or outsiders, a contest that provokes powerful community allegiances among fans. The second level of competition in baseball is the contest between the batsman at home plate and his opponents arrayed on the field. It is here that the game most vividly reflects the American dilemma: reconciling ideas of community and fair play with those of privacy and heroic individualism.

At the third level the teams disappear altogether, and baseball becomes a showdown between pitcher and batter, who face off in a mythic shoot-out scenario, each struggling to control the ball and unnerve the other. This dimension of the game has been greatly amplified by the advent of television, which in more ways than one has brought baseball home. By zooming in on the batter and the pitcher, televised baseball blocks out the fielding game for all but a few action-packed moments and is almost exclusively confined to the intimate battle taking place between the mound and the plate.

Finally there is a fourth level, where not only the teams fade from view but also the game, the season and the decade. At this level, through statistics, each player enters into a kind of ongoing universal supergame, beyond time and space, in which each is pitted against every other player who has ever worn a uniform. The lure of the "stats" has been perhaps the most commonly noted distinctive aspect of baseball. As Angell has written, a host of statistics "swarm and hover above the head of every pitcher, every fielder, every batter, every team, recording every play with an accompanying silent shift of digits." Thus Ty Cobb's .367 career batting average (the all-time standard) has merged with his name, his dates of birth and death and the memory of his irascible disposition.

An obsession with batting average, RBI, ERA and such is characteristic of a society at once democratic and individualistic, egalitarian and fiercely competitive, a nation preoccupied with enforcing a vision of community upon a vastly heterogeneous population. What statistics do for baseball, polls and elections do for society at large. As Rousseau noted long ago, in *A Discourse Upon the Origin and Foundation of the Inequality Among Mankind*, in a democracy the general will of the people can never really be general. It can only be manifest through the assertion of numerical superiority—the will of the majority.

30   Thus it is altogether fitting that the stats are an important way in which the spectator can participate in a professional's game. If gradations in players' skills can be translated through statistics into a quantitative hierarchy of value, so too can differences in skill and devotion among fans be ranked through a contest that engages their knowledge of the numbers. This is meta-baseball; one can be bored with the actual events of a game—yet relish the ongoing Pythagorean drama of numbers piling up against numbers in the mind's own ballpark.

Children enter early into this cosmic contest through baseball cards. In their incarnations as cards, players can be lifted out of their local team context and placed into the wider marketplace of baseball, their stats compared, their value calculated. When my seven-year-old son, his box of baseball cards tucked under his arm, sets off to close a deal with a boy down the block, he joins the ranks of baseball owners. Through a combination of shrewd business savvy and raw hero worship he connects with the most atomistic dimension of baseball.

The central Christian rite of Communion involves confronting and momentarily overcoming basic theological contradictions: life and death, body and spirit, god and human being. Whether religious or secular, ritual thrives on such paradoxes, crystallizing for the participants a fleeting reconciliation of opposites. As a civic ritual baseball enacts tensions between domestic, private and individual concerns, on the one hand, and social, public and communal concerns, on the other. Americans often use the language of the game metaphorically to represent other activities that involve the problematic nexus of self-interest and social responsibility, and no activity is more frequently so described than sexual behavior. Consider these expressions: "I can't get to first base"; "making a hit with him"; "he struck out with her"; "going all the way"; "I scored last night." Along the same lines American schoolboys commonly liken a sexual interlude to an epic dash around the base paths, in which they achieve more daring levels of physical intimacy with every base—and, with any luck, go all the way.

At first glance one might assume that baseball terminology is applied to all realms of sexual endeavor. Yet "My wife and I went all the way last night" and "I couldn't get to first base with the prostitute" seem jarringly inappropriate. Evidently, the baseball metaphor doesn't apply to sex when sex either is fully domesticated and private or is a fully public and commercial transaction. Baseball lingo is linked to sexual adventurism in dating behavior, in which a male must negotiate a perilous field of play with at least the possibility of coming home to score.

Like all games, baseball has rules to govern the competitive relationships between players. But possibly because it is a game that calls into question issues of individual freedom and social regulation, the attitude toward rules in baseball is notoriously ambivalent. Behind home plate, at the very apex of the infield, stands the embodiment of the rule book: the umpire, whose judgments represent the final authority in the game. But while umpires hold absolute power, managers, coaches and some players regularly treat their decisions as if they are open to protracted, sometimes violent negotiation. Such legendary figures as John McGraw, Leo Durocher and Billy Martin earned folkloric niches as much for their profane, dirt-kicking, tobacco-spewing debates with arbiters as for their managerial skills. This venerable ritual of challenging authority endures even though umpires rarely change decisions — certainly not in response to abuse by a player or a coach.

This leitmotiv of rebellion extends from the field to the grandstand: In no 35 other American sport is there any counterpart of the traditional cry to kill the ump, a recurring ritual rebellion aimed not only at a particular call but also at the dominion of the rule book itself. In the nineteenth century, club owners encouraged their patrons to humiliate the umpires. As Albert Spalding suggested, fans who harassed umpires were merely expressing a democratic right to protest tyranny. In fact, nineteenth-century fans were called cranks, an appropriate sobriquet, given their predilection for razzing and, on occasion, rioting.

The same reckless spirit can be found within the game itself. Spitters and brushback pitches, phantom double plays and the hidden-ball trick: these moments of petty villainy have a revered place in the sport. A reputation for insouciance has followed baseball almost from the start: as Harvey Frommer notes in *Baseball: The First Quarter-Century of the National Pastime*, Cincinnati's Red Stockings — models of Victorian property in their daguerreotypes — were loved in the 1860s not just for their on-field adventures but for their rowdy off-field antics.

For the most part the challenge of baseball to social order has always had an endearing tameness about it: it is the schoolboy playing hooky or swiping penny candy from a glass jar at the sweet shop, not the darker sins of elders. The authentic hero of American baseball is not the rapacious Hun but the errant knight — not the man but the Babe. Thus, as Paul Gardner points out in his 1975 book, *Nice Guys Finish Last: Sport and American Life*, George Herman Ruth was the perfect embodiment of the game's ambiguous relation with the idea of order:

> He had come up the hard way. He had reached the top without special training, without a college education; he was a graduate of "the school of hard knocks." He was a big man, with big appetites. He was irreverent and scornful of authority. He liked kids. And he made a lot of money. . . . He drank and he ate enough for two men, ignored the training rules and curfews, yet he played baseball better than anyone else around. . . . Ruth,

it seemed, could get away with anything, while Americans chuckled and muttered in envious admiration, "That Babe. . . ."

For its millions of devotees baseball, though obviously a game to be played, is also a ritual to be observed; and ritual, by most definitions, is religion in motion, constituted by activities directed toward the sacred. In his book *The Savage Mind,* the French anthropologist Claude Lévi-Strauss reflects on the relation between games and rituals:

> Games thus appear to have a *disjunctive* effect: they end in the establishment of a difference between individual players or teams. . . . At the end of the game they are distinguished into winners and losers. Ritual, on the other hand, is the exact inverse; it *conjoins,* for it brings about a union . . . between two initially separate groups.

For Lévi-Strauss the crucial difference between games and rituals hinges on the relation between the fixed rules, or structural forms, and the unpredictable events to which they give rise. In games the structure of play is taken for granted and recedes into the background like the bass line in a piece of music: a barely perceptible but deeply resonant grounding on which the melody dances with illusory freedom. Games use the rules to create disequilibrium between players and teams that ostensibly started out as equals. Rituals, on the other hand, bring the shared framework of forms and rules forward into consciousness. A ritual can serve as a kind of public social memory, an enacted recollection of shared experience. It brings us together.

An oft-noted characteristic of games is that they are not for real: they are "just play." All games take place within an agreed-upon "play frame" that suspends to some extent the seriousness of ordinary activity. The play frame is defined by both time and space, so that suspension of workaday reality is understood to be in effect only within the confines of the park, or game space, and only for as long as the game is in play.

40   Ritual shares with games this framing of reality. Often, however, a ritual is assumed to be more important than everyday behavior. Whereas games seem to operate on a level just below ordinary business, rituals rise transcendently above it, largely because ritual—particularly religious ritual—is frequently believed to be the repetition of sacred primal events. To devout worshipers, the rites of their faith may fairly be characterized as more real than reality or, at least, part of a higher reality. At the same time, ritual draws much of its power from the interplay of its immutable forms and the possibility that a real event may chance upon the scene. At the edge of performance, ritual flirts with reality: Rites of passage can come unnervingly close to bodily experience, whether for novices in New Guinea or fraternity pledges on college campuses. Real pain, authentic dan-

ger and, not infrequently, body mutilation figure prominently in such rites, throwing into doubt their status as performance.

Baseball, it seems, is neither game nor ritual alone but both at once. Our experience of the sport as player or spectator exemplifies what might be called — to use a musical metaphor — the polyphonic mind. That is, a thick, complex texture of conscious experience is made possible by the simultaneous interaction of several layers of knowledge. From our box at the ballpark our immediate attention may be riveted on the flow of the events of the game. But the total experience of baseball includes the embodied awareness of the recurrent forms and traditions of the game, which have a resonance all their own.

The interplay of game, ritual and reality in baseball was brought into sharp relief last fall, when a major earthquake struck before the third game of the World Series between the San Francisco Giants and the Oakland Athletics. There is no more sacred event in American sport than the Series, in which two major league titlists duel for what is a bit jingoistically called the World Championship. Feats accomplished during this festival are transcendent, and those who achieve them are enshrined in myth. When the earthquake struck the Bay Area, game, ritual and reality collided violently. We were jolted, confused by the sight of uniformed players huddling with their wives and children in Candlestick Park, reacting to an all too real intrusion from beyond game space. In the aftermath the reality of leveled buildings and of cars crushed on a freeway bridge seemed at first to render baseball absurdly insignificant. Even at World Series time, it *was* only a game. Or was it? As bodies were being pulled from wreckage, questions of when, where and whether or not the Series should resume were being hotly debated. And when, after what was deemed a respectable interlude, the Giants and the Athletics took to the field, the restoration of baseball, game and ritual, was for many like awakening from a nightmare to look again on the real world.

TALKING ABOUT IT

Seeing Metaphor: Revealing and Concealing

1. What images from other experiences does Shore use to talk about baseball? How do they work to reveal other ways of understanding the game? What's lost and what's gained by these metaphors?

2. In "Loading the Bases," Shore quotes the French anthropologist Claude Lévi-Strauss on the relationship between games and rituals:

    > Games thus appear to have a *disjunctive* effect: they end in the establishment of a difference between individual players or teams. . . . At the end of the

game they are distinguished into winners and losers. Ritual, on the other hand, is the exact inverse; it *conjoins*, for it brings about a union ... between two initially separate groups.

Why does Shore tell us that?

Seeing Composition: Frame, Line, Texture, Tone

1. How does Shore's depiction of the relationship of players to the game compare or contrast with concepts of "team" that we carry with us every day?

2. As he develops his argument, Shore calls on different voices. What are they? How do they contribute to his argument and to the overall tone of the piece? Are you more sympathetic to his point of view because of the different voices? Which voice do you find most effective for you, and why?

Seeing Meaning: Navigating and Negotiating

1. Shore quotes Jacques Barzun's observation that "whoever wants to know the heart and mind of America had better learn baseball." Do you agree? Or do you think another game or sport better represents the American character?

2. Shore sees baseball as "neither game or ritual alone, but both at once." He doesn't seem to feel that other sports share the aspect of ritual. Why? Do you agree?

WRITING ABOUT IT

1. Write about a women's sport in which you argue like Shore that it is both a game and a ritual. Tell how the game embodies values important to women of a particular culture or subculture. How do these rituals and associated values compare to those Shore attaches to American baseball? What do you make of the differences?

2. Write about another, less nationally visible or widely popular sport that could be said to represent the character of a particular subculture or social group in certain ways — for example, a car, bike, boat, or animal race; demolition derbies; animal fights; darts; chess; bowling. How might these be, like bases, "loaded" too?

Crossword Puzzles

MARGARET VISSER

Margaret Visser is the author of The Rituals of Dinner *(1991) and* Much Depends on Dinner *(1986). "Crossword Puzzles" originally appeared in her* Saturday Night *column, "The Way We Are," and is also in Visser's collection of essays* The Way We Are *(1994).*

Ever since mastery of speech proved we were human, people have loved mind-stretching word puzzles: questions like "What is it that walks on four legs in the morning . . . ?" or meaning-laden names, as in "Thou art Peter and upon this rock. . . ." To all the double-entendres constructed of pure sound, written letters have added acrostics (letters in the verses of a poem which, read vertically, make a word), palindromes (phrases that read the same backwards and forwards, like the one with which Adam introduced himself to Eve: MADAM, I'M ADAM), anagrams (convert JAMES STUART, and get A JUST MASTER), and homomorphs (as when SEWER can mean a needle, not a drain).

Crossword-puzzle addicts are people obsessed with language. Many of them love filling in a grid with letters that make up words answering simple definitions. Others are a more twisted breed altogether: having understood that words are patterns which can be reshaped and reinterpreted, they cannot resist playing about with that fearsome power. There are now more than fifty million regular cruciverbalists, representing every alphabetically written language on earth. Yet the form of this particular word mania, ancient as are its roots, was set only in 1913 when Arthur Wynne printed a clued and numbered "Word-cross," in the shape of a diamond with a blank centre in the form of a cross, in the Christmas edition of the Sunday *New York World.*

In 1924 the first crossword puzzle book was published, and the craze took off. That same year crosswords arrived in England, where the cryptic version of the puzzle would soon emerge, with its riddles, its poetry, and its compilers' rules ("Always say what you mean, though you don't always mean what you say"). By the 1940s, crosswords were known to be so irresistible in Britain that in January 1945 the Nazis scattered propaganda puzzles in English from a buzz-bomb. A typical clue: "We hear that this is a rare commodity in England (3)" (EGG). In the Soviet Union, magazine readers were invited to "unravel" even more blatant, politically correct messages, such as "American puppet in Bonn circus (8)" (ADENAUER).

The puzzle's popularity has never abated since it became a world-wide obsession in the twenties. For those who like them, crosswords can absorbingly fill in the time we spend in waiting rooms, lining up, commuting, travelling, or unwinding after stressful work that leaves the brain stimulated but hungry. Only puzzle, pencil, and solver are required. Great stretches of our lives, especially our waiting hours, are lived alone these days, and crosswords are solitary pursuits.

5   They are perfect examples of "closed system" thinking, the chief strategies of which are extrapolation and interpolation. This type of thinking is different from much scientific, artistic, and even everyday discursive thought; it requires logic, memory, and a particular kind of agility and tenacity of mind. A person with a combination of such characteristics delights in carefully framed occasions for setting them all in operation.

Sometimes puzzlers are rewarded with flashes of insight, when they "just know" a solution to a cryptic clue, even before they consciously understand the reasoning; it is an exciting and satisfying sensation. Solving at record speed, in the intense competitions which are now common, requires a large dose of this ability to leap over the intervening (but always present) logical steps. (Eight and a half minutes has been clocked for *The Times* of London's contest; the record set at three and a half minutes in 1970 still stands — but the puzzle became much more difficult soon after that date.)

What is "cut and run" in seven letters? (OPERATE.) Leather moved from side to side, by the sound of it (5)? (SUEDE.) What makes dat guy's appearance no longer dat guy's (8)? (DISGUISE.) Crosswords love abbreviations (L is left, V is five), and conventions like "the French (LE, LA, LES), O for "love," or PP, "very soft." Crossword country is full of tors and heather (ling), and overrun with emus, asps, lions, imps, saints (ST, SS), and people with Old Testament names (Eli, Amos, and Eve). Cryptic clues may involve puns, allusions, anagrams, hidden words, ambiguous definitions, charades, reversals, rebuses, deletions, containers, combinations: solvers must spot which tricks are being played before they can see through them.

The compiler is the unseen fiend with whom they do battle. Some of these trap-setters have achieved immortality, like the great Torquemada (Edward Powys Mathers) of the *Observer,* who would sit cross-legged on his bed "very like a somewhat relaxed Buddha," smoking and gazing into the distance until something clicked, whereupon, "with a contented smile or discontented shrug," he wrote down his clue. (His wife performed the more mundane but possibly even more difficult task of constructing the grid, with words he supplied.)

Torquemada once devised a "Knock-knock. — Who's there?" crossword, made up of clues like "Blank fool and caught a cold (8)": ABINADAB. Afrit of *The Listener* made a grid in which his own face lurked, with Q's for eyes. Compilers with minds like these rejoice in demonic pseudonyms: Mephisto and Afrit (A. F. Ritchie) are both devils, while Torquemada, Ximenes, and Azed (reversed) were leaders of the Spanish Inquisition.

REFERENCES

Tony Augarde, "Crosswords," in *The Oxford Guide to Word Games.* New York: Oxford University Press, 1984.

Sir Frederic Charles Bartlett, *Thinking: An Experimental and Social Study.* London: Allen and Unwin, 1958 (esp. pp. 63–66).

Roger Millington, *Crossword Puzzles: Their History and Cult.* London: Nelson, 1974.

Colin Parsons, *How to Solve a Crossword.* London: Hodder and Stoughton, 1988.

TALKING ABOUT IT

Seeing Metaphor: Revealing and Concealing

1. List the metaphors that Visser uses to describe the puzzlers and the puzzle-makers. What do they reveal about the author's and/or others' attitudes toward them?

2. How can the phrases "mind-stretching" (paragraph 1) and "closed-system thinking" (paragraph 5) both refer to the act of solving crosswords? How are these metaphors used?

Seeing Composition: Frame, Line, Texture, Tone

1. What does Visser's tone reveal about her own attitude toward crossword puzzles, the players, and the compilers? Is she neutral, favorably biased, or critical?

2. Outline this short essay by topic sentences, paragraph by paragraph. What is the logic in the progression of ideas?

Seeing Meaning: Navigating and Negotiating

1. Of some crossword-puzzlers, Visser remarks that "having understood that words are patterns which can be reshaped and reinterpreted, they cannot resist playing about with that fearsome power." To what extent do you agree that the ability to reshape and reinterpret word problems is a "fearsome power"?

2. Make up some examples in class of palindromes, anagrams, and homomorphs (paragraph 1). Are these fun for you to construct or not? Why?

WRITING ABOUT IT

1. "Great stretches of our lives, especially our waiting lives, are lived alone these days, and crosswords are solitary pursuits." Imitating Margaret Visser's piece, write the history and appeal of another game that can be played

alone. What kind of thinking skills are involved? What types of personalities might be attracted to the game so much so that it becomes "an obsession and can absorbingly fill in the time"?

2. Argue for the greater appeal of a word game that is not played alone but with other players. What kinds of thinking skills are privileged in team-played word games that are different from those in games played alone?

The Search for Marvin Gardens

JOHN MCPHEE

John McPhee is the author of Assembling California *(1993), among other books, and a regular writer for the* New Yorker. *"The Search for Marvin Gardens" originally appeared in the* New Yorker *and can also be found in McPhee's* Pieces of the Frame *(1972).*

Go, I roll the dice—a six and a two. Through the air I move my token, the flatiron, to Vermont Avenue, where dog packs range.

■   ■   ■

The dogs are moving (some are limping) through ruins, rubble, fire damage, open garbage. Doorways are gone. Lath is visible in the crumbling walls of the buildings. The street sparkles with shattered glass. I have never seen, anywhere, so many broken windows. A sign—"Slow, Children at Play"—has been bent backward by an automobile. At the lighthouse, the dogs turn up Pacific and disappear. George Meade, Army engineer, built the lighthouse—brick upon brick, six hundred thousand bricks, to reach up high enough to throw a beam twenty miles over the sea. Meade, seven years later, saved the Union at Gettysburg.

■   ■   ■

I buy Vermont Avenue for $100. My opponent is a tall, shadowy figure, across from me, but I know him well, and I know his game like a favorite tune. If he can, he will always go for the quick kill. And when it is foolish to go for the quick kill he will be foolish. On the whole, though, he is a master assessor of percentages. It is a mistake to underestimate him. His eleven carries his top hat to St. Charles Place, which he buys for $140.

■   ■   ■

The sidewalks of St. Charles Place have been cracked to shards by through-growing weeds. There are no buildings. Mansions, hotels once stood here. A few street lamps now drop cones of light on broken glass and vacant space behind a chain-link fence that some great machine has in places bent to the ground. Five plane trees—in full summer leaf, flecking the light—are all that live on St. Charles Place.

■   ■   ■

Block upon block, gradually, we are cancelling each other out—in the blues, the lavenders, the oranges, the greens. My opponent follows a plan of his own devising. I use the Hornblower & Weeks opening and the Zuricher defense. The first game draws tight, will soon finish. In 1971, a group of people in Racine

5

Wisconsin, played for seven hundred and sixty-eight hours. A game begun a month later in Danville, California, lasted eight hundred and twenty hours. These are official records, and they stun us. We have been playing for eight minutes. It amazes us that Monopoly is thought of as a long game. It is possible to play to a complete, absolute, and final conclusion in less than fifteen minutes, all within the rules as written. My opponent and I have done so thousands of times. No wonder we are sitting across from each other now in this best-of-seven series for the international singles championship of the world.

■   ■   ■

On Illinois Avenue, three men lean out from second-story windows. A girl is coming down the street. She wears dungarees and a bright-red shirt, has ample breasts and a Haden-doan Afro, a black halo, two feet in diameter. Ice rattles in the glasses in the hands of the men.

"Hey, sister!"

"Come on up!"

She looks up, looks from one to another to the other, looks them flat in the eye.

10   "What for?" she says, and she walks on.

■   ■   ■

I buy Illinois for $240. It solidifies my chances, for I already own Kentucky and Indiana. My opponent pales. If he had landed first on Illinois, the game would have been over then and there, for he has houses built on Boardwalk and Park Place, we share the railroads equally, and we have cancelled each other everywhere else. We never trade.

■   ■   ■

In 1852, R. B. Osborne, an immigrant Englishman, civil engineer, surveyed the route of a railroad line that would run from Camden to Absecon Island, in New Jersey, traversing the state from the Delaware River to the barrier beaches of the sea. He then sketched in the plan of a "bathing village" that would surround the eastern terminus of the line. His pen flew glibly, framing and naming spacious avenues parallel to the shore — Mediterranean, Baltic, Oriental, Ventnor — and narrower transecting avenues: North Carolina, Pennsylvania, Vermont, Connecticut, States, Virginia, Tennessee, New York, Kentucky, Indiana, Illinois. The place as a whole had no name, so when he had completed the plan Osborne wrote in large letters over the ocean, "Atlantic City." No one ever challenged the name, or the names of Osborne's streets. Monopoly was invented in the early nineteen-thirties by Charles B. Darrow, but Darrow was only transliterating what Osborne had created. The railroads, crucial to any player, were the making of Atlantic City. After the rails were down, houses and hotels burgeoned from Mediterranean and Baltic to New York and Kentucky. Properties — building lots — sold for as little as six dollars apiece and as much as a thousand dollars. The original investors in the railroads and the real estate called themselves the Camden & Atlantic Land Company. Reverently, I repeat their names: Dwight Bell, William Coffin, John DaCosta, Daniel Deal, William Fleming, Andrew Hay, Joseph Porter, Jonathan Pitney, Samuel Richards — founders, fathers, forerunners, archetypical masters of the quick kill.

▪ ▪ ▪

My opponent and I are now in a deep situation of classical Monopoly. The torsion is almost perfect — Boardwalk and Park Place versus the brilliant reds. His cash position is weak, though, and if I escape him now he may fade. I land on Luxury Tax, contiguous to but in sanctuary from his power. I have four houses on Indiana. He lands there. He concedes.

▪ ▪ ▪

Indiana Avenue was the address of the Brighton Hotel, gone now. The Brighton was exclusive — a word that no longer has retail value in the city. If you arrived by automobile and tried to register at the Brighton, you were sent away. Brighton-class people came in private railroad cars. Brighton-class people had other private railroad cars for their horses — dawn rides on the firm sand at water's edge, skirts flying. Colonel Anthony J. Drexel Biddle — the sort of name that would constrict throats in Philadelphia — lived, much of the year, in the Brighton.

▪ ▪ ▪

Colonel Sanders' fried chicken is on Kentucky Avenue. So is Clifton's Club 15 Harlem, with the Sepia Revue and the Sepia Follies, featuring the Honey Bees, the Fashions, and the Lords.

▪ ▪ ▪

My opponent and I, many years ago, played 2,428 games of Monopoly in a single season. He was then a recent graduate of the Harvard Law School, and he was working for a downtown firm, looking up law. Two people we knew — one from Chase Manhattan, the other from Morgan, Stanley — tried to get into the game, but after a few rounds we found that they were not in the conversation and we sent them home. Monopoly should always be *mano a mano* anyway. My opponent won 1,199 games, and so did I. Thirty were ties. He was called into the Army, and we stopped just there. Now, in Game 2 of the series, I go immediately to jail, and again to jail while my opponent seines property. He is dumbfoundingly lucky. He wins in twelve minutes.

▪ ▪ ▪

Visiting hours are daily, eleven to two; Sunday, eleven to one; evenings, six to nine. "NO MINORS, NO FOOD, Immediate Family Only Allowed in Jail." All this above a blue steel door in a blue cement wall in the windowless interior of the basement of the city hall. The desk sergeant sits opposite the door to the jail. In a cigar box in front of him are pills in every color, a banquet of fruit salad an inch and a half deep — leapers, co-pilots, footballs, truck drivers, peanuts, blue angels, yellow jackets, redbirds, rainbows. Near the desk are two soldiers, waiting to go through the blue door. They are about eighteen years old. One of them is trying hard to light a cigarette. His wrists are in steel cuffs. A military policeman waits, too. He is a year or so older than the soldiers, taller, studious in appearance, gentle, fat. On a bench against a wall sits a good-looking girl in slacks. The blue door rattles, swings heavily open. A turnkey stands in the doorway. "Don't you guys kill yourselves back there now," says the sergeant to the soldiers.

"One kid, he overdosed himself about ten and a half hours ago," says the M.P.

The M.P., the soldiers, the turnkey, and the girl on the bench are white. The sergeant is black. "If you take off the handcuffs, take off the belts," says the sergeant to the M.P. "I don't want them hanging themselves back there." The door shuts and its tumblers move. When it opens again, five minutes later, a young white man in sandals and dungarees and a blue polo shirt emerges. His hair is in a ponytail. He has no beard. He grins at the good-looking girl. She rises, joins him. The sergeant hands him a manila envelope. From it he removes his belt and a small notebook. He borrows a pencil, makes an entry in the notebook. He is out of jail, free. What did he do? He offended Atlantic City in some way. He spent a night in the jail. In the nineteen-thirties, men visiting Atlantic City went to jail, directly to jail, did not pass Go, for appearing in topless bathing suits on the beach. A city statute requiring all men to wear full-length bathing suits was not seriously challenged until 1937, and the first year in which a man could legally go bare-chested on the beach was 1940.

■   ■   ■

20   Game 3. After seventeen minutes, I am ready to begin construction on overpriced and sluggish Pacific, North Carolina, and Pennsylvania. Nothing else being open, opponent concedes.

■   ■   ■

The physical profile of streets perpendicular to the shore is something like a playground slide. It begins in the high skyline of Boardwalk hotels, plummets into warrens of "side-avenue" motels, crosses Pacific, slopes through church missions, convalescent homes, burlesque houses, rooming houses, and liquor stores, crosses Atlantic, and runs level through the bombed-out ghetto as far — Baltic, Mediterranean — as the eye can see. North Carolina Avenue, for example, is flanked at its beach end by the Chalfonte and the Haddon Hall (908 rooms, air-conditioned), where, according to one biographer, John Philip Sousa

(1854–1932) first played when he was twenty-two, insisting, even then, that everyone call him by his entire name. Behind these big hotels, motels — Barbizon, Catalina — crouch. Between Pacific and Atlantic is an occasional house from 1910 — wooden porch, wooden mullions, old yellow paint — and two churches, a package store, a strip show, a dealer in fruits and vegetables. Then, beyond Atlantic Avenue, North Carolina moves on into the vast ghetto, the bulk of the city, and it looks like Metz in 1919, Cologne in 1944. Nothing has actually exploded. It is not bomb damage. It is deep and complex decay. Roofs are off. Bricks are scattered in the street. People sit on porches, six deep, at nine on a Monday morning. When they go off to wait in unemployment lines, they wait sometimes two hours. Between Mediterranean and Baltic runs a chain-link fence, enclosing rubble. A patrol car sits idling by the curb. In the back seat is a German shepherd. A sign on the fence says, "Beware of Bad Dogs."

Mediterranean and Baltic are the principal avenues of the ghetto. Dogs are everywhere. A pack of seven passes me. Block after block, there are three-story brick row houses. Whole segments of them are abandoned, a thousand broken windows. Some parts are intact, occupied. A mattress lies in the street, soaking in a pool of water. Wet stuffing is coming out of the mattress. A postman is having a rye and a beer in the Plantation Bar at nine-fifteen in the morning. I ask him idly if he knows where Marvin Gardens is. He does not. "HOOKED AND NEED HELP? CONTACT N.A.R.C.O." "REVIVAL NOW GOING ON, CONDUCTED BY REVEREND H. HENDERSON OF TEXAS." These are signboards on Mediterranean and Baltic. The second one is upside down and leans against a boarded-up window of the Faith Temple Church of God in Christ. There is an old peeling poster on a warehouse wall showing a figure in an electric chair. "The Black Panther Manifesto" is the title of the poster, and its message is, or was, that "the fascists have already decided in advance to murder Chairman Bobby Seale in the electric chair." I pass an old woman who carries a bucket. She wears blue sneakers, worn through. Her feet spill out. She wears red socks, rolled at the knees. A white handkerchief, spread over her head, is knotted at the corners. Does she know where Marvin Gardens is? "I sure don't know," she says, setting down the bucket. "I sure don't know. I've heard of it somewhere, but I just can't say where." I walk on, through a block of shattered glass. The glass crunches underfoot like coarse sand. I remember when I first came here — a long train ride from Trenton, long ago, games of poker in the train — to play basketball against Atlantic City. We were half black, they were all black. We scored forty points, they scored eighty, or something like it. What I remember most is that they had glass backboards — glittering, pendent, expensive glass backboards, a rarity then in high schools, even in colleges, the only ones we played on all year.

I turn on Pennsylvania, and start back toward the sea. The windows of the Hotel Astoria, on Pennsylvania near Baltic, are boarded up. A sheet of unpainted plywood is the door, and in it is a triangular peephole that now frames an eye. The plywood door opens. A man answers my question. Rooms there are six, seven, and ten dollars a week. I thank him for the information and move on, emerging from the ghetto at the Catholic Daughters of America Women's Guest House, between Atlantic and Pacific. Between Pacific and the Boardwalk are the blinking vacancy signs of the Aristocrat and Colton Manor motels. Pennsylvania terminates at the Sheraton-Seaside — thirty-two dollars a day, ocean corner. I take a walk on the Boardwalk and into the Holiday Inn (twenty-three stories). A guest is registering. "You reserved for Wednesday, and this is Monday," the clerk tells him. "But that's all right. We have *plenty* of rooms." The clerk is very young, female, and has soft brown hair that hangs below her waist. Her superior kicks her.

He is a middle-aged man with red spiderwebs in his face. He is jacketed and tied. He takes her aside. "Don't say 'plenty,' " he says. "Say 'You are fortunate, sir. We have rooms available.' "

25   The face of the young woman turns sour. "We have all the rooms you need," she says to the customer, and, to her superior, "How's that?"

▪   ▪   ▪

Game 4. My opponent's luck has become abrasive. He has Boardwalk and Park Place, and has sealed the board.

▪   ▪   ▪

Darrow was a plumber. He was, specifically, a radiator repairman who lived in Germantown, Pennsylvania. His first Monopoly board was a sheet of linoleum. On it he placed houses and hotels that he had carved from blocks of wood. The game he thus invented was brilliantly conceived, for it was an uncannily exact reflection of the business milieu at large. In its depth, range, and subtlety, in its luck-skill ratio, in its sense of infrastructure and socio-economic parameters, in its philosophical characteristics, it reached to the profundity of the financial community. It was as scientific as the stock market. It suggested the manner and means through which an underdeveloped world had been developed. It was chess at Wall Street level. "Advance token to the nearest Railroad and pay owner twice the rental to which he is otherwise entitled. If Railroad is unowned, you may buy it from the Bank. Get out of Jail, free. Advance token to nearest Utility. If unowned, you may buy it from Bank. If owned, throw dice and pay owner a total ten times the amount thrown. You are assessed for street repairs: $40 per house, $115 per hotel. Pay poor tax of $15. Go to Jail. Go directly to Jail. Do not pass Go. Do not collect $200."

▪   ▪   ▪

The turnkey opens the blue door. The turnkey is known to the inmates as Sidney K. Above his desk are ten closed-circuit-TV screens — assorted viewpoints of the jail. There are three cellblocks — men, women, juvenile boys. Six days is the average stay. Showers twice a week. The steel doors and the equipment that operates them were made in San Antonio. The prisoners sleep on bunks of butcher block. There are no mattresses. There are three prisoners to a cell. In the winter, it is cold in here. Prisoners burn newspapers to keep warm. Cell corners are black with smudge. The jail is three years old. The men's block echoes with chatter. The man in the cell nearest Sidney K. is pacing. His shirt is covered with broad stains of blood. The block for juvenile boys is, by contrast, utterly silent — empty corridor, empty cells. There is only one prisoner. He is small and black and appears to be thirteen. He says he is sixteen and that he has been alone in here for three days.

"Why are you here? What did you do?"

"I hit a jitney driver."   30

    ■ ■ ■

The series stands at three all. We have split the fifth and sixth games. We are scrambling for property. Around the board we fairly fly. We move so fast because we do our own banking and search our own deeds. My opponent grows tense.

    ■ ■ ■

Ventnor Avenue, a street of delicatessens and doctors' offices, is leafy with plane trees and hydrangeas, the city flower. Water Works is on the mainland. The water comes over in submarine pipes. Electric Company gets power from across the state, on the Delaware River, in Deepwater. States Avenue, now a wasteland like St. Charles, once had gardens running down the middle of the street, a horse-drawn trolley, private homes. States Avenue was as exclusive as the Brighton. Only an apartment house, a small motel, and the All Wars Memorial Building — monadnocks spaced widely apart — stand along States Avenue now. Pawnshops, convalescent homes, and the Paradise Soul Saving Station are on Virginia Avenue. The soul-saving station is pink, orange, and yellow. In the windows flanking the door of the Virginia Money Loan Office are Nikons, Polaroids, Yashicas, Sony TVs, Underwood typewriters, Singer sewing machines, and pictures of Christ. On the far side of town, beside a single track and locked up most of the time, is the new railroad station, a small hut made of glazed firebrick, all that is left of the lines that built the city. An authentic phrenologist works on New York Avenue close to Frank's Extra Dry Bar and a church where the sermon today is "Death in the Pot." The church is of pink brick, has blue and amber windows and two red doors. St. James Place, narrow and twisting, is lined with boarding houses that have wooden porches on each of three stories, suggesting a New Orleans made of salt-bleached pine. In a vacant lot on Tennessee is a white Ford station wagon stripped to the chassis. The windows are smashed. A plastic Clorox bottle sits on the driver's seat. The wind has pressed newspaper against the chain-link fence around the lot. Atlantic Avenue, the city's principal thoroughfare, could be seventeen American Main Streets placed end to end — discount vitamins and Vienna Corset shops, movie theatres, shoe stores, and funeral homes. The Boardwalk is made of yellow pine and Douglas fir, soaked in pentachlorophenol. Downbeach, it reaches far beyond the city. Signs everywhere — on windows, lampposts, trash baskets — proclaim "Bienvenue Canadiens!" The salt air is full of Canadian French. In the Claridge Hotel, on Park Place, I ask a clerk if she knows where Marvin Gardens is. She says, "Is it a floral shop?" I ask a cabdriver, parked outside. He says, "Never heard of it." Park Place is one block long, Pacific to Boardwalk. On the roof of the Claridge is the Solarium, the highest point in town — panoramic view of the ocean, the bay, the salt-water ghetto. I look down at the rooftops of the side-avenue motels and into swimming pools. There are hundreds of people around the rooftop pools, sunbathing, reading — many more people than are on the beach. Walls, windows, and a block of sky are all that is visible from these pools — no sand, no sea. The pools are craters, and with the people around them they are countersunk into the motels.

▪   ▪   ▪

The seventh, and final, game is ten minutes old and I have hotels on Oriental, Vermont, and Connecticut. I have Tennessee and St. James. I have North Carolina and Pacific. I have Boardwalk, Atlantic, Ventnor, Illinois, Indiana. My fingers are forming a "V." I have mortgaged most of these properties in order to pay for others, and I have mortgaged the others to pay for the hotels. I have seven dollars. I will pay off the mortgages and build my reserves with income from the three hotels. My cash position may be low, but I feel like a rocket in an underground silo. Meanwhile, if I could just go to jail for a time I could pause there, wait there, until my opponent, in his inescapable rounds, pays the rates of my hotels. Jail, at times, is the strategic place to be. I roll boxcars from the Reading and move the flatiron to Community Chest. "Go to Jail. Go directly to Jail."

▪   ▪   ▪

The prisoners, of course, have no pens and no pencils. They take paper napkins, roll them tight as crayons, char the ends with matches, and write on the walls. The things they write are not entirely idiomatic; for example, "In God We Trust." All is in carbon. Time is required in the writing. "Only humanity could know of such pain." "God So Loved the World." "There is no greater pain than life itself." In the women's block now, there are six blacks, giggling, and a white asleep in red shoes. She is drunk. The others are pushers, prostitutes, an auto thief, a burglar caught with pistol in purse. A sixteen-year-old accused of murder was in here last week. These words are written on the wall of a now empty cell: "Laying here I see two bunks about six inches thick, not counting the one I'm laying on, which is hard as brick. No cushion for my back. No pillow for my head. Just a couple scratchy blankets which is best to use it's said. I wake up in the morning so shivery and cold, waiting and waiting till I am told the food is coming. It's on its way. It's not worth waiting for, but I eat it anyway. I know one thing when they set me free I'm gonna be good if it kills me."

※   ※   ※

How many years must a game be played to produce an Anthony J. Drexel   35 Biddle and chestnut geldings on the beach? About half a century was the original answer, from the first railroad to Biddle at his peak. Biddle, at his peak, hit an Atlantic City streetcar conductor with his fist, laid him out with one punch. This increased Biddle's legend. He did not go to jail. While John Philip Sousa led his band along the Boardwalk playing "The Stars and Stripes Forever" and Jack Dempsey ran up and down in training for his fight with Gene Tunney, the city crossed the high curve of its parabola. Al Capone held conventions here — upstairs with his sleeves rolled, apportioning among his lieutenant governors the states of the Eastern seaboard. The natural history of an American resort proceeds from Indians to French Canadians via Biddles and Capones. French Canadians, whatever they be at home, are Visigoths here. Bienvenue Visigoths!

※   ※   ※

My opponent plods along incredibly well. He has got his fourth railroad, and patiently, unbelievably, he has picked up my potential winners until he has blocked me everywhere but Marvin Gardens. He has avoided, in the fifty-dollar zoning, my increasingly petty hotels. His cash flow swells. His railroads are costing me two hundred dollars a minute. He is building hotels on States, Virginia, and St. Charles. He has temporarily reversed the current. With the yellow monopolies and my blue monopolies, I could probably defeat his lavenders and his railroads. I have Atlantic and Ventnor. I need Marvin Gardens. My only hope is Marvin Gardens.

※   ※   ※

There is a plaque at Boardwalk and Park Place, and on it in relief is the leonine profile of a man who looks like an officer in a metropolitan bank — "Charles B. Darrow, 1889–1967, inventor of the game of Monopoly." "Darrow," I address him, aloud. "Where is Marvin Gardens?" There is, of course, no answer. Bronze, impassive, Darrow looks south down the Boardwalk. "Mr. Darrow, please, where is Marvin Gardens?" Nothing. Not a sign. He just looks south down the Boardwalk.

※   ※   ※

My opponent accepts the trophy with his natural ease, and I make, from notes, remarks that are even less graceful than his.

※   ※   ※

Marvin Gardens is the one color-block Monopoly property that is not in Atlantic City. It is a suburb within a suburb, secluded. It is a planned compound of seventy-two handsome houses set on curvilinear private streets under yews and cedars, poplars and willows. The compound was built around 1920, in Margate, New Jersey, and consists of solid buildings of stucco, brick, and wood, with slate roofs, tile roofs, multimullioned porches, Giraldic towers, and Spanish grilles. Marvin Gardens, the ultimate outwash of Monopoly, is a citadel and sanctuary of the middle class. "We're heavily patrolled by police here. We don't take no chances. Me? I'm living here nine years. I paid seventeen thousand dollars and I've been offered thirty. Number one, I don't want to move. Number two, I don't need the money. I have four bedrooms, two and a half baths, front den, back den. No basement. The Atlantic is down there. Six feet down and you float. A lot of people have a hard time finding this place. People that lived in Atlantic City all their life don't know how to find it. They don't know where the hell they're going. They just know it's south, down the Boardwalk."

TALKING ABOUT IT

Seeing Metaphor: Revealing and Concealing

1. As McPhee jumps from the world of the game to the world of Atlantic City, how does he change your prior perceptions about the game of Monopoly?

2. What does he reveal about the relationship between the game and the place it represents? What does he conceal?

Seeing Composition: Frame, Line, Texture, Tone

1. Describe how McPhee structures the essay and the effect of the structure on your understanding of his search.

2. How does McPhee provide a line of continuity through his essay?

Seeing Meaning: Navigating and Negotiating

1. Describe how a board game you know mirrors life. What goals might game-makers have — even in games for children three to five years old — that mirror life? (Consider games like Chutes and Ladders or Candyland, for example.)

2. What significance is there for where McPhee locates Marvin Gardens compared to where he locates other places on the Monopoly board?

WRITING ABOUT IT

1. Imitate the general structure of McPhee's essay by writing about a board game in which you juxtapose the playing of the game and the life (events,

beliefs, attitudes, values) behind the game. What do you accept as true, good, valuable, and so forth when you play this game?

2. Monopoly is a game about capitalism in which players act out middle-class American values regarding property and ownership. Write about another board game in which you argue that the players act out values (social or political) particular to a culture or subculture.

Song

Brigit Pegeen Kelly

Brigit Pegeen Kelly is a poet who teaches in the creative writing program at the University of Illinois at Urbana-Champaign. She is the author of two collections of poetry, To the Place of Trumpets *(1988), for which she won the 1987 Yale Series of Younger Poets Prize, and* Song *(1995), which was the 1994 Lamont Poetry Selection of the Academy of American Poets. Her poems have appeared in many journals and anthologies, as well as in* Best American Poetry *and* The Pushcart Prize.

Listen: there was a goat's head hanging by ropes in a tree,
All night it hung there and sang. And those who heard it
Felt a hurt in their hearts and thought they were hearing
The song of a night bird. They sat up in their beds, and then
5   They lay back down again. In the night wind, the goat's head
Swayed back and forth, and from far off it shone faintly
The way the moonlight shone on the train track miles away
Beside which the goat's headless body lay. Some boys
Had hacked its head off. It was harder work than they had imagined.
10   The goat cried like a man and struggled hard. But they
Finished the job. They hung the bleeding head by the school
And then ran off into the darkness that seems to hide everything.
The head hung in the tree. The body lay by the tracks.
The head called to the body. The body to the head.
15   They missed each other. The missing grew large between them,
Until it pulled the heart right out of the body, until
The drawn heart flew toward the head, flew as a bird flies
Back to its cage and the familiar perch from which it trills.
Then the heart sang in the head, softly at first and then louder,
20   Sang long and low until the morning light came up over
The school and over the tree, and then the singing stopped. . . .
The goat had belonged to a small girl. She named
The goat Broken Thorn Sweet Blackberry, named it after
The night's bush of stars, because the goat's silky hair
25   Was dark as well water, because it had eyes like wild fruit.
The girl lived near a high railroad track. At night
She heard the trains passing, the sweet sound of the train's horn
Pouring softly over her bed, and each morning she woke
To give the bleating goat his pail of warm milk. She sang

Him songs about girls with ropes and cooks in boats. 30
She brushed him with a stiff brush. She dreamed daily
That he grew bigger, and he did. She thought her dreaming
Made it so. But one night the girl didn't hear the train's horn,
And the next morning she woke to an empty yard. The goat
Was gone. Everything looked strange. It was as if a storm 35
Had passed through while she slept, wind and stones, rain
Stripping the branches of fruit. She knew that someone
Had stolen the goat and that he had come to harm. She called
To him. All morning and into the afternoon, she called
And called. She walked and walked. In her chest a bad feeling 40
Like the feeling of the stones gouging the soft undersides
Of her bare feet. Then somebody found the goat's body
By the high tracks, the flies already filling their soft bottles
At the goat's torn neck. Then somebody found the head
Hanging in a tree by the school. They hurried to take 45
These things away so that the girl would not see them.
They hurried to raise money to buy the girl another goat.
They hurried to find the boys who had done this, to hear
Them say it was a joke, a joke, it was nothing but a joke. . . .
But listen: here is the point. The boys thought to have 50
Their fun and be done with it. It was harder work than they
Had imagined, this silly sacrifice, but they finished the job,
Whistling as they washed their large hands in the dark.
What they didn't know was that the goat's head was already
Singing behind them in the tree. What they didn't know 55
Was that the goat's head would go on singing, just for them,
Long after the ropes were down, and that they would learn to listen,
Pail after pail, stroke after patient stroke. They would
Wake in the night thinking they heard the wind in the trees
Or a night bird, but their hearts beating harder. There 60
Would be a whistle, a hum, a high murmur, and, at last, a song,
The low song a lost boy sings remembering his mother's call.
Not a cruel song, no, no, not cruel at all. This song
Is sweet. It is sweet. The heart dies of this sweetness.

TALKING ABOUT IT

Seeing Metaphor: Revealing and Concealing

1. What does Kelly's narrative reveal about the sense of "song"? What does it
   conceal? How might we understand "song" and "singing" in this poem?

2. The boys say, "It was a joke, a joke, it was nothing but a joke." Wherein lies the "joke" for them? Where was the fun? What, then, does their sense of "game" reveal about them?

Seeing Composition: Frame, Line, Texture, Tone

1. Kelly begins the narrative at the climactic center: the goat head singing in the tree. And she ends it there. Why begin with the most dramatic part of the story only to end on the same note?

2. How would you describe the tone in which the speaker tells her tale? How does it affect your response to "Song"?

Seeing Meaning: Navigating and Negotiating

1. There is none of the usual talk about guilt and punishment in the poem. The boys do not claim remorse, nor are they required to pay retribution through fines or community service, for example. Instead, they hear the goat's song, night after night. The speaker says, "Not a cruel song, no, no, not cruel at all. This song / Is sweet. It is sweet. The heart dies of this sweetness." What are the boys haunted by?

2. James P. Carse, a professor of religion and author of *Finite Games and Infinite Games,* claims that "no one plays a game alone." How might this statement apply to the joke that the boys play?

WRITING ABOUT IT

1. What some people call "only a joke" may be no joke at all to the victims. And as most everyone knows, it needn't be as cruel as what the boys do in "Song" to be painful. Depending on the player, the intended victim, and the occasion, even the mildest practical joke can cause harm.

   In your journal or in class discussion, list memories of pranks that you have observed or read about. Choose a story to tell in which you are an outsider, not a player or victim. You could, like Kelly, begin at the climactic center of the story, then go back and tell the story from the beginning. Then answer these questions: where was the fun for the player(s)? What did their sense of "game" reveal about them? Why do you remember this story?

2. Kelly reminds us that guilt and retribution can take mysterious, surprising forms. What someone may fear for herself or may wish for as revenge doesn't happen. Write about a time either you or someone else experienced a mysterious or surprising consequence for bad behavior. What did you expect to happen? What did happen? What did you make of the consequence and why?

You could exchange these stories with two other writers in class. Ask each to respond with another interpretation of the surprising consequence for bad behavior. After reading their responses, write about what you make of the similarities and differences in your classmates' and your interpretations.

The Killing Game

JOY WILLIAMS

Joy Williams is an essayist, short-story writer, and novelist whose books include Breaking and Entering *(1988) and* The Changeling *(1978). "The Killing Game" was first published in* Esquire *in 1990.*

Death and suffering are a big part of hunting. A big part. Not that you'd ever know it by hearing hunters talk. They tend to downplay the killing part. To kill is to put to death, extinguish, nullify, cancel, destroy. But from the hunter's point of view, it's just a tiny part of the experience. *The kill is the least important part of the hunt,* they often say, or, *Killing involves only a split second of the innumerable hours we spend surrounded by and observing nature* . . . For the animal, of course, the killing part is of considerably more importance. José Ortega y Gasset, in *Meditations on Hunting,* wrote, *Death is a sign of reality in hunting. One does not hunt in order to kill; on the contrary, one kills in order to have hunted.* This is the sort of intellectual blather that the "thinking" hunter holds dear. The conservation editor of *Field & Stream,* George Reiger, recently paraphrased this sentiment by saying, *We kill to hunt, and not the other way around,* thereby making it truly fatuous. A hunter in West Virginia, one Mr. Bill Neal, blazed through this philosophical fog by explaining why he blows the toes off tree raccoons so that they will fall down and be torn apart by his dogs. *That's the best part of it. It's not any fun just shooting them.*

Instead of monitoring animals — many animals in managed areas are tagged, tattooed, and wear radio transmitters — wildlife managers should start hanging telemetry gear around hunters' necks to study their attitudes and listen to their conversations. It would be grisly listening, but it would tune out for good the *suffering as sacrament* and *spiritual experience* blather that some hunting apologists employ. *The unease with which the good hunter inflicts death is an unease not merely with his conscience but with affirming his animality in the midst of his struggles toward humanity and clarity,* Holmes Rolston III drones on in his book *Environmental Ethics.*

There is a formula to this in literature — someone the protagonist loves has just died, so he goes out and kills an animal. This makes him feel better. But it's kind of a sad feeling-better. He gets to relate to Death and Nature in this way. Somewhat. But not really. Death is still a mystery. Well, it's hard to explain. It's sort of a semireligious thing . . . Killing and affirming, affirming and killing, it's just the cross the "good" hunter must bear. The bad hunter just has to deal with postkill letdown.

Many are the hunter's specious arguments. Less semireligious but a longstanding favorite with them is the vegetarian approach: you eat meat, don't you? If you say no, they feel they've got you — you're just a vegetarian attempting to impose your weird views on others. If you say yes, they accuse you of being hyp-ocritical, of allowing your genial A&P butcher to stand between you and reality. The fact is, the chief attraction of hunting is the pursuit and murder of ani-mals—the meat-eating aspect of it is trivial. If the hunter chooses to be *ethical* about it, he might cook his kill, but the meat of most animals is discarded. Dead bear can even be dangerous! A bear's heavy hide must be skinned at once to pre-vent meat spoilage. With effort, a hunter can make okay chili, *something to keep in mind,* a sports rag says, *if you take two skinny spring bears.*

As for subsistence hunting, please . . . Granted that there might be one 5 "good" hunter out there who conducts the kill as spiritual exercise and two others who are atavistic enough to want to supplement their Chicken McNuggets with venison, most hunters hunt for the hell of it.

For hunters, hunting is fun. Recreation is play. Hunting is recreation. Hunters kill for play, for entertainment. They kill for the thrill of it, to make an animal "theirs." (The Gandhian doctrine of nonpossession has never been a big hit with hunters.) The animal becomes the property of the hunter by its death. Alive, the beast belongs only to itself. This is unacceptable to the hunter. *He's yours . . . He's mine . . . I decided to . . . I decided not to . . . I debated shooting it, then I decided to let it live . . .* Hunters like beautiful creatures. A "beautiful" deer, elk, bear, cougar, bighorn sheep. A "beautiful" goose or mallard. Of course, they don't stay "beautiful" for long, particularly the birds. Many birds become rags in the air, shredded, blown to bits. *Keep shooting till they drop!* Hunters get a thrill out of seeing a plummeting bird, out of seeing it crumple and fall. *The big pheas-ant folded in classic fashion.* They get a kick out of "collecting" new species. *Why not add a unique harlequin duck to your collection?* Swan hunting is satisfying. *I let loose a three-inch Magnum. The large bird only flinched with my first shot and began to gain altitude. I frantically ejected the round, chambered another, and dropped the swan with my second shot. After retrieving the bird I was amazed by its size. The swan's six-foot wingspan, huge body, and long neck made it an impressive trophy.* Hunters like big animals, trophy animals. A "trophy" usually means that the hunter doesn't deign to eat it. Maybe he skins it or mounts it. Maybe he takes a picture. *We took pictures, we took pictures.* Maybe he just looks at it for a while. The disposition of the "experience" is up to the hunter. He's entitled to do what-ever he wishes with the damn thing. It's dead.

Hunters like categories they can tailor to their needs. There are the "good" animals—deer, elk, bear, moose—which are allowed to exist for the hunter's pleasure. Then there are the "bad" animals, the vermin, varmints, and "nuisance" animals, the rabbits and raccoons and coyotes and beavers and badgers, which are disencouraged to exist. The hunter can have fun killing them, but the pleasure is diminished because the animals aren't "magnificent."

Then there are the predators. These can be killed any time, because, hunters argue, they're predators, for godssakes.

Many people in South Dakota want to exterminate the red fox because it preys upon some of the ducks and pheasant they want to hunt and kill each year. They found that after they killed the wolves and coyotes, they had more foxes than they wanted. The ring-necked pheasant is South Dakota's state bird. No matter that it was imported from Asia specifically to be "harvested" for sport, it's South Dakota's state bird and they're proud of it. A group called Pheasants Unlimited gave some tips on how to hunt foxes. *Place a small amount of larvicide* [a grain fumigant] *on a rag and chuck it down the hole . . . The first pup generally comes out in fifteen minutes . . . Use a .22 to dispatch him . . . Remove each pup shot from the hole. Following gassing, set traps for the old fox who will return later in the evening . . .* Poisoning, shooting, trapping—they make up a sort of sportsman's triathlon.

10   In the hunting magazines, hunters freely admit the pleasure of killing to one another. *Undeniable pleasure radiated from her smile. The excitement of shooting the bear had Barb talking a mile a minute.* But in public, most hunters are becoming a little wary about raving on as to how much fun it is to kill things. Hunters have a tendency to call large animals by cute names—"bruins" and "muleys," "berry-fed blackies" and "handsome cusses" and "big guys," thereby implying a balanced jolly game of mutual satisfaction between the hunter and the hunted—*Bam, bam, bam, I get to shoot you and you get to be dead.* More often, though, when dealing with the nonhunting public, a drier, businesslike tone is employed. Animals become a "resource" that must be "utilized." Hunting becomes "a legitimate use of the resource." Animals become a product like wool or lumber or a crop like fruit or corn that must be "collected" or "taken" or "harvested." Hunters love to use the word *legitimate.* (Oddly, Tolstoy referred to hunting as "evil legitimized.") *A legitimate use, a legitimate form of recreation, a legitimate escape, a legitimate pursuit.* It's a word they trust will slam the door on discourse. Hunters are increasingly relying upon their spokesmen and supporters, state and federal game managers and wildlife officials, to employ the drone of a solemn bureaucratic language and toss around a lot of questionable statistics to assure the nonhunting public (93 percent!) that there's nothing to worry about. The pogrom is under control. The mass murder and manipulation of wild animals is just another business. Hunters are a tiny minority, and it's crucial to them that the millions of people who don't hunt not be awakened from their long sleep and become antihunting. Nonhunters are okay. Dweeby, probably, but okay. A hunter *can respect the rights* of a nonhunter. It's the "antis" he despises, those *misguided, emotional, not-in-possession-of-the-facts, uninformed zealots who don't understand nature . . . Those dime-store ecologists cloaked in ignorance and spurred by emotion . . . Those doggy-woggy types, who under the guise of being environmentalists and conservationists are working to deprive him of his precious right to kill.* (Sometimes it's just a *right;* sometimes it's a *God-given* right.) Antis can be scorned, but nonhunters must be pacified, and this is where

the number crunching of wildlife biologists and the scripts of *professional re-source managers* come in. Leave it to the professionals. They know what numbers are the good numbers. Utah determined that there were six hundred sandhill cranes in the state, so permits were issued to shoot one hundred of them. Don't want to have too many sandhill cranes. California wildlife officials reported "sufficient numbers" of mountain lions to "justify" renewing hunting, even though it doesn't take a rocket scientist to know the animal is extremely rare. (It's always a dark day for hunters when an animal is adjudged *rare.* How can its numbers be "controlled" through hunting if it scarcely exists?) A recent citizens' referendum prohibits the hunting of the mountain lion in perpetuity — not that the lions aren't killed anyway, in California and all over the West, hundreds of them annually by the government as part of the scandalous Animal Damage Control Program. Oh, to be the lucky hunter who gets to be an official government hunter and can legitimately kill animals his buddies aren't supposed to! Montana officials, led by K. L. Cool, that state's wildlife director, have definite ideas on the number of buffalo they feel can be tolerated. Zero is the number. Yellowstone National Park is the only place in America where bison exist, having been annihilated everywhere else. In the winter of 1988, nearly six hundred buffalo wandered out of the north boundary of the park and into Montana, where they were immediately shot at point-blank range by lottery-winning hunters. It was easy. And it was obvious from a video taken on one of the blow-away-the-bison days that the hunters had a heck of a good time. The buffalo, Cool says, threaten ranchers' livelihoods by doing damage to property — by which he means, I guess, that they eat the grass. Montana wants zero buffalo; it also wants zero wolves.

Large predators — including grizzlies, cougars, and wolves — are often the most "beautiful," the smartest and wildest animals of all. The gray wolf is both a supreme predator and an endangered species, and since the Supreme Court recently affirmed that ranchers have no constitutional right to kill endangered predators — apparently some God-given rights are not constitutional ones — this makes the wolf a more or less lucky dog. But not for long. A small population of gray wolves has recently established itself in northwestern Montana, primarily in Glacier National Park, and there is a plan, long a dream of conservationists, to "reintroduce" the wolf to Yellowstone. But to please ranchers and hunters, part of the plan would involve immediately removing the wolf from the endangered-species list. Beyond the park's boundaries, he could be hunted as a "game animal" or exterminated as a "pest." (Hunters kill to hunt, remember, except when they're hunting to kill.) The area of Yellowstone where the wolf would be restored is the same mountain and high-plateau country that is abandoned in winter by most animals, including the aforementioned luckless bison. Part of the plan, too, is compensation to ranchers if any of their far-ranging livestock is killed by a wolf. It's a real industry out there, apparently, killing and controlling and getting compensated for losing something under the Big Sky.

Wolves gotta eat — a fact that disturbs hunters. Jack Atcheson, an outfitter in Butte, said, *Some wolves are fine if there is control. But there never will be control. The wolf-control plan provided by the Fish and Wildlife Service speaks only of protecting domestic livestock. There is no plan to protect wildlife . . . There are no surplus deer or elk in Montana . . . Their numbers are carefully managed. With uncontrolled wolf populations, a lot of people will have to give up hunting just to feed wolves. Will you give up your elk permit for a wolf?*

It won't be long before hunters start demanding compensation for animals they aren't able to shoot.

Hunters believe that wild animals exist only to satisfy their wish to kill them. And it's so easy to kill them! The weaponry available is staggering, and the equipment and gear limitless. *The demand for big boomers has never been greater than right now, Outdoor Life crows, and the makers of rifles and cartridges are responding to the craze with a variety of light artillery that is virtually unprecedented in the history of sporting arms . . .* Hunters use grossly overpowered shotguns and rifles and compound bows. They rely on four-wheel-drive vehicles and three-wheel ATVs and airplanes . . . *He was interesting, the only moving, living creature on that limitless white expanse. I slipped a cartridge into the barrel of my rifle and threw the safety off . . .* They use snowmobiles to run down elk, and dogs to run down and tree cougars. It's easy to shoot an animal out of a tree. It's virtually impossible to miss a moose, a conspicuous and placid animal of steady habits . . . *I took a deep breath and pulled the trigger. The bull dropped. I looked at my watch: 8:22. The big guy was early. Mike started whooping and hollering and I joined him. I never realized how big a moose was until this one was on the ground. We took pictures . . .* Hunters shoot animals when they're resting . . . *Mike selected a deer, settled down to a steady rest, and fired. The buck was his when he squeezed the trigger. John decided to take the other buck, which had jumped up to its feet. The deer hadn't seen us and was confused by the shot echoing about in the valley. John took careful aim, fired, and took the buck. The hunt was over . . .* And they shoot them when they're eating . . . *The bruin ambled up the stream, checking gravel bars and backwaters for fish. Finally he plopped down on the bank to eat. Quickly, I tiptoed into range . . .* They use decoys and calls . . . *The six point gave me a cold-eyed glare from ninety steps away. I hit him with a 130-grain Sierra boat-tail handload. The bull went down hard. Our hunt was over . . .* They use sex lures . . . *The big buck raised its nose to the air, curled back its lips, and tested the scent of the doe's urine. I held my breath, fought back the shivers, and jerked off a shot. The 180-grain spire-point bullet caught the buck high on the back behind the shoulder and put it down. It didn't get up . . .* They use walkie-talkies, binoculars, scopes . . . *With my 308 Browning BLR, I steadied the 9X cross hairs on the front of the bear's massive shoulders and squeezed. The bear cartwheeled backward for fifty yards . . . The second Federal Premium 165-grain bullet found its mark. Another shot anchored the bear for good . . .* They bait deer with corn. They spread popcorn on golf courses for Canada geese and they douse meat baits with fry grease and honey for bears . . . *Make the baiting site redolent of inner-city doughnut shops.* They use blinds and tree stands and mobile stands. They go out in groups, in gangs, and employ "pushes" and "drives." So many methods are effective. So few rules apply. It's fun! . . . *We kept on repelling the swarms of birds as they came in looking for shelter from that big ocean wind, emptying our shell belts . . .* A species can, in the vernacular, be *pressured by hunting* (which means that killing them has decimated them), but that just increases the fun, the *challenge.* There is practically no criticism of conduct within the ranks . . . *It's mostly a matter of opinion and how hunters have been brought up to hunt . . .* Although a recent editorial in *Ducks Unlimited* magazine did venture to primly suggest that one should *not fall victim to greed-induced stress through piggish competition with others.*

But hunters are piggy. They just can't seem to help it. They're overequipped 15 . . . insatiable, malevolent, and vain. They maim and mutilate and despoil. And for the most part, they're inept. Grossly inept.

Camouflaged toilet paper is a must for the modern hunter, along with his Bronco and his beer. Too many hunters taking a dump in the woods with their roll of Charmin beside them were mistaken for white-tailed deer and shot. Hunters get excited. They'll shoot anything — the pallid ass of another sportsman or even themselves. A Long Island man died last year when his shotgun went off as he clubbed a wounded deer with the butt. Hunters get mad. They get restless and want to fire! They want to use those assault rifles and see foamy blood on the ferns. Wounded animals can travel for miles in fear and pain before they collapse. Countless gut-shot deer — *if you hear a sudden, squashy thump, the animal has probably been hit in the abdomen* — are "lost" each year. "Poorly placed shots" are frequent, and injured animals are seldom tracked, because most hunters never learned how to track. The majority of hunters will shoot at anything with four legs during deer season and anything with wings during duck season. Hunters try to nail running animals and distant birds. They become so overeager, so *aroused,* that they misidentify and misjudge, spraying their "game" with shots but failing to bring it down.

The fact is, hunters' lack of skill is a big, big problem. And nowhere is the problem worse than in the new glamour recreation, bow hunting. These guys are elitists. They doll themselves up in camouflage, paint their faces black, and climb up into tree stands from which they attempt the penetration of deer, elk, and turkeys with modern, multiblade, broadhead arrows shot from sophisticated, easy-to-draw compound bows. This "primitive" way of hunting appeals to many, and even the nonhunter may feel that it's a "fairer" method, requiring more strength and skill, but bow hunting is the cruelest, most wanton form of wildlife disposal of all. Studies conducted by state fish and wildlife departments repeatedly show that bow hunters wound and fail to retrieve as many animals as they kill. An animal that flees, wounded by an arrow, will most assuredly die of the wound, but it will be days before he does. Even with a "good" hit, the time elapsed between the strike and death is exceedingly long. *The rule of thumb has long been that we should wait thirty to forty-five minutes on heart and lung hits, an hour or more on a suspected liver hit, eight to twelve hours on paunch hits, and that we should follow immediately on hindquarter and other muscle-only hits, to keep the wound open and bleeding,* is the advice in the magazine *Fins and Feathers.* What the hunter does as he hangs around waiting for his animal to finish with its terrified running and dying hasn't been studied — maybe he puts on more makeup, maybe he has a highball.

Wildlife agencies promote and encourage bow hunting by permitting earlier and longer seasons, even though they are well aware that, in their words, *crippling is a by-product of the sport,* making archers pretty sloppy for elitists. The broadhead arrow is a very inefficient killing tool. Bow hunters are trying to deal with this problem with the suggestion that they use poison pods. These poisoned arrows are illegal in all states except Mississippi (*Ah'm gonna get ma deer even if ah just nick the little bastard*), but they're widely used anyway. You wouldn't want that deer to suffer, would you?

The mystique of the efficacy and decency of the bow hunter is as much an illusion as the perception that a waterfowler is a refined and thoughtful fellow, a *romantic aesthete,* as Vance Bourjaily put it, equipped with his faithful Labs and a love for the solitude and wild places. More sentimental drivel has been written about bird shooting than any other type of hunting. It's a soul-wrenching pursuit, apparently, the execution of birds in flight. Ducks Unlimited — an organization that has managed to put a spin on the word *conservation* for years — works hard to project the idea that duck hunters are blue bloods and that duck stamps with their pretty pictures are responsible for saving all the saved puddles in North America. *Sportsman's conservation* is a contradiction in terms (We protect things now so that we can kill them later) and is broadly interpreted (Don't kill them all, just kill most of them). A hunter is a conservationist in the same way a farmer or a rancher is: he's not. Like the rancher who kills everything that's not stock on his (and the public's) land, and the farmer who scorns wildlife because "they don't pay their freight," the hunter uses nature by destroying its parts, mastering it by simplifying it through death.

20   George ("We kill to hunt and not the other way around") Reiger, the conservationist-hunter's spokesman (he's the best they've got, apparently), said that the "dedicated" waterfowler will shoot other game "of course," but *we do so much in the same spirit of the lyrics, that when we're not near the girl we love, we love the girl we're near.* (Duck hunters practice tough love.) The fact is, far from being a "romantic aesthete," the waterfowler is the most avaricious of all hunters . . . *That's when Scott suggested the friendly wager on who would take the most birds . . .* and the

most resistant to minimum ecological decency. Millions of birds that managed to elude shotgun blasts were dying each year from ingesting the lead shot that rained down in the wetlands. Year after year, birds perished from feeding on spent lead, but hunters were "reluctant" to switch to steel. They worried that it would impair their shooting, and ammunition manufacturers said a changeover would be "expensive." State and federal officials had to weigh the poisoning against these considerations. It took forever, this weighing, but now steel-shot loads are required almost everywhere, having been judged "more than adequate" to bring down the birds. This is not to say, of course, that most duck hunters use steel shot almost everywhere. They're traditionalists and don't care for all the new, pesky rules. Oh, for the golden age of waterfowling, when a man could measure a good day's shooting by the pickup load. But those days are gone. Fall is a melancholy time, all right.

Spectacular abuses occur wherever geese congregate, Shooting Sportsman notes quietly, something that the more cultivated Ducks Unlimited would hesitate to admit. Waterfowl populations are plummeting and waterfowl hunters are out of control. "Supervised" hunts are hardly distinguished from unsupervised ones. A biologist with the Department of the Interior who observed a hunt at Sand Lake in South Dakota said, *Hunters repeatedly shot over the line at incoming flights where there was no possible chance of retrieving. Time and time again I was shocked at the behavior of hunters. I heard them laugh at the plight of dazed cripples that stumbled about. I saw them striking the heads of retrieved cripples against fence posts.* In the South, wood ducks return to their roosts after sunset when shooting hours are closed. Hunters find this an excellent time to shoot them. Dennis Anderson, an outdoors writer, said, *Roost shooters just fire at the birds as fast as they can, trying to drop as many as they can. Then they grab what birds they can find. The birds they can't find in the dark, they leave behind.*

Carnage and waste are the rules in bird hunting, even during legal seasons and open hours. Thousands of wounded ducks and geese are not retrieved, left to rot in the marshes and fields . . . *When I asked Wanda where hers had fallen, she wasn't sure.* Cripples, and there are many cripples made in this pastime, are still able to run and hide, eluding the hunter even if he's willing to spend time searching for them, which he usually isn't . . . *It's one thing to run down a cripple in a picked bean field or a pasture, and quite another to watch a wing-tipped bird drop into a huge block of switch grass.* Oh nasty, nasty switch grass. A downed bird becomes invisible on the ground and is practically unfindable without a good dog, and few "waterfowlers" have them these days. They're hard to train — usually a professional has to do it — and most hunters can't be bothered. Birds are easy to tumble . . . *Canada geese — blues and snows — can all take a good amount of shot. Brant are easily called and decoyed and come down easily. Ruffed grouse are hard to hit but easy to kill. Sharptails are harder to kill but easier to hit* . . . It's just a nuisance to recover them. But it's fun, fun, fun swatting them down . . . *There's distinct pleasure in watching a flock work to a good friend's gun.*

Teal, the smallest of common ducks, are really easy to kill. Hunters in the South used to *practice* on teal in September, prior to the "serious" waterfowl season. But the birds were so diminutive and the limit so low (four a day) that many hunters felt it hardly worth going out and getting bit by mosquitoes to kill them. Enough did, however, brave the bugs and manage to "harvest" 165,000 of the little migrating birds in Louisiana in 1987 alone. *Shooting is usually best on opening day. By the second day you can sometimes detect a decline in local teal numbers. Areas may deteriorate to virtually no action by the third day* . . . The area *deteriorates.* When a flock is wiped out, the skies are empty. *No action.*

Teal declined more sharply than any duck species except mallard last year; this baffles hunters. Hunters and their procurers — wildlife agencies — will *never* admit that hunting is responsible for the decimation of a species. John Turner, head of the federal Fish and Wildlife Service, delivers the familiar and litanic line. Hunting is not the problem. *Pollution* is the problem. *Pesticides, urbanization, deforestation, hazardous waste,* and *wetlands destruction* are the problem. And drought! There's been a big drought! Antis should devote their energies to solving these problems if they care about wildlife, and leave the hunters alone. While the Fish and Wildlife Service is busily conducting experiments in cause and effect, like releasing mallard ducklings on a wetland sprayed with the insecticide ethyl parathion (they died — it was known they would, but you can never have enough studies that show guns aren't a duck's only problem), hunters are killing some 200 million birds and animals each year. But these deaths are incidental to the problem, according to Turner. A factor, perhaps, but a *minor* one. Ducks Unlimited says the problem isn't hunting, it's *low recruitment* on the part of the birds. To the hunter, *birth* in the animal kingdom is *recruitment.* They wouldn't want to use an emotional, sentimental word like *birth.* The black duck, a very "popular" duck in the Northeast, so "popular," in fact, that game agencies felt that hunters couldn't be asked to refrain from shooting it, is scarce and getting scarcer. Nevertheless, it's still being hunted. *A number of studies are currently under way in an attempt to discover why black ducks are disappearing, Sports Afield* reports. Black ducks are disappearing because they've been shot out, their elimination being a dreadful example of game management, and managers who are loath to "displease" hunters. The skies — *flyways* — of America have been divided into four administrative regions, and the states, advised by the federal government coordinator, have to agree on policies.

25   There's always a lot of squabbling that goes on in flyway meetings — lots of complaints about short-stopping, for example. Short-stopping is the deliberate holding of birds in a state, often by feeding them in wildlife refuges, so that their southern migration is slowed or stopped. Hunters in the North get to kill more than hunters in the South. This isn't fair. Hunters demand equity in opportunities to kill.

Wildlife managers hate closing the season on anything. Closing the season on a species would indicate a certain amount of *mis*management and misjudgment at the very least—a certain reliance on overly optimistic winter counts, a certain overappeasement of hunters who would be "upset" if they couldn't kill their favorite thing. And worse, closing a season would be considered victory for the antis. Bird-hunting "rules" are very complicated, but they all encourage killing. There are shortened seasons and split seasons and special seasons for "underutilized" birds. (Teal were very recently considered "underutilized.") The limit on coots is fifteen a day—shooting them, it's easy! They don't fly high—giving the hunter something to do while he waits in the blind. Some species are "protected," but bear in mind that hunters begin blasting away one half hour before sunrise and that most hunters can't identify a bird in the air even in broad daylight. Some of them can't identify birds in hand either, and even if they can (#%! *I got me a canvasback, that duck's frigging protected . . .*), they are likely to bury unpopular or "trash" ducks so that they can continue to hunt the ones they "love."

Game "professionals," in thrall to hunters' "needs," will not stop managing bird populations until they've doled out the final duck (*I didn't get my limit but I bagged the last one, by golly . . .*). The Fish and Wildlife Service services legal hunters as busily as any madam, but it is powerless in tempering the lusts of the illegal ones. Illegal kill is a monumental problem in the not-so-wonderful world of waterfowl. Excesses have always pervaded the "sport," and bird shooters have historically been the slobs and profligates of hunting. *Doing away with hunting would do away with a vital cultural and historical aspect of American life,* John Turner claims. So, do away with it. Do away with those who have already done away with so much. Do away with them before the birds they have pursued so relentlessly and for so long drop into extinction, sink, in the poet Wallace Stevens's words, "downward to darkness on extended wings."

"Quality" hunting is as rare as the Florida panther. What you've got is a bunch of guys driving over the plains, up the mountains, and through the woods with their stupid tag that cost them a couple of bucks and immense coolers full of beer and body parts. There's a price tag on the right to destroy living creatures for play, but it's not much. *A big-game hunting license is the greatest deal going since the Homestead Act,* Ted Kerasote writes in *Sports Afield. In many states residents can hunt big game for more than a month for about $20.* It's cheaper than taking the little woman out to lunch. It's cheap all right, and it's because killing animals is considered *recreation* and is underwritten by state and federal funds. In Florida, state moneys are routinely spent on "youth hunts," in which kids are guided to shoot deer from stands in wildlife-management areas. The organizers of these events say that these staged hunts *help youth to understand man's role in the ecosystem.* (Drop a doe and take your place in the ecological community, son . . .)

Hunters claim (they don't actually believe it but they've learned to say it) that they're doing nonhunters a favor, for if they didn't *use* wild animals, wild animals would be useless. They believe that they're just *helping Mother Nature control populations* (*you wouldn't want those deer to die of starvation, would you?*). They claim that their tiny fees provide *all* Americans with wild lands and animals. (People who don't hunt get to enjoy the animals all year round while hunters get to enjoy them only during hunting season . . .) Ducks Unlimited feels that it, in particular, is a selfless provider and environmental champion. Although members spend most of their money lobbying for hunters and raising ducks in pens to release later over shooting fields, they do save some wetlands, mostly by persuading farmers not to fill them in. *See that little pothole there the ducks like? Well, I'm gonna plant more soybeans there if you don't pay me not to . . .* Hunters claim many nonsensical things, but the most nonsensical of all is that they *pay their own way.* They do not pay their own way. They *do* pay into a perverse wildlife-management system that manipulates "stocks" and "herds" and "flocks" for hunters' killing pleasure, but these fees in no way cover the cost of highly questionable ecological practices. For some spare change . . . *the greatest deal going* . . . hunters can hunt on public lands — national parks, state forests — preserves for hunters! — which the nonhunting and antihunting public pay for. (Access to private lands is becoming increasingly difficult for them, as experience has taught people that hunters are obnoxious.) Hunters kill on millions of acres of land all over America that are maintained with general taxpayer revenue, but the most shocking, really twisted subsidization takes place on national wildlife refuges. Nowhere is the arrogance and the insidiousness of this small, aggressive minority more clearly demonstrated. Nowhere is the murder of animals, the manipulation of language, and the distortion of public intent more flagrant. The public perceives national wildlife refuges as safe havens, as sanctuaries for animals. And why wouldn't they? The word *refuge* of course *means* shelter from danger and distress. But the dweeby nonhunting public — they tend to be so literal. The word has been reinterpreted by management over time and now hunters are invited into more than half of the country's more than 440 wildlife "sanctuaries" each year to bang them up and kill more than half a million animals. This is called *wildlife-oriented recreation.* Hunters think of this as being no less than their due, claiming that refuge lands were purchased with duck stamps (. . . *our duck stamps paid for it* . . . *our duck stamps paid for it* . . .). Hunters equate those stupid stamps with the mystic, multiplying power of the Lord's loaves and fishes, but of 90 million acres in the Wildlife Refuge System, only 3 million were bought with hunting-stamp revenue. Most wildlife "restoration" programs in the states are translated into clearing land to increase deer habitats (so that too many deer will require hunting . . . you wouldn't want them to die of starvation, would you?) and trapping animals for restocking and study (so hunters can shoot more of them). Fish and game agencies hustle hunting — instead of conserving wildlife, they're killing it. It's time for them to get in the business of protecting and preserving wildlife and creating balanced ecological systems instead of pimping for hunters who want their deer/duck/pheasant/turkey — animals stocked to be shot.

Hunters' self-serving arguments and lies are becoming more preposterous 30 as nonhunters awake from their long, albeit troubled, sleep. Sport hunting is immoral; it should be made illegal. Hunters are persecutors of nature who should be prosecuted. They wield a disruptive power out of all proportion to their numbers, and pandering to their interests — the special interests of a group that just wants to kill things — is mad. It's preposterous that every year less than 7 percent of the population turns the skies into shooting galleries and the woods and fields into abattoirs. It's time to stop actively supporting and passively allowing hunting, and time to stigmatize it. It's time to stop being conned and cowed by hunters, time to stop pampering and coddling them, time to get them off the government's duck-and-deer dole, time to stop thinking of wild animals as "resources" and "game," and start thinking of them as sentient beings that deserve our wonder and respect, time to stop allowing hunting to be creditable by calling it "sport" and "recreation." Hunters make wildlife *dead, dead, dead.* It's time to wake up to this indisputable fact. As for the hunters, it's long past checkout time.

TALKING ABOUT IT

Seeing Metaphor: Revealing and Concealing

1. In this essay, we enter a realm of games that are considered sport only by a segment of a given population. How might "sport" be defined differently by hunting enthusiasts than by antihunting groups? How do the criteria for defining "sport" differ? What are some other activities that, like hunting, are debatable as sports?

2. One definition of game is "prey." We talk about "hunting game," in which "game" refers to the object of our pursuit. We also use "game" to mean "play" or "sport." How does Williams play on both of these senses of "game" in her title? What is revealed about her point of view in choosing "killing" rather than "hunting"?

Seeing Composition: Frame, Line, Texture, Tone

1. Beyond how you personally feel about hunting, discuss the strength of Williams's examples to support her argument. How do various terms used by conservationists and hunters serve Williams's own argument about the sport of hunting?

2. How does the use of italics function in this essay? For what audiences is it most effective?

Seeing Meaning: Navigating and Negotiating

1. To the extent that "game" as "prey" has a literal application in hunting, how does it affect the way you see it in contrast to board games, computer games, or games we play as children in which hunting is an imagined event? How might those kinds of games affect your response to real hunting as "game" or "sport"?

2. Describe a game, sport, or recreation that you cannot sanction. Give reasons and illustrations to support your belief.

WRITING ABOUT IT

1. Hunting is not the only debatable sport. Argue against labeling some other activity a "sport" or a "game." In your argument, you'll need to define those terms from the opposing point of view and from your own. You might argue, for example, that staging animal races or fights is cruel, or that bungee-jumping and other such risk-taking activities are not sports. If you can, try to play on the terms used by enthusiasts of the sport to serve your own argument, the way Williams does in her essay.

2. Instead of arguing to persuade a particular audience that one point of view is superior to another, try to present both sides of the issue for the purpose of understanding. Choose a sport or game over which there is some debate. This might be a good opportunity for collaborative writing: in pairs, each writer could take one stance. After each has written a draft of reasons and support for one point of view, the authors could work together to balance each other's argument and to form, therefore, a synthesis of views.

The Hitchhiking Game

MILAN KUNDERA

Milan Kundera is a Czech author now living in France whose novels include The Unbearable Lightness of Being *(1984) and* Immortality *(1990). "The Hitchhiking Game" appeared in his first collection of stories,* Laughable Loves *(1984).*

1

The needle on the gas gauge suddenly dipped toward empty and the young driver of the sports car declared that it was maddening how much gas the car ate up. "See that we don't run out of gas again," protested the girl (about twenty-two), and reminded the driver of several places where this had already happened to them. The young man replied that he wasn't worried, because whatever he went through with her had the charm of adventure for him. The girl objected; whenever they had run out of gas on the highway it had, she said, always been an adventure only for her. The young man had hidden and she had had to make ill use of her charms by thumbing a ride and letting herself be driven to the nearest gas station, then thumbing a ride back with a can of gas. The young man asked the girl whether the drivers who had given her a ride had been unpleasant, since she spoke as if her task had been a hardship. She replied (with awkward flirtatiousness) that sometimes they had been *very* pleasant but that it hadn't done her any good as she had been burdened with the can and had had to leave them before she could get anything going. "Pig," said the young man. The girl protested that she wasn't a pig, but that he really was. God knows how many girls stopped him on the highway, when he was driving the car alone! Still driving, the young man put his arm around the girl's shoulders and kissed her gently on the forehead. He knew that she loved him and that she was jealous. Jealousy isn't a pleasant quality, but if it isn't overdone (and if it's combined with modesty), apart from its inconvenience there's even something touching about it. At least that's what the young man thought. Because he was only twenty-eight, it seemed to him that he was old and knew everything that a man could know about women. In the girl sitting beside him he valued precisely what, until now, he had met with least in women: purity.

The needle was already on empty, when to the right the young man caught sight of a sign, announcing that the station was a quarter of a mile ahead. The girl hardly had time to say how relieved she was before the young man was signaling left and driving into a space in front of the pumps. However, he had to stop a little way off, because beside the pumps was a huge gasoline truck with a large metal tank and a bulky hose, which was refilling the pumps. "We'll have to wait," said the young man to the girl and got out of the car. "How long will it take?" he shouted to the man in overalls. "Only a moment," replied the attendant, and the young man said: "I've heard that one before." He wanted to go back and sit in the car, but he saw that the girl had gotten out the other side. "I'll take a little walk in the meantime," she said. "Where to?" the young man asked on purpose, wanting to see the girl's embarrassment. He had known her for a year now but she would still get shy in front of him. He enjoyed her moments of shyness, partly because they distinguished her from the women he'd met before, partly because he was aware of the law of universal transience, which made even his girl's shyness a precious thing to him.

2

The girl really didn't like it when during the trip (the young man would drive for several hours without stopping) she had to ask him to stop for a moment somewhere near a clump of trees. She always got angry when, with feigned surprise, he asked her why he should stop. She knew that her shyness was ridiculous and old-fashioned. Many times at work she had noticed that they laughed at her on account of it and deliberately provoked her. She always got shy in advance at the thought of how she was going to get shy. She often longed to feel free and easy about her body, the way most of the women around her did. She had even invented a special course in self-persuasion: she would repeat to herself that at birth every human being received one out of the millions of available bodies, as one would receive an allotted room out of the millions of rooms in an enormous hotel. Consequently, the body was fortuitous and impersonal, it was only a ready-made, borrowed thing. She would repeat this to herself in different ways, but she could never manage to feel it. This mind-body dualism was alien to her. She was too much one with her body; that is why she always felt such anxiety about it.

She experienced this same anxiety even in her relations with the young man, whom she had known for a year and with whom she was happy, perhaps because he never separated her body from her soul and she could live with him *wholly*. In this unity there was happiness, but right behind the happiness lurked suspicion, and the girl was full of that. For instance, it often occurred to her that the other women (those who weren't anxious) were more attractive and more seductive and that the young man, who did not conceal the fact that he knew this kind of woman well, would someday leave her for a woman like that. (True, the young man declared that he'd had enough of them to last his whole life, but she knew that he was still much younger than he thought.) She wanted him to be completely hers and she to be completely his, but it often seemed to her that the more she tried to give him everything, the more she denied him something: the very thing that a light and superficial love or a flirtation gives to a person. It worried her that she was not able to combine seriousness with lightheartedness.

5   But now she wasn't worrying and any such thoughts were far from her mind. She felt good. It was the first day of their vacation (of their two-week vacation,

about which she had been dreaming for a whole year), the sky was blue (the whole year she had been worrying about whether the sky would really be blue), and he was beside her. At his, "Where to?" she blushed, and left the car without a word. She walked around the gas station, which was situated beside the highway in total isolation, surrounded by fields. About a hundred yards away (in the direction in which they were traveling), a wood began. She set off for it, vanished behind a little bush, and gave herself up to her good mood. (In solitude it was possible for her to get the greatest enjoyment from the presence of the man she loved. If his presence had been continuous, it would have kept on disappearing. Only when alone was she able to *hold on* to it.)

When she came out of the wood onto the highway, the gas station was visible. The large gasoline truck was already pulling out and the sports car moved forward toward the red turret of the pump. The girl walked on along the highway and only at times looked back to see if the sports car was coming. At last she caught sight of it. She stopped and began to wave at it like a hitchhiker waving at a stranger's car. The sports car slowed down and stopped close to the girl. The young man leaned toward the window, rolled it down, smiled, and asked, "Where are you headed, miss?" "Are you going to Bystritsa?" asked the girl, smiling flirtatiously at him. "Yes, please get in," said the young man, opening the door. The girl got in and the car took off.

3

The young man was always glad when his girl friend was gay. This didn't happen too often; she had a quite tiresome job in an unpleasant environment, many hours of overtime without compensatory leisure and, at home, a sick mother. So she often felt tired. She didn't have either particularly good nerves or self-confidence and easily fell into a state of anxiety and fear. For this reason he welcomed every manifestation of her gaiety with the tender solicitude of a foster parent. He smiled at her and said: "I'm lucky today. I've been driving for five years, but I've never given a ride to such a pretty hitchhiker."

The girl was grateful to the young man for every bit of flattery; she wanted to linger for a moment in its warmth and so she said, "You're very good at lying."

"Do I look like a liar?"

"You look like you enjoy lying to women," said the girl, and into her words 10 there crept unawares a touch of the old anxiety, because she really did believe that her young man enjoyed lying to women.

The girl's jealousy often irritated the young man, but this time he could easily overlook it, for, after all, her words didn't apply to him but to the unknown driver. And so he just casually inquired, "Does it bother you?"

"If I were going with you, then it would bother me," said the girl and her words contained a subtle, instructive message for the young man; but the end of her sentence applied only to the unknown driver, "but I don't know you, so it doesn't bother me."

"Things about her own man always bother a woman more than things about a stranger" (this was now the young man's subtle, instructive message to the girl), "so seeing that we are strangers, we could get on well together."

The girl purposely didn't want to understand the implied meaning of his message, and so she now addressed the unknown driver exclusively:

15   "What does it matter, since we'll part company in a little while?"

"Why?" asked the young man.

"Well, I'm getting out at Bystritsa."

"And what if I get out with you?"

At these words the girl looked up at him and found that he looked exactly as she imagined him in her most agonizing hours of jealousy. She was alarmed at how he was flattering her and flirting with her (an unknown hitchhiker), and *how becoming it was to him*. Therefore she responded with defiant provocativeness, "What would *you* do with me, I wonder?"

20   "I wouldn't have to think too hard about what to do with such a beautiful woman," said the young man gallantly and at this moment he was once again speaking far more to his own girl than to the figure of the hitchhiker.

But this flattering sentence made the girl feel as if she had caught him at something, as if she had wheedled a confession out of him with a fraudulent trick. She felt toward him a brief flash of intense hatred and said, "Aren't you rather too sure of yourself?"

The young man looked at the girl. Her defiant face appeared to him to be completely convulsed. He felt sorry for her and longed for her usual, familiar expression (which he used to call childish and simple). He leaned toward her, put his arm around her shoulders, and softly spoke the name with which he usually addressed her and with which he now wanted to stop the game.

But the girl released herself and said: "You're going a bit too fast!"

At this rebuff the young man said: "Excuse me, miss," and looked silently in front of him at the highway.

4

25   The girl's pitiful jealousy, however, left her as quickly as it had come over her. After all, she was sensible and knew perfectly well that all this was merely a game. Now it even struck her as a little ridiculous that she had repulsed her man out of jealous rage. It wouldn't be pleasant for her if he found out why she had done it. Fortunately women have the miraculous ability to change the meaning of their actions after the event. Using this ability, she decided that she had repulsed him not out of anger but so that she could go on with the game, which, with its whimsicality, so well suited the first day of their vacation.

So again she was the hitchhiker, who had just repulsed the overenterprising driver, but only so as to slow down his conquest and make it more exciting. She half turned toward the young man and said caressingly:

"I didn't mean to offend you, mister!"

"Excuse me, I won't touch you again," said the young man.

He was furious with the girl for not listening to him and refusing to be herself when that was what he wanted. And since the girl insisted on continuing in her role, he transferred his anger to the unknown hitchhiker whom she was portraying. And all at once he discovered the character of his own part: he stopped making the gallant remarks with which he had wanted to flatter his girl in a roundabout way, and began to play the tough guy who treats women to the coarser aspects of his masculinity: willfulness, sarcasm, self-assurance.

This role was a complete contradiction of the young man's habitually so- 30 licitous approach to the girl. True, before he had met her, he had in fact behaved roughly rather than gently toward women. But he had never resembled a heartless tough guy, because he had never demonstrated either a particularly strong will or ruthlessness. However, if he did not resemble such a man, nonetheless he had *longed* to at one time. Of course it was a quite naive desire, but there it was. Childish desires withstand all the snares of the adult mind and often survive into ripe old age. And this childish desire quickly took advantage of the opportunity to embody itself in the proffered role.

The young man's sarcastic reserve suited the girl very well — it freed her from herself. For she herself was, above all, the epitome of jealousy. The moment she stopped seeing the gallantly seductive young man beside her and saw only his inaccessible face, her jealously subsided. The girl could forget herself and give herself up to her role.

Her role? What was her role? It was a role out of trashy literature. The hitchhiker stopped the car not to get a ride, but to seduce the man who was driving the car. She was an artful seductress, cleverly knowing how to use her charms. The girl slipped into this silly, romantic part with an ease that astonished her and held her spellbound.

5

There was nothing the young man missed in his life more than lightheartedness. The main road of his life was drawn with implacable precision. His job didn't use up merely eight hours a day, it also infiltrated the remaining time with the compulsory boredom of meetings and home study, and, by means of the attentiveness of his countless male and female colleagues, it infiltrated the wretchedly little time he had left for his private life as well. This private life never remained secret and sometimes even became the subject of gossip and public discussion. Even two weeks' vacation didn't give him a feeling of liberation and adventure; the gray shadow of precise planning lay even here. The scarcity of summer accommodations in our country compelled him to book a room in the Tatras six months in advance, and since for that he needed a recommendation from his office, its omnipresent brain thus did not cease knowing about him even for an instant.

He had become reconciled to all this, yet all the same from time to time the terrible thought of the straight road would overcome him — a road along which he was being pursued, where he was visible to everyone, and from which he could not turn aside. At this moment that thought returned to him. Through an odd and brief conjunction of ideas the figurative road became identified with the real high-way along which he was driving — and this led him suddenly to do a crazy thing.

35   "Where did you say you wanted to go?" he asked the girl.

"To Banska Bystritsa," she replied.

"And what are you going to do there?"

"I have a date there."

"Who with?"

40   "With a certain gentleman."

The car was just coming to a large crossroads. The driver slowed down so he could read the road signs, then turned off to the right.

"What will happen if you don't arrive for that date?"

"It would be your fault and you would have to take care of me."

"You obviously didn't notice that I turned off in the direction of Nove Zamky."

45   "Is that true? You've gone crazy!"

"Don't be afraid, I'll take care of you," said the young man.

So they drove and chatted thus — the driver and the hitchhiker who did not know each other.

The game all at once went into a higher gear. The sports car was moving away not only from the imaginary goal of Banska Bystritsa, but also from the real goal, toward which it had been heading in the morning: the Tatras and the room that had been booked. Fiction was suddenly making an assault upon real life. The young man was moving away from himself and from the implacable straight road, from which he had never strayed until now.

"But you said you were going to the Low Tatras!" The girl was surprised.

50   "I am going, miss, wherever I feel like going. I'm a free man and I do what I want and what it pleases me to do."

6

When they drove into Nove Zamky it was already getting dark.

The young man had never been here before and it took him a while to orient himself. Several times he stopped the car and asked the passersby directions to the hotel. Several streets had been dug up, so that the drive to the hotel, even though it was quite close by (as all those who had been asked asserted), necessitated so many detours and roundabout routes that it was almost a quarter of an hour before they finally stopped in front of it. The hotel looked unprepossessing, but it was the only one in town and the young man didn't feel like driving on. So he said to the girl, "Wait here," and got out of the car.

Out of the car he was, of course, himself again. And it was upsetting for him to find himself in the evening somewhere completely different from his intended destination—the more so because no one had forced him to do it and as a matter of fact he hadn't even really wanted to. He blamed himself for this piece of folly, but then became reconciled to it. The room in the Tatras could wait until tomorrow and it wouldn't do any harm if they celebrated the first day of their vacation with something unexpected.

He walked through the restaurant—smoky, noisy, and crowded—and asked for the reception desk. They sent him to the back of the lobby near the staircase, where behind a glass panel a superannuated blonde was sitting beneath a board full of keys. With difficulty, he obtained the key to the only room left.

The girl, when she found herself alone, also threw off her role. She didn't feel ill-humored, though, at finding herself in an unexpected town. She was so devoted to the young man that she never had doubts about anything he did, and confidently entrusted every moment of her life to him. On the other hand the idea once again popped into her mind that perhaps—just as she was now doing—other women had waited for her man in his car, those women whom he met on business trips. But surprisingly enough this idea didn't upset her at all now. In fact, she smiled at the thought of how nice it was that today she was this other woman, this irresponsible, indecent other woman, one of those women of whom she was so jealous. It seemed to her that she was cutting them all out, that she had learned how to use their weapons; how to give the young man what until now she had not known how to give him: lightheartedness, shamelessness, and dissoluteness. A curious feeling of satisfaction filled her, because she alone had the ability to be all women and in this way (she alone) could completely captivate her lover and hold his interest.

The young man opened the car door and led the girl into the restaurant. Amid the din, the dirt, and the smoke he found a single, unoccupied table in a corner.

7

"So how are you going to take care of me now?" asked the girl provocatively. "What would you like for an aperitif?"

The girl wasn't too fond of alcohol, still she drank a little wine and liked vermouth fairly well. Now, however, she purposely said: "Vodka."

"Fine," said the young man. "I hope you won't get drunk on me."

"And if I do?" said the girl.

The young man did not reply but called over a waiter and ordered two vodkas and two steak dinners. In a moment the waiter brought a tray with two small glasses and placed it in front of them.

The man raised his glass, "To you!"

"Can't you think of a wittier toast?"

65   Something was beginning to irritate him about the girl's game. Now sitting face to face with her, he realized that it wasn't just the *words* which were turning her into a stranger, but that her *whole persona* had changed, the movements of her body and her facial expression, and that she unpalatably and faithfully resembled that type of woman whom he knew so well and for whom he felt some aversion.

And so (holding his glass in his raised hand), he corrected his toast: "O.K., then I won't drink to you, but to your kind, in which are combined so successfully the better qualities of the animal and the worst aspects of the human being."

"By 'kind' do you mean all women?" asked the girl.

"No, I mean only those who are like you."

"Anyway it doesn't seem very witty to me to compare a woman with an animal."

70   "O.K.," the young man was still holding his glass aloft, "then I won't drink to your kind, but to your soul. Agreed? To your soul, which lights up when it descends from your head into your belly, and which goes out when it rises back up to your head."

The girl raised her glass. "O.K., to my soul, which descends into my belly."

"I'll correct myself once more," said the young man. "To your belly, into which your soul descends."

"To my belly," said the girl, and her belly (now that they had named it specifically), as it were, responded to the call; she felt every inch of it.

Then the waiter brought their steaks and the young man ordered them another vodka and some soda water (this time they drank to the girl's breasts), and the conversation continued in this peculiar, frivolous tone. It irritated the young man more and more how *well able* the girl was to become the lascivious miss. If she was able to do it so well, he thought, it meant that she really *was* like that. After all, no alien soul had entered into her from somewhere in space. What she was acting now was she herself; perhaps it was the part of her being which had formerly been locked up and which the pretext of the game had let out of its cage. Perhaps the girl supposed that by means of the game she was *disowning* herself, but wasn't it the other way around? Wasn't she becoming herself only through the game? Wasn't she freeing herself through the game? No, opposite him was not sitting a strange woman in his girl's body; it was his girl, herself, no one else. He looked at her and felt growing aversion toward her.

75   However, it was not only aversion. The more the girl withdrew from him *psychically*, the more he longed for her *physically*. The alien quality of her soul

drew attention to her body, yes, as a matter of fact it turned her body into a body for *him* as if until now it had existed for the young man hidden within clouds of compassion, tenderness, concern, love, and emotion, as if it had been lost in these clouds (yes, as if this body had been lost!) It seemed to the young man that today he was seeing his girl's body for the first time.

After her third vodka and soda the girl got up and said flirtatiously, "Excuse me."

The young man said, "May I ask you where you are going, miss?"

"To piss, if you'll permit me," said the girl and walked off between the tables back toward the plush screen.

8

She was pleased with the way she had astounded the young man with this word, which — in spite of all its innocence — he had never heard from her. Nothing seemed to her truer to the character of the woman she was playing than this flirtatious emphasis placed on the word in question. Yes, she was pleased, she was in the best of moods. The game captivated her. It allowed her to feel what she had not felt till now: a *feeling of happy-go-lucky irresponsibility.*

She, who was always uneasy in advance about her every next step, sud- 80 denly felt completely relaxed. The alien life in which she had become involved was a life without shame, without biographical specifications, without past or future, without obligations. It was a life that was extraordinarily free. The girl, as a hitchhiker, could do anything, *everything was permitted her.* She could say, do, and feel whatever she liked.

She walked through the room and was aware that people were watching her from all the tables. It was a new sensation, one she didn't recognize: *indecent joy caused by her body.* Until now she had never been able to get rid of the fourteen-year-old girl within herself who was ashamed of her breasts and had the disagreeable feeling that she was indecent, because they stuck out from her body and were visible. Even though she was proud of being pretty and having a good figure, this feeling of pride was always immediately curtailed by shame. She rightly suspected that feminine beauty functioned above all as sexual provocation and she found this distasteful. She longed for her body to relate only to the man she loved. When men stared at her breasts in the street it seemed to her that they were invading a piece of her most secret privacy which should belong only to herself and her lover. But now she was the hitchhiker, the woman without a destiny. In this role she was relieved of the tender bonds of her love and began to be intensely aware of her body. And her body became more aroused the more alien the eyes watching it.

She was walking past the last table when an intoxicated man, wanting to show off his worldliness, addressed her in French: "*Combien, mademoiselle?*"

The girl understood. She thrust out her breasts and fully experienced every movement of her hips, then disappeared behind the screen.

9

It was a curious game. This curiousness was evidenced, for example, in the fact that the young man, even though he himself was playing the unknown driver remarkably well, did not for a moment stop seeing his girl in the hitch-hiker. And it was precisely this that was tormenting. He saw his girl seducing a strange man, and had the bitter privilege of being present, of seeing at close quarters how she looked and of hearing what she said when she was cheating on him (when she had cheated on him, when she would cheat on him). He had the paradoxical honor of being himself the pretext for her unfaithfulness.

85   This was all the worse because he worshipped rather than loved her. It had always seemed to him that her inward nature was *real* only within the bounds of fidelity and purity, and that beyond these bounds it simply didn't exist. Beyond these bounds she would cease to be herself, as water ceases to be water beyond the boiling point. When he now saw her crossing this horrifying boundary with nonchalant elegance, he was filled with anger.

The girl came back from the rest room and complained: "A guy over there asked me: *Combien, mademoiselle?*"

"You shouldn't be surprised," said the young man, "after all, you look like a whore."

"Do you know that it doesn't bother me in the least?"

"Then you should go with the gentleman!"

90   "But I have you."

"You can go with him after me. Go and work out something with him."

"I don't find him attractive."

"But in principle you have nothing against it, having several men in one night."

"Why not, if they're good-looking."

95   "Do you prefer them one after the other or at the same time?"

"Either way," said the girl.

The conversation was proceeding to still greater extremes of rudeness; it shocked the girl slightly but she couldn't protest. Even in a game there lurks a lack of freedom; even a game is a trap for the players. If this had not been a game and they had really been two strangers, the hitchhiker could long ago have taken offense and left. But there's no escape from a game. A team cannot flee from the playing field before the end of the match, chess pieces cannot desert the chess-board: the boundaries of the playing field are fixed. The girl knew that she had to accept whatever form the game might take, just because it was a game. She knew that the more extreme the game became, the more it would be a game and the more obediently she would have to play it. And it was futile to evoke good sense and warn her dazed soul that she must keep her distance from the game and not take it seriously. Just because it was only a game her soul was not afraid, did not oppose the game, and narcotically sank deeper into it.

The young man called the waiter and paid. Then he got up and said to the girl, "We're going."

"Where to?" The girl feigned surprise.

"Don't ask, just come on," said the young man.   100

"What sort of way is that to talk to me?"

"The way I talk to whores," said the young man.

10

They went up the badly lit staircase. On the landing below the second floor a group of intoxicated men was standing near the rest room. The young man caught hold of the girl from behind so that he was holding her breast with his hand. The men by the rest room saw this and began to call out. The girl wanted to break away, but the young man yelled at her: "Keep still!" The men greeted this with general ribaldry and addressed several dirty remarks to the girl. The young man and the girl reached the second floor. He opened the door of their room and switched on the light.

It was a narrow room with two beds, a small table, a chair, and a wash-basin. The young man locked the door and turned to the girl. She was standing facing him in a defiant pose with insolent sensuality in her eyes. He looked at her and tried to discover behind her lascivious expression the familiar features which he loved tenderly. It was as if he were looking at two images through the same lens, at two images superimposed one upon the other with the one showing through the other. These two images showing through each other were telling him that *everything* was in the girl, that her soul was terrifyingly amorphous, that it held faithfulness and unfaithfulness, treachery and innocence, flirtatiousness and chastity. This disorderly jumble seemed disgusting to him, like the variety to be found in a pile of garbage. Both images continued to show through each other and the young man understood that the girl differed only on the surface from other women, but deep down was the same as they: full of all possible thoughts, feelings, and vices, which justified all his secret misgivings and fits of jealousy. The impression that certain outlines delineated her as an individual was only a delusion to which the other person, the one who was looking, was subject — namely himself. It seemed to him that the girl he loved was a creation of his desire, his thoughts, and his faith and that the *real* girl now standing in front of him was hopelessly alien, hopelessly *ambiguous*. He hated her.

105   "What are you waiting for? Strip," he said.

The girl flirtatiously bent her head and said, "Is it necessary?"

The tone in which she said this seemed to him very familiar; it seemed to him that once long ago some other woman had said this to him, only he no longer knew which one. He longed to humiliate her. Not the hitchhiker, but his own girl. The game merged with life. The game of humiliating the hitchhiker became only a pretext for humiliating his girl. The young man had forgotten that he was playing a game. He simply hated the woman standing in front of him. He stared at her and took a fifty-crown bill from his wallet. He offered it to the girl. "Is that enough?"

The girl took the fifty crowns and said: "You don't think I'm worth much."

The young man said: "You aren't worth more."

110   The girl nestled up against the young man. "You can't get around me like that! You must try a different approach, you must work a little!"

She put her arms around him and moved her mouth toward his. He put his fingers on her mouth and gently pushed her away. He said: "I only kiss women I love."

"And you don't love me?"

"No."

"Whom do you love?"

115   "What's that got to do with you? Strip!"

11

She had never undressed like this before. The shyness, the feeling of inner panic, the dizziness, all that she had always felt when undressing in front of the young man (and she couldn't hide in the darkness), all this was gone. She was standing in front of him self-confident, insolent, bathed in light, and astonished at where she had all of a sudden discovered the gestures, heretofore unknown to her, of a slow, provocative striptease. She took in his glances, slipping off each piece of clothing with a caressing movement and enjoying each individual stage of this experience.

But then suddenly she was standing in front of him completely naked and at this moment it flashed through her head that now the whole game would end, that, since she had stripped off her clothes, she had also stripped away her dissimulation, and that being naked meant that she was now herself and the young man ought to come up to her now and make a gesture with which he would wipe out everything and after which would follow only their most intimate love-making. So she stood naked in front of the young man and at this moment stopped playing the game. She felt embarrassed and on her face appeared the smile, which really belonged to her — a shy and confused smile.

But the young man didn't come to her and didn't end the game. He didn't notice the familiar smile. He saw before him only the beautiful, alien body of his own girl, whom he hated. Hatred cleansed his sensuality of any sentimental coating. She wanted to come to him, but he said: "Stay where you are, I want to have a good look at you." Now he longed only to treat her as a whore. But the young man had never had a whore and the ideas he had about them came from literature and hearsay. So he turned to these ideas and the first thing he recalled was the image of a woman in black underwear (and black stockings) dancing on the shiny top of a piano. In the little hotel room there was no piano, there was only a small table covered with a linen cloth leaning against the wall. He ordered the girl to climb up on it. The girl made a pleading gesture, but the young man said, "You've been paid."

When she saw the look of unshakable obsession in the young man's eyes, she tried to go on with the game, even though she no longer could and no longer knew how. With tears in her eyes she climbed onto the table. The top was scarcely three feet square and one leg was a little bit shorter than the others so that standing on it the girl felt unsteady.

But the young man was pleased with the naked figure, now towering above   120 him, and the girl's shy insecurity merely inflamed his imperiousness. He wanted to see her body in all positions and from all sides, as he imagined other men had seen it and would see it. He was vulgar and lascivious. He used words that she had never heard from him in her life. She wanted to refuse, she wanted to be released from the game. She called him by his first name, but he immediately yelled at her that she had no right to address him so intimately. And so eventually in confusion and on the verge of tears, she obeyed, she bent forward and squatted according to the young man's wishes, saluted, and then wiggled her hips as she did the Twist for him. During a slightly more violent movement, when the cloth slipped beneath her feet and she nearly fell, the young man caught her and dragged her to the bed.

He had intercourse with her. She was glad that at least now finally the unfortunate game would end and they would again be the two people they had been before and would love each other. She wanted to press her mouth against his. But the young man pushed her head away and repeated that he only kissed women he loved. She burst into loud sobs. But she wasn't even allowed to cry, because the young man's furious passion gradually won over her body, which then silenced the complaint of her soul. On the bed there were soon two bodies in perfect harmony, two sensual bodies, alien to each other. This was exactly what the girl had most dreaded all her life and had scrupulously avoided till now: love-making without emotion or love. She knew that she had crossed the forbidden boundary, but she proceeded across it without objections and as a full participant — only somewhere, far off in a corner of her consciousness, did she feel horror at the thought that she had never known such pleasure, never so much pleasure as at this moment — beyond that boundary.

12

Then it was all over. The young man got up off the girl and, reaching out for the long cord hanging over the bed, switched off the light. He didn't want to see the girl's face. He knew that the game was over, but didn't feel like returning to their customary relationship. He feared this return. He lay beside the girl in the dark in such a way that their bodies would not touch.

After a moment he heard her sobbing quietly. The girl's hand diffidently, childishly touched his. It touched, withdrew, then touched again, and then a pleading, sobbing voice broke the silence, calling him by his name and saying, "I am me, I am me . . ."

The young man was silent, he didn't move, and he was aware of the sad emptiness of the girl's assertion, in which the unknown was defined in terms of the same unknown quantity.

125   And the girl soon passed from sobbing to loud crying and went on endlessly repeating this pitiful tautology: "I am me, I am me, I am me . . ."

The young man began to call compassion to his aid (he had to call it from afar, because it was nowhere near at hand), so as to be able to calm the girl. There were still thirteen days' vacation before them.

TALKING ABOUT IT

Seeing Metaphor: Revealing and Concealing

1. How does the experience of hitchhiking enable the young woman to reveal parts of her personality that beforehand had been concealed, perhaps even to her?

2. James P. Carse, a professor of religion and author of *Finite Games and Infinite Games,* claims, "No one can play a game alone. One cannot be human by oneself. . . . We do not relate to others as the person we are; we are who we are in relating to others." How does the hitchhiking game enact this idea? How do the young man and woman develop their own personal game from what they understand hitchhiking to be about?

Seeing Composition: Frame, Line, Texture, Tone

1. How do the breaks function in the story? On one level, they're like small chapters, but why break the text at all? Another way to think about the frame is to ask how the sections connect.

2. How does tone change as the story proceeds? How can you see that from the way Kundera describes what the characters are thinking and feeling?

Seeing Meaning: Navigating and Negotiating

1. As you read this story, at what point would you want to stop the game, and what would you say to the characters? Why?

2. Why is it hard, if not impossible, for one or the other character to stop playing the game? What's at stake beyond their relationship with each other?

WRITING ABOUT IT

1. Write alternative dialogues for these two characters at the point where you would stop the game. Read these to each other in class. Explain to each other why you stopped the game where you did.

2. By not naming the characters, Kundera universalizes the experience of role-playing. If you've ever agreed to role-play, what conflicts arose when you or the other(s) tried to disengage from an accepted role? Consider roles within a circle of friends, a family, a club, a workplace, even within the classroom community.

Bone Yard Stretch

KIRA SALAK

Kira Salak received her MFA from the University of Arizona. The following essay appeared in Witness *(1994) and was her first publication.*

He doesn't know English, only Portuguese, yet he speaks to me. He stands by the filthy, white stucco wall of the building, his mouth smirking in between words. I pretend not to hear him. His AK-47 leans against his leg like a walking stick. He stops speaking to me for a moment so that he can wipe his dark, sweaty face with the red bandanna around his neck.

"No speak Portuguese," he says, mockingly.

I look to my side. I see nothing but others like him, smirks on their faces. They are young. Fifteen, seventeen, eighteen.

My backpack is being gutted beside me. The soldiers' campfire is fed with pages from my paperback. Walt Whitman's *Leaves of Grass.* Every time his words are added, the new blaze momentarily lights up the trunk of the baobab beside me. Rather than staring into the darkness beyond it, I look at the width of the smooth gray trunk. The height of the short, stubby branches. I concentrate on how old the tree must be. It is a giant, here for centuries. Here long before any of—

5   Simmias screams out in Chichewa, pleads to them in English. They don't know either language. They have never been to Malawi, except, maybe, for raids across the border. And English, England, they have never been anywhere near there.

Simmias crawls across the dust towards me, and a soldier kicks him back behind the giant tree. He is conscious again, and the beating will continue. I wonder why they have left his brown pilot's hat on his head. The earflaps hang down over his ears, the wool bloody. There is nothing I can do for him. I can barely move. I have strips of car inner tube bound about my hands and legs.

The other two drivers start to stir. Their blood paints the side of the building, and they smear it into even more grotesque designs as they try to stand. They are like marionettes. Their legs bend where there are no joints. The soldiers have formed a semi-circle around the drivers to watch them try to get up. Every time a leg bows, they laugh. One soldier nudges a driver with his foot and the man collapses against the other. They fall into the dust and lie there sprawled, their chests heaving.

And Simmias has started to scream again.

"You're animals!" I shout at the soldiers and they laugh and circle like hyenas, laughing because it is their noise, their sound.

10   I look at the soldier in front of me. I look into his eyes. One of the black eyes is slightly smaller than the other. It twitches uncontrollably, the eyeball lopsided and looking off into the darkness. The other one is centered on my eyes.

The whiteness is sickly. It reminds me of an egg gone bad, invaded by a moldy brown patch of infection.

His lips mutter in Portuguese to me, his camouflage pants bulge in the middle, right under the belt. I know why they have hardly beaten me. I know what they want.

A hazy Midwestern sun faded into the top of the distant maple trees. Cicadas hummed and droned. Denise and I walked through the pet cemetery. Her decision. She'd never been to one but always wanted to stop. And tonight she invited me with her so we could say goodbye. Like my family, she wouldn't try to stop this dream I'd been saving a year and a half for. But like my family, Denise, my best friend, wasn't sure she'd see me again, that I'd ever come home.

We stopped beside each little tombstone. A lot of Fluffys. And Blackies. A lot of Tigers, too, with circular photos of orange cats encased under clear plastic and stuck right above the names.

I looked up above the graves and stared at the orange sun. Denise glanced at me, at the distance in my stare.

"Aren't you scared, Christi?" she asked me.   15

I listened to a plane rush by above the clouds and remembered past journeys. To Egypt, Poland, Israel. Always by myself for the independence — and the fear. My philosophy was that it is the good and the bad that make an experience memorable. It is important to live like an animal at times, sleeping in filthy beds with fleas and mosquitoes. Drinking whatever water you can find when thirsty. Ignoring your dirty, oily hair and hands. Taking only cold showers, or just bucket showers. And surviving. If life isn't hard, then it isn't worth living, I believed. And backpacking in Africa, alone: that was the hardest thing I'd be doing yet.

"No, I'm not scared," I lied, not wanting to explain. "Just sentimental. Africa is a long way from Illinois."

We walked up to a large mausoleum, easily big enough for a human being. It was dedicated to a dog called Sergeant, a dog that supposedly saved five lives. A huge picture of a Saint Bernard looked amiably at me.

I touched the photo and thought of my early morning departure the next day.

"You can always judge a country," I whispered to the photo, "by how they   20 treat their animals."

I have never before heard such a sound. The sound of bones cracking is a snap snapping like the wind-blown, water-logged canvas of a circus tent on a stormy day. I am surprised that this comparison lodges in my mind. This memory of a gray Midwestern day and muddy roads and chained circus animals being pulled against their will towards the darkness of the big tent.

Simmias has stopped screaming, his bones have stopped cracking. Jeremiah has pissed his pants.

He's next, he's the last of the drivers. The others must be dead. They don't move. I remember how excited Jerry had been to get back to Zimbabwe, to give his sister the baby shirt he bought for her in Lilongwe. I look at him now, his face contorted in fear. His wide Zimbabwean nose swells in a fast rhythm with his breathing. His sharp black cheekbones twitch every time a soldier walks past. He's next. He's the last one.

Then me.

25   The soldier watching me takes off his red beret, walks up and brushes it across my face. Across my chest. Laughs.

"*Señorita*," he says, his one eye rolling off. My legs are tied together out in front of me. He straddles them until his pelvis is an inch from my face.

"No speak Portuguese," he says, smirking, shoving his bulge against my face. I feel my chin start to tremble. I start to cry. The other soldiers, who are hauling Simmias away, drop him in order to watch.

The soldier tries to get me to open my mouth. I turn my head to the side but he grabs my face and holds it forward. His fingers burrow between my clenched lips. His thumb breaks through and I taste dirt on his oily hands. His smile glows brilliant white as he reaches in to grab my tongue. Another soldier walks up to him and hands him my Swiss Army knife. And I squeal and writhe.

"Will someone take me through Mozambique?" I humbly asked. It was nine at night. The last of the trucks leaving Blantyre, Malawi, for the Mozambique border were revving their engines. The writing on their doors told me that the drivers were South Africans, Zimbabweans, Malawians. A few from Tanzania and Botswana. Simmias, a Malawian, walked up to me and introduced himself. He was a cute little man, with a face that was peaceful and sincere. He wore on top of his head a brown pilot's hat with the woolen earflaps down. He smiled pleasantly at me.

30   "Aren't you afraid of getting shot?" he asked, the only one of the drivers stopping to speak to me.

I didn't know that I was afraid of anything at the moment, and certainly not death. I was actually alive, standing there, a twenty-year-old in the middle of a place called Malawi, living out of the backpack in her hands. It was a whole college year of putting away a dollar a day. A summer of sixty-hour-a-week workdays in a factory basement packaging bread. Fifteen-minute breaks of emerging from the oven rooms to read travel guides on places with names like Zimbabwe and Madagascar. Telling myself every minute of every day that next summer I'd see the places in those books, that I'd show everyone that I could get to Africa and back. That through my own volition I could go just about anywhere in the world.

Even Mozambique.

"No," I said to Simmias. "I'm not afraid. Everybody dies sometime. I always travel alone, so I'm used to giving my life to the Fates."

The little man looked at me with his pale brown eyes, staring, hushed, as if waiting for a curtain to go up.

"Ask Jerry," he said finally. "Jerry's my best friend." 35

I threw my backpack onto one shoulder and he led me over to a tall man in khaki shorts, his back to me, inspecting his truck.

"Jerry, will you take her with you? She wants to go through Mozambique."

"Why do you want to do that? There's buses from here to Zambia that go on to Zimbabwe."

"I already got the transit visa, and . . . if I didn't it'd take three times as long and cost three times as much. Through Mozambique, I can get to Harare in one day."

"If you don't get shot," he said, his back still to me. His arm hung over the 40 open truck door as he stretched to look at the back of his truck.

Then Simmias spoke to him in Malawian Chichewa. It's unlike Swahili and I couldn't make out any of it. Frustrated, I put my pack down, listening to them exchange sentences for a minute.

"Yeah, fuel injector," I heard Jerry say in English. "I don't know if it will make it."

Finally, Jerry turned to look at me. I noticed that he wasn't much older than me. A flash of thought registered that he was good-looking. He rested his back against the open truck door, sighing, staring. Not unkind eyes looked out of a broad, black Zimbabwean face.

"I'll take it through. The fuel injector's broken," he said to Simmias. "It could die along the way."

He wiped the sweat off his forehead and sighed again, this time looking 45 sharply at me.

"You scared?" he asked.

Before I could answer he told me to get in.

Machine gun fire. The soldier above me puts his beret back on, pockets the knife. He turns to listen to the gunfire in the distance that's followed by whoops and screams. Orders in Portuguese thrash the night. The soldiers around me bound off like swaggering hyenas with their guns, smiles on their faces.

Jerry crawls towards me. Like me, his hands are tied behind his back and his legs are bound. The bottom of his chin scrapes the rocky ground as he inches forward.

"Turn around," he says. "Quickly!" 50

The machine gun fire gets closer. We sit upright, back to back, fumbling with each other's wrists. Tears rage down my cheeks. My nails are shredded and bent backwards undoing the rubber knots. But in what seems like a moment, I am free. I run off behind Jerry into the darkness. I am out of breath, but I run. My legs are weights some god is mechanically moving—and halting, by a baobab tree. And Jerry is trying to climb it.

"Why are you climbing it? They'll see us!" I say, my voice not the same, my voice a gasping wail. He doesn't seem to hear me.

The ancient tree has split itself open, burst a gaping slit on one side, and he climbs the wound into the stubby branches and reaches a hand down to help pull me up. I wrap my arm around a fat branch and grab his hand. My arm muscles swell, my hiking boots slip on the smooth bark until they catch on one of the mushroom-like growth rings on the trunk, and I make it up into the branches.

I climb over the thick branch and press it tightly against me, feeling warmth from the cold, gray skin. I look up, expecting to see leaves but there are none. This is the winter season, I remind myself, but I wonder if the trees ever get leaves in Mozambique. The baobabs. I even wonder why they're still standing. The civil war destroyed everything else in the country but left the baobabs. *Why?* Old tribal taboos? New ones? Maybe they have become beacons. The only reminders that something can thrive through seventeen years of war and hunger and death. I don't know. All I wonder is if I'll be left standing. Survive.

55   And I see the lion.

The "Bone Yard Stretch" of the road towards Tete.

"This is where the most people die."

Jerry popped a Bob Marley tape into his truck stereo and leaned back nice and cool. Simmias passed us on the right, smiling and honking his horn.

"He is my best friend," Jerry told me, motioning to him. "We met in Zimbabwe. We always go to the same places."

60   Jerry slowed his truck for a moment as the big tires plunged from the asphalt into a two-foot-deep land mine crater.

"Have you ever driven this road when a land mine went off?" I asked.

"Yes. Many times. I have seen a truck passing me get blown from the road. Killed two people."

Another two trucks passed us on the right. The drivers waved and honked their horns at us.

"The Renamo put the mines on the sides of the road, right?"

65   "Yes."

"Then why do people pass?"

Jerry tipped a bottle of orange drink to his lips, his fingers tapping to the beat over the gear shift knob.

"You die you die, you know?" he said.

I looked out at the landscape. There was nothing green. Lining the road were burnt grass and four-foot-high tree stumps that were hastily severed: an attempt, Jerry had said, to destroy hiding places for ambushes. In the distance, the land rose, scattered with tufts of bushes that carried yellow leaves. The winter season in Africa, yet no wind to dispel the intense heat that settled on your skin. And no people, either. No typical rural villages with waving children and thatched huts and gardens of corn like the ones I'd seen in Kenya and Madagascar. The land oozed decay, like the occasional blown-apart buildings abandoned by the road, their shattered cement bleeding in the yellow grass.

Yet the trucks passed through. Six days a week, every week. The guarded convoys took the road each morning to get their loads through to Zimbabwe in a day, and then down to South Africa and their bosses. I was told that it was "business," this Bone Yard Stretch and its harsh tolls. Just business. If you went safely through Zambia, Jerry had said, you'd be fired for being too slow.

"How many times have you driven this road?" I asked.

"Many, many times," he said.

"Have you ever been ambushed by rebels? Shot at?"

I glanced at myself in the big passenger side mirror and thought I looked like a child again.

"Yes, oh yes. One place is coming. I will show you where."

"Aren't you afraid?" I asked.

He laughed loudly, raising his sandaled foot from the clutch onto the dashboard, the toes curling in and out like a cat kneading its claws.

"We all die sometime," he said, smiling.

"There could be rebels hiding in those bushes over there right now, about to shoot you."

He sighed impatiently.

"And it doesn't scare you?"

He shook his head, and this time I laughed with him. I couldn't help it. There was something funny about driving through the Bone Yard Stretch of a country in the middle of a long civil war, chatting about death while glancing at the remains of vehicles lying like bleached bones in the sunlight. Something perversely funny, like the actor who plummets off the stage by accident and you laugh, telling yourself it was just part of the show.

I stopped thinking about rebels hiding in the brush long enough for my eyes to close. A moment later, I heard Jerry's voice.

"There. That is where nineteen people died a few days ago. It was a bus."

I opened my eyes to see a huge crater and shattered glass. The truck ahead of us in the convoy splattered through the window glass and stained bits of clothing. The wind from its exhaust pipe caused a book, lying on the side of the road, to pulsate its yellowed pages in the sun. It was hot. I wiped the sweat from my brow and closed my eyes again, listening for guns.

A shot to the head could kill it. Or to the heart. Jerry moves deeper in between two branches, watches the soldiers shoot the lion. They fire into its legs. Their laughs seem louder than the animal's roars.

The lion is old, failing as it runs. It carries its shredded hind leg behind it as though it were attached by children as a prank. Its eyes are wide and white, and it never blinks. It rushes at the soldiers, its dark brown mane flying up. And it growls and spits out froth. In the darkness from atop this tree, all I can see really well are its white teeth and those crazy eyes.

Lions don't belong *here,* I think. Maybe to the north, in Zambia. Or to the west in Zimbabwe. But not here. There is nothing alive in Mozambique except people, starving people.

I look at the gaunt tawny body of the lion. At the ribs pushing out the skin like dull knives. And I know that it is starving, too. I saw ones like it in the Serengeti. The old ones, forgotten by the pride, left to starve and then die.

90   I stare at the tattered leg, wondering how it got that way. Land mine?

Jerry motions for me to climb higher, nearer to where he is. I pull myself up and crouch on a branch beside his, push my sweat-covered hair behind my ears as the lion staggers, drooling, growling.

"They'll see us here," I say.

"No they *won't,*" he insists, taking his eyes off the soldiers for the first time to look at me. "They are not smart. They only look for things on the ground. They don't think of climbing trees."

I think of one of my cats being up a tree, of a stomping, barking, whining dog making futile attempts to get to it. But those were just animals. I look at the soldiers circling the collapsed lion. Wiping my nose on my arm, I look above me.

95   The sky is cloudless. The constellations glow as though the window of the earth were cleaned. I see Orion, the Big Dipper. I think that perhaps in another half of the world, in a place called America, they can see them, too.

The truck had no pick-up. The fuel injector was getting worse and worse. Trucks in the convoy kept passing us on the side, and the sun was past its mid-point and descending.

Hills were the worst. We went up them doing only about ten miles an hour, the truck gasping, the tachometer hand lurching each time Jerry hit the ac-celerator. Jerry punched out his Bob Marley tape and stopped the truck on the side of the road. Simmias, who'd been following us, stopped and jumped out of his truck.

"Fuel injector," Jerry said to me quietly.

Simmias stood so that his tiny head peeped through Jerry's window, his pilot's hat hanging just above his eyes.

100   "Hi," he said to me, smiling. Then he looked at his best friend and they talked in Chichewa and Jerry shook his head, motioning to the RPM gauge. Truck after truck passed on our right but none stopped. I bit my lower lip, chewed on it.

Jerry leaned over towards me and said that we'd eat lunch now, and he'd think what we should do. We got out of the truck into the intense heat of the sun and sat on large rocks beside the road. He took out his portable gas heater and filled a pot with flour and bottled water. Simmias brought over some tomatoes to crush in a pan. Jerry concentrated on stirring the boiling flour for the *mili-mili* as diesel motors ground past us, horns screaming. To our surprise, two trucks approaching us slowed to a stop and the drivers got out. They spoke in Chichewa to Jerry.

"They'd like to help us," Simmias explained to me. Jerry put more flour into the pan for them, and they chatted away, occasionally glancing at me. One of the drivers was from East Africa, apparently, because whenever he'd gesture to me I'd hear him say, "wazungu," taken from Swahili: white person. I knew all too well how out of place I was. I pushed my damp blond hair behind my ears, blinked away the sweat burning my blue eyes. Looking down the slope of the road, I tried to pretend I wasn't there. That I could fade into the landscape.

But Simmias wouldn't let me. He shifted so that he could face me.

"Are you a student?" he asked as he mashed his tomatoes.

"Yes. I have one more year of college." 105

"That's good. I studied for a year, then I had to stop to become a driver. My parents died and left behind two little ones. My sister is watching them, so she can't work. I give her half my salary."

As Simmias continued his story, I was graciously taken away from Mozambique with him. I traveled back to Malawi, to his sister's house in Blantyre. To the little house with the tomato patch out back. I met the two little children. David and Audrey. Watched as Simmias' pale brown eyes looked at them with love and pride as Audrey tells him she'd like to be a lawyer.

"There are only a couple female lawyers in all of Malawi," Simmias said to me, breaking the vision.

In the distance, coming up the slope, was a jeep filled with government soldiers. Waves of heat shuffled the image, made it seem like a hallucination as it traveled up the hill.

The jeep stopped beside us. Several soldiers got out while a couple of cam- 110
ouflaged men stayed behind and sat around the mounted machine guns, their hands resting casually on the stocks. We looked back and forth at each other, their eyes scanning me, their mouths creeping smiles. Their guns made me feel safe from the bushes about us. The bushes where the rebels hide, the cheetah-like Renamo hunting our large convoy of trucks, waiting for the weak or crippled ones to fall behind as easy prey.

I turned to Jerry and interrupted his conversation.

"The rebels can't get us," I said. "The soldiers guarding our convoy are here. You can tell them that the truck's not working. Maybe they'll take us to the border or something."

Jerry scoffed, his eyes glaring at a couple of soldiers as they walked slowly around his truck, tapping the muzzles of their guns against the sides.

"Don't tell them anything," he said.

115   The lion lies dead in the grass. The soldiers poke their gun barrels against it, take trophies from it. The ear or the tail. The heart. The body is cut open and the meat brought over to the fire where the baobab is—where we're supposed to be.

The night and the silence of it return again, and I am scared to breathe. I curse my white skin which seems almost luminescent in the darkness. I try to conceal any part that is not covered by my flannel shirt. Angry Portuguese ex-clamations make my body shudder. I know that now they will come looking for me. It is a warped kind of children's tag. A Ghost in the Graveyard of the Bone Yard Stretch of Mozambique. And no goal to run to. No Kool-Aid waiting for those out of breath. I pant and bury my face against my shoulder, pressing my eyes into my skin.

I hear the sounds of an argument among several of the soldiers. I hear the crunch of their black boots on the rocky ground. The footsteps are quick and la-bored. The stocks of their guns rattle. Metal slides into metal. Bolts are pulled back. The ground crunches louder and louder. Stiff leather creaks. Breaths suck in, push out.

One of the soldiers howls and the others laugh, and the laughs sound as if they are right below me, yet far off. I ask the clenched darkness behind my closed eyes to save me. A rock is kicked below me and I hear it collide with the tree trunk. The grass swishes, crunches around me. A zipper is undone and a trickle of water peters against some bushes. Machine gun fire blasts into the night and I jump and shake until Jerry's warm palm covers my cheek and I lie still again. I concentrate on how my eyelashes brush against his skin. Concen-trate on the buzzing insects of the night and on dying and coming back again. Or never coming back. On my bones, broken, lying somewhere in Mozambique. On anything but the soldiers.

And . . . finally . . . the footsteps move away.

120   I knew something was wrong from Jerry's look, a kind of side-long glance at Simmias. The two drivers, seeing him, would widen their eyes and stop chewing.

I dipped my ball of boiled flour into the pan of tomato sauce and raised it to my lips. Just before I opened my mouth, I saw two soldiers staring at me from under the truck. Smiling. Another four soldiers walked beside the trucks of the two drivers who'd just joined us, opening the doors to the rig and looking inside, peeking under the tarpaulin strapped over the goods in back. One of the drivers knew Portuguese and spoke harshly to the soldiers. They immediately backed away like accosted dogs.

Fewer and fewer trucks passed us, I noticed. Most were probably nearing the town of Tete on the Zambezi River, the end of the Bone Yard Stretch. The goal. Crossing the Zambezi meant you'd most likely live: it was said that there weren't as many Renamo on the other side to kill you.

Jerry started to speak in Chichewa to the others and their eyes flitted to the soldiers. Then a soldier approached us. Like all the others, he was tall and skinny, his camouflage pants hanging on his body like shredding snake skin. He said something in Portuguese to all of us and pointed at me.

"He wants to see your passport," one of the drivers said. I pulled my money belt out from where it was lodged down my pants, and removed my passport. Trying to appear polite, I smiled and handed it to him.

"Como esta usted," stumbled out of my mouth, remembered from my year 125
of Spanish. He looked at me and smiled, one of his eyes twitching, the eyeball rolling to the side.

"No speak Portuguese, aye?"

I don't know how many hours have passed. I can't tell. I watch the moon as I would the sun, wondering when it will take off its mask and light up the earth again.

Every sound seems in front of a microphone. It is like there are a thousand speakers aimed at my ears. I stare at the distant fire by the baobab. I watch the three soldiers sitting there talking to one another. Their unintelligible conversation rushes to my ears in sprints and jumps.

"They will leave before the sun rises," Jerry whispers. "They will have to escort a new convoy."

"What about your truck . . . the drivers? Simmias?"   130

"They will say the rebels did it. They will take everything they want, then blame it on the Renamo."

I lower my head against the trunk and shiver, the night cool against my body. Jerry moves close to me and speaks in my ear.

"During the day they fight for the government. At night, they join the rebels."

I remember how relieved I was to see them pull up beside our trucks when we were eating the *mili-mili*.

"There is no one to help us," I say. "The soldiers and the rebels are the same."   135
Jerry softly sighs.

"I know. But the morning will. Now, shhhhh."

It was the first time a gun was ever pointed at me. This one was shoved against my chest, some cheap-looking machine gun with the stock folded in so it looked compact, like something a gangster would hold. I stared at the metal, stared at it as I'd stare at a snake twisted about my feet. Fear isn't the right word. This was beyond fear. This was an ache that seemed to form a bridge between life and death itself. A precarious tightrope walk of fear.

"Tell them to take everything!" Jerry yelled to the driver who knew Portuguese. "Tell them to just take it all and let us go."

140   The man rattled off the translation to the soldiers. They laughed at him and turned to watch as the trucks were being driven off the road by four soldiers. The inexperienced drivers made the vehicles clamor over the rocky terrain like they were herding ornery cattle.

The one who held the gun on me leaned forward and grabbed my hair, yanking my head to the side. He spoke sharply to the other soldiers while fingering my blond hair. Stroking it.

"He says," said the driver, "that he wants to keep you, too. What will you give him if he lets you go?"

"What will I give him?!" Simmias walked up to me, ignoring the soldier's gun against his back.

"Give them your bag," he said to me softly, leaning up against me. "Your rucksack. Give it to them. And all your money. Then walk away, just walk away until you get over that slope — "

145   "What slope?" my voice implored. "Where?"

"In front of you — don't look up — in front of you. When you get there, run. *RUN.*"

He walked back beside Jerry and the other drivers, being held at gunpoint against a white-washed wall that emerged from the rubble of a blown-up building.

"The soldiers say that you must give them something now."

I walked over to the truck, the gun pushing me forward. Behind me, I could hear Simmias and the others talking quickly in Chichewa, the soldiers' Portuguese overpowering them until an argument broke out in scattered tongues.

150   I opened the door to the rig and pulled out my backpack. The soldier grabbed it from me and hoisted it onto his thin shoulder. As we walked back around the truck, I heard a loud whack and Simmias was sprawled on the ground. Jerry and the drivers were kneeling down, pleading, and the soldiers were nudging them with their feet.

"Señorita," the soldiers all said in turn as I walked towards them. I looked at their eyes and smiles. So identical. To my side I saw the slope that Simmias had talked about, like a distant mirage. Mirage or not, as soon as the soldier put down my pack, I ran towards it.

I made it halfway up before machine gun fire spattered the ground before me and I fell. Just collapsed. The soldiers dragged me back across the rocky dust.

Somehow, the morning.

The eastern horizon turns from a black to a blue. The blue starts to fade into a grayish orange light. It is like watching the feet glide under a closed curtain, moving into place.

155   The three soldiers are still awake and have just started putting out the fire. They look out in the distance, for the others who have not returned, but noth-

ing distracts their view. They pull the drivers' bodies away from the rubble of the building and drop them between two of the trucks.

I recognize Simmias, stiff in their grasp, pilot hat hanging down over his eyes. They yank it off as they toss him down and make a last-minute search of his body.

"Simmias is dead," I whisper. Jerry shakes his head, a tear running down the dirt on his cheek. He quickly wipes it away.

They load the contents of my backpack into a jeep parked nearby. They strip the trucks of anything worth carrying. Jerry's stereo is ripped out. His clothing and tapes all removed. I see the light green baby shirt he'd never be able to give his sister.

The East is making the night lose its darkness, and the soldiers are still here. I prepare to leap from the tree, to run faster than I ever have before. I tell myself that there is no such thing as guns. This is a dream, and by running, I will wake up back home.

The soldiers take a dirty plastic container over to the trucks and pour fluid   160
on the hoods and on the seats. Then they drive further away in their jeeps.

I do not know where the others are, the ones stalking us. I am waiting for them to return, having finally sniffed us out.

Jerry closes his eyes, rests his head against the limb like he's sleeping. The sound of several gunshots and the howl of an explosion rouse him. He looks out just as flames spread in billowing ringlets over the trucks and parched earth, over the bodies of the drivers.

The three soldiers jump into the jeep and turn on the engine. Now it is our turn. They are coming for us, they are driving right for us. *Mom, Father, Marc, Denise, I love you . . .* The engine roars towards our baobab, the heat from the fire covering my skin, engulfing me. I close my eyes . . .

The jeep plummets past. I watch its back bump up and down as it flies over the yellow grass, the bodies of the soldiers bobbing. White dust swirls around us in the branches. We are a couple of cats, watching the dogs going away. Then the sun breaks free over the horizon, a mother's palm on my cheek, a jewel shining through a throbbing gray stream.

Jerry tells me to climb down fast. I do, and he follows me. And we run.   165
"To the road," he says. "This way."

The convoy came by at midday. Jerry leaped from the bushes and waved the trucks down. The first few groaned by without stopping, but one driver slowed.

"Ambushed!" Jerry said to him, and pointed at me huddled beneath some bushes. The driver motioned us to get in, and I crouched in the back of the rig with Jerry. That was how I got to the border. That was how I finally got through.

I sit in some grass in a void between the two countries. I sit in the grass because it's too green, because no one from Mozambique could have planted it.

170   They won't actually let me enter Zimbabwe since my passport is gone. Everything's gone. Jerry left me to fill the curious Zimbabwean ears with his story. Our nightmare together. His eyes moisten when he mentions Simmias, but we are suddenly strangers again. All we saw together, his hand on my cheek— gone. We are alive now, safe. He stands with his back to me, talking to them.

     A man in the Zimbabwe customs house is going to call the American Embassy. He assures me that I'll be cleared to get through.

     "Don't worry, you won't have to go back," he says, smiling uncomfortably. "But we cannot let you go through without authorization." I don't protest. I am too tired because I know the dream will actually end. I am patient, numb, as though in an alpha state. And in my mind, the lion reappears . . .

     I can hear its harsh growls, see the shredded leg. I convince myself that in its long wanderings into this land, the lion stepped on one of the Renamo's mines. Its leg saved a bus of Mozambique peasants from being blown apart, giving the Bone Yard Stretch yet another metal skeleton to add to the road. It saved a Simmias or Jerry from being killed, too. And another me.

     Simmias. The only way to remember him is to forget. To forget his sister called Audrey. The one who wanted to become a lawyer. To forget his brother, David. To forget that for one short moment I had seen their smiles as Simmias stood above them, proud, in the house with its own tomato patch in a Malawian city called Blantyre.

175   Out past the void the soldiers stand in three groups, kept in Mozambique by the chain-link fence of the border. Their fingers clasp the metal circles like long claws. They smile at me. Their eyes grate up and down my body like nails. A soldier stands apart, one of his eyes lolling off to the side, the other fixed upon me. He opens a Swiss Army knife and holds it straight out, below his belt, wiggling the blade.

     I close my eyes. *Close close close* . . .

     When I open them again, they are gone.

     The customs man is motioning me into the town of Nyapamanga. Into Zimbabwe. He gives me Zimbabwean dollars loaned to me from the Embassy. I feel the pretty money as I walk forward, look at the balanced rock designs drawn on the front of the bills. At the red gazelles and the blue zebras, the elephants. At the only Africa I thought I would ever see. I press the money to my nose, smelling the crisp bills, hating to spend them: they are my tickets out of the void, the purgatory.

     "Take this bus waiting for you. It's going to Harare," he says. "When you get there, go straight to the American Embassy."

180   *Then home?* I try to remember a place called Home.

     A clean white bus waits by a Coca-Cola sign. Women in bright *kangas* sit on board, fanning their faces with smooth black hands. A woman wearing wire-rimmed glasses reads *East of Eden*, jean legs crossed, gold earrings gleaming in the sunlight. She looks at me over her lenses, pensive, while I stand outside and read the sign in the window. HARARE. As I get on, everyone stares at my appearance in surprise and I smile, wanting to thank them. Delightfully conscious of my tangled blond hair, I twist my fingers through it and sit down.

The bus starts and the door swings shut. It glides on bright asphalt roads. The countryside is green crops and waving children and zebu herds. And baobabs, too. It is everything as it should be. It is Zimbabwe. Mozambique vanishes, with each swishing yellow stripe on the road, to wherever it came from.

TALKING ABOUT IT

Seeing Metaphor: Revealing and Concealing

1. What kind of game did Salak play when she embarked on this and other such trips? What kinds of cultural games did she have to play to get her ride into Mozambique?

2. Describe the game that the soldiers play. What significance does it have for you?

Seeing Composition: Frame, Line, Texture, Tone

1. How does Salak handle time in this essay, and what is the effect? How does she use space breaks in this essay? What is the effect on the story line?

2. Examine a passage or two where Salak uses sentence fragments. Rewrite one such passage in complete sentences. What differences do you hear? What does that exercise show you about the impact of fragments on the tone of the passage?

Seeing Meaning: Navigating and Negotiating

1. What specifically does Salak tell about herself that helps you empathize with or understand her perception of the adventure? How might your response be different without that self-revelation?

2. When you finish reading this piece, do you imagine her doing anything like this again? Why or why not?

WRITING ABOUT IT

1. Out of your own experience, list some independence games that you've played and read these to each other in class. Choose one to elaborate in an essay and tell what you learned from the experience about placing metaphorical boundaries or limits on such games.

2. Some adventures people choose carry serious risks not only for themselves but also for those left behind as well as those who are needed so that the adventure can take place. What may seem to the adventurer as compelling reason to ignore caution can seem to others irrational and irresponsible. Try to see one such risk-taking activity from both sides. Write about it from two points of view, without judging one right or wrong. Let the two points of view stand. This writing can also be done collaboratively in pairs. Each writer represents one point of view, then the writers work together to see that each view is given the fairest representation.

Baseball — A Mirror of Japanese Culture

YUKIKO OKA

Yukiko Oka, an advanced student from Saga University in Japan, studied English at the University of Richmond for one year. She then returned to Saga, planning to complete her undergraduate degree and later teach English to Japanese high school students. Enrolled in the first-year writing course, Yukiko taught the class much about Japanese cultural values through her study of conceptual metaphor.

In "Loading the Bases," Bradd Shore states, "baseball is both a game and a ritual that appeals to particular cultural notions of space, time, and social relationships." This claim is valid for Japanese baseball games too. In particular, high school baseball can be said to be one of the most ritualistic and cultural sports in Japan.

A big tournament is held every spring and summer. The summer one is especially large and more popular than the spring because only the winning team in each prefecture tournament can participate. In spring, however, there is no prefecture tournament and some strong teams are picked at random. As a result, it is the fulfillment of a dream and an honor to participate in the summer tournament. Each of the forty-nine teams is seen as representative of their prefecture and are highly respected. The players take great pride in themselves and do their best to meet people's expectations. They also try to play a good baseball game, of course.

As evidence of their best, they perform several rituals which are characteristic only for this tournament. These rituals have no relation to the game itself, but they are one of the most important elements that make high school baseball popular and fascinating. Within them, we can find hidden Japanese cultural values and ideas; it is as if baseball were a mirror of Japanese society.

One example is the ritualistic haircut that players get in mid-July at the start of the summer tournament. Their hair is cut very short, and it's not too much to say that they are almost bald. No player ever refuses the haircut. As Bradd Shore says, "A ritual is assumed to be more important than everyday behavior." And it is also true here that this is no ordinary haircut. It carries meaning beyond the idea of a unified look for the players.

First, it is honorable to join the tournament, so it is thought a kind of 5 courtesy to cut one's hair. The effect is to cleanse oneself in the act of having a haircut. Players should be clean or pure to participate in the game. Second, as representatives of the prefectures, the players also represent a standard or ideal for other people. They offer a fresh, clean image and the promise that they are deserving of the honor to play. There are practical reasons, too, of course, for the haircut, and these are the most obvious: players can see better and risk fewer distractions if their hair is short. They won't be combing or touching their hair while in play.

The courtesy that the players show by their haircuts is also shown in other ways toward the other players, the spectators, and even the very ground of the stadium. For example, before and after the game, both of the teams bow to each other, taking off their caps. The bow before the game suggests that they will play fair, while the bow after the game suggests appreciation for the opposing team. Even though one team defeats the other, both teams play their best. They should not regret a loss or think ill of the other team. Bowing to one another reminds them of this culturally valued attitude.

Bowing to the ground is also an act of courtesy and appreciation. Players could not have their opportunity without the ground, and it is where they may play their best game. In that sense, the ground is sacred. We should appreciate it. Within the act of bowing, there lies another hidden idea for Japanese: even a lifeless thing has a soul or a value. A typical example is the popular idea that there is a god in each grain of rice and it is, therefore, impolite to leave even a grain of rice in the rice bowl because it means one abuses or kills a god. We can find almost that same idea in the ritual of bowing to the ground. The ground is not a god, but represents something sacred. Thus, the players should show their courtesy by bowing.

Another significant ritual is the song. The winning team is given the right to play and sing the school song. It's an award for the team, similar to the gold medal winner singing his or her national anthem in the Olympic Games. By singing their song, the players demonstrate pride in themselves as representatives of their school and prefecture. Moreover, singing is also joyful; the players feel they will surely win the next game in order to sing again. The song gives them confidence. It also has the effect of uniting the players and the crowd. The players sing to show their appreciation to the audience who has cheered for them, and in turn, the fans sing along with all their heart to show their own appreciation to the players and to share the delight of victory. The song inspires patriotism.

Just as the song is a reward to the winning team, there is too a reward for the losing team. The players are permitted to take some sand from the ground. Though it is not special sand and has the same quality of ordinary sand, players of the losing team pick up some grains and take them home. This ritual is a remembrance of the summer tournament, the honor of playing. The sand is like a picture which represents a precious moment in the current time. As described earlier, only forty-nine teams can play on this ground each year. The number of people who can scoop up some sand is limited, and hence, the sand is valuable. It is not just sand, but metaphorically, traces of the players' efforts, games, and memories. We can find in this ritual the same Japanese notion that a lifeless thing is important.

We can see yet another aspect of Japanese culture in high school baseball   10 where the players are male and where the support of the team is female. Girls contribute to a team by keeping score, aiding an injured player, carrying balls, and so forth. In a sense, it's not too much to say that they are important members of the team. Nevertheless, these girls are never permitted to enter the playing field nor the bullpen. They have to sit in the stands like the fans. It is an idea that baseball is a man's world where women should not take a step or push themselves forward. In other words, women belong to men. When we consider that no woman, even today in the age of feminism, can enter the playing field, it is obvious that this idea still has power in Japan. In recent news stories, we can see how many female students have difficulty finding a job. We cannot help admitting that most people, especially the older generation, still think that women are inferior to men whenever we see high school baseball. It's a sad reminder.

Bradd Shore's belief that baseball is not just a game, but a symbolic way of expressing central cultural ideas, can be supported by a study of Japanese high school baseball too. There we can see both positive and negative values as implied in the meaning of various rituals and traditions. The game is like a miniature of Japanese society, a mirror of cultural values. Through this symbolic mirror, Japanese people reaffirm their own traditions, and other people too can see them. We can, as Shore says, "construct a view of reality" by examining high school baseball in Japan.

PERMEABLE BOUNDARIES: WRITING WHERE THE READINGS MEET

1. Kira Salak describes how the soldiers treat the lion in "Bone Yard Stretch." How do the soldiers differ from the hunters in "The Killing Game"? How much difference does context make in the degree to which you accept the game of hunting the lion as similar to the hunting that Joy Williams describes in "The Killing Game"?

2. Argue that some of the cultural values, traditions, or rituals that are described in "Loading the Bases" can be connected to other games or sports described in other chapter selections.

3. To what extent do "Bone Yard Stretch" and two others in this chapter serve as an illustration of the idea that selfhood is constructed by community? That is, how might you argue that we are socially constructed by our culture's tendency to find identity through games, either traditional games or those we invent for ourselves?

4. Milan Kundera, Brigit Pegeen Kelly, and Kira Salak describe risk-taking adventures that claim a price from the players. What similar stakes are in the games they play? What similar consequences? How might you argue that seeing one thing in terms of another is not just a way of thinking but a way of acting/behaving?

5. Examine the metaphors on the sports page of your local newspaper. What do they reveal about the beliefs, attitudes, and values attached to particular games and their players? Are any of these evident in selected readings here?

6. The concept of capitalism is important in understanding how Monopoly and thus American capitalism put things at "stake" for other "players" in the game as well as for people in real life who are incapable of getting outside the capitalistic system. What other board game or video game do you know that depends on understanding another social or political concept, one that also puts things at stake for players? Write about it in comparison to "The Search for Marvin Gardens." As an exercise in genre and organization, you could imitate the general structure of John McPhee's essay by juxtaposing the playing of the game and the real-life events, attitudes, and values the game suggests.

7. What kind of games do you play that could be seen as a form of social acceptance, and how might these be tied into two or three of the readings in this chapter? You might begin by making a list in your journal or in class of the activities, games, or rituals in which you've taken part.

8. Write about two films that you have seen in which games are featured: one involving a traditional or official game; and the other, a game played with

one's life. What similar social or cultural values do you notice in both? What differences? Where are the boundaries of the game, both literal and metaphorical? What do you make of your findings that concern significance beyond mere game?

Acknowledgments

TEXT CREDITS

ATWOOD, MARGARET, "The Female Body" from *Good Bones and Simple Murders* by Margaret Atwood. Copyright © 1983, 1992, 1994, by O. W. Toad, Ltd., A Nan A. Talese Book. Used by permission of Doubleday, a division of Bantam Doubleday Dell Publishing Group, Inc.

BAKER, NICHOLSON, "Changes of Mind" from *The Size of Thoughts* by Nicholson Baker, pp. 3–9. Copyright © 1982, 1983, 1984, 1989, 1991, 1992, 1993, 1994, 1995, 1996 by Nicholson Baker. Reprinted by permission of Random House, Inc.

BEGLEY, SHARON, "Commandos of Viral Combat" from *Newsweek,* May 22, 1995, pp. 50–51. Copyright © 1995, Newsweek, Inc. All rights reserved. Reprinted by permission.

BOSLOUGH, JOHN, "Black-Hole Encounter" from *Stephen Hawking's Universe* by John Boslough, pp. 59–67. Copyright © 1985 by John Boslough. By permission of William Morrow & Company, Inc.

BUTLER, ROBERT OLEN, "Crickets" from *A Good Scent from a Strange Mountain* by Robert Olen Butler, pp. 59–64. Copyright © 1992 by Robert Olen Butler. Reprinted by permission of Henry Holt and Company, Inc.

CHEUSE, ALAN, "Writing It Down for James: Some Thoughts on Reading towards the Millennium" from *The Antioch Review,* the Glorious Essay, vol. 51, no. 4, Fall 1993, pp. 487–501. Reprinted by permission of the author.

COHN, CAROL, "Wars, Wimps, and Women: Talking Gender and Thinking War" from *Gendering War Talk,* Miriam Cook and Angela Woollacott, eds. Copyright © 1993 by Princeton University Press. Reprinted by permission of Princeton University Press.

CONNIFF, RICHARD, "What's in a Name? Sometimes More Than Meets the Eye" from *Smithsonian,* Dec. 1996, vol. 27, no. 9, pp. 66–70. Copyright © 1996 Richard Conniff. Reprinted by permission of the author.

DUBISCH, JILL, "You Are What You Eat: Religious Aspects of the Health Food Movement." Reprinted by permission of the author.

DUFF, KAT, "Towards an Ecology of Illness" from *The Taos Review,* 5, Summer 1991, pp. 30–43. Reprinted by permission of the author.

JAMISON, KAY REDFIELD, "Speaking of Madness" and "A Life in Moods" from *An Unquiet Mind* by Kay Redfield Jamison, Alfred A. Knopf, Inc., 1995, pp. 179–184, 210–216. Copyright © 1995 by Kay Redfield Jamison. Reprinted by permission of Alfred A. Knopf, Inc.

KAYSEN, SUSANNA, "Girl, Interrupted" from *Girl, Interrupted* by Susanna Kaysen, pp. 137–159. Copyright © 1993 by Susanna Kaysen. Reprinted by permission of Random House, Inc.

KELLY, BRIGIT PEGEEN, "Song" reprinted from *Song* by Brigit Pegeen Kelly, with the permission of BOA Editions, Ltd., 260 East Ave., Rochester, NY 14604.

KLOSS, CAROL, "Fat." Reprinted by permission of the author.

KUNDERA, MILAN, "The Hitchhiking Game" from *Laughable Loves* by Milan Kundera, translated by Suzanne Rappaport. Copyright © 1974 by Alfred Knopf, Inc. Reprinted by permission of the publisher.

LAMOTT, ANNE, "Shitty First Drafts" from *Bird by Bird* by Anne Lamott, Pantheon Books, 1994, pp. 21–27. Copyright © 1994 by Anne Lamott. Reprinted by permission of Pantheon Books, a division of Random House, Inc.

LAWLER, JOHN M., "Metaphors We Compute By." Lecture delivered in 1987; available at http://www-personal.umich.edu/~jlawler/meta4compute.html_. Reprinted by permission of the author.

LE GUIN, URSULA K., "The Rule of Names," first appeared in *Fantastic,* from *The Wind's Twelve Quarters,* pp. 101–116. Copyright © 1964, 1992 by Ursula K. Le Guin. Reprinted by permission of the author and the author's agent, Virginia Kidd Agency, Inc.

LEWIS, C. S., "Bluspels and Flalansferes: A Semantic Nightmare." First published in *Rehabilitations and Other Essays* by C. S. Lewis. Copyright © 1939 C. S. Lewis Pte. Ltd. Reprinted with permission from Curtis Brown Group Ltd.

LIGHTMAN, ALAN, "Einstein's Dreams" from *Einstein's Dreams,* Pantheon Books, 1992, pp. 3–7, 23–27. Copyright © 1992 by Alan Lightman. Reprinted by permission of Pantheon Books, a division of Random House, Inc.

MCPHEE, JOHN, "The Search for Marvin Gardens" from *Pieces of the Frame.* Copyright © 1975 by John McPhee. Reprinted by permission of Farrar, Straus & Giroux, Inc.

NAITO, HATSUHO, "My Body Will Collapse Like a Falling Cherry Blossom" adapted from *The Thunder Gods: The Kamikaze Pilots Tell Their Story* and appeared in *Air & Space/Smithsonian,* April/May, 1991, pp. 38–42. Reprinted by permission of Air & Space/Smithsonian.

NJERI, ITABARI, "What's in a Name?," from "Has-Beens Who Never Were" in *Every Goodbye Ain't Gone* by Itabari Njeri, pp. 336–340. Reprinted by permission of Miriam Altshuler Literary Agency on behalf of Itabari Njeri. Copyright © 1990 by Itabari Njeri.

NORMAN, DONALD, "Turn Signals Are the Facial Expressions of Automobiles," from *Turn Signals Are the Facial Expressions of Automobiles* by Donald Norman, Addison Wesley Longman, 1992, pp. 117–134. Copyright © 1992 by Donald Norman. Reprinted by permission of Addison Wesley Longman.

NORMAN, MARSHA, "Say Amen to Somebody." Originally published in *Mirabella,* Vol. VII, Number 1, No. 73, September/October 1995, pp. 117–119. Copyright © 1995, 1998 by Marsha Norman. Reprinted with permission from The Tantleff Office, Inc.

PARK, EDWARDS, "I Moved Far Away from Soaring Ideals — I Became a Warrior" from *The Smithsonian,* Dec. 1992, pp. 85–95. Copyright © 1992 by Edwards Park. Reprinted by permission of the author.

PRESTON, RICHARD, "Back in the Hot Zone" originally published in *The New Yorker,* May 22, 1995, pp. 43–45. Copyright © 1995 Richard Preston. Reprinted by permission of the author.

RAYMO, CHET, "The Ink of the Night" and "The Revenge of the Yokyoks" from *The Virgin and The Mousetrap* by Chet Raymo, Viking Penguin, 1991, pp. 123–131, 173–182. Copyright © 1991 by Chet Raymo. Used by permission of Viking Penguin, a division of Penguin Putnam Inc.

ROSEN, MARJORIE, "New Face, New Body, New Self," *People Weekly,* April 26, 1993. Copyright © 1993 Time Inc. Reprinted by permission.

SALAK, KIRA, "Boneyard Stretch" first appeared in *Witness,* Vol. 8, No. 1, 1994, pp. 140–155. Reprinted by permission of the publisher.

SANER, REG, "Naming Nature" from *The Four-Cornered Falcon: Essays on the Interior West and the Natural Scene,* pp. 104–121. Copyright © 1993 by Reg Saner. Reprinted by permission of Johns Hopkins University Press.

SHORE, BRADD, "Loading the Bases: How Our Tribe Projects Its Own Image into the National Pastime" from *The Sciences.* This article is reprinted by permission of *The Sciences* and is from the May/June 1990 issue. Individual subscriptions are $28 per year. Write to: The Sciences, 2 East 63rd St., NY, NY 10021.

SINGER, NATALIA RACHEL, "Nonfiction in First Person, without Apology" from *Creative Nonfiction,* 6, The Essayist at Work, 1996, 93–102. Reprinted by permission of the author.

SONTAG, SUSAN, "AIDS and Its Metaphors" from *AIDS and Its Metaphors* by Susan Sontag, Farrar, Straus & Giroux, Inc., 1988, 1989. Copyright © 1988, 1989 by Susan Sontag. Used with permission from the publisher.

STERNBERG, ROBERT J., "Love Is a Story," *The General Psychologist,* 30:1 Spring, 1994, pp. 1–11. Reprinted by permission of the author.

THORNE, KIP, "Black Hole Birth: Deeper Understanding" from *Black Holes and Time Warps: Einstein's Outrageous Legacy* by Kip Thorne, W. W. Norton, 1994, pp. 254–257. Copyright © 1994 by Kip S. Thorne. Reprinted by permission of W. W. Norton & Company, Inc.

ULLMAN, ELLEN, "Getting Close to the Machine." First appeared in *Harper's,* pp. 13–17, June 1995. Copyright © 1995, 1997 by Ellen Ullman. Reprinted by permission of City Lights Books.

UPDIKE, JOHN, "The Female Body" from *Odd Jobs* by John Updike. Copyright © 1991 by John Updike. Reprinted by permission of Alfred A. Knopf, Inc.

VISSER, MARGARET, "Crossword Puzzles" from *The Way We Are: The Astonishing Anthropology of Everyday Life* by Margaret Visser. Copyright © 1994 by Margaret Visser. Reprinted by permission of Faber & Faber, Inc., a division of Farrar, Straus & Giroux, Inc.

WADE, TED, "Walkabout: A Perplexatron Asks an AllKnowaBot a Few Things about Human Nature and CyberSPACE" from article posted on the Web, 1995 at http://www.uchsc.edu/sm/pmb/cybspce/space.htm. Reprinted by permission of the author.

WILLIAMS, JOY, "The Killing Game" first published in *Esquire,* 1990. Copyright © 1990 by Joy Williams. Reprinted by permission of International Creative Management, Inc.

WOLFF, TOBIAS, "Close Calls" from *In Pharoah's Army* by Tobias Wolff, Alfred A. Knopf, Inc., 1994, pp. 87–98. Copyright © 1994 by Tobias Wolff. Reprinted by permission of Alfred A. Knopf, Inc.

WRIGHT, JAMES, "Autumn Begins in Martins Ferry, Ohio" from "The Branch Will Not Break," in *Collected Poems* by James Wright. Copyright © 1971 James Wright. Reprinted with permission of Wesleyan University Press.

PHOTO AND ART CREDITS

Chapters 1, 7: Stockbyte

Chapters 2, 3, 4, 5, 6, 8: Image copyright © 1997 PhotoDisc, Inc.

Page 147: Cover drawing by Eugene Mihaesco. Copyright © 1988 The New Yorker Magazine, Inc. All rights reserved.

Index of Authors and Titles

thursday
Next building.